Henry Clay

HENRY CLAY

THE MAN WHO WOULD BE PRESIDENT

JAMES C. KLOTTER

OXFORD
UNIVERSITY PRESS

OXFORD
UNIVERSITY PRESS

Oxford University Press is a department of the University of Oxford. It furthers
the University's objective of excellence in research, scholarship, and education
by publishing worldwide. Oxford is a registered trade mark of Oxford University
Press in the UK and certain other countries.

Published in the United States of America by Oxford University Press
198 Madison Avenue, New York, NY 10016, United States of America.

© Oxford University Press 2018

Library of Congress Cataloging-in-Publication Data
Names: Klotter, James C., author.
Title: Henry Clay : the man who would be president / James C. Klotter.
Description: New York, NY : Oxford University Press, [2018] | Includes bibliographical references and index.
Identifiers: LCCN 2017053284 (print) | LCCN 2017053862 (ebook) | ISBN 9780190498054 (updf) |
ISBN 9780190498061 (epub) | ISBN 9780190498047 (hardback : alk. paper)
Subjects: LCSH: Clay, Henry, 1777–1852. | United States—Politics and government—1815–1861.
Classification: LCC E340.C6 (ebook) | LCC E340.C6 K57 2018 (print) | DDC 973.6092 [B]—dc23
LC record available at https://lccn.loc.gov/2017053284

1 3 5 7 9 8 6 4 2

Printed by Sheridan Books, Inc, United States of America

Frontispiece: Engraving by A. Sealy of Henry Clay from a daguerreotype by Root.
Wilson Family Photographic Collection, University of Kentucky. Special Collections

CONTENTS

———◦◦◦———

ACKNOWLEDGMENTS

BOOKS ARE THE PRODUCTS OF many hands, though only one person's name may appear on the title page, for without the work of others, the finished work would be a poor product, indeed. Most acknowledgments start with an obligatory nod to repositories of information, which is as it should be, for it is in those places where the real work begins. This book is no exception, so my thanks go to many people, some of them no longer at these institutions—Terry Birdwhistell, William J. Marshall, and others at the University of Kentucky library system; Mark Wetherington, James Holmberg, and Rebecca Rice at the Filson Historical Society; Sara Elliott, Darrell Meadows, and Louise Jones of the Kentucky Historical Society; B. J. Gooch of the Transylvania University Library; Greg Decker and Susan Martin of the Georgetown College Library; and various others at the Kentucky Library at Western Kentucky University, the Kentucky Department for Libraries and Archives, and the University of Louisville Library. Outside the commonwealth, much aid particularly came from staffs at the Library of Congress, the National Archives, the US Senate Historical Office, the Virginia Historical Society, the University of Chicago, the Newberry Library, the Southern Historical Collection of the University of North Carolina at Chapel Hill, and the Tennessee State Library and

Archives. (And I would be amiss if I did not thank Henry Clay for having such good penmanship; that made reading his manuscripts much easier than examining those of the typical leaders of his age.)

Individuals who supported this work in many different ways include those who either owned Clay letters and images or pointed the way to Clay-related items: Betty Jones of Richmond, Kentucky; Caroline Miller of Bracken County, Kentucky; Chris and Nan Mosher of Washington, DC; Harold Tallant of Georgetown College; Glen Taul of Georgetown, Kentucky; Kim Gelke of Illinois; and Cassandra Trimble of Washington State. Other aid was provided by Eric Blair, Braden Blankenship, Celisa Bowen, Jessica Brown, Ann Cothran, Dana Edgerton, Ian Ellis, Greg Haynes, Ron Klotter, Sarah and Rebekah McIntosh, Travis Mazurek, John Sosbe, and Catherine Taylor. A special thanks to Ollie Puckett. My appreciation also goes to Eric Brooks and Avery Malone of the Ashland Estate and Amy Elizabeth Burton of the Senate Curator's Office. And it goes without saying—but I will say it anyway—that the editorial and production team from Oxford University Press deserves much praise, including Elda Granata, Julia Turner, and Elizabeth Vaziri. Many thanks especially go to Nancy Toff, for her guidance throughout the project.

Research support was provided through a Goode Grant and a Summer Research Grant from Georgetown College, a Mellon Fellowship from the Virginia Historical Society, a Breaux Fellowship for the Filson Historical Society, and a research grant from the Kentucky Historical Society. Part of the results of that work already appeared in print in 2012, in an article in the *Register of the Kentucky Historical Society* and as a chapter in *Kentucky Renaissance*. My thanks go to the Kentucky Historical Society and the University Press of Kentucky and for permission to use parts of those works herein.

But in so many ways, an author's greatest thanks should go to those who take time off from their own projects and work, and critique a manuscript. I have been extremely fortunate in having excellent historians and editors who have commented in depth about this book. It is much better because of the suggestions made by two anonymous readers of Oxford University Press; retired Georgetown College professor Lindsey Apple, himself author of a book on the Clay family; Thomas H. Appleton Jr. of Eastern Kentucky University, editor extraordinaire; and John David Smith of the University of North Carolina, Charlotte, a special historian. And to my long-ago dissertation director, the late Holman Hamilton,

I beg forgiveness for offering a harsher view than did he of his favorite subject, Zachary Taylor.

And finally, I have dedicated previous books to my spouse, our children, and our grandchildren, but in truth they are an important part of all my work. For they help me better understand the human condition and make it all worth living.

PROLOGUE

———❦———

THE PRESIDENTIAL CAMPAIGN OF 1844 had ended. Now Henry Clay awaited the results. Twice before he had received electoral votes for president; twice he had been defeated. Another time he had sought his Whig Party's nomination and had failed to receive it, only to see the nominee win the office of chief executive. Now, however, his friends agreed that this race represented his best opportunity to lead the nation.

Because states held their elections on different days, news of the results trickled in over a period of almost two weeks. But as more returns became known, it seemed clear that if New York voted for Clay, he would become president. If it did not, he would taste bitter defeat once more.

In that atmosphere, Clay and his wife attended a wedding as they waited for the fateful news. Any day a dispatch might bring jubilation or dejection. In Illinois, Lexington native Mary Todd Lincoln received a letter written by her stepmother, telling what had transpired:

> As the hour approached for the arrival of the mail, I saw several gentlemen quietly leave the room, and knowing their errand, I eagerly watched for their return. As soon as they came in the room I knew by the expression of each countenance that New York had gone Democratic. The bearers of the news consulted together a moment,

then one of them advanced to Mr. Clay who was standing in the center of a group, of which your father [Robert Todd] was one, and handed him a paper. Although I was sure of the news it contained, I watched Mr. Clay's face for confirmation of the evil tidings. He opened the paper and as he read the death knell of his political hopes and life-long ambition, I saw a distinct blue shade begin at the roots of his hair, pass slowly over his face like a cloud and then disappear. He stood for a moment as if frozen. He laid down the paper, and, turning to a table, filled a glass with wine, and raising it to his lips with a pleasant smile, said: "I drink to the health and happiness of all assembled here." Setting down his glass, he resumed his conversation as if nothing had occurred and was, as usual, the life and light of the company.[1]

Three years later, a New York newspaper termed Clay "The Great Rejected."[2]

PREFACE

━━━◦◦◦◦◦━━━

ON THE FOURTH OF JULY 1861, in the early stages of the Civil War, a crowd gathered in Kentucky not to advocate for one side or the other but, rather, to dedicate a monument to honor their state's most famous political leader, a man who had tried to avoid the war now raging around them. Henry Clay had died almost a decade earlier, but only now the tall memorial to honor him had been completed. At the top, 130 feet from the ground, stood an imposing statue of the man many called the Great Compromiser. It faced Clay's home of Ashland and it majestically surveyed the scene around it. Even then, it would be another three years before the body of Henry Clay would be secured in its final resting place, in a sarcophagus at the base of the edifice.

For years, the monument stood as a quiet testament to the man who had helped guide the nation in the crucial years of its history. But some forty years later, a storm over Lexington unleashed thunder, high winds, and lightning bolts. The howling tempest hurled the head of the statue to the ground below, where the stately stone broke into several fragments. For seven more years, the Clay sculpture remained headless. Then, in 1910, the old statue was taken down, to be replaced by a newer representation of the man buried below. But in its damaged state, the older figure shattered upon its removal. Workmen buried the pieces in a corner of the mausoleum.

Soon a new symbol of Clay looked down on the world of the twentieth century and the old one seemed forgotten.[1]

Like the statue in Lexington Cemetery, Clay's reputation rose and fell during the years after his death, sometimes looming large and imposing, sometimes appearing broken, the man largely forgotten. Initially, the pendulum of history seemed to swing Clay's way.[2] But during Clay's lifetime, his two bitter rivals were Democrats Andrew Jackson and John C. Calhoun, and in the struggle for historical attention, they began to win out once more. Decades later, with the hard days of the Great Depression, with the business and bank failures, and with the party of Andrew Jackson ever more popular, the hero of the common man began to appeal more to Americans. Even though Franklin D. Roosevelt's New Deal owed much of its philosophical basis to Clay's belief in the role of the central government in economic planning, Jackson's words and image resonated louder. Jackson Day dinners and new books about the general left Clay either the villain or a bit actor in the pageant. Jackson ruled. Later yet, in the Cold War era, readers likewise seemed more attracted, for a time, to Calhoun's absolutism and abstract reasoning than to Clay's pragmatism and compromises[3]

But scholars abhor historical vacuums. During the last three decades, that pendulum began to swing back and writers started, once more, to give Henry Clay greater prominence in the history of his era. As it became clear that both current American parties owed part of their ancestry to Clay's Whig Party, books have focused increasingly on those past partisans. At the same time, changes in American society dimmed the appeal of Jackson and Calhoun. The South Carolinian's obstructionist stands and his unyielding defense of slavery seemed less noble in the era of civil rights resistance in the South. And scholars began to present the war hero in a much less heroic way, given Jackson's racist views, his treatment of Native Americans, his laissez-faire philosophy, and his arbitrary actions. By contrast, Clay now appeared more modern, more progressive, and more valued.[4]

By the twenty-first century, discordant party rhetoric also may have caused Clay to grow more appealing and more vital as a subject of study. His ability to rise, on occasion, above state or section or party, his capacity to produce workable compromises, and just his sheer talent caused people to focus attention on him. The views of Henry Clay range from that of one writer who called him "an LBJ-like figure" to that of a critic who looked at his policies and labeled him, of all things, "a National Socialist." More commonly, a greater number of Americans have agreed with the journalist who

At over 130 feet tall, the Clay Monument in Lexington Cemetery was dedicated in 1861. More than four decades later, a storm knocked the head off the statue of Clay, and the decapitated body remained in place for seven more years. In 1910, the replacement statue was erected but was also damaged in a storm. Like his memorial, Clay's reputation suffered over the years. *Clay Lancaster Slide Collection, University of Kentucky Special Collections Research Center, 2008ms020*

perused contemporary politics and stressed "our need for another Henry Clay." So, is there anything more to be said about Henry Clay?[5]

When this project was begun, the question motivating it was a simple one: Why did Clay not win the presidency? A corollary query involved another issue: Why did Clay's contemporaries continue to support him for the nation's highest political office despite his many defeats? In short, this project started as a study of Clay and the presidency. And so this is not a biography, per se, of Henry Clay. Instead, it focuses on the aspects of his life and his career that had an impact on his presidential searches and races. But very quickly into the study, it became clear that it must contain extensive biographical elements, for a person's life may well shape the formation of him as candidate. Beyond that, no political entity exists only in the maelstrom of a campaign. Clay's career, his compromises, his policies, his lifestyle—all became subjects of intense scrutiny and debate. That made this work not only a political story but also a social, intellectual, economic, and family one.

As with current political candidates, everything Clay did had the potential to become part of a race. A possible presidential candidate for at least a quarter century, he stood always "in the gaze of millions." Usually half of those voters praised him while the other half damned him. Yet every casual word, each private conversation, any thoughtless action could be used against him. Whenever he left the relatively safe confines of his estate, supporters flocked to him and enemies scorned him. As one journal noted, Clay could not move in public "without having to harangue a deputation of political friends, and stand to be kissed by ladies and pump handled by men, and hide the enormous bane of it beneath a fixed smile." Even in his home, he could not separate himself from public life: enormous amounts of mail demanded answers, as he posed for artists, talked to journalists, revealed himself to biographers, and regaled with stories the numerous domestic tourists and foreign travelers who appeared at his door. He might enjoy some quiet moments with his family, but even then sorrows tormented him. Should he devote more time to his wife, children, and grandchildren, or should he pay more attention to the model farm that helped him meet his constant financial obligations, or should he continue to serve in Congress and do more to advance his presidential ambitions? Clay's private life was seldom private and usually could not be separated from his public person. This story, then, is about the making of a person and a politician, as well as the unmaking of a presidential candidate.[6]

An 1847 journalist asked, "How come it that if Mr. Clay, unquestionably the greatest statesman of America, is also the most popular—how come it that his efforts for the Presidency have invariable ended in inglorious defeat?" Or to put it another way, "Why did Clay not win the presidency?" That question seemed relatively simple and straightforward. After all, for most candidates for the presidency, one defeat is usually the death of any future hopes for the office. As one twentieth-century politician explained, "A defeated candidate is a kind of pariah. They never ask him to the party anymore." Among major candidates, only Henry Clay and William Jennings Bryan three times received electoral votes for the highest political post in the nation and lost all three times. Two other candidates—Martin Van Buren and Grover Cleveland—also ran three times, but they both won at least one time. What was it that caused Clay's losses?[7]

After all, Henry Clay seemed to have it all. He pointed to his humble origins and his support from the masses, yet he also owned a plantation and ran in aristocratic circles. He lived in an agricultural area, yet he called for industrial growth. He won acclaim for his passionate oratory and his ability to convince in the heat of debate, yet he formulated a policy, a system, that appealed primarily to voters' reason. He supported the start of the then-popular War of 1812, yet he helped make the peace that concluded a then-unpopular contest. He rose to prominence as a spokesman of the West, yet he became most identified as a stalwart of the Union, beyond sectional divides. He spoke with slaveholders as one of them, yet he also publicly voiced antislavery sentiments. He stood up forcefully for his stated principles, yet he gained fame for his compromises.

Democrat and aristocrat, agrarian and businessman, War Hawk and peacemaker, sectionalist and nationalist, slaveholder and antislavery advocate, man of principle and man of compromise, Clay could appeal to various constituencies. But he also seemed a paradox, given the different sides he showed the public. His career appeared made for the presidency—US senator before the age of thirty, Speaker of the US House of Representatives on the first day of his service to that body, diplomat and secretary of state, forger of famous compromises to defuse sectional tensions, leader of his party, formulator of the American System—this man of great charisma appeared to have the needed experience and to possess all the qualifications. In antebellum America, everywhere one looked, there was the hand of Henry Clay.

Yet despite his strengths, Clay could not win the political office he most coveted. Posterity would name him one of the nation's most important

US senators and one of the hundred most influential Americans. A 1990s survey of hundreds of historians and political scientists asked which candidate they would vote for now, who ran in the presidential races of the past. In that survey, Clay outpolled his opponents in two of his three presidential races, yet voters did not so reward his services with election to that office. Both his contemporaries and modern-day commentators have pointed to myriad reasons for those defeats. The almost bewildering variety of answers became almost contradictory. Clay was too political; he was not political enough. Clay was too proslavery; he was too antislavery. Clay was too dictatorial in Congress; he was too much of a compromiser. Clay was too sectional; he was not sectional enough. Clay was too devoted to principle: he was too unprincipled. Clay was too tied to the old republican ideals of his youth; he was too much in advance of his times. Others have argued that Clay expressed his opinions too openly and too often, that he made serious strategic mistakes, that he reacted badly in the heat of battle. Some critics pointed to Clay's duels, his character, and his moral makeup as explanations for the losses. A few note that he simply suffered from bad luck and bad timing. In short, Clay had so many gaps in his political armor that opponents could easily find a weak spot to exploit.[8]

Most of the answers fault the error-prone Kentuckian for being the unwitting architect of his own downfall. And when I started this project, I admittedly had a more critical view of Clay. The story I expected to tell was one that would have criticized Clay more for not being true to his instincts, for being a compromiser when he should have taken a stronger stand, for being all fluff and no substance, for being a waffler—in short, an example of what a political leader should not be. But I was forced to modify those views. Another look at Henry Clay and the American presidency suggested that while the conventional wisdom may not necessarily be wrong, the best answer is found beyond that. That is, no single factor explains Clay's defeats. Each chapter in his search for the presidency had its own story line, and what appeared important in one race might be less important in the next. If there is one answer, it would be that the many cuts he suffered bled the political lifeblood from the candidate. But going beyond that explanation, and focusing on Clay and the presidency, revealed how some of the strengths he brought to his candidacy also proved to be weaknesses. As a compromiser, he angered both extremes, and so lost votes. As a nationalist, he upset those who chiefly spoke for one section. As an antislavery slaveholder, he alienated both camps. As a person with a specific program, a man who voted on controversial bills, an individual who took open stands on issues, he was a target for political attacks. Yet all those factors reveal much about politics, then and now. If electing key leaders is crucial to making democracy work, then citizens must continue to learn from history.[9]

The question of one Clay ally, after his hero's defeat in 1844, still echoes across the years: "And shall we never more hear that deep, melodious voice in the Senate or before our people? Never see that beaming countenance, that flashing eye, illuminated with the radiant gleamings of his great soul? Who will take his place?"[10] Perhaps no one could or has taken his place, but the Clay story, in both positive and negative ways, has meaning and importance for us, even now.

HENRY CLAY

I

Preparation

IN MARCH 1840, HENRY CLAY returned to the place of his birth. Born on April 12, 1777, in an area of eastern Virginia known as the Slashes, he had not seen that home for almost a half century. In that time, politically oriented biographers had crafted their accounts of his early years, and others would continue to add to the story. They told of the early demise of Clay's poor and pious clergyman father, whose passing left the family in abject poverty, and the widow with little more than seven children. That tragic death had made son Henry "a poor and friendless orphan boy" at the age of four, and he had received limited education as a result. Instead, he would work the fields, and the shoeless, sunburnt boy would mount an old horse and take corn to a distant mill to help provide for the family. In the biographers' portrayal, this "Millboy of the Slashes," born in poverty and obscurity, had raised himself by force of his brilliance and had risen to become "the self-made man of America."[1]

Clay reinforced those elements of his life story with his own words. When a caustic critic condemned him in 1824 for his lack of learning, Clay responded that he knew his weaknesses: "I was born to no proud patrimonial estate; from my father I inherited only infancy, ignorance, and indigence. I feel my defects." Later, when supporting aid for public education, he dramatized again his humble origins, stressing that he had been left an orphan, "too young to have been conscious of a father's smiles and caresses, with a widowed mother, surrounded by numerous offspring, in the midst of pecuniary embarrassments, without a regular education, without fortune, without friends, without patrons." Given all that, he would reasonably conclude: "I have reason to be satisfied with my public career."[2]

And well he might, for by 1840, he had been a state representative, US representative, US senator, diplomat, secretary of state, the "Great Compromiser," and twice presidential candidate. But many of his most important years lay ahead.

In 1840, Henry Clay returned to the memories of a past that he had left behind so many years earlier. Here, in "the spirit of a pilgrim," he came to see people and places from his past. Here, his heart returned to cherished spots. Here, he came home. Marveling at what he saw, he wrote his wife, "Every thing was changed." No stone marker but, rather, a field of wheat covered his father's and grandparents' graves, long leveled by the plow. A fondly remembered hickory tree now stood in decay. His old homestead between Black Tom Slash and Hanover Courthouse had been greatly modified, and he barely recognized the room of his birth. The old St. Paul's Church where he had attended school for two years seemed on the verge of collapse. The whole experience strengthened Clay's sense of his own mortality and of his place in history.[3]

Yet his remembered origins and his political present did not always completely coincide. The invented life and the historical one could diverge considerably. But sometimes they did not. As Clay noted, he *had* been orphaned at the age of four, and he never really knew his father or grandfather. John Clay had been a little over forty years old when he died, leaving Elizabeth Hudson Clay a widow in her thirties. At almost the same time, the family experienced further trauma. As Henry Clay noted later, he was "rocked in the cradle of the revolution." That became reality when Sir Barreste Tarleton's British troops came to the Clay household, seized food, destroyed furniture, confiscated slaves, and then plunged their swords into the fresh graves of Clay's father and grandfather, thinking the family had buried valuables there. That image of desecration would later affect Clay's political actions, and he clearly remembered the event six decades later. Death and violence were a recurring part of Clay's childhood.[4]

But other parts of the Clay story as told by early biographers, as well as Clay himself, did not reflect reality. That struggle between fact and fiction would infiltrate Clay's entire public life. In contrast to the image of Rev. John Clay as a poverty-stricken minister of the Old Dominion, in truth Henry's father came from a distinguished family that had been in Virginia almost from the first English settlement. "Sir John," as he was called by contemporaries, held sizable landholdings of over 450 acres and owned at least twenty slaves. Most of that estate went to his widow, leaving the family in a comfortable situation. Her remarriage at age thirty-three to the considerably younger Henry Watkins, a planter, militia captain, and brother of her sister's husband, brought further stability to the household and helped shape the boy and would-be president. Well-to-do in his own right, Watkins turned out to be a kind stepfather to young Henry and an important influence.[5]

Still, Clay did not live a life of ease. His first memory involved walking behind a plow. Moreover, the family experienced hardships of another kind. Of the nine children of John and Elizabeth Clay, only three lived to become adults. Henry's mother also bore more children in her second marriage, for a total of sixteen. His father's death, his mother's remarriage, his new stepfather, the death of siblings, an influx of half-brothers and sisters—all shaped the man and the politician he became.[6]

During his subsequent career, Henry Clay left a sizable record through his printed speeches, manuscripts, and recorded conversations. Yet in all those words he said remarkably little about his parents and siblings, except concerning his formative years. In the early 1790s, his mother, her husband, and their expanding family moved to the new frontier of Kentucky, but Henry remained behind. The fourteen-year-old's feelings at the time about that kind of virtual abandonment remain unknown. Perhaps the choice was his. But a paucity of familial love may have been a factor in forming the public man who searched for the nation's affection.[7]

If the orphaned Millboy of the Slashes representation grew out of a factual basis, and the poor, penniless image did not, Clay's educational accomplishments tell a more mixed story. In 1820, John Quincy Adams thought his rising opponent had a mind "very defective in elementary education." And a congressman who knew Clay called him "not a man of much study." In some ways, they both were correct. Clay did have little formal schooling—three years in his home county. But he was not as uneducated as his detractors sneered, or even as he sometimes suggested. He admitted that he had never learned Latin or Greek and that he studied too little and relied too heavily on "the resources of my genius." But all that masked the fact that the raw boy and then the adult man continued to learn, to grow intellectually, to read, long after the classroom bell last rang.[8] As a youngster, Clay memorized poetry while studying history and science. Later in life, he purchased numerous books, including a set of Shakespeare's works. Clay advised a son to read history and noted his own appreciation for such authors as Plutarch, Socrates, Gibbon, Hume, Hallam, and Marshall—suggesting a reasonably well-read man. Clay also proved to be a voracious consumer of newspapers. In 1823, he received a half-dozen on a regular basis and six years later, the list had grown to almost twenty, from ten different states.[9]

People in politics might fault Clay's education, but few faulted his intelligence. In fact, Adams, in the same sentence in which he derided Clay's deficiencies, approved the man's "vigorous intellect"—high praise indeed from the often-disparaging New Englander. Another Clay critic, John Tyler, grudgingly admitted that Clay had "an intellect of the highest order." Of course, intellect does not always transfer into intelligent actions. And though smart, Clay made mistakes, often. But if neither as well educated nor as well read as some leaders of his generation, he seldom took second place to anyone in the intellectual give and take of debate. He could constantly draw out relevant examples from memory, could formulate appropriate answers quickly, and could win over his auditors with his ideas and the force of his argument. In private settings or public courtrooms, few could out-argue him. To some, Clay might be better read in men than in books; as Adams noted, "His school has been the world." But when that "street sense" combined with a mostly underappreciated intellect, it belied the ill-educated image often attributed to Clay.[10]

In fact, the entire self-made-man image propagated by Clay and his supporters stressed how Clay rose from obscurity on the force of his talent. Much of that was correct. Yet at the same time, he might not have accomplished what he had if he had not had much help along the way. His stepfather recognized Clay's possibilities early and secured the fourteen-year-old a position as a clerk in a store in Richmond. Then he obtained a post for him in the Office of the Clerk of the Chancery. Soon after that, the Clay family ventured to Kentucky and left Henry to deal with life as a young teenager, almost alone in what seemed to be a big city. He and his fellow clerks played cards, placed bets on the thoroughbreds, and courted the ladies. But more important for Clay's future, his duties meant that he observed the many talented Virginia leaders at work. He listened to their oratory, watched their debates, and digested their arguments. Perhaps the highlight of his time in the Old Dominion was when Clay twice heard Patrick Henry speak. The great orator from his home county so impressed Clay that he said he never forgot the ringing tones of that fiery voice.[11]

His stepfather's aid got Clay started down a career path. But Henry's real opportunity came when the legendary George Wythe, Sole Chancellor of the High Court of Chancery and the state's foremost legal mind, met the young clerk. Clay's abilities impressed the aged man who had taught Thomas Jefferson, John Marshall, James Monroe, and others. A signer of the Declaration of Independence, the unimpressive-looking Wythe had helped craft the US Constitution as well. Now he asked Clay to be in essence his private secretary, his amanuensis—a particularly important task, since Wythe barely could use his hand. But more than that, Wythe became Clay's mentor, perhaps his father figure.[12]

For some four years following his sixteenth birthday, Clay worked closely with Wythe. He took dictation, copied decisions, and researched cases. But the work was far from one-sided. If Wythe mentioned a book Clay should peruse, the young scribe usually examined it, to his profit. Clay felt heavily his inability to read Greek and Latin, but Wythe would read passages to him, to Clay's delight. The chancellor also would explain his decisions and the reasoning behind them, and Clay's legal awareness grew. In turn, Clay idolized Wythe. Near the end of his own life, after meeting famous people on two continents, Clay lovingly remembered the "plain, simple, and unostentatious" Wythe as, "one of the purest, best, and most learned men" that he had ever known. Wythe's instruction helped the boy; his advice aided the student; but his example, most of all, shaped the man.[13]

Wythe rewarded Clay for his loyalty by arranging for him to read law with the Virginia attorney general, former governor Robert Brooke. Once more, Clay found himself allied to a major player in the political game. Under Brooke's guidance, Clay learned his lessons quickly, and in November 1797, "Henry Clay Gentleman" qualified to practice law. At the age of twenty, Henry Clay may not have overcome as much as the legend would later indicate, but he had, nevertheless, faced much adversity and had seized his opportunities. He now had the prospects of a fine future before him. But where would that future be?[14]

As the end of the eighteenth century neared, more and more Virginians had left their increasingly worn-out lands for the rich soil of the Kentucky frontier. Some had departed seeking more religious freedom. Others sought greater political and professional opportunities. But for almost all of them, the place across the mountains represented hope—for a better life. In 1797, new attorney Clay looked westward as well, as he questioned whether he should join his family in what some called a New Eden, others a New Hell. Originally part of Virginia, now a state for barely five years, the Commonwealth of Kentucky had already attracted many talented immigrants. Lawyers, like Clay, had gleefully noted that the new state's use of the old Virginia land system had resulted in many vague and overlapping "shingled" claims—ones that produced numerous lawsuits, and much income for attorneys. Ambitious men like George Nicholas and John Breckinridge saw the limits to advancement in the more closed Virginia society, with its plethora of talented political leaders, and instead sought their fortunes in the West. The Kentucky myth of plenty motivated many.[15]

At the same time, if Clay did depart Virginia, he would leave behind the politically important support groups from which he had benefited in Richmond. And while many who left found better lives in Kentucky, many did not. Movement westward did not mean automatic success, and it could involve failure, especially given all the talent Clay would compete against, at the bar of justice. In the end, perhaps it was simply the spirit of the new land that enticed him to make the move. The fledging state was in transition, moving to a society that more replicated the cultural and class situations of the mother state but that also contained elements representing freer forces, born of its earlier experience. That appealed to Clay as well. The struggle between the democratic forces of the frontier and the aristocratic might of the established gentry, the contest between the mass of the population and the elite, would be a long-continuing one in American history. In Kentucky, separated from the Atlantic seaboard by mountains and forged out of the conflict with native peoples, the mentality of the old order clashed with the ethos of the new order. Out of that, a different force emerged, one unlike that of the East. Kentucky became the First West. Shaped as well by those from both the agrarian South and the commercial North, the resulting society represented a mix of influences, different from them but tied to them. As it turned out, functioning in that society would produce in Henry Clay an outlook that combined elements of various cultures, classes, and sections. Whether that would be an asset for him remained to be seen.[16]

The new state matched the temperament of the new man, this young attorney, and he would make Kentucky his home for the rest of his life. It would prove to be a fortuitous choice, for from the moment in 1797 until Clay's death, the commonwealth took its place as one of the nation's most important states. In that time, the state would help shape Clay's beliefs and positions during his political career.

At a time when agriculture provided much of the wealth of a people or of a commonwealth, Kentucky would, by 1840, stand first in the nation in the production of hemp and wheat, second in tobacco and corn, and fourth in rye. Its diversified crops made the Bluegrass State a breadbasket for the young country. Moreover, the commonwealth ranked first in good horse-flesh and second in its number of mules and hogs. From the earliest times, that agricultural promise, plentiful animals, and good land attracted a large and diverse population; people surged to the commonwealth. By 1840 also, Kentucky's 780,000 souls stood sixth in population among the then thirty states of the nation. And in the presidential elections between 1824 and 1860, a Kentuckian was on the ballot for either president or vice president in eight of the ten races. Put simply, antebellum Kentucky would form a key part of the federal Union.[17]

At the core of that state was its symbolic heart—the central Bluegrass. There it was that Clay settled. When he arrived on horseback, Lexington was the largest city in Kentucky and would retain that title for almost the first four decades after statehood. In 1800, it had a larger population than Pittsburgh and twice as many people as Cincinnati. The city would more than double in size a decade later and then increase more slowly through 1820—still the largest place in the state. By 1830, Louisville would surpass it in size. But through all those decades before the Civil War, the central Bluegrass continued to tout its many strengths.[18]

After Harvard-educated clergyman Timothy Flint visited the area in 1816, he wrote of what he found in the Bluegrass: "Lexington," he said, "is a singularly neat and pleasant town . . . [that] has an air of leisure and opulence. . . . In the circles where I visited, literature was commonly the topic of conversation. . . . The best modern works," he continued, "had generally been read. . . . There was generally an air of ease and politeness in the social intercourse of the inhabitants of this town, which evinced the cultivation of taste and good feeling. In effect Lexington has taken the tone of a literary place, and may be fitly called the Athens of the West."[19]

Almost everyone who visited Clay's new hometown commented favorably on the beauty of the land and the fertility of the soil. And if the countryside and the agrarian ethos enthralled visitors, the city itself often enchanted them, as it had Clay when he first arrived. An English barrister called it "the neatest country town I had yet seen in the United States," and pointed to its spacious roads and "delightfully shaded" streets. Harry Toulmin, in his influential, London-published *A Description of Kentucky in North America* (1792), had barely been able to find words to praise the land, calling it "a country beyond description," an "extensive garden" with no forbidden fruit, a place so rich that "it is impossible that we can experience anything like poverty, for no country . . . upon this globe is so rich in the comforts and necessaries [*sic*] of life."[20]

But more than the strengths of the physical city itself, observers stressed again and again the positive aspects of the people and their culture. Visitors pictured a cosmopolitan, exciting, vibrant city and region, with strengths in business, education, religion, science, medicine, society, and culture. At the beginning of the nineteenth century, the state also stood at the center of a new national religious rebirth, the Great Revival. It reached its visual apex in 1801 at Cane Ridge, near Lexington. There, as many as twenty thousand people—a tenth of the commonwealth's population—came together to be part of one of the most important gatherings in all of American religious history. An aspect of the Second Great Awakening, the Cane Ridge Camp Meeting in Bourbon County espoused a more egalitarian Christianity, a new social equality, and a more inclusive, less structured worship service. Out of the Great Revival emerged a fresh democratic culture, as did a more welcoming spirit for new religions. In that area, as in others, central Kentucky seemed to be at the forefront of change, the kind of place where a man like Clay might excel.[21]

At the same time, the state showed its continuing ability to reconcile religion with racing, red-eye whiskey, and retailing. The antebellum market revolution found a happy home in old Kentucky. An 1811 traveler found shops "piled with goods," while another noted the numerous "men of enterprise" in this new Athens. City newspapers printed the currency exchange in New Orleans, New York, and London, for Lexington was part of a global economy. Advertisements in the 1810s and 1820s offered consumers books from London, dinner plates from Liverpool, tea from India, rum from Jamaica, iron from Sweden, wallpaper from France, and linen from Ireland, all found, according to a traveler, in "great profusion" in Lexington shops.[22]

Merchants had first begun to gain considerable wealth by selling supplies to the armies on the frontier, and the area soon grew to become a distribution center for Kentucky and the West. In contrast to many of their Virginia brethren, Kentucky merchants often reinvested their profits in their businesses, not in displays of wealth. In fact, at first the city's remoteness basically protected its economy from competition. As a result, Lexington developed markets, industries, and businesses that thrived—and that made numerous men very wealthy. Some of them thus found this New West liberating and argued that it judged entrepreneurs and immigrants like Clay more on their actions than on their class or religion or past.[23]

Yet of all the aspects of central Kentucky that travelers and observers praised—the land, the town, the businesses, and more—they most applauded the society, culture, and education. One man who grew up there titled a section of his memoirs "A Reading Population." And so it was. A visitor went to a reading room in a coffeehouse and found that it subscribed to forty-two different newspapers, many of them from overseas. Little wonder that a Cincinnati paper in 1820 called the city "the headquarters of *science and letters* in the western country," or that English traveler J. Lewis Peyton wrote of his time in the area in the 1840s: "The more I saw of Kentuckians, the more agreeably was I impressed by them. Remarkable for intellectual activity," he noted, "they are eminent in urbanity and real politeness." Clay fit the mold perfectly and such attributes would help make him an attractive political candidate.[24]

Educational strengths and achievements formed the axis around which so many of those societal strengths revolved. Transylvania University was, during part of the antebellum era, one of the best schools in the nation. In its golden age under President Horace Holley, people called it the "Harvard of the West." With a law school, medical school, and undergraduate program, the institution received city and state support, and it became the early center of western and southern education. When French aristocrat and American Revolutionary War hero Lafayette visited in 1825, his secretary wrote that the establishments for public instruction in Lexington "rival the most celebrated college and universities in the principal towns of Europe." Those eager to learn flocked to the city. By the time one of Transylvania's former students, Jefferson Davis, went to Congress, seven other senators—13 percent of the total—had graduated from there. Central Kentucky had become the educational heart of the South and West.[25]

Students and visitors alike enjoyed Lexington because Kentucky hospitality proved to be very real and very welcome. One person who first arrived in 1815 wrote: "I have never found a more kind and hospitable people than those in Kentucky, generally, and I have travelled in most all States of the Union." Moreover, Lexington, according to one student, was "a fun place for amusements, to get into frolicks, visit the girls, and all such things." The most exciting place, with the most talented people, it seemed to one study, "like a Renaissance city of Italy."[26]

Quite a picture. But that portrait of a city conceals as much as it reveals. Like an artist's canvas that has been painted over, a ghost image lurks beneath the painting. That hidden view has darker hues and fewer bright points of light. Yet, in many ways, the ghost image better represents the real Athens, a city with deep flaws and dark secrets as well. For in truth, the "Athens of the West" was a place of many contrasts and contradictions—like Henry Clay.

For example, this place of such fertile land, this region that offered so much promise to those who came, this area of so much wealth represented something else to so many. Some may have migrated and discovered a liberating and open West, but others found a more restrictive one, with the best land already taken, their hopes shortly ended, their promise quickly destroyed. In 1800, fewer than half the people in Kentucky owned any land—approximately the national average. Across the state, more than a hundred individuals held more than ten thousand acres. Some 1 percent of the people controlled one-third of the total acreage. The rich had gotten richer while many of the poor remained poor. Some did achieve their dreams, and their stories would be trumpeted abroad. But too many remained landless and voiceless. Could—or would—the increasingly wealthy Clay speak for them, too?[27]

Kentucky's universal white male suffrage caused citizens to tout their democratic spirit. Yet this learned society, this place open to change, firmly embraced slavery, provided few legal rights to women, and employed young children in hard labor. The region may have been economically strong, but it also proved morally weak. Few listened to the voices of protest around them. Most could not cast off the racial and gender blinders and endorse changes in their society.[28] By 1810, half of the white families in Fayette, and three-fourths of those in the city of Lexington, held people in slavery. Ads for runaway slaves, sales of divided families, and the cries of the oppressed reminded people daily of the system and what it did to all those it touched. Slave merchants sold humans; owners whipped slaves. A visitor watched all that and wrote: "Their screams soon collected a numerous crowd—I could not help saying to myself: 'These cries are the knell of Kentucky liberty.' "[29]

Although a society of violence, economic disparities, and racial and gender inequities, Lexington did produce significant positive accomplishments; its sophistication, cosmopolitan spirit, and cultural strengths were real. Yet at the same time, like America, it had a soft underbelly of narrow views and reactionary responses that could quickly become exposed. Transylvania University's president, Horace Holley, would quickly discover the existence of such outlooks. With the support of Clay and others, he had made the university great. But the Holley urbanity that engaged Clay produced antipathy in other quarters. A journal in 1823 criticized Holley, saying, "The theatre, Ballroom, the Card table, and all those places to which the vain and dissipated resort . . . are places to which he resorts." Under siege for going to "large parties and to the public races," the unhappy leader resigned in 1827. Within a decade, what had once been the jewel of education in Kentucky and in the South stood as only a faint glimmer of its former self.[30]

Holley's resignation marked the beginning of a period of decline from the earlier days of glory. In the first three and a half decades after statehood, the city had deserved its high reputation. It rose to glory at the same time Clay had. But a series of events, some of which Lexington could control and some of which it could not, began to have an effect. Lexington's death knell did not toll loudly. Symbolic death came in stages, softly, over time—with the quiet whisper of Holley's quill pen as he wrote his resignation; the distant whistle of a steamboat on the Ohio River; the dying sighs of cholera victims; the muffled sobs of slaves on the auction block; the sounds of businesses closing their doors in a depressed time—each of these chipped away at the columns of past glory, frustrating Clay's hopes for a brighter future and leaving increasingly tarnished artifacts of fading grandeur and lost greatness.

The first crack in the façade came with a financial depression, which seriously damaged the economic health of the region. Then began a transportation revolution and steamboats started to ply the Ohio. Lexington's lack of a navigable watercourse soon made it more and more vulnerable. Very early, the city—and Clay—tried to compensate by advocating internal improvements such as turnpikes, and by supporting construction of a railroad to Frankfort and then to Louisville, one of the first such roads in the United States. But that railroad progressed only slowly and that option helped little in the antebellum years. And so as the riverboat bypassed Lexington, the city settled into a waterless economic backwater. When an English barrister visited in 1832, he said the city stood as the "only place of note in the United States, whose prosperity, for several years, has been on the decline."[31]

Events in 1833 added to the decline of the city. A cholera epidemic struck in June, and before it ended two months later, some 500 citizens had died, of a population of 6,000—1 of every 12 people. A survivor remembered that "it came like a sudden and awful clap of thunder upon us—the whole community was stunned and paralyzed." Travel stopped. Businesses closed. Schools ceased. Henry Clay, Mary Todd, Jefferson Davis, and John C. Breckinridge all resided in the city then; remarkably all survived, but others died so fast that not enough coffins could be built and not enough labor could be procured to bury the bodies fast enough. Another epidemic struck in 1849 and left nearly 350 more dead.[32]

All those events took their toll on the city in so many ways. As the deaths mounted, as the next generation of potential new leaders moved to the better promise of the trans-Mississippi West, as the economy stagnated, as the educational institutions declined, as the spirit of innovation faded, the central Bluegrass —like its chief citizen— lost some of its luster. But, in truth, Lexington died a series of slow deaths over the years, and each blow saddened Clay. He had cast his lot with the city and had seen it prosper. Lexington, in turn, had inspired and shaped him in ways both big and small. For over a half century, the city and the man would be tightly intertwined.[33]

When he arrived in Lexington in 1797, Clay found the city much to his liking. As he participated in its lively social life, a young woman soon gained his affection, and within a year and a half he married her, in April 1799, one day before his twenty-second birthday. Their match would also prove important to both his financial and his political career, and Clay likely knew it.[34]

Eighteen-year-old Lucretia Hart came from a wealthy family and brought a comfortable dowry with her. Moreover, the Harts had numerous kin who linked Mr. and Mrs. Clay to key national figures. Lucretia's sister married James Brown, later a senator from Louisiana, and Mrs. Clay's first cousin was the mother of later Missouri senator Thomas Hart Benton. Family connections also stretched to Isaac Shelby, the first governor of Kentucky. Marriage thus gave Henry Clay easier entry into elite social and political circles, some of which might otherwise have been denied to the newcomer.[35]

As for his spouse, the exact role she played in Clay's political life remains something of an enigma. Though she was not deemed physically attractive by the standards of her time, neither was this slender, lively girl with auburn hair and blue eyes simply a "plain-looking woman." Over the years, those who met her described instead her easy dignity, referred to her as "one of the best-hearted women I have ever known," and called her "a fine woman," one who inspired respect. A close friend characterized Lucretia Clay as a kind, friendly, religious, discreet person who played music and occasionally danced, but chiefly enjoyed family. At the same time, even her admirers found that the increasingly quiet spouse took little part in conversation and preferred to stay out of the political and social spotlight.[36]

Clay's relationship with his wife also continues to be mostly hidden from history. His letters to her reveal his emotions, but almost none of those she wrote to him remain extant, and she did not write many. Her brother-in-law referred to her "repugnance to writing" and Clay complained in 1849 that she "never writes." Her husband's comments about Lucretia tell of an unselfish, "cheerful and happy" woman who provided stability to the household and cared little for societal demands on her. Instead, she preferred to focus on home. But after the deaths of many of her children, she withdrew ever more and Clay worried in 1825 that "she has been so much out of society that I am afraid it will be difficult to renew her taste for it." It was. Raising eleven children and numerous grandchildren, with a husband absent to tend to legal or political affairs, she retreated to her safe haven of the new estate they called Ashland. Unlike some other political wives, she created no controversies, as did Rachel Jackson or Peggy Eaton, nor did she get involved in political quarrels, as John C. Calhoun's wife did. As one society member noted, Mrs. Clay made no enemies. Overall, in more than fifty-three years of marriage, Lucretia Hart Clay provided her husband with welcome serenity, quiet strength, and perhaps even love. He needed all that.[37]

Clay had married well. He had made an excellent choice in selecting a place to practice his profession. Matrimony may have opened some doors, but could Clay's talents take him through them? Now, the time had arrived to see if he could actually be successful as an attorney. It was far from a given that such would be the case. Future President James Buchanan came to the new state and later recounted his experience: "I went to Kentucky expecting to be a great man there, but every lawyer I met at the bar was my equal, and more than half of them my superior, so I gave up." Had Clay had the same reaction, then he might have spent a career scrambling to make a living, rather than engaging in politics. But Henry Clay possessed some advantages that lawyers like Buchanan did not enjoy. Clay's education in Virginia under Wythe and Brooke granted him instant credibility, tied him to other leading lawyers who had trained under them, and provided him with a solid legal background. Perhaps the three most prominent attorneys near him were George Nicholas, John Breckinridge, and Clay in-law James Brown. All had ties to the College of William and Mary, where Wythe had taught. Furthermore, Clay's father-in-law used his high standing in Lexington to help the new couple. But, most of all, more than Buchanan and others, Clay had something else operating in his favor. Clay had exceptional talent.[38]

Critics stressed that Clay's successes in the law came more from the fact that he was more a man of action than of legal scholarship. Some indicated

This portrait of Henry and Lucretia Clay in their old age—perhaps taken on their fiftieth wedding anniversary in 1849—reveals a serious couple, but both were more carefree in their youth. Over time, the death of many of their children took its toll. Still, throughout her life, Lucretia gave Henry much-needed support in both good times and bad. A private person, she left few letters and remains somewhat hidden from history. *Kentucky Historical Society, SC1474_1*

that he was not a profound attorney, nor one who studied much. They stressed that his personal attributes in the courtroom hid his legal deficiencies and won his cases. Clay himself often made jests about his abilities, adding to the developing image. And enough truth existed in that picture to give it some basis in fact. But when Clay appeared in a courtroom, his client would have an excellent chance of success. In the informal, sometimes confusing state legal system—often based on personalities, relationships, friendships, and even antipathies—Clay learned how to win, as he would later in Congress.[39]

At a time when, as one observer noted, "there were *Gentlemen*, attending the Courts, who studied Hoyle, more than they did Blackstone," Clay made as many allies for his out-of-courtroom "studies" as he did before the bar of justice. That lesson would prove useful in the political arena. Other attorneys liked the Clay of the courtroom as well. He had power, presence, and style. Once, in arguing a case against later political rival William T. Barry, Clay stopped and offered his beleaguered opponent a glass of claret, which Barry accepted. But the courteous Clay did not always dominate. Another later political enemy, Tom Marshall, recalled how he had tried to anticipate every argument his opposing counsel Clay would make, then demolished them one by one. He sat down, pleased with "spiking Clay's guns." But as Marshall recounted: "Imagine my mortification when Clay concluded a splendid speech without even alluding to anything I had said." Clay's arguments won.[40]

Most often, the young attorney simply used the force of his words to persuade, as he would later in Congress. In a case in which future US senator John J. Crittenden opposed him, an observer noted how Crittenden's side had all going for it. The general impression seemed clear to all: "Mr. Clay's cause was lost—that he could have nothing effective to say, and that he was beaten . . . by his great comrade Crittenden." But then Clay rose and gave the courtroom the feeling "that he knew his power." Then he spoke: "Scarcely ever was before such a toppling over of a beautiful, logical and rhetorical structure which Mr. Crittenden had raised." With the legal edifice gone, the case collapsed and Clay's client won.[41]

Even near the end of Clay's life, he could still move a jury and a courtroom to tears by his eloquence, could still almost intuitively understand how jurors felt, and could still appeal to their sympathies. A woman who attended a trial in 1849 recounted how the seventy-two-year-old Clay had demolished witnesses under cross-examination. He even mimicked some answers, which "amused everybody very much," and he then complimented other witnesses in such a way that "it was expressed most beautifully, and said in such a simple way that it made the impression on every one who heard him." The courtroom filled with those who came simply to savor his excellence. In his summation, he spoke "so simply and lucidly that a child might have understood it, yet so beautifully and forcibly that every one felt the cause their own." Clay even noted that the word on the street was that money had been used to secure a hung jury, but he knew that before him were honorable and honest men who would not stain the honor of their city by such unfaithful actions. That represented the typical Clay approach—and not just in the courtroom—of stressing emotions, emphasizing reason, anticipating problems, appealing to the better nature of those before him. But Clay, who also studied Hoyle with regularity, could bluff and use other tactics in different situations.[42]

In short, Clay learned to use the devices he needed to win. The nature of early Kentucky justice sometimes meant that appeals to emotion, or pressure tactics, or some other approach gave the best opportunity for victory. Involved legal reasoning, based on precedents, common law, or statutes, often did not advance the cause the same way. Clay chose the best means to the end. In so doing, he often left the impression that he appealed more to the emotions than to the law. But had Clay simply been a good orator in the courtroom, senator and then US attorney general John Breckinridge would not have left his cases with the twenty-three-year-old lawyer when Breckinridge departed for Washington. Nor would US Supreme Court justice Thomas Todd of Kentucky have selected Clay to be his personal counsel for a trial (which Clay won). Nor would Thomas Jefferson have engaged Clay for a major case. Nor would James Morrison, one of the wealthiest men in Kentucky, have made Clay his executor. Nor would Transylvania University have made the twenty-eight-year-old a law professor at the school (where he taught for three years). Nor would President John Quincy Adams have offered Clay a seat on the Supreme Court (which Clay declined). That does not mean that Clay matched the best legal minds of his generation. But Clay was not an ill-informed lawyer who relied only on his oratory to win. His knowledge of the law served him well in several areas.[43]

Clay proved to be particularly well-versed in the legal quagmire of Kentucky land law. One early visitor had noted that Kentuckians "would hardly know how to buy a piece of land without involving themselves in a lawsuit, often ruinous, always long and wearing." A study that appeared the same year Clay came to the commonwealth concluded that land grants had been issued for twice as much land as existed in the state. Such a "complicated calamity" meant much work for attorneys, and much income for good ones. Clay quickly prospered—so much so that in 1805 a brother-in-law wrote him that "some accounts assure us that you are acquiring money as fast as you can count it." That seemed only a slight exaggeration. Generally, attorneys took land cases in exchange for a percentage of the property, if successful. Through his land cases, Clay received a large portion of the over ten thousand acres he owned by 1808. Such wealth could provide security should he choose to pursue a political career.[44]

If lawsuits over land initially represented the most important part of his practice, they did not prove to be the only lucrative cases he accepted. Clay spent much time collecting fees owed to businessmen back in the East, usually taking 5 percent of anything he gained for them, while also winning their goodwill for his own later political efforts. He also qualified as executor of his father-in-law's sizable estate, and similarly served as executor of James Morrison's even larger estate. In the latter situation, Clay kept 5 percent of any continuing receipts gathered on behalf of the estate. By July 1827, for instance, he had earned $2,901 from just those efforts, in a time when he calculated that the most successful attorneys in the state made from $4,000 to $5,000 from all their cases in a single year.[45]

Clay's rising stature as a lawyer, as well as his frequent trips to Washington, DC, later, made him a favorite choice as an attorney to take appeals to the US Supreme Court. He first appeared before the justices in 1807, at the age of thirty, and still had cases before them forty-five years later. In between, Clay appeared on a regular basis and won many of his appeals. It did not hurt that he and Chief Justice Marshall both had been students of Wythe. Clay apparently was also the first person to appear before that body as a friend of the court. Those Supreme Court cases usually provided particularly good remuneration, and Clay's fees rose in proportion to his prominence. By the 1840s, Clay could collect a fee of $5,000 for a successful appeal of a case, and later won a decision that brought $8,000.[46]

Clay also took selected criminal cases, almost always in defense of a client. While some debate exists as to whether he ever lost a capital criminal case, it does seem clear that in the last forty-seven years of his life, he never did. A person who could persuade—and pay—Clay to take his or her case had an excellent chance of securing a dismissal, a hung jury, or a "not guilty" decision. Actually, no matter the kind of case involved, Clay won. In his home area of Fayette, Clay seemed almost invincible. In a random selection of cases, he won twenty-nine of thirty he argued between 1798 and

1811. Given those statistics, the comments later recounted in the *Lexington Reporter* seemed to be a commonplace perception: "Well neighbor, the court has decided against you?" asked one man. His friend answered: "Yes, but if I could have got Henry Clay on my side things would not have been so." In fact, by 1806, knowledgeable observers recognized Clay, not even thirty years old, as the best lawyer in the state. Attorneys George Nicholas and John Breckinridge had died by then, James Brown had moved to Louisiana, and another rival, Felix Grundy, would leave for Tennessee two years later. One lawyer acknowledged Clay's status when he wrote, "It gives me real pleasure to hear from every quarter that you stand in Kentucky at the head o[f our] profession."[47]

By the first decade of the nineteenth century, then, Clay had already accomplished a great deal. He had earned an education, had married well, and had forged a successful law practice. Clay and his growing hometown seemed well matched for one another, with each reflecting some of the other's strengths and weaknesses. At the same time, a kind of legend had already begun to form around the larger-than-life persona that was Henry Clay. It was time now to take those talents to another arena, at last.

2

Politics

SOMETHING IN THE VERY ATMOSPHERE of Kentucky and in the very blood of an attorney seemed to produce a need to run for office. Almost as soon as he arrived in his new home, Henry Clay breathed that heady air and soon became intoxicated with public life. Once in that rarified world, he never really could leave it. Like other young men of his era, Clay had seen the path of the law as the surest route to political success. But, like them, he also found politics could prove to be a tortuous and tricky road, in Kentucky and in the United States.

By the time of Clay's arrival in 1797, aspects of the more egalitarian attitudes of the frontier, which could elevate talented members of that rougher society, such as Daniel Boone, to leadership positions, still remained strong. At the same time, many of those attitudes warred with outlooks prevalent in the second wave of settlement, in which lawyers, planters, and professional men dominated. Through the state's early period, both elements had always been present, for rising aristocratic types had been in Kentucky from the start, claiming the land, seeking to lead, trying to build a new state. But those on the frontier initially supported leaders who could defend them, rather than those who could lecture them. They selected natural leaders over self-proclaimed ones and listened to political voices that defended the rights of the common man over the rights of the wealthy. That frontier never rejected the beliefs and cultures from which it sprang, yet at the same time, Kentucky's history had produced a hybrid society, with roots firmly planted both in America's past and in its future.

Almost immediately, Clay stepped into that evolving political debate. Some Kentuckians favored a revision of the state's first constitution, which provided for indirect election of the senate and governor and a nonelective judiciary. Voters sought a stronger voice in government; some even called for emancipation of the slaves. To established leaders like John Breckinridge and George Nicholas, no convention should occur. Such demands threatened to unleash what Breckinridge called "the halcyon dogs of anarchy." He warned former Governor Isaac Shelby that discontented, "beardless boys" with "little to risque" advocated those dangerous changes.[1]

Clay seemed to be in that category of the discontented. Writing as "Scaevola" in the April 1798 *Kentucky Gazette*, the just-turned-twenty-one-year-old Clay placed himself squarely in the reform camp. Some aristocrats warned that convention delegates could do "wicked" things, said Clay, but such talk paid "poor compliment to the discernment and integrity of the people." Trust their voice, modify corrupt institutions, and institute change, he counseled. Clay supported a gradual emancipation of slaves, for the institution produced evil for the bondsmen, the master, and the state. Beyond that, Clay called for the abolition or reform of the state senate, a body that he considered contrary to republican ideals. "The spirit of democracy" did not require a body that spoke for the nobility; one house should represent all people. Vote for a convention, he concluded. In May, Kentuckians did just that. The next year, as the voting neared for the selection of delegates to the convention, "Scaevola" wrote again, in more general terms, though still calling for gradual emancipation and for a bigger share for "the poorman" in government.[2]

In the end, both sides won out in the eventual convention of 1799. A spirit of accommodation and compromise prevailed. In the new document, both the governor and the senator would now be popularly elected, the chief executive's powers would be more limited because he could serve only one term, and the judiciary would be subject to greater controls. However, the senate had not been abolished, the slave system was continued, and the county court system had actually been made less democratic. In the end, the constitution quieted the discontented, but it left power basically with the same people who had controlled political life when the debate started. Clay watched those unfolding developments and learned.[3]

In his second public stand on a political issue, the youth who had criticized elder statesmen Breckinridge and Nicholas soon found himself supporting them in another controversy. Federalist passage in the US Congress of the Alien and Sedition Acts in June and July 1798 brought near-instant opposition in Kentucky. Clay heard angry citizens criticize the broad arrest powers, the sweeping limits on free expression, and the repression of civil liberties as unconstitutional and dictatorial actions from an authoritarian government. That opposition assumed a face when George Nicholas addressed a large gathering and denounced the acts. The movement found its voice, however, when the cries of "Clay!" brought him forward to give the first of many political speeches. His arguments energized his audience, but the force of his words almost stunned them. When Clay finished, only silence followed. It was as if the masses wanted more and they could not believe the magical moment had ended. Then they began to applaud, then cheer, then roar their approval. The crowd put their heroes Nicholas and Clay on their shoulders, carried them to a waiting carriage, and paraded them through the streets for all to honor. Heady stuff at age twenty-one.[4]

All those events marked the culmination of a very busy and important 1798 for Clay. He had gained admission to the Kentucky bar, penned a major address during the constitutional revision question, and earned the accolades of the populace for his forceful speech on the Alien and Sedition Acts. Over the next five years, he would marry, build up his law practice, and solidify his place in his new hometown. The only foray into formal politics came in 1800, when Clay sought to fill a vacancy in the clerkship of the state senate, though he failed in the pursuit. But in those years, he was building his base, his goodwill, and his fortune.[5]

The first major biography of Henry Clay appeared in 1831, on the eve of his second presidential race. In it, author George Prentice told the story of how Clay first achieved political office. In his telling, Clay had gone to Olympia Springs in Bath County in 1803. Relaxing there, men might play cards into the evening, sleep late the next morning, enjoy a leisurely breakfast, converse with the ladies, fish, go on carriage rides, take the mineral springs, eat some more, then dance in a spacious ballroom, before the cards called again. According to Clay's biographer, in that stress-free time of rest and relaxation, Clay learned that in his absence from Lexington, and unknown to him, his friends had entered his name as a candidate for the legislature. At that time, polling took place over three days, and Clay returned to Lexington for the third day of voting. He found himself trailing the other candidates, who had attacked and conspired against him. It so angered Clay that he made a few cutting remarks about them and a few positive ones on his own behalf. He admitted to his youth—age twenty-six—and inexperience, and stressed that he had not sought the office. But he also indicated that since his name had been entered into the fray, he did not seek to lose. He appealed to those who had not yet voted and, said his biographer, "was subsequently carried, almost by acclamation." He had won thanks to "his political virtue."⁶

Such an account fit perfectly with the times. Voters did not want candidates to be ambitious and seek the office but, rather, wanted the office to find the virtuous man. In the biographer's story, Clay's friends nominated him and he had no desire for the post, but when unfair tactics aroused him, honor declared that he speak out. No questionable electioneering tactics, no overwhelming ambition, colored his canvas. The innocent youth won by the clear vote of a proud people. In the America of republican virtue and democratic spirit, that narrative held great appeal.

But was it true? Clay did earn deep friendships and his compatriots might have nominated him without his knowledge. And victory in a Kentucky election might conceivably result from one speech on the final day of polling. But more often, a much more complex set of circumstances and strategies brought victory. Clay knew that, for while an oligarchical county court system controlled the election apparatus, the elections them-selves were among the broadest and most democratic in the United States. Many celebrated the openness of the system, where basically all free white males could pay the poll tax and then declare their preferences at an elec-tion. With votes cast orally, in the presence of one's peers, in essence all present knew a man's choice. At the same time, recorders of the votes kept a running total, so at any time during the three-day election the candidates or their allies could know how the vote stood. Both of those factors con-tributed to voter irregularities. Candidates who trailed going into the third day—as Clay had—might make special efforts to bring in voters from the hinterlands of the precinct—or even beyond. The length of voting made it easy for "floaters" to cast votes in several counties. Some candidates treated citizens to free drinks, or more. A newspaper editor noted that over the three days of the election, "whiskey and apple toddy flew through our cities and villages like the Euphrates through ancient Babylon." After some elections, voters' eyes would be "reddened for months to come." All that made it easier for Clay to believe accounts of voter irregularity used against him in his later national races.⁷

A disgruntled and unsuccessful candidate for office described a typical Kentucky election of the era. As the defeated man explained it, candidates usually appealed to "the passions and prejudices, not the reason of the voter." They used flattery and false facts, and "the most shameful political and religious hypocrisy" to gain sympathy. Some told jokes and acted almost as jesters. But what bothered the writer most of all was that "a pack of cards, a keg of whisky, and a game cock, have on some occasions . . . been a good electioneering apparatus." All that might push the legal envelope, for such tactics could result in the recording of more votes for a candidate than there were registered voters in a county. In the 1832 presidential race, for example, Oldham County would achieve unwanted notoriety and some kind of Kentucky record for casting a herculean 163 percent of its potential vote.[8]

Candidates seldom just showed up and won. The process usually spread over a much longer period. One losing candidate averred that the successful politician had to start campaigning a year before, to the neglect of any private life or business. Moreover, office-seekers usually sought to build up an undercurrent of support by trying to attend every county court session, every public barbecue, every militia muster. Given the existing system, the story that Clay's biographer told of his hero's election in 1803 seems even more remarkable, for it included no political campaigning over time, no solicitation of the important city systems or county courts, no "treating" of voters, no appeals to militia groups. Perhaps the biographer's tale, as told in 1831, represented a retelling of the history of Clay's first election to fit the image Americans wanted of their leaders. Or perhaps Clay had been too confident of winning and had to rush back to secure his victory. Or perhaps the story might even be true.[9]

Whatever the case, the twenty-six-year-old Henry Clay was elected to the Kentucky House of Representatives in 1803, and that marked the beginning of almost a half century of political life. In that time, he would never be defeated in his home district or in an election in his adopted state. The next year, Clay won reelection to the one-year term and did so again in 1805. He resigned during that session to take another political post, then returned to reclaim the seat in 1807. The following January, members voted him Speaker of the Kentucky House. Two years later, Clay left state office behind for good and shifted his attentions to the national scene. But during his years of service in the state capital, Clay learned many useful political lessons.[10]

First, Clay learned a lesson about the art of the possible. In the selection process for US senator in the 1804–1805 session, Clay's own decision seemed easy, for the incumbent, John Brown of Frankfort, was his brother-in-law's brother. Beyond such family ties, Brown had served well as president pro tempore of the US Senate just the year before. Selected by the legislature rather than by popular vote, he now needed a majority in the General Assembly to return him for a third term. But regionalism and power politics quickly complicated the race. Those outside the central Bluegrass sought a greater voice in state decision making, and they united to support the candidacy of a man more favorable to their cause, former Speaker of the Kentucky House John Adair. The entry of Judge J. Buckner Thruston of Lexington further splintered the central Kentucky bloc. For six ballots, the issue remained deadlocked, with Adair leading each time and Thruston a poor third. Clay could see the political handwriting on the election wall, and realized his candidate Brown could not win. But he did not want the opposition to take the prize and leave Clay and his allies without influence. So on the seventh ballot, Clay threw Brown's support to Thruston and his fellow Lexingtonian then won. People praised the "artful management of H. Clay." Clay had emerged on the winning side, had earned Thruston's support for his switch in time, and had learned how to bargain for votes.[11]

Clay's second foray into the morass of Kentucky politics showed the clear importance of understanding the opposition, both its strengths and its weaknesses. It also demonstrated to Clay that a change in tactics, even late in the game, could seize victory out of defeat. When critics, led by Felix Grundy, sought to repeal the charter of the state's first bank—saying

The earliest-known image of Clay (about 1805, age twenty-eight) shows some of the charm and appeal that won him friends and allies throughout his life. *Courtesy of Ashland, the Henry Clay Estate*

it corrupted republican virtues and aided the commercial classes over the yeoman farmers—Clay arose as the bank's champion. He held stock in the lucrative financial institution, and his father-in-law sat on its board. But Clay also spoke for its interests as one who argued that properly constituted banks were crucial to the growth and betterment of society. Moreover, he considered repeal unconstitutional. Clay matched Grundy's passionate words with ones of equal fervor, as one satirist noted: "Thus did Felix and Henry assail the chiefs of the people with cunning speeches for many days." The bank survived by a single vote. But the next year, with a different General Assembly, Grundy won repeal. The governor, however, vetoed the act as an unconstitutional attack on the sanctity of the charter. The lower house overrode the veto and the bank seemed doomed to defeat.[12]

At that moment, card player Clay pulled out his trump card. Many of the supporters of repeal came from the section of Kentucky called South of Green River. Heavily settled by squatters, the "Southside" had been the beneficiary of a 1795 legislative homestead act that gave them the right to purchase that land at a very low price. But even that created payment problems for many of the poorer settlers. Southsiders united in getting the time to pay up extended to four years, then twelve. Over and over they avoided paying the state by restructuring their debt. The amount owed Kentucky had become sizable. That situation gave Henry Clay the opening he needed. As the legislature awaited the Senate's action on the veto, Clay introduced a bill to compel immediate payment of the Green River debt. He made his message clear: if you override the veto, we have the votes to use on the debt issue. Given that option, the Southsiders chose their land over the bank. The veto remained in force, the debt continued, and so did the bank. Clay's cloakroom maneuvering had staved off defeat by one vote in the first instance. In the second, his knowledge of the weakness in his opponents' armor allowed him to change the focus of the debate and thus break up the majority coalition. The rising politician had learned valuable lessons. Now he would take that knowledge to the national level, for in early 1810 he was going to Washington as US senator.[13]

It was not the first time Clay had served in the Senate. In November 1806, the General Assembly had selected him to fill the remaining few months of the term vacated by the resignation of John Adair. That post would provide travel funds for a trip to the capital, where he could use his free time to argue lucrative cases before the Supreme Court as well. Clay had accepted the opportunity. But, once in the District, Henry Clay had

found that he liked the national spotlight and had looked for the right opportunity to return.[14]

But that brief senatorial stint in 1806–1807 would later haunt presidential candidate Clay. The US Constitution requires that "no person shall
be a Senator who shall not have attained the age of thirty years." When
Clay had produced his credentials and had taken his seat in the Senate on
December 29, 1806, he had fallen 105 days short of meeting that qualifica-
tion. As his grandson noted, "This disability seems not to have occurred
to him, or to his friends in the Kentucky legislature." Or if it did occur to
them, they seemed to think it unimportant in the general scheme of things.
Clay himself would later remark defensively that he never took an oath
regarding his age and that he stood only "a few months" short of the re-
quirement, after all. When an ally quizzed him about the discrepancy, Clay
laughingly answered, "I think, my young friend, . . . we may as well omit
any reference to my supposed juvenile indiscretions." That statement reveals
much about Clay. As an attorney, he certainly knew the Constitution and
its requirements. Yet he chose to ignore that, accept the seat, and go to
Washington, despite any potential consequences. To those who would later
say that Clay would do anything to satisfy his ambition, that action just
seemed in character.[15]

In later Congresses, when senators or representatives were selected before reaching the required age, they generally were permitted to take the
seat only after their birthdays made them constitutionally eligible to serve.
Had that practice been followed in Clay's case, he never would have served,
for the unexpired term ended before his April birthday. But in the few
months that he did sit in the Senate, Clay had acquired a taste for national
politics. He told those back home that he had been very well received by
his new peers and that various members had praised his stands in debates.
Already sure of himself by his Kentucky legislative experience, he had not
stood by quietly as a first-time member. At the same time, the new senator
had admitted that the session had not been as interesting as he had hoped.
In March 1807, he had ended his first service in Congress and returned to
Kentucky.[16]

But the lure of political office remained and so, more than two years later,
in December 1809, the political paths of Buckner Thruston and Henry Clay
crossed again. Thruston had resigned as US senator to take a judicial post,
and his vacant seat beckoned to Clay. Perhaps a grateful Thruston gave his
support in the legislature to the man who had helped elect him; the record
remains silent. But in January 1810, the *Kentucky Reporter* noted that Henry

Clay had been easily selected to fill Thruston's unexpired term, to end in March 1811. When Clay finally took his seat in February 1810, it would mark the real start of his career in Washington. Over the next forty-two years, he would be either in Congress or in the diplomatic service for all but a decade.[17]

As it turned out, just getting to Washington, DC, proved taxing. Without steamboats or railroads, and with limited good roads, the trip from Kentucky took some three weeks. An English traveler of the era described the "frequently intoxicated" stagecoach drivers as "rough and reckless." Accidents proved frequent, discomfort constant. But once a traveler overcame all that, he found a capital city that seemed almost like America itself—a place of high expectations and great promise, but still raw, unfinished, and growing. Charles Dickens called it a "City of Magnificent Intentions." Another visitor at the same time termed it "a struggling village." It was both. Arriving by stage, Clay went down wide, unpaved streets, some already partly overgrown with weeds. Few sidewalks existed, no lamps lit the way at night, and cow paths often offered the only connections across deep ravines or from one place to another. Lexington had better roads and sidewalks than the nation's capital. Amid Washington's dusty avenues, in dry weather, or muddy streets on wet days, pigs, cows, and other animals wandered the roads.[18]

Those streets divided and united a different city. A congressman in the 1820s called it "the city of a *Great Nation*, . . . [but] by no means a *great city*." He praised the capitol and other public edifices, but carped at the distances between buildings "scattered over a great space." Similar words came over a decade later from the Englishman Lord Carlisle, who called it a strange place, a "city of magnificent distances." To his mind, "it looks as if it had rained houses at random," yet at the same time "very handsome" government offices stood all around. The grand, unfinished capitol dome stood over a mile away from the President's House, for example, with little in between except thickets and moors. Those marshes here and there around the city, when combined with the familiar flooding and poor sanitation, provided good breeding grounds for flies and mosquitoes and homes for rats and disease. All that made for an unhealthy place for some thirteen thousand people in 1820. As one Englishman concluded, "The capital wants a city."[19]

Once in the nation's political heart, Clay had to find a place to stay. Because few congressmen brought their families, the place took on the all-male atmosphere of a fraternity. An Englishman described the members of Congress "packed together in large and very inferior boarding houses."

The close quarters, the heat or cold, the sameness of companionship, the sometimes bad food, the absence of families—all could create a volatile mix. In that small world, whether in boardinghouses or in Congress, angry outbursts, words uttered in haste, and bitter barbs would all be remembered and magnified.[20]

For Clay and others, a few outside distractions provided variations in the daily theme. Congressmen might entertain themselves by attending the races, or going to the theater, or visiting gambling and other houses, few of repute. In that transient society, most formal social activities centered on politically inspired gatherings, such as what Clay called the "gay and agreeable" Wednesday evening parties of Dolley Madison. (She later would write to her brother-in-law and former US representative Richard Cutts, "Send my love to Mr. Clay. . . . He, whose wisdom, delicacy, and friendship I know well.") In such settings, unattached women might be present and gallant gentlemen would escort them, all done in total innocence—or not. The combination of gambling, liquor, and boredom did challenge the morality of many. A member of Congress found life there "a continual round of dissipation and gaiety," while a clergyman visited the District and wrote home despairing of "this hotbed of politics & sin."[21]

For most congressmen, the main form of entertainment centered less on sin and more on the ungodly politics in Congress. In the dead space between political battles, solons would recount in their boardinghouses or in taverns each argument, each jest, each slight. They also discussed the physical setting and its challenges. The capitol itself, though incomplete, could be impressive at first glance. Lord Carlisle found the classic little senate chamber "handsome and convenient." But on closer observation, flaws soon appeared. One observer noted the tobacco-covered floor of the rotunda, while another pointed out each congressman's "spitting-box, to which he does not always confine himself." Clay and one-time messmate John C. Calhoun both tried to avoid night sessions in the chambers, for the languid, smoke-filled air seemed almost impossible to breathe and produced what Clay termed "serious injury to health." Fireplaces and chimneys generated numerous dangerous blazes. The House of Representatives had a leaky roof and poor acoustics—"the worst room for hearing I ever was in," a visitor commented. Adding to that situation, congressmen did not have offices, so they used their desks for that purpose. As debates went on, some members wrote letters, others spoke with friends, and a few even rested their eyes. The disarray, noise, and poor acoustics challenged even the most dedicated listeners. In that complex, yet simple world of Washington politics, newcomer Henry Clay thrived, once again. He excelled in the small gatherings or at the social parties, and he did not find the halls of Congress much different from what he had known in Frankfort.[22]

Mr. Clay also found himself in Congress at a particularly momentous time, and that allowed him to become a spokesman for a cause. Engaged in the Napoleonic Wars, Great Britain and France both interfered with American shipping and ignored neutral rights. But with Britain the dominant naval power, most transgressions fell on its shoulders. As the United States struggled to find a way to balance concerns about rights and honor with its desire to avoid war, Clay increasingly began to offer his thoughts. In a major address in February 1810, less than three weeks after he took his seat, a confident Clay stressed that the unusual times demanded atypical actions. For years America had sought to protect its rights, he noted. Nonimportation acts, embargo acts, nonintercourse acts—all showed sincere attempts to avoid war. But when those fail, when the nation's reputation falters, then, he proclaimed, "I am for resistance by the *sword*." Though calling himself a man desiring harmony, Clay admitted he now preferred "the troubled ocean of war, demanded by the honor and independence of the country, . . . to the tranquil putrescent pool of ignominious peace." Britain's lawless and arbitrary acts on the high seas required different action.[23]

Some said the nation could not carry on a war, that it lacked the funds to do so. "Are we," Clay asked, "to be governed by the low, groveling parsimony of the counting room?" Others cried out that nothing could be gained from war with such a power. Nothing? "The conquest of Canada is in your power." He boasted it would be an easy thing, for "the militia of Kentucky are alone competent to place Montreal and Upper Canada at your feet." The Indian threat to the West must also be ended, just as the threat to maritime liberties must be met. A spirit of militarism might result, he noted, which could "eventuate in the aggrandizement of some ambitious chief" who would prostrate American liberty. But he did not expect that. Some military ardor might be needed to wash away what he viewed as a rising "spirit of avarice." No conservative speaking there. Then Clay strongly stated the core of his argument, in ringing words: "If we surrender without a struggle to maintain our rights, we forfeit the respect of the world, and what is infinitely worse, of ourselves."[24]

Clay thus strode to the forefront of the emerging group known as the War Hawks. He had demonstrated by the power of his words and the vigor of his arguments that this new senator from Kentucky would be a force on the national stage, perhaps even presidential material in the future. Later, Clay called on the United States to focus also on Spanish Florida, for the nation should include all territory east of the Mississippi River, "and some of the territories north of us also." He further suggested that Cuba should not be held by foreign powers, because its position in the Gulf would place American trade from New Orleans at the mercy of that nation. At this stage of his career, Clay's vision of America included a nation that stretched from the icy north of Canada to the warm southern climates of Cuba and westward into the Louisiana Territory. Over the next two years, he would push hard to redeem national honor against Britain, while not coincidentally furthering his dream of a greater America, one that would stand tall among its peers—if indeed, it would have any peers, in his view of the future.[25]

Given Clay's rising success in the Senate, many observers expected him to seek the full term in the fall of 1810, and to win. Clay himself doubted he would even have any opposition. But, to the surprise of many, in May of that year Clay announced instead that he would seek a seat in the House of Representatives. Publicly, he promised voters only two things: that he would follow his previous political principles and "promote the welfare of the nation." When queried by friends about his decision, Clay confessed his partiality for the "turbulence" of the House over the "solemn stillness" of the upper chamber. He acknowledged the likelihood of his Senate election by legislators he knew, as opposed to risking himself before the vote of the people in his district. As it turned out, Clay won his race in August, unopposed. Then, when the new representative stepped on the floor of the House, something historic happened.[26]

When the first US Congress assembled in 1789, none of its members, of course, had served in that body. In selecting a Speaker, they by necessity chose a neophyte to the House. In the subsequent history of the House of Representatives, that has happened only two other times. The second occurred on November 4, 1811. On the first day he set foot in the House as a member of that body, Henry Clay was selected Speaker of the House, the most important position in that body. By a sizable first-ballot majority, fellow representatives chose the thirty-four-year-old to preside. Almost immediately he transformed the office of Speaker.[27]

Over the next fourteen years, he served almost continuously in that post, winning reelection with virtually no opposition much of the time. For well over a century, no Speaker held the office longer than Clay did.

Even his enemies conceded that Clay discharged his duties in an exemplary fashion. John Tyler recalled of those times: "Over the House . . . presided one who seemed formed for the station, and the station made for him. To commanding talents he united an urbanity with a decision of character, which commanded the respect of the House." Though his colleagues might get angry with Representative Clay, they trusted and respected Speaker Clay.[28]

With a membership that ranged from 143 to 213 during the time Clay served as Speaker, the House seemed huge compared to the 34 person Senate he had left. Moreover, it often appeared rudderless. With no majority or minority leaders, the body needed guidance and Clay—willingly—supplied that. In past Congresses, the Speaker had mostly functioned simply as a parliamentarian. But the new Speaker now served as party leader as well. Clay did not just preside; he led. And if he could lead that body well, perhaps he could lead the nation.[29]

Clay's success as Speaker resulted from several factors. First, he displayed firmness and courage when challenged. Second, Clay proved to be, indeed, a fine parliamentarian with an excellent grasp of the details of the rules. None of his decisions from the chair was overridden. He followed the advice he later gave another Speaker: do not explain the reasons for your rulings. "The House," he emphasized, "will sustain your decision, but there will always be men to cavil and quarrel over your reasons." But Clay did not just follow the established rules of debate; he initiated new tactics as well. No limits on discussion existed until 1841, so endless talk seemed all too often the rule. The House had difficulty getting things done. Clay as Speaker got Congress to approve the practice of limiting debate by using the device of Calling the Previous Question. If approved, that effectively closed discussion and started the vote. Such actions brought even his frequent critic Thomas Hart Benton to compliment Clay as "one of the most skilled parliamentarians . . . in America or Europe."[30]

But Clay's greatest strength as Speaker centered on the perception that he acted fairly in his rulings and in his committee assignments. The Speaker, Clay said, must be impartial, patient, firm, courteous, good-tempered, "cool and unshaken amidst all the storm of debate." He largely achieved those goals. Congressman Willie Mangum of North Carolina explained Clay's recurring selection as Speaker as a result of the Kentuckian's "superior qualifications and transcendent abilities" in conducting the office. Clay's adroit manner of managing the deliberations, together with "manners most dignified & yet the most fascinating & popular," wrote Mangum, made him an excellent Speaker. That popularity might prove useful, should the House ever be called on to be a part of the presidential decision-making process.[31]

If Clay as Speaker did not overtly use the powers of his office for his own programmatic or personal gain, that does not mean that he did not frequently benefit from his actions. Selecting people from various board-inghouse blocs or from different sections of the country might help build diversity in committees, but it also broadened Clay's ties and potential base. Similarly, picking freshman members to sit in those councils might give committees a nice mix of young and old, but it also afforded the Speaker a way to reward protégés or make others converts to his cause. Nor did Clay completely ignore politics in his committee selections. In some instances, supporters of his view might well be underrepresented, but in others they could be overrepresented. Often on some important committee, Clay would make certain that a majority favored his stand when a key question arose. He could remain truly impartial most times, garnering political popularity as a result, but in other instances could be subtly partial to his politics while retaining the impression of evenhandedness. When all those elements are combined with the fact that Clay insisted on his right to speak on issues as a member—apparently the first Speaker to do so—and thus often engaged in vigorous debates that could end in hurt feelings, Clay's success as Speaker becomes even more remarkable.[32]

Through the force of his will, the power of his personality, the strength of his parliamentary skills, and the fairness of his actions, Clay became one of the greatest Speakers in the history of the House of Representatives and one of the most powerful leaders of the nation between 1811 and 1825. And as Speaker, he won one of the most prized rewards given by Congress—its esteem.[33]

Both through his prerogatives as Speaker in 1811 and his abilities as a member of the House, Henry Clay used the office and the moment to lead the House of Representatives. Because almost half its members had not been present in the previous Congress, that gave the Speaker an even greater opportunity to mold them, but at the same time, as he later recalled, they represented the greatest galaxy of "eminent and able men" ever assembled in that body. Men such as Richard M. Johnson of Kentucky, John C. Calhoun of South Carolina, John Randolph of Virginia, and Felix Grundy, now of Tennessee, would not follow Clay without reason. Yet most did ally with him on the key issue of whether to declare war, because his beliefs and theirs coincided. They went down the war road together.[34]

Clay continued to speak out for more forceful resistance to British actions. If such national degradation took place, then "war . . . becomes a blessing, and peace a curse." To continue to act passively invited only "disbasement, dishonor, and disgrace." Britain's goal was to humiliate America, humble a rival, and destroy the nation's spirit. The United States, stressed Clay, must secure the respect of all countries, and not fear fighting to do so: "What are we to gain by war, has been emphatically asked? . . . What are we not to lose by peace? Commerce, character, a nation's best treasure, honor!" An insulted nation cried out for redress, for justice, for its rights. Clay agreed with the sentiments expressed by Kentucky governor Charles Scott in his call for war: "We have nothing so much to fear as from ourselves."[35]

Clay understood the possible terrible outcome of a conflict, but as he told a Maryland ally, war seemed the only alternative except submission. Clay saw his efforts bear fruit when a divided Congress declared war in June 1812. A month later, Clay responded to the first of seventeen after-dinner toasts and summarized why he had supported the then-popular declaration of war: "Our multiple wrongs—the peaceful farmer bleeding beneath the tomahawk—the mariner no longer finding sanctuary under our national flag—the shackles imposed on our commerce, imperiously called upon him to act." At that moment, Henry Clay stood very high in the political affections of his countrymen. It seemed a major step forward for someone with ambitions for higher office.[36]

Then the war came. Clay anticipated that several things would happen. While disappointed in the prewar efforts to build up the military forces, he nevertheless expected the American military to perform well and achieve much. Given Britain's continuing battles with Napoleon, he did not envision England's sending many troops to the New World, just some naval forces. In that scenario, America would be victorious on the land, the Kentucky militia would seize Canada, the army would defeat the Indians, and national honor would be redeemed. But, in the end, little of that turned out as Clay foresaw.[37]

Clay would emphasize that leadership failed at several levels. He greatly admired the soft-spoken, diminutive president James Madison, but found the emotionless and intellectual commander-in-chief better suited to peace-time pursuits: "Mr. Madison is wholly unfit for the storms of war. Nature has cast him in too benevolent a mould." Those the administration picked to lead the army also concerned Clay. He warned Secretary of State James Monroe that General William Hull, commander of American forces in Detroit, should be replaced. Hull, he said, had lost the confidence of the soldiers, had doubtful fidelity to the cause, and had few attributes of leadership. Unfortunately, Hull proved Clay correct and surrendered his large army to the British in August, almost without firing a shot. That "disgrace of Detroit" confounded Clay's expectations for the western campaign. After that, a series of defeats and victories followed. Clay lost a brother-in-law at the bloody River Raisin, an event that reflected his state's involvement in the conflict in the West. Two of every three eligible men from the commonwealth participated in the fighting. Many lost their lives. According to one estimate, of all Americans killed in the War of 1812, some 64 percent of the dead had served from Kentucky. Clay's state eventually played a major role in helping clear the Northwest of British and Indian influence, but the conquest of Canada remained a dream.[38]

Clay had also anticipated the nation would unite behind the war effort. That did not occur, either. Soon after the start of the conflict, Monroe worried about the "inveterate toryism" of the New England states, while the next January Clay harshly criticized "the parasites of opposition." They plotted dismemberment of the Union, he alleged. Nor was all that just partisan wordsmithing. Bankers in the Northeast often bought British bonds, not American ones. They traded with the enemy. And continuing American defeats brought threats of disunion. As Governor Isaac Shelby, Clay's relative, wrote in April 1814, the United States should pursue peace forcefully, because the "ruinous" war meant "we are literally, 'a house divided against itself.'"[39]

Disgrace and defeat in military matters, and disloyalty and disunion in civil ones, meant that Clay's hopes for victory could not stand. Then the final leg of his tripartite expectations collapsed when Napoleon abdicated in April 1814, ending the European war and freeing up the large and battle-hardened British forces to concentrate on America. It was symbolic that, while Congress and the executive branch fiddled away, Washington burned under the British torch in August 1814. The United States had achieved some victories, but the future looked bleak, both for the nation and for War Hawk Clay's future political hopes.

Yet Clay quickly recovered and got the political best of both worlds: he helped start a war that was popular in some circles, and now he helped end one that was unpopular in most. On January 19, 1814, Henry Clay stepped down as Speaker of the House and began preparations to serve in a new position, as one of eventually five peace commissioners sent to negotiate with their English counterparts. Some of the Federalist press immediately derided the selection, calling Clay "a back-woodsman, a determined war-hawk, who knows, nor cares anything about 'sailors' rights.'" They doubted such a person could procure peace, and if he did, it would be a dishonorable, "disgraceful" treaty. As it turned out, Clay's selection would prove to be very important to the outcome—and for Clay himself.[40]

A month after his resignation as Speaker, Clay and fellow commissioner Jonathan Russell sailed from New York and after a sea voyage of more than six weeks, they arrived in Gothenburg, Sweden, the expected site of meetings, just after Clay's thirty-seventh birthday. There, Clay learned of Napoleon's sudden abdication. In London, another peace commissioner, the capable Albert Gallatin, wrote of the shocking "total change in our affairs," for Britain's large and battle-tested army stood ready to meet America's poorly prepared forces, to chastise their American cousins. Negotiations might begin, but Gallatin indicated his belief that the English would not make concessions and would not be concerned if the talks failed. Clay, who had hoped some American victories before he left would strengthen the US position, now quickly recognized the implications of France's surrender. And so, after fifty fruitless days in Sweden, Clay set out through Germany for the new negotiation site, British-held Ghent. There he met the man most expected would be the spokesman and leader of the American commissioners.[41]

At age forty-seven, John Quincy Adams had lived a decade longer than Clay and had experienced much more of the world of diplomacy. Yet the seasoned veteran and the neophyte diplomat would each become key leaders of the American delegation. The two differed greatly. Adams kept a detailed diary, which has endeared him to historians ever since, but which also allowed his viewpoints to be better represented in those accounts. Many have found it hard to step back from the Adams account and look at the overall story. As a result, Clay's motivations and beliefs remain more hidden from history. But in his diary, Adams indicated that he had heard Clay called one of the "finest temper'd men." If so, he soon questioned his sources, for the two men's temperaments ran to the extremes. Clay considered Adams too much a diplomat, too poor a politician, too little of an advocate for the cause. Adams thought the clearly political and more emotional Clay not diplomatic enough. Both were correct. On the one hand, a delegate noted Adams's pessimism and "gloomy cast" regarding the possibilities of peace. The ever-optimistic Clay, on the other hand, remained much more hopeful. Even the personal habits and schedules of the two seemed vastly different—Clay would play cards, relax, and retire in the early morning hours, whereas Adams prayed, worried, and rose before daybreak.[42]

Yet the two in combination and by accident made a good team. In a sense they acted, sometimes unwittingly, as a kind of hardliner/softliner duo in the negotiations. To the British, Clay would bluster and threaten, Adams would reconcile and reassure. Then they would reverse positions on other issues. It worked. In the end, they won a major, bloodless victory, and Clay added to his stature as a rising politician and statesman.[43]

Clay's knowledge of the political art of compromise, and of human nature, revealed itself clearly at Ghent. While, as one of his fellow peace commissioners said later, Adams and Gallatin seemed willing to have "peace at any rate," Clay made it known that without compromise no peace would result. How much of that represented his real views and how much of that simply was "brag" or bluff is hard to gauge. At times, he had to convince not just the British that he meant what he said but some of his own delegates as well. As Adams noted, "Mr. Clay actually beat again a majority by outbragging [bluffing] us." Tactics learned in the card rooms, the courtroom, and in Congress all helped. In the end, Clay might have retreated from some of his stands, had the British held firm, for he wanted peace also. But better than his fellow commissioners, the Kentuckian sensed that the British had more problems than the others discerned. Yes, the British might hold fast to their demands, in the hope that military victories would gain them further bargaining chips in the diplomatic poker game. But Clay could also both bluff and recognize bluffs, and he could be patient if it meant a winning hand in the end. He recognized that a war-weary and heavily taxed British people needed peace as much as the United States did.[44]

Finally, on Christmas Eve 1814, the American and British peace commissioners signed the Treaty of Ghent, ending the War of 1812. Clay told Monroe that given the "very unfavorable" conditions facing the American delegates, he considered it a good document: "We lose no territory, I think no honor." In truth, what one French diplomat called the "Treaty of Omissions" did little more than return matters to where they were before the war and conclude hostilities. That was about as much as the United States could have expected. The treaty mostly reflected the battle-field stalemate and home-front fatigue. Clay had taken a chance in agreeing to serve as a peace commissioner, for if he failed in that attempt and disaster followed in war, his almost unbroken string of successes would be shattered. As it was, news of the treaty arrived in America soon after the euphoria accompanying the accounts of Andrew Jackson's victory at the Battle of New Orleans. That sequence made it seem that the United States had won the war, and as a result, Clay earned mostly accolades, not jeers, for his role. But, more than that, Henry Clay had surprisingly demonstrated that he could transfer his considerable skills to the diplomatic table. He had been lucky in that his temper and bluffs represented the right tactics at Ghent; that would not always be the case. But, although he and Adams still did not like each other very much, they at least had learned to respect each other's abilities. All that would prove crucial in later decision making, with a presidency at stake.[45]

Clay's diplomatic labors had not ended on Christmas Eve, however. The peace commissioners had decided to defer the difficult discussions of a commercial agreement between the two nations. Now Clay, Gallatin, and the new minister to the Court of St. James, John Quincy Adams, would represent the United States in those talks, in England. The resulting commercial convention of July 3, 1815, ended discriminatory duties and allowed US trade in the East Indies, but remained silent on the more lucrative West Indies trade. Through it all, diplomat Clay had fiercely opposed British demands. But now visitor Clay began to find the English not quite the devils he had portrayed. Ironically, one-time Anglophobe Clay, who would continue to speak against British power and for American hegemony, would become to the English perhaps the most praised of all American leaders during the early years of the republic. While in England, Clay met with royalty and others, seemingly charmed them all, and made many friends. His European encounters soon brought some to refer to him as "Prince Hal." Afterwards, when important British travelers ventured to the United States, many sought out Clay and visited him at his Lexington home. It helped Clay that he had been extremely well compensated by his government. That allowed him to live comfortably in Britain and to entertain well. For the some twenty-one months that Clay served overseas, he received almost $32,000, a princely sum indeed when most congressmen made less than $1,000 per year.[46]

With his second mission accomplished, Clay eagerly headed home. When he returned to Kentucky in November 1815, he had been absent from Lexington for almost two years. But those had been important years for his career. He had seen Europe, met key leaders, forged a peace, and succeeded as a diplomat. All of those would be important assets for a rising politician.[47]

What occurred during the War of 1812 drastically changed Clay. Even before the conflict, he had spoken of the need for the government to be more active in aiding the national economy and growth. But the experiences of the war strengthened that attitude greatly. The poor financial situation of the country, the weak transportation system, the lack of a centralized authority, the divisions within the nation—all told Clay that serious internal weaknesses existed in the infrastructure of the Union. America had been lucky not to lose that war, or to lose its liberty. Clay never modified his belief that the war was a necessary and just one. But the fighting had taught the Kentuckian much, and he never again would be the War Hawk he had been in 1812. He now saw the human costs of war. He knew firsthand the sorrows of widows and children, the losses of friends and neighbors, and the emotional price of conflict. Yet even more, he recognized the dangers war brought to American liberties and the unforeseen circumstances that could arise out of the confusion of strife. Even before the declaration of hostilities, Clay had warned of the threat of executive despotism in emergency situations. But more than that, he worried about the rise of a military dictator leading an army forged out of the crucible of combat. The War of 1812 thus created a whole new Henry Clay, one who now sought compromise over conflict, who advocated territorial expansion by purchase or diplomacy and not war, who supported a stronger national effort to build unity, who defended congressional prerogatives against executive encroachments, who feared militarism. It was also a Clay who recognized that a new, positive spirit prevailed in peacetime America, and that attitude sparked in him great ambitions for his country—and for himself.[48]

Voters had sent Clay back to Congress in 1814, even while he negotiated in Europe. Members of the House immediately chose him once again as Speaker. With Federalists discredited by their wartime actions, Clay's party faced little opposition. He and the Fourteenth Congress then achieved a very strong record of accomplishments. Near the end of his presidency, Madison even offered Clay a position in the cabinet, which he declined. Given the Speaker's power, that would have been a step down. Clay's career instead seemed upward bound without pause. Then he made an almost fatal mistake.[49]

Clay entertained few doubts, he declared, that the Compensation Bill under consideration in Congress represented the best approach. Instead of paying congressmen a per diem and travel expenses, it gave them a retroactive annual salary of $1,500. While that represented a sizable raise from the average of $800 to $900, he deemed it necessary. Otherwise, only the wealthy could afford to run; none of the "poor and the middling classes" could serve. Moreover, increased compensation gave members more independence from the enticements of the executive branches, provided an incentive to end a session sooner rather than just prolong it for the per diem, and reduced legislative turnover. His rational appeals found a receptive audience, and the bill passed. Then all sorts of electoral hell broke loose. Deferential politics would no longer satisfy, as angry voters considered the act a salary grab. Once politically safe congressmen suddenly found themselves facing serious voter antipathy, perhaps for the first time.[50]

So it was with Henry Clay. The campaign of 1816 marked his most serious electoral challenge in Kentucky. Defeat could end his career, or at least seriously impede it. Very soon after passage of the controversial bill, Clay discovered the growing opposition to it, and a new challenger. Attorney John Pope—the brother-in-law to, of all people, John Quincy Adams— had served in the US Senate and represented a serious threat. He and his allies appealed to voters to throw off this man who had given himself a raise, "when the people were burdened with taxes . . . from a war which he himself approved and prompted." The *Western Monitor* criticized the law, passed without consulting voters on the matter. Clay was no republican, it asserted, but rather a spoils man, "fattening on . . . the people."[51]

Clay answered those attacks first with a defense of his actions and then with an offensive outburst. In a July speech he admitted, "We have sinned . . . in making the law retrospective," and later vowed to repeal the law once returned to Congress. But he also stressed his record of service to his constituents and to his country. Once more, however, Clay seized on his opponent's weakness, for Federalist-leaning Pope had supported the hated Alien and Sedition laws. Even worse, Pope had as senator voted against the declaration of war, for which citizens burned him in effigy. Mercilessly presenting Pope almost as a traitor, Clay verbally pummeled him in a joint debate: "[Pope] fell gradually back till he was pressed against the wall and there his conqueror dealt blow after blow upon his defenseless head, till the scene became intensely painful to the spectators. Mr. Clay, finding that it would be inglorious to prolong the strife, turned with dignity away from his fellow foe." But Clay won votes through different approaches as well. A story retold many times recounted how Clay met an old huntsman and longtime supporter who admitted he now opposed Prince Hal because of "that miserable compensation bill." Clay asked him if, as a hunter, he had killed many animals. He had. When your weapon failed to fire, the candidate inquired, "Did you take that faithful rifle and break it all to pieces . . . or did you pick the flint and try it again?" Understanding the point, the hunter agreed, "I'll try you again, give me your hand." Such a combination of appeals made Clay seem unbeatable, even when strapped with an unpopular issue and a strong opponent. In the second-highest turnover in the history of Congress, of the eighty-one congressmen who voted for the Compensation Bill, only fifteen returned to Congress the next session. Clay was one of the fifteen, capturing almost 58 percent of the vote. He had survived. And he would fight on.[52]

Reminded once more that he served at the people's will, but emboldened by his margin of victory, Clay returned to a Congress that included many fresh faces. He also returned under a new president. The first man who would serve as president who had traveled extensively in the West, James Monroe had been governor and US senator before he became secretary of state. Now Monroe came to power amid almost one-party rule in the "Era of Good Feelings." But the new president's actions soon meant that as far as Clay was concerned, few good feelings existed.[53]

Clay had hoped, perhaps had been led to expect, that he would be offered the position of secretary of state in the new administration, a cabinet post that had been the stepping stone to the White House for Jefferson, Madison, and Monroe. Clay thus did not accept with magnanimity the subsequent (and excellent) appointment of New Englander John Quincy Adams. He quickly declined Monroe's peace offering of the post of secretary of war, and then another as minister to the Court of St. James in Britain. Policy differences with the chief executive soon surfaced. The Speaker began to stand more and more as independence advocate and less and less as administration spokesman. In March 1818, Clay told Congress that he would not be compliant with the chief executive just because of Monroe's long service: "I am no groveling sycophant, no mean parasite, no base supplicant at the foot of authority." Few would ever accuse Clay of being any of those things, at any time, to any president. Not for the last time, Clay found himself in frequent opposition to his party's leader. That same year, a Supreme Court justice surveyed the political landscape and concluded that as Monroe lost strength, the House, under Clay, "has absorbed . . . all the effective power of the country." Adams attributed his rival's rising opposition to Clay's desire for higher national office. That may well have been true. But even before a worried Adams penned in his diary those words about a potential competitor, Clay had written to a friend back home, telling how he was "seriously" debating leaving public life. The tranquility of the country meant he could do so without "abandoning my post in an hour of danger." Family responsibilities, "the strong desire to spend more of my time in Kentucky," and the sacrifices he had made to serve the public—all pulled him in that direction, he said. But very soon the nation's tranquility vanished, the hour of danger tolled, and the sacrifices of service increased.[54]

By 1819, a combination of economic events and actions came together to produce a major depression. Only two years before, Clay had written of the "greatest prosperity" and of the "buoyancy in the spirits of the public." That quickly disappeared. Overseas, the end of the Napoleonic Wars had lessened demand overall for exported US goods. Poor crops in Europe had temporarily offset that loss by creating higher agricultural prices. But with a rebound in crops overseas, and more British use of cotton from India, American agricultural prices started to fall. At the same time, as Clay had predicted, the British began to dump their surplus goods on the nearly unprotected American markets, which hurt emerging national manufacturing. Just as those events began unfolding, the immediate postwar prosperity fueled a spirit of unchecked enterprise. The "Great Bubble of 1817–1819" grew and grew. Land values soared as speculators—including Clay—expected rising prices to provide the profits to pay off their increasing loans. If not a market revolution, at least a market metamorphosis seemed in the making. But then, as the effects of the overseas events began to influence the false prosperity of America, the nation's major financial institution, the Bank of the United States (BUS), hastened and then deepened the depression with poor decisions regarding credit and other matters. The resulting panic of 1819 represented the first major exposure of the nation to the caprices of business cycles, and it shook the people to their core. As Clay stressed, the financial and moral suffering "plunges its victims into hopeless despair. It poisons, it paralyzes the spring and source of all useful exertions." Prices declined, fortunes fell, and debts rose.[55]

Every part of the Union felt the effects. In Kentucky, a drought only added to the economic distress, and prices fell to half their level of two years earlier. As eastern merchants sued for payments and as state banks failed, debtors conveyed land and other property to meet obligations on mortgages and loans. Almost overnight, a third of the people's wealth in the state had been transferred from them to banks, businessmen, and other creditors to satisfy claims. Clay shared their hurt, for he too suffered mightily. In fact, in some ways he never fully recovered the relative wealth he had in 1818. Clay paid taxes on some $75,000 in property that year; four years of depression reduced that figure to almost a third—$28,000. Moreover, he had cosigned loans for some in-laws, to a "considerable sum," and now had to pay off some of those loans. Payment of those debts, the decline in income on his properties, the inability of his debtors to pay him, and the need to meet his own obligations all caused Clay to execute a sizable mortgage. It would take him almost a decade to extinguish that debt. But unlike some of his contemporary congressmen, Clay took seriously the need to deal with such concerns through his own agency. That meant, however, that he had to derail some of his political plans—or, at the very least, spend less time on politics—in order to meet his financial needs.[56]

When Clay became the legal advisor, then lead counsel, for the BUS in Ohio, he knew full well that working for that unpopular institution would not help him politically. People blamed it for a variety of economic sins, and being the attorney who brought lawsuits in its name would not win sympathy, or votes. Still, his crucial need for the financial security the job offered and the presumably favorable loan terms the bank advanced, overrode such concerns. He accepted a $5,000 annual retainer as "just and liberal" compensation for his work. But, at the same time, politician Clay tried to limit the negative effects of his decision by following what he called the course of moderation in pursuit of debts owed the institution. In short, he attempted to tread the middle path of representing his client—the bank—fairly while patiently giving the defendants much leeway. Even then, he won every contested case. A contemporary author cried out that "the bank was saved, and the people were ruined." Clay certainly made enemies, but he made fewer than might be expected. Of more than a hundred cases that Clay prosecuted in Cincinnati, almost half of those defendants eventually supported Clay when he first ran for major national office.[57]

On occasion, a crisis can bring some unexpected political benefits. In Clay's case, one of his chief rising rivals in Kentucky was Richard M. Johnson. The two had agreed on some issues—involvement in the War of 1812, for example—but increasingly found themselves on opposite sides. Each would soon become leaders of his respective party in the commonwealth. But Clay's actions regarding Johnson's financial issues during the panic of 1819 and after would soften Johnson's subsequent attacks and keep him from being a more vocal Clay critic. The two would continue to work to defeat each other politically, but the dialogue remained respectful. Clay's kindness to Johnson during that time helped mute a potentially aggressive critic. Immensely popular and a good orator, Dick Johnson served in the US House of Representatives for twenty years and the US Senate for a decade, and he had gained a reputation as the poor man's friend—despite being the author of the ill-fated Compensation Bill. He led the campaign to continue to keep the mails operating on Sunday (despite religious opposition) and to "keep church and state disunited." Johnson also sought a law to abolish imprisonment for debt. Such stances won him support from the laboring classes.[58]

But all those attributes and activities paled in comparison to the other source of his great political popularity. Colonel Richard Mentor Johnson became known as the slayer of the great Indian leader Tecumseh, at the Battle of the Thames in the War of 1812. In truth, much controversy surrounded that question, for others challenged whether Johnson should be given credit for that act. What was not in dispute was that during the battle, he took three bullets in the thigh, two in the arm. He suffered from stiffness and inflammation as a consequence of those wounds and limped for the rest of his life. During the confusion of the brief battle, Tecumseh had been killed, perhaps by Johnson. The "scar-covered Hero" accepted the accolades given him and that reputation, more than anything else, later earned him the vice presidency of the United States under Martin Van Buren.[59]

Clay, who had known the Johnsons "long and intimately," respected Dick Johnson's talents and sacrifices, but not the military-based source of his success. Over the years, he emphasized that Johnson had an "insatiable thirst for office" and would do almost anything to attract votes. Clay, who tended to denigrate the motivations of anyone who might provide a challenge to gaining offices *he* sought, also derided Johnson's ambitions and stances. Not surprisingly, then, when the BUS approached Clay regarding Johnson's massive debt to the institution, he initially hesitated to get involved, for he feared if he did, Johnson "might entertain the opinion of a favorable disposition toward him, on my part." Whether due to Johnson's entreaties for aid, or just a change of heart, Clay did get involved in what was a very messy financial situation. Money matters would plague Dick Johnson and his brothers for the rest of their lives. Like others, they had speculated during the boom period and now harshly felt the effect of the bust. As the panic of 1819 worsened, the Johnsons owed the BUS between $50,000 and $400,000 at various times.[60]

Bank attorney Clay could have influenced the bank to foreclose on Johnson. That he did not caused Johnson to call Clay "an honorable man" and to remember those relative kindnesses. He eventually supported Clay's first presidential bid, though he soon became a staunch advocate of the opposition. But the two men extended various courtesies to one another over the years, and in 1843 Johnson publicly asserted that Clay had no equal in the nation: "He is a great man, a very great man."[61]

Yet what makes Clay's support even more interesting, and Johnson's support in Kentucky even more surprising, were the circumstances surrounding Johnson's personal life. While various slaveholders across the South took slave mistresses, often clandestinely, those actions remained an open secret or were hidden from public view. Johnson flaunted such mores and frankly admitted that his mulatto slave Julia Chinn functioned in his household as a wife would. No hypocrite in that regard at least, he apparently loved her and the two children she bore him. Julia presided over his dinner table; she ran the farm in his absence. He raised their daughters as equals to those in white society, and gave them sizable dowries when they both married white men. After one girl's early death, Johnson described her as his source "of inexhaustible happiness." It was not the act of having a slave mistress and children that angered white southern sensibilities. Rather, Johnson's elevating his family's status and his open recognition of their place in his life brought him much criticism in that society.[62]

In 1835, his domestic arrangement became public knowledge in the nation when a Virginia newspaper referred to vice presidential candidate Johnson and his "mulattoes, wooly head, wench, and all." By then, Julia Chinn had actually died during a cholera epidemic and another slave ran the household, but the attacks continued, coming often from political enemies within his own party as they sought to deny his nomination. An ally of Andrew Jackson wrote Old Hickory, for example, that a Johnson selection would be "affirmatively odious" to every slaveholder, for such claims to equality were loathed by all. But Johnson did get the nomination, did find scurrilous attacks on his life continuing, and did have to go before the Senate to be selected, because some southern electors withheld their votes from him. Johnson would still be a major contender for national office for most of his life, but that one issue likely kept him from attaining even greater success—and from posing a greater challenge to Clay in Kentucky.[63]

The effects of the financial depression caused Clay to take two other political actions. Citing the need to repair his family fortunes, he announced in the late spring of 1820 that he would not seek reelection to Congress. Clay indicated he would serve out his term, but because of business and legal responsibilities, he would delay his return to Washington. He also asked to be relieved of his position as Speaker of the House.[64]

As it turned out, the nation needed his presence and political skills, for another crisis loomed. Clay had made his plans to step down because he believed he had just ended a congressional confrontation that had vividly revealed the hidden cracks in the edifice of the Union. In 1818, before the panic had hit hard and brought economic sectional tensions to the forefront, a move to admit Missouri as a new state had produced the platform for controversy. On a February day in 1819, the talented and unpredictable James Tallmadge of New York introduced legislation that would prohibit slavery, over time, in Missouri. That proposal reawakened an ever-present but often-dormant sectionalism. Seeing its system of racial control, its "peculiar institution," its dominance, under attack from without, the white South coalesced and warned of dire consequences should slavery be restricted in Missouri. A Georgia representative declared that "we have kindled a fire which all the waters of the ocean cannot put out, which seas of blood can only extinguish." Tallmadge heard the responses and cried out, "If dissolution of the union must take place, let it be so! If Civil War . . . must come, . . . let it come!" The resolution passed the House despite a solid southern vote in opposition. The Senate, however, failed to pass the bill, and in early 1819 Congress adjourned without a Missouri bill.[65]

When a new Congress assembled in late 1819, the unresolved issue emerged once again, producing an equally furious and divisive debate. Then-Speaker Clay reportedly advised Missouri to insert a provision in its constitution for gradual emancipation, but when the territory showed little inclination to do that, he had to find another way to end what he saw as a very real and very growing threat to the existence of a country not a half century old. In January 1820, he wrote that the debate had been started "for the purpose of arraying one portion of the U. States against another; and there is some reason to apprehend that this sinister design may be effected." That same month, he concluded that the Missouri question dominated all conversation: "The words, civil war, and disunion, are uttered almost without emotion."[66]

When Senator Jesse Thomas of Illinois proposed a compromise that same month, Clay began to hope that the controversy might end, even if he did not agree with much of what Thomas proposed. But if no solution arose, the "ultras" of both sections would begin to form the "worst of all parties," a sectional one, and disunion would soon become a reality. The Thomas Compromise offered Missouri's admission as a slave state, Maine's as a free one, while it made all the rest of the territory north of 36°30′ free, the part south of the line slave. Clay predicted that with "the subject of *disunion* . . . discussed in circles with freedom and familiarity," the compromise bill would fail. It did. Then, with members exhausted by the all-consuming debates, Clay took charge. Now, for the sake of conciliation, he turned to support what Thomas proposed. Openly, Clay made an emotional speech that, according to a New York newspaper, left "half the House in tears." Behind the scenes, the Kentuckian lobbied, manipulated, and persuaded. One congressman reported, "He begs, entreats, adjures, supplicates, & beseeches us." As he had as a lawyer back in Kentucky, Clay did what the situation demanded to win. And as he had learned earlier in the state legislature, he also changed tactics as needed. When conflicting bills passed each house, he arranged for a joint conference committee of moderate members favorable to a settlement. With the need to switch only a few votes, Clay successfully piloted a resolution to the impasse. If Thomas had provided the vehicle for the compromise, Clay had driven it through. His will and his skill resulted in passage of the compromise in March 1820. The crisis seemed over. A fatigued Speaker wrote a Kentucky friend that he had "employed my best exertions to produce this settlement of the question. . . . The question thus put to rest will I hope leave no bad consequences."[67]

Those events had occurred as the panic raged around Clay and as he had fought for his own financial life. So, flushed with the victory of the compromise, a tired Clay had made his May 1820 announcement that he would not seek reelection. But the Missouri question had not been settled, after all, and seemingly would not rest. When Missouri inserted a section into its constitution that would prohibit the migration of free blacks once it became a state, it reopened the entire issue of statehood and the compromise itself, and began what became an even more serious threat to the health of the Union.[68]

Article 4, Section 2, of the US Constitution declares, "The Citizen of each State shall be entitled to all Privileges and Immunities of Citizens in the several States." Because free blacks were citizens (if often second-class ones), Missouri's restrictions on them seemed to violate that federal protection clause. Moderates who had agreed to the earlier compromise felt betrayed. A Washington journalist advised the still-distant Clay back in Bluegrass country that "the second Missouri Campaign has begun." Watching from afar, Clay indicated that Missouri's actions "could hardly be defended" and considered them an insult to Congress. Moreover, by including that offending section in its constitution, Missouri brought its own legal status into question. Was it already a state, or still a territory? Could Congress stop the process and rescind its earlier action? Adding to the confusion, with Clay having stepped down as Speaker, the House seemed leaderless. It had taken the body twenty-two ballots just to select his successor. Adams had written earlier that "the Missouri question is indeed a flaming sword that waves round on all sides and cuts in every direction." Sectionalism continued rampant, as southerners called for admission of Missouri, to fulfill the first compromise, based on the Thomas amendment. In turn, northerners called for rejection of the statehood act, since the compromise had been violated.

Congress seemed on the verge of voiding all the months of earlier effort. Harsh threats once more echoed through the capitol. But how long could that go on without the threats of disunion becoming reality?[69]

On January 16, 1821, Henry Clay finally took his seat in Congress and found a chaotic situation. Immediately, he tried to resolve the crisis. With, in Clay's words, the "cup of conciliation" seemingly empty, he came in almost like a last-minute savior. Years later, in a private letter, Clay recounted what he found and what then occurred: "All efforts had been tried and failed to reconcile the parties. . . . Both parties appealed to me; . . . I went to work." He quickly realized that he had to propose some compromise "which should involve no sacrifice of principle" by either group. In a good explanation of how he succeeded, then and over the years, he related how he had labored very hard: "I coaxed, soothed, scorned, defied them, by turns as I thought the best effect to be produced." Moreover, Clay engaged in "long, arduous" debates, speaking almost every day over the course of several weeks. His major, four-hour speech, which some considered the best one he ever gave, would not be recorded for posterity. But it had the desired effect of breaking down the barriers to reconciliation.[70]

Meanwhile, and perhaps with Clay's blessing, another Kentucky representative offered a bill that would repeal the recent 36°30' restriction on slavery. In a sense, that action shocked antislavery northerners who realized that if the earlier compromise died, so too might the limits on the expansion that it contained. A Clay proposal used deliberately equivocal language to state that Missouri would now declare by "a solemn public act" never to restrict citizen rights. Each side could read it to match its own desires. The almost meaningless resolution diffused the debate. That approach, coupled perhaps with the scare tactic regarding 36°30', worked. Both houses of Congress soon passed what became known as the Second Missouri Compromise.[71]

Contemporaries and historians alike have almost unanimously praised Clay's role in crafting that congressional peace. An antislavery man concluded that Clay's conduct "has been extremely honorable to himself & useful to the country," while an opponent of Clay's grudgingly noted how Clay had outmaneuvered his side, showing what "unexampled perseverance" could do. Chief Justice John Marshall said of his fellow Virginian, by birth: "I think him entitled to particular credit for having brought the Missouri conflict to a peaceful termination." Since then, historians have echoed those conclusions. One said the crisis demanded a magician to solve it, and found one in Clay.[72]

Not all agreed, however, that Clay should be honored. Clay himself noted how "persons on both sides of the question" would be dissatisfied. Antislavery activists blamed Clay for what one later termed an "unholy compromise" that allowed a new slave state into the Union, while fire-eating southerners criticized him for yielding on the question of restricting slavery expansion. And, in truth, in this preview of the coming decades of sectional debate, Clay had fashioned a compromise that closed the curtain on only that particular act. But amid the thunderous applause that greeted his actions, he understood that the sharpness of the debate likely meant there would be more parts to the unfolding script, for the Union rested on a fragile foundation and required constant vigilance.[73]

In his era, however, Clay's role in the two Missouri Compromises stamped him as a statesman of the first order and earned him the title of "the Great Pacificator." With accolades won, Clay retired from Congress in March 1821, at the age of forty-three. By that time he had been successful in virtually every public endeavor he had undertaken—as attorney, as state representative, as US senator, as member of the House of Representatives, as Speaker, as diplomat, as compromiser. But two other elements constituted the growing Clay image—his personal attributes and his programs. And they provided a more mixed effect.

3

Personality

WHO WAS THE REAL HENRY CLAY? Was it the man his supporters pictured—a great orator, a charismatic figure, a person offering a unified system to help America grow, a constructive leader, a caring individual devoted to his country, a man above section or party? Or was it the Clay his enemies depicted—a man who drank heavily, swore habitually, gambled recklessly, whored repeatedly, and lusted for office constantly? Was it this man—an irreligious, amoral partisan, consumed by ambition, who used his seductive oratory on behalf of perilous programs that would endanger the republic and divide the people? Or was the real Clay none of these things? Or all of them?

Elements in the makeup of Henry Clay both added to his political persona and took away from it. His personal attributes, his civic skills, and his legislative programs all contained parts that made Clay so appealing to so many as both a person and a presidential candidate. At the same time, components of all those areas carried the capacity to bring about his defeat.

Clay's contemporaries agreed that no portrait of Clay did him justice, for no artist fully captured the man's vigor, spirit, and charm. Those who met Clay could agree that the most skilled renderings did get some things right. At six feet, one inch tall, Clay towered over most of his contemporaries and looked even taller. His lengthy and lithe form—he weighed around 165 pounds all his adult life—and his erect bearing added to the sense of impressive height. Most artists got right his light, tow-colored hair that turned quickly white, his high forehead, his prominent nose, his long, loose arms, his graceful gestures.[1]

Other aspects of Clay's physical makeup attracted special attention from those who observed him—especially his eyes, his bearing, and his mouth—but portrait painters could never quite translate all that onto canvas. In repose, for example, Clay's brilliant blue-gray eyes might twinkle with mischievousness. But put Clay on the debate floor or out among the voters, and his eyes expressed the intense emotions, the fiery heart inside. They might glare with contempt in one instance, then, as a contemporary noted, "pierce the utmost soul of those whom he addresses" in the next moment. Before Clay would even utter a word, he could make the audience feel his passion and fear his power, just with the fierce sweep of his eyes over a crowd.[2]

Similarly, Clay's entire bearing and overall presence could not be preserved in art. One of his female friends said that when Clay threw himself "gracefully into a recumbent position," all seemed so natural and relaxed. His courtly movements, his captivating manners, his "wholly unpretentious" demeanor impressed friends and enemies alike. Not handsome—one of his own campaign songbooks called him "monstrous ugly"—he almost never left that feeling with those he met. That same person who termed him ugly then added, "But for all that, he's the best-looking man I ever saw." The intangibles Clay brought with him allowed the inner man to dominate the outer shell. When that not-so-handsome face "glowed with the fire of inspiration," when those eyes blazed, when that body flowed, it all came together to make Clay seem the most attractive man on earth.[3]

And then there was a mouth so uncommonly large that a contemporary observer deemed it "gigantic . . . certainly it was huge." Stories circulated that his mouth was so wide that he could never spit properly, and that when kissing the adoring ladies, he could "rest one side of it while the other side was doing active duty." But the size of the mouth did not alone make it special; Clay's manipulation of it made it distinctive. At one moment, he might present an appealing, almost sensual impression; at another, he might turn to an opponent with a sardonic, satanic snarl that could devastate. Then, in an instant, Clay could offer a warm and winning grin that melted hardened hearts. One person declared, "When he smiled, he smiled all over." That said it all.[4]

But more than anything else, a voice that people called magnificent and moving was responsible for his initial success and for much of his later fame. It helped him rise in Virginia, it aided his legal success in Kentucky, and it gained him national attention in Washington. Though a grandson insisted that Henry Clay had inherited his wonderful voice from his minister father, in truth Clay had worked hard to develop his oratorical skills. Late in his career, he told some law students, "I owe my success in life, I think, chiefly to one singular fact, . . . that at the age of 17, I commenced and continued for years the process of daily reading and speaking upon the contents of some historical or scientific book." With a stump as a platform and the field, forest, or horse as his listener, he practiced and improved. "There is no power like that of oratory," he told the students, and it, he said, "shaped and molded my whole subsequent destiny." Then Clay had come to Kentucky, where he almost had to grow as an orator to survive. As a Texan recalled of that society, "Them Kentuckians . . . [are] the speakin'est people I ever seen." At a wedding, funeral, or camp meeting, they would offer resolutions and make talks, he said: "To tell the truth . . . they cain't cut a watermelon without a speech." From the time in 1798 when he addressed the Lexington crowd on the Alien and Sedition Acts until his death well over a half century later, Henry Clay absolutely excelled as a speaker. Almost all who heard him agreed that no one did it better.[5]

Clay's talks nearly enchanted the willing listener, who did not want the hypnotic moment to end. To some the clear, captivating, convincing words completely charmed them. Others recounted how the melodious, moving, magical tones totally mesmerized them. A contemporary described Clay's "penetrating and far-reaching" excellence, while a Kentuckian simply called Clay's "the finest voice that I ever heard." The doorkeeper of the Senate acknowledged that Henry Clay eclipsed all the speakers he had heard in his many years there: "There was a fascinating grandeur and charm in his eloquence that was simply indescribable, and that . . . could never be equaled." In short, in an age of great orators, allies and adversaries alike simply praised the richness of the voice itself.[6]

But Henry Clay's success as a speaker did not just result from fine powers of expression. He knew how to use that voice in many effective ways. Clay understood crowd psychology, and he could almost immediately establish a rapport with his audience. In one instance, he started out asking if he needed, after all these years, to explain his position on the issues. The crowd roared back, "No!" Did he need to tell them his opinions on matters? They again answered, "No!" That back and forth continued and gave the talk spirit and movement, uniting speaker and audience. On other occasions, Clay might alternate moods, with words of compromise following defiant language, or with kind expressions accompanying harsh ones, or with humor matching pathos. A Georgia editor described how Clay could "put you in a rage at one moment, and make you laugh and cry the next, at will." Clay's "sweet and soft" voice had no superior, a magazine declared, but Clay could abruptly leave those floating, soothing intonations behind and then his voice would shake the Senate, "filling the air with its absolute thunders." Similarly, in 1831, a writer referred to Clay's eloquence—"sometimes whispering to the heart . . . and then calling to the passions with the mingled voice of earthquake and whirlwind."[7]

Clay's rhetorical greatness came not just from his voice and his presentation. It also came about because of the passion that burned within. When people discovered that Clay would be addressing Congress on a subject of interest to him and of importance to the nation, they flocked to hear him, for they anticipated that his fervor could produce electrifying results. Clay's utterances and actions left those who heard him fully persuaded that he earnestly believed in the cause and convinced them that the words came from his heart. One senator explained that Clay's eloquence could not be described because of all the intangibles that made it so successful: "It must be *seen* and *felt*." He stressed how the eyes, the tears, the words, the expressions, the movements, were only part of the effect. More than that, "because *he* felt . . . he made *others* feel." The result "was something greater and higher than eloquence; it was *action*—noble, sublime, God-like." While others could entertain an audience, Clay, by his power and passion, could also motivate and persuade people. His emotions became their emotions, his heart their heart, his will their will. Clay's sentences breathed "the soul of humanity into the measure of the state."[8]

Perhaps the most impressive thing about the speeches that Clay delivered and that virtually all praised so highly was that they were not written out, nor did they always represent the product of much preparation. Clay said he wrote out beforehand only two or three speeches, that he preferred to speak extemporaneously. If anything, he tended to use an outline with a few notes attached, occasionally glancing at them over the course of several hours. But most of what Clay said came from the magic of the moment—well-organized, fresh, unrehearsed, and original. Nor did Clay usually revise his speeches for publication. By contrast, Daniel Webster spent hours adding or subtracting from the talk he had just given. That resulted in much more readable end products, with quotable phrases never used in debate, but also speeches that sometimes varied considerably from those actually delivered. By contrast, Clay let stand the words he spoke in Congress or elsewhere. But the result proved somewhat unfortunate for him. As a writer for the

Southern Literary Messenger noted, "Clay impresses more when he speaks—Webster more when he is read." At a time when voters learned much of what they knew about a candidate from reading speeches, not hearing them, Clay's failure to rewrite hurt him in that regard.[9]

Clay's unrevised, published speeches remain mostly flat, tepid, and lifeless when read. Nineteenth-century critics recognized that and said the words "repel readers by their dullness," while those in the next century echoed such thoughts, calling the Great Pacificator's printed talks "prolix, imprecise, and often shallow." Yet in Clay's era, the accounts of those same talks tell how the audience cheered, cried, laughed, and termed the speeches the best they had ever heard. The disconnect appears because the words on paper could not convey what Clay's personality—his fire, his spirit, his charm, his effect on people—contributed. Ironically, some of Clay's best speeches were never recorded because they so entranced that, as Abraham Lincoln noted, "the reporters . . . dropped their pens, and sat enchanted from near the beginning to quite the close. The speech now lives only in the memory of a few old men."[10]

Like a great actor with a bad script, Clay could make what might seem dead words come vividly alive, through the inflection of his voice, the gestures of his body, and the spirit of his soul. Some in his era disparagingly dismissed him as a habitual thespian and not much else. That description does contain some elements of truth. Oratory demanded theatrical flourishes, and Clay certainly practiced well that craft. But, more than that, politicians must, at times, function as actors in other situations. Though angry, they may need to appear calm; if tired, seem fresh; and if discouraged, be optimistic. At times in his career, Clay did all that. The problems arise when the leader cannot separate acting from life, when the person is always acting and is never real, when the individual stands for nothing and continually lives the lie of the moment. In Clay's case, he used his abilities to emphasize and dramatize points, to help his speeches speak to the core of those who heard them.[11]

When people went to hear Clay speak, when he served in Congress, they did so perhaps secretly hoping that he would spark a reaction among his fellow members, because in the give and take of spontaneous debate, Clay truly dominated and often delighted. As one representative noted, "These set speeches don't take here." Instead, the free-flowing discussions, the questions and responses, the "grand intellectual sparring expositions," made reputations—or broke them. In that atmosphere, Clay quickly made it clear that an opponent could seldom beat him in debate. He was almost always prepared, and his responses showed real substance. His quick recall, good mind, and agile oratory served him well. In numerous instances, when an opponent brought out a name in a discussion, Clay rapidly responded with an appropriate (if frequently mangled) quote from that person. Similarly, when a senator challenged Clay, saying Clay had misquoted him, the Kentuckian relied on his memory, asked for a copy of the official journal of four years earlier, and then proved his reference correct by reading the passage aloud. And, finally, after John C. Calhoun had spent three weeks preparing his two-hour reply to a Clay speech, Clay rose immediately, replied that he did not need such a time to concoct *his* response, and as John Quincy Adams recorded in his diary, subsequently "had manifestly the advantages in the debate." Clay's forty-five-minute rejoinder completely destroyed the foundation that Calhoun had so carefully laid.[12]

At the same time, such success may have made Clay too confident in his course of action, too sure of himself. Constant vanquishing of the opposition did not encourage humility in Clay and fed his already considerable ego. Nor did it endear him to those who found themselves oratorically defeated, time after time. Clay's tactics in debates added to his appeal, but also contributed to his political problems. His use of humor, for example, frequently further endeared him to his listeners, whether in Washington or across the nation. When addressing a crowd in Nashville once, he learned that Felix Grundy, his one-time Kentucky adversary now turned Tennessee attorney and politician, was not present because he had gone to campaign for Clay's opponents. Clay observed, with a smile, "I had hoped . . . to have the pleasure of meeting and renewing my acquaintance with my old friend Grundy, but I understand that he is in East Tennessee, at his old business— *defending criminals!*" Even the opposition joined in laughter.[13]

Similarly, in Congress, Clay's remarks often enlightened a dull debating day and warmed both enemies and allies. One of his most-quoted comments (with several variations) concerned a long-winded member who had been advised to conclude his talk so the House could move on to other business. The speaker haughtily replied that he was speaking not to politicians of the present but to posterity. To which Clay remarked, "Yes, and you seem resolved to continue speaking until your audience arrives." Pennsylvania's James Buchanan bore the brunt of many of the Kentuckian's gibes, partly because he accepted such comments in the right spirit and because Clay liked him personally, even though they represented different political sides. Once Buchanan told Congress that he had served in a volunteer military company during the War of 1812 that had marched to the relief of

Baltimore. The group learned on the march, however, that the British had been repulsed and it then returned home. That, Buchanan said, had concluded his military service. Clay then arose and blandly expressed the desire to ask the speaker a question. Buchanan immediately replied that he would allow it. The Kentuckian, with what was described as a twinkle in his eye, then inquired "whether the gentlemen marched to the relief of Baltimore because he learned that the British had left, or whether the British left because they heard the gentleman from Pennsylvania was coming?"[14]

But Clay's words in debate did not always bring forth humor. Even genuine expressions of mirth could leave lingering scars in the memory of their victims. As one member of Congress explained, "It was poison in jest." In Buchanan's case, for example, when Clay commented about the Pennsylvanian's "well-known eloquence and melodious voice," that was in fact oratorical irony, for Buchanan's stuttering and sharp tones represented the opposite of melodious. On another occasion, Clay offered a clever comment that gained laughter, but also represented a cutting remark to a man with a muscular disability in one eye. Clay could go too far in his attempts at humor.[15]

If Clay could unintentionally injure feelings, there remained no doubt of his intentions when he actively sought to ridicule opponents in debate. Not overly cautious in his choice of words, and not particularly concerned about their effects, at times Clay could orally eviscerate an opponent. He used blunt words that left no question of intent or outcome. When a new member assailed Clay on a personal matter, Clay turned, wrote George Prentice, and "with a tone and manner of half pity and half indignation" began to pummel and ridicule him. Clay's anger almost seemed to come because the neophyte had dared to challenge him in the first place. The result was that the man never stood up to Clay again and, in fact, seldom ever spoke in Congress again. His spirit had been broken.[16]

Numerous opponents, and even a few friends, felt the fury of such verbal assaults. Clay might stand on his toes, then stomp his foot, then march across the House or Senate floor, his eyes darting around at one enemy after another, full of contempt or disdain for them. What one contemporary referred to as "the sarcastic tone, the withering look, and the scornful gesture" completed the armory of weapons used. And his frankness in expressing his views, his directness in presenting his points, and his openness in showing his emotions made his feelings even clearer than in most men. But that also meant that his candid words could easily produce anger in those who did not forget. An opponent who verbally jousted often with Clay noted that one of Clay's "very provoking" verbal assaults left "a wound . . . more painful than death . . . . The barb was steeped in venom," he continued, "and the venom was in the affected candor which hung on the barb." Audiences loved to hear Clay in debate, with his sharp responses and humorous replies. His opponents, however, had different reactions. At a time when society demanded that gentlemen defend attacks on their honor, whether they came in physical or verbal form, the fear of responding to Clay, yielding mastery to him, and facing defeat at his hands, ate away at any good feelings some might have entertained toward the talented and funny Mr. Clay. Instead, his very brilliance would create enemies. Clay thus seemed a contradiction. He carefully scrutinized people, cultivated them, watched them, pulled them over to his circle of ideas. Yet at the same time, in the heat of debate Clay would antagonize those same individuals and turn them away with his relentless sarcasm and deadly wit.[17]

Clay constantly apologized for the fervor of his words, and asked for pardon for his ardent temper, his too-warm nature, and his "offensive" language. He offered those words fully expecting that he would be forgiven and the harsh comments forgotten. To Clay, there was no contradiction in his actions, because he saw politics partially as a game, with the players moving from one side to the other on different issues. As in a game, once the contest concluded, those involved in the fray should all be friends again, in the camaraderie of politics. They could come together and share drinks around a table. In a sense that reflected part of his Kentucky frontier influence, where people might exchange harsh words, perhaps even fight, but on the morrow they would laugh about it all, slap each other on the shoulder, and face a hostile world together. Yet even Clay recognized that his political game was a very important one, affecting the fate of a nation and its people. When Clay made his verbal thrusts as part of that process, he expected others to see them in that light. Yet he was so good in the attack, with opponents who held a different view, that forgiveness seldom came. And when those same people styled themselves to be his superior and antagonized Clay with their own words, he too found it difficult to quench the resulting anger. At such times, Henry Clay did not seem presidential material.[18]

But if Clay's oratory was a weapon that could cut both ways, overall it proved to be one of his greatest strengths, a force that touched almost all who heard him speak. Even Andrew Jackson conceded that his enemy "is the most plausible speaker that ever opened his mouth. . . . If you listen to him, he will make you believe." That represented a key part of Clay's power.

Ben Perley Poore, a journalist who observed the national scene for more than forty years, recalled Clay with great admiration: "No such voice was ever heard elsewhere. . . . It was equally distinctive and clear, . . . rich, musical, captivating. . . . Every thought spoke; the whole body had its story to tell." Similarly, Robert Winthrop of Massachusetts later served in Congress with Clay and heard some of Clay's greatest speeches, but he most remembered a small gathering in 1833, when some sixty people assembled in the drawing room of a hotel to present a gift to the famous Mr. Clay. With no reporters present, the occasion had no public bearing on Clay's political hopes. A small thank-you would have sufficed. But when Clay rose to speak extemporaneously in response to the gift, "the fire burned" and the walls vibrated with the resulting "soul-stirring eloquence." With no notes, Clay still enthralled the group. "After the lapse of forty-six years," wrote Winthrop, "the tones still ring in my ears, and can only bear witness to an impressiveness of speech never exceeded, if ever equaled, within an experience of nearly half a century." But perhaps the greatest compliment to Clay's special talent came when a great-granddaughter was doing her research for an article on Clay and asked an elderly blind man who had heard Clay speak to describe the spell of that voice: "He tried to convey to me . . . an impression of the magic of Mr. Clay's power, and finally broke off; 'You cannot do justice to him, child. No one can. It is impossible.' "[19]

If people praised Clay's speaking abilities and agreed that his strengths there helped define candidate Clay before the voters, there was considerable debate regarding his personal attributes and habits. Friends and enemies seemed to emphasize very different aspects of the same person. Was Clay captivating or seducing, active or exploitative, proud or conceited, fast-acting or rash, confident or arrogant?[20]

Virtually everyone conceded that Clay exuded great charisma. To his harshest antagonists, that made him even more dangerous. But to most others, that made him exceedingly interesting and appealing as a person. Editor Horace Greeley explained how readers in future centuries could "scarcely realize the force of his personal magnetism," while a Kentuckian wrote that Clay's friends looked to him "with an admiration almost Divine." Opponents, of course, viewed him in a decidedly less celestial way. Still, something about Clay inspired supporters to adulation, almost love. And the key, for them, seemed to be the inner man. Clay had "a heart that flows like water," declared later US senator Charles Sumner in 1844. Many found that the more they talked with Clay, the more they liked him. Sam Long used to "clown around" in Lexington and supported the party opposed to Clay. Long happened to be riding a mule in a procession at the same time Clay was. Trailing Clay's carriage, Long yelled out, "Here we are, fellow-citizens, Wisdom led by Folly." The crowd laughed, as did Clay. The next night Clay sent Long a bottle of "the finest wine I ever tasted." With it came a note: "From the poorest fool to the best clown in the United States." Such self-deprecation, kindness, and action transformed doubters into supporters, allies into disciples.[21]

When people met Clay in person, it grew even harder to resist becoming part of the Clay orbit. More than one individual called Clay a brilliant, captivating conversationalist and the most fascinating person they had ever known. Such reactions resulted, in part, from the host's almost intuitive ability to understand human character and treat each visitor differently, as an individual. A sculptor who spent much time with Clay and Jackson compared the two and concluded: "Clay knows infinitely more of what every Boddy [sic] is about & has the far greater genius to fit every fellow in his place." As Thurlow Weed, no Clay ally, grumbled to a man who had fallen under the Clay spell, "Yes! That was like Henry; he always sent everybody from him charmed, because he made them think he was charmed by them."[22]

Clay could do that with young and old, male and female, wealthy and poor. Washington, DC, society matron Margaret Bayard Smith started out antagonistic to Clay, but ended up as a great admirer. She wrote a friend in 1829 that Clay had more "intellectual power" than anyone else she had met, and she had known Jefferson, Madison, Monroe, and Adams. But more than that, Clay had "a natural power and force of mind, beyond any I have ever witnessed." His irrepressible "elasticity and buoyancy of spirit," his openness, his warmth, his kindness, she found absolutely captivating: "He is a very great man." The Oxford-educated member of the Privy Council, and later Lord Lieutenant of Ireland, George Howard, Viscount Morpeth, found Clay's society "most attractive, easy, simple, and genial, with great natural dignity." But perhaps the clearest example of how Clay made people feel at ease involves, once again, a rather simple act. Josephine Russell recalled how as a young girl eating with her family at the Clays', she ended up sitting by the great man himself. She very much disliked the artichokes placed before her but was eating them as a courtesy, or was trying to, at least. Host Clay noticed her discomfort, quietly slipped the offending vegetables to his plate, and relieved her suffering. When the child later showed the group an autograph album she kept, Clay immediately took pen in hand and wrote how honored he was to sign the album. Whereas others might have done nothing, signed nothing, said nothing to a young girl who could never vote for them, Clay genuinely cared, and in that caring, won her affection, as he did with so many others—who could vote.[23]

Reading such words of praise over and over from Clay's contemporaries almost produces a sense of hagiography. Clay was far from a saint. But at the same time, the evidence makes it clear that he had a tremendously appealing manner. Charles Dickens called Clay a "perfectly enchanting and irresistible man." Later presidential hopeful and cabinet member Edward Bates wrote his wife that the "manly & bold" Clay "grows upon me more & more, every time I see him." A new Georgia congressman, from the party opposing Clay, was asked if he would like to be introduced to the famous Henry Clay. "No, sir!" he quickly responded. "I am his adversary, and choose not to subject myself to his fascination."[24] He knew the power of Clay's magnetism. But perhaps the fullest and fairest summary came from the man who spent many days with Clay as he cast a bust of him. Sculptor Joel Tanner Hart wrote in his diary:

Clay, at home is as kindly as mortal can well be & attends in person upon his guests,—is the first to observe, and serve them at table— neglects no one at his own house,—sees, & hears every thing, and replies only to that which has point.—Elegant and forceful when with the Strong, and intelligent;—dictatorial to those whom he can not lead—Gentle to old ladies—courteous to young ones,—fond of children,—cordial to his friends,—polite, with great ease and dignity to strangers—loves a good joke makes it short,—quizzes with great acuteness . . . —gets impatient at a long story, scarcely ever tells a long one himself—attends in person to his own affairs,—attends to little things, as well as great ones,—disappoints no boddy [sic],—kind to his wife & children, indulgent to his servants,—hospitable to the Stranger,—cuts light matters short, is what he seams [sic] to be, earnest, ardent,—is often eloquent.[25]

Such attitudes brought political opponent and historian George Bancroft to write of Clay: "Never in public nor in private did he know how to be dull." Many people would be satisfied with that as an epitaph.[26]

Numerous leaders have the ability to charm in small groups; fewer have the special facility to convey their charisma before larger audiences. Clay could do both. In his presence, few could adequately explain what happened, but the flowing eloquence, the crackling wit, and the sparkling personality all combined to sweep over the multitudes and leave them certain that they had been a part of greatness. And then as he walked through the crowd, or even sometimes before the entire group, Clay demonstrated another talent very useful to a politician—an excellent memory. One man met Clay again after a first introduction a year before: "He recognized me at once, being possessed of a marvelous memory and recollection of names—he never forgot a face and never failed in courtesy towards any one that he knew." In another, even more public instance, Clay stopped in Mississippi briefly and a crowd gathered. A one-eyed man approached Clay, after telling his friends he wanted to see if Clay would remember him.

"Where do I know you?" Clay asked the man, thought for a minute, then inquired further.

> "Have you lost that eye since I saw you, or had you lost it then?"
> "Since," the man answered.
> Clay viewed the man's profile for a moment, then exclaimed. "I have it! Did not you give me a verdict, as a juror, of Frankfort, Kentucky . . . twenty-one years ago?"
> "I did, I did," the happy man responded
> "And is your name Hardwicke?"
> "It is, it is! Didn't I tell you that he would know me, though I have never seen him from that time to this? Great men never forget faces."[27]

Examples like that one just added to the Clay legend, and helped explain why, by the time of his death, the *New York Times* would stress that the adulation of Clay "shared all the fervor of personal love. . . . He was . . . nearly *worshipped* by the great mass of the American people." Such sentiments by a sizable segment of the voters illustrate one reason why Clay endured so long as a candidate and had such an influence on the American political scene. Yet at the same time, that also explains some of his problems. Most of the voting public never saw him or heard him. His success before the voters in a personal sense skewed his "read" of the situation. Clay proved excellent one-on-one or in crowds. And although Clay was an actor at times in his public appearances, his allies perceived that, at his core, their hero was not acting his affection for the masses. Clay *needed* them. For if he loved the people, Clay had to have their adulation in return. But if he had their affection, did he also have their trust—and their votes?[28]

If Clay's eloquence and charisma represented significant strengths that he brought to the electoral table, other aspects of his makeup provided much more controversial elements to the repast. The opposition denounced him as ambitious and temperamental, as well as being a duelist, drunkard, profligate, philanderer, boozer, and blasphemer. Such attacks certainly damaged Clay, for they raised questions, in the mind of some voters at least, about his moral fitness for the presidency. Given that the opposition, on both sides, seized on and spread any rumor of wrongdoing in an attempt to smear the cause of their rivals, how much of the criticisms reflected the truth and how much depicted fiction?[29]

Take the question of Clay's ambition. Many accepted that as a given, and the charge followed Clay all his life. In 1822, rival John Quincy Adams deemed Clay's ambition "too ardent"; six years later a newspaper referred to the Great Pacificator's "mad, reckless ambition." In the 1840s, a magazine stressed the "ever-straining" ambition of a man devoured by that demon. So obsessed with winning that he would do anything to ensure his ascendency, Clay, in those accounts and in the words of Jackson, stood as a selfish, un-principled demagogue.[30]

Clay *was* ambitious, and he constantly worked to win the prize. Yet, how many successful politicians—indeed, successful people—are not am-bitious? A better question might be whether Clay's ambition was fueled by the right motives. Did he seek the presidency because he desired the prestige and power of the office, or because he wanted to use that position to enact programs that would help the nation? On that basic question, his enemies and allies would disagree. Clay's sin was that his eagerness showed through and that he pursued his goal too openly. As a result, critics pictured his every action as motivated by his quest for the presidency.[31]

On the charge that he had a strong temper, Clay may well have pled *nolo contendere*. He admitted that he had an "ardent" temperament and apol-ogized often for that. But many in his era were not so willing to forgive. They said Prince Hal lacked the coolness, the judgment, the self-restraint needed to lead a nation. To them, his "mercurial" temper raised issues of trust and suggested that he acted more from willfulness than from wisdom. Moreover, they argued, that produced in the so-called Great Pacificator an anger and arrogance that made him insolent and dogmatic. Even members of his own party sometimes agreed. Daniel Webster called Clay "irritable, impatient, & occasionally overbearing," and referred to his "resentful, vio-lent, & unforgiving" temper. Yet he led better, had a larger following, and produced more compromises than Webster ever did. Over time, some of Clay's impetuosity also gave place to more tranquility. Still, Clay's temper hurt him at times.[32]

On the criticisms that he drank, gambled, swore, and smoked, Clay likely would have debated the details of the charges while admitting to the basic premise. He also probably would have questioned why that mattered. If he did those things, did not much of male society, especially in the West and South, to some degree? Besides, Clay pointed out that he did none of those to excess, except on rare occasions. And, finally, as Clay's allies correctly noted in his defense, Clay mitigated those vices later in his life. As a magazine writer remarked, Clay came to Washington "a gambler, a drinker, a profuse consumer of tobacco, and a turner of night into day. He overcame the worst of those habits very early in his residence at the capital." But by then the perception had been formed, the stories circulated, and the damage done.[33]

An abolitionist traveling in Kentucky in the late 1830s recorded that profanity was common in western America. As a creature of that region, and shaped by it, Clay reflected that part of the mores of the lingering frontier. But even away from the West, men in and out of public life swore freely and often. When Clay once supposedly said openly, "Go home damn you, where you belong," his political enemies seized on that phrase and used it against him when he ran for office, conveniently forgetting the proclivities of their own leaders, such as Jackson, for similar language. Yet, to some, what might seem a rather innocuous issue became part of a bigger one. Antislavery leader Lewis Tappan called Clay a "duelist—a gambler—a profane swearer" and asked, "How can a Christian justify himself in voting for such a man?" Each issue became another building block in the edifice that political opponents fabricated and labeled "Clay's immorality."[34]

Another brick in that edifice involved Clay's drinking. When Amos Kendall arrived in Kentucky in 1810 from New England, he wrote that to be popular in Kentucky required only two things—"Drink whiskey and talk loud." Similarly, future US senator William Pitt Fessenden of Maine visited the commonwealth as a young man and discovered "hailstorms" (brandy juleps) and "snowstorms" (weaker ones): "The way they drink those things in Kentucky is a caution to sinners." Clay, perhaps a sinner, and certainly popular, readily and willingly adapted to that Kentucky culture. And if a good host in Kentucky, he proved equally pleasing in Washington, where Clay found few politicians who did not drink on a regular basis. In 1838, for instance, he and a South Carolina senator hosted a dinner party for sixteen people, at which they consumed eight bottles of Champagne and twelve more of Madeira wine. In fact, supposedly Clay introduced bourbon to the nation's capital and mixed the first mint julep there, at what is now the Willard Hotel. If so, then politicians since then have well honored his memory.[35]

Accounts of Clay being actually inebriated, however, are rare. An early description in the disapproving Adams's diary tells of Clay being "gay, and warm with wine," but nothing else. One account written some three decades after the fact told how Clay came late to a card party, "leaning on the arm" of a fellow senator, and how Clay then insulted Winfield Scott, a man he felt had helped deny him a presidential nomination. If that event did occur, that represented an anomaly, for in most accounts Clay drank often but moderately, generally favoring wine. But even that hurt him politically, especially in later races. For as the years passed, the nation became more devoted to temperance, culminating in Maine's statewide prohibition law a year before Clay's death. By the 1830s, one in every eight novels focused on the evils of drink, and more and more people judged candidates in that regard. Drinker Clay, who favored voluntary enactment of temperance but not forced legislative action regarding private matters, might seem in retrospect little different from most politicians of his time, but increasingly voters sought someone else—or at least someone whose habits were not as well known.[36]

The issue of gambling presented even more of a concern to some of the electorate. They did not seem to be bothered particularly by Clay's involvement in horse racing, for that, after all, was the sport of kings, if not democrats. Like Jackson, Clay kept fine thoroughbreds and even built a racetrack on the grounds of his estate. But most criticisms of his gambling inclinations centered on his card playing. That Clay enjoyed a game of cards, few disputed. In one of Clay's early sessions in Congress a fellow member noticed that the Kentuckian "gambles much," and Adams called him a "gamester" both in public and private life. That label stuck to Clay all his days. He enjoyed playing the more respectable game of whist (which resembles bridge or spades), but passionately loved to join a group engaged in "brag" (similar to poker). In whist, men and women often played—even John Quincy Adams—but the slower play and the lack of table stakes made it less appealing to Clay. Sources vary on whether Clay was actually very good at these games. Once, when asked if it was not a shame her husband gambled so much, Lucretia Clay reportedly replied, "Oh, I don't know. Mr. Clay usually wins." Often, young attorneys on the circuit made more money from cards than from their cases, and Clay reputedly did so as well. But in 1820, Adams recounted that Clay had "embarrassing losses." A much later account tells how Clay would hold the cards several feet apart and fly them from one hand to another in the shuffle, "without a single card falling." When he put his mind to it, he could also name what cards remained to be played. But the apparent "card shark" did not play well, according to that same report. Clay more enjoyed the companionship, the risk-taking, and the excitement of the game, and as a result played carelessly and apparently worried little about the end result. The observer did notice one characteristic of Clay: "He used to bluff a great deal."[37]

Winner or loser, Clay probably gained several ways from the knowledge gathered at the table. At Ghent, for instance, he played cards frequently with the British commissioners and likely learned as much about diplomatic matters from the conversations around that table as he did in formal discussions. Moreover, his ability to bluff often helped him both in foreign missions and in American legislative halls. At the same time, Clay eventually recognized that he enjoyed brag more than was good for him, or for his reputation. Even though card-playing represented a common social vice followed by many of that day, it could also be the vehicle for more insidious results, such as lobbyists using brag as the way to bribe congressmen, by purposely losing a bet to them. As a result, Clay vowed to limit his involvement in that "seductive passion." And he apparently largely succeeded in doing so. By 1839, he advised a son never to take up the game, for it could create an addiction and (probably speaking from experience) could cause the loss of "money, time, sleep, health, and character." But Clay himself did not have the discipline to give up cards completely. Yet even if he had the requisite will, he probably would not have stopped playing, for the savvy politician used the game to gain knowledge of people, to construct political deals, to relax, and simply to enjoy the company of others.[38]

Clay's involvement in the controversial practice of dueling also brought into serious question his fitness for higher office, especially among some religious or reform groups in the North. They called for rejection of the "infamous" and notorious "brawler *Henry Clay*," a "professed duelist," a man "whose hands are stained with blood." To elect him, said the Reverend Lyman Beecher, would reward the murderer for his actions. The problem with many of those characteristics concerned their fidelity to the truth. Clay's hands were barely stained with blood, if at all. He seldom ever brawled, and he certainly never killed anyone—unlike Jackson, who did fight several duels, did kill an opponent, and did engage in numerous fights. Yet as with other attacks on his moral character, such charges against Clay cost him votes.[39]

Clay certainly erred in fighting his two duels. Both involved harsh words spoken in the heat of debate in hallowed legislative chambers, and could have been ignored for that reason. Or if Clay knew his actions were beyond reproach, then as the best judge of his own honor he could have ignored such comments. Or given Clay's verbal abilities, he could have reacted to perceived insults and have bloodied with his words anyone who attacked his honor. But he could not do that, for his temper, need for mastery, and southern sense of honor all dictated otherwise. For while the Code of Honor represented a set of external, ethical rules understood by southern gentlemen and yeomen alike, it also involved certain community expectations, as men often fought to prove their manhood and place in society. Clay's actions not only in Congress but also on the dueling ground thus brought description of him as "bold, chivalrous & manly." At another level, it all also involved mastery of others and of oneself. Honor could not be arbitrated. A person either had it or did not: "Honor required courage; cowardice meant shame; insults could not be tolerated. Action must follow, for only blood could cleanse the stains of honor." Clay had a high sense of honor and self-worth, and a low threshold for insults. Duels resulted. But they came at a time when the nation increasingly saw such duels as anachronistic and archaic, part of an irrational code that contradicted an American value system emphasizing the intrinsic worth of each individual life. Given that, and with the growing religious spirit in the United States, Clay's dueling may have won him some individual respect and personal satisfaction, but it came at significant cost politically.[40]

Henry Clay prosaically described the fruits of honor in a January 1809 letter, as he told of his recently completed duel, sparked by words in the legislature, with fellow member Humphrey Marshall, the brother-in-law of the chief justice of the United States: "I have this moment returned from the field of battle. We had three shots. On the first I grazed him just above the navel—he missed me. On the second my damned pistol snapped, and he missed me. On the third I received a flesh wound in the thigh, and owning to my receiving his first fire &c., I missed him. My wound is no way serious." Yet Clay did not return to the legislature for some three weeks. The rising politician had been injured and had risked sacrificing a promising career on the altar of honor. The irony was that the man who became known as the Great Pacificator and the Great Compromiser fought duels.[41]

Clay's second duel seemingly could have been easily avoided, with little risk to his honor. That was because it involved one of the strangest men to sit in the US Congress—John Randolph of Roanoke, Virginia. Brilliant and talented but arbitrary and arrogant, witty and wealthy but unstable and maniacal, Randolph owned more than eight thousand acres of land and almost four hundred slaves. He defended his way of life without apology: "I am an aristocrat. I love liberty. I hate equality." A proponent of states' rights and slavery, he termed Yankees great scoundrels but promiscuously attacked all parties and sections in Congress. After 1818—when he was in his forties—Randolph's dementia started to become more obvious, and he also became addicted to opium later in life. As a result, Adams termed Randolph a "jumble of sense, wit and absurdity." Another contemporary wrote that if Randolph's bizarreness "did not border on insanity, [it] also separated from it by a very slight partition"; a congressman called the Virginian crazy and "wild as a maniac."[42]

Not surprisingly, the two strong-willed men clashed in Congress over issues small and large almost from the start of Clay's service in the House. Although Randolph apparently admired Clay's frankness, he bitterly opposed the Kentuckian's programs and loved to taunt him in regard to those and his political ambitions—"Clay's eye is on the Presidency, and my eye is on him." It would be only a matter of time before Randolph's often rambling and discordant talks, or his quick repartee in debate, resulted in some devastatingly clever and cutting remark that would deeply offend Clay. That day came near the end of March 1826. Clay, who was not in Congress at the time but was in Washington, heard a somewhat erroneous report that stressed how Randolph had sarcastically accused Clay of forgery and corruption. Friends tried to dissuade Clay from issuing a challenge to a duel, noting that Randolph's mental status meant he could be ignored, and that a duel would hurt Clay's political fortunes. Clay considered all that, but nevertheless felt compelled to send a challenge for the "unprovoked attack on my character." Perhaps appropriately, on April Fool's Day 1826, Randolph accepted.[43]

A week later, the two men faced off at ten paces. Randolph had told a friend beforehand that he would not try to harm Clay, because he did not want to leave Clay's children fatherless. Now, on the command of "Fire," Clay's first shot barely missed him. In the heat of the moment, Randolph did shoot, yet he did not hit his target. On the second exchange, Clay's bullet went through Randolph's coat, harmlessly. The man from Virginia then raised his weapon, fired into the air, and exclaimed, "Mr. Clay I came upon the ground determined not to fire at you, but that vexatious accident changed my purpose for a moment, which I sincerely regret. I give you my hand." They shook in reconciliation, and then Randolph playfully said, "You owe me a coat, Mr. Clay." The Kentuckian responded, "Mr. Randolph, I thank God that I am no deeper in debt." (Clay's friend Rebecca Gratz, on hearing of those comments, remarked that it would have been better if Clay had given Randolph a straitjacket.) The two men parted as they had arrived, not as friends but as talented opponents.[44]

Yet in satisfying his honor, Clay had again erred terribly. He had first hesitated to act, owing to the "state of Mr. Randolph's mind," and had he simply left it at that, few would have questioned that response. Clay should have just symbolically walked away from the insult. Even though he regretted turning to the "pernicious practice" of dueling, he did confess afterward that the affair had left him composed and satisfied, "which I should not have enjoyed, if the occasion had not occurred. We are strange beings!" But while some of his friends approved a reflective Clay's actions as the only corrective for Randolph's "evil propensities," others mildly rebuked him for reacting to a "madman" and putting himself in harm's way, as a family man. (For, after all, if dueling satisfied a personal need and might be done to preserve the family honor, at its core it still represented a selfish action.) In the end, more of Clay's correspondents criticized him than praised him. From Paris, his brother-in-law James Brown warned him that the increasingly "unfashionable" practice of dueling would damage him in the East. A Rhode Island ally seconded that, saying that New Englanders saw the practice as a "horrible" thing; a New Yorker echoed that the duel would hurt Clay "with a large class of our people." And Clay knew the results of his actions would offend many in the religious and moral community, yet he seemed unable to resist the call of honor. That southern-oriented aspect of his core value system lured him into actions that hurt him politically, and his opponents would capitalize on that.[45]

Randolph and Clay finally reconciled some six years later. On his way through Washington, Randolph went to the Senate chamber he had haunted for so long, just as Clay was speaking. Weak and feeble, Randolph called to a friend, "Raise me up! I want to hear that voice again!" After Clay finished, he noticed his old antagonist, "looking as if he were not long for this world," and went to him. Clay offered his hand and expressed the hope that Randolph was better. Randolph replied that he was dying, but he had come there to hear Clay and talk with him. They shook hands and, amid tears, made peace. Randolph openly called Clay "a braver man . . . , a consistent man . . . , an independent man and an honest man." Still, the stories surfaced that Randolph had asked to be buried facing west, "so it was said, that he might still keep an eye, even after death, on Henry Clay."[46]

In fact, Clay and Randolph stories of dubious validity circulated long after the demise of both. The marvelous imagery of Randolph's comment about an opponent—"He shines and stinks like rotten mackerel by moonlight"—likely was directed at Edward Livingston, not Clay, but over the years Clay's name became attached to it. Similarly, a century after the Kentuckian's death, US vice president Alben Barkley told how Clay and Randolph had been strolling down opposite sidewalks, and unknowingly both ventured at the same time across a plank walkway laid over the muddy DC streets. Suddenly they confronted each other in the middle. Randolph fumed, "I never get out of the way of a damned scoundrel!" Clay smirked and said, "I always do," and stepped aside. Yet, when it had mattered to his political future, Clay had not stepped aside, but had fought instead.[47]

But the one duel that caused as much public damage to Clay as any did not even directly involve him. In February 1838, congressman Jonathan Cilley of Maine questioned an editor's honesty. Kentucky representative William Graves conveyed the editor's subsequent challenge to Cilley. But the man from Maine refused to accept the note, indicating the editor was not his equal. That response, in turn, offended Graves, for it supposed that he, as the bearer of the challenge, was no gentleman, either. The written Code of Honor required in such circumstances that the second, Graves, offer himself instead. He did. After several further notes, the duel between the two congressmen took place. Cilley chose rifles, with the agreement that after each exchange the two parties would move closer. On the third fire, at around eighty yards, Graves killed Cilley. Great censure fell on the Kentuckian, who told a companion, "The hand of Cain is upon my brow." But he ran for reelection and won. Meanwhile the ensuing, detailed congressional investigation and numerous newspaper stories did not even mention Clay.[48]

Then politics reared its hostile head. Some four years after the duel, as Clay geared up for another presidential race, political opponent (and Cilley's second) Henry A. Wise suddenly charged Clay with having instigated the duel. The stories later escalated: "Mr. Clay was the cause of Cilley's murder." Accomplice Clay, the accounts stressed, had rewritten Graves's response in such a way as to make it impossible to reach a settlement. A perplexed Clay explained that he *had* rewritten an early note, but for the reverse reason—he wanted to *soften* the language to help bring about an amicable result. The Great Pacificator had even told the police about the upcoming duel in an effort to get it stopped. But he had failed. Perhaps Clay could have taken an even more active role in trying to end it, but he should bear no blame for aiding and abetting it. In that duel, at least, Clay stood as an innocent victim.[49]

Dueling, drinking, gambling, swearing—all those may have been signs of Clay's manliness to masculine America. Yet at the same time, Clay had the rare ability in his era to be viewed by men as manly and by women as sensitive and caring. The female population of Washington frequently turned out in large numbers to listen to well-known political figures address the House or Senate. But when Clay spoke, women especially came to hear him, and they often occupied all the available seats. And once the Whig Party formed, women— or at least the middle and upper-class women who left more of a record— flocked to the party of Henry Clay. In 1844, one man wrote him to report that 70 percent of women favored that party. A Richmond, Virginia, newspaper declared, "The ladies are Whig, almost universally." Three years later, a magazine article indicated that women had become "generally attached" to the Whig standard. More religiously oriented and less traditional in regard to women's role, the Whigs encouraged the participation of women at their rallies. Women attended political gatherings for Clay in large numbers, often composing a fourth or more of the audience. They also gave him memberships in their organizations and presented Clay with vases, silver pitchers, and other gifts. At a time when women sought to allay social ills by more active involvement in society through the support of orphanages, asylums, temperance groups, and other betterment activities, many of those same reformers supported Henry Clay. Ironically, for all the attacks on Clay's moral failings, the most moral and religious part of American society overwhelmingly and unabashedly endorsed Henry Clay. The group at the core of the temperance crusade venerated Clay; those who advocated higher moral standards applauded Clay; many who disapproved of gambling and profanity approved of Clay. Why? Perhaps because he represented the party they supported, or perhaps because they could separate the private man from the public one they endorsed, or perhaps it was because he symbolized harmony over conflict. But some supported Clay also because his oratory enthralled them, his manners charmed them, and his charisma convinced them—as they did many American men. Even a Democratic politician's wife openly admitted: "I am a *Clay* man; in fact, the ladies are all Clay men."[50]

Had women been able to vote, Clay likely would have been elected president more than once, as one writer suggested when she welcomed Clay to a Ladies' Fair: "Welcome again! thrice welcome to our city! / And mark among your presidential notes / How sorrowful it is, and what a pity, / That women may not rulers choose with votes!" But whether they had the ballot or not, Clay simply seemed to genuinely enjoy talking to women. In private settings, a relaxed Clay often showed a very different side of his being than that offered to masculine America. Margaret Bayard Smith had initially cared little for the Clay of reputation. Then she heard him give an eloquent, witty talk and saw the power of his "soul-speaking eye." Later, as she got to know Clay better, she found him absolutely fascinating, for he combined a natural intellect with a soft, revealing tenderness. Once at a party, soon after Clay had experienced bitter defeats and much personal sadness, she saw him being gracious and courteous, but knew the hurt he felt. He came to her, inquired about her husband, and instinctively asked why she seemed so sad. Her good friend, Lucretia Clay, would soon be leaving Washington for Kentucky, Mrs. Smith explained. He took her hand, his eyes filled with tears, and he simply said, "We must not . . . talk of such things *now*." He wiped his eyes and rejoined the crowd, "as if his heart was bright and easy." Another woman praised Clay's kindness and his ability to lose "all thought of himself in his desire to give pleasure to others." With women, Clay felt comfortable revealing a sensitive, caring person, one far removed from the image enemies painted of him, and women who knew him appreciated that frankness, that side of what they saw as a feeling, emotional, compassionate man, not a designing politician.[51]

That does not mean, however, that in an age that stressed language and manners, Clay did not use flattery and suavity to charm some women he met, as he also did with some men. One woman asked Clay, "You do not remember my name?" His answer made eased the situation: "No, for when we last met long ago, I was sure your beauty and accomplishments would very soon compel you to change it." Such examples broke down many barriers and made Clay so appealing. To a later generation, Clay in his era combined all the elements of a motivational speaker, a stand-up comedian, a motion picture actor, and a rock star. And like those, he attracted the attendant attention. A woman beckoned to a Senate page, after one of Clay's speeches, and asked him to go to Clay "and say that a lady wishes to kiss him for that speech." Such displays disgusted William H. Seward, who complained of women fawning over Clay: "Young ladies insist on kissing him in public assemblies." Little doubt exists that Clay had, as William Henry Harrison expressed it, "great admiration of female beauty." And when Clay came into a room, a reporter noted that many women wanted to say they had been kissed by Clay. But really more than the mischievous pleasure of all that, Clay simply enjoyed the company of women, of all ages and all political persuasions. Less a ladies' man than a man for the ladies, Clay delighted in their society and their conversation.[52]

Clay's attractiveness to women generally was not the issue for him politically. The criticism of Clay came from charges that he liked women too much. Some observers noted what was an inconvertible truth—that numerous women showed public affection for Clay, and that he, in return, took obvious pleasure in their presence—and made the leap from that certainty to the assumption that he thus had affairs with some of those women. After all, other American leaders supposedly had illicit liaisons in the past—Benjamin Franklin, Aaron Burr, and Thomas Jefferson, for example—so would not Clay as well, given his reputed immorality, his public actions, and his many opportunities? Opponents thus attacked this notorious, "*habitual libertine*," this "grossly immoral" individual, this man who "*spent his days at the gambling table and his nights at the brothel.*" And all those words came in just one year of vitriol, from one section. A reporter concluded that there was "scarcely any known species of vice and profligacy that he has not been said to be guilty of."[53]

But was he guilty as charged?[54]

The problem lies in that the scanty evidence emanates almost totally from his political enemies. Several contemporaries made reference, for example, to the "looseness of his morality," but in the context usually of a discussion of his political morality. In an election year, a Mississippian wrote he had uncovered a story that Clay had fathered a child by a former slave, and that he had sent both mother and child south. The letter writer indicated that the information should be used to Clay's political detriment. In an era when every rumor or scandal made opposition headlines, that one apparently did not, suggesting that after even a cursory examination, it held no basis—even for a rumor. Other charges made by political opponents similarly never gained credibility—except among those who would believe anything bad about Clay. Because of his own sexual offenses, South Carolina congressman and governor James H. Hammond tended to accept similar rumors and repeat them. He indicated that Webster and Clay—both of the opposite party—were "addicted to loose indulgences with woman." Of course, such language can have different meanings. A woman told her sister how a woman whom Clay loved "in a *paternal* way" would not permit him to take "the familiarities which so many ladies seem proud to have him take." What sounds salacious becomes something else when the next line in the letter reveals the scandalous activity being fought off was simply one of Clay's typical kisses of greeting.[55]

In contrast, extant letters to and from Clay offer little support for the charge of infidelity. Not that some women did not make veiled offers to Clay. For example, a self-described "eccentric" married woman from Philadelphia wrote to him in 1828, asking for a patronage post for a nephew. She told of her admiration for Clay, then recounted how she had made love to Aaron Burr: "A great man may love as much as he pleases." The woman gave her address and then indicated that she sensed Clay had many of Burr's traits, including his "electric fire." A single woman from Baltimore similarly asked for a position for a friend and closed her letter saying, "*I am still in the blessed state of celibacy,* and if you know any one *worthy of me*, let me be apprized, as I intend coming down this session." The object of her patronage request did not get the job. In fact, there is no evidence that Clay responded to either letter.[56]

Clay did carry on an extended, warm, and witty correspondence with several other women, almost all of them married and most of them the spouses of his political friends. Eliza Johnston, the wife of Transylvania-educated Louisiana senator Josiah S. Johnston, told Clay, for instance, how she missed him "terribly" after he left their home, and hoped he would only see "ugly old maids" rather than "handsome ladies." But she probably enclosed that playful note in a letter her husband sent Clay, and Clay typically wrote her husband some clever comments for him to relay to Eliza. In like spirit, Clay called Mary Bayard, the wife of a Delaware senator, "my truest, best, and faithful friend." They too exchanged amiable words and heartfelt comments. Clay also wrote warmly to Octavia Walton LeVert, who spoke three languages and hosted a well-attended, multinational salon in Mobile, Alabama. As Clay explained to Mary Bayard, who had just met Octavia, Mrs. LeVert had little "personal beauty" but possessed a kindness and "affability" that made her very attractive as a person. And in truth, that latter description fit most of Clay's female correspondents. His attraction was not sexual but, rather, emotional. He found many women interesting and personable, the kind of individuals, male and female, that he liked to know and be around.[57]

Given the proclivity of Washington female society to shun those it deemed guilty of sexual indiscretions (Peggy Eaton, for example), and given the increasing religiosity of the United States, would such women have welcomed Clay into their home and confidences if they had any firm suggestion of impropriety on his part? In fact, the extant sources suggest that no woman who met Clay and wrote about it intimated that Clay had made improper advances. If the evidence for and against the rumors were placed on the scales of justice, the predominance of weight lies heavily on the side of fidelity.[58]

Having said that, this does not mean Clay *was* faithful. Surrounded by female slaves, men like Richard M. Johnson sought them out for companionship; absent from family on long diplomatic missions, some men, like Henry's cousin Cassius Clay, had affairs; away from spouses for months at a time while serving in Congress, other men went to brothels. Clay may have as well. But accepting uncritically the rumors and politically based charges made against Clay flies in the face of most existing evidence.[59]

Still, whether Clay was innocent of the charges did not matter. All his opponents had to do was create a suspicion of guilt in the minds of the undecided or the "soft" supporters. If they did not vote for Clay or went with some third-party candidate, then Clay's enemies had won. Enough truth existed on such questions as drinking, gambling, and dueling to suggest smoke, if not fire, in the forest of morality. Believing those truths, it did not take many steps to accept the allegations of sexual improprieties and other more debatable charges. Supporters might testify to Clay's "integrity . . . beyond the reach of reproach," while opponents might swear to Clay's "reckless contempt [for] . . . every moral and religious injunction." Would the rumors about his lifestyle raise enough reservations concerning his persona to defeat him? Or would the voters disdain such unsavory tactics, look at the facts of the man, at his history, and vote for those reasons? The answers might be troubling, and the basic questions raised might not end in Henry Clay's era.[60]

4

Programs

IN 1828, A LETTER WRITER from Boston remarked sadly that Clay's envious enemies in the United States seemed determined to damage his reputation forever. Ironically, he noted, patriots across South America praised Clay as their firmest friend and foremost ally. People in other countries recognized Clay's greatness, he concluded, even if Americans did not. Those fighting for freedom abroad read Clay's speeches to revolutionary forces, and to them, his reputation remained unsullied. Almost a century later, while US citizens seemingly paid little attention to the sesquicentennial of Clay's birth, in Latin America they still praised Clay's support for their independence and Venezuela erected a statue of Clay to honor his contribution.[1]

Clay's leadership efforts sprang both from his deeply held philosophy that "the great cause of human liberty" must prevail around the globe and from his belief that the continents must be tied together in spirit and in commerce. As the best hope of democracy, the United States must be the beacon lighting the way for the rest of humanity. To do that, said Clay, it had to be free and prosperous. His political outlook, his philosophical underpinnings, his economic plans all sought to make that vision a reality.[2]

In 1810, the first of a series of revolts against Spanish colonial control had broken out in South and Central America. A dozen years later, the United States would be the first nation to recognize the independence of those emerging new nations. But in that interim period, Henry Clay vehemently pushed for recognition of the struggling republics. By leading the American effort he earned the sympathy of the revolutionaries and the antipathy of many at home.

In those dozen years before recognition, America's guarded foreign policy—formulated chiefly by James Monroe and John Quincy Adams—first resulted in a proclamation of neutrality. Cautiously, the nation wanted to make certain the revolts succeeded and that it did not act rashly. At the same time, the United States did not want to anger Spain unduly. Engaged in delicate, ongoing negotiations regarding the US purchase of Spanish-owned Florida, American diplomats sought to continue the discussions and give Spain no reason to break off talks. All in all, their position represented a reasonable approach to what some deemed the best policy for the long-range interest of the United States.[3]

None of that reasoning satisfied the impatient Henry Clay. As early as 1816, the Kentuckian noted that the actions taking place to the south had made a "serious impression" on his mind. By the next year, he came out fully in support of recognition, despite accusations that he was acting in an "imprudent" way. "I care not," Clay responded, "when the independence, the happiness, the liberty of a whole people is at stake." Over the next half decade, Clay made a series of strong speeches in support of their independence. Opponents criticized Clay, saying the former War Hawk would risk an American war with Spain with early recognition. John Randolph charged that when visiting Europe, Clay had ventured too near Waterloo and "had sniffed the carnage and caught the infection." But Clay answered that he had seen enough of death and dying and would give "no just cause for war." Clay thundered that the United States must simply do the right thing, at the right time.[4]

Some congressmen used the argument that the rebels were too "ignorant" and too "superstitious" (that is, Catholic) to enjoy democratic freedoms and thus should not be self-governing. Even Adams indicated that the revolutionary rulers did not meet American standards of virtue. Clay gave such polemics short shrift. More optimistic than these critics, he termed such pessimistic outlooks "the doctrine of thrones, that man is too ignorant to govern himself." As to the supposed superstitions of the people, they worship the same God, said Clay, as Americans do, and only when religions are united with governments do they become inimical to free expression. Otherwise, if separated from government, they remain compatible with liberty. Besides, in some ways, said Clay, those peoples stood in advance of the United States, for they had emancipated their slaves. Such patriots had fought for freedom, had won it, had deserved it, and now should be given the opportunity to enjoy it. They might make mistakes in the future, but they would do so as free people. Crucial to his vision of the future was making certain the republics of the two Americas shared common forms of government, similar commercial ties, and comparable destinies. If the United States led in recognizing the new nations, that objective could be achieved.[5]

That stance, however, put Clay in an awkward, antagonistic position with the Monroe administration. After an 1818 dinner, Secretary of State Adams wrote that Clay "came out with great violence against the course pursued by the Executive." (The suspicion exists that Clay frequently overstated his views when with Adams, just because he knew they would vex him.) Some slaveholders also apparently opposed Clay's course on South America because they feared the example of a more dark-skinned people guiding their own fortunes and emancipating their slaves. Both groups would thus find fault with Clay when he looked to higher office.[6]

Yet Clay also succeeded in certain ways. Had the United States taken more of a leadership role earlier, the acclaim given Clay the person by the people of South America could have been the spirit shown the American nation as well. Whether Clay hastened recognition or not, he took a stand that resonated with many, abroad and at home. He reached them as a democrat, as a spokesman for the aspirations of human freedom, as an opponent of tyranny. Clay expressed views that reflected his own feelings regarding the struggles and rights of a people. And if such views grew increasingly popular politically, Clay did not mind that at all.[7]

Clay took a similar stand regarding the Greek War of Independence against Turkey. Once more, critics charged that his rash proposals would hurt American commerce, risk war with a foreign power, and involve the United States in European affairs. In a powerful 1824 speech, he answered those attacks: "Are we so humbled, so low, so despicable, that we dare not express our sympathy for suffering Greece, lest, peradventure, we might offend some one or more of their imperial and royal Majesties?" Nor should the trade question be a factor: "What shall it profit a nation to save the whole of a wretched commerce, and lose its liberties?" Instead, the key question for Clay was one of humanity. The United States, as "the sole, the last, the greatest depository of human hope and of human freedom," must take a stand in favor of liberty for "suffering and bleeding Greece."[8]

The actions of Henry Clay regarding Greece and South America reflected his strong Jeffersonian faith in democracy and in the power of the people. Over and over, he stressed that the United States must lead, for if it failed and the light of liberty dimmed, then human society would descend into "one universal darkness." But who determined the best course toward a bright future? To Clay, the surest guide was a single one: the majority of the people. After one of his presidential defeats, he expressed regret on the outcome of the vote, but he emphasized that the people had spoken and his republican duty had called him to obey. John C. Calhoun once correctly summarized Clay's view of government and of the majority: "The Senator from Kentucky . . . maintained that the people of these States constitute a nation; that the nation has a will of its own; that the numerical majority of the whole was the appropriate organ of its voice. . . ." Clay heard loudest not the sounds of the states but the voice of the people.[9]

Having grown up amid the teaching of Revolutionary War republicanism, with its emphasis on concessions, consensus, and the common good, Clay never abandoned those core beliefs. Some of those who had crafted the Constitution had also called for limited powers for the executive; so did Clay. Once more expressing his belief in the people as the fount of rightness, he favored the legislative branch as the dominant one in government. It represented the voters' will more directly and more often than the executive branch did. Moreover, an ambitious president could use patronage, popularity, and power to woo and awe the people and, bit by bit, take away their liberties. As early as 1819, Clay warned Congress that they must keep "a watchful and steady eye" on the executive. And once Andrew Jackson became president, that admonition became a virtual mantra.[10]

Yet, at the heart of Clay's political philosophy beat another republican theme: compromise. "All society is an affair of moral concession," he declared in 1820, and government was no different. After all, Clay reminded his audience again and again that the US Constitution—"that greatest of all compromises"—showed the fruitful benefits of such an approach. There, the various sections, the diverse concerns, the different viewpoints had all come together, made mutual sacrifices, and taken moderate actions. If that spirit prevailed, then no question "in human affairs, so weak or so strong . . . could not be approached by argument and reason."[11]

Clay saw a growing nation of many and varied interests—East versus West, North versus South, rural versus urban, agricultural versus manufacturing. Add to that ethnic, religious, and class divisions, then mix in the combustible elements of slave labor versus free, and the Union was filled with competing stakeholders. With minority elements present on most questions, not all could be satisfied. Clay's answer to the problems posed by the nature of America and of democracy consistently focused on the use of compromise. His role in that arena did not come naturally, however, for his temper, stubbornness, and pride all mitigated against that. Yet he saw himself as the model for compromise—sacrificing his own feelings, as the founding fathers had done, for the good of the country. Compromise had to involve reciprocity, with each concerned group yielding something while keeping something. But when groups made those sacrifices and the national interest benefited as a result, then the act of compromise itself would further cement all to the nation.[12]

People were inconsistent and imperfect, Clay concluded (and he knew of what he spoke). Therefore, what individuals produced in the political world likely would not be perfect, either. Change would occur over time. The key to success, he suggested, would be to understand and accept imperfection and to formulate the best answers that the times allowed. Comparing the United States to "one common family," he noted that, as in families, arguments and disputes arose. Anger and harsh words could be exchanged. At times such institutions could even become dysfunctional. But if both those in the family and those in the family of states acted "in the spirit of brothers" and put the peace and welfare of all above any petty emotions, then they could act constructively, forgive and forget, and go on to even greater things.[13]

But Clay also worried that those on both extremes of a question would not compromise. If their numbers remained small, such obstinacy mattered less. But if the extremes grew, so did the chance of unresolved conflict and an open rupture. Clay spoke for moderation in a nation increasingly moving away from that center, and his stands would cost him votes. Yet to him, the issue was clear: "Extremes . . . are ever wrong. Truth, and justice, sound policy, and wisdom always abide in the middle ground." Those of partisan spirit "must find some common ground, on which both can stand."[14]

During his public career, Clay tried to use his sensitivity to the concerns of all groups and his faith in the future of the United States to find that common ground, to keep the nation standing. He was the best in his generation at doing so.[15] Yet compromise came at a price. For Clay often lost as much as he gained from the compromises, big and small, that he forged. As one government building sign explained more recently, "Blessed are the peacemakers for they catch hell from both sides." Those on each extreme may feel anger at the person who forged the compromise that denied them their goal. Others may see the act of compromise itself as a sign of moral weakness or a failure to take a firm stand. Like many politicians then and since, he faced the difficult choice: Do you remain firm to your beliefs and perhaps produce stalemate, or do you compromise your principles and possibly create productive results? No satisfactory answer exists. Politicians are expected to be consistent *and* to compromise; not surprisingly, they may be pilloried for whatever action they take. Perhaps Edmund Burke expressed it best in 1775: "All government . . . is founded on compromise and barter," he explained, but no one should barter away "the jewel of his soul." That outlook would produce key questions for Henry Clay: What if one of the extremes holds the moral high ground? Is compromise always desirable? When do you stop compromising and follow the dictates of your soul? The answers would affect his presidential races and would prove troubling throughout his life.[16]

While Clay's support for the concept of compromise as a key part of national policymaking brought forth a mixed but generally positive reaction, his advocacy of another constitutional interpretation elicited stronger emotions and harsher criticism. To Clay, the country's continued growth required a flexible construction of the US Constitution and the creation of a strong central government. Like most men of his generation, Clay revered America's governing document—what he called "the sheet-anchor of the national safety"—but he disagreed with those who sought to limit it by a strict-construction, states' rights reading. They would so restrict actions as to make the Constitution a dead letter, "an inanimate Skeleton." Following their reasoning, said Clay, would head the United States down a fateful road that would end in the wreck of a weak, squabbling government that could do little, much like the ill-fated and little-lamented Articles of Confederation.[17]

Instead, to Clay, a flexible, living Constitution must guide the nation. Fallible people, different contingencies, and varying circumstances meant that the rules and actions of the present might not, and should not, be the guide for future generations. After all, "a new world has come into being since the Constitution was adopted," and no reason existed to think that such would not be the case in distant years. If the nation wanted to prosper and lead, it must have the constitutional discretion to adapt to "the exigencies of the times." Clay admitted that earlier in his career he had taken a more restrictive view regarding such limits. But "events of the utmost magnitude"—the War of 1812—had transformed his thinking. Now he more feared atrophy than the abuse of federal power. Change would occur, whether people wanted it or not, and only by adjusting to that change, and legislating to reflect it, could the nation grow and prosper. Otherwise, it would wither and die.[18]

At the same time, Clay realized that dangers existed in that controversial interpretation. A broad constitutional view could lead an unscrupulous executive to try to assume powers not delegated or granted, as in the Alien and Sedition Acts he had earlier protested. But if power resided primarily in the legislative branch with its many voices, if those leaders used common sense, vigilance, and discretion, if they limited application to those things "tending to the general benefit" of the nation, if the will of the majority ruled, those conditions should overcome most concerns and well serve the country. Clay's views reflected the future in that regard, though he did not anticipate the role a strong president could play in advocating the national interest in the years ahead. But most of all, his concepts harkened back to his belief in the importance of compromise. The Constitution had to be continually readjusted to meet changing times, and the power within it had to be constantly reallocated in response to new situations. National greatness demanded nothing less.[19]

If people accepted Clay's views of a flexible constitution with a broad construction of the "necessary and proper" clause, the natural result would be increased power for the federal government. His doctrines implied that while individuals might manage their personal concerns better than the government could, only positive federal involvement could bring the diverse individual forces together to provide the needed aid to benefit the larger community. As Clay would later express it, the duties of a "parental" government required it "to lift up the depressed, to heal the wounds, and cheer and encourage the unhappy man who sees in the past . . . nothing but ruin and embarrassment, and in the future nothing but gloom and despair."[20]

However, Clay's clearly stated beliefs made him a pariah to many Americans, who damned his theory, detested his subsequent programs, and denied his political hopes. The *United States Magazine and Democratic Review* criticized Clay's "bold and elastic latitudinarianism of construction" regarding the Constitution, as a doctrine that would "revolutionize our beautiful federative system into a consolidated and unrestrained energy of central government." To those who closely guarded state prerogatives and considered the Constitution almost perfect at inception, such federal encroachment on their powers and their liberties had to be stopped. And they must defeat Henry Clay. On several fronts, they attacked the man who spoke such dangerous words. Opponents noted Clay's earlier comments favoring a more limited government and threw them back at him. Others accused Clay of changing his principles "as a man of many suits changes his clothes" and of saying "one thing to-day and the opposite to-morrow." A South Carolinian charged the Kentuckian with accommodating his doctrines to "the temper of the times." (Clay might not have greatly disagreed with that critique, for he did feel the need to change his views on occasion, not necessarily to the temper of the times but to the changing circumstances that demanded fresh answers.) But on a larger scale, most of his critics simply opposed Clay's support for a stronger federal government.[21]

If Clay's abstract principles of government engendered much fierce debate, his programs based on those creeds produced white-hot anger and equally charged praise. Indeed, the fact that Clay had a stated program, a specific plan, differentiated him from most other politicians of his generation, and even from later ones. In the after years, some presidents would become associated with concentrated, developed blueprints for their domestic policies, but few presented such overreaching ideas before they filled the office. Clay did so—and that both helped and hurt him politically.

Clay's American System owed much to the thoughts and theories of those who came before him, but he took the various concepts, unified them, added to them, and most of all, expressed them in a national forum in a clearly stated, easily understandable way. Clay offered a sweeping conception of what America could be, should be, would be, and how it should get there. He would fight most of his political life to convince his fellow citizens that his vision should become their destiny. In that, he had a more accurate understanding of what would actually unfold in the future than did most politicians of his era. But would anticipating future directions mean that he would be so far in advance of his followers that he would be a lonely leader? Would he be heralded for a stronger approach to governmental involvement in the economy, or would he be ignored because of it?[22]

While Clay first used the term "American System" in 1818, he gave it widespread national attention two years later, when he cried out, "Let us become real and true Americans, and place ourselves at the head of the American system." In major speeches then and in 1824–1825, he outlined the shape and substance of his economic nationalism. It rested on four pillars: a set of high tariff duties that would protect fledgling American manufacturing and certain agricultural interests in the home market, and thus produce more jobs; a financial system that would provide a reliable currency, national banking stability, and safe loans for growth; a system of support for internal improvement—for roads, rivers, and canals—that would make trade easier and better bind the country together; and a policy of selling unoccupied lands in the federal domain under a pricing structure that would manage and control growth while raising funds for other projects, such as education and emancipation. Clay recognized that his proposals would require sacrifice by certain groups. Some people might experience temporary inconvenience, but in the spirit of compromise and "for the good of the whole," they should submit for their future benefit. After all, he declared, "We are the same people. We have the same country."[23]

Clay envisioned his American System to be the final step in the consummation of independence. A war had restored honor in a second revolution, and now a similar economic result could occur through legislative action. After all, almost from the earliest English settlements, local governments had been involved in the economy and the community, whether by building roads and dams, regulating tavern rates, or aiding the needy. Clay would take that outlook and transpose it to the national scene. In his view, national wealth should be more important than individual wealth; the common good should subsume the private good; the prosperity of the whole should dominate the prosperity of the particular. In the end, all would then benefit, all would gain, all would prosper.[24]

Adopting that approach would require an almost seismic shift in American thinking. Utilizing a broad construction of the enacting clauses, Clay's activist federal government would institute a planned national economic system and distribute benefits across the nation. That might take the shape of stimulating growth through land grants, tax exemptions, charters, franchises, and subsidies. Commercial and transportation networks, for example, would be constructed with federal support and would integrate the various sectional economies into a national economy of "affinity and consanguinity." Those receiving such benefits would be obligated "to the fountain head, and to the support and strength of the Union." In short, Clay wanted to transfer first loyalty from the individual states to the United States. While some cohesive features bound people together—language, law, and history—other natural tendencies separated them. Fearing such sectional disunity and such economic divisions, Clay sought to build a national mindset, one that acted for the welfare of all. His program would, he argued, foster development and harmonize the interests of capital and labor, agriculture and manufacturing, North and South, East and West. Doing that, the government could achieve its primary goal, the union of the states. In that way a more patriotic people and a more self-sufficient nation could meet the challenges of a new industrial age and different market demands.

A popular 1844 campaign engraving symbolizes Clay's American System and his commercial and agricultural background with the anvil, plow, cows, and ship. He points to the flag, recalling his support for the Union, and to a globe with South America displayed, as a reminder of his fight for recognition of those countries as they sought their independence. *Library of Congress, LC-DIG-pga-04108*

The United States would then emerge as the greatest moral, political, and economic force in the world.[25]

Clay's successes in executing his American System testify not only to the elements of the plan itself but also to his ability to persuade others to work in pursuit of those goals. In the end, he never saw all the elements of the American System in place at once. He asked much of America, but for some the required sacrifices seemed too great, the mindset changes too difficult, and the opposition too strong.

On many fronts and for many years, critics attacked "Clayism" with its "false and fetal heresies" of dangerous fiscal policies and "absurd" commercial restrictions. Others found it difficult to do as Clay expected and put their personal interests behind national ones. They might often help in local communal activities at times, but they inevitably retreated to the ideal of an autonomous family farm, free from restrictions. While Clay asked for the regional economies to complement each other, if farmers of limited means saw themselves receiving lower prices for their crops and paying higher prices for their clothes as a result of a high tariff, they often found it difficult to grasp the logic and value of that to the nation. Many people in the land of plenty resisted Clay's ideas of self-sacrifice for the good of all.[26]

Sectionalism also reared its hostile head in the debate over Clay's American System. While the Kentuckian's plans had appeal to some individuals in all sections of the nation, certain farmers across the country, and especially certain planters in the South, complained that Clay's plans for a protective tariff favored eastern manufacturing interests and little benefited the country overall. A Macon, Georgia, newspaper's declaration that the tariff taxed the labor of the South for the benefit of the North reflected a common view in that region. Clay's opponents argued that a protective tariff kept out cheaper foreign items and brought higher prices for domestic products. Meanwhile, in the West, Clay's calls for high prices for public land and slower, controlled development met resistance as well. And some in the East opposed that policy also, charging that it would damage the chances that poor easterners could make a fresh start by farming cheap lands in a new environment. Critics in all sections assailed any national legislation that did not affect them directly as special-interest actions that, as a New Jersey paper argued, conferred privileges on the few and produced inequalities for the many. Editorial writers and politicians alike decried what they saw as Clay's naiveté in giving special rights to favored groups. Such preferential treatment subverted liberty and freedom of action, they said. In short, many in Clay's America viewed the world chiefly through their own individual, state, or sectional glasses. To Clay, such myopic vision represented the very thing he sought to overcome. Whether his dream of sections united by a shared vision of greatness would become chimera or reality remained to be seen.[27]

Besides sectional antagonism to various aspects of his program—which translated into political opposition—Clay faced severe challenges from those who feared giving more power to the federal government, just as he envisioned. Some of that antipathy sprang from historical roots. After all, the American Revolution had partly resulted out of anger over the growing consolidation of British power. Such republican resistance to centralization remained strong. Yet at the same time, the Revolution had unleashed unexpected new forces and fresh ways of looking at government. Those two worlds of old republicanism and new outlooks collided in the American System. In 1823, in a letter to his old friend, Virginian Francis Brooke told the Kentuckian that Clay's bold, broad doctrine of federal authority would create political problems for Clay in the Old Dominion. The next year, John Randolph made the case explicitly when he warned that if Congress possessed the expanded power sought in a bill on the floor, then that same power could be used to emancipate all slaves. And in that same decade the *Charleston Mercury* linked Clay's American System to dangerous notions that threatened "the liberties . . . of the white people of the Southern States." The Missouri Crisis of 1819–1821 had not been a "firebell in the night," suddenly awakening southern fears regarding slavery, for such sounds had been tolling for decades. But the crisis had increased the volume of the debate, and Clay's declaration in the 1820s regarding federal power thus coincided with those rising tones of worry. A growing southern-siege mentality threatened to erupt into a crescendo of fury. Sectional interests thus combined with philosophical concerns to challenge Clay's plans for America—and his political hopes for greater office.[28]

Despite the attacks on his programs, Clay hardly hesitated in his continued advocacy of his economic vision. As early as 1810, for example, he had spoken strongly in favor of a tariff that would protect fledgling US industries. Duties on imports, Clay declared, could free the United States of all dependence on foreign countries. Referring to the largest American woolen mill, he cried, "Others may prefer the cloth [of] Leeds and London but give me those of Humphreysville." But his appeals gained few followers that year. After the War of 1812, however, as English goods began to flood the American market, more and more people agreed with his analysis. At the same time, many misstated Clay's stance. While he generally supported the idea of broad protection, he actually called for selective use of the principle. Protect those things that needed governmental intervention to survive, he argued, but do not apply such remedies to those less in need. Furthermore, Clay did not necessarily endorse the idea of a protective tariff as a permanent policy for the young nation. He saw it as a reasonable, short-term response to the problem of cheap foreign products underselling American ones. Clay expected high duties to stimulate the economy and encourage domestic manufacturing. But once that stability and economic independence occurred, he said, a different policy with reduced duties could well follow. Passage of the nation's first real protective tariff in 1816 seemed to mark the country's acceptance of those principles.[29]

With New England divided and the South opposed, an 1820 effort to revise that tariff failed. But four years later, in the election year of 1824, conditions once more pushed the tariff discussion to the forefront. Early on, Clay cautioned that the debate should not bog down in minutiae. Everything under discussion, he argued, affected all the Union, not just the part directly involved: "The happiness of a nation is the happiness of the several states that compose it; . . . the protection of the several parts of a nation is the protection of the nation." Otherwise, Clay noted, the debate becomes the Union versus Kentucky, or Pennsylvania, or some other state, dividing all regions even more.[30]

As the arguments intensified and the words grew harsher, Clay took to the House floor in late March 1824 and delivered one of his longest and most reasoned addresses. In it, he said some politicians wanted a low tariff to produce revenue and would leave American industry on its own, as part of the "natural progress." Others sought instead a protective policy that would lessen the nation's dependence on foreign powers. Both held sincere beliefs, he acknowledged. But the economic distress after the panic of 1819 had produced deep suffering in the populace. Should leaders just sit back and watch as events unfolded? Or should they try to relieve the tribulations by positive action? He spoke for action—a tax on foreign imports to promote American growth. To those naysayers who contended a high tariff would harm commerce, reduce revenue, abolish competition, raise wages, favor one group or section over another, and exceed constitutional authority, Clay answered them point by point. Regarding southern opposition, for example, he warned that those views would produce a country of jealous rivals and competition, not a company of friends. Clay again pointed out that it might be a nation of many interests, but all stood aboard the same ship of state, "with a noble crew." If the nation prospered, then all

won. Moreover, he did not accept the view that the South would not produce manufacturing establishments. Who could say that its future would
not include industry, owing to the tariff's protection? He ended with an
appeal for an action that would lead the nation down the road "to riches, to
greatness, to glory."[31]

At last, Clay's views won out. The resulting actions of 1824 significantly
raised tariff duties. The Kentuckian's principles on protection seemed to
reflect the national mood. A high tariff also served his home region well.
Lexington still had thriving industry in 1824. A decade earlier, it had had
more cotton factories than any city and had made more cotton bagging
than the rest of the nation. Kentucky, in turn, in 1810 had stood among the
top three in the United States in distilleries, gunpowder mills, cotton looms,
naileries, tanneries, and salt manufacturers. So when Clay told the South
it could become a manufacturing place, he could point to a close model.
Yet at the same time, England produced 70 percent of the goods consumed
in Kentucky, and its products challenged the state's own commodities for
dominance. Clay knew firsthand the problems America had to overcome in
that regard. But most of all, he understood the need for protection because
of a crop he grew—industrial hemp. By mid-century, Kentucky growers
would produce more than half the nation's crop. But that hemp—used
for clothing, rope, and cotton bagging—constantly faced serious overseas
competition from the lower-priced Russian hemp. So "the Prince of Hemp"
made certain his own and his constituents' interests were protected through
the tariffs he advocated. Clay's words and actions philosophically supported
the policies he pursued as those best for the nation, but the fact that such
tariffs also helped him and his community did not hurt, either.[32]

A sound national financial system provided a second foundation for the
American System. But Clay's philosophical and political journey to get to
that part of his program proved much more arduous, with a significant de-
tour. First, the West needed banks. With few such institutions in existence,
those who required credit had to get it through accounts at stores, or in
bartering arrangements, or by private deals. Moreover, since the US government issued only coins (hard specie), actual money remained scarce in
many cases. Some of the individual banks that finally did emerge issued
their own paper money to meet the need for a flexible, available currency, but
the value of those funds depended in large part on the strength of the issuing
bank. Not legal currency per se, that bank-backed paper might be accepted
at face value or, for financial institutions with weaker assets, at a discount.
Behind that paper was a promise to pay in specie, on demand. When hard

times struck, and the discounts rose, individual requests for coins in exchange for notes might not be met, and the banks and their depositors might experience distress. The BUS provided some stability to the system, but it had problems itself.[33]

Clay, who served for a time as a director of the Bank of Kentucky, chartered in 1806, knew firsthand the problems the West faced. But when the vote came in 1811 to renew the charter for the BUS, he opposed the effort. A US senator at the time, he had been elected by vote of the legislature, and it now instructed him to oppose that Federalist edifice. Clay indicated that he felt bound by its directive. But his hostility to the recharter effort sprang from deeper roots. Contrary to his earlier support for state-chartered banks in Kentucky, now he alleged that the national institution represented a threat to democratic beliefs. "Wealth is power," he averred; and in the BUS, a favored class, invested with special privileges from governmental actions, wielded that immense power. Moreover, 70 percent of its capital came from foreigners, chiefly the hated English. That endangered liberty. But beyond that, Clay in 1811 offered a much more restrictive view of the Constitution than he would in subsequent years, stating that the proposed recharter was not justified by the implied powers of that document. With widespread support for that interpretation and in an anti-British atmosphere, the effort to recharter the BUS failed.[34]

Perhaps Clay truly considered state banks better suited to deal with financial matters. Perhaps he considered himself bound by the legislative instructions. Perhaps, with his youthful views, he saw the institution as unconstitutional and antidemocratic. But whatever he felt, his vote on the matter, and especially the words he spoke in that debate, would come back to haunt him in later years. For very soon, Clay realized that he had erred. The War of 1812 quickly revealed the weakness of the existing financial system, lacking a national bank. With limited credit, financial disarray, and fiscal confusion everywhere, Clay's nation faced a crisis. As he later noted, he viewed the postwar situation with "the most serious alarm" and recognized the "urgent necessity" for change. But as new attempts emerged in 1816 to recharter the BUS, what should he do? Voters valued consistency. Clay had called the BUS unconstitutional, had openly opposed it, and had voted against it. Could he now repudiate what he had said only five years before?[35]

During Clay's lifetime, Ralph Waldo Emerson wrote that "a foolish consistency is the hobgoblin of little minds, adored by little statesmen, philosophers, and divines." Clay would not be of little mind. He knew that consistency would be the safest course politically, for change would bring censure in some circles. But to his credit, he now took the action he felt was necessary for the national well-being. Rising to talk to fellow members of Congress, Clay admitted his earlier errors. He told how he once considered the BUS unconstitutional and how he charged that it had abused its powers. To adhere to that view would be the easiest course of action, he admitted. But he would rather be right than consistent. Why had he modified his views? Clay explained that a total change of circumstances and "events of the utmost magnitude" had made the need for change obvious. The people now favored a central bank. As for his constitutional objections, he simply answered that what had seemed not "necessary and proper" in 1811 now he deemed it so. He voted for the BUS.[36]

As Clay had expected, his actions brought him political grief almost immediately. In the crucial 1816 election fight with John Pope, following the Compensation Bill brouhaha, Pope had hammered Clay on his inconsistency. An unknown author writing as "Pitt" had noted in a local paper that to Clay the Constitution was "one thing today and the opposite to-morrow." Though Clay survived that battle, other national opponents would continue to remind the electorate of that vote. They would print Clay's 1811 speech side by side with his 1816 words to support their argument that Clay was a political chameleon, willing to change his philosophical skin to match the prevailing color of the electorate. The expedient thing would have been to remain tied to the earlier views; but as Clay saw it, that was not the best course for a struggling nation. It is difficult for a public figure to admit error, openly and unabashedly. Clay did so. And it cost him.[37]

At the same time, Clay's support for the BUS became an important part of his American System, and thus helped him with those who followed that program. A tariff would protect American industry and some agriculture; a bank would provide the credit and currency for secure growth. And funding internal improvements would supply the transportation and infrastructure to make it all work. Clay knew firsthand the problems of the transportation system in America. He had crossed the Appalachian frontier many times; as an attorney, he had traveled the backroads of the state, plying his trade. But he had found even the most-frequented thoroughfares had presented problems. In the mire of winter, the sometimes six-inch-deep mud meant that it could take all day—eight hours or more—to traverse the twenty-eight miles from Clay's home to the state capital. Most stagecoaches did not even run for several months a year because of the almost-impassible nature of the roads. Moreover, early in his career, when Clay made the trip from Lexington to Washington, DC—a straight-line distance of some four hundred miles—it took him three weeks. No steamboats, no railroads, and few good highways existed. But beyond the physical comfort and the speed of movement that better transportation could give Clay the individual, it could be part of a larger internal improvement system that would mean much to the nation.[38]

As Clay well knew, local and state efforts had long supported such activities, by either funding or subsidizing roads, canals, bridges, lighthouses, and harbor improvements. They granted the rights to dam streams, to collect tolls, and to take lands through eminent domain, all for the public good. Governments approved lotteries in some states for the money to improve navigation or roads, to build bridges or waterworks, and to pave streets. Whether by direct public funding or support for private efforts (such as the purchase of stock), the authorities endorsed some governmental involvement in internal improvements. Even at the federal level, limited steps had been taken in support of that principle. The 1802 act providing for Ohio's admission to the Union had dictated that a portion of the sale of public lands be used to construct a road across the state. Four years earlier, Congress had approved initial funding for the Cumberland or National Road, which would eventually extend from the Potomac River into Illinois.[39]

Almost from the beginning of his political career, Clay had endorsed such an expansive governmental role in support of internal improvements. That stance would prove to be controversial, but he seldom faltered in its advocacy. As early as 1804, in the state legislature, he had voted for an act that incorporated the Ohio Canal Company, to construct a way around the Falls of the Ohio at Louisville. Three years later, Clay's first vote as a US senator apparently had been in favor of a bill granting the right to build a toll bridge across the Potomac. But before 1812, very few federal funds went to internal improvements. Clay, however, saw increased national action as absolutely necessary for widespread success. State and local governments were very limited in what they could do and how they would cooperate; private actions were inconsistent, weak, and piecemeal. He argued that centrally planned and coordinated federal action, by contrast, could remove obstacles to commerce and unite diverse interests. Moreover, the existence of such a system could prove vital in wartime.[40]

Once again, the War of 1812 had revealed serious weaknesses in the existing system. If, as Clay said, battles were won by "celerity and rapidity of movement," then the American situation presented major obstacles. Localism inhibited national defense measures. Angry divisions showed a disunited nation. And poor transportation confirmed fears that soldiers could not be supplied adequately nor could armies maneuver quickly. By war's end, the United States had overcome some of those disadvantages, but just barely. Many who observed that state of affairs determined to remedy the situation. And so Henry Clay would be at the forefront of that battle, although his leadership made him a clear political target.[41]

In 1816, a ton of goods could be moved across the Atlantic from Europe to the United States for about the same cost as it took to move that same amount of material thirty miles inland on American roads. It then cost seven times that amount to get the goods to Kentucky. Such conditions motivated Clay to call that same year for a series of turnpike roads "to bind and connect us together." As others would do later, he partly defended the move as a military one, for "in peace we ought to prepare for war." But in truth, that appeal masked the larger purpose: "the great work, too long delayed," of a national policy of internal improvements.[42]

The continuing debate over federal support for roads and canals erupted in full political bloodshed the next year, when then-nationalist and, at the time, Clay ally John C. Calhoun proposed putting the BUS's future dividends into an internal improvement fund. He used the same arguments as had Clay—the war had shown the national weaknesses in that area, and the fund would be used to bind the republic closer. When opponents furiously began attacking the plan as a dangerous example of the consolidation of power, Clay left the Speaker's chair and spoke in support of Calhoun, of multi-state projects, and of actions that promoted the welfare of "our common country." Progress and expansion, he declared, demanded federal intervention in order to conquer "space itself."[43]

The bill passed, and it appeared that the nation would adopt a systematic, ongoing plan of public works. Then, President James Madison vetoed the act as unconstitutional. A surprised and furious Clay attacked the veto. When the next president, James Monroe, pursued a modified, but similar constitutional course, that only added to the Kentuckian's growing disdain for Monroe. In March 1818, Clay responded to the critics who said Congress had no power to cut canals or construct roads except with state consent. He first denounced what he called the "old theme of 'State rights'" with its narrow and limiting views, and once more openly advocated a broad interpretation of the Constitution, giving the document vigor and vitality. Look to the "necessary and proper" clause, look to the power to create postal roads, look to the sections regarding national defense, and there was justification for internal improvements, he proclaimed. But even more than those, he underscored in an election-year speech in 1824, something even greater than the Constitution dictated such a course of action: the "greatest object, the Union of these States." Passage of a river and harbor bill that year gave some support to his goals. But to many of his critics, his words on that and other occasions seemed utterly subversive, even traitorous. They wanted a strict construction of the Constitution; he did not. They wanted the state government, not the federal, to dominate; he did not. They wanted to keep patronage in local hands; he did not. Adding to their fears was the growing recognition that Clay, more than most politicians, had the prestige and power to put those doctrines into practice through legislative or—if he were ever president—executive action. To them, that made Clay even more dangerous.[44]

Whig and later Republican politician William H. Seward of New York would remember Clay as a man who "from the day on which he entered the public service until that on which he passed the gates of death, . . . was never a follower, but always a leader." That trait separated Clay from many of his peers at the national level. Most could speak well in favor of one issue; some could control a select group of supporters on a limited concern; but few could do both—and then persuade still others to join them. Over and over, observers pointed to Clay's leadership abilities as one of his greatest strengths. But his real talents in that regard also contributed to one of his greatest weaknesses.[45]

Of Clay's flair for leadership, there was little debate. In assessing his skills, the *New York Herald* used such words as "powerful intellect," "bold spirit," "courage," and "perseverance." Abraham Lincoln pointed to the rare combination of Clay's soaring eloquence, excellent judgment, and indomitable will as keys to the Kentuckian's success. Another nineteenth-century observer noted that Clay "had a bold and commanding spirit which imposed its will upon those around him. He carried all before him by the irresistible force of his nature." Even his political enemies sometimes admired those traits. Cabinet member William Barry privately attacked fellow Democrat Martin Van Buren in a letter, contrasting him to Clay, whom he called "an open, fearless, and brave man." In short, leader Clay would take clear stands, speak out forcefully for them, and work tirelessly to enact them.[46]

Clay's ability to lead manifested itself in ways both small and large. A congressman once walked with Clay to the capitol and was amazed that Clay seemed to know everyone along the way and in the halls of power, including the slaves. He recognized them by name, offered them warm words of greeting, and drew them into his orbit of friendship and power. They, in turn, could help keep him informed of people and actions around him, which could prove useful over time. Little kindnesses won political allies, as well. When Senator Thomas Ewing of Ohio made a tariff speech early in his career, the already-famous Mr. Clay came up to him afterwards, noted his longtime study of that issue, and complimented a very pleased Ewing on bringing out, as Ewing recalled to his wife, "points of light wholly new to him." Later, Clay sent Ewing some beet seeds to mail home. Step by step, Clay drew many to become ardent allies. But it often went beyond that, for Clay's personal qualities and leadership abilities frequently forged a devotion that bordered on political love. As one national observer wrote, a large number of those in Congress "would rather do wrong than estrange themselves from Henry Clay." In times of uncertainty, they looked to him for direction, and he willingly provided it.[47]

Clay's ability to lead successfully and, more important, his belief in his ability to do that would also contribute to his political weaknesses. His confidence in his capacity to bring about a resolution to an issue often caused him to underestimate the difficulties involved, often with awkward results. Moreover, his faith in his political talents could necessitate needless strategies. One woman wrote that "Mr. Clay, even in so small a matter, never works without an object."[48]

Furthermore, Clay's certainty about the correctness of his course of action could induce him to become too assertive, too resolute, and too inflexible in his pursuit of those goals. That determination might achieve positive results, often needed ones, but at a price with long-range consequences. His words and actions might turn one-time political friends into lukewarm allies at best, or quiet enemies at worst. But even more damaging, in some ways, was the effect Clay's demanding and exacting actions produced among those who remained loyal to him. They would continue to support him, vote with him, and honor him. But as Ewing noted, "Mr. Clay has such influence over the mind of men, that very few, perhaps not one in ten thousand, will in conversation with him, venture to advance anything which he knows will be personally disagreeable." That combination of affection for Clay and fear of angering him thus denied Clay wise counsel when he most needed it. For if an attorney who defends himself has a fool for a client, then a politician who listens only to friendly counsel has a similar weakness. If Clay's friends would not tell him his errors, who would?[49]

Still, despite some problems and certain negatives, by 1822 Clay had been successful in almost every public endeavor he had undertaken—as lawyer, state representative, US senator, member of the US House of Representatives, Speaker of the House, compromiser, and diplomat. By the age of forty-five,

Clay had achieved more than almost anyone of his generation. Highly talented, with great charisma, almost matchless speaking ability, and recognized leadership qualities, he depended not just on those things for his appeal. Clay spoke for the aspirations of liberty for those in foreign lands. He also articulated a vision for America's future, and unusual for that time, a clearly stated program to achieve that vision, his American System. Clay thus seemed almost to have it all. But he did not have the greatest political prize that nation had to offer—the presidency of the United States.

5

Presidential Candidate I

FATE PLAYED ITS FIRST OF many tricks on Clay's presidential aspirations in the 1824 campaign. At first, it gave him hope; then it introduced a new element into the mix, one that helped shatter Clay's high expectations. Finally, it showed Clay just how tantalizingly close he had come.

Clay had left Congress in 1821, following his much-praised actions in the Second Missouri Compromise, and since then had worked to repair his crippled financial fortunes. Not coincidentally, that time also gave him the opportunity to plan his political future. He sent out numerous letters, seeking advice on how to craft a winning strategy. Allies agreed to work for his cause, and journalists began to tout the abilities of the Great Pacificator. In late 1822, a grateful Missouri legislative caucus nominated Henry Clay for the presidency. Soon Kentucky and then Ohio followed suit. The race was on.[1]

It would, however, be a very crowded field, full of political thoroughbreds. The acknowledged front runner in 1822 was William H. Crawford. The Georgian used the patronage of his post as secretary of the treasury to advance his political agenda and, alone among the candidates, had what the president of the BUS called an "*Organised Party*." But beyond that, Crawford possessed personal attributes that made him appealing. Though dressed in the old style and usually wearing a wig, the tall and sturdy Crawford often impressed people with his pleasant, affable, and gregarious nature. But another part of his makeup offered a more negative counterbalance. For many of those who met Crawford used the same word to describe him: "intriguer." When combined with his use of office for political purposes, these two elements caused many to question Crawford's fitness for the high position he sought.[2]

Clay had a generally favorable impression of Crawford, however. During the latter part of the War of 1812, he—like Clay—had been a diplomat, serving as minister to France and aiding the American delegates at Ghent. The Kentuckian had observed to a friend that the Georgian had been particularly kind to him. Yet, considerable differences on matters of policy continued to divide them. Crawford represented the states' rights view and generally opposed federal support for internal improvements, thus further placing himself in opposition to Prince Hal. Several states of the Southeast looked to Crawford as their defense against the dangerous heresies of Mr. Clay. With a cadre of party followers—such as Martin Van Buren in New York—with access to patronage, with a proven record of achievements, and with the support of a states' rights core, Crawford had a broad base from which to work, and he had many advantages. But two factors slowed his ascendancy as the favorite.[3]

If Fate would deal Clay a bad hand in the 1824 race, it gave Crawford a terrible one. In September 1823, a newspaper referred to the Georgian's "vigorous mind." But that same month, the fifty-one-year-old Crawford suffered an apparent stroke. The medical treatment given him likely complicated his recovery, for doctors "bled" him almost two dozen times and introduced a series of drugs into his system. In combination, these treatments left Crawford partly paralyzed and physically debilitated. But—and this would prove to be a key factor in the election—few people knew of this. Almost immediately a newspaper referred to Crawford's "indisposition," but many accounts went little beyond that vagueness for the longest time. Even among the informed, not many knew exactly what had occurred. Rumors abounded. By January 1824, Clay heard stories that Crawford was "dangerously ill" and almost helpless. Crawford supposedly sat in a dark room, for he could not see, could not speak clearly, could not walk well. Two months later, John Quincy Adams talked to a man who had seen Crawford and termed Crawford's chances of survival uncertain. Yet others told a different story, of how Crawford had recovered and would soon be his old self.[4]

Then in May 1824, with the election only six months away, Crawford either suffered a relapse or, likely, another stroke. He displayed "paralytic symptoms" and existed in a "living death," according to several private accounts. Crawford could not read, had memory lapses, and spoke with difficulty. His candidacy should have been at an end. But the continued confusion about his condition allowed his supporters to keep his name before the electorate: "Mr. Crawford's friends almost to a man are determined never to give him up." They had too much to lose if he withdrew, and they had hopes that Crawford would regain his health in time to govern as president. Stories circulated about his recovery. Yet the doubts, the rumors, the realization about his actual condition began slowly to have an effect on his support. That brought about a second factor that damaged Crawford's chances.[5]

In earlier years, congressional caucuses had selected presidential candidates. But a growing democratic spirit caused increasing resentment of "King Caucus." A variety of state caucuses had begun to replace that approach. But Crawford's friends, sensing his slipping chances, pushed the congressional caucus idea once more. Yet the resulting rump gathering in February 1824 proved something of a political fiasco. When only 66 of the 261 members of Congress attended, almost all of them Crawford supporters, that desperate attempt highlighted what Adams called Crawford's "forlorn hope." Still, because of the states pledged to him and the supporters still tied to his now-fading star, Crawford remained a factor in the race. In September 1823—the month of Crawford's stroke—a New London, Connecticut, newspaper had called the race a two-person affair. One was Crawford. The other was John Quincy Adams.[6]

The relationship between Clay and Adams had not appreciably warmed since their chilly encounter at Ghent almost a decade earlier. In the time since then, the two had clashed when Secretary of State Adams's Spanish policy had conflicted with Clay's demand for quick recognition of the emerging South American republics. But in truth the two did not stand too far apart on most matters of public policy. Where they differed chiefly was in personality. For in some ways, Adams was a great man. But great men and great women may not be lovable human beings, or even likeable ones. People loved Clay, but might not respect him; they respected Adams, but did not love him. Individuals found Clay charismatic, but questioned his honesty; they liked Adams's directness, but hated his haughtiness. Folks enjoyed Clay's warmth, but doubted his morals; they praised Adams's character, but criticized his aloofness.

In many ways, Adams seemed particularly well prepared for the presidency. From childhood, he had been told he was an agent for greatness. Yet he had to overcome that "hereditary notoriety" and his connections to his now-disliked Federalist father, while knowing those same ties helped him in New England and elsewhere. He had the advantage of learning, as well. Fluent in several languages, he knew seven as a result of his time in the diplomatic corps. A reporter found that Adams "seems to have read every newspaper in the country." Yet one congressman admitted that he first thought Adams "a mere man of books," while a letter writer derisively called Adams "*The Professor.*" Learning and a sense of duty were two-edged swords in Adams's America. Still, John Quincy Adams seemed perfectly made for the office of president—except for his personality.[7]

The inner Puritan in Adams meant that he constantly questioned his own motives. Even Clay confessed that Adams was almost always right in exact matters of fact. But that trait, combined with a spirit that seldom doubted its correctness on issues of interpretation, meant that Adams was frequently unyielding and uncompromising, even on small points. All too often, he left the impression of having a fault-finding, demanding, suspicious, ir-ritable, passionless personality—and such words came from his allies. As one contemporary wrote, "He knew little of the human heart." In truth, Adams could be witty and even warm at times in the company of friends. But Adams, the longtime diplomat, surprisingly did not feel comfortable in the presence of those he did not know. Hardworking, intelligent, and cos-mopolitan, the insecure and shy Adams most often sought solitude. Only when alone could he converse with an intellect and personality worthy of him—and often not even then. Yet that call within him to serve his country, and an ambition that he refused to recognize openly, warred with his natural instincts. The continuing conflict for the soul of John Quincy Adams would cause him great political pain, while also motivating him to great political actions.[8]

Crawford's health issues left him vulnerable; Adams's personality traits could be exploited as well. Surveying the field, Clay had reason to believe that, like the Kentucky thoroughbreds, he could come off the pace from behind and win. But there were also a few other runners in the starting gate to consider, and he had to keep a wary eye on them as well.

Initially, at least three other candidates seemed to harbor serious presi-dential intentions. In populous New York, De Witt Clinton sought to use his political connections to build a base beyond his home state. Nephew of a former governor and vice president, he had been US senator and governor in his own right, and had barely lost the presidency in the 1812 race. As early as 1820, John Quincy Adams had predicted a coalition between the wes-terner Clay and the easterner Clinton. That combination never occurred. As it turned out, divisions within his home state doomed Clinton's candidacy, he made no real push for office, and while Clinton backed another candidate, most of his forces gave their support to Adams.[9]

Clay knew another serious contender very well. John C. Calhoun had been a fellow War Hawk and an ally in the bank fight, but by 1823 the Carolinian was seemingly moving away from that nationalist phase of his career. Many political observers—perhaps including Calhoun himself—were not yet certain of what he was, what he believed, or what he sought. Five years younger than Clay, the secretary of war, like Adams and Crawford, had the advantages of a cabinet post as he sought office. For a time, he was seen as a serious contender. But Calhoun needed to be more than a regional candidate, and he based his hopes on gaining the support of Pennsylvania. When that vote went elsewhere in 1824, so too did his prospects. He wisely turned instead to the relative certainty of election as vice president.[10]

Both of those candidacies had concerned Clay. Clinton could have garnered many votes in New York State, where the Kentuckian had high expectations, while Calhoun might have challenged Clay for ballots in the Southwest. Clay worried less about a third minor candidate, Andrew Jackson. He might carry Tennessee, a state Clay would otherwise win, but Clay and most other observers early on predicted that Jackson would do nothing beyond that. Many expected him to drop out eventually, as Clinton and Calhoun did. After all, Jackson was a mere general. So, given that cast of characters—Crawford, Adams, Clinton, Calhoun, and Jackson—Clay was more than willing to play the cards circumstance had dealt him, for if he played correctly, he might well win the political pot of gold.

Part of the story of Henry Clay's races for the presidency involves strategies mishandled, mistakes made, and opportunities lost. But in the 1824 campaign, he actually formulated a rational and reasonable plan for winning. As it turned out, many factors negated that strategy, but at the start it had promise. After all, and as Clay certainly saw it, he enjoyed several important advantages.

First, he had the experience and qualifications for the presidency, as did Adams and Crawford, but he could argue he had better overall credentials than either. As Clay's friends wrote in a Boston newspaper, "Let us then elect a man whose long political career has been marked by an undeviating attachment to his country." Clay's allies—and their hero—expected his career to speak for itself with the voters.[11]

But less lofty sentiments also came into play. The man who stressed his national programs and who sought to unify the regions based his strategy chiefly on sectionalism. Once that minor irritant Andrew Jackson dropped out, as expected, then Clay would be the only real western candidate in the race. As the first major spokesman for that region, he fully anticipated getting its entire support: "Of that I entertain no doubt." By mid-summer 1822, Clay noted the "highly favorable" reports already reaching him regarding his regional chances. He expected the West and Southwest to unite behind his candidacy. Adams, in another sectional vote, would take New England, and Crawford would have some of the South Atlantic states. The voters in Clay's nine states would take him halfway to the majority needed to win the Electoral College. Those votes would surpass the New England bloc and Crawford's core states. Clay viewed the main battlefield as the Middle Atlantic States, especially New York and Pennsylvania, which would have none of their own candidates in the mix at the end. If Clay could just break even in these places, he might win an outright majority. But even if he should falter there, the electoral stars might still align for him. Add the Old Dominion to those western state votes and pick up a few in the Middle Atlantic states, and he would be close enough to the magic majority number to ride the bandwagon to victory. Once he gained momentum, others would flock to him. In June 1823, a Philadelphia paper predicted that Clay would win a majority of voters, assuming that Jackson and Calhoun dropped out as expected.[12]

Clay did make mistakes early on that tempered the optimism, however. He misread the support for his policies and the extent of his name recognition across the nation. But most of all, he seriously misjudged the appeal of Andrew Jackson.

At least by the late summer of 1821—more than three years before the election—supporters in Tennessee had begun to suggest Jackson for president. That reflected, in part, a response to the state political scene, but it also indicated that some recognized Jackson's nascent national appeal. Early the next year, rumors reached Clay of a possible Jackson candidacy. By August 1822, that had become reality, when the Tennessee legislature put forth Jackson's name for president.[13]

Some biographers of Clay have suggested that he did not take Jackson's candidacy seriously until it was too late. In fact, the Kentuckian almost immediately recognized the possible problems such a candidacy presented. Within days of Jackson's nomination by Tennessee, Clay wrote an ally asking how the "injurious effect" of that move could be counteracted. Given the narrow margin for error in Clay's mentally constructed plan to win the presidency, the loss of even one state would injure his chances for an outright victory. Prescient observers, like Calhoun, quickly noted that Jackson's presence in the race particularly hurt Clay. But as Clay polled others, an early consensus seemed to form, one that lessened Clay's initial concerns. The governor of Tennessee, for example, told Clay that he did not expect Jackson to get support outside of the Volunteer State, and once that became clear, then Jackson would drop out and Clay would carry the state. Others saw the Jackson candidacy more as a tactic by Clay's national enemies to try to divide his core of western support and weaken him, but not as a credible threat in itself. And so Clay confidently—or perhaps not so confidently—told allies that Jackson might hurt Clay's chances briefly, but would likely not even be in the field by the time 1824 rolled around.[14]

Part of Clay's confidence resulted from what he heard and knew of Jackson. A few years earlier, Clay had admitted he had a "very limited" acquaintance with him, though his contacts had all been amicable. While that might have been true on a personal level at that time, Clay did not engender such warm feelings by 1822. Even setting individual emotions aside, Clay just did not view Andrew Jackson as a credible candidate, for he seemed to have neither the background nor the personality to be presidential material. After all, by 1822, Jackson had shown limited interest, little service, and less distinction in the political field. He seemed almost unable to remain engaged in the work of the few posts he had held, serving as a member of the US House for three months only and of the US Senate for a little over six months and having been appointed governor of the Florida territory for a controversial four months. Such a political record paled in comparison to anyone else in the race. Since George Washington, no president had been elected who did not have a distinguished record of service.[15]

Even more than that, Jackson's personal traits seemed hardly likely to cause voters to think him qualified for the high office. While Clay was no saint in that regard, he seemed almost seraphic by comparison. Jackson supporters portrayed their hero as a man who had not transgressed "a single moral principle" and whose meritorious life invited no whisper of calumny. But in truth, Jackson had youthful issues with drinking and gambling. And while Jackson eventually had a long and loving relationship with his spouse Rachel, they began that connection while she remained another man's wife, and Rachel and Andrew both knew it. Later, Jackson engaged in some questionable land dealings as a speculator, profited from slave trading, and killed a man in a duel. But more than his history and his actions, Jackson had a fiery temper and displayed a vindictive rage that caused some people to find him overbearing and tyrannical. John Quincy Adams termed Jackson "incompetent both by his ignorance and by the fury of his passions"; Clay indicated that the irascible, inflexible, and impulsive Jackson would be a rash and dangerous leader because he "always follows the lead of his passions." But even more neutral observers, including former president Thomas Jefferson, stressed that aspect. Speaking of the presidency, Jefferson termed Jackson "one of the most unfit men I know of for such a place." Numerous political observers, then, did not consider Jackson qualified for the presidency, either by experience or by temperament. Initially, Clay fully expected the voters to offer the same judgment. But he, like others, underestimated the strength of Andrew Jackson. They did so at their peril.[16]

The tall, gaunt, cadaverous Jackson might not look physically imposing at first glance, and his poor speaking ability—one congressman thought him "the Roughest Man in his Speech [sic] I ever heard"—might not impress in an initial encounter, but when the Furies touched Andrew Jackson, when he felt the passion of right rising within him against the forces of evil, when Jackson was fully roused to action, he would become a fearsome, impressive leader. Then a buoyant spirit, a great charisma, and a powerful will would dominate the decayed teeth, the rheumatism, the headaches, the bullet in his body. At various times, he could be politically astute or carefully calculating or shrewdly careful. But overriding all those moderating considerations was Jackson's firm confidence in the correctness of his course of action. In that sense, his enemies were right—he would follow his passions and beliefs, no matter what. But they did not see that such singleminded intensity and fierce zeal formed the core of his being, as well. With the power of one who does not doubt himself or his cause, Jackson could concentrate all his will and all his efforts toward a desired end. Unlike Clay, he would not lose sight of the prize or of the way to victory. Loyal to his friends, even if they erred, he would reward such fidelity, inspire devotion from his supporters, and demonize any who did not follow the true cross. And if he grew convinced of the base wickedness of the opposition, then his resolve took on even greater force. In such moments, that emaciated body would stand straighter and appear like a pale, avenging ghost, riding to haunt his enemies.[17]

At first, Jackson's political enemy Henry Clay did not fully understand the power of his character or the grassroots appeal of his candidacy. But he should have perceived some of that at least, for the two men were, in some ways, much alike. Both had become slaveholding, horseracing planters and had built fine mansions. Both were attorneys. Both supported the ideal of union. Both had ambition. Both had supreme confidence in their abilities. Both displayed charisma. Both engendered great affection from their supporters. Both could be arbitrary at times. Both held a high sense of personal honor. Both wanted the presidency. And, in the end, both hated each other.

The differences between the two, as Clay saw it, outweighed any similarities. Clay felt that he had long prepared for the presidency through political leadership and statesmanship, and that Jackson had not. In fact, Clay seemed the antithesis of the hero when it came to policy decisions. The Kentuckian instinctively sought to reconcile contrasting views, to conciliate, to compromise; the Tennessean saw it all as a question of right or wrong, black or white, for or against. Henry Clay tried to understand both sides in crafting legislation, even though he might produce partisan results; Andy Jackson, on the other hand, tended to see his side as the only side. To Clay, that oversimplification of issues, that inability to compromise, that passion made Jackson very dangerous indeed. Clay's actions and worldview, in turn, made Jackson see his opponent as a political demon. And on top of all that was the issue of the military man in politics, which divided them even more.

Many people in Clay's era genuinely feared a sizable standing army in peacetime and worried about the potential for abuse in such a force. Clay showed less concern on that topic, because following the War of 1812 fiasco he better understood the need for at least a small, well-trained military force, ready to react to crises: "These halcyon days of peace, this calm, will yield to the storm of war," he predicted a year after the War of 1812 had ended. Clay supported military academies and praised the wartime achievements of many heroes, including Andrew Jackson. But what Clay did fear was a large army and the appearance of another Napoleon Bonaparte. He could applaud the symbolic historical example of Cincinnatus returning to the plow, or George Washington refusing the crown, but he considered the Caesar or Napoleon model more likely. As a result, Clay had a genuine, if erratically applied, lifetime apprehension of military men in politics, particularly if they displayed warning signs of egotism and excess. In short, he feared an Andrew Jackson.[18]

Clay's initial dismissal of candidate Jackson suggests that he saw Jackson more as a minor irritant, like a buzzing insect that would soon fly away to political oblivion, rather than a serious threat to his control of the West. In fact, Clay's early opposition to Jackson came less from sectional rivalries than from Clay's open concern that here stood a military leader who later called Napoleon "a great & good man." If not curbed and controlled, such a person might be dangerous to republican liberty and national independence. Long before Jackson came on the national scene, Clay had warned that war could produce what he called "the cherishing of a martial spirit" and cautioned citizens not to aggrandize "some ambitious Chief" who could prostrate the liberties of America.[19]

The later actions of Andrew Jackson fed those existing fears. In the Battle of Horseshoe Bend, Jackson's army had slaughtered nearly eight hundred Red Stick men, women, and children. Then during the time surrounding the Battle of New Orleans, Jackson had summarily executed six mutinous militiamen. All the while, Clay said nothing. In 1818, during the First Seminole War, Jackson invaded Spanish Florida—likely without authorization—illegally convened a court-martial to try two British subjects for aiding the Indians, and executed them both. Many Americans, particularly in the South and West, again ignored the unconstitutional moves and high-handed approach, and instead roundly applauded those various deeds. This time Henry Clay did not remain silent. Such egomaniacal actions had to be curbed or this home-grown Bonaparte might continue his march toward military despotism.[20]

In January 1819, Clay arose on the floor of the House to begin a long discussion of the question of whether to censure Jackson. One biographer spared no fury in calling the resulting attack on Jackson "one of the most foolish things Clay had ever done in his life," in that it greatly angered Jackson. But why? The passion of Clay's words might be questioned, but given his long-stated views about embryonic Caesars, it is more surprising that Clay waited to criticize as long as he did. If he truly feared the action of a military chief—like Jackson—he *should* have spoken out on the matter. And he did. But Clay did mince few words in making his concerns known. In the Seminole War, where perhaps "fault was on our side," Jackson had used dishonorable means to deceive and capture key Indian leaders and had summarily hanged them without a trial. Was the United States not a civilized nation of laws? asked Clay. Some in Congress, he noted, had said that Indian atrocities required such a response. He knew of "the tomahawk and scalping knife" and had lost friends to the Indian Wars, Clay sadly noted. "But I love my country, and its constitution; I love liberty and safety, and I fear military despotism more."[21]

As for Jackson's execution of the two foreign nationals in the Seminole War, Clay admitted that both men might well have been guilty. But they still should have been tried in civil courts. Do not let the passions of the moment or the sympathies for the result cause the nation to forget fundamental principles, he warned. No army commander should have such power over the life and death of civilians, Clay said; American law must be followed. A legally constituted trial should have occurred in Florida, Clay concluded, not a tyrannical execution. He conceded that Jackson undoubtedly had pure and patriotic motives. Still, America must hold the high ground in that "great moral battle" for human rights and virtue, justice, and a "greatness of soul" must guide the country's actions. People might not heed his words and prefer instead to honor the hero, Clay admitted, but they would be honoring, if they did, the triumph of the military over the civil laws, over the constitution, over the liberties of the people: "Remember that Greece had her Alexander, Rome her Caesar, England her Cromwell, France her Bonaparte, and, that, if we would escape the rock on which they split, we must avoid their errors."[22]

As those words echoed in the House chamber, a wave of wild applause followed. Wherever he was, Andrew Jackson was not applauding. In fact, that speech alone earned Clay the enmity of Jackson. When the two next met, "Old Hickory" virtually ignored Clay. Even though the resolution of censure had failed, despite Clay's speech, the Kentuckian had impugned Jackson's judgment, honor, and reputation, and Jackson seldom dismissed such words easily. And he almost never forgot them. Still, by the fall of 1823, when it appeared the two men might need each other in the developing presidential race, friends of Jackson approached Clay, and he felt a reconciliation had occurred: Jackson "has buried the hatchet and we are again on good terms." A wiser Clay would have realized that Jackson rarely buried the hatchet with an opponent he so disliked—unless it was in that person's body.[23]

At the same time that the supposed reconciliation took place, Clay began to recognize Jackson's growing appeal. If he had not viewed Old Hickory as a legitimate contender a year before, he began to do so now—and that changed all his calculations. An almost shocked Henry Clay gradually saw that a rising flood of pro-Jackson sentiment threatened to engulf his presidential plans. The Kentuckian had recognized the potential appeal of the hero of New Orleans, but had expected better of the voters. He had supposed they would judge men and issues, not react to symbols. But Clay slowly realized the powerful emotional forces that Jackson evoked. Here was an outsider working against privileged and established politicians. Here was a savior—for those hurt by the panic of 1819—seeking to throw out of the political temple those responsible for their distress. Here was a hero on horseback leading his forces to victory over various enemies, real or·imagined. By contrast, the diplomat signing a treaty or the politician forging a compromise just could not challenge the Jackson graven image, so easily envisioned and understood. Clay's world seemed a staid one of words and debates, rules and regulations, laws and compromises; Jackson's was one of decisions and actions, right and might, strength and force. Jackson appeared aggressively masculine. That worked well in much of America.[24]

Jackson had immediate name recognition as a result of his hero status, and he had an outsider's appeal to the disaffected and the disenchanted. But with the help of his friends he also ran a good race. That made him even more likely to destroy Clay's ambition.[25]

Despite his forceful, often dominating, personality, Jackson recognized some of his weaknesses as a candidate and allowed key advisors to shape the story given to the voters. Throughout his career, Jackson attracted astute aides who knew well the political world. In the 1824 election, senator John H. Eaton and William B. Lewis, in particular, filled that need. In 1823, for example, Eaton's anonymous letters appeared under the byline of "Wyoming" in a Philadelphia newspaper and were reprinted the next year in a hundred-page pamphlet. The "Letters of Wyoming" argued that Jackson's lack of political experience was a strength, for it meant he had not exploited an office to advance his fortunes. Eaton presented Jackson as the embodiment of a dying Revolutionary past, one that should be revived and revered. Free of foreign influence, tested by war, uncorrupted by the power of office—unlike Clay, Adams, and Crawford—the virtuous Jackson represented the Revolutionary republicanism the nation needed. To Eaton, his candidate offered the best hope for overthrowing the entrenched, privileged interests and reclaiming the mantle of Washington.[26]

The Jackson camp employed other avenues to get their message out and, in so doing, used a basic but effective political machine to do so. Various newspapers republished favorable stories, such as the Louisville *Advertiser's* 1823 "Philo Jackson" letters, which also appeared in pamphlet form. The militia musters also provided a natural source for support of one of their own. But most of all, in whatever form or forum, the image of Jackson that emerged from various sources would be one hard to overcome. Jackson was many things: He was an aristocrat, but a spokesman for democracy. He was a conservative, but was seen as the agent of change. He was a businessman who had speculated freely and prosecuted debtors, but was viewed as a friend of the workingman. He was a cotton planter, but had supported the tariff of 1824. Jackson's image continued to win fights, for when Calhoun dropped out, much of his southern support went to Jackson, not Clay. Still, Clay had hopes that Jackson's growing appeal had limits. A year or so after the race had ended, a congressman summarized the view he said many had held: "We admitted the advantages of General Jackson's position; his splendid services, his force of character, his strength of judgment, his ardent patriotism but still we believed that . . . Mr. Clay . . . was his superior." Clay had counted on such attitudes to elect him president.[27]

The changing electoral scene in America, however, complicated the picture. The expected etiquette for presidential candidates demanded that they should not campaign openly for the office, but could write letters to supporters as a way to offer their thoughts on issues for public consumption. Perhaps they might even give a speech or two, but going around the country to appeal for votes was deemed both ungentlemanly and unseemly, beneath a person seeking the presidency. But that existing electoral protocol had the result of negating the advantages of a charismatic orator and debater like Clay. Such static conduct by the candidates and the lack of strong party machinery at the close of the Era of Good Feelings thus did little to energize the electorate. Furthermore, in many cases, personalities, not issues, dominated discussions regarding which candidate to support. With the power of party only sometimes present, individuals became the main lamppost around which the politically active gathered. Given the fact that many states still disfranchised numerous citizens by various property or taxpaying requirements, many potential voters could not go to the polls. And, finally, six states—New York, Vermont, Delaware, South Carolina, Georgia, and Louisiana—continued to cast their electoral votes for president by a ballot of their legislatures, removing the voters in one-fourth of the states from a direct voice in the matter. An extremely low turnout in the election of 1824 resulted. Only one in four potential voters would bother to go to the polls. Even in Clay's home state of Kentucky, which had no property restrictions on voting, the governor's race produced a much greater turnout than the national one (69 percent vs. 25 percent turnout). Presidential apathy reigned. But alterations were beginning to occur. Between the spring of 1823 and the fall of 1824, five other states had modified their methods of selecting the president from the legislative system to a direct selection of electors. Several states had begun to end lingering restrictions on white male voting and had increased the size of the electorate. The race in 1824 would be the first in which no "founding father" asked for votes. It symbolized the appearance of a new generation. And a growing democratic spirit was waking them.

GEN. ANDREW JACKSON.

THE HERO OF NEW ORLEANS.

Clay early on saw potential political problems when Andrew Jackson entered the 1824 presidential race, but he underestimated the tremendous appeal of the "Hero on Horseback" image. After 1824, the two would become lifelong enemies and eventually the leaders of their respective parties. *Library of Congress, LC-USZC2-2421*

Ironically, Clay's controversial actions in the aftermath of the 1824 race would help mobilize those sleeping forces.[28]

Clay had pinned part of his hope for victory on the appeal of his record. The Kentuckian expected the electorate to recognize that he had an established plan of action and to reward him accordingly. As it turned out, what he saw as a strength would be, to many, a weakness. The economic nationalism of his still-developing American System troubled some, for example, who objected to its pro-bank stance or protective tariff aspects or internal improvements emphasis—or to all three. Even though other candidates supported parts of each of those, Clay alone had a widely articulated, clearly comprehensive, all-inclusive program. Crawford and his spokesmen, in particular, criticized the Clay system and its broad central powers. One paper called Clay suspect because his tariff policy would prove to be "so injurious to the whole Southern section." Grudgingly, Clay seemed to accept the fact that such attacks showed his program might cost him some votes. But what bothered him more was that he did not correspondingly gain support in pro-tariff states—such as Pennsylvania—for his open stand. Why was he losing much and not gaining more?[29]

Virginia, the state of Clay's birth, home of many personal friends, and place of his high electoral hopes, seemed to exemplify the various concerns about him and, as a result, never warmed to him. To Clay, Virginia should have embraced his American System. Since it was declining from its earlier height of prominence and influence in America, Clay expected an enlightened citizenry to explore new answers in an attempt to reverse the pattern and correct the problem. But instead, Virginia seemed to cling to its safe and secure states' rights abode and to reject, in large part, Clay's framework. Its people generally looked nostalgically to the golden age of their past and disdained much change. A Hanover, Virginia, critic complained that the Kentuckian had abandoned the tried-and-true agrarian way and instead had encouraged corporations and manufacturing by the use of "exclusive privilege and monopolies." In a place, then, where he had natural advantages, Clay made little headway in gathering support. Not for the first or last time, his program, policies, and pronouncements cost him politically.[30]

Those sentiments in Virginia reflected the larger sectional concerns both for and against Clay across the nation. His successful compromise regarding the Missouri question earned him great support there, for example, but it hurt him some in those places that blamed him for bringing a slave state into the expanding Union: "Were it not the recollection of the

Missouri question then [there] would scarcely be a dissenting voice" in Ohio, wrote a correspondent from that state. However, Clay's pro-bank stance hurt his cause in the western United States, including Missouri and Ohio. Moreover, Clay's earlier attacks on the popular Jackson and on the general's actions regarding Indians in the Lower South injured Clay in states like Mississippi, Alabama, and Louisiana, where Jackson's activities had been generally popular. And the broad jealousy between sections continued to operate as well. A letter writer told Clay that some in the North still doubted whether the West was yet "entitled" to the presidency. In turn, a friendly newspaper editor in Kentucky indicated the big question in the election centered on "whether this or that section of the Union has been more perfectly represented in the executive department of the government." Sectionalism already threatened to make the Union, as a Boston paper worried, "a rope of sand." For unionist Clay, that left him little to grasp.[31]

Other problems arose for Clay. With newspapers a key element in spreading a message or answering a criticism, Clay found it difficult to make inroads in the Atlantic papers. Efforts to establish a major Clay newspaper failed, and other candidates garnered a much more favorable hearing as a result. Thus, when the opposition termed Clay too young to be president—with one paper erroneously making him six years younger than he was—he found it hard to correct errors or ease apprehensions, whether on age, programs, or something else. That left Clay to rely on an organization to get out the word and the vote. But with little party apparatus already in place, Clay faltered there as well. The patronage powers of the cabinet officials—Crawford and Adams especially—helped them, while the Jacksonians outdid everyone in organizational prowess. By contrast, a Rhode Island paper noted, "No measures have been taken to rally the friends of Mr. Clay." The strengths that Clay showed in Congress and the appeals he displayed in drawing rooms were moot if he lacked the organization, patronage, and press needed to proclaim his talents and to tout his presidential abilities.[32]

Clay understood that weaknesses in those areas were hurting his chances for victory. But even more important, he recognized the extreme danger of the Jackson ascendancy to his hopes. As early as 1821, John Quincy Adams had confided to his diary his belief that the presidential election, then three years away, would likely be decided by the vote of the House of Representatives. Under the provisions of the Twelfth Amendment to the Constitution, if no candidate received a majority of the electoral votes, then the three highest candidates would be sent to the House, where each state would have one vote. With various candidates in the field, the likelihood now of one getting the majority needed in a general election seemed slim. By November 1822, the president of the BUS told Clay that such an outcome also seemed to him "the most probable event." But Clay had reasonable hopes for his outright election if all the pieces fell right, as he anticipated. As late as April 1823, a newspaper in his hometown saw little chance that the election would be decided by the House and not the nation. Then, the growing Jackson movement destroyed any expectations Clay might have held for a clean majority win.[33]

Clay compiled his campaign information from the many newspapers he received, from the various correspondents he encouraged, and from the many congressmen he encountered when in the District. An inkling of the spreading Jackson "contagion" came from Alabama in June 1823, when a writer informed Clay that "your friends here have at present a difficult part." They did not think Jackson a viable candidate and did not want to alienate his allies (who could later support them), yet the Jackson men were "inimical both to you and Mr. Crawford." Given that Jackson men increasingly believed their hero could carry the state, the Clay candidacy there seemed bleaker than just weeks before. Despite those gloomy words, Clay continued to receive contradictory reports. His kinsman and not-yet-enemy Thomas Hart Benton wrote that after two months in Tennessee "there is hardly anyone who thinks he [Jackson] has any chance." With Jackson out, as Benton expected, Tennessee would go to Clay as well.[34]

By fall 1823, however, the warning signs had become too obvious to disregard. In August, a Pennsylvania observer of Clay's interests despairingly noted that the Jackson nomination "has so possessed the public mind & the disorder has broken out in so many fresh places that your friends have been unable to make much headway." Without Jackson in the field, the man concluded, Clay would have overwhelmingly carried the Keystone State, but most people now (correctly) expected the general to do so. Then the next month, Clay's correspondent in Alabama now confirmed that Jackson would dominate the field there. Given the unexpected scope of Jackson support, Clay revised his thinking. Clearly he could not win an outright majority if he could not forge a united West. Nor could he count on a rising tide of support to carry him, for outsider Jackson seemed to have stolen the bandwagon. With the South and West thus divided among Clay, Crawford, and Jackson, Adams seemed to have the brightest prospects, since he represented a more united region and had broad national support.

Clay's new strategy would thus focus on making certain the election actually did go the House—*his* House—and ensuring that his name would be one of the three presented to the representatives there.[35]

To help strengthen his chances, Clay reentered Congress and in November 1823 was easily selected as Speaker of the House. Again in the capitol, Clay began talking to his fellow congressmen to gauge the political scene. What they told him reinforced the view that Jackson represented a real political threat and that the election would probably go to the House for a decision. Four days after Christmas, Clay wrote a son-in-law that he now recognized Jackson might keep him out of the final electoral mix, but if he did not, then, Clay said, "there is a moral certainty of my election." Throughout the next two months, the Kentuckian repeated that analysis to friends and allies. Jackson would be a force and might carry four states, but Clay was "absolutely certain" he would win six states, plus votes in several that selected by the district system. He would thus outpoll the general and then join Crawford and Adams as one of the three candidates before the House. If that occurred, he predicted, his election would be "secure" and "safe." In March 1824, Clay concluded, "All agree that if I enter the House I shall be elected."[36]

How much that statement represented reassuring words to questioning followers, or just false bravado, or his genuine expectations is difficult to know. But Clay, once more, had read the signs wrong. After Calhoun dropped out in March and Pennsylvania clearly supported Jackson, Clay's tone finally changed. Now, with a sense of urgency, he pressed his friends to work hard to ensure that he would indeed be one of the three chosen ones. By September, Adams indicated privately that he considered Jackson the leader for the nation's votes. Clay almost could not bring himself to that same realization. He could not believe the citizens of his America would favor such a man in a field filled by men with such distinguished records of service to the nation. And what of Crawford? The persistent efforts for the Georgian also perplexed Clay. How could Crawford's allies continue to support an incapacitated man? It all was a volatile, confusing situation where rumors abounded—rumors that further damaged Clay's fading hopes.[37]

Perhaps part of the reason Crawford's illness received less attention than it should have was that earlier stories regarding Clay's own health had already spread across the nation. In October 1822, newspapers falsely proclaimed that Clay was dangerously ill or even dead. Then, in December 1823, a Connecticut newspaper reported that Clay "is still in a dangerous situation, and that surgeons had given up all hope of his recovery." In that time, Prince Hal had suffered some illnesses, but nothing particularly unusual. But while Crawford battled serious health issues, Clay battled mostly false rumors regarding his robustness and fitness for office.[38]

Even more damaging to Clay's prospects, however, were the political rumors he had to face and fight, again and again. In the early months of 1823, Clay had to write to a New York ally, stressing that it was a "base calumny" that he and Clinton had allied. The Kentuckian emphasized that he would form no alliances and would win or lose on his own merits. But stories of some kind of alliance with the Crawford forces surfaced and would continue throughout the campaign. Early on, Jackson told a friend that he expected such a union of political armies to occur. As the Crawford camp saw their candidate's chances fading with the growing health concerns, and as they saw Jackson's rising orb begin to eclipse Clay's hopes, they initiated such talk themselves. In early 1823, Crawfordite Martin Van Buren sounded out Clay on a merger: "If I had . . . said anything very explicitly encouraging to him," said Clay, "his zeal would have been given a different direction." But Clay would personally make no promises, no combinations. Still, he did not want to alienate the Crawford camp, for should their candidate drop out, Clay wanted their goodwill—and their votes. His allies continued discussions. By January 1824, desperate Crawford forces recognized their weakness and offered Adams the vice presidential spot on their ticket. When he refused, they tendered the same post to Clay, who also declined. But then, after Calhoun's withdrawal from the race to run for vice president, and with many of his supporters favoring Jackson, the talk of Clay as vice president again spread. Apparently keeping his options open, Clay neither encouraged nor discouraged such talk—a mistake. But by late October 1824, Clay told an Ohio ally that friends of Crawford had once more proposed to make Clay the vice presidential choice. But the Kentuckian refused the entreaty: "I have felt it my duty to abstain from every species of comprominent; to reject every overture looking to arrangement or compromises; and to preserve my perfect freedom of action whether I am elected or not. . . . If I am elected, I shall enter office without one solitary promise or pledge to any man to redeem; and," he added, "if I am not elected, I will at least preserve unsullied that public integrity and those principles which my friends have supposed me to possess."[39]

When Adams heard rumors of Clay joining forces with Crawford, Adams discounted them; he did not think Clay's personality would allow him to be subservient to another. In the long term, Adams was wrong, as Clay would serve loyally and well under the next president. But in the present case, the man from Massachusetts had it right. Clay considered his candidacy as strong as the fading Crawford's and his principles even stronger. Why should he give up his beliefs and his race to work with a lesser man? For Clay, the answer was easy. Crawford, not he, should drop out. But should Clay have taken a different course? As he saw his chances fading, should he have folded his political cards and sought a new deal? While in retrospect that would have been a better career move, perhaps, at the time it just did not represent a likely scenario or real option for Clay. He could not merge forces with Jackson; his personality clashes with Adams meant no combination there. Besides, in some places the Adams and Jackson forces seemed to be working together. That left only Crawford. Together the Crawford-Clay forces would have a greater chance of success, perhaps even of victory. He could have hitched his hopes to the Crawford camp, with the expectation that a Crawford victory would make him the heir apparent. But he could not support a man whose principles so differed from his own, nor yield in order to put a sick man in office. Crawford's condition, to Clay's eyes, meant that he could not lead and should not win. Still young, Clay preferred to take his chances, hope for a House election, and win there in his own right. At the very least, he would fight with honor and, if he were not the winner, would fight again.[40]

But each rumor of illness, or of dropping out to run for vice president, made Clay appear a more unlikely choice, a weakening candidate. Then came even more damaging stories that further crippled a fading candidacy. As early as March 1824, rumors spread about Clay's withdrawal from the race. He termed those "ridiculous," for his withdrawal without any merger of forces might help Jackson win, and that must not occur. By September and October, such continuing stories caused several Clay friends to ask if he had withdrawn, as they had heard. One noted that many Clay supporters, on hearing those reports, had already gone over to other candidates. Just days before the election, a Massachusetts paper announced that Clay had dropped out to run for vice president, while others indicated he had simply withdrawn. Coming as those did on the heels of the other Crawford rumors, they could easily have been believed by some of the electorate. And without much of a friendly press in the East to speak up quickly to counter such claims, Clay's candidacy ended in confusion in many locales.[41]

In late October 1824, the candidate from Kentucky faced the electorate and wrote that he was "Clay in the potter's hands. And that potter is the public." Now, how would the potter shape Clay's future? Given that voting took place over a five-week period, from late October to early December, reports from different states would dribble in, each one a cause for celebration or despair. A good showing in early returns could thus influence voters whose decision time might still be weeks away. Moreover, the one-fourth of states that selected electors by legislative action added to the complicated mix. And to muddle matters further, in the haphazard system of nominating candidates and getting them on ballots, various leaders would not even appear on the ballots of some states. Clay, for instance, received no votes or virtually none in ten of the states, and received less than 4 percent of the vote in three more. Of the eighteen states with popular voting, he thus had no chance in over two-thirds. Others faced the same problem to lesser degrees—Crawford gained almost no votes, or none at all, in eight states, Jackson in five (all in New England), and Adams in three.[42]

With only some 350,000 popular votes cast—one-fourth of them in Ohio and Pennsylvania—a relatively small number of people decided the election. In that atmosphere, deals and "understandings" and "arrangements" were being made right and left by friends of all the candidates. The groups might change from state to state, and the goals as well, but many worked behind the scenes to maximize their man's chances. And as in all elections, local matters played a role as well. For example, Ohio, then the fourth largest state in the Union, saw sectionalism, ethnicity, and anger fuel the vote there. On the one hand, those favoring the policy of internal improvements preferred a western candidate—Clay or perhaps Jackson. Those in Ohio who had New England roots, on the other hand, opposed the Missouri settlement and supported northerner Adams. The Scotch Irish tended to vote for Jackson, who had defeated the hated British in battle. And some of those hurt badly by the panic of 1819 struck out at bank attorney Clay, and looked more to outsider Jackson. In Ohio, the popular vote showed Clay with 19,255, Jackson 18,489, Adams 12,280, and Crawford none. Ohio's 16 votes went to Clay, barely, by a plurality of 766. And so it went in state after state—personalities sometimes dominating, issues occasionally a force, regionalism usually important, and uncertainty always present.[43]

Over and over, to numerous people, Clay had reiterated that he would win six western states—Kentucky, Ohio, Indiana, Illinois, Missouri, and Louisiana. Together they would give him 46 votes. He expected to receive some significant electoral recognition from New York as well, and perhaps a vote from Maryland, with its district-by-district selection process. That should be more than enough, he surmised, to beat out either Jackson or Crawford. But as it turned out, the "safe" states that Clay thought he had were not so safe after all. By late November, he had still not heard the results from Indiana or Illinois. Then, when that news trickled in, Clay grew worried. He had received no electoral votes from either state: "Events on this side of the mountains have surprised me," he confessed. A Jackson wave had engulfed the 5 votes of Indiana, where the hero won 7,444 votes, Clay 5,316, and Adams 3,071. In Illinois, an almost even vote among four candidates occurred, ranging between 847 and 1,516 each. Adams carried that state by 244 in the popular vote, but the district system gave Jackson 2 votes and Adams 1. Clay was shut out. He did win Kentucky's 14 votes handily and narrowly carried Ohio's 16 into his column. As expected, Missouri also went with "the Great Pacificator." But with the loss of two of his "safe" states, now his hopes increasingly depended on two very dissimilar states—New York and Louisiana. And both selected electors by legislative action, meaning that pressure politics, individual manipulation, and personal preferences all came into play.[44]

New York had 36 electoral votes, more than one-fourth of the 131 needed to win the presidency. But factional battles between Van Buren's Albany Regency forces and DeWitt Clinton's "People's Party" made the state a chaotic political battleground. With no candidate of its own in the mix, the state made Richard M. Johnson's analysis prescient: "No man can tell who will be the result." In 1823, Clay's chief organizer and key point man in the Empire State, Peter Porter, had predicted that Adams had one-fourth of the state's votes, Crawford had the same, and the rest remained open for the seizing. However, Porter would prove to be a less than perfect judge of the New York political scene, offering not always dependable advice. He seemed a good choice—he had married into the Kentucky Breckinridges, had served in Congress with Clay, had won distinction in the War of 1812, and had been New York's secretary of state. But his optimistic words caused Clay to see "highly encouraging" signs in that state by August 1823. But Josiah Johnston's analysis almost a year later represented a more accurate view. He said the state remained so divided that no prediction could be made regarding its ultimate course.[45]

As that situation became clearer to all concerned, discussions began between the friends of various contenders. When asked to sanction a deal with the Adams forces, Clay demurred, saying that he had personally pledged to avoid "any interposition by me in respect to such an arrangement." But, he noted, his friends could act as they wished and thought best, in essence giving them free rein but no guidance. Acting in Clay's stead, Porter reported in October 1824, just before the popular voting started across the nation, that the Adams forces had offered to join with the Clay allies to defeat Crawford, with a two-to-one Adams and Clay division of the resulting electoral vote spoils. If that agreement occurred, that would likely give Clay enough electoral votes in New York to ensure he would be among the valued three, should the election go to the House. But Porter rejected the deal, he reported, because he thought they could do better. He was wrong.[46]

By the time of the New York legislature vote, results elsewhere had made clear already that Jackson and Adams led in the national count. The fight centered on who would be the third person. Crawford would have 36 electoral votes, Clay 33, with New York and Louisiana still out. Van Buren sought to rally his forces for Crawford, master manipulator Thurlow Weed his for Adams, and others for Clay. The initial voting seemed to suggest that Adams would come out with 25 electoral votes, Clay 7, and Crawford only 4. If that count stood, Crawford and Clay would each have 40 votes nationally, with Louisiana expected to be pro-Clay. Then came deals and rumored deals. Apparently Weed persuaded Clay leaders to form an Adams-Clay ticket to defeat Crawford and maximize the Adams vote. Trusting Clayites expected that outcome to give Clay enough votes to ensure his place in the next stage of the race, in the US House. But when the final vote came in, they cried "Betrayal!" On the December 1, 1824, joint ballot, Weed's bargain broke down and Clay lost out. Van Buren, another master of behind-the-scenes maneuvering, had made some last-minute arrangements to get Crawford more votes. In the end, the final New York vote stood at Adams 26, Crawford 5, Clay 4, and Jackson 1. If Clay had gotten the 7 or 8 votes expected in either the preliminary vote or in the later deal, he would have had 40 or 41 electoral votes, matching or surpassing Crawford, with one state to go.[47]

What had happened? Clearly, the Clay forces had been outmaneuvered by both Van Buren and Weed. But more than that may have been involved. Later, a Clay advocate explained the switch in votes as due to "corrupt bribery," while a biographer in the same era attributed the defeat to "bad faith . . . treachery." That may well be the case, but Clay's friends missed early opportunities for an agreement even before the election. And once the national votes became clear, it is not at all unlikely that the Adams forces worked the vote to get the maximum count for their candidate and the minimum one for Clay, once they realized that Adams would certainly have a better chance of winning if Crawford, not Clay, went to the House for the vote. As Speaker, Clay had great popularity, and they knew that. Ironically, Clay, the politician who was so "hands-on" as Speaker, by not getting more involved in the politics in New York, may have cost himself the election.[48]

But Louisiana and its five electoral votes even more clearly doomed Clay. If the Millboy of the Slashes won four of those, he would tie Crawford; if he gained them all, he would go into the House contest. Clay had great expectations. He had family members working for him there, had supported the high protective tariff sugar growers sought, had visited the state, and had attacked Jackson's martial-law actions. However, that same tariff had angered cotton growers, while his critique of the hero of New Orleans had displeased those who saw Jackson as their savior. Still, the overall signs and the overwhelming analysis seemed good. In 1822, Louisiana governor Thomas B. Robertson, who disliked the "Despot" Jackson, confidently informed Clay, "You may count on the votes here." The next year, a legislative caucus declared for Clay. Little wonder, then, that the Kentuckian had "*no doubt*" in 1823 that the Louisiana legislature would give him the state's electoral votes. In 1824, the governor again assured Clay that the candidate would do well there, and with Governor Robertson unfortunately leaving office that year, the governor-elect further stressed that Clay would win Louisiana. With such words coming from the highest officials in the state, Clay had good reason to feel confident.[49]

Yet by the first week of December, with Louisiana increasingly representing his last hope, a worried Clay wrote that "the fabrication of tales of my being withdrawn—the discouragement of my friends . . . which nearly lost Ohio and have occasioned the loss of Indiana, may reach Louisiana and deprive me of the vote of that state." Rumors—correct ones—reached him of a compromise between the Jackson and Adams forces to unite and deprive him of the vote. (In fact, a Jackson ally told the general that the coalition had been formed to keep Clay "from receiveing [*sic*] the vote of the State.") By the second week of December, as Clay still awaited the results, he seemed resigned to the worst: "I am prepared . . . to receive unfortunate intelligence." Still, he hoped and even expected to be able to muster at least a 31–27 legislative majority, and get the votes needed. Then, a little over a week before Christmas, the news arrived in Washington, DC.[50]

Clay had lost Louisiana. The legislature by a 30–28 count had given 3 electoral votes to Adams, 2 to Jackson, and 0 to Clay. That vote, coupled with the New York news, meant that Crawford, not Clay, would be the third candidate before the House. Throughout the 1824 campaign, Clay had committed many mistakes and missed many opportunities. He had failed to develop a strong organizational base and a cadre of sound advisors; he had faltered in setting up a newspaper informational base in the East; he had ignored the Jackson warning signs for too long; he had discouraged, or not encouraged, any alliance with Crawford forces, or others. But in the case of Louisiana, he seemingly had done things right. He had good counsel from knowledgeable sources and appeared to have the ballots he needed. With Louisiana's vote, Clay would still have crafted a successful strategy and achieved his goal of being one of the three finalists. A senator-elect from that state wrote Clay and explained what had occurred to deprive Clay of his victory, and Clay sadly repeated the analysis to an ally: "Two of my friends in the legislature were upset in a gig the day before & thusly prevented from attending [the vote]; two other votes [who] were expected did not arrive & three were seduced." Had Clay gotten those seven votes, it would have been 35 legislative votes for Clay, 27 for the others. Even with his losing the three "seduced" votes, had the four others arrived as expected, Clay would have won the Louisiana electoral vote, 32–30. And if those four had not shown up, had the three supposed bribed votes remained loyal, Clay would still have won the count, 31–27. But none of those scenarios had unfolded. Instead, the combined votes of Adams and Jackson forces had been enough to defeat him; but in truth, they would not have done that, if bad luck—and perhaps bribery—had not occurred.[51]

Clay attributed his loss to two factors. First, the false rumors of his withdrawal caused some of his friends to desert him. Second, as he concluded the next month regarding the Louisiana vote, "*accident* alone prevented my return to the H. of R., and, as is generally now believed, my election." Contemporaries added other elements. One indicated that the legislative vote was called when the opposition knew of the absence of the Clay allies. In short, he had once more been outmaneuvered. But another chronicler wrote that Clay had been "unfairly deprived" of the vote, suggesting bribery in the luring of the three voters. But at that moment, in late 1824 when the news reached Clay of the Louisiana vote, the reason mattered less than the outcome. He would not be president in the 1824 race. But he might be president-maker.[52]

6

President Maker

GIVEN THE MANNER IN WHICH Clay had seen his presidential hopes dashed and the way in which his solid chances had evaporated, he could have been resentful and bitter. Instead, he remained remarkably cheerful. Clay's buoyancy of spirit and his usual optimism served him well in the nadir of his career to that point. He shook off the defeat, looked to the future for redemption, and turned to the matter at hand—selecting a president.

Ironically, the original draft wording of the Twelfth Amendment to the Constitution had indicated that the top five vote-getters in the Electoral College would go before the House—the same language as in Article II, Section I, of the original Constitution. In fact, then-US senator John Quincy Adams had spoken, fruitlessly, in favor of keeping the number at five. That 1803 decision had now left Clay wandering in the presidential wilderness. He had been in the capital for more than two weeks and had already been elected Speaker by the time the news of the Louisiana vote reached Washington, DC. Had Clay been one of the three electoral leaders going before the House, many observers, both then and since, have argued that he would have been the eventual choice for president. But now, he would have tremendous influence in the selection of the chief executive. That power might eventually make him president. Or it might seriously injure such hopes. Though Clay had been the enemy of each of the three men before the House, at the same time he had not burned all his political bridges. In a light-hearted fashion, Clay wrote in late December 1824, "I enjoy the rare felicity, whilst alive, which is experienced by the dead—that of hearing every

kind of eulogium and panegyric pronounced upon me." Those kind words
came because almost everyone realized what two congressmen expressed at
the time: "The election I think will depend upon the course that Mr. Clay
may take," wrote Congressman Willie Mangum. Another simply noted, "It
is in fact very much in Clay's power to make the President."[1]

But before that occurred, Clay had another duty to perform. The Marquis
de Lafayette had arrived in the United States some months before the election had concluded. As the last surviving Revolutionary War regular army
general, and as the hero from abroad, he took a grand tour that occasioned
much interest. Clay and Lafayette, in fact, had corresponded ever since Clay
had met him in Paris, following Ghent. Over the course of the next years,
they would exchange more than a dozen letters. Now it fell to a pleased Clay,
as Speaker of the House, to introduce his friend to Congress on December
10, 1824. He told the old patriot in his welcoming speech that since the
time the general had fought in the United States, much had changed—
"the forests filled, the cities built, the mountains leveled, the canals cut, the
highways constructed"—but what had not changed was the nation's devotion to Washington and to liberty. Clay then stepped from the Speaker's
chair and saluted Lafayette. The other members followed Clay's lead. It was
a touching moment, one Clay cherished. But as Lafayette continued his tour
around the nation, at the same time the deliberations for the presidency were
occurring, Clay grew concerned that the adulation for another general hero
might aid the cause of Jackson. Even the welcome diversion of Lafayette's
visit could not avoid the world of politics, a sphere growing increasingly
contentious.[2]

The first vote for president among the three remaining contenders would
take place on February 9, 1825. For almost two months, then, the various candidates and their friends discussed strategy, offered options, and
suggested deals. Each man's allies had made "arrangements" during the
campaign; that process continued now, with the presidency within even
closer reach. At the center of all that activity stood "an Eagle among Crows,"
Henry Clay. In a situation he found "very amusing," the Speaker discovered
that each contender believed Clay's "friends" could decide the election and
that he could control those supporters: "Really the friends of all the three
Gentlemen are so very courteous, and affectionate, that I sometimes wish
it was in my power to accomodate [sic] each of them." But if Clay had that
wish, he did not have it long.[3]

Still, Clay enjoyed the situation as much as he could. His continuing charm and his mischievous nature in such a tense time were fully

displayed at a mid-January dinner, with Adams, Jackson, Calhoun, and others in attendance. Neither of the two presidential claimants, Adams and Jackson, seemed very comfortable or very sociable amid the tensions and machinations surrounding them. Clay, however, had no such reaction. As one who was present told it, "Clay was in fine spirits, and amused himself a little at the expense of the rivals." Jackson and Adams stiffly sat near each other, with a vacant chair in between. Clay rose from his seat on the opposite side of the table, sat in the space between the two men who had beaten him, and said, perhaps with a twinkle in his eyes, "Well gentlemen, since you are both to[o] near the chair, but neither can occupy it, I will step in between you and take it myself." The loud laughter that followed filled the room and showed those assembled that had Clay been one of the three still in the fight, he might well have filled the presidential chair. The contrast between the delightful, defeated Clay and the dour, discomforted candidates seemed particularly great at that moment. Whether Jackson and Adams joined in the laughter is not recorded.[4]

But more serious matters awaited, as the gaiety died down and the decision neared. Which of the three candidates would get Clay's perhaps president-making support? Would it be Crawford? After all, the friends of the two men had been discussing possible alliances even before the election process had started. Moreover, Clay probably harbored more favorable personal feelings toward Crawford than for either of the other two. In early January, a congressman commented that "Clay & his friends" actually preferred Crawford, "but they still more prefer success." Crawford supporters were not going to abandon their candidate, but as James Buchanan recognized, the seemingly still-confident Crawford forces really had little chance of winning unless a deadlock occurred. Very early on, Clay had made it clear that he, too, saw little prospect of a Crawford presidency. By the third week of January, he told several allies that Crawford's health problems might present "an insuperable objection" to picking him. Later, Clay explained that the "unfortunate condition" of the Georgian had almost made his selection "out of the question." To Clay, it seemed that Crawford could not win, and the Kentuckian would not ally with a lost cause.[5]

If not Crawford, then, could Clay possibly support Jackson? Though Clay had criticized the general, the two now seemed to be on reasonably good terms as they socialized in DC. Besides, if Clay wanted his western world to be represented in the halls of power, only Jackson among the three candidates would allow that. As Clay later noted, "There were a succession of wooing advances from Jackson and his friends to me and mine." He indicated that he did not object to a military man per se and would support one who demonstrated "prudence, temper, and discretion." However, in Clay's eyes, Jackson still displayed few of those qualifications. Earlier, Clay had been discouraged at seeing voters so "intoxicated & deluded by a little military glory." Now, he told a friend in December 1824, he could not support a person "whose sole recommendation rests on military pretensions." The next month, he wrote that the election of a mere "military chieftain" would be "fraught with much danger" to the republic. The matter seemed clear to Clay: "I cannot believe that killing 2,500 Englishmen at N. Orleans qualifies for the various, difficult and complicated duties of the Chief Magistracy." In short, Clay's consistent response to the question of backing Jackson seemed to go beyond a simple "No" to an emphatic "Hell, no!"[6]

But could Clay support Adams? After all, according to Clay's enemies, he had called the man from Massachusetts "an Eastern puritan" and a "political hypocrite." The two had disagreed at Ghent and had taken different sides on the issues of Spanish Florida and South America. In the eyes of some observers, Adams's forces in both New York and Louisiana had worked to keep Clay out of the final House vote, and Adams appeared closer to Jackson than Clay was. To many, then, any coalition with John Quincy Adams would be an "unnatural," unholy alliance.[7]

Because of Clay's concerns and conflicts with all three candidates, the partisans of each considered they had a chance to persuade Clay to support their man as the least of the three evils. "His real policy is known to no living being," a Virginian had written earlier. Advocates thus hoped to influence his ongoing thought process and bring him eventually to their cause. If Clay did little to encourage some of that with certain candidates, neither did he discourage it. It all became part of the new political game in town, and he enjoyed playing a central role. He sought to delay announcing his choice as long as possible, for he knew full well that once that choice became known, major criticism would fall on him from the other two candidates, no matter how he decided. But in truth, Clay had long before made up his mind, and in fact, he had not been very secretive about that decision.[8]

Henry Clay would support John Quincy Adams for president of the United States. In remembrance perhaps of Adams's previous treatment of him, he toyed with Adams for a time, stringing out the process. But Clay had made the decision that he would support the man from Massachusetts even before he left Kentucky to face the intrigues of Washington politics.

At least a half-dozen men put in writing their assertions that Clay had either told them that he could not support Jackson or that he would support Adams. Those names included a Kentucky congressman, a respected doctor, Thomas Hart Benton, and the almost-irreproachable John J. Crittenden. Clay's comments had been uttered as early as October 1824 and had extended until the time he left the state. Once in the capital, Clay reiterated that choice over the next two weeks, informing Lafayette, a Virginia senator, and a Louisiana lawmaker, among others, of his intention. By the end of 1824, then, numerous people knew that Clay would support Adams, and rumors so informed many others. Thus, when Crawford and Jackson supporters expressed shock after Clay eventually made his choice public, their words represented more of a political tactic than a sudden realization that Clay had rejected them. They knew that already, or should have known. Perhaps they had hoped he would change his mind, but nothing had shifted since Clay made that decision back in Kentucky. It was almost inevitable that he would go for Adams, after all. Clay could not support Crawford because of his health concerns; nor would he support an inexperienced, militaristic man. That left only Adams. It was a match made in neither Heaven nor Hell but, rather, was one of expediency and principle, cemented in Washington politics.[9]

Although Clay had long made up his mind, and had casually told several people of his inclination, as the new year dawned he had not yet informed the worried Adams, nor made his choice official. Already his allies had contacted Adams, and Adams, in turn, had campaigned for their support. As soon as it had become clear that Clay would not be in the presidential mix, Kentucky congressman and later governor Robert P. Letcher visited Adams's home. Gregarious, popular, and witty, "Black Bob" Letcher became the chief conduit between the two camps. When the man from Massachusetts spoke to the man from Kentucky, he knew his words would go to Clay. At a December 17 meeting, Adams wrote that "Letcher wished to know what my sentiments toward Clay were, and I told him without disguise that I harbored no hostility against him." That was what Letcher, who lodged with Clay, wanted to hear. He assured Adams that Clay held no ill feelings toward him, either. Then Letcher broached a delicate subject. If Clay supported Adams, could Clay's friends (including Letcher) expect to have "a prominent share" in any subsequent administration? Adams's diary remains silent on his answer, but Letcher apparently did not leave disappointed. He returned six days later, and in a long conversation, suggested that Clay might support Adams and secure a first-ballot House victory, something Adams doubted. Less than a week later, Letcher visited again.[10]

By January 1, 1825, Clay finally decided that he had enjoyed the spotlight long enough, and he would make his decision known to Adams. That day, both men attended a dinner at which Clay asked Adams for a "confidential conversation." Exactly a month before the decisive vote would take place in the House, Clay visited Adams. For some three hours they talked. Clay had already told his then-ally Francis Preston Blair the day before that he would support Adams for "the public good." Now, he informed Adams that he had delayed speaking to him "to give a decent time for his own funeral solemnities as a candidate." That time gone, Clay sought final confirmation that he and Adams agreed on key Clay policy matters, as articulated in the American System. Once satisfied on that score, Clay finally gave Adams his explicit endorsement, support, and promise to work to elect him. Adams provided few details in his diary. Later critics would say the two struck a bargain at that meeting. But Clay did not need such assurances; he had already made his choice and, in a sense, had no other choice, as he saw it. If Adams became a Clay ally in the White House, that would be helpful. Of course, if Clay gained politically from an Adams victory, that would be acceptable as well. For the good of the nation—or at least for the expected political good of both men—they reconciled.[11]

Still, they had to secure a difficult and elusive victory on the floor of the House. Clay's decision to support Adams did not magically guarantee that Adams would win. After all, Jackson had won electoral votes in as many states as Adams, and the Crawford forces appeared determined to hold fast to their candidate. Adams seemed certain of only the six New England states, and a victory required the votes of thirteen of the twenty-four states. Clay had won three states. That combination still made only nine states, even if Clay could carry all of his for Adams—not at all certain, for Missouri looked doubtful. The battleground would take place in divided states, ones that had given significant electoral and/or popular votes to both Adams and Jackson—Illinois, Louisiana, Maryland, and New York. If all four could be persuaded to go for Adams, he would win. A defection of just one, and the vote would be deadlocked and drawn out. The Speaker's skills would be tested, and the fate of the presidency and of the nation depended on the outcome.

Just two days after the Clay-Adams meeting, Adams told an ally in Congress of Clay's decision to support him. Presumably that represented part of a plan to persuade others to be part of a victorious movement. But on that same day, the Kentucky legislature passed a resolution that could change the electoral equation again and partially negate Clay's actions. The General Assembly instructed its representatives in the House to vote for Andrew Jackson, their fellow westerner. One gleeful congressman predicted that would be "a heavy blow for Clay." However, Letcher, Clay, and others had expected that action for almost a month. That was one reason Letcher wanted assurances that Clay's friends would be rewarded, if need be. Should they go against those instructions, they might lose their seats before an angry electorate. Now that possibility of legislative involvement had become reality. Would the Kentucky members of Congress follow the dictates of their legislature, or of their judgment, or of their Prince Hal?[12]

Clay had something of a mixed record on whether legislators should follow such instructions. In 1816, in the BUS debate, Clay explained that he had opposed the earlier recharter in part because he had been instructed to do so. As he was elected senator by the legislature, not by the people directly, he felt some obligation to listen to its dictates. However, he noted later that year, "But there may be cases, when it would be the duty of a representative to disobey an instruction." In short, Clay had indicated that if elected by the legislature, as senators were, then the will of the legislators should be followed more than if elected by the people directly. The people's instructions would come through the electoral process, not a vote in the General Assembly. Still, in either case, the elected officials should take under serious consideration those instructions. But in the end, the senator or representative must do what he saw as his duty and his responsibility. Conscience must be the final guide.[13]

In the Kentucky delegation caucus on how they would vote on the upcoming presidential ballot, Clay expressed his views, informed them how he would vote, and indicated they should do as they thought best. Some of the Kentucky members felt more sympathy to the westerner Jackson than to Adams. However, Letcher had likely made it known that Adams had spoken warmly of supporting Kentuckians—perhaps even Clay—for recognition. The vote went 10–4 in favor of Adams and against the legislative instructions. Clay's influence had won out. Thus, two weeks before the final presidential ballot, Kentucky had made known its course—and Clay's. After that vote, all the rumors of a Clay-Adams coalition seemed verified. And with that, all kinds of political hell broke loose. Depending on the candidate they supported, newspapers quickly either praised or damned Clay's course. In Washington, a correspondent expressed astonishment that Clay would disregard the wishes of the people of the West and go with Adams. A paper in Nashville opined that an act of "such shameless inconsistency" proved that Clay did not want a western rival to win. In response, a Boston letter writer stressed that if critics felt Clay should support Jackson instead of Adams, all they had to do to make their case was to show that the general was better qualified to serve than Adams. If they could not do that, he asked, how could they criticize?[14]

In a town already overrun with rumors, Washington filled with even more accusations and charges. Almost as soon as the Clay-Adams alliance became public knowledge, the Jackson and Crawford forces began discussions about their own coalition to counter that one. But the Jackson men found out what Clay had discovered during the campaign—the Crawford forces would neither withdraw nor compromise. Once that became clear, the supporters of those two candidates turned their full fury on the kind of arrangement they had sought but could not fashion. One Crawford supporter in Congress decried the "scound[r]ell" Clay for his "unnatural, preposterous" union. That Delaware senator found the Jackson men "violent & implacable" in their anger and agreed with them that Adams must have sanctioned corruption: "I have always told you, there never lived an honest Yankee."[15]

The fury of an angry Jackson also knew few bounds. While his political handlers had been doing pretty much the same thing as had the other two camps—probing for alliances, seeking deals, arranging for votes—Andrew Jackson remained either ignorant of those actions or, more likely, had chosen to interpret them in a different light than more neutral observers would. He filled his letters with seemingly genuine sentiments that stressed how he remained above all that and would sanction no dealmaking or bargaining. During the campaign, for instance, he had referred to Clay's attempts to form some kind of coalition in New York as proof of Clay's corruption, but he remained silent when his friends arranged a similar alliance in Louisiana. Convinced that he remained above the fray as a different politician, he saw the action of the opposition as reprehensible and anti-republican. Moreover, as the recipient of the largest number of popular votes, Jackson expected the representatives in the House to follow what he saw as the will of the people—a not illogical view. But those beliefs thus made Jackson furious when his chances began to wane, because of the "deep intrigue" of Clay. The possibility of a defeat infuriated him, especially one produced by the union of John Quincy Adams and Henry Clay. "Such an unexpected course," said the general five days after the Kentucky delegate voted, had to result not from pure motives but from "corruption, and sale of public office." By then, he had no doubt that Clay had sought to bargain with him, and once he had rejected Clay's corrupt entreaty, the villainous man had then sold himself to another bidder. But as it turned out, Jackson erred in his reconstruction of events and his interpretation of them. That mistake would have long-term political repercussions.[16]

Some two and a half years later, when pressed to substantiate his version of Clay's corrupt offer of support in exchange for office, Jackson pointed to the actions of James Buchanan. According to the general, at the end of December 1824, Buchanan had come to him after talking with Clay. He had then informed Jackson that the friends of Adams had been asking Clay for his support in exchange for the secretary of state post. When Buchanan had asked Jackson if he would make the same offer to Clay, Jackson recalled that he responded by saying "I would see the earth open & swallow both Mr. Clay & his friends, and myself with them" before he would be a part of "such means of bargain and corruption." As the *New York Times* later summarized, "Buchanan's conversation with Jackson made such impression on the latter as to lead him to charge, if not to believe that the Secretaryship was the sole consideration of *Mr. Clay's* ultimate preference for his rival." The Clay-Jackson break would have occurred no matter what the circumstances, but the Buchanan conversation with Jackson fed the division and made it more bitter.[17]

The problem was that Jackson had badly misunderstood Buchanan. When asked to confirm Jackson's version of their talk, a very surprised and somewhat embarrassed Buchanan tried to respond in an ambiguous way. After all, by then he was a firm ally of Jackson. Yet his response refuted Jackson's account completely. Over the next thirty years, the story unfolded gradually and more details emerged, but in essence, Jackson had it backwards. Without consulting the general, Buchanan had gone as Jackson's emissary and had approached Clay, asking if he would accept the secretary of state offer from Jackson. The man from Pennsylvania had said to the Kentuckian that the Jackson camp would not go out of the room for a secretary of state, as he looked directly at Clay. The Kentuckian playfully laughed off the suggestion, saying the only cabinet timber he saw in the room was Buchanan. Buchanan had left and told Jackson of the conversation and offer as they walked down a DC street. And so Jackson apparently heard what he expected to hear, not what Buchanan actually told him. It confirmed his conspiracy theories that his enemies sought to thwart the will of the people.[18]

In fact, when Buchanan made his statement and openly averred that he never made any proposition from Clay to Jackson, and rather sought to bargain on Jackson's behalf, the general refused to believe it. His ally had to be in error. By then, Jackson had already staked out a position based on his charges of corruption, and he could not retreat. In a private letter he termed Buchanan's answer "unaccountable," but also asked his journalistic ally Amos Kendall to treat the matter "with delicacy." In a later public letter, Jackson accused Buchanan of "a want of moral courage," saying he had not done justice to Jackson in his "exposé." Yet even then, he stated that Buchanan "never gave any exonerating testimony in there [sic] favour." Selective amnesia helped justify the anger.[19]

But all that lay in the future. In January 1825, Jackson firmly believed that Clay had approached him through Buchanan, and when rejected had sold his services to Adams. The Kentucky delegation's vote now confirmed the coalition. Something had to be done to expose such nefarious behavior. Perhaps the public outcry would sully the political reputations of those involved, defeat the alliance, and let the people's voice win. What was needed was someone who would give voice to the rumors. So, on the day after the news of the Kentucky delegation vote, a congressman penned a letter that appeared in the January 28, 1825, issue of a Philadelphia newspaper subsidized by pro-Jackson men. The unsigned missive informed readers of a "disgraceful transaction . . . a bargain." Repeating Jackson's interpretation of what he thought Buchanan had told him, the letter indicated that Adams had approached Clay; offering him the secretary of state appointment in exchange for Clay's support, and that friends of Clay had asked Jackson for the same offer, but had been rebuffed: "None of the friends of Jackson would descend to such mean bargain and sale." Still, the Jackson supporters had not expected honorable men to take such actions, but now Adams and Clay had done so, in one attempt, to subvert "the will of the Nation." That combination, said the writer, must not succeed.[20]

On reading the letter, Clay could not restrain himself. He had been accused of a dishonorable act; he had to respond. Perhaps silence would have been the better course, in the hope that the letter would receive little attention, but that seemed unlikely in the heated atmosphere. Silence might also be interpreted as guilt. A gentleman could not ignore a wrong, and Clay clearly considered himself wronged. And so three days after the letter appeared, Clay's "card" in the *National Intelligencer* termed the writer "a base and infamous calumniator, a dastard, and a liar." If he would show himself, Clay wrote, he would deal with him by "the laws which govern and regulate men of honor"—in short, a duel. Up until the appearance of those two letters, surprisingly little news had appeared about the election controversy. A few rumors had been repeated, but it had been a fairly quiet scene. Now that all changed.[21]

A few days later, George Kremer, a member of Congress from Pennsylvania, announced that he had signed the letter. Few believed that he had authored it, at least on his own. Something of a laughing-stock in Congress, Kremer dressed eccentrically, displayed little of the learning shown in the letter, and earned few positive comments from those who knew him. One person described him as "a strange, broad-shouldered, awkward, coarse-looking, Pennsylvania farmer. . . . He is sometimes called *George Screamer*." On learning the writer's identity, Clay did not challenge him to a duel, for Clay was convinced (correctly) that Kremer was simply a tool for others. Adams recorded that the often-intemperate Kremer "scarcely knew whether he had written the letter or not." According to Clay, Kremer later told the secretary of the navy that he had not penned the letter. By then Clay considered Jackson's close advisor John Eaton responsible and asked him to confirm or deny that accusation. Eaton admitted he had met with Kremer the night before the letter had been sent—people had seen them together—but refused to answer the query, in several masterfully dodging replies.[22]

Unable to confirm the real author of the letter, and unwilling to duel the ungentlemanly George Kremer, Clay turned to the only option left to redeem his honor—the truth. The day Kremer declared himself the author, Clay asked for a congressional committee to investigate the charges. But such an inquiry was not what Jackson's supporters wanted. Whether the charges were true or not, they needed the public to believe them. Thus, when called to testify under oath before the investigating committee, Kremer declined, claiming it was a personal matter over which the House had no authority. He said he wrote his earlier letter "under a conviction of its truth," thus again making the charge indirectly. But, presenting him-self as "a humble member" of Congress under "unexpected" attack from the powerful Speaker, Kremer refused to give the committee any evidence supporting his charge of a bargain. With his stance, a frustrated committee concluded they could take no further steps. Later, Clay himself called Kremer's refusal to testify "a miserable subterfuge" and said that it showed Jackson would rather hang a man than try him first.[23]

The Jackson managers, through the Kremer letter, had achieved their goal—they put the Adams-Clay forces on the defensive and made the debate a public one. Over the two weeks between the appearance of the letter and the vote for president, the same stories appeared in most newspapers—Kremer's letter, Clay's response, an anti-Clay letter, and a few other accounts. It was open war, and pro-Jackson and pro-Crawford papers criticized the "most unnatural and the most corrupt coalition," one where Clay had "sold himself to Mr. Adams." All this brought Clay to conclude, the day after the Kremer letter appeared, that the Jackson forces "with the most amiable unanimity" sought to vituperate him: "The knaves cannot comprehend how a man can be honest." A few days after that, he told a friend in Virginia how Crawford-Jackson supporters wanted to drive him "from the course which my deliberate judgment points out," while Calhoun and Clinton "want to remove me as an obstacle to their [future] election." But, he wrote, such intimidation would not work.[24]

Clay's duty, as he saw it, involved electing Adams and keeping Jackson from the White House. On the same day the Kremer investigating committee issued its report, or nonreport, the House of Representatives met to cast its first ballot for president. On the one hand, each state, no matter the size of its delegation, had only one vote. Thus, while more than one-third of the representatives came from the three states of New York, Pennsylvania, and Ohio, those seventy-four men controlled only three votes. On the other hand, in numerous less-populated states a small number controlled a more sizable bloc of votes. Only some fifteen representatives commanded the votes of eight states. In four states, in fact, one person would make the entire state decision; in four other states, three or fewer did. Particularly in those single-delegate states, the various sides exerted great pressure on that representative. John Scott of Missouri, for example, did not like Adams (who received few votes in that state) and indicated that he would not vote for him. But since his friend Clay had been instrumental in getting that state admitted into the Union, Scott would follow the Great Compromiser's lead. As one observer noted, "Clay has power to persuade him to vote for Adams." (Ironically, Clay's Missouri Compromise actions, which hurt Clay somewhat in the North during the campaign now worked to the benefit of the northerner Adams.) In divided Illinois, which had given two of its three electoral votes to Jackson, its lone representative, Daniel Cook, had supported Adams but did not want to go against the western tide if it went for Jackson. Many pressured Cook. But "the moment he learned the course of Mr. Clay," he indicated that he would vote for Adams. (In return, a grateful Adams administration would reward both men once they left Congress. Cook received a lucrative and semi-secret appointment as "confidential agent to Cuba," while Scott became examiner of land offices.) On and on went the jockeying for votes.[25]

In the midst of a heavy February snowstorm, with visitors flocking to the capital city to observe the historic proceedings and to cheer the victor, whomever he might be, the voting began. Some two weeks earlier, a glum Adams (even for Adams) had confided to his diary that he did not expect to win. One of Jackson's key advisors, only two days prior to the vote, predicted that Jackson and Adams would each get ten states, and Crawford four, on the first ballot. He envisioned a scenario where, with a deadlock continuing, eventually three of the Crawford states would go to the general, giving him the victory. Many other observers, however, saw the obstinacy of the Crawford forces preventing any such coalition or compromise, and they foretold a long, bitter struggle, with no foreseeable conclusion. Meanwhile, Clay searched to produce a different outcome and continued to work the aisles.[26]

In one sense, Clay's most successful maneuvering in his entire congressional career may have been his efforts to get Adams elected on the first ballot. That represented at least as important a compromise as others Clay crafted over the years. He got Louisiana, which had failed him earlier, to vote two-to-one for Adams; he, Adams, and Daniel Webster persuaded a small majority of Maryland's representatives to disregard Jackson's 7–3 electoral vote there, and go for Adams. Illinois and Missouri gave their votes to him. Using his "great influence" in the House, Clay capitalized on individual feelings, on personal contacts, and on power politics. And it soon became clear that the Clay-Adams forces had garnered an unexpected twelve votes—just one short of the needed majority. The key became badly divided New York, where prognosticators predicted that Adams would fall one short of a majority there. If that occurred, a second ballot would follow, and one Adams state had already planned to desert him for Jackson. As it turned out, it all came down to one man's vote—again. The sixty-year-old, Harvard-educated, former War of 1812 general Stephen Van Rensselaer had served in the New York statehouse and had been in Congress for some three years. Crawford forces, led by Van Buren, expected Van Rensselaer to vote with them. Much later an outmaneuvered Van Buren told a fanciful, colorful story of how the undecided Van Rensselaer had prayed for guidance and, looking down, had seen an Adams ballot, and so voted. The truth seems more prosaic. As early as 1822, Clay had received word that "your friend," the New York general, looked favorably on the Kentuckian's candidacy, though he doubted Clay could win. The two men had long known each other. Regarding that crucial swing vote, Clay thus knew from experience when to push, and he played that political game perfectly. A tearful Van Rensselaer, fearing a deadlock and chaos, and knowing that he would be vilified for his vote, cast his ballot—and thus New York's—for John Quincy Adams. He said later that he wanted to cut short "the long agony" and also that "Mr. Clay's combination could not be resisted." Contrary to most expectations, Adams now had a majority and would be the next president of the United States. "May the blessings of God rest upon the events of this day!" a surprised winner wrote. God and Henry Clay. "All agreed it was Mr. Clay who had decided it," an observer concluded. For once, the Jackson forces had been out-generaled.[27]

Clay's success in getting Adams elected on the first ballot represented a major accomplishment. The Speaker basked in the glory of victory. But in that success lay the foundation for Clay's political damnation. Three days after the House selected him as president, Adams met with Clay and, as expected, offered to nominate him for secretary of state. Clay "made light of the threatened opposition," recorded Adams, but said he would talk with his friends and take the offer under consideration. Perhaps without knowing it, Clay faced one of the most important political decisions of his life, a defining moment for his later electoral hopes.[28]

Two years before, in the early stages of the presidential race, Clay had told a confidant that he would participate in no intrigues, make no arrangements, offer no promises or pledges. "If not elected . . . I will at least have the satisfaction of preserving my hands unsullied and my heart uncorrupted." But now, in the last month, the opposition had accused him of intrigue, arrangements, pledges, and corruption. To accept the post would seem to confirm their charges. But if he refused, the West might not be properly rewarded, the critics would announce he lacked confidence in the government he had supported, and the opposition could say their charges had kept him from accepting. Besides, if he did not take the office, the man who would do so thus could become next in line to sit in the President's House. A year earlier, long before any bargain charges, a congressman had said that only two men deserved consideration for secretary of state, no matter who won—Clinton or Clay. Could Clay let the Jacksonians and their attacks keep him from serving the nation? Could they dictate his course? But could he accept, knowing the political costs of that choice?[29]

Clay did consult with his friends. Letters went out to such trusted advisors as Francis Brooke in Virginia and John J. Crittenden in Kentucky, literally asking, "What shall I do?" Within a couple of days of the offer it became public knowledge, and other letter writers offered unsolicited advice to the conflicted Clay. The normally astute Crittenden told Clay he should accept, or otherwise intimidation would win. In a sense, he saw that Clay's honor had been challenged and the Kentuckian should not back down—an argument that would have had great effect on Clay. Besides, Crittenden suggested, once the appointment had occurred, "All will be quieted in a moment." Others, however, supported rejecting the offer, to prove the bargain charges false on the face of it, even if it was false in reality. Overall, Clay's friends were divided in their opinions. He could find support, and an equal amount of criticism, for whatever course he took. Clay openly stated that he knew to leave the House of Representatives would remove him from his post of great influence. However, as the right-hand man of President Adams, he could greatly influence foreign policy. Still, acceptance of the post would mean abuse; but "they would abuse me at any rate." Finally, Clay told Adams he would join the administration as secretary of state. On March 5, 1825, he was formally nominated and two days later, in a 27–14 vote, he was confirmed.[30]

With that action, a political controversy engulfed the nation. Even before Adams's inauguration as president and Clay's confirmation as secretary of state, a Nashville paper announced Andrew Jackson's candidacy for president four years hence. There would be no honeymoon for the president-elect. The campaign of 1828 had started. Speculation began immediately about candidates and platforms, alliances formed and reformed, attacks started and changed. But in 1825, the candidates for the next race had essentially been decided and the charges already formulated. Clay observed, "Immediately after my vote, a rancorous war was commenced against me, and all the barking dogs let loose upon me." The Jackson supporters clearly sought to cast the next election around the corrupt bargain accusation. That represented a brilliant, unifying electioneering tactic. For many voters, it tarred Clay's character in such a way that the stain could never be erased during Clay's lifetime. Moreover, while the charge used innuendo, not evidence, it crafted the account in such a way that it "made the people believe." It also produced a new partisanship and, eventually, a new party. As early as February 1825, an aging New York congressman noted that "a party is forming itself to oppose Mr. Adams' administration." The alleged Era of Good Feelings had passed. An era of very real bad feelings had returned.[31]

The specific attacks came on two fronts. First, Jackson allies criticized Clay and Adams as "the upholders of corruption and the enemies of

In a painting depicting the signing of the Treaty of Ghent in 1814, American delegate John Quincy Adams stands at the forefront and Clay in the background. Though they would oppose each other in the 1824 presidential election, they later developed not only mutual respect but also friendship. However, when Clay accepted the office of secretary of state from President Adams, the resulting charge of a "corrupt bargain" would follow him for the rest of his career. *Oil on canvas by Amedee Forestier, Smithsonian American Art Museum, 1922.5.2*

freedom." The two men sought to establish a dynasty through their dishonorable alliance. The second stage of the criticisms centered on a more elemental, philosophical argument: Clay and Adams had gone against the will of the people and had deprived the electorate of their rightful choice for president. Of Clay specifically, the *Washington Gazette* wrote that "he has gambled away the rights of the People." Such bold and shameless antirepublican actions, said South Carolina congressman George McDuffie, represented a "gross and palpable" violation of the spirit and principle of the nation's Constitution.[32]

To support their point about subverting the people's choice, Jacksonians pointed to the fact that the general had won 41 percent of the popular vote, versus Adams's 31 percent, Clay's 13 percent, and Crawford's 11 (with 4 percent for others). Clay had little use for that argument, noting that if the people's will was that Jackson be president, they would have voted him into office outright. In fact, if Clay's percentage was combined with Adams's, they had a larger figure than did Jackson. Did their coalition thus represent the voters' choice? But in reality none of those counts really reflected the elusive will of the people, for six states had selected electors by legislative action, and thus no popular vote occurred in those places. What would the count have been if those states had conducted a poll for president? Without those six states' votes, it remains impossible to say what the overall will of the electorate really was regarding the candidates.[33]

One of those affected by the charges was Andrew Jackson himself. Probably seething inside at the increasingly clear trends, he nevertheless publicly kept his temper in check for much of the early period of the political negotiations—in part, perhaps, to silence attacks on his reputation for rash action. But when the Clay-Adams agreement became open knowledge, and particularly after the formal vote defeated him, Jackson threw off any restraints. Old Hickory quickly called Clay "the Judas of the West." Now the hero would lead a holy political war of extermination against the foe. After 1825, to Jackson the name Clay was indeed a four-letter word.[34]

The effective propaganda from the Jackson camp struck a political nerve with many voters. They did not want an intriguer as leader but, rather, an open fighter. Thus, by March 1825, all the core elements of a developing opposition image were set. To them, Clay was an immoral man, a woman-izer, a gambler, "a colossal cheat," a duelist, a blasphemer, a slanderer, and a slaveholder (or antislavery man, depending on the section). Clay, in their presentation of him, favored a central government over the rights of the states, the rich over the poor, one section over another. The Great Pacificator would easily compromise his principles, they argued, for the sake of office, would do anything to win, and would follow his insatiable ambition and "political prostitution" into the arms of the elite instead of the people. A few new elements would be added over the years, and it would be refined and redefined as needed, but in essence the 1825 decision gave birth to the image that Clay would fight the rest of his life. Yet it was like a wandering wisp of fog that he could never grasp, nor really ever dispel.[35]

But Clay tried mightily to do so. At first, he genuinely seemed to think that the charge would go away soon and have little long-term effect. In fact, as the attacks continued and intensified, Clay's reaction was silence. When called on to respond to more charges, Clay would often refuse, noting that if he answered the accusation, others "in endless succession" would follow. An ally told him that for every "one lie contradicted two new ones are im-mediately got up." But silence in the face of such attacks went against much of Clay's being and he could not long endure that course.[36]

Next came anger. Clay saw his action as noble, not ignoble. He had conferred a favor on Adams by accepting the post, rather than being the recipient of a gift exchange of office. Ambition had certainly influenced Clay's decision to become secretary of state, for that office had traditionally been the steppingstone to the presidency. But another factor may also have motivated him. Clay knew the likely problems that Adams's personality would create for his presidency. If he could help the chief executive overcome those problems, the administration and the nation might succeed and flourish. Clay expected the bargain charge to fade, and with his talents at work in the cabinet, he could be part of a glorious administration. And then he could run for president on a greater record of achievement. What Clay did not see was that his very presence in the government precluded that success from occurring.[37]

After going through the steps of denial, silence, and anger, Clay next reacted to the attacks on his character and his honesty by vigorously defending himself. Yet that tactic meant that it now put the burden of proof on Clay. His enemies had no evidence of corruption, just the appearance of evil to bolster their case. Clay, though, had to prove a negative in his response. And each time he did that, the attempt reminded voters once again of the charge. Clay continued to offer a defense of his action because he considered himself innocent. What he overlooked was that the opposition presented a case too, and many accepted that version because it fit well with their negative worldview of politics and politicians. Clay had a difficult time understanding that sometimes image trumps reality. He thus faced a dilemma. If he did nothing, the electorate might interpret silence as guilt; if he responded fervently and often to the attacks, those who cast ballots might think there must be something to the charge. Clay could protest too much or too little—and never win.[38]

"Wanton and groundless" attacks appeared almost daily; a spirit of "crimination, denunciation, and abuse" filled the opposition; whispers circulated clandestinely; "artful men" deceived the uninformed. In Clay's view that situation could not continue. When Andrew Jackson fired his opening salvo, in a letter published the day before Clay received the official nomination as secretary of state, he sneered, adding how "Mr. Clay never yet has risked himself for his country . . . or made an effort to repel an invading foe. . . . No midnight taper burnt by me; no secret conclaves were held, or cabals entered into." On hearing that the war hero had thrown the gauntlet in Clay's face, attacking his manhood and honor, an angry Clay could not stay silent. Within a few weeks he responded publicly, in a bitter barb: "Gen. Jackson fights better than he reasons." Did he mean that only generals should be president? Clay admitted he had not fought, but if he had, "I should have left to others to proclaim and appreciate the deed."[39]

Tired of hearing all the attacks, Clay decided to counter. In a widely reprinted "Address to the People of the Congressional District," on March 26, 1825, he appealed to voters' sense of justice. He first told of the warm "sunbeams" of kindness lavished on him by the Jacksonians before his course had been announced. When they heard his decision, that all changed. But he knew his preference before he left Kentucky, for a choice based on "military idolatry" would be injurious to the public good. He recognized that the people of his district preferred a western man as president, but a state must not act "within the narrow selfish limits of its own section." Instead, the common good of the whole must guide decision makers. The resolution of the legislature calling on him to vote for Jackson he earnestly considered, but he found it "incompatible with my best judgment." Voters had selected him to use his reasoning powers when representing them; he had done so. If they disagreed with his stance, they could show their displeasure by defeating him in the next election. Turning to the charge of bargain, Clay's prose thundered: "I entered into no cabals; I held no secret enclaves; I enticed no man to violate pledges given."[40]

Friends immediately congratulated Clay on his "masterful address." Lewis Cass of Michigan Territory called it a "triumphant refutation of the vile slanders," and others responded in similar terms. A happy Henry Clay reported that the "wonderful" effects of the defense had surpassed his most sanguine hopes. Determined to press what he saw as his advantage, Clay accepted a series of invitations to public dinners in his honor, when he returned to Kentucky in late May. Emboldened by the frequent praise of his "manly" actions, he defended himself against those who sought to destroy his political character. As he returned to DC in July, Clay also spoke in Cincinnati. A man who was present later recalled Clay's passion: "I was fairly startled by the speech, which was the most eloquent one I ever heard, in fiery utterance and energetic action. . . . He had . . . real soul." But others never heard Clay's voice or saw into his soul, and they remained unconvinced.[41]

Over the years, most observers have agreed that Clay made a reasonable, rational decision in supporting Adams. For that he has received little criticism. But most historians have also concluded that Clay's acceptance of the office of secretary of state constituted one of his gravest errors, in a life of many errors. Critics, confederates, and historians all would come to that conclusion—as perhaps Clay would.

In Clay's era, the effects were clear as well. An ally wrote a political confidant in 1825 that Clay's taking the cabinet post "can contribute nothing to his fame" and could cost him much. A key figure in the charge—James Buchanan—perhaps provided the best assessment of all. In 1844, he wrote to Robert Letcher that it was "unfortunate" that Clay had accepted Adams's offer of office: "To be sure there was nothing criminal in it; but it was worse, as Talleyrand would have said, it was a great blunder." Without that, said Buchanan, Clay would have served two terms as president. A year after Clay's death, an article in the *Southern Literary Messenger* deemed Clay's acceptance "a fatal error . . . a most inexcusable blunder, . . . [political] suicide."[42]

Historians have echoed and repeated those conclusions. Merrill Peterson termed Clay's taking of the post "the worst error of his political life." An editor of the published papers of Henry Clay suggested that the charge "was a political millstone that Clay carried to his grave." In short, virtually all agree that Clay made a fateful and disastrous mistake in 1825, one that would seriously injure his future prospects. But it is also a measure of the man that Clay could recover from such an almost mortal political wound, one that would have killed the hopes of other politicians.[43]

If there is much agreement as to the negative effect of Clay's acceptance of the cabinet position in the Adams administration, there is more debate on the basic question: Was there a bargain? Pointing to the fact that most expected Clay to be secretary of state, no matter who won, John Quincy Adams pronounced the charge totally unfounded, a conclusion repeated by others involved in the decision-making process in 1825. Since then historians have generally supported Adams's statement, though often in imprecise and loose language. For the first century after Clay's death, the conclusions were very clear. In 1887, Clay biographer Carl Schurz wrote that "nobody believes that lie now." More recently, however, the words have been less clear-cut, the conclusions more cautionary. The comments range from the damning "it certainly gave the *appearance* of a deal," to the uncertain "probably not," to the careful "no solid proof," to the simple "We shall never know," to the qualified "Both Adams and Clay were too sophisticated to strike any explicit bargain." Those comments all reflect the more refined awareness that political coalitions are often necessary to produce results. If no specific words of bargain took place at the national level, clearly the two men needed each other to defeat Jackson, and they understood that alliance at some level. But the fact that Clay asked the opinion of others before accepting the office supports the idea that it certainly was not a *fait accompli*. Simply stated, no "corrupt bargain" of buying the presidency by an offer of office took place. While Adams would not be above doing questionable things, if he could convince his conscience he was right, a corrupt bargain would have caused his mind to forever be tortured by the ghosts of his puritan ancestors. And all the evidence clearly shows that Clay made his decision for Adams even before he left Kentucky, and certainly before any offer could have been made. He and Adams later needed no formal, stated agreement; they understood the stakes of the game, the rewards of success, and the costs of failure.[44]

Perhaps Clay's best answer to those who charged him with corruption came some years later, as he spoke to thousands of his fellow Kentuckians. In his talk, he had mentioned the charge, with some disdain, and someone in the crowd cried out the name of a person whose testimony had supported Clay's version. Clay paused, then with quiet emotion and feeling, touched his heart, as he said, "I want no testimony: here-here-HERE-here is the best of all witnesses to my innocence."[45]

All of his life, Clay maintained that his motives and actions had been untainted, unsullied, and uncorrupted. And for a time it did not seem the charges would hurt him. After all, in the next election, the Adams faction retained a higher proportion of their seats than did the Jackson supporters. The electorate did not immediately punish congressmen who had voted with the "corrupt" Clay for Adams. But very quickly, Clay began to realize the serious long-term effect his decision had on his career. Writing to Crawford in 1828, he admitted that "it is quite possible that I may have erred." That admission cost much. Some fourteen years later, Clay again concluded that he had made a mistake in accepting the post of secretary of state, for he had underrated "the power of detraction and the force of ignorance." Confident of his own integrity in the matter, he had erroneously expected others to see the correctness of his course. Finally, near the end of his life, Clay offered a "frank confession" to a small gathering of politicians. Had he the ability to change the past, he would not have taken the post offered by Adams: "By doing so I injured both him and myself; . . . often have I painfully felt that I had seriously impaired my own capacity for public usefulness." Clay had only by then recognized that the public memory of what had occurred had become submerged in the myth of a "corrupt bargain," and the truth lost out.[46]

If Clay paused to look back at the 1824 campaign and its aftermath, he could view it in two very different ways. In one scenario, he could fault himself for running for the office too soon. Before then, his career featured success on success. He had critics but few enemies. However, by running for president and losing, and in acting toward Adams as he did, that all changed. Clay now had many real and lasting enemies. But in Clay's eyes, perhaps, if he had not run, then the opportunity to be president might be eight years away—a lifetime in politics. Clay could have faulted himself in other ways, as well. In retrospect, he might confess that he ran a bad campaign—he organized poorly, anticipated the Jackson bandwagon badly, handled the Crawford situation awkwardly, and provided for journalistic support weakly. In that critical look, he lost as a result of mistakes.

Another school of thought, however, could portray 1824 as one of Clay's best opportunities for the presidency. In that year, he had no electoral baggage—the "corrupt bargain" charge—weighing him down, as in later races. Nor did strong party loyalty skew the outcome. If Clay been one of the three who went before the House for the vote, he would have had an excellent chance for victory. Luck, fate, and Louisiana decreed that Clay would not have that opportunity, however. But Clay might well have indulged in wistful thoughts of what could have been, with just a slight shift of fortune. Had he been in the three-man race, rather than Crawford, a deadlock would probably have occurred. Over time, the frustrations of an impasse would have created an atmosphere where a true bargain, corrupt or not, would have emerged as a compromise solution. And in a Congress friendlier to him than to any of the three, President Clay could have emerged from the stalemate.

Perhaps it is well that such a possible outcome never occurred in 1825. A drawn-out fight, complete with deals and even greater charges than those that actually emerged, would have put tremendous pressure on a still-developing, fledging American democracy. Had Clay won the presidency after getting only 13 percent of the popular vote, the fury of a spurned electorate might have been dangerous, even disastrous. As it turned out, Clay's successful efforts in securing Adams's selection on the first ballot precluded such an extended, bitter fight. The system had worked. Yet in working the system, Clay had taken actions that tormented him politically for all his days. But in 1825, he looked forward to serving as secretary of state and, in doing so, going to the front of the line to be the next president.

7

Protagonists

IN 1825, CLAY EXPECTED TO spend many years in Washington—perhaps eight as secretary of state, followed by eight more as president. Then, at the age of sixty-three, he could retire to his beloved Ashland estate to enjoy accolades and grandchildren. For that reason, the Clays kept their house and farm but placed most of their livestock and furniture at auction. Clay did retain his supply of wine and liquor, and directed a friend to fill a 120-gallon barrel with "old whiskey" from Kentucky distillers and ship that to his new address. By July, the family had made the move to Washington, DC, first to a boardinghouse, then to a rented, three-story brick home on F Street, between Fourteenth and Fifteenth Streets. About a year and a half later, the Benjamin Latrobe–designed residence of the deceased Commodore Stephen Decatur became available. Calling it the best house in the city, Clay willingly paid the very high rental expense ($800 a year). Whether Clay saw any irony in living in the home of a military hero is unknown.[1]

When the Clays arrived in the capital city, Congress had adjourned for the summer, leaving a calm, tranquil place. One man later described Washington at such times as almost deserted, but also very pleasant: "No electioneering, no politics, but stillness & quiet sociability." After the trauma of the previous session, such an atmosphere would be welcome. It gave Clay time to learn his duties and start his work without the extreme partisan spirit ever-around him. Then and later, he and Mrs. Clay hosted parties and smaller gatherings. At other times, Clay used the quiet time to become better acquainted with the departments he might one day oversee as president. For Clay, now the nation's diplomat, could never fully leave behind the political life. Nor did he want to, for he enjoyed, even lived for, that world as well.[2]

The new secretary of state found himself supervising a diverse organization. On the diplomatic side, he had to administer some fourteen American missions overseas, as well as 110 consulates in foreign cities. At home, Clay's office dealt with the foreign diplomats to the United States, issued passports, and compiled lists of passenger arrivals. Beyond all that, the office of the secretary of state handled numerous domestic matters. Clay supervised the unorganized territories; operated the patent office; recorded the laws and pardons; guarded the congressional journals, the Declaration of Independence, and the Constitution; and conducted the census every ten years. Those important patronage powers outside the capital had proved useful to previous secretaries as they had become president, and might again for Clay in the future. But in the here and now of Washington itself, Clay found his staff extremely small in size and heavily overworked in practice. He had only a dozen clerks, two messengers, and two guards to conduct all those duties. Clay repeatedly asked for more help for the everyday work, but not until his last year in office did it arrive. He also suggested dividing the duties and forming a "Home Department"—later, the Interior Department, created in 1849—to handle the domestic work.[3]

Given the many duties of the office and the small support staff, Clay had to labor long hours. He had worked hard before, as a struggling attorney and as a congressman, especially during crisis situations, but those periods usually had occurred in short spurts. Now, Clay rose early, walked or rode several miles before breakfast, then went to the State Department to work twelve- to fourteen-hour days. Not surprisingly, within a month of taking office he called the work "very severe"; that analysis did not change during the entire time he held the post. Daniel Webster warned him not to try to do too much; a brother-in-law predicted that Clay would find his job confining and limiting.[4]

In fact, Clay's acceptance of the secretary of state post may have been another of his greatest mistakes, because the office's many duties kept him away from doing more of what he did best—operate in the political sphere. Overworked, he could not fully use his skills to help the administration advance its programs in Congress. For someone who loved the action and activity of the political arena, who reveled in the excitement and exhilaration of the fight, the slow, often-dreary, and cautious diplomatic life did indeed confine him like "a lion in a cage." Clay would become a much more rounded, better-trained leader as a result of his efforts in the office, should he become president. But by removing him somewhat from politics, the position became not a steppingstone to higher office but, rather, a stumbling block.[5]

Frustrated and overworked, Clay found several things helped him endure the duties and better accept his responsibilities. First, the position paid very well. Federal government positions were highly sought because they offered a regular, well-paying job at a time when uncertainty was the norm. In Clay's case, he could live off his government salary, even with the cost of hosting parties and renting expensive houses. That allowed him to use his Kentucky income to pay off debts that arose out of the panic of 1819. A second factor that made the job bearable was that few major foreign crises erupted. He operated in a relatively quiet time. Third, he had the advice, when needed, of President John Quincy Adams, himself a seasoned diplomat. Surprisingly, and by all accounts, the two men worked well together. If the president and his secretary of state never really understood each other at a personal level, they respected each other's abilities, and that support grew over time into something approaching friendship. Adams had long honored Clay's political principles; Clay had long appreciated Adams's intellect and talents. Within a month of taking office, Clay had written about the confidence existing between the two, the "entire harmony" prevailing on public matters. When Clay asked for Adams's suggestions on some state matter, he usually accepted the offered comments. The two would differ on the politics of the presidency, but altogether they had a strong working relationship, probably something neither of them had anticipated.[6]

Another thing that made Clay continue as secretary of state, despite his many disappointments, was the fact that he accomplished much—also perhaps a surprise to most observers. In fact, Clay completed more foreign commercial treaties than had any of his predecessors. At a time when it usually took a month or more for instructions to get to a foreign mission, and the same time to get a reply, each of those treaties represented much time and effort, much patience and waiting. A realist in diplomacy, a man who understood balances of power, Clay by his actions also signaled the kind of president he might be. He showed vision in that he approached the minister to the United States from the Central American republics and officially asked for his cooperation in a canal project through present-day Nicaragua. Similarly, he sought to defuse a dispute that a later president would use as a pretext for war—the Mexican boundary. Clay authorized negotiations and payment of a suitable amount to secure the line not at the Sabine River, closer to US territory but, rather, at the more distant Rio Grande. Inept diplomacy at the scene doomed that. But the effort indicated Clay's attempt to use peaceful means to anticipate potentially troublesome issues. And finally, Clay kept a close eye on nearby Cuba. He dispatched an observer there on a secret mission, to gauge conditions. Any change might warrant invoking the Monroe Doctrine to keep foreign hands from the island. American purchase of Cuba stood as an option should its status change.[7]

What became the greatest failure of American diplomacy during Clay's watch resulted from actions taken abroad in response to moves made, or not made, by Adams when he had been secretary of state. Since the end of the War of 1812, the British had sought to restrict the West Indian trade to British ships, and the United States had worked to overturn that restriction. Some cracks in the English colonial wall had appeared, but a stubborn Secretary Adams had pushed for more American rights. The angry British retreated to their earlier position and in essence again closed all their West Indian ports. With negotiations frustrated by the opposition in Congress, Adams had retaliated by closing American ports to British ships from the West Indies. Thus he effectively ended the lucrative West Indies trade. Jacksonians blamed the administration, and the matter quickly became a major campaign issue in the next election. In subsequent presidential years, Clay would see the question arise again and again, as opponents blamed him for "losing" the West Indies trade.[8]

The other major diplomatic controversy during Clay's time as secretary of state evolved into what some considered Clay's greatest failure and others deemed his greatest success. It involved race and politics, but more than that, it introduced issues that would long resonate in debates about America's place in the world. Should the nation be involved in cooperative ventures, or should it remain removed from the outside world? Should the country be a leading actor on the world stage, or should it only stand in the wings, watching events? Should it be an activist or a passive government?

Clay saw the emerging Central and South American nations as places of great promise. He sought economic partnerships with those new countries, but most of all Clay wanted to see them as free republics, not dissimilar to the United States. They then could all be part of a Western Hemisphere without the monarchical ways of the Old World. Given that outlook, Clay was delighted when his nation received an invitation to send delegates to a multinational gathering scheduled to meet in June 1826. Adams appointed two delegates, both friends of Clay, to represent the nation at the Panama Congress.[9]

Then it became a partisan political issue. In late December, Adams submitted his choices to the Senate for confirmation. By February 1826, it had become clear to Clay that the opposition had chosen to make the Panama Congress its rallying point. For different reasons, the Crawford, Jackson, and Calhoun forces all could agree to oppose the appointments and withhold funds. Some complained of the cost. Some decried Adams's acceptance of the invitation without consulting the Senate. Some opposed sending delegates who would associate with dark-skinned people, who also seemed sympathetic to ending slavery. Some argued that the United States should stay neutral and uninvolved in any conference involving foreign nations. Some sought simply to frustrate the administration, no matter what the issue. Certain historians have seen the ensuing debate as the event that crystallized the opposition into a united force. But in truth that had basically occurred when the House voted Adams in as president. A political campaign had started that day and, as a result, every subsequent Adams action became political fodder for the growing antiestablishment rhetoric. The Panama Congress debate represented just another chapter in that growing story of opposition to the administration.[10]

The debate turned vicious and moved far from the issue at hand. South Carolina's George McDuffie used the occasion to remind his auditors once again of the "corrupt bargain" charge. His talk in a sense showed the real reason for the debate. McDuffie said that the political gambler Clay, "a man notorious for the looseness of his morality and the versatility of his political doctrines," had held back waiting for the best offer and "as the reward for his treachery" had been named secretary of state. The acid-tongued Carolinian stressed that he could never support such a dishonorable, "sulking manager." Equally harsh words echoed from Virginian John Randolph, who also resurrected old charges. In his sarcastic, inimitable way, he termed the Clay-Adams union an alliance of "the old sinner and the young saint," the combination of "the puritan and the black-leg." Moreover, he seemed to suggest that Clay had even forged the document inviting US participation. Randolph saw it all as a "Kentucky cuckoo's egg laid in a Spanish American nest." Those attacks symbolized the growing lack of middle ground between the two sides.[11]

The tactics of the opposition successfully stalled the appointments long enough so that the congress had concluded before the American delegates could even arrive. Clay's vision would not be realized. The whole affair was a fiasco. Yet in connection with the debates and the eventual dispatch of the delegation, Clay had created perhaps his finest state paper. Virtually all his own work, the eighty handwritten pages of instructions to the representatives voiced his—and his nation's—progressive principles.[12]

Clay had long sought to connect Latin America and the United States in a closer association, based on similar political and commercial principles. His instructions thus emphasized the need for a "new epoch in human affairs," one in which hemispheric nations would come together as good neighbors in peaceful conferences and work out issues regarding conflict, neutral rights, commerce, and more without resorting to war. "Peace is the true interest of all Nations," he stressed. The delegates should work for a joint declaration of reciprocity in commerce, where the rights extended to one should go to all. The United States did not desire special privileges, he said. Clay instructed the delegates to try to secure a joint declaration from all involved to support the Monroe Doctrine, and he made it clear that European attempts at colonization would be viewed as an "inadmissible encroachment." They should seek to get nations to agree to unite behind the issue of a canal to connect the oceans, one that would be open to all countries. Finally, Clay advised them to work diligently to persuade the congress to proclaim religious freedom and promote the "cause of free institutions." As it turned out, the delay meant none of that would occur, and the Senate even vengefully refused to publish his forward-looking instructions. Many could not separate Clay the potential presidential candidate from Clay the diplomat. Yet his words spoke to what could be, and what the nation should be. Clay had tried to make his vision a reality and had failed, but in the attempt he had stood tall.[13]

Clay had another, unofficial, duty as a member of the administration: to advise the president on political matters. In that regard, fundamental differences divided the two men. The secretary of state usually took a more practical approach to politics, the president a more idealistic one. If Adams considered the political Clay to have too little control over his emotions, Clay viewed Adams as having too much. But no matter how much Clay advised or cajoled, Adams remained determined to hold true to his ideals of what a president should be and should do. For a man who had acted in an astute political manner during the campaign, a different Adams operated once in office. To him, a chief executive must act in a nonpartisan fashion, retain officeholders, and promote a grand vision. Even if it meant political suicide, President Adams would not abandon that outlook. Would-be president Clay, in turn, considered plans and principles important, but cautioned that they did not mean a great deal if they remained only words on paper. Concrete action and specific results must follow. Adams sought government by consensus, Clay by compromise.

The president had the knowledge, the foresight, and the programs needed to be an exceptional executive, but he desperately lacked leadership skills and political wisdom. Clay could have supplied more of those, but he remained in the background, as the president made misstep after misstep. Clay tried to be a louder voice, a stronger influence, but he would not push Adams to the brink on controversial matters. A perfect example of the two men's differences arose regarding Adams's first annual message. Clay advised him not to recommend anything that would not succeed before Congress. As a minority president, his administration needed early victories. Adams, however, produced a visionary, philosophical document. It included many elements that had little chance of success, others that unified the states' rights opposition, and a few that just earned ridicule, such as his reference to "Light Houses of the Skies." By not listening more to Clay, Adams died a slow but noble political death.[14]

The president did face many obstacles. An organized opposition made it increasingly difficult to get bills through Congress, for example. Still, Adams's own actions continued to frustrate Clay and his allies. Nowhere was that clearer than in regard to patronage. Clay wanted to rid the administration of its political enemies, reward its friends, and use the resulting goodwill to build a supportive political base that could succeed in the next election. Adams would have none of that. He would not discharge officeholders unless evidence of corruption appeared; he would appoint men to positions regardless of the side they supported. Angry Adams allies, hungry for office, told Clay how the president was "passing by his friends and promoting his enemies." From South Carolina, an Adams man complained that every federal office there remained in the hands of the opposition: "I cannot understand this policy." Neither could the leadership. Daniel Webster grumbled that the lack of patronage to friendly newspapers had effectively neutralized them, while the lucrative customhouse appointments had gone to the opposition. It seemed to many allies that the way to get a job was to join the Jacksonians. Little wonder, then, that supporters of the administration became more inactive and less organized. Yet the nonpartisan policy did not change.[15]

If Clay could grudgingly muster at least a modicum of sympathy for Adams's principled stance on patronage, he could not grasp the president's lack of action regarding an enemy within the cabinet itself. Postmaster General John McLean performed well in his post, but he did so as a loyal ally of Calhoun and Jackson. When the secretary of state learned of that perfidy, Clay quickly urged the president to discharge McLean; Adams refused to do so, even though he accepted the truth of the charges. McLean would remain because he ran the office efficiently (efficiently for the enemy, an infuriated Clay fumed). Over and over, Clay urged Adams to remove the cancer within their political body. After all, the postmaster general sat in on cabinet meetings and could relay sensitive political information to the other side; he manipulated the building blocks of patronage; he appointed hostile postmasters across America, and reports reached Clay that some of them opened the letters of the president's allies. As the next election neared, it became obvious that McLean was using the franking privilege—the right to send materials through the mail at no cost—to advance Jackson's cause. In the end, most of the expenses of that campaign were borne not by Jackson supporters but by post office subsidies. Those issues of patronage and the postmaster general created more differences between Clay and his president than any other matters. They reflected how Clay envisioned the office. They also showed, however, that Clay remained loyal to the administration. He wanted it to succeed, but increasingly feared it would not.[16]

Various other controversies occurred during the Adams presidency—important Supreme Court decisions, what Clay called "a civil war with Georgia about the Creek Indian lands," and the contentious tariff of 1828—but overshadowing them all were the increasingly divisive political wars. Jacksonians prepared early for the battle of 1828 and began purchasing newspapers. Attack stories appeared, charges surfaced, and rumors proliferated. A woman in Tennessee sighed that "Jackson, Clay, & Adams are the topic of the day, pollitick will never die—and party spirit Make controversy."[17]

At the center of the political maelstrom was the bargain and corruption accusation regarding the aftermath of the election of 1824. It seemingly refused to die, and like a political vampire it continued to suck the lifeblood from the administration. The president referred to "the load of obloquy, slander, and persecution" heaped on the secretary of state. Under attack, an angry Clay finally struck back in another lengthy defense of his actions in a thirty-page *Address to the Public*. It is possible that the response was a mistake which might have receded from public view had Clay not brought it up again. But it is more likely that Clay's opponents would have used that controversy no matter what Clay did. He could protest to his dying day that the charges were "devoid of all truth and destitute of any foundation what-soever," and use evidence to support that defense, but it mattered not. The appearance of evil proved hard to combat.[18]

Partly to offer a defense of his actions regarding the charge, Clay returned to Kentucky in the summers of 1826 and 1827. That meant taking needed time from his State Department duties. But the quiet of Washington in summer gave him the opportunity to step out and touch his Kentucky base once more. He desperately needed to do so, for his cabinet work had kept him away too much, and far-ranging events were taking place in the commonwealth.

What became known as the Old Court–New Court struggle would, in the end, split Kentucky politically, create chaos in the state judiciary, and damage Clay's prestige. It would also form the genesis of the Second Party System in America. The origins of the controversy lay in the panic of 1819 and its results. In 1818, just before the depression hit, Kentucky created some forty-six independent banks, with little regard for their potential stability. Those "Forty Thieves," as they were called, issued their own notes (paper money backed by their own deposits) and furthered speculation and inflation. Then came the panic, and many banks closed. For others, their notes depreciated wildly. Bank-issued money that might have been worth its face value earlier now would be exchanged for much less. In 1821, a letter writer said the bank notes circulated at one-fourth their level; the next year, a diarist complained that "the Commonwealth's money is now passing two dollars for one." That financial instability combined with the economic stress to produce confusion, uncertainty, and anger. A father told his son, away at college, of the effects: "You will upon your return find this town greatly changed for the worst. . . . Business of every kind is almost at a stand[still]—our mechanics nearly out of employment. . . . Our storekeepers are unable to keep an assortment of goods & many of those who were considered as our most wealthy citizens are so overloaded with Debt, that the interest alone is sufficient to eat up their remaining property." But the hardest hit were the struggling farmers, the country's yeomen, the agrarian heartland.[19]

The 1820 Kentucky General Assembly had surveyed the financial bedlam and the economic turmoil and sought to help those who seemed unable to pay their debts and who might lose all they had worked for over the years. Like other states, Kentucky passed replevin laws to aid those in distress. Basically, the acts gave debtors a year's extension to pay off their debts. At the end of that time, they could close their accounts by paying in the depreciated bank notes. If creditors refused that, then the debts would not be due for another year. Finally, another law stated that property under forced sale could not be put under the auctioneer's hammer for less than three-fourths of its appraised value. For those who had borrowed money, these laws gave them relief for two years, or allowed them to pay their creditors with money that might be worth only half of what they had borrowed. Angry creditors, who had their own debts to pay, called the actions unfair and unconstitutional. This "predatory war upon property" pitted class against class, divided rural interests and urban ones, placed in opposition entrepreneurial types and anti-entrepreneurial constituencies, and alienated small farmers from businessmen. Various circuit judges voided the replevin laws in 1821. It now became a question of checks and balances, of majority versus minority rights, of the limits on judicial review. When the state's highest court sustained the lower courts' decisions two years later, then things really grew divisive.[20]

In the middle of that muddle, in 1824, Kentuckians elected Joseph Desha as governor. Poorly schooled and distrustful of the educated elite, he had once ridiculed Clay for not fighting "the savages" but instead "pouring over his books in a closet." During the governor's term of office, he helped force out the progressive president of Transylvania University, and that school, so dear to Henry Clay, never regained the same level of prominence. And when Desha's son was convicted of a brutal murder, the governor—his father—pardoned him. The chief executive also backed very controversial actions by his pro-relief forces regarding the judiciary.[21]

Faced with the various court rulings that declared the replevin laws unconstitutional, the new, pro-relief legislative majority first tried to impeach and remove the offending judges, who in essence served for life; but the General Assembly could not muster the necessary votes to do so. Spurred by their followers' demands to do something to help them survive the panic, and by their opposition to the idea of an activist court, the legislators turned to a more radical solution: they abolished the state's highest court and created a new body, this time with their own appointees. Now, Kentucky had the farcical situation of two high courts. The Old Court refused to cease operating and called the legislative moves unconstitutional; the New Court insisted it spoke for the republican majority and had taken correct legal actions. Debtors and relief forces would appeal to the New Court to sustain them and the laws favoring their cause; creditors and anti-relief men would take their cases before the Old Court and receive its favorable rulings. Legal chaos followed.[22]

Clay observed all of this sadly. Concerned initially with his own 1824 presidential race and then, once it concluded, with his duties as secretary of state, he had watched the quarrels from afar. He even wrote, "I mean to abjure K. politics." But of course he could not. Looking at the Old Court–New Court imbroglio through his attorney's eyes, he concluded that both the replevin laws and the creation of the New Court were unconstitutional. Clay quietly advised his friends to "repeal bad laws" and restore the Old Court to its rightful legal place. But he only slowly went beyond that.[23]

Away from the furor of the controversy for much of the time, Clay did not grasp the changes taking place, nor what they meant for American politics, nor for him personally. From Kentucky, various allies warned him that something significant was afoot. William T. Barry wrote that "the bitterness of party is without example"; Francis P. Blair became clerk and advocate of the New Court; Amos Kendall told Clay that "ferocious feelings" had arisen, ones which might even endanger the public peace. In fact, the crisis would turn all three men against Clay. Their change reflected a grassroots reorganization, a reformation of alliances that would soon grow into parties. The roots of the Second Party System ran strongest and deepest in Clay's Kentucky.[24]

The divisions grew firmer and clearer. By 1826 it had become obvious that the New Court relief forces of Desha and others had successfully organized for Jackson, while the Old Court anti-relief group had mostly gone to Adams and Clay. The secretary of state recognized that his stance had alienated the relief party and had produced a formidable opposition for the future. In a sense, out of that struggle emerged the Jacksonian Democratic Party that would fight Clay the rest of his political life. As it turned out, within a few years, in Kentucky the Old Court forces triumphed and voided all the actions of the New Court. The immediate crisis ended. But the effect of "almost one continued Scene of high party excitement" lived on. It all symbolized deep divisions within American society, and did not bode well for Clay and Adams in the upcoming 1828 election.[25]

As the 1828 race unfolded, the charges that would make this campaign so memorable, in a negative way, began to fly from the editorial pens of both camps. Regarding Adams, some attacks portrayed him as an elitist intellectual who had engineered a "corrupt bargain." Others incorrectly accused him of purchasing a billiard table for the White House using public funds, and even of having been the pimp for the czar in Russia. Regarding Jackson, critics called him a slaveholder, a murderous duelist, a conspirator with the disgraced Aaron Burr, and a lawless general in Florida. But some Adams supporters went well beyond that and termed Jackson's mother a mulatto and her son a literal bastard. And from the press of Clay's friend Charles Hammond came the salacious charge that Jackson's wife had committed bigamy by living in sin with Jackson before her divorce was granted. This "profligate woman" and this "seducer of other men's wives" deserved public censure, said the Adams press. All that together produced one of the dirtiest elections in American history.[26]

That last charge, regarding his wife, infuriated Jackson more than any other, perhaps so much so because he was not innocent in that regard. In fact, the two clearly lived together before the divorce proceedings had even been started, and many citizens of Nashville had known that. But those attacks on his now-saintly spouse cut her husband to the core. Since the later divorce proceedings had taken place in Kentucky, and since the originator of the story was a known Clay ally, the general not illogically saw "the finger of Clay" in the whole affair. He dispatched his right-hand man, John Eaton, to confirm those suspicions. A few days before Christmas 1826, Eaton reported that he had confronted Clay directly on the issue and that Clay had "frankly declared" that he had played no role in the attacks. Eaton related to Jackson that he believed Clay— something the general neither expected nor perhaps wanted to hear. Eaton also queried Hammond, who likewise denied the Clay connection and, in fact, reported that when he had asked Clay what he knew about it all, the Kentuckian "expressed his opinion that the subject ought not to be brought before the public." But despite Eaton's findings, the general continued to hold Clay responsible for the "base attempt" to damage his wife's name and her womanly virtue. First, Clay had harshly criticized his actions in Florida, then he had corruptly kept him from the presidency, and now this. Nothing Clay could say or do would convince Jackson that Clay was not an evil, venal, dangerous man. In short, the two men held similar views about each other. With various permutations, that hatred would largely shape much of American political history over the next two decades.[27]

How much of the dirty campaign tactics actually emanated from Clay remains unknown. He did send Hammond information regarding Jackson's expenses when governor of Florida, to use to counter the billiard-table expense charge. But that marks the known extent of Clay's involvement, based on existing records. Clay's vitriol tended to involve an opponent's programs or politics, or some sarcastic personal comment, not character assassination. That came from others. But the squalid campaign soiled all it touched, the innocent as well as the guilty. And it forewarned Clay what he could expect should he should run again for the office.[28]

All the focus on the election's harsh personal attacks can obfuscate the greater truth: that the Jacksonians were more organized, more spirited, and more energetic. As an antebellum writer noted, the Jacksonians aroused public sentiment in their favor by portraying the issue as one of "the honest old soldier circumvented by two conniving politicians." This man of integrity, this frontier hero, this man of the people, this person of rare republican virtues, this leader who opposed the growing "rage for diplomacy & inter-national connection" now sought the seat rightly his. It became a race not of programs and politics but of personalities and perceptions. One man summarized his shock at the success the Jacksonians had in presenting their picture of affairs: "Good God! Can the American people know so little of character as to permit themselves to be persuaded that Mr. Adams, whose whole life has been one of unostentatious republican simplicity, is a proud, arrogant aristocrat, whilst his competition, who travels with the retinue of the Chieftain of a Scottish clan, is made to pass for a plain and exemplary Democrat?" That represented the outlook of an older political style; in the new, emerging political world, image often became just as important as programs, men just as crucial as measures. Clay the political man would find it hard to adapt to such change.[29]

At another level, Clay and Adams operated at a disadvantage as well. Martin Van Buren had led the Crawford clique into the Jackson camp, and now the unified group began to meld the particularistic, state-centered parties into one organized whole. The web of Jackson newspapers then got the message out—by the 1820s, half of the nation's households subscribed to a paper. And an expanded electorate changed the dynamics of elections, as well. By 1828, only two states still chose electors by legislative ballot and that, coupled with the changed campaign and the organizational efforts, brought forth greater voter interest and turnout. One Jacksonian in Kentucky told Governor Desha that "the state is thoroughly organized I believe & almost every Jackson man ticketed & invited to the polls."[30]

Part of their confidence resulted from the absence of enthusiasm among Adams supporters. The president's lack of support for their patronage requests, his own pessimism regarding reelection, and his weak administration were reflected in their passionless actions. As one Massachusetts ally told Clay, the president was tolerated but not fervently supported: "He had admirers, but not friends." Clay, Webster, and others tried their best to counter that feeling by taking to the campaign trail and by organizing some newspaper counterattacks. But they faced an uphill struggle, and they knew it.[31]

As it turned out, Clay's Kentucky would be a key state in the election, and most commentators saw that as well. If the secretary of state and the administration he served could not win Henry Clay's home state, it would send a negative message to the rest of America. A vote for the Jackson party would signify a vote not only against Adams but against Clay as well. The slanders, the "shameless and relentless warfare against your absent friend," represented attempts not just to defeat the current president but also to keep Clay from the office in the future: "Friends of the persecuted man!—now is the time to rally around him."[32]

But the time that the "absent man" spent in Washington and away from Kentucky politics showed. He had not stemmed that Jacksonian tide rising out of the Old Court–New Court struggle, and the results reflected that. In 1828, the vote for state offices would precede the fall elections for president. Political eyes turned to Kentucky for a sign. Emboldened by "truly encouraging" news from home, Clay wrote a son-in-law that if the state supported Adams, he thought the president would win, for, as he told an ally soon after, its news would influence the vote in several key undecided states. As political operatives warned Clay, "Kentucky is necessary to us," and "if that state is gone, the election is over." When the results of the governor's race came in, Clay's group had elected the governor, but by only a few hundred votes; Jacksonians got their man as lieutenant governor and won a majority in both houses of the legislature. Clay had done too little, too late. He had failed to deliver his constituency. And that symbolized what the general election results would be in Kentucky and the nation.[33]

In the end, Jackson won an overwhelming victory. Adams had carried only two states outside New England and had split the vote in two others. Jackson had won the entire West and South, including Clay's Kentucky. With four times as many people voting as four years earlier, Jackson received some 56 percent of the ballots—a percentage that would not be exceeded for the rest of the century. It seemed a tremendous victory, and it was. Yet, had some eight thousand or fewer votes shifted in each of the three large states of New York, Ohio, and Kentucky—and had New York delegated its entire electoral vote to the winner instead of splitting it—the final results would have favored Adams. Despite huge disadvantages, Clay had actually come close to crafting a winning strategy—one that would have made Adams a minority president for a second time. But in real life, Jackson had won. The "great calamity" that Clay feared had become reality.[34] The election of 1828 taught the observant politician several lessons, including the importance of a widespread and partisan newspaper effort, a well-funded and well-organized campaign, a concerted and united opposition party in Congress, and a dedicated and devoted cadre of aides. Clay would observe, and would learn the lessons, though sometimes slowly and often imperfectly.[35]

Following the election, Clay seemed to accept the results. Friends found him in an agreeable mood and enemies remarked on his buoyant spirits. He even managed to speak of Jackson "in a good humour'd, sprightly way." That optimistic, positive side typified many of the attributes that made Clay so popular. But perhaps a woman who knew him well discovered the truth better. She noted how he kept on "the mask of smiles." The results hurt him, but he would hide behind a veil of cheerfulness. Perhaps in one way, though, he did feel a sense of relief, for he now would be free of the daily drudgery of the State Department, would not be serving under someone else, and would be once more his own, independent political man. That formally occurred on March 3, 1829, when Clay resigned his post. In what had been both a frustrating and a rewarding time, he had demonstrated a firm grasp of diplomacy, had learned much, and had displayed good vision in his efforts. Yet the politics of the Adams presidency left him feeling impotent and disappointed. In the end, the administration had been rejected by the voters, and that wounded Clay.[36]

Four days after his resignation, at a farewell dinner in his honor, Clay finally released some of that pent-up bitterness. He stated that the people had chosen a man with no qualifications save military valor, a person who had done the speaker many injustices, all for the purpose "of gratifying private resentments, and promoting personal ambition." But Clay then asked all those present to discard such feelings. Jackson was president and every citizen had the duty to support him. (Or, as Clay would phrase it in another talk less than two weeks later, even if he was not in command of the ship of state, "we should most anxiously wish it a prosperous voyage, under its newcomer.") Clay closed his talk by commenting that he could leave Washington "with a spirit unconquered." Later he had an emotional parting with the man he had served loyally and well for four years. The next day, as they left town in their carriages, the two men happened to pass each other, and they exchanged one last, distant greeting. It was over. Clay departed, uncertain of his future. But despite his words, it would not likely involve much long-term support for Andrew Jackson.[37]

After what Clay called a triumphant march across the mountains, with friends cheering them all along the way, the family returned home to

Kentucky on April 6, 1829. A vacant house awaited them, and much work needed to be done to bring the estate back up to Clay standards. The patriarch had already decided not to run for Congress and had told a relative that he wished to remain in retirement, "and I shall do so, if I can." When Clay wrote those words, he meant that his supporters would pull on him to reenter the political field. But in truth, the question centered on whether *he* could withstand the call. Politics was a drug that he could resist for a time, but he could never break the habit.[38]

Clay licked his political wounds and watched with a mixture of disgust and satisfaction as his predictions regarding Jackson seemed to come true—at least to his eyes. If one accepted Clay's view and premise—that Jackson sought to consolidate power and become a military dictator—then the unfolding events seemed to support that, bit by bit. In truth, Jackson did consolidate and add to the power of the presidency, but his beliefs never took him far down the road to despotism. In that regard, Clay was again wrong. However, the threat existed, as even Jackson's strong ally Thomas Ritchie admitted. The editor confessed that he rarely went to bed "without apprehension that he should wake up to hear of some *coup d'état* by the General." Like Clay, others feared Jackson would quickly take more extreme measures if he believed the "people's will" threatened. It would not need a long step to protect the people from a corrupt Congress, or a dangerous monopoly, or

One of the first examples of the daguerreotype in the United States was displayed in Clay's hometown of Lexington. In this rare image of an elder statesman, Clay's eyes and slight smile define him. *Wilson Family Photographic Collection, University of Kentucky Special Collections Research Center, pa62w8*

a rogue state by taking extraordinary actions. Viewing Jackson as irrational and vindictive, Clay worried that this side of the general would win out. And his opposition operated at several levels, for he disliked Old Hickory's challenge to his western dominance, Jackson's attacks on his honesty, and the new president's party politics. But at the basest level, Clay's antipathy grew out of the fear of what Jackson *might* do.[39]

Even before Clay left Washington, Crittenden had advised him that he should stay out of the political limelight and "remain quiet for a time." Clay could let passions cool, rebuild his Kentucky base, and return to Congress later, if he desired. Clay followed that sound advice for exactly three months. The superficial spark that brought Clay out of his brief shell of political inaction involved what Jackson called the principle of rotation in office and others termed the "spoils system." Prince Hal saw all that as an open attempt to build a loyal, unquestioning fiefdom, peopled by the soldiers of the president's civilian army of officeholders. Moreover, Jackson filled the leadership of that force with the enemies of Henry Clay. It was open war.[40]

Even worse for Clay, former allies also turned to Jackson. Two of the most visible were Missouri senator and Clay kinsman Thomas Hart Benton and a former Clay friend, Postmaster General William T. Barry. The Benton defection hurt worst. A cousin of Lucretia Hart Clay, Benton had once been on friendly terms with her husband. After all, Clay could not be angry with a man who had once been engaged in a pistol and knife brawl with Jackson in Tennessee. Five years younger than Clay, Benton had eventually moved to Missouri and represented that state in the US Senate for thirty years after 1821. With a retentive memory and an iron will, he struck many as a man of several talents and constituted a powerful political force. But he had another side, one that brought him many enemies. His egotistical and overbearing nature caused one person, on first meeting him, to write of "feelings of disgust and aversion which I have seldom experienced." Fellow Democrat James K. Polk noted Benton's "violent passions"; the two did not speak for over a year. Later in life, Clay complained how the man from Missouri frequently produced his "casket of calumnies."[41]

By then, Clay and Benton had long been estranged. Later, Clay tried to rebuild the friendship of a man once "sincerely attached" to him, but to no avail. Over the years, Clay respected and even maintained friendly social relations with some of his bitterest political critics. But as Benton increasingly became an outspoken enemy and defender of Jackson, Clay could not bring himself to respect Benton in that same way. In his eyes, Benton had been family, had betrayed him for Jackson, and had committed a dishonorable act that could not be forgiven.[42]

The actions of William T. Barry, on the other hand, did not produce the same sense of loss and regret. The course of that one-time ally caused Clay to pity the postmaster general more than anything else. A neighbor of Clay's, Barry had been, noted Clay, "once, both my personal and political friend." He had given Barry some of his law cases when he was absent in Washington, had cosigned some loans that Barry had taken, and had served with him in Congress. The small and wiry Barry had arrived in Kentucky from Virginia a year before Clay, had won the lieutenant governor's post in 1820, and had served as a justice of the New Court. Defeated for governor, the almost insolvent Barry asked for a reward for his service to the cause. John Pope wrote Jackson that the mild-mannered Barry "is not fit for any station which requires great intellectual force or moral firmness—but he is a gentleman in his deportment & amiable in his personal relations." That very mixed recommendation apparently satisfied the president, who made Barry the postmaster general, in charge of eight thousand employees. Not one to stand up to the chief executive, Barry willingly supported the removal of postmasters for political purposes, saying they were "right and politic to encourage and reward friends." He would prove to be a good party man but a poor administrator. Clay saw him as another example of Jackson's taking less competent men and bending them to his will.[43]

As those developments unfurled, Clay decided he could not be silent any longer. The leading national figure for what people increasingly called the National Republican Party, he sounded the alarm. Clay spoke at Fowler's Garden near Lexington on May 16, 1829, to a crowd of more than three thousand people. Describing to the multitude how he had come to them many years before as "an orphan boy, penniless, a stranger," Clay explained how he had been accepted by Kentuckians and they had eventually honored him with office. Now he came to warn them of the dangers before them: "In a monarchy, all power and authority, all offices and honors, proceed from the monarch. His interests, his caprices, and his passions influence and control the destinies of the kingdom." "King Andrew" sought to gratify his favorites with rewards and jobs, not because of their good civil services but simply because of their fidelity to the king. Defending the actions of Adams, Clay contrasted them to those of Jackson. He did not impute to the president designs on American liberties (though, of course, he did), but he noted that if an ambitious president sought the overthrow of government, then that person would take actions similar to those undertaken by the current chief executive. Such a threat meant that the people must defend their liberties. Clay made clear that he did not want political office at the moment and preferred retirement at the age of fifty-two, but if voters saw the need for his services in the future, "I will promptly obey any call." Clay followed that talk with similar addresses across Kentucky. The gauntlet had been thrown. Just as Jackson had spent four years running against Adams, Clay had begun to do the same thing regarding the successor or, as he saw it, the intruder.[44] Given the Jacksonians' recent campaign attacks on Clay's personal and political morality, the object of those charges likely observed with a smile what became known as the "Petticoat Affair." When Jackson confidant (and Clay enemy) John Henry Eaton married Margaret "Peggy" O'Neale Timberlake on New Year's Day 1829, he set into motion a series of events that would have important political repercussions, some helpful to Clay and some hurtful. Before the evolving scandal ended, it would irrevocably split the administration forces, alienate John C. Calhoun from Andrew Jackson, and transmute Martin Van Buren into Jackson's political favorite.[45]

Scandal already surrounded Peggy Timberlake by the time of her wedding. The daughter of a Washington tavern keeper, she had early on been associated with rumors of unchaste behavior before her marriage to a Navy purser. During his subsequent long absences, gossip continued to link her to other men. In April 1828, Peggy's husband committed suicide at sea. A scant nine months later, the attractive and vivacious thirty-year-old widow exchanged wedding vows with the thirty-nine-year-old, up-and-coming Jackson confidant John Henry Eaton, an act that horrified and surprised proper Washingtonians. Clay, still in the capital city as secretary of state, had made humorous comments regarding her virtue, but he was far from alone. A later Jackson cabinet minister wrote that Eaton had "just married his mistress & the mistress of 11-doz. others!!" An Ohio attorney, soon to be US senator, stressed that the former Mrs. Timberlake had not possessed "a reputation entirely unblemished" while her former spouse still lived. A Jacksonian editor privately called her "a woman of equivocal character."[46]

Peggy Eaton had her defenders, however, and none was more important than the president of the United States. Jackson was apparently one of the few people in Washington who believed Mrs. Eaton morally chaste. That may or may not have been the case, but it might have remained just a battle of conflicting opinions, and not a political issue, had the new Mrs. Eaton remained quietly out of the public eye and in private society. But

Peggy made an official call on Vice President Calhoun. Her husband John absent, Floride Calhoun received Mrs. Eaton politely. The rules of society now required her to return the call. But well-bred southern spouses did not associate with courtesans. Honor, morality, and decorum dictated only one course. Mrs. Calhoun would not return the call on Mrs. Eaton. Other wives of cabinet members reacted similarly; even Jackson's beloved nephew and his wife refused to do so. Such actions incensed Jackson. Word spread of the split and it became an open secret.[47]

Characteristically, Jackson first blamed Henry Clay for the situation. When a minister wrote the president warning the chief executive about supporting Peggy's virtues, he gave specific examples of her moral looseness, then closed, saying, "She will do more to injure your peace and your administration than one Hundred Henry Clays." A furious Jackson responded five days later, and just three weeks after Clay's resignation as secretary of state, he saw the hand of Clay in it all. Jackson defended Eaton and said, "I have not the least doubt but that every secret rumour is circulated by the minions of Mr. Clay." Given the fact that most of his cabinet, and probably most of the people in Washington, believed the charge valid, Jackson's assertion reflects once more how he almost instinctively blamed Clay for any ill. By May, Jackson repeated that the stories reflected "the act of *Clay*, whose project it was."[48]

Jackson was seeing conspiracies where none existed. Clay certainly reveled in the president's political discomfort and the scandal's effect on the administration—and his own political possibilities. But he said and did nothing a whole host of others were not saying or doing, including many in Jackson's official circle. (The only difference perhaps was that Clay often said it in a more quotable way. As for Peggy Eaton, for example, he remarked at one party, "Age cannot wither nor time stale her infinite virginity.") For two years, Clay watched the whole matter drag on. Finally, in April 1831, a series of resignations within the administration separated the sides and, to Jackson, punished the offenders. Vice President Calhoun had broken from Jackson and would resign his post before his term ended. The administration stood in disarray. To Henry Clay, it seemed as if events had favored his cause at last. The scandal had split the Jacksonians and had seemingly damaged that party's prospects for victory in 1832.[49]

By then, Clay needed some sense of hope to sustain him, for Jackson had continued to oppose not only Clay personally but Clay's programs as well. One of the Kentuckian's pet projects had long been the National Road running from Cumberland, Maryland, westward into the Midwest. A few years before, Clay had defended federal expenditures on that highway, pointing out that it provided a "bond of union" that knitted the sections together. Moreover, it stimulated growth, increased property values, and reduced travel time—in one section lowering trips from ten days to three. In 1830, a bill had passed that would strengthen those sectional bonds even more. Funds would go to support part of a southern branch—going from the National Road at Zanesville, Ohio, to Maysville, Kentucky, then to Lexington. Later support was expected to extend it through Tennessee to northern Alabama and perhaps even to New Orleans.[50]

But on May 27, 1830, Andrew Jackson vetoed the Maysville Road Bill. The president and his advisors masterfully called the bill purely local, an unwise use of scarce funds, and an action beyond what the constitutional fathers had envisioned. Moreover, excess federal monies should go to pay off the debt, not support internal improvements. The message struck a sympathetic chord among the populace, especially in the states' rights South.[51]

Clay saw the veto message in a somewhat less sympathetic light. King Andrew was at it again. Pointing to the inconsistencies of the president's action, Clay noted that Jackson had approved the appropriation to improve a seven-mile stretch of the almost-unknown Conneaut Creek. That was national, but the Maysville Road, with its ten thousand travelers per month and its connections southward, was not? Just three days after the veto, Jackson had approved funds for the extension of the National Road. Was not the Maysville Road an extension, too? In fact, during his presidency Jackson signed legislation that doubled the previous amount spent on that highway. His various Congresses appropriated more money for internal improvements than any other body over a similar period during the entire antebellum era. Yet the canny veto message had stamped Jackson in the minds of many as a strict states' rights constructionist, and a foe of federal support for such improvements.[52]

While Jackson may have gained politically from the veto overall, it may not have been as wise a move as many thought, then and later. In the wake of the Old Court–New Court struggle, Kentucky seemed to be moving to the Jackson camp. The general had easily carried the state in 1828. But since then Clay had begun to rebuild his base. The veto now helped Clay's cause immensely. It showed Jackson's disdain for the state; Clay thought it had sealed Jackson's fate in the commonwealth. Another state politician cried out that the president "will never appropriate one dollar for internal improvements in Kentucky." Neither of the two Jacksonian senators from Kentucky, both of whom had voted to sustain the veto, ran for reelection. Within a few years after the Maysville Road veto, Clay's party would dominate the state and do so for the next two decades. Any question about Kentucky's loyalty to Clay would soon be mostly dispelled.[53]

The veto, coupled with the political fallout from the Petticoat Affair, roused Clay once more to open action. In the first three months of 1830, he had visited family members in the warmer climes of New Orleans; the next year, he repeated the visit, but after the veto experience he paid more attention to politics there. In between, he made several speeches in Ohio. In the manner of the time, Clay seemed to be campaigning for some future office.[54]

John Crittenden had advised Clay to remain quiet, and Daniel Webster had counseled him to "stay at home." But Clay had a tendency to return to Congress just before beginning a presidential race, as in 1823, in order to make personal connections and build support among political leaders. Perhaps he also expected to gain attention and publicity from public debates on the floor of Congress. In retrospect, that outlook may not have been the wisest one politically. It put him, once more, in the position of having to speak out and vote on controversial actions—actions that could help him little but hurt him much. But, after over two and a half years of being away from the exciting, intoxicating action in Washington, after a time of relative quiet, after the continued attacks by Jackson, Clay reentered the arena. On November 20, 1831, in one of the closest elections in his career, he defeated the Jacksonian Richard M. Johnson for the position of US senator. Clay was returning to the halls of power. And he was running for president of the United States.[55]

8

Presidential Candidate II

TWO MONTHS AFTER HIS INAUGURATION in 1829, President Andrew Jackson repeated to Martin Van Buren the analysis given him by a general from Massachusetts: "Mr. Clay has sunk never to rise again." That represented one viewpoint on Clay's future. But neither Jackson nor Van Buren fully held that opinion about their rival. They agreed more with the writer in *American Monthly Magazine* who noted that same year that "it is hardly probable that Mr. Clay is destined to pass the remainder of his life in his retreat at Ashland." The chief question seemed to be not if Clay would run again, but when.[1]

After Adams's defeat and even before Jackson's inaugural, Clay sounded like a candidate for the presidency in the next race. In January 1829, the Kentuckian told a friend in Virginia that he was encouraged about his chances over three years hence, for he could unite the National Republicans behind his candidacy. By April, a Georgia newspaper reported that Clay "is again taking the rounds, eating great dinners, drinking great toasts, and making great speeches; and, for ought we know, making great numbers of proselytes." Already an almost four-hundred-page collection of his speeches had appeared in book form—said to be the first such volume published in the United States. And in 1830, Clay's friends decided a biography of the Millboy of the Slashes would help his expected candidacy. Accordingly, a quiet, young, Brown University–educated New Englander gave up his editorship of a literary magazine and came to Kentucky to undertake the biography. He and his subject would be intertwined politically for the rest of Clay's life.[2]

George D. Prentice arrived in Lexington in mid-summer 1830 and completed his biography in November—a feat other biographers might either envy or disparage. The book arrived on the scene the next year, in time for readers to digest the work before the upcoming presidential race. It apparently sold well. By then, Prentice had also established the *Louisville Journal*, which became one of the leading newspapers in America, avidly read by the public and prominent politicians alike. Prentice's brief and biting editorials favored Clay and then the Whig Party generally and gave Clay's candidacies a needed and significant voice to counter the growing Democratic press supporting Jackson. Meanwhile, Prentice's biography told Clay's full story to a national audience for the first time. Openly done "to influence an approaching political election," the three-hundred-page work presented its subject in a friendly light, but surprisingly did not hesitate to note some of Clay's less admirable traits. It marked a good start to the outpouring of political biographies that would follow over the next two decades.[3]

Yet if many people expected Clay to run for president in 1832, and if Clay himself seemed to support that expectation, the matter was not as clear-cut as some thought. For three years after 1829, Clay experienced many doubts and questioned exactly what his course should be. The immediate matter concerned whether Andrew Jackson would run for reelection in 1832. Many observers did not expect the president, who would be sixty-five years old that year, to seek a second term. "Enfeebled by age and debility," he would instead anoint Martin Van Buren as his successor, some predicted. Key Clay advisors saw that issue as paramount. Throughout 1829 and 1830, one counselor frankly told Clay that if Jackson ran, "I doubt whether you can beat Old Hickory." If Jackson did not run, however, then Clay had excellent prospects for success. Almost everyone gave the excellent advice that the Kentuckian should wait for Jackson's action before formally entering the electoral fray. But an impatient Clay replied that if he waited too long, that might encourage other challengers, such as Ohio's John McLean. Accordingly, in December 1830, a Kentucky convention nominated Clay for president. That might well have been the deciding factor for Andrew Jackson, for a little more than a month later, the *Washington Globe* announced that the hero would run again. As one political leader noted, Clay's enemies, including Jackson, "seemed to be haunted by continual fear" that Clay might win. They wanted him stopped, and Jackson was the best way to do that.[4]

Surveying the political situation, Henry Clay and numerous national observers expected the Kentucky general election of August 1831—a year after the Maysville Road veto—to give some indication of the temper of the times. If Clay forces won handily in the divided state, it would speak well of his chances; if they lost, his hopes could be dashed. Daniel Webster reminded Clay how much depended on that vote, writing that "you cannot conceive our anxiety abt. Kentucky." Traveling the country, future Mississippi governor John A. Quitman found more excitement about the race in the Bluegrass state than anywhere else in the nation.[5]

The results disappointed both sides, each of which had sought a clear decision. Pro-Clay forces carried the state legislative seats, but Jacksonians won the congressional delegation. While a Baltimore paper tried to put a positive spin on the results for the National Republicans, saying how the vote dispelled the idea of Jacksonian invincibility in the state the Tennessean had carried in 1828, most Clay allies saw the outcome differently. The failure to win a decisive victory produced much pessimism about the upcoming presidential race. A Boston paper angrily declared that Kentucky deserved only contempt for the stigma it had attached to the noble man who sought to defeat "the broken down dotard" now at the head of affairs. Clay agreed with that assessment. His state's results greatly discouraged him: "I have been disappointed & mortified with the issue of our elections," he told an ally. He asked if there was someone else better able to lead the party to victory over Jackson. Over the next two months, he repeated that analysis to several others. With "very much against us," should he continue the search for the presidency, or step away?[6]

Several factors influenced him in either direction. On the one hand, Clay's instincts warned him that many of the letter writers might be right. He could see the unfavorable results of the Kentucky vote; he could discern the political trends enough to perceive that Jackson presented a formidable foe; he could understand that he faced a very difficult fight. A one-time ally told a Clay supporter to tell him that with the general in good health and high spirits, Clay could not prevail in a race between the two. Another person could taste defeat in 1832, and then Clay could run against someone not named Jackson four years hence, perhaps with brighter prospects.[7]

But could Clay abandon the field of victory to General Jackson without a battle? Besides, several factors suggested that the president might be vulnerable, especially given the great confusion within Democratic ranks following the mass cabinet resignation of 1831 and the Petticoat Affair. At the same time, John C. Calhoun, a one-time Jackson ally, let it be known that he might seek the presidency in 1832 as well, further fragmenting the Jackson bloc. Perhaps a three-man race would throw the election once again to the House. But even if Calhoun did not run, his followers might turn to Clay; certainly South Carolina would not give its electoral votes to Jackson. That helped even the odds. It all boded well for the opposition.[8]

Besides his ever-present ambition, Clay continued his search for the presidency in 1832 mainly because of the specter of Andrew Jackson. Clay pictured Jackson's spoils system as a response to those party masses calling out to him, like French revolutionaries, "Give us bread! . . . Give us our reward!" Moreover, said Clay, "the military principle has triumphed." The president's party comprised his troops, the opposition his enemy. How could the nation advance with such an outlook? Thus, a Maysville Road veto, when other internal improvements received support, showed the power of party over principle, of vindictive hypocrisy over need, of despotism over democracy. Most of all, however, Clay wanted to defeat Jackson because he feared what might occur in the future. While in his public pronouncements the Kentuckian sometimes exaggerated the Jackson threat or actions, in private letters he made it clear that his fears were deeply held, not just campaign rhetoric. Jackson was building a political army, and it required only a spark to merge that with a military force and produce a dictatorship. A friend had written Clay: "You are the only person they fear." If Clay waited until 1836, he would be fifty-nine years old and perhaps less physically fit for the office. But more crucially, if Jackson served four more years there might not be a presidency at all, or at the least, the Jackson political machine would be so dominant that no one could successfully challenge it. Given that view of the political world, Clay hardly hesitated, despite the warning signs.[9]

In December 1831, the National Republican Party met in Baltimore and held the first major-party nominating convention. Newly elected Senator Clay kept up with activities from nearby Washington. In a spirit of "much harmony & good feeling," and with little debate, the delegates unanimously selected Clay for president and John Sergeant of Pennsylvania for vice president. The nomination for the second place on the ticket surprised Democrat Richard M. Johnson—"Sergeant who no one thought of as V. President!!!" Yet, the Princeton-educated attorney, humanitarian, and former congressman represented an important state. The slate was made. On December 13, Clay formally accepted the nomination.[10]

Clay was perhaps overconfident in the 1832 race. But his correspondence reveals that when he made the decision to seek higher office again, he was aware of the problems he faced. Just a few days after the nomination, John Tyler wrote his daughter that Clay could not defeat Jackson, "and I am incline[d] to believe that he has no expectations of doing so." But Clay also had a reasonable chance for victory, given what had occurred within the Jackson camp. Once the Kentuckian made his decision, he did begin uttering more optimistic words—his usual trend. Perhaps it reflected Clay's need to convince himself, or just his intention to persuade others, that he could indeed win. Either way, some events in the next year added to his hopes—a still-high new tariff angered some southerners, while the president's actions regarding Indian removal upset some northerners. But the appearance of a new factor, an organized third party based on one-issue politics, soon complicated the race.[11]

To many Americans, but especially evangelical Americans, Freemasonry, with its secret rituals and oaths, seemed exclusive, aristocratic, anti-republican, and unchristian. Equating it with popery, critics attacked both Catholics and Masons as restricting members' freedom of conscience and action. Both seemed to adhere to a higher authority, outside of American law and government. A kind of crusading, cultural, religious mass movement arose, just at the wrong time for Henry Clay. That moralistic, somewhat anti-party opposition, soon coalesced into a formal party, the Anti-Masons, which proved especially strong in New England, the Mid-Atlantic States, and Ohio. The party introduced a new, unexpected factor into the 1832 equation. Generally anti-Jackson, the group might be expected to support Clay. But the religious context of the new party meant that it would be difficult for members to go to either Clay or Jackson, for both were viewed as slaveholders, duelists, and men of questionable morals. By drawing its core of strength from National Republicans, the Anti-Masonic Party greatly complicated Clay's already difficult chances of winning.[12]

To make matters worse, both Clay and Jackson were Masons. The president remained an active member and thus drew fire for having instituted "a consolidated Masonic government." In Clay's case, his Masonic ties brought anti-Masonry newspapers to castigate him as a "pliant tool of masons," a "professed duelist and habitual libertine," a man "objectionable in a moral point of view." But such attacks based on Clay's Masonic ties ignored part of the reality. Clay had been a Mason in Lexington Lodge No. 1, and had even been elected Grand Mason in 1820. But he seldom attended meetings and in November 1824 withdrew as an active member. That action, taken before the anti-Masonic movement had even really begun, now gave Clay an advantage and a perfect opportunity to gain the support of the rising third party. Richard Rush, a leading advocate of anti-Masonry, told Clay on June 1, 1831, that if he wrote a letter denouncing Masonic "mischief," then he would get the nomination of both the Anti-Masonic Party and the National Republican Party and would win the presidency. John Quincy Adams also concluded that if Clay would renounce Masonry, he could win.[13]

Henry Clay, the man so often criticized for being such a political animal that he would do anything to win, now—once more—took a stand based on principle over politics. He rejected writing such a letter. Even though Clay stressed that Masonry "practically does neither much good nor harm," and even though he noted in 1831 that "I care not a straw for Masonry," he still said he would not renounce it, even "to be made President of the US." The reason was simple. Clay did not think personal issues such as Masonry or temperance should be interjected into politics. Such matters should be private, individual decisions and thus "principle and policy are both opposed to my meddling with it [Masonry]." To Clay, the Anti-Masonic Party with its "exclusive, pro-scriptive" aspects had its own evils: "An Anti-Masonic President for Jackson would be a mere exchange of one tyranny for another." In a public letter he declined to be the nominee for the new party. Non-Mason John C. Calhoun also refused to let his name be used, for similar reasons. The Anti-Masonic Party thus turned to former Mason William Wirt of Maryland as its nominee, and there was now a three-man race.[14]

A divided opposition to Andrew Jackson did not hold much hope for those seeking the general's defeat. Clay's reluctance to unite with the emerging cultural reform forces in America would have long-running consequences, but in this election it threatened to derail any hopes for victory. Clay predicted that the Anti-Masonic Party would be "troublesome," especially in New England and New York. His allies agreed. One reported that the Anti-Masonic Party would receive 50,000 votes in the Empire State; another New Yorker cursed the new party, which "defects all attempts at systematic operation against the common enemy"; a third New Yorker railed against "the demon of Anti-Masonry," and on and on the warnings came. Webster told a friend that the party was growing in Pennsylvania "like an Irish rebellion." This was the first third-party movement in American history, and no one seemed to know exactly how to deal with it. Clay's refusal to denounce Masonry had ended any national attempts at coalition. It would be left up to each state to work out whether it would shape fusion arrangements to unify the opposition to Jackson. Without any central guiding authority or organization, it all became very haphazard—and it showed.[15]

It was a chaotic political world. Democrats remained openly united behind one party and one man. Opponents, however, shifted to one group and then back to another, coalitions were formed and dissolved, strategies emerged and changed. Die-hard anti-Masons did not want to be part of any fusion ticket with Clay at the head, fearing that "Masonry will be the soul of the coalition" should that occur. Anti-Masons instead called on Clay to unite with their movement, withdraw from the canvass, and support Wirt. Only then, they argued, could Jackson be defeated. But more moderate anti-Masons placed defeat of the president higher on their list of priorities, and noted that both the National Republicans and their Anti-Masonic Party shared similar platforms and goals. For them, as one newspaper expressed it, "the question comes home to every man's bosom, whether he would save his country, or his party." The moderates seemed more willing to agree on some honorable union to curb Jacksonians.[16]

In the end, in three major states with significant anti-Masonic strength—New York, Pennsylvania, and Ohio—fusion tickets of some sort emerged. The desire to defeat Jackson, or the recognition of a certain loss without fusion, overcame philosophical scruples. In crucial New York, the forces of anti-Masonry, led by rising editor Thurlow Weed, formed a fusion ticket. As one political observer noted, "I am told that our friends in New York will all jog along together—Masons, Antimasons, National Republicans . . . and their hopes are high." Similar fusion tickets finally materialized in Pennsylvania and Ohio, no thanks to Clay, who continued to take a mostly neutral stance while his supporters worked to craft agreements. Still, the unions brought Calhoun to conclude that "Jackson's defeat is almost certain."[17]

Yet the fusion tickets came with a high price tag. As in the case of Clay's own compromises, such actions caused feelings of anger and disillusionment among those with strong views—the most dedicated Masons and most fervent anti-Masons. A real danger existed that many of those voters would simply decide to sit out the contest. One Clay advisor warned that some "obstinate" Masons would not support the Ohio ticket, while a Wirt newspaper expressed the view of the other extreme: "For either of the other presidential candidates, we cannot as antimasons, nor shall not, vote." More than that, though, the fusion tickets allowed the Democratic press to resurrect its favorite tactic against Clay. It gleefully denounced one of the "outrageous, barefaced, corrupt, and unprincipled BARGAINS and COALITIONS that ever disgraced the records of our political history." Other papers referred to the Ohio merger of forces as "a SECRET BARGAIN," or the New York one as "the corrupt coalition." In truth, without the fusion agreements the Clay forces in those states would have had little opportunity for victory. They made political sense in that way. But the gains would be balanced with some significant costs, as well. Anti-Masonry would continue to damage Clay's campaign in numerous ways.[18]

Another factor that caused Clay to lose advantages he had accrued earlier involved an old issue, one that had already brought Clay major political headaches: the BUS. Henry Clay had strenuously opposed the recharter of the First BUS in 1811; the War of 1812 had transformed his views on the issue, however, and five years later he had strongly favored the recharter of a BUS, which was ultimately successful. Since that action, the institution had initially experienced some managerial problems, had not performed well during the panic of 1819, and had become something of a scapegoat for that depression. But more recently, the Second BUS had become a sound and crucial part of the US financial system. The only nationwide institution and the largest American corporation at the time, it offered and controlled credit, conducted the exchange of foreign funds, and helped limit financial fluctuations. Perhaps most important, because the national mint produced only hard-money coins (specie) and not paper currency, the bank's paper issuances served as the closest thing to a national legal tender. Far from having monopolistic control over the nation's finances, the bank in 1830 held one-fifth of all US loans, one-fifth of all notes in circulation, one-third of all specie, and one-third of all deposits. It had become like a modern central bank. Though it had structural issues and control questions—the government held one-fifth of the stock and private investors held the rest—the BUS still arguably provided the soundest banking system the United States would have until the creation of the Federal Reserve System in the early twentieth century.[19]

In Clay's view, those qualities made the BUS absolutely critical to continued growth for the United States. It reflected a nationalistic economic part of Clay's American System, and he seemingly never regretted his decision to reverse his earlier stance and support the Second BUS. Since then, Clay had become intimately involved with the bank. In 1816, he had purchased shares of BUS stock (making him one of its four thousand stockholders), but two years later he had declined to sit on its board, citing a conflict of interest. He had, however, secured a branch of the bank for Lexington, had

A POLITICAL GAME or BRAG.
Or the best hand out of four.

In an 1831 game of brag (a form of poker), Clay (left) has three aces, labeled "US bank," "internal improvement," and "Domestic Manufactures." Saying, "O damn me!," President Jackson (right) has three of a kind as well, but the three knaves in his losing hand are entitled "Intrigue," "Corruption," and "Imbecility." The Anti-Masonic Party candidate ("I bolt.") and John C. Calhoun look on as Clay wins. In real politics, Jackson held the winning hand. *American Antiquarian Society*

borrowed money from it, and had served for a time as superintendent of the bank's legal affairs in Kentucky and Ohio, when he desperately needed funds following the panic of 1819. That business arrangement had ended when he became secretary of state in 1825. So by the time Clay was running for president in 1832, he had some loans with the bank but no formal ties, and had not for some time. He did retain a deep interest in its affairs. Moreover, he respected its young, confident, and assertive president. The Princeton-educated attorney and former Pennsylvania legislator Nicholas Biddle had served the institution ably as a banker. Now his—and Clay's— political skills regarding the bank would be severely tested.[20]

For if Clay, Biddle, and many others in antebellum America saw the BUS as an important modernizing force in national economic development, Andrew Jackson and many of his allies did not. Although the president had used banks and even purchased some bank stocks, he never fully trusted those institutions, and especially so the BUS with its vast power. Moreover, he disliked paper currency and favored hard money. Given Jackson's outlook, Nicholas Biddle feared the worst.[21]

In his first annual message in 1829, President Jackson had raised the issue of the bank's recharter, due to occur in 1836. That marked the beginning of a quandary for Clay, the BUS directors, and its other supporters. Should they wait until its old one expired to recharter, or should they seek a renewal early? By waiting, a more favorable president—perhaps Clay himself—might be in office. But delaying could mean that the current congressional majority in favor of the bill might dissolve over time. Additionally, postponing actions until the last minute could leave a cloud over the nation's finances and hurt the economy. Finally, should the issue be part of the presidential campaign of 1832 or not?

By the end of 1830, key pro-bank players seemed to be in agreement. In September, Clay wrote Biddle that he had heard the bank president might try to push the recharter early. Clay discouraged that "unwise" approach, noting that even if the bill passed, Jackson might veto it. Moreover, that would make the bank a political issue in a presidential year and would, Clay predicted astutely, "play into the hands of that party." Only if Biddle received assurances from the administration that no veto would follow should he proceed, Clay advised. In a return letter, Biddle agreed. Had the matter remained there, it would have been better for Clay's presidential hopes.[22]

Clay's subsequent role remains murky. Perhaps he saw the BUS recharter (and possible veto) as an issue that could propel him into the presidency, and thus pushed Biddle into seeking a premature recharter. Or maybe Biddle, Webster, and their allies made the determination to push for an early fight, and Clay only reluctantly agreed to go along. Something in between those two views most likely occurred. After the 1831 Kentucky election results, Clay's campaign was faltering. Still, he had not then advised Biddle to try to recharter early. But meantime, the bank president had received mixed messages from those within the Jackson circle. At least some implied that a properly crafted bill might actually be signed, owing to election pressures, or could become law without a signature. Daniel Webster, who had much closer ties to the BUS than did Clay, pushed Biddle toward recharter as well. They had the votes to pass the bill now, and he doubted Clay would win the race for president, so why wait?[23]

As Biddle pondered his course, he received contradictory advice from key advisors. Maryland senator Samuel Smith recounted a conversation with Clay in which the Kentuckian advised moving forward with a bill immediately: "However glittering the prize of ambition may be, he [Clay] is remarkable for the habitual exercise of dispassionate judgment and clear perception." The next day, Webster followed with his own suggestions to Biddle. He urged an application for renewal of the charter without delay. But four days later, Biddle's agent in the capital provided a different perspective. The secretary of the treasury, a friend of the bank, had advised waiting, telling him that if a bill appeared in the current session, the president would interpret that as a partisan act in a presidential election year and would veto it. But by January 4, 1832, Biddle had decided. He would apply for a recharter; four days after that, Webster informed Clay. The "Bank War" had begun.[24]

From the start of his tenure, Nicholas Biddle had clearly expressed the desire to keep the bank out of politics. The one-time Federalist had voted for Jackson in 1828 and had declared that he cared for no party except the bank "and the Bank alone." In his words, the bank had been "straight and neutral" in the last presidential race. Of course, Biddle did not note that through favorable loans, sizable retainers, and frequent fees, the bank had tied itself to certain key leaders, at least indirectly. However, even before the new chief executive took office, Jackson supporters had asked Biddle to appoint more Democrats to bank boards. He expressed his "extreme unwillingness" to play politics with the institution. But men very close to the president pressured Biddle to take more partisan actions, including the appointment of a presidential ally to a Nashville bank board. Failing in those attempts to politicize the institution, said Biddle, they instead had turned to "breaking it down." Such warning signs, coupled with Jackson's first message regarding the BUS, convinced Biddle that the Jackson forces sought to destroy the bank and use it as an electioneering tactic. Now, despite his earlier, nonpartisan approach, Biddle would also make the issue a political one.[25]

Some westerners, such as Thomas Hart Benton, opposed the bank because of its restrictive policies regarding paper currency; some easterners, like Martin Van Buren, attacked it because they sought to make New York, rather than the bank's home of Philadelphia, the financial center of the nation; some, like the New York Working Man's Advocate, later challenged the BUS as a matter of "whether the Bank or the People shall rule," whether the "PEOPLE'S PRESIDENT" or "the moneyed Aristocrats" should dominate. But Congress passed the bill and sent it to the president. What would Jackson do?[26]

As he waited, Clay seemed to have the better of two political worlds. If the BUS bill was signed, then a major part of his program would be saved and extended. If the act was vetoed, Clay expected a popular outcry against that action, especially in Pennsylvania, where the institution was located; a Jackson veto might win Clay that crucial state. But as it turned out, the actions of two of his former allies would play a crucial role in upsetting his calculations.[27]

By 1832, Amos Kendall hovered over the political scene like some ever-present, never-seen spirit, sucking the political life force from the enemies of Jackson. From his shadow world, he manipulated men, influenced leaders, and shaped destinies—or so the opposition seemed to think. He even looked the part. Sickly, slight, and stooped, the prematurely white-haired but "dark-minded man" could be shrewd, shy, and sensitive to some observers, but others reserved harsher words for him. A Frankfort, Kentucky, editor compared Kendall to a "famished wolf": "It makes one hungry just to look at his lean, lank jaws, his restless, eager eyes, and his voracious, hooked nose." Both critics and allies alike recognized that Kendall's frail, cadaverous body masked a strong, larger-than-life presence within. Both understood him to be a crucially important part of the government of Andrew Jackson. Both feared him.[28]

Henry and Lucretia Clay knew a different Amos Kendall—or at one time thought they did. In 1814, the twenty-four-year-old New Englander had made his way to Kentucky. Massachusetts born, Dartmouth educated, and legally trained, Amos Kendall set out for the promise of the New West, expecting to become the tutor of a Kentucky senator's children. With few funds, he fortuitously received help from William T. Barry as they made their way down the Ohio River to the promised land of Kentucky. But on arrival, Kendall found his anticipated position had fallen through. Forlorn and penniless, he was relieved from his plight when the thirty-three-year-old Lucretia Clay engaged him to tutor the Clay children for $300 a year, plus room, board, and use of the Clay library. By all accounts, he did well in that task, and Lucretia also aided the awkward young man by instructing him in the ways of a gentleman in polite society. After a year, Kendall struck out on his own, setting up a legal practice, then a publishing venture, in nearby Georgetown. But when a serious illness brought him "to the brink of the grave," Mrs. Clay once more took him in, and she restored him to health at Ashland. Later, he finally met her husband, who had been overseas. Kendall soon moved to Frankfort, where he became the editor and later owner of the *Argus of Western America,* an important newspaper.

He and his new wife also found themselves involved in a grist mill, slave-holding, and debt. Then the panic of 1819 arrived.[29]

Though he struggled financially, Kendall did find that he had a real talent for editorial writing. His self-righteous morality produced ethical arguments, his active mind constructed critical ones, and his ardent spirit crafted emotional appeals, all of which combined with his caustic invective and sharp pen to make him a welcome ally or a dangerous enemy. And initially his words supported the policies of Henry Clay. Early in his news-paper career, Kendall praised the Second BUS, internal improvements, and other aspects of what became known as the American System. Clay helped the *Argus* win a government printing contract, loaned Kendall a sizable amount of money, and aided in other ways. Only days after it appeared that Clay might be made secretary of state, Kendall asked his mentor if he could find a patronage job that "you could turn to my advantage" and help him financially again.[30]

By that time, however, Kendall's political loyalty to Clay seemed in question. In the Old Court–New Court struggle, Kendall's editorials more and more supported the New Court cause. Himself a debtor to the tune of $10,000, he increasingly advocated the relief outlook. Clay frankly told Kendall he considered that stance to be in error, but continued to try to help him. Kendall took the opportunity to tell Clay that if he were em-ployed in the Adams administration, he would "certainly not write against it" and with proper funding would take a quieter role in the relief con-troversy. Whether for political reasons or personal ones, Clay overlooked his one-time ally's critical words and in the fall of 1825 offered Kendall a government job, as requested. But the editor considered the salary too low and asked for one paying 50 percent more. Clay had nothing to offer at that level, however. The moment had passed. A contemporary wrote Clay later, warning him not to trust Kendall: "He is a political swiss. Money is his object and he will write for that man, or that party, which pays him best." As Kendall continued to criticize the Adams administration and the Old Court forces, Clay finally chastised him by ending the government printing contract. Soon the split widened. In October 1826, Kendall openly came out for Andrew Jackson. Richard M. Johnson wrote to Martin Van Buren on Kendall's behalf, asking for funds that could allow Kendall to pay off his loan to Clay and free him from any obligations. Only then did Clay finally conclude, sadly, "I have been deceived by Mr. Amos Kendall."[31]

In the election of 1828 between Adams and Jackson, Kendall was on the winning side. His editorials on the bargain and corruption charge, while mostly full of well-written sound and fury and presenting little evidence, had attracted national attention and the new president's praise. Kendall expected—and received—a reward for his services. As the new fourth auditor in the Treasury Department, he made three times the salary that Clay had offered him earlier. Moreover, what he termed "very light" duties allowed him to earn significant extra money writing editorials favoring the Jackson cause.[32]

Kendall's influence within the administration quickly grew. The rapidity of that rise added to the aura surrounding Kendall. He helped edit the administration newspaper, used the Treasury and then the Post Office for patronage purposes, and served as one of Andrew Jackson's key advisors. The behind-the-scenes influence of Kendall and a few others brought forth references to a secret cabal, a "Kitchen Cabinet," that opponents said controlled the elderly president and manipulated the government. Just weeks after Clay had stepped down as secretary of state, he had predicted that "secret, unseen, unworthy, and irresponsible advisors" would direct the proscription of "men of tried capacity and integrity" and replace them with sycophants. The years since had done nothing to change Clay's opinion. And he saw Amos Kendall, his one-time supporter, the man Lucretia had brought into his home, the reader of his books, as the leader of those hidden mentors. In fact, by 1832, Kendall had become the chief organizer of Jackson's campaign for the presidency. His words, his advice, and his strategy provided the kind of national leadership that Clay's campaign always lacked.[33]

To make things even worse for Clay's presidential hopes, Kendall placed his chief journalistic ally as the editor of the Jackson administration's main party organ, the *Washington Globe*. That choice aided the president's cause greatly, for favorable editorials soon issued from the pen of the capable new editor. And that man had been at one time another key Clay supporter, an even closer Clay friend, back in Kentucky.

Francis Preston Blair came from a political family. His father served many years as Kentucky's attorney general. After the son received his legal training from Transylvania University, he added to those political connections through marriage to a stepdaughter of a governor; his wife's sister married the wealthy Benjamin Gratz. Blair, the new graduate and new husband, quickly secured a post as circuit court clerk in the state's capital city, where he met numerous political figures, including Clay, who knew Blair's father and Gratz as well.[34]

The man Clay saw before him did not impress physically. In some aspects, he resembled Clay—he was taller than average for the time (about 5′10″), and had a fair complexion, sandy hair, and blue eyes. But though Blair had great charm, like Clay, the resemblances stopped there. Most described Blair as a bit odd-looking, with a large head, a thin face "of the hatchet kind," and an even thinner body. A friend said Blair "looks like a skeleton, lacks little being one." Yet that frail body contained a strong mind, one that could master political invective.[35]

Clay's relationship with Blair paralleled, in some ways, his association with Amos Kendall. He had praised both men, calling Blair "very worthy and intelligent" in 1821. Clay also considered them allies. But when the relief struggle began, he and they eventually supported opposite sides. In Blair's case, he, like Kendall, had significant debts as a result of the panic of 1819, and eventually aided the New Court. But whereas Clay saw Kendall as someone who deceived him and then betrayed him, a man who now corrupted the nation's capital with his polluting political actions, he held a different opinion of Blair, who had followed a similar path. Part of that resulted from a deeper respect for Blair. But part also came about because during the Old Court–New Court struggles, Blair was open and frank with Clay about his course of action and why he took it. Clay appreciated such candor. Early on, Blair admitted that Clay's opposition hurt the New Court cause Blair supported, and he asked Clay to try to reconcile the two sides. While that did not occur, the younger man's letters remained respectful and friendly. Over and over, Blair stressed that while their political faiths had diverged, he remained a sincere admirer of Clay. He even apologized for his new party's tactics regarding Clay in the mean-spirited 1828 race. Blair continued to close his letters with "affectionate regards" to Clay. In turn, Clay in his letters constantly referred to his own friendship with Blair. Even though their political differences caused him great pain, said Clay, he held Blair in continued esteem, had never imputed bad motives to him, and hoped that their mutual regard would not be sacrificed on a political pyre. He called Blair's actions toward him "manly and honorable." For that reason, perhaps, when the "corrupt bargain" charge arose before the 1828 election, Clay could have published a letter from Blair that would have hurt Blair politically. Blair implored, almost begged, Clay not to release that letter, which would reveal "one heart exposed naked to the world." Although Clay could have injured a member of the then-opposition, and perhaps aided his own cause, he respected Blair's request.[36]

When Amos Kendall got President Jackson's approval to bring in Francis Preston Blair as editor of the *Washington Globe* in December 1830, that put further strains on the Clay-Blair relationship. But with Blair's move, a trio of one-time Clay supporters from Kentucky now stood at the forefront of the fight to defeat Clay in 1832. Physically, the fellow slaveholders and westerners Barry, Kendall, and Blair all looked like their leader in their gaunt appearance. Andrew Jackson had surrounded himself with men who had a lean and hungry look. In Clay's case, such men were dangerous.[37]

As it turned out, that trinity of avenging angels (or demons) would not remain united in their vilification of Clay for very long; in fact, they would later turn their denunciations on each other. Most of the differences centered on Kendall. He would eventually alienate his key allies—except for Andrew Jackson. But such later divisions in the ranks of Clay's new enemies did not matter in 1832. In that year, Clay found the three men aiding Jackson as the president prepared his response to the bill rechartering the BUS.[38]

Bank president Nicholas Biddle had made it clear early on that he would gladly compromise on several issues if that would make the proposed bill more acceptable to the chief executive. Biddle told his principal lobbyist: "The President and the Bank do not disagree in the least about the modifications he desires. He wishes some changes and the Bank agrees to them." Two weeks later, he had reiterated that he saw no stated change desired by Jackson that he could not support. Yet he received few signs that modifications to the bill would suffice, and in the end, only a few emerged in the finished legislation. Instead, anti-bank opponents had instituted a fruitless investigation of the BUS. Jackson's opposition had hardened over the weeks, as he heard the voices of those Kentucky New Court relief advisors much clearer than he did those of the pro-bank forces in his administration. Despite what some pro-Jackson newspapers in some pro-bank states later asserted, little indication came from the Jackson presidency that it would look favorably on any BUS bill. Still, supporters had held out hope.[39]

President Jackson received the bank bill on the Fourth of July, 1832. Six days later, he vetoed it. With input from the president, Attorney General Roger Taney, and several other advisors, the masterful message had chiefly emerged from the potent pen of Amos Kendall. He crafted a polemical, powerful, and in some ways path-breaking message, one that spoke directly to the people, not to the politicians.[40]

The president in his veto justified the action in several ways. But the keys to it all were the words he used. Clay might be brilliant in offering arguments in the heat of debate, but Kendall proved a special wordsmith in crafting phrases that could be readily understood and grasped by those who read them in newspapers or pamphlets. In the veto, Jackson's arguments varied widely. First, he called the act unconstitutional; it was not, he said, "necessary and proper." Although the courts had ruled otherwise already, he did not consider them the final arbiters of the Constitution: "The opinion of the judge has no more authority over Congress than the opinions of Congress have over the judges, and on that point, the President is independent of both." Read one way—as by Clay, for example—Jackson seemed to say that he could interpret the governing document as he saw fit, no matter how the courts had ruled.[41]

A second argument in the veto message used xenophobic and sectional appeals. Pointing to the fact that foreigners held about one-fourth of BUS stock, Jackson said that kept Americans from benefiting from the bank's success and gave aliens control over the finances, especially in times of war: "It should be purely American." He also used states' rights and sectional arguments, stressing that the East, especially New England (where he had less political support), dominated bank counsels and stockholders. That deprived the Midwest and the South from sharing the wealth. Benefiting from centralized power and free from taxation—unlike state banks—the BUS was "principally a debt to the Eastern and foreign stockholders."[42]

But the political brilliance of the veto came from its open class appeals. The president represented a living person, the bank a faceless corporation. He embodied the people, the BUS typified the moneyed power. He voiced the simple, republican, yeoman ideals of the past; the bank epitomized the special, privileged, corporate present. The symbolism and the clarity of the words made the veto message all the more powerful. A monopoly, "dangerous to the liberties of the people," had the exclusive favor of the government. That should not be. Guided by a few designing men who acted behind closed doors and held concentrated power in their hands, the bank represented a threat to national self-determination: "The rich and powerful too often bend the acts of government to their selfish purposes" and use artificial, federally supported advantages "to make the rich richer and the potent more powerful." Instead of equal protection and equal benefits, the wealthy had used congressional action for their personal gain, thus arraying "section against section, interest against interest, and man against man." Instead, the message stressed, Jackson defended the humble and the oppressed. Such words appealed directly to the people, especially those in less fortunate circumstances, those who believed the corporations were responsible for their ills, those who saw Jackson giving vent to those frustrations through his presidential voice.[43]

Some parts of the veto were misleading at best: foreign stockholders held no voting rights, and the suggestion that the president had not been consulted about the bill and might have agreed to one that met his objections does not seem supported by the evidence. The veto narrative basically ignored all the good things the BUS did for the economy and the country's financial system. Jackson did not favor the bank, or probably any national bank, and certainly did not favor one supported and advocated by Clay. In fact, the veto signified a political attempt to redefine the 1832 presidential race—and it did.[44]

For all its omissions, questionable logic, and faulty reasoning, the veto message resounded with some voters because certain charges rang true. The bank did have great power and influence, with few outside controls. It did operate beyond the light of public scrutiny. It did have politicians under its control through loans and retainers. It did have the potential to use its vast resources for or against a political candidate. Clay, Webster, Biddle, and other bank advocates saw clearly the positive effects of the BUS on the economy, but they were almost blind regarding the real concerns about the institution. Webster, for instance, haughtily rejected the president's constitutional arguments: "If that which Congress had enacted and the Supreme Court has sanctioned, be not the law of the land, then the reign of individual opinion has already begun." Clay, in turn, quickly denounced the veto with "deep alarm," especially for its errors regarding foreign control, its "unlawful" constitutional doctrines, and its creation of "general disorder and confusion" in financial circles. Both men made excellent rational, legal arguments. Both expected the people to rally to their interpretation. And both for the longest time failed to grasp the power of the emotional appeals inherent in the veto. Vulnerable on the spoils system, the divisions within his party, the growing corruption, the Indian issue, the tariff, and more, Jackson had turned attention elsewhere in the presidential contest by focusing on the bank. In that war of words and images, Clay could not win. The veto gave Jackson an issue more recent than the "corrupt bargain" charge, and produced a kind of temporary amnesia about the administration's problems. The Jackson newspapers took up the new attack strategy in earnest.[45]

Francis Preston Blair's *Globe* led the charge. In a series of widely reprinted stories, it pointed out the dangerous financial powers held in the monarchial hands of one man, the BUS president. Accounts emphasized how, for example, the US government prostrated itself before the British lion, while the "vampyres of England" fed off "the rich veins of young America." Others portrayed Clay as the supporter of "aristocratic money changers" and pampered monopolists. This "monied monster," this political cancer, this buyer of men's votes, must not be allowed to enslave the workingman. The Jackson press delighted in printing in parallel columns Clay's speeches, calling one "Henry Clay in 1811," the other, "Henry Clay in 1832." Another variation included columns reading "Henry Clay without a fee" and "Henry Clay with a fee of $30,000." They suggested, not very subtly, that Clay had sold his political soul to Adams in 1825 in exchange for office, and now he had bartered away his financial self to the highest bidder.[46]

That argument ignored the fact that Clay had voted for the Second BUS before he came into the employ of the bank, and that he had voiced pro-bank sentiments years before the current campaign. But the perception of fault seemed the stronger image. Jacksonian rhetoric now referred not to the National Republican Party but, rather, to "the Clay Bank party." In truth, the bank veto itself may have won Clay as many votes as he lost in some states. But where the issue did hurt him was that the attention focused on that subject took away from other potential issues. It caused Clay to be defensive and reactive, and it cost him the opportunity to gain votes over the course of the campaign. By September, letter writers to him had made it clear that voters had generally given the veto message a favorable reception. Clay knew by then that, regarding his gamble on that issue, he had been outplayed.[47]

By July 1832, with the bank veto, all the major elements of the campaign were in place. Now the race settled down into a typical format of support for one side, criticism for the other. Not surprisingly, the Jackson forces continued to proclaim the president's hero status. Of all the candidates, only he had risked his life fighting for the nation, they noted. Moreover, as the chief executive, he had protected the treasury and stopped legislative excesses by such actions as the Maysville Road veto. Turning criticisms of Jackson around, his allies proclaimed that his dismissal of public officials had ended corruption and fraud and had saved millions of dollars. By fighting off the bank with its foreign, "monied oligarchy," he had kept it from controlling Congress. His supporters also stressed that he had nearly paid off the national debt, had reopened the West Indian trade, and had even rid the nation of the "great evils" of Indians in their midst through a series of treaties they called "highly advantageous" to the native peoples. As a result of his actions and his states' rights views, only Andrew Jackson could unite the nation, for Clay's philosophical views made him unacceptable in the South.[48]

But most of all, the honest and patriotic Jackson deserved reelection because he alone stood as the defender of the humble citizen, the foe of aristocracy, and "the tried friend of the poor man." Uncorrupted by the bank, he had reformed government, stabilized domestic and foreign relations, and protected the people's rights. He should be given a second term.[49]

The administrative press did not so much cover Jackson as attack Clay. Papers brought up the usual charges of the "corrupt bargain" and his "unprincipled alliances and glaring inconsistencies." That tied in with his supposed questionable morality. "A gambler and a duelist," as well as a brawler and a bully, Clay stood in stark contrast, the president's press said, to their hero and his high morals. Such statements required rather remarkable historical blinders by the authors, since Jackson had killed a man in a duel, had ordered the execution of others, and had fought many more fights. But readers of antebellum newspapers, with their party's own interpretation the only one that often appeared in accounts, had no desire to be fair and balanced. Even when Clay spoke in favor of a day of fasting and prayer in response to the cholera epidemic raging across parts of America, the Jackson press criticized him. Calling him hypocritical, they declared he had "violated every moral and religious junction."[50]

More forceful criticism of Clay centered on his public life. Jacksonians first tried to tar him with the Federalist Party brush, saying that this "old-fashioned '98 Federalist and Hartford Conventionist" now led that party in its new guise. His programs they found equally awful. The American System depended on central power, which would annihilate state sovereignty. It would raid the treasury for internal improvement projects favorable to his friends, would institute massive expenditures, and would raise tariff rates. Most of all, however, Clay led an unprincipled faction that sought only power and plunder. He wanted to break down the people: "Remember the Aristocrat at the Polls."[51]

Supporters of Clay, a man no more aristocratic than Jackson in personal life, responded in kind. They attacked the "totally incompetent—wicked, unjustifiably wicked—and profligate and corrupt" administration. As opposed to the Jacksonians, they found the president was responsible for more wasteful spending, more corruption, and more scandals than his predecessors. He had also oppressed "the hapless Cherokees." Jackson's temper, obstinacy, and ignorance of government disqualified him, they argued. He followed only his ideas and his intents, except when dissuaded by his shadow advisors, who had their own concerns in mind.[52]

All that resulted from the most dangerous aspect of the Jackson presidency—his "pure despotism." Daniel Webster said that the chief executive's actions so resembled those of a French monarch that he should just announce, "I am the state." A Connecticut paper referred to Jackson as "the Caesar with the imperial purple." Political cartoons showed "King Andrew the First" on his throne, surrounded by the shreds of the Constitution. By using bribes in the form of jobs, by playing to the passions of the mob, by disregarding the courts, Jackson had—said his enemies— shown himself a threat to American liberties. Clay, not Jackson, stood for the people's rights.[53]

In contrast to the Jackson press, Clay allies tended more to praise their candidate and attack his opponent a bit less. In their view, a comparison of the two men showed that one clearly stood out as being qualified for the presidency. This man of untarnished honor, who openly expressed his frank sentiments, had a long and patriotic career. A statesman, he had championed the Constitution, "which *he* has never violated." Whatever he did, Henry Clay had done for the national good. His collected speeches, new biography, and new song, "Freedom and Clay" all proclaimed that, as the song called out, "Huzza! To the man of the West . . . who has stood every test . . . Henry Clay is the man." But did voters agree?[54]

Observers of the American political scene held varied opinions. In 1830, many Clay allies had predicted victory. The next summer, various commentators had concluded that "the present miserable administration will go down." But the 1831 Kentucky elections had soured many, and by December, Calhoun was "almost certain" Clay would lose. By February 1832, several politicians concluded that nothing could stop the march of the Jackson army. The July bank veto encouraged a Maryland newspaper to predict a Clay victory, and Clay later suggested that Jackson would now lose the key states of New York and Ohio, and probably Pennsylvania. A Massachusetts businessman hoped that analysis was correct, for if Jackson won, "We shall never have another presidential election."[55]

As the election results arrived in Lexington, it quickly became clear that Clay had suffered a crushing defeat. Jackson carried sixteen states outright and divided Maryland with Clay; Clay won only five states; the Anti-Masonic Party took Vermont; and renegade South Carolina threw its electoral votes to John Floyd in protest of the candidates. The final electoral count gave Jackson a 219–49 margin over Clay. The popular vote reflected

Clay hoped for victory in 1832, thanks to Jackson's perceived weaknesses. As the president sits in a collapsing chair, his "Altar of Reform" and a pillar with the words "Public Confidence . . ." tumble around him. At his feet, rats representing his resigned cabinet secretaries scurry away from "a Falling House." *Library of Congress, LC-DIG-ds-00853*

the totality of the Jackson triumph, as well. The incumbent won 54 percent of the ballots cast, Clay more than 37 percent, and William Wirt almost 8 percent. About the only bright spot for the Kentuckian came when his adopted state reversed its damaging earlier votes and handily supported Clay. Otherwise, he carried outright only three New England states and Delaware (and that by only a plurality of 166 votes). West of the mountains, in the Midwest and the South, he performed abysmally. Clay carried no state south of Kentucky while Jackson won 81 percent of the vote in the slave states. Even in pro-tariff Louisiana, which Clay had considered safe, the pro-Jackson tide there had led both major pro-Clay papers to abandon him.[56]

Moreover, Clay carried none of the Midwestern states. His natural, western constituency had deserted him. Beforehand, Clay had also identified three states as crucial to his hopes—New York, Pennsylvania, and Ohio. Not coincidentally, his forces had tried to forge an alliance with the strong Anti-Masonic Party in each. In the end, such coalitions failed to achieve the desired purpose, and Clay lost all three states. The strategy of unification may have been necessary to bring together divided forces, but it also apparently kept some voters from choosing to exercise their franchise for the Mason Clay, or, conversely, an Anti-Masonic Party ticket. Openly, the new party cost Clay Vermont's electoral vote; covertly, it may have cost him more elsewhere. On the one hand, after the Jackson victory, the third-party advocates often seemed almost embarrassed that their decision to run a candidate, or not to vote at all, had helped elect a man most opposed—Andrew Jackson. On the other hand, the effects of the bank veto remain more difficult to gauge. Supposedly pro-bank Pennsylvania gave Jackson a sizable 58 percent of its votes, but that also represented an almost 10 percent drop in his margin from four years before. Nor did Jackson's coattails extend to Congress, for the opposition had a Senate majority in the next session. It seemed more a personal victory than a party one.[57]

While it is often easy and tempting to attribute a loss to a single issue, usually several factors decide a race. In this case, the third-party movement certainly divided the anti-Jackson forces and the bank veto obviously redefined the race, to Clay's loss. But beyond that, in various states different influences operated. In the South, for example, the tariff and Clay's identification with the American System hurt greatly, while Jackson's Indian removal policy helped the incumbent. Across the nation, Clay principles or programs did not excite the public overall. Nor did a majority of voters perceive Jackson as the potential military dictator that Clay pictured. Instead, they saw the masculine hero, the friend of the humble yeoman, the protector of their liberties from the monster bank and from centralized power. They voted for that personality instead of for the professional politician. Coupled with the fact that the Jacksonians out-organized, out-mobilized, and out-propagandized the Clay forces, the combination proved unbeatable. Calhoun noted that with materials aplenty to destroy half a dozen administrations, Clay partisans seemed unable to form a forceful opposition. The Great Pacificator's lack of an organizer like Kendall or a communicator like Blair showed. But basically, Clay's judgment is most at fault for his loss in 1832. He well understood the difficulty in defeating a well-prepared, still-popular incumbent who could use the power of the office to help win reelection. It probably mattered little what Clay did or did not do in that race, for he likely would still have lost, third party or no party, program or no program, bank or no bank. And when the veto turned Clay into the defender of monopolies and Jackson into the ally of the common man, the deal was sealed.[58]

When Clay learned of the results, he lamented that "whether we shall ever see light, and law and liberty again, is very questionable." Still, despite the gloom and doom, he had duties yet to perform as senator, and a despondent Clay arrived in the capital by mid-December. By then, various pro-Jackson newspapers had once more written Clay's political obituary. Like a dazzling meteor, Clay had blasted through the political air, a New Hampshire paper noted, but now he had fallen, like Lucifer, from the heavens, "never to rise again." Yet, even as Clay languished in the depths of deep despair, unfolding events would bring him to one of his greatest congressional achievements. Over the next several months, Clay would defy predictions and rise again, emerging once more as a revered statesman, a respected leader, perhaps even a presidential possibility.[59]

And the controversy, at its core, grew out of a subject that neither Clay, nor the South, nor the nation, could readily solve.

9

Peculiar Institutions

ALL HIS LIFE, HENRY CLAY had known slavery. He grew up in a slave society. He operated in a slave culture. He owned slaves. In fact, almost from his earliest years, he technically had been a slaveholder in that world. When Clay's father died, the will left four-year-old Henry two slaves. A grandfather's bequest gave him another. The exact eventual disposition of those bondsmen remains uncertain, but Clay apparently came to Kentucky not owning any slaves. That situation quickly changed. Marriage probably brought into the new household either slaves or the funds to purchase slaves, and prosperity as a lawyer made that option more financially possible. Later, ownership of a landed estate furthered the perceived need for slaves to operate the farm. By 1800—three years after Clay's arrival in Kentucky and a year after his marriage—the tax lists indicated that he owned slaves for the first time in the commonwealth. Those three slaves had become six by the next year, then nineteen on the eve of the War of 1812. Less than twenty years later, Clay held fifty-two humans in bondage, a number that put him among the half-dozen largest slaveholders in Lexington, among the sixty biggest in Kentucky, and among the top 5 percent of all southern slaveholders. For many voters, those figures alone made Clay anathema as a presidential candidate.[1]

When Clay arrived in the fluid, still-frontier state of Kentucky in 1797, it had already addressed the question of whether it would be a slave state like Virginia or break free of the mores of its past. In the first constitutional convention readying the land for statehood, in 1792, Kentucky had retained slavery by a 26–16 vote. By then one of every six people in the region lived in perpetual bondage. A massive influx of slaves soon followed that decision. It is estimated that more slaves came to Kentucky in the two decades before 1810 than to any other state. By 1830, almost one in four Kentuckians lived as slaves. In Clay's Lexington in 1802, more than 40 percent of the households held slaves; a half century later, the county had more blacks than whites. Yet those numbers both reflect the strength of slavery and, at the same time, conceal the fragile nature of that institution in the Upper South. Throughout Clay's lifetime, some in the commonwealth continued to question the wisdom of the institution and to voice doubts about its long-term existence. At times, those words became mere whispers; at other times they grew loud enough to frighten slavery apologists. Clay would operate both in the world of the slaveholders and, improbably, in the sphere of slavery's critics. That duality would prove crucial in his presidential races.[2]

That conflicted view of slavery emerged early on for attorney Clay. The US Constitution seemed to suggest that Congress had no power over slavery where it existed. On the one hand, with no constitutional amendment likely to change that, the matter would be a state issue, pure and simple, according to Clay's reading of the law. On the other hand, he also knew that slaves were people, not property. Like so many in the antebellum era, Henry Clay had great difficulty in trying to reconcile those clashing views. Yet, he did produce an approach that attempted to do just that, and his views remained basically consistent. Clay would change his tone and his emphasis over time, but overall, the points he made as a youth of twenty-one in 1798 would be those he would present fifty years later. Crucially, at various times in his presidential bids, he chose to emphasize more openly either his antislavery or, conversely, his proslavery views, often to his political detriment. And at the same time, his overall views remained static while the national mindset increasingly intensified and changed.[3]

Like most Americans of his era, Henry Clay was no racial egalitarian. Few were. To his view, Caucasians had superior intelligence, but that still did not justify the existence or continuation of slavery. According to one account, as a youth in Virginia, Henry had seen a runaway slave, a slave he had known and liked, killed in his attempt at freedom. That left a vivid impression. Clay himself said that he had been taught from childhood that "every man, no matter what was his color or his condition, was entitled to freedom." And to respect. That attitude emerged in an incident later in Clay's life. According to a recollection that appeared fifteen years after

Clay's death, Clay had been on board a riverboat on the Ohio when he heard a commotion. He found angry slaveholders threatening to harm two black men (one of whom, as it turned out, was Frederick Douglass) after the men sought to sit down in the dining room. One observer remembered that Clay "spoke warmly and even eloquently" in favor of allowing the men to take their seats, and persuaded the crowd to allow that. As Clay told the spectator, such racially motivated treatment of free citizens and respectable men represented "a disgrace to civilization."[4]

Those sentiments had appeared early in Clay's life. Soon after his arrival in his new state, he found that Kentuckians had begun to discuss in earnest whether to call a new constitutional convention to address defects in the existing document. Once more, the debates partly focused on whether to keep slavery. Writing as "Scaevola" in the *Kentucky Gazette* in 1798, Clay had taken a clear and forthright stand. How, he asked, could a person countenance such an institution when he sees slaves on the auction block, "when he beholds the anguish and hears the piercing cries of husbands separated from wives and children"? Deprived of the things that made life desirable, slaves found themselves herded like cattle and treated little better. The proposed constitution, Scaevola urged, should give the legislature the power to abolish slavery in the future. It was not a radical stand, but it was a courageous one for a young attorney. When the convention gathered the next year, however, proslavery forces carried the day, and even strengthened the peculiar institution in the state. It was the first of several disappointments for Clay regarding emancipation.[5]

That defeat did not cause Clay to drop or play down his antislavery sentiments, despite what some historians have suggested. A quarter century later, when queried on his beliefs on the slavery issue in the midst of a presidential race, Clay still pointed to his 1798 letter and wrote, "My opinions are unchanged." A little over another quarter century after that, he penned a public letter that essentially repeated the stands he had taken in his youth, even using similar words.[6]

Throughout his career, Clay declared that slavery represented the greatest evil facing America. In 1827, he told a national audience that this deepest stain on American honor, this "foul blot" of slavery, stood as "an universally acknowledged curse." He stated that viewpoint even more forcefully later: "*I consider slavery as a curse*—a curse to the master, a wrong, a grievous wrong, to the slave." Clay had little use for those who later defended slavery as "an ordinance of Heaven," a positive good, an uplifting of an inferior race. He would call such revisionist interpretations "indefensible, unintelligible."

Had those been Clay's only words regarding the institution, he would have found allies in at least one section of the nation.[7]

Yet, like many southerners who opposed slavery in theory, Henry Clay held slaves. In public life, Clay could look at matters through the eyes of others, a trait that helped him craft his compromises or push through legislation. But he had a moral blind spot to aspects of the slavery issue. Clay did understand, on one level at least, what he called "the injustice of slavery." He pointed out that slaves were "rational beings like ourselves." Given that, they had a soul that yearned for liberty and an intellect that knew the unfairness of their situation. Forced to America through the slave trade—"the most abominable traffic that ever disgraced the annals of the human race"—the bondsmen found themselves unwillingly thrust into an evil system that took away not only their freedom but also their humanity. But slavery could not take away such things in the end, said Clay in an 1827 speech. For those who advocated slavery's triumph, he stressed, they must "repress all tendencies towards liberty. . . . They must blow out the moral lights around us, and extinguish that greatest torch of all which America presents to a benighted world. . . . They must penetrate the human soul, and eradicate the light of reason and the love of liberty."[8]

That love of liberty would continue to drive slaves to seek freedom, Clay predicted. They had done so in the bloody 1791 rebellion in Saint-Domingue (Haiti), and had sought to do so in real or supposed insurrections in Virginia and South Carolina in 1800, 1822, and 1831. The names Gabriel, Denmark Vesey, and Nat Turner brought fear to many white southerners. To them, slavery must continue in order to control the dangerous race in their midst. But to Clay, those revolts also reminded him that the desire for freedom burned within slave bodies and would grow over time. After all, as he told one bondsman, "If I was a slave, I would walk across the sea barefoot . . . for freedom." Given Clay's view of slaves as rational, feeling beings, he understood that attempts at freedom would be almost inevitable. He supported the patriots in South America as they rose up to break free of their colonial oppressors, and he held similar philosophical sympathies for those who might rebel in America against their own oppressors. Clay hoped that would not happen; he would work to ensure it did not. Yet he did not fear black leaders heading black republics. Clay would introduce a petition for the recognition of Haiti (an act that would not come to pass until a decade after his death) and would support the independence of Liberia in Africa. After all, Clay considered the freedom of all men and the extinction of slavery as inevitable: "It may by law. It may by sword. It may by the operation of natural causes." But slavery would end. An outmoded institution, a relic of an earlier time, a stain on the American record, it had no place in the modern world.[9]

Yet, Clay continued to hold slaves, despite his comments about freedom. The situation in Kentucky perhaps made it easier for him to rationalize the day-to-day continuance of slavery, even as he foresaw its eventual end. Many travelers and observers of the state's conditions called slavery more permissive and benevolent there than elsewhere, and the state's politicians and public embraced that fiction. By the 1830s, several commentators expected citizens to end the institution within their borders. James Freeman Clarke, no friend of slavery, came to the state and wrote how Kentuckians considered the slave system a curse: "Slavery mild. People said 'All wrong, inexcusable; Kentucky will emancipate.'" Later he recalled: "Public sentiment in Kentucky, in 1835, was almost unanimous against the continuation of the system." Abolitionist James G. Birney, a former Alabama slaveholder, returned to his native state of Kentucky in the 1830s because "I looked upon it as the *best side in our whole country for taking a stand against slavery*." Even antislavery man William H. Seward later concluded that slavery in the Bluegrass State took its least repulsive form.[10]

Those who congratulated themselves on the mildness of slavery in Kentucky noted that while Kentucky had a large number of slaveholders—third highest in the South by 1850—average size holdings were small, the third lowest in the region. By their thinking, the larger, faceless slave gangs of the hot, fever-ridden Deep South would be a harsher environment than the small, individual holdings in temperate Kentucky. Laws also seemed to reflect that more moderate treatment: unlike most southern states, Kentucky did not prohibit educating bondsmen; it forbade the importation of new slaves into the commonwealth from 1833 to 1849; and it had a court system that recognized enslaved persons had certain natural rights. In this "world between" the extremes, various commentators concluded that slavery wore a mild face in Kentucky. Or so many believed.[11]

But small holdings in Kentucky did not necessarily equate to better treatment. More often, slaves would be in an owner's home, under constant supervision and on call, with less free, independent time than field slaves in their quarters after work. The small numbers of slaves held by individuals also meant that, with a restricted marriage pool in the area, slaves might marry partners in more distant places. In times of financial stress, slave sales and the separation of families might occur more frequently in small holdings, as well. One historian has estimated that one in every three

Kentucky slaves would be sold at some time. The original title given the song "My Old Kentucky Home" makes it clear that the song represented the lament of a slave: "Hard Times comes a knocking at the door," and the slave is sold south, away from the "happy and bright" Kentucky home, to a harsher place. Many of the enslaved in Kentucky knew that feeling, for the state became a center for selling slaves to the developing southern sugar and cotton fields. But most of all, the debate over whether slavery was compassionate in Kentucky was specious. Slavery was still slavery, a system of virtually unlimited control by one person over another. Those in human bondage knew that freedom remained a distant dream, that the psychological tyranny of slavery surrounded them daily, that the threat of sale and separation from loved ones loomed over them always. Mental and physical abuse condemned the system, no matter the degree or frequency. Those who heard the cries of slaves being punished by whipping in the public square knew the falseness of the claim of benevolence. Clay himself wrote that "Here in Kentucky slavery is in its most mitigated form, *still it is slavery.*" Jared Stone expressed that sentiment even more forcefully: "Kentucky, no doubt, exhibits slavery in its mildest form, but even here there is enough to cause the very heart to sicken." Clay might rationalize that he lived in the mildest slave society in America, but he knew the sickening evils of the system around him. He knew, yet he remained a slaveholder. And that condemned him.[12]

Like most slaveholders, Clay considered himself a "good" master. When he referred in letters to "my own family," he paternalistically meant his family free and slave, white and black. Existing documentation suggests he made adequate provisions for the slaves' physical well-being—clothing them, feeding them, giving them medical care. On occasion they received pay for extra duties undertaken at crucial times, such as the hemp harvest or hog killing. When Clay purchased new slaves, he seemed to try to keep families intact, frequently purchasing both husband and wife or mother and children. He ultimately freed at least eight slaves, including his body servant "my friend Charles" and the nurse of his children. Most stayed with Clay after securing their freedom, and some worked as wage laborers. In Clay's mind, their loyalty reaffirmed his belief that he treated his slaves well and fulfilled his duty to those humans entrusted to his care.[13]

Yet in truth, how the Clay slaves were treated remains largely unknown. At one level, it is only a matter of degree, since they remained slaves, subject to all that entailed. At another level, Clay may have had only sporadic influence on that treatment, no matter his intentions. His long absences on the legal circuit, on trips across the country, in Congress, in Europe, and in the cabinet meant that in some years he was not present at Ashland, and in most years he was gone for several months. Thus, Clay's overseers often set the tone for treatment, though Lucretia and her sons sometimes updated Clay on situations on the estate. One overseer had problems with drink, and on at least one occasion an overseer whipped one slave to excess. Political opponents later suggested that a slave died violently as a result of a whipping, but some evidence suggests the slave, in ill health and despondent, committed suicide. Either way, at Ashland or on slave farms and plantations across the South, the costs of enslavement ran high.[14]

What took place in the slave quarters at Ashland remains mostly hidden from history, and the stories that survive are often mired in the quagmire of politics. Opponents would find little firm evidence they could use regarding Clay's treatment of his slaves, but some still produced negative references, usually based on unconfirmed rumors. In 1828, for example, Jacksonians criticized Clay for holding a freed slave in illegal bondage. Clay responded that the slave in question, Jerry, was, by his owner's will, to be freed on reaching age twenty-eight. Not yet at that age, and thus still a slave, Jerry had asked Clay to purchase him until then (which suggests that Clay had a reputation among other owners' slaves as a kind master). Clay had done so, and Jerry would be freed and paid thirty-five dollars on his twenty-eighth birthday.[15]

On at least two later occasions, the northern antislavery press printed stories from slaves who had either run away from Clay or seen him sell a slave's wife and children. In the first case, Clay angrily replied that he never owned a slave by that name, and in the second, when runaway Lewis Hayden said Clay had sold his wife Ester and their children, Clay said that he never owned those slaves in question. Hayden's response gave potentially convincing details, yet no extant record shows Clay bought or sold a slave woman by that name. Two years after that, abolitionists gleefully told how Clay's body servant had left him in New York, seeking freedom. Clay wrote that if that was the case, then no measures should be taken to bring him back. "It is probable that in a reversal of our conditions I would have done the same thing." As it turned out, the slave said he had been offered $300 by abolitionists to defect from Clay's service, but he had reconsidered after a day, and then rejoined Clay. Such examples make it difficult to separate political propaganda from the reality regarding slave-owner Clay.[16]

On one other matter, however, a clearer picture emerges, for Clay bought and sold slaves. Overall, he purchased more than sixty individuals, at an average price of more than $400 each, and he sold at least a dozen. The Kentuckian's own response to a query about whether he sold human beings was qualified and careful: "I never sold, in my life, any woman or child to go down the river or to go South." That statement concealed the fact that he did sell slaves for use in the state. But on the question of buying or selling slaves, once more the perspective on such matters is often missing. Clay, for example, purchased a slave, Daniel, for $450 in 1808. But he did so because Daniel's brother, who was free, wanted to buy his sibling's freedom. When Clay later received those funds, he emancipated Daniel. In another instance, Clay apparently sold his cook Rachel because she desired to be closer to her slave husband. Again, without that perspective, the transaction seemed a simple case of Clay the slave seller. So Clay sold slaves, and for that he would be criticized by his political enemies, but the story remains more complicated.[17]

Less defensible were Clay's actions regarding those of his slaves who sought immediate freedom. At a time when Clay could not control his own political fate, he could control the fate of others—the slaves at Ashland. When a young male slave fled in 1814, Clay sought his capture; three years later, another runaway brought forth a reward notice in a Washington paper for his return. One freedom case gained much national attention and injured Clay politically. Ironically, it involved one of the most respected slaves in the family. Charlotte (Lottie) nursed the Clay children; she was married to Clay's personal servant at that time, Aaron Dupuy. (Their son Charles would follow his father in the role.) But in 1829, Lottie had gone to visit relatives in Maryland, with Clay's permission. After talking with them, she then filed suit in the District of Columbia, petitioning for a judgment that she and her children were free. Clay fought the action, asked that Lottie be imprisoned for her "insubordination," and showed that while Lottie's mother had indeed been a free woman at one time, she had been a slave when Lottie was born. Because slavery followed the status of the mother, Lottie had thus been born, and remained, a slave. Accordingly, so were her children, under the law. Twenty-three years earlier, he had purchased her so that she and her husband could be together. Clay noted that the purchase was thus legal and that she remained his property. The court agreed.

All that proved very embarrassing to Clay, not only politically but also personally, for it challenged his authority and questioned his evaluation of himself as an understanding owner. After the case ended, an angry master sent Lottie to his daughter in New Orleans for two years' exile from her family. Yet the story did not end there. Some eight years after that, Clay emancipated Lottie and one of her children. Later, he freed another of her offspring, Charles. But these actions came on his terms, at his choosing. Clay did not like to lose, even when it involved breaking the bonds of the slave system.[18]

Politics and slavery mixed in one additional aspect of Clay's life. Given his reputation, it was perhaps not unexpected that political opponents would spread rumors that he had affairs with slave women. Yet, once more, little extant evidence supports such charges. The best source is a newspaper story that appeared almost forty years after Clay's demise. It told of the death of a light-skinned ex-slave named Phoebe Moore. According to the account, she had been bought by Thomas Hart Benton and then sold to Clay. She became his mistress, it said, bore him two children, and finally received her freedom from him. But problems appear in the story. In the existing accounts, there is no record of Clay either purchasing or emancipating a slave named Phoebe. The story also related how she had letters that Clay wrote to her. Most slaves were not literate; even if she was, it is doubtful Clay would have written to her. No such letters have surfaced. It is not impossible that Henry Clay had such liaisons, but the existing evidence does not lead there.[19]

Even while living in a slave state, Clay realized that the slave system needed to end. As he wrote a friend in the 1830s: "That slavery is unjust & a great evil are undisputed axioms. The difficulty always has been how to get rid of it."[20]

How indeed? Clay's answer to that quandary—gradual emancipation and then colonization—would hurt (and perhaps help) him politically all his career, and it was shaped by several assumptions and conclusions. First, he saw the hand of racism touching everything. Clay understood that slavery represented a method of racial control more than any economic system. He also recognized that white racism existed throughout the United States, in the free North and the slave South alike. No new state since 1819 allowed blacks to vote. African American citizens might be forbidden to travel in stagecoaches in some parts of the North; they might see interracial schools sacked; they might be seated in segregated sections of churches; they might have to post cash bonds to ensure good behavior; they might even be attacked by mobs, as in Cincinnati. And in the South under slavery, such attitudes and fears developed to the extreme.[21]

Clay looked at the free blacks of the slave South—less than 1 percent of Kentucky's population in 1830 but almost 21 percent of Delaware's—and at

Slaveowner Clay and antislavery advocate Clay represented two sides of the same politician, and anything connected with this issue and the candidate became news. According to one version of the story, Clay's slave Aaron Dupuy had angered Mrs. Clay and she sought to have him whipped as punishment. Dupuy has fooled the overseer, taken the whip from him, and has commenced whipping him instead as Clay enters the room. Clay did not reprimand Aaron, who remained Clay's personal servant. *From* The Kidnapped and the Ransomed *by Kate E. R. Pickard (1856), courtesy of Ashland, the Henry Clay Estate*

the same population in the North, and he saw a "debased and degraded" group of a third of a million people. Harshly describing them as "corrupt [and] depraved," "useless and pernicious," "improvident and thoughtless," he seemingly held little sympathy for free men and women of color. Yet, he also noted that the existing situation did not result from their inherent inferiority or natural conditions but, rather, from their "unfortunate situation." That emphasis on environment over innate racial characteristics signified an important step for a slaveholder to take. Because of white prejudice and racism, said Clay, the dominant population would never give free blacks equal privileges. Moreover, because most whites, like himself, saw amalgamation of the races as something unnatural, "revolting, . . . offensive to God and man," Clay concluded that irreversible racial differences meant that large numbers of free blacks could never achieve equivalent rights or reach their full potential in racist America.[22]

That viewpoint led Clay to a second, crucial conclusion that also shaped his ideas on the best way to end slavery. The bloody example of the Haitian slave revolt, the few domestic slave conspiracies, and Clay's own belief that as rational, feeling beings, freed slaves would strike out in revenge against their longtime white oppressors all caused him to expect—as many slaveholders did—that an immediate emancipation of the slaves would produce terrible results: "Carnage, pillage, conflagration, devastation, and the ultimate extinction or expulsion of the blacks. Nothing is more certain." As the races competed under freedom, a bloody race war would result, one particularly fierce in areas of sizable slave numbers, such as South Carolina with its 54 percent slave population in 1830. The more numerous whites of America would never allow black dominance and control, for that would "make us the slaves of slaves," said Clay. In his view, then, if all African Americans were freed at once, the determination of whites to maintain control assured that the black race would never be treated fairly in America. No model of a real, multiracial system existed to challenge Clay's assumptions. His own racism added to the mix, as well. Given his analysis that the two races could not exist together in equality and in harmony, he could argue that for the good of the black race, the immediate abolition of slavery, with its expected sinister results, was not practical, and another option must be found.[23]

Clay's assumptions were of course flawed. Multiracial societies would exist. Race warfare by American ex-slaves would not occur. Attitudes would change over time. Yet, he correctly perceived the powerful role that racism played, and plays, in various societies. Given his views, and given the difficulty in persuading slave owners to give up their property, Clay supported a plan that he hoped could result in a workable, peaceful way to end slavery. But that too would be steeped in controversy.

Clay proposed, in his words, *"the final extinction of slavery"* through voluntary emancipation over time and movement of most freed slaves to overseas colonies. A systematic form of social engineering, his plan sought to deal with a special American problem through collective action. His ideas appeared to many to be the only proposals that had any opportunity for success in an increasingly entrenched South. Clay's commitment to an active government, his optimism, his belief in the humanity of slaves as people, his compromising spirit—all came together in his program. If he were successful, he could remove a divisive debate that threatened to tear the nation apart and could eventually rid the nation of the slave system. Yet, his plan would be pilloried by some as too openly abolitionist, by others as too proslavery, by some as promoting a too-activist federal government, by others as not being activist enough, by some as a diversionary, impractical scheme with no hope of success, by others as all too likely to achieve its aims.

Controversy dogged Clay's proposal from the start, but he never publicly retreated from it and never overly questioned its correctness. Thus, while slaveholding presidents like Andrew Jackson and James K. Polk voiced few serious antislavery sentiments, and while other chief executives seemed seldom inclined to challenge the peculiar institution, Clay did both. He openly took a stand and presented a program in support of that stand. But once again, his specificity and his principles cost him politically, on both sides of the voting spectrum.[24]

Clay's specific solution to ending slavery came in the form of the American Colonization Society (ACS). When a group of advocates met in a small room in a Washington, DC, tavern to plan the organization, Clay was there. Over the years, he became the best-known spokesman for the ACS, and he served as its president for more than a dozen years. Its cause became his cause, its hopes his hopes. At its most basic, Clay's ACS sought to take freed blacks and transport them to Africa, where they could get a fresh start and live as free men and women. That would also decrease the black population at home and reduce racism. But two important points formed the basis of that solution. First, Clay did not suggest shipping all blacks "back to Africa." He proposed sending only enough ex-slaves to reduce the percentage of blacks in the overall population, so that whites in America would no longer see them as a threat. That would preclude the race warfare he and others feared. Second, Clay saw racial removal as a positive force for free blacks, who existed with second-class status in America. In Africa, he predicted, they could rise to a prominence never attainable in the United States: "There, they would be in the midst of their [other free black] friends . . . and elevated above the natives . . . as much as they are degraded here." Diffusion overseas would not produce the world proslavery advocates wanted but, rather, a biracial, free society in America, albeit a limited one.[25]

More than that, however, the ACS proposed nothing less than the re-demption and regeneration of Africa. The racism behind the plan was mixed with a religious and republican spirit. Clay and others in the organization saw the new African settlements as models for a new continent, helping free it of "ignorance and barbarism." The nation, said Clay, owed a moral debt to those whose ancestors were brought to America against their will and thus should redress those wrongs and repopulate the continent: "Every emigrant to Africa is a missionary carrying with him credentials in the holy cause of civilization, religion, and free institution." And unlike the naysayers who proclaimed that blacks could not govern themselves, Clay and the ACS vehemently disagreed. Once freed of the racial animosity of America, ex-slaves could lead "a great republic," forged from their determi-nation, their hard work, and even their blood. The Pan-African movement of Marcus Garvey and others in the next century could recognize much of their rhetoric in the words of the ACS a hundred years earlier.[26]

What had to happen to put the plan in place? In Clay's best of worlds, enlightened slaveholders would free their slaves once they saw that the freedmen would be sent overseas. Eventually, the resulting small ratio of blacks to whites in the United States would produce a system of free labor, he predicted. However, for Clay's plan to work, it almost required either federal financial action or massive philanthropic donations. States could help, as Kentucky did for a time by providing a small fund to support ACS actions. But limited state resources and meager private aid had not met the need. Thus, the federal government had given over $250,000 in aid to the ACS. To Clay, that represented a hopeful start. Then in 1830, Jackson stopped that rather restricted support.[27]

For colonization represented another, more forgotten branch of Clay's American System. He considered slavery's end an important element in unifying and modernizing the nation. But at the same time, he continued to speak from the white perspective more than from the black. To Clay, the South would never accept an immediate end to slavery, with its expected attendant horrors, and he thus called for a gradual system of emancipation.

That outlook meant, however, that millions of slaves would spend their lives in bondage. Generations might pass before the system changed. Clay wrote of the end of the peculiar institution at a "very distant . . . day," perhaps not even in his lifetime, or in a century or more. That would be a slow remedy, he recognized, but he said that slavery had taken root over the centuries and thus required time to be removed: "I do believe it is better that slaves should remain slaves than be set loose [immediately] as free men among us." Those gradualist views would hurt him in some northern circles; that he voiced them at all harmed him politically in southern ones.[28]

Once freed, by whatever means, slaves then had to be transported to the new colony of Liberia. The overall approach of the ACS, but especially that aspect of their plan, garnered criticism both then and since. Clay heard those attacks in his time and took considerable pains to answer them with specific numbers. Because he did not seek to send all blacks to Africa, his plan proposed only to ship a number equal to the annual national increase in the slave population. That would freeze the number in America by sending overseas some 50,000 freed slaves per year. Clay estimated that the cost to do that would be under $25 per slave. The ACS thus needed a little over $1 million each year to move those numbers of free people to their new home. About one-ninth of the nation's shipping would need to be involved in the enterprise. Should all that occur, over a sixty- or seventy-year period the issue would be moot, he argued. By that time, the nongrowing black population and the expanding white population would produce a racial ratio whereby blacks represented no rational threat to white fears. (In fact, had Clay's plan gone into operation, the US black population, free and slave, would have declined from under 20 percent in 1830 to under 4 percent within sixty years.) Clay argued that the US government could thus peacefully end a divisive moral and political issue that had plagued the nation almost from its very first days. Moreover, it could stop the suffering, under slavery, of millions of humans. Observing that Kentucky in the early 1830s seemed to be moving toward emancipation, seeing that Britain stood ready to end slavery in the Caribbean, advocating a plan that he considered reasonable and fair to the slave South, Clay had high hopes as that decade dawned.[29]

The lone existing impediment to success, wrote Clay to a friend, was "the want of money, money, money." But he knew, too, that the South feared federal intervention. So Clay came up with what seemed to him a reasonable solution. Using an indirect, trickle-down, revenue-sharing approach, he proposed that a portion of the sales of federal land be redistributed to the states, to be used for specific purposes—mainly for education, internal improvements, and colonization. That approach removed the federal onus and allowed the states to deal with the matter, while moving forward aspects of Clay's beloved American System. But so far, he had not been able to get that option through Congress, either. Still, Clay perceived that he had a workable plan of attack and a sound strategy to achieve it. Now he needed only to win some battles.[30]

Clay expected opposition to his plan from the slaveholding South; he did not expect much resistance in the North. To many southerners, especially in the Deep South, such colonization plans "set off alarm bells." Because the Kentuckian came as a supposed friend, as a fellow slaveholder, that almost seemed to make him more suspect, his advocacy more dangerous. Those in the region might attack the ACS plan as impractical and quixotic, but in truth the opposition had deeper roots. Colonization would be built on the freedom of slaves, and that raised a stench of abolitionism that hit the nostrils of southerners. Clay understood that attitude and resistance, and he expected that the example of other nations, the passage of time, and the growing benevolent views would gradually make inroads into the southern mindset.[31]

Clay did not anticipate the ferocity or hostility to his plan that came from a growing abolitionist movement in the North. Opposition in that region to the ACS and Clay's colonization plans not only surprised him but also eventually angered him, to his political detriment. One criticism, however, did not surprise or shock Clay, because he realized the correctness of the barb. When opponents called Liberia a death trap, they were correct. In a little over two decades after 1820, more than a third of the American ex-slaves who went to Africa died within a short time. Malaria killed one in every six immigrants, and some left the unhealthy colony, a few even returning to the States. Clay knew about the high fatality rate, but he pointed out that, given the choice of freedom and possible death overseas, slaves chose to throw off their shackles and risk death to be free. Besides, he pointed out, English settlers at Jamestown had experienced even greater mortality rates, but out of that had come a dynamic new nation.[32]

For many free blacks in the North, Clay's approach and the ACS program held little appeal, however. Frederick Douglass's newspaper would later reprint stories critical of the Great Compromiser and would repeatedly editorialize against the colonization plan. Calling the ACS the "deadliest foe to the colored man," both stories and editorials noted that colonization rested on the assumption that the two races could not live together on terms of equality. Instead, it sought to manipulate a people and "dump free Negroes into the savage wilds of Africa." Even if treated badly in America, said Douglass, free blacks in the United States still saw it as their country, too, for they had been there longer than many more recently arrived whites. Why should free blacks support such an impractical plan, built on gradualism and what Douglass's *North Star* termed a "bitter and revengeful spirit"?[33]

Douglass also turned his attention to Henry Clay specifically, as president of the ACS. Reprinting a story from another antislavery organ, the paper stressed that by placing so many conditions on the end of slavery, by supporting property rights first and human rights second, Clay removed the argument from "the court of conscience where alone it can be decided absolutely and without appeal" and placed it at the mercy of political economy. Clay wanted to captain the vessel of state but, said Douglass, he put the slavery issue "out of sight, in the rear of the ship." That was an astute and correct conclusion. Like many of his generation, Clay saw confrontations over slavery as dangerous to party and to union. He promoted the colonization approach as the safest, most likely way to appeal to a South teetering on the edge of a defense of slavery as a positive good.[34]

Clay argued that gradual emancipation and partial slave removal represented the only approach with any success of ending slavery peacefully. But southerners seldom freed their slaves and abolitionists increasingly leveled harsh attacks on slaveholder Clay and his answers. The *Liberator* termed him the "haughty despiser of the colored race" and a strong prop to the slave system. In the 1830s, abolitionist Lewis Tappan, a one-time friend of Clay, criticized him for standing aloof from the fight. Another friend, the former slaveholder James Birney, called on Clay to promote antislavery more openly and wholeheartedly, but privately worried that Clay had "no conscience about the matter." Some of the later abolitionist critiques applied stronger words to Clay, labeling him a "slave breeder," a "manstealer," a "human-flesh monger." This "arch-enemy of the colored race" daily heard the cries of women and children under the lash on his farm, said one newspaper. Some of those critiques had much truth to them, for Clay did not truly empathize with slaves at the most basic level. He could have done much more regarding abolition. Yet, he also feared a too-forceful attack would provoke the opposite reaction in the South and cause the region to turn inward, in defense. But Clay did recognize the human, moral part of the debate, did oppose slavery, and did seek its end. His answers, as it turned out, were the wrong ones. But he did speak out, when many others did not.[35]

The growing abolitionist onslaught on Clay took its toll, and he gradually began to strike back. As in other instances, he should have remained silent, but his fiery spirit did not allow that, especially when he considered himself wronged and his plans threatened. By the 1830s, Clay concluded that "public opinion is on the march" regarding slavery, especially in some slave states, like Kentucky. A letter to a Boston paper noted, "There is hardly a true born Kentuckian who will not make exertions and sacrifices to get rid of slavery in any moderate and practical manner. . . . We are the pioneers of emancipation south of Mason and Dixon's line." Another immigrant to the state indicated that a majority of the citizens there had tired of slavery and predicted an end to it in Kentucky within a few years. However, that letter writer warned his father back in Pennsylvania that the rising spirit of abolitionism "tends to retard the desirable event and engender animosity and strife. . . . I can already see the extremes of evil with both parties."[36]

That analysis coincided with Clay's own fears about the "fatal consequence" of calls for immediate emancipation. Such "misguided" efforts came from "a fanatical class" of zealots, and Clay feared extremes at either end: "Time, Providence will cure all—abolition nothing. It may ruin all." His carefully planned house of reform seemed to be crumbling before his eyes. He saw most abolition societies disappear in the South, one by one. He heard the voices of change in Kentucky grow fainter, despite the brave words. He read the words of his correspondents, like the abolitionist who warned him in the 1830s, that "we may dismember the Union[,] we may wade through seas of blood, but it must come to this at last." Increasingly, Clay perceived proslavery advocates and antislavery abolitionists as equal threats to the harmony of the Union. As he later remarked in Congress, he saw the greatest danger to the nation as "the ultraism of the South on the one hand . . . and the ultraism of Abolition on the other." In fact, he told the Colonization Society of Kentucky that immediate emancipation with its expected race warfare posed a greater evil than slavery itself. Abolitionist agitation moved the conservative side of Henry Clay to dominate his reform side.[37]

That often-quiet, usually small voice of antislavery conscience within Clay still recognized that the moral argument behind abolitionism had validity. Even though he was bitterly attacked by abolitionists, Clay respected their right to make their appeals; he just considered their solutions wrong. Yet despite his war with abolitionists, after Ohio congressman Joshua Giddings was censured for his antislavery stands, Clay met him, extended his hand, affirmed that Giddings had the absolute right to utter his views, and expressed outrage at the action taken. Clay would also support the antislavery John Quincy Adams, who combined moral criticisms of slavery with a "sense of the possible in politics." Moreover, Clay signed a petition for the pardon of a Kentucky abolitionist caught aiding slaves to escape, and apparently was willing to help secure the release of archenemy William Lloyd Garrison when the editor was imprisoned. Clay defended the right of abolitionists to send their materials through the mail, a stand opposed by most southerners. In short, he recognized abolitionists' rights and even the moral force of their cause, while at the same time viewing their solutions as extremely dangerous ones.[38]

Slavery did not suddenly arise in the national consciousness because of the growth of abolitionism in the 1830s. The peculiar institution had lain dormant in public discussions at times, but it seemed ever-present in the minds of those living in antebellum America, as their diaries and letters reveal. If it had not been the growth of abolitionism, something else would have eventually unleashed the debate, for the ropes of reaction could not restrain the moral power of antislavery. Clay may have been partly correct in his view that the growing spirit of immediate emancipation was creating a fortress mentality in a South under attack. But the crack of the whip, the cry of the auctioneer, the wails of the separated families made it difficult to wait patiently for the evil to end in some far-distant future. Clay expected slavery's demise, some day. But the actions of those in his generation, and even his grandchildren's, suggest that slavery and some form of regulated race relations were deeply ingrained in the southern white psyche. Clay might fear that abolitionists would hasten a bloody, destructive war, but they also abetted the freedom of millions of their fellow humans. That moral outrage, that sense of urgency, did not burn as deeply within Clay as with them. He understood it, sometimes voiced it, occasionally lived it, but other values mattered more and consumed him with greater force: the devotion to order, the rule of law, the importance of compromise, and, most of all, the emphasis on union.

Clay's political armor always had many chinks and weak spots, but none proved more vulnerable than his stance on slavery. The things that he valued as his overall strengths all had defects regarding that issue. His support for conservative reform, for example, produced the dilemma for him that when he tried to answer the divisive question of slavery, he faced the issue of how to end it in an orderly way. His advocacy of compromise stressed moderation in action, but that conflicted with the view that, in some cases, there could be "no compromise with dishonor," or with evil. His focus on preserving the Union meant that ending slavery might take second place to that greater goal. And so as Clay took his stands against slavery and for colonization, he also was limited in how far he would go.[39]

Clay tried to reconcile being both a slaveholder and an antislavery man, just as many increasingly saw those positions as irreconcilable. He hoped to appeal, on both counts, to the better nature of each section; he sought to have it both ways. Torn between the existing wrongs of slavery and the possible dangers of race war or future secession, Clay chose to compromise on slavery. He saw no easy choices before him. Acceptance of one option doomed people to perpetual bondage and suffering. The other option might take the nation down the bloody path of conflict—perhaps even a civil war with hundreds of thousands of deaths. Clay thus tried to diffuse that explosive issue through compromise or concessions, to keep the matter from tearing the nation apart. But the problem would not stay quiet. Nor should it have. The slavery issue demanded a response, and both slaveholders and abolitionists gave their answers. As a slaveholder, Clay tried to allay the fears of the South, but he would anger the North because of his conciliatory words and actions. An antislavery man, Clay sought to convince northerners of his fidelity to the cause through his plans, but he would infuriate southerners who feared even one step down the emancipation road. Clay tried to appeal to the sections, but over and over he alienated the rising numbers of those who eschewed the middle ground. He thus got the worst of both political worlds: "The abolitionists are denouncing me as a slaveholder, and the slaveholders as an abolitionist."[40]

Clay remained true to his views regarding slavery and the need to end it, even though that stand hurt him politically at times. Yet, Clay made the wrong choice. He considered his plan of gradual emancipation and colonization the only realistic hope to achieve the overall aim of freedom. It was not that his plan would not have produced the result he sought. But the approach was wrong, the assumptions were false, and the underlying beliefs were erroneous. If Clay instead had taken a more revolutionary approach in still-proslavery Kentucky, he might well have forfeited hopes for political victory. Yet, Clay had so many skills that perhaps he could have led in transforming opinion through his forceful words and brilliant oratory. It remains tantalizing to wonder what would have occurred had Clay moved beyond his conservative reform agenda and had grown in regard to his racial views. Could he have used a stronger antislavery stance to gain widespread northern support, even to presidential victory? Or would that have made Clay such an electoral pariah in the South that he might not even have received another nomination at all? In one sense, Clay himself answered those questions, for he seemed determined to be a national candidate, not a sectional one. He did not desire to be Henry Clay, choice of the North, or Clay of the South but, rather, Clay as the choice of all the people of the *United* States. But his era increasingly judged presidential candidates by their stance on slavery and voted in sectional ways. Slavery thus damaged not only Clay's moral compass but also his chance to hold the Union together as a nationalistic president. It was his great hamartia. As much as any other issue, Clay's stance on slavery killed his presidential hopes. But if it did, it was a self-inflicted wound.[41]

Despite the efforts of politicians like Henry Clay to bury the slavery issue and keep it out of national debates, the matter would not remain buried. It stood ready to spring forth to disrupt any question before the people. And even if it was not always presented openly as the motivating factor behind some particular stand, slavery often stood in the shadows of the discussion, directing actions and shaping stances. That would be true in the next crisis Clay faced, one that emerged full-blown in late 1832, just after his presidential defeat.

Leading one side in the emerging controversy was a man Clay knew well, and a peculiar institution in his own right. At one time John C. Calhoun and Henry Clay had been allies. The two men had pushed as War Hawks for the war with Great Britain, had supported the Second BUS together, had spoken for aspects of what would be called the American System.[42] Both men held slaves, both loved their landed estates, both practiced law, both developed a devoted core of followers, both confidently pushed plans and philosophies they felt crucial to national survival, and both despised Andrew Jackson. Yet over time, the two had grown apart. Calhoun abandoned his nationalism but Clay never did. Their respective states took different paths, as well. But the core of the resulting division between the one-time collaborators grew out of differences centered on personality, approach, and outlook.

Calhoun appealed more to men's intellect, Clay more to their emotions. The Carolinian spoke for absolute principles, the Kentuckian for flexible compromises. Calhoun lived a self-disciplined life, Clay a more undisciplined one. The man from Fort Hill produced careful, measured, analytical addresses in Congress; the man from Ashland offered quick, reactive, moving talks. One presented theoretic generalities, the other pragmatic specifics. Whereas Calhoun often appeared stiff and aloof, Clay proved personable and relaxed. Whereas John C. Calhoun could be an earnest and forceful, but not strong, speaker, Henry Clay would be the master orator. Whereas Calhoun had an unblemished, if not affectionate, personal life, Clay had one filled with rumors and innuendos. And most of all, John C. Calhoun offered a legalistic, mechanical, and limited approach to government, whereas Henry Clay had a flexible, positive, optimistic one. One wanted to protect the status quo, the other to challenge it more. The Carolinian feared the future; the Kentuckian welcomed it.

Clay and Calhoun differed not just on how they did things or on their personal traits but also on issues and mindsets. The "cast-iron man," Calhoun seemed never to relax and his mind "never slept." He was always thinking, always fearing, always agitating. But Calhoun's theoretical answers to real issues produced disdain in Clay. The Great Pacificator had absolute contempt for what he saw as his opponent's abstract and impractical logic. Carefully constructed theories that would not work in actual life held little appeal for realist Clay when a crisis required action. Clay at those times needed something that would produce results, not more unworkable theories. As the Kentuckian observed, Calhoun "will theorize you to death." Another politician referred to a Calhoun speech as "metaphysical nonsense and absurd abstractions." But Calhoun would offer an initial premise as accepted fact, or capitalize on a single weakness in the opposing viewpoint; and his great mind could then craft an elaborate, seemingly logical argument that excluded all other principles and possibilities save his own. If reason prevailed, it would be *his* reason. Couple that with the zeal of an advocate who spoke with "a fire in his eyes, the fire of a soul that seemed to burn within him," and Calhoun could hold great appeal for similar true believers. Others, however, such as Daniel Webster, had a different reaction as they looked at Calhoun from another perspective. Webster sneered that Calhoun could not make "a coherent, able, argumentative speech," while Georgian Howell Cobb later referred to the mad, evil genius of the South Carolinian.[43]

Calhoun, from the intellectual security of his own insular little world, saw little need to compromise, for he spoke from a heart that held fast to absolute rights and wrongs. The press of that era noted that Calhoun displayed "the very genius of abstract reasoning, calmly and deliberately adding link after link to the iron chain of his logic." He piled rapid syllogism on syllogism, "leaving his audience bewildered by the subtly [sic] of his metaphysics." When people heard Calhoun speak, even his supporters sometimes noted that he seemed like a harsh schoolteacher lecturing with glee about some new dissertation on negative powers. Men might call Calhoun brilliant, but to Clay true brilliance lay not in words on paper but in concrete, constructive action that accomplished something of value, something that lasted.[44]

If Clay had total contempt for Calhoun's approach to politics, he had similar disgust for Calhoun's specific theories of government. In fact, it is somewhat surprising that so many writers since Clay's time have praised Calhoun for his original, innovative thinking, particularly regarding majority rule versus minority rights. Calhoun certainly produced such tracts, but his solutions generally would not work in practice, nor probably solve the core problems they sought to address. To Clay, anyone could formulate theories; only a few could produce plans that might actually work. For many writers, what contemporaries called the "practical wisdom" of Henry Clay seemed less exciting and less valued than Calhoun's critical but flawed thoughts. But most people living in Clay's time recognized the greater importance of Clay to the nation.[45]

Calhoun's conception of how American government had been formed and how it should operate differed considerably from Clay's vision of the American Union. To the South Carolinian, ultimate sovereignty rested not with the people of America as a whole but, rather, with each state. Unlike Clay, Calhoun's United States did not function as one nation and one population; instead, it was a partnership of separate, sovereign "interests." His chief concern seemed almost as old as government itself: How can minority interests be protected in a government of majority rule? The founders of the Constitution and the early national leaders had eventually answered that question with a system of checks and balances (with the Supreme Court, two houses of Congress, a presidential veto, and more). Moreover, ensuring freedom of speech gave minority dissent a voice, and giving states the power to decide strictly state issues helped as well. That model Clay adopted. To him, majority rule represented the only fair, sustainable approach. After all, over time, minorities could become majorities. The "interests" of Calhoun would be addressed through the compromises that formed the basis of government. Clay envisioned a very different kind of union than did Calhoun.[46]

Calhoun rejected the Supreme Court as the final arbiter of the law and proposed that each state or interest (perhaps the slave-owner interest) would have a veto right of sorts over congressional laws. His solution to the question of minority rights almost seemed to harken back to the failed Articles of

Confederation model, in which a single state could halt any federal action. Calhoun's answer to an oppressive majority—perhaps an antislavery majority one day—involved giving each state or interest the right to declare a congressional action void. If three-fourths of the states agreed, then the act of nullification would be overridden and the law would be operative once more. In that case, the state that had nullified the act would then have the choice of either accepting the law or of regaining its sovereign powers by peacefully leaving the Union. If the vote failed to procure a three-fourths margin to overturn the nullification ordinance, then the law in question would be declared everywhere inoperative and void, and the state action would stand over the federal one. Thus, one-fourth of the states could negate the vote of the majority. States whose wishes were not supported could withdraw from the union of states—one state over one issue, another state over another matter. Much later, Calhoun even proposed a dual presidency, with one chief executive representing northern interests, one southern interests, and each with a veto power over acts taken. Such was Calhoun's theoretical approach to a workable federal government.[47]

Henry Clay, James Madison, and others then and since found such arguments and such theories impractical at best and dangerous at worst. Minority dominance would replace majority rule under Calhoun's plan, they warned. Based as it was on questionable assumptions, oversimplified analyses, convoluted premises, and selective examples, it did not even protect all minorities (such as slaves or poor whites), just selected ones. And where did the veto rights stop—at the state borders? What about the minority within the minority? Critics noted that almost no legislation would pass muster without some state's objection, and possible nullification, under Calhoun's proposal. States could choose which laws to accept or to ignore. Anarchy would rule. To John Quincy Adams, nullification would mean "organized civil war," would produce a sectional party based on narrow interests, and would make government unworkable. Clay agreed. In 1828, he wrote that if nullification theory operated, "the union may indeed as well be dissolved; for it would not be worth preserving." Much later, he called Calhoun's plan "a novel and strange doctrine."

It was little wonder that in 1831, to his political detriment, presidential candidate Clay had rebuffed allies' attempts at a political alliance with the also anti-Jackson Calhoun, for as Clay wrote, "Their principles are directly opposed to ours." The Kentuckian worried that Calhoun would push his radical ideas to their extremes, sowing seeds of dissention and disunion. The South Carolinian appeared ready to do anything to protect slavery, which he termed a fundamental right and, later, a positive good. While Clay and Calhoun could agree on the expected dangerous results of immediate emancipation, Calhoun could not envision a southern world without slavery. Clay could. If needed, Calhoun would destroy the Union to save slavery, as one historian noted. But, if needed, Clay would sacrifice slavery to save the Union.[48]

Calhoun's whole sense of self, his every theory, his worldview—all appeared predicated on the issue of protecting slavery. He might form political plans to protect minority interests and couch them in philosophical terms, but in the end they revolved around slavery. He might criticize central power, but rarely did he refuse the use of federal force in regard to upholding the institution of slavery. Yet more often, he and other southerners worried that the expansion of government powers—the very thing Clay supported—might eventually be applied to the matter of abolition. As a result, almost any political issue held the potential to be the one that would ignite that smoldering concern.[49]

By the 1830s, that issue was the tariff. As a former congressman wrote, "The whole of our Southern Opposition to the tariff may be traced to the principle of slavery." Calhoun was consumed by slavery and each issue seemed connected to it, in his mind, in some irreparable nexus. In early 1832, Congress had once more taken up that charged subject of the tariff, and the words had grown more strident and the debates more confrontational. Clay, even in an election year, did not avoid the subject and gave one of his most masterful (and most reprinted) speeches on the issue. Over three days, he declared that tariffs had protected infant American industries and had thus saved thousands of jobs. Calhoun countered that a free-trade policy would push Americans to innovate in order to compete and would better stimulate the economy by open competition. In turn, Clay stressed that governmental protection of US manufacturing would foster greater American entrepreneurship. Calhoun responded that he wanted no part of an activist federal government. When the man from South Carolina pointed out that his state and region suffered from the effects of the tariff, the man from Kentucky asked that if the nation was prosperous overall (as it was), why was South Carolina upset? "I stand here," the advocate of the American System later said, "as the humble but zealous advocate, not of the interests of one state . . . but of the whole union." Were we not all one people, one nation, working for one common good?[50]

Of course, that was the question. Was it one country or a collection of sovereign states? South Carolina may well have suffered somewhat from the effects of a high tariff—the matter remains under debate—but it also had greater internal problems, such as a paucity of land, overproduction, exhausted soil, overextended finances, and outmigration. The state faced a crisis of confidence as a result, and the tariff made a convenient scapegoat. The tariff of 1832 that finally passed did reduce rates over the previous incantation. But its moderate duties failed to satisfy extremists in South Carolina. A potential disaster threatened the Union, and Henry Clay soon found himself again in the middle of it all.[51]

Step by step, South Carolina escalated its opposition to matters federal, and specifically to tariff issues. By April 1832, a US senator wrote that the state acted as if it expected, or even wanted, war. With passage of the tariff act, Carolina's wrath intensified and the earlier worries seemed all too real. Just after Jackson's reelection and Clay's defeat, the South Carolina legislature passed a series of resolutions nullifying the new tariff as of February 1833. That action meant that if nullification succeeded, then Congress could never pass effective antislavery legislation. But if nullification did not find support, then secession could be the next step, so South Carolina provocatively began building an army, just in case. That charged atmosphere caused reasonable men to fear for the nation's future. A young Democratic congressman from New York found on his arrival at the Capitol that fellow representatives from South Carolina were "full of fire & vengeance." After two weeks in Washington, he saw the nation "standing upon the brink of an awful precipice—a single rash step, or a timid one, may plunge us into a civil war." With that, the scene now shifted to the White House. President Jackson could salute that flag of nullification—or tear it down.[52]

Jackson's previous actions offered support to either option. At times, the president had sympathized with actions limiting federal power and had ignored existing constitutional standards (as with Supreme Court decisions on Indians). But now Jackson saw his South Carolina protagonist Calhoun as ambitious, anti-Jackson, and a threat to the Union. He thus submerged any previous views in order to squelch South Carolina's insubordination and challenge to his authority. In 1832, the president responded with a Nullification Proclamation, which spoke the words of Henry Clay: the government was of the people, not of the states, and the states had no right to nullify a federal law or to secede. To support the words, Jackson called for passage of what became known as the Force Bill. The tariff would be enforced and troops would be used if South Carolina seized federal property or sought to nullify national law. Those words angered states' rights supporters across the South, hastened the departure of some from the ranks of Jackson to the Clay side, and expanded the debate beyond one state. John Randolph expected Jackson to invade and start a civil war. A New York Democratic congressman voiced the concerns of many, in and out of Congress: "It is vain to reason with them [nullifiers]. . . . The bloody flag is hoisted." The Force Bill would give Jackson the power to use the army against Americans.[53]

That possibility worried Clay greatly. He could support strong executive action in a crisis, but he also feared the overall expansion of executive power—unless perhaps the executive happened to be Henry Clay. The broad presidential powers in the proposed Force Bill could give Jackson the ability to establish a military dictatorship, all in the name of squelching South Carolina's threatened insurrection. Near the end of 1832, Clay considered the president bent on the destruction of the "rash and intemperate" state, but called Jackson's statements "able and eloquent." These were strange words coming from Clay about Jackson, but in truth, the chief executive had spoken the words Clay would have uttered and had taken the course Clay would have followed in the end. In some ways, it was Jackson's finest political moment. But it was Andrew Jackson who had acted, and that greatly concerned Clay, given his fears about the military man. As a magazine writer noted of the general later, "swords not words were *his* arguments. . . . He had neither the temper nor the abilities to parley." By mid-January 1833, an apprehensive Clay despaired of any "amicable and permanent settlement of this question." He understood the power of history behind the forces at work and perceived the difficulty in producing a solution. America faced another dangerous crisis.[54]

As he prepared to act, Clay knew well that the fires of secession and separation could burn brightly in America. He did not see Calhoun's words as just some philosophical threat. His own state's earlier history told him otherwise. Separated from the East by mountains, with a distant government seemingly unconcerned with their problems, Kentucky's frontier leaders had discussed not only statehood but also independence or alliance with another foreign power. Before Clay came to the Bluegrass State, some prominent Kentuckians, seeking a trade outlet down the Mississippi through Spanish Louisiana, had given support to what would be termed the Spanish Conspiracy. In early 1786, Thomas Jefferson worried that Kentucky might separate from the Confederation—which would be "a most calamitous event." Some Kentucky leaders conspired with Spain; several took foreign money, or like General James Wilkinson, remained in the pay of Spain for years. In the end, ties of tradition and language won out and

Kentucky became a state in the federal Union. But for years it remained an unhappy one.[55]

Just a few years before Clay's arrival in Lexington, the French envoy Citizen Genet sought to recruit a Kentucky volunteer army to invade Spanish territory. That so-called French Conspiracy also failed. Then in 1798 and 1799, anger over Federalist action brought forth the Kentucky Resolutions, later used as a basis for nullification theory. In 1803, when it appeared that Spain had closed the vital shipping port of New Orleans to Kentucky goods, the state once more prepared to send men there. A young, eager Henry Clay got appointed as aide to a general: "I shall go with that crowd to endeavor to share the glory of the expedition." But Jefferson's Louisiana Purchase ended such war talk and finally gave Kentuckians some hope that the distant government might have their interests at heart, after all.[56]

Yet only three years later, Aaron Burr arrived in Kentucky. Disgraced elsewhere by his killing of Alexander Hamilton in a duel, he found more sympathy in anti-Federalist, pro-dueling Kentucky. And he also, once more, began to get the state's citizens involved in another scheme that perhaps involved disunion. What exactly Burr envisioned remains unclear, but at the least, he expected to use Kentucky volunteers to seize parts of foreign territory in Mexico. Or, he may have sought to establish a western empire, one that might include Kentucky. When word of Burr's efforts reached officials, some in Kentucky sought to halt him in court. That brought Clay into the equation, for he spoke with the charming, persuasive former vice president, got assurances that Burr had no designs to dissolve the Union or separate states from it, and then agreed to defend him pro bono. Clay proved successful, and Burr went free. Only later did Clay hear words that caused him to suspect Burr's guilt, to feel "deceived" by him, and to worry about what they could mean politically. By February 1807, he admitted, "We have been much mistaken about Burr." But in the end, Burr would not be found guilty of treason (owing to a narrow definition of the term), and Clay would be only lightly tainted by his association (as would Jackson). Clay saw in the support for Burr the continuing fragile nature of the federal Union in the West. Yet, that episode marked the high-water mark of separatist feeling in Kentucky. By then, the state had grown more attached to the Union it once had questioned. As a Kentuckian wrote about Burr in 1807, "he may have in contemplation the disunion of the American States, but . . . the people of the western country are too much opposed to it." A friendlier president in Thomas Jefferson, the popular purchase of Louisiana, and, later,

Kentuckians' sacrifices in the War of 1812 all cemented the attachment to the Union.[57]

At the same time, Clay saw separatist sentiment lurking in other American corners. Federalist New England's anger in the War of 1812 had brought further rumors of disunion. The war's end stopped those discussions, but the spirits lingered. Then came the Missouri Crisis and still another section bandied about words of disunion. Clay worried that if the South followed up on its threats and left, so too would the West, for he saw there "natural causes, tending toward disseverance." If those ropes that bound the nation together should be severed, then the once-proud nation would be "sent into miserable petty states, and those convulsed by perpetual feuds and wars." But New England, the West, and the South—indeed, all parts of the Union—seemed imbued at one time or another with that separation virus. Internal threats might imperil the still-new Union more than external ones, as the Spanish and French Conspiracies, the Kentucky Resolutions, the Burr Conspiracy, the New England issue in the War of 1812, the Missouri Crisis, and now South Carolina all showed. The balancing of the scales of union required constant effort.[58]

From his Kentucky experiences and from his years in Congress, Clay knew firsthand that the seeds of disunion could sprout from dormancy almost overnight. Throughout his career, he would work to kill them before they could bloom. For to Henry Clay, while politics or his presidential hopes often dictated his actions, so too did his continuing devotion to the federal Union. In fact, that would be the most consistent aspect of his life.[59]

Dissolution of any part of the Union troubled Clay because he feared that such a move would seriously threaten "all the bright and animating anticipations of mankind." Clay strongly urged, then, that the nation must develop a community of interests, must be tied together tightly by "mutual kindness, the feelings of sympathy, the fraternal bonds," and must have harmony among the sections. His American System sought to do that. Conversely, to Clay, alarming talk of nullification or even secession would result in unconstitutional actions adverse to union, no matter the protestations of Calhoun and others. A clash of arms would follow.[60]

Over the years, Clay made it very clear where he stood regarding the dissolution of the Union. In 1830, two years before Jackson's call for force, he told an ally that if civil war resulted, the general government should use all its forces to quell any rebellion. Later, he warned of the separation of states from the Union: "I cannot see the remedy for any evil. . . . Nothing, nothing can be gained—all would be lost by it. By the dissolution of the Union, I see introduced with it all the calamities, all the misfortunes, and all the horrors of civil war." In the 1830s, Clay made his choice clear: "I go for the union as it is, one and indivisible. . . . I will neither voluntarily leave it, nor be driven out of it by force." In the next decade Clay spoke the words that explain the reasoning behind his most crucial actions, that reveal his very core, that define Henry Clay: "If any man wants the key to my heart, let him take the key of union, for that is the key to my heart." Clay acted to ensure that the "tough and strong cord" of union remained intact. If he did not, the next president—perhaps one Henry Clay—might not be head of the *United* States.[61]

In looking at the situation before him in 1833, it seemed that two irresistible forces—the federal government and the state—and two uncompromising men, Andrew Jackson and John C. Calhoun, made reconciliation unlikely. But on closer inspection, that was not the case. Calhoun, whom Adams said swayed with the prevailing breeze, could see that he did not have widespread support outside his home state. To many southerners, he seemed too extreme. Alone, South Carolina would lose before the power of the federal government. At the same time, Jackson—despite his words of action—seemed willing to find a peaceful solution. His administration thus proposed a compromise tariff bill. Each side had tried hard to avoid a confrontation, a spark that could set off a political explosion. Given all that, the possibilities for a solution might be better than Clay had first thought. But if Congress did nothing, as one member predicted, "Somebody [might] get hanged and some killed."[62] Numerous public men stressed that only Clay could step into that situation and craft a compromise that could end the crisis. A master mediator and negotiator, he had the respect of many for his force of character and wisdom of counsel. John Randolph proclaimed that "there is one man and one man only, who can save the Union—that man is Henry Clay." Similarly, Martin Van Buren later wrote that Clay was the "only man who had it in his power" to extricate South Carolina from the mess it had made. At the time, in January 1833, John Tyler saw no hope for a settlement, "except through Clay . . . from him I still have hope." Tyler later explained that Clay saw the dangers to the Union: "I appealed to his patriotism. No man ever did so in vain."[63]

Clay may have delighted in the irony of the situation, even as he recognized the severity of it. After all, in the last election the Jackson press had praised their leader as "a firm friend of the rights of the states," and had pilloried Clay and his programs as a threat to the South. Now those same Jacksonians defended the president's use of federal power, and southerners saw Jackson, not Clay, as the threat. But if Clay reveled in Jackson's discomfort, he did so only briefly. He had work to do, to avert a conflict, and it would not be easy.[64]

How could Clay end the crisis and also protect his programs, his union, and his presidential hopes? The tariff represented the surface issue of discontent, and the president's actions on that matter concerned Clay a great deal. An administration bill introduced by outgoing congressman Gulian Verplank of New York would lower duties to the 1816 level. To Clay, that would mean a "total sacrifice" of his policy of protection of American industry, and would injure national manufacturing. Because of its low rates, the proposed Verplank tariff might not pass in the present "lame duck" Congress. But in the upcoming one, the Jacksonian majority would be greater, and it would probably pass there. So on the one hand, Clay saw the likelihood that eventually his policy of protection would be gutted. But on the other, if the bill did not pass in the present session, some southerners' discontent over what they called the "cruel, unnecessary extortion" might produce the dissolution of the Union. Clay seemingly faced an unsolvable dilemma—if he supported the bill, he might end the problem. But it would also end his policy of protection of industry. How could he get a tariff passed that would satisfy the South's demand for low rates and the North's for protection? How could he end the crisis?[65]

On February 12, 1833, only twenty days before Congress was due to adjourn, Henry Clay rose from his seat in the Senate and, to the shock of many, produced a proposal for a compromise to end the impasse. Though it would be roundly criticized in many circles, it was a brilliant plan, given the circumstances. It was also a surprising plan. Clay proposed nothing less than a dismantling, over time, of one of his cherished aspects of the American System—the protective tariff. He had not arrived at that decision easily or quickly. Two months earlier, he had prepared a draft, and a month after that had admitted that he was "far from sanguine" that any such plan would pass. He hoped he would not have to act. But events finally forced him to stand up and speak. Accordingly, he proposed that tariff duties be gradually lowered. That would give immediate general protection to American industry and some agricultural interests, and would provide stability and the breathing room—a decade—for them to become stronger against overseas competition. Yet the proposed compromise would also meet the long-term goal of South Carolina for lower tariff rates. To Clay, those reciprocal actions would placate the passions, remove the divisive issue from the table, and heal the wounds "of our distracted country." As he concluded, "Let us have peace and become more united as a band of brothers."[66]

As soon as Clay sat down, Calhoun rose to address the body. He immediately approved the principles of the plan. The gallery applauded and cheered in support; an astonished Congress realized that Clay had forged yet another coalition; he had made a bargain, not one for political gain per se (though that might result) but, rather, one to end the divisions in the nation. Moreover, some northern manufacturing interests soon spoke out in favor of Clay's proposal as well, an equally surprising turn of events. In the case of those who favored protection, Clay had quietly met with some of them in Philadelphia, had hinted at what he planned, and had convinced many that in his option lay their best hope, given the prospect of a pro-Jackson majority reducing duties shortly.[67]

Calhoun's unexpected support represented both diplomacy and good fortune on Clay's part. The two men had not spoken to each other for some time. Yet they both disliked Jackson and, for different reasons, both wanted to end the confrontation. The president would have nothing to do with the Carolinian; Clay, however, had kept the dialogue open through friends, and that would prove crucial in the crisis year of 1833. An Ohio attorney who observed the action had noted months earlier how the men who had once roundly criticized Clay's alleged "corrupt bargain" during the recent presidential race now treated him differently in the heat of danger: "Mr. Clay is on terms of the most cordial friendship with Hayne, Tazewell & many others who now when party rage has exhausted itself recognize in him the veteran American patriot which they so admired in the most perilous crisis." Clay and Calhoun disagreed on philosophy, but Calhoun needed to end the confrontation with Jackson and escape with honor, while Clay needed to diffuse the military threat of the Force Bill and protect the tariff. Thus, the two men Jackson most hated politically, and the two who did not particularly like each other much as well, made their political bed together and conceived a coalition that might end the crisis. Jackson, as expected, saw the "evil" cohabitation as a wicked design to dupe the people. But he also wanted to resolve the dispute and did not overtly oppose the Clay plan.[68]

Despite the Clay-Calhoun understanding, passage remained "very uncertain," wrote Clay. The Kentuckian recognized that he had alienated some key allies with his proposal and that had "personal consequences and personal risks." While his actions might help him in the South, a greater identification with that region might damage him in the North; while his plan sought to "gain time" for protection, opponents to that proposal said he had sold them out to the demands of the Carolinians; while he gained support as a compromiser, he lost it for the specifics of the compromise. Yet, in principle, Clay had yielded some of his most cherished beliefs in order to save that issue about which he would not yield—the Union.[69]

As Clay explained later, he had two immediate objects: "One was to avert a Civil War. The other was to preserve the policy of protection." Clay could have added a third, longer-term objective that he sought—the decade-long cession of a divisive issue before the body politic. He sought to keep off the table any conflicts that might produce sectional diversity and disunion, in the hope that national harmony would grow in the absence of argument.[70]

Soon after Clay's address and Calhoun's comments, a Clay ally, the Kentuckian Robert Letcher, had moved to replace the Verplank bill with Clay's proposal. Daniel Webster, John Quincy Adams, and other Clay allies from New England opposed what Webster called "Clay's pretty little bill," as its creator had expected and feared. But the Great Pacificator of the Missouri Compromise again worked both sides of the aisles hard, and in the end the high-tariff Middle Atlantic states joined the low-tariff South in support of Clay, while Democrats voted with him two-to-one (as opposed to his own, New England–based party's two-to-one opposition vote). The Force Bill also passed and South Carolina symbolically nullified it, to no effect but for show. The tariff bill stood at center stage and its passage brought down the curtain on the crisis.[71]

As usual, statesman Clay paid a political price for his compromise. At one end of the spectrum, a New York congressman saw the "artfully executed" plan as the sacrificing of manufacturing "at the shrine of ambition." Another observer criticized the "calculating" Kentuckian for killing his own political child by joining Calhoun. At the other end of the spectrum, Calhoun would later term the compromise "a full surrender on the part of Clay" on the issue of protection, while Jackson viewed it as another Clay bargain designed to hurt him.[72]

In truth, Clay may well have understood that he might gain politically in the South from Jackson's course and his own. A contemporary indicated that "Henry Clay may yet be, South of the Potomac, what Andrew Jackson *has been*, the most popular man in the land." That outcome would be all right with Clay. But his talks, his correspondence, and his actions at the time offer no real support for that as a reason for his course. It seemed all about saving the Union. In words that could be echoed across generations, Clay noted that he would be criticized for his plan: "But what is a public man worth who will not sacrifice himself if necessary for the good of his country?"[73]

A more forgotten aspect of the Compromise of 1833 involved the issue of the sale of public lands. By 1830, one-tenth of all US revenue came from the funds generated by those transactions. The relatively moderate rates helped fill federal coffers. Opponents argued that the higher prices restricted settlement, and they sought reduced rates or even free land. Clay understood the hopes that had once driven people like him to the promise of the New West, but he had also seen the haphazard settlement of Kentucky and preferred a more orderly process. Besides, as he saw it, the present system had worked well. But Clay's words would not make him especially popular in developing western areas. Moreover, land-sale revenues had been an important source of funds to pay off the national debt, and soon that debt would be liquidated. Many western leaders argued that when that occurred, there would be no further need for high land prices, and thus sought low ones to encourage migration to their states. In that atmosphere, Jackson had called for reduced rates in a December 1832 message. Earlier, Clay had spoken against that policy, saying it would be "the squandering of the public domain." The land constituted "a common fund, purchased by the common blood, and as the common property of all." Later, he criticized Jacksonians for trying to sell a national resource "for a mess of pottage; to surrender it for a trifle—a mere nominal sum."[74]

Clay had grander visions. His Land Distribution Bill sought to use the land revenues that had once gone to pay off the debt for more constructive purposes. By keeping rates at the existing level, the continuing surplus funds could be distributed to the states, chiefly in proportion to their population. The states would then be required to use them for a specified set of purposes—education, internal improvements, debt reduction, and even African colonization. Clay had pushed hard for passage of his bill, but in January one observer saw little hope for it: "Congress is not ready." But that opinion underestimated the power of a Clay who was aroused and in action. The bill soon passed the Senate, and two months later it went through the House as well. That represented a major success for Clay, for it gave several key parts of his program the funding to go forward. As Clay had explained, that would settle the issue not only of the tariff but also of public lands and internal improvements—and, perhaps, slavery. Many also saw it as an important part of the evolving compromise—Jackson got his Force Bill, Calhoun got the principle of tariff reduction, Clay got his protective tariff for almost a decade and now his land bill, and the Union got its peace.[75]

But Jackson did not sign the land bill. By pocket veto—since Congress had passed it so late in the session, it could not vote to override—he thus killed Clay's best chance to get regular federal funding, through the states, for education, internal improvements, and colonization. To the Kentuckian, it was an act of betrayal, a rejection of a part of the compromise. A furious Henry Clay now had yet another reason to hate Andrew Jackson.[76]

Still, despite his extreme disappointment over the land bill, Clay felt that he had accomplished a great deal. Others agreed. A Delaware senator later noted how the crisis was put down "not by the sword or musket, not by proclamation: but by the will and sagacity of Henry Clay." Democrat Stephen A. Douglas, in the midst of another crisis, one that would break up the Union, pointed to Clay's actions of 1833 as an example of how, despite political differences, politicians could make common cause: "The voice of partizan strife was hushed in patriotic silence." In the end, the Nullification Crisis gave Clay what he most required after his recent defeat—a sense of worth. In November 1832, he had been filled with disappointment and had even contemplated leaving public life. But he had quickly thrown off such thoughts when he perceived that the country needed him. As a result, by the following March he had become widely known as the Great Compromiser, a man who had gained much respect. And those actions had once again made him a player in the presidential game.[77]

IO

Party

IN EARLY 1833, HENRY CLAY was absolutely furious. As Clay saw it, Jackson's "high-handed and daring violation of the Constitution," in the form of a pocket veto of Clay's land bill, stymied the will of the populace and undid a vital part of the compromise that had ended the recent crisis revolving around the tariff controversy. And, to the view of the Great Pacificator, Jackson had done so simply because he so despised Clay that he could not give him even that one victory. But Jackson's actions did not surprise the Kentuckian. After all, as Clay would soon see it, the chief executive was "ignorant, passionate, hypocritical, corrupt, and easily swayed by the basest men who surrounded him." Jackson had done nothing constructive in his public career or in his presidency itself: "He goes for destruction, universal destruction." Any ephemeral positive feelings that Clay held for his president as a result of Jackson's nationalist, unionist stance in the South Carolina crisis soon dissipated. The veto of the land bill reignited the war between the two men, and other events soon erected a new party as a vehicle for that opposition.[1]

One event that solidified some of that opposition involved Jackson's policy toward the American Indians. Before the 1832 election, the president's efforts on that subject had angered Clay; over the next two years, the chief executive's moves would infuriate him. In the Kentuckian's rhetoric, those actions were yet another example of Jackson's imperious, imperial, and dangerous tendencies.

Clay supported the cause of the American Indians for humanitarian reasons, not racial ones. These "poor children of the forest" should be treated with kindness, he said, for American actions had stripped them of many of life's rights and hopes. Clay did expect those "wretched people" to die out as a race eventually. But should the nation therefore hasten that action? Instead, the United States should protect the freedoms of this "miserable remnant" of a noble race, and should be guided by kindness and "every duty of religion, humanity, and magnanimity." In the case of South American rebels, Greek patriots, and black slaves, Clay had called for the nation to help the less fortunate, whether through official recognition of their efforts or support for colonization. Now, in the case of Indians, he appealed for protection of their remaining rights. Despite his pessimistic views about the eventual fate of the Indian nations, Clay took stands not shared by most of his contemporaries in the South and West. For a politician who sought more votes from those places, he could have said nothing and thus angered few. In those particular sections—where he needed to increase his support in any presidential race—Clay had little to gain for his eventual actions in support of Native Americans. Still, he took his stances openly and forcefully. It may have been bad politics, but it was good policy.[2]

Clay's open opposition had begun in earnest in 1830, with the passage of Jackson's Indian Removal Bill. With land-hungry settlers eagerly eyeing the rich lands of the native peoples in the South, Jackson chose to interpret the act in ways that would hasten the removal of Indians from those lands and relocate them to less desirable lands farther west. Politically, his popularity rose in the region. However, Clay found nothing good in the "abominable" law. He became the voice of these "helpless and unfortunate aborigines." This "foul and lasting stain" on American honor violated numerous established treaties with the Indians, emphasized Clay. Worse, it went against the principles of fair play. When the president then announced that he would refuse to enforce an 1802 treaty that protected Indian lands from intruders, that seemed to Clay just another example of Jackson's disregard for the law.[3]

That sentiment soon intensified. Originally the US Supreme Court had ruled that it had no jurisdiction over cases involving Indians because they were neither citizens nor foreign nations but, rather, a domestic, dependent nation. As a result, Georgia had continued to spread the blanket of its state laws over the contested lands within its borders. But in 1832, the court's ruling in *Worcester v. Georgia* declared the Cherokee a sovereign nation and proclaimed Georgia's actions unconstitutional. The state disregarded the ruling, a defiant act that, if not challenged, said Clay, would produce "a virtual dissolution of the union." In a sense, Georgia had nullified the decision, and Jackson had encouraged that action by refusing to enforce the court ruling. That presidential inaction would embolden the South Carolina nullifiers the same year. But more than that, it seemed to Clay that Jackson's Indian policy was the height of hypocrisy. To the president, Georgia's nullification was acceptable on the issue of Indian land, but South Carolina's on the tariff was not. Moreover, while many in the South opposed Clay's broad policies as an expansion of the powers of the national government, when it came to the Indians many of those same people favored the use of federal authority to force removal, in a kind of ethnic cleansing.[4]

Following his defeat in 1832, Clay grew even more vocal in his criticism. Two years later, he called Jackson's dereliction of duty and specific actions a "horrible grievance . . . inflicted upon the Indians, by that arbitrary policy which trampled upon treaties and the faith of the nation." After the Black Hawk War in the Northwest and the beginning of the process involving removal of the Cherokees in the South, Clay asserted in 1835 that the Indians experienced the same emotions, pleasures, and pains as all other humans. They had the universal rights to have happiness, to live under their own customs and laws, to control their own land. Instead, an unrepentant region and an unsupportive federal government had forced them to give up those dreams and hopes. Clay, motivated, he said, by feelings of grief, sorrow, and regret, and with tears in his eyes, forcefully presented the plight of the Indian: "Thrust out from human society, without the sympathies of any, and placed without the pale of common justice, who is there to protect him, or defend his rights?"[5]

That protector would not be the president of the United States, certainly. As one biographer noted, Jackson's "affection for the Indian about equaled his affection for Henry Clay." Eventually, the costs of the chief executive's policy resulted in the removal of some forty-six thousand Indians westward and the deaths of thousands of others in the later "Trail of Tears" (which ironically would run through Clay's Kentucky). But Jackson's actions in that regard made him more popular among many voters in the South and Northwest. While Clay's support of the Indian cause won him some accolades from the Cherokee nation and from mostly eastern reformers, it also would cost him dearly, especially when he sought the presidency again. Potential candidate Clay would have much work to do if he wanted to extend his electoral appeal.[6]

If Clay found Jackson's actions toward the Indians deeply distressing, he considered the president's fiscal plans completely deplorable. While the chief executive had vetoed the BUS charter in 1832, that institution still had nearly three years of existence, according to the law. Jackson's view of the BUS as evil and venal caused him to worry (with much justification) that the bank would try to use its considerable financial clout to defeat his party and eventually gain passage of a recharter bill. The president determined that the bank had to be stopped.

Advisors Amos Kendall and Francis P. Blair and Attorney General Roger Taney all suggested that future deposits of federal funds be halted, taking away the bank's core of cash and reducing its reserves. If that occurred and the BUS became a bank with little money, it soon would be a toothless threat. However, many other Jackson cabinet members and advisors opposed the move on the simple grounds that it seemed illegal or at least unwise. The existing law ordered the secretary of the treasury to deposit federal funds in the BUS so long as the bank was sound—and a congressional investigating committee had recently deemed it so. Thus, despite the veto, the statute stood until the charter expired. But the president proposed, and a new secretary of the treasury executed, what was termed the Removal of the Deposits. That seemingly unlawful taking of the federal monies from the BUS in itself caused great consternation. But when the administration then put the funds in favored and unregulated state banking institutions—"pet banks"—a political firestorm erupted. To a significant number of Americans, that action seemed to confirm Clay's long-held charge that Jackson sought to act illegally, unconstitutionally, and unilaterally to build a political machine to support his efforts.[7]

The furor over the Removal of the Deposits and the bestowing of those funds in state "pet banks" grew and grew. Numerous observers, including former Jackson supporters, questioned whether the president had the constitutional authority to take those actions. US senator Willie Mangum of North Carolina referred to the "tyrant" Jackson's insolence and arrogance of power. In a private letter, the president's own postmaster general, William T. Barry, who had earlier seen a banking crisis in his home state, now wrote of "the foolish plan of the Secretary of the Treasury . . . ; the consequent derangement of the currency and suffering of the community, are making deep and lasting impressions on the public mind." Not unexpectedly, Clay did not long remain silent about what he termed the financial delusions of the administration. Eventually attacking the growing "yoke of despotism," he pointed to the power of Jackson's cabal of "individuals, lean, lank, lantern-jawed, hollow-hearted, and with empty purses." Clay stressed how the "pet banks" (which increased from seven to over ninety) were in the pocket of the chief executive, willing to do his bidding, "always ready to fly to the succor of the source of their nourishment." By late December, he assumed the floor of Congress for a major speech in which he spared no words in taking the president to task.[8]

With an eye as usual on politics, Clay sought resolutions of censure for Jackson's activities: "We are . . . in the midst of a revolution, hitherto bloodless, but rapidly tending toward a total change of the pure republican character of the Government, and to the concentration of all power in the hands of one man." If something did not change, warned Clay, the presidency would soon be transformed into an elective monarchy. By his efforts to unite "the sword and the purse," Jackson would gain such power that "there will be but one will in the State"—his will. As it already stood, people spoke not in the "fearless tones of manly freemen, but in the cautious whispers of trembling slaves." Would the nation oppose Jackson and support "the bleeding constitution of my country"? Would it throw off the shackles of political despotism? Clay saw his motion for censure as the first step in answering those questions. The debate on that motion continued over the next three months.[9]

Meanwhile, the actions of BUS president Nicholas Biddle confirmed Jackson's concerns about the power of the monopoly. In January 1834, Biddle explained to an ally that nothing short of "the evidence of suffering abroad will produce any effect in Congress." Partially as a result of the Removal of the Deposits, but also as a deliberate policy to create stress on the system, the bank restricted its borrowing and called in loans. As the BUS president sarcastically stated a month later, "This worthy President thinks that because he has scalped Indians and imprisoned judges, he is to have his way with the Bank. He is mistaken." But Biddle erred again. The president would prevail—though at much political cost, as it turned out. Jackson had the power, and he seldom questioned the correctness of his course. In that same month, the chief executive wrote that Clay's reckless actions regarding censure resembled those of "a drunken man in a brothel" and would have no effect on him: "The Deposites [*sic*] will not be removed nor the Bank rechartered. This mamoth [*sic*] of power and corruption must die. . . . I have it chained, *the monster must perish*."[10]

Actions taken by the BUS did add to the financial uncertainty that produced a panic in 1834. Jackson had been right to fear its power. But the president's policies and those of the "pet banks" also helped induce the resulting economic distress. Some critics pointed out how politicians used the "pet banks" for their personal advantage, despite having criticized the

BUS for so doing. Richard M. Johnson, for example, approached one financial institution in Lexington and indicated he would support its application to receive federal largesse as a "pet bank" if it would provide him with a new line of needed credit. But more than that, the influx of federal funds to the favored state banks gave them surplus money, without any regulation or much oversight. Overexpansion and an overextension of credit caused inflation—prices rose 50 percent between 1830 and 1839—fueled speculation, and brought about affliction.[11]

Amid the rising financial crisis, Clay rose from his seat in the Senate, turned to Vice President Martin Van Buren, the presiding officer and Jackson's chosen successor, and dramatically appealed to him to tell his president "the actual condition of this bleeding country. Tell him it is nearly ruined and undone by the measures which he has . . . put into operation." Tell him, said Clay, of the falling property values, of the growing stagnation of business, of "the heart-rending wretchedness of thousands." Tell him, thundered Clay, about "the tears of helpless widows . . . and of unclad and unfed orphans," about how "the wicked counsels of unprincipled men" had misled him, about the ruinous course he had pursued. Unless the president reversed himself, Clay concluded, awful consequences would follow. Soon, the Senate passed Clay's resolutions of censure of the president—for the first and only time in history. A symbolic vote, it changed nothing in practice. But it did show that Jackson's Removal of the Deposits had coalesced the opposition into a more formal, organized foe. The Whig Party was forming.[12]

New York politico Thurlow Weed would later say that the Whig Party "had been in existence for years before its birth." In truth, the political embryo had long been growing; now the reaction to Jackson's actions brought into being a party. A mixed and sometimes motley crew came together in opposition to the president and his followers, with Clay as their chief. The core changed over time, but initially the new forces were a diverse combination that included such disparate groups as Clay nationalists and Calhoun secessionists, antislavery northerners and proslavery southerners, businessmen and planters, ex-anti-Masons and ex-Democrats, and more. Before, the leader of the opposition to Jackson had clearly been Henry Clay. But he had not been an organizer, outside of Congress, and the opposition forces had remained catatonic. But Jackson's spoils system, his vetoes, his Force Bill, his Indian policy, his Removal of the Deposits, and his use of "pet banks" now had almost forced the opposition to coalesce into a party. By 1832, some had suggested the name "Whigs" in opposition to King Andrew's

PLAIN SEWING DONE HERE

SYMPTOMS OF A LOCKED JAW

In the aftermath of Clay's successful congressional attempt to censure Jackson—in this case, by sewing up his mouth as a "cure for calumny," as a slip of paper in Clay's pocket reads—the long adversarial relationship between the two grew even worse. That division in large part defined the politics of the age. *Library of Congress, LC-DIG-ds-00856*

"Tories." Only slowly did others follow that lead. In a March 1834 speech, Clay first used the term, and it stuck. Whether or not he was present at the conception, Clay was certainly one of the political midwives assisting in the birth of what became the Second Party System. The fact that the resulting Whig coalition of convenience held together as long as it did, and achieved the successes it enjoyed, was due in no small part to the intellectual and political nourishment furnished by the man who formed the party's heart and soul—Henry Clay.[13]

Who, then, supported the two emerging parties, Democratic and Whig? Who voted for Clay or for Jackson? Some cast ballots for one party or another for more localized reasons—power politics, family ties, neighborhood rivalries, and regionalism. But others supported Whigs or Democrats on broader grounds—ethnic and cultural ones, racial reasons, economic matters, worldviews, and national issues. Obviously, exceptions exist to almost any statement regarding party composition in the antebellum period. What was true in one region or state or community might not be true in another. In some parts of the United States, substantial differences between the two forces might not exist; in other locales, very real divisions took place. Still, some generalizations do emerge. Some Whig voters, for example, voted as they did for cultural reasons. Local questions—that could expand to become national ones—might shape their Election Day responses. On some of those morally and religiously oriented matters, "the sober and discreet" Whigs gathered more of their votes from those with Protestant backgrounds in the British Isles, evangelical (pietistic) religious views, and Yankee reformer orientations.[14]

Conversely, Democrats garnered greater support from Catholics, Dutch-Germans and other immigrant groups, and more ritualistic religions. Yet, in that era of Bible politics, those party compositions held truer in the North than in the South, where other issues might seem more crucial. In other places as well, there were no strong divisions based on ethnic or religious grounds. Still, for some Whig and Democratic voters, such questions highly motivated their electoral behavior. Because Clay tended to view those moral issues as best left to individual consciences, rather than state or federal actions, that outlook sometimes put him at odds with many of the most vocal parts of his new party.[15]

Clay had more interest in the economic issues that induced many people to vote for his party. He identified with those voters, and his programs appealed more to them. Overall, his Whigs wanted to expand the market economy; many Democrats feared that such expansion would leave them behind. Whigs came more from cash-crop agricultural and growing manufacturing areas; dispossessed Americans, little touched by industry and commerce, tended to go with the Democrats. Voters in more prosperous areas, who had higher expectations, chose the Whigs; those in less successful places, who had but fleeting hopes and saw little promise for them in the American System, cast Democratic ballots. Whether in Virginia, whose Whigs lived in towns and commercial areas while Democrats operated tobacco farms, or in New Hampshire, where the party of Jackson gained its support more from poor farmers and the inhabitants of small villages while the Whigs dominated in larger towns, a person's view of the world and his place in it often led a voter to choose one party or the other.[16]

Once voters decided on an affiliation, most stayed in that party. In Virginia, for instance, some 90 percent of the voters never changed their party support from one election to another, even on local matters. But at times, certain voters did change parties. The particular issue might vary from place to place and from time to time—Jackson's Force Bill and subsequent strong executive action caused some states' rights southerners to go to the party of the nationalistic Clay, for example. The president's bank policies drove other southern planters, who operated in a world economy, into the arms of the Whigs. Jackson's Indian policy caused some northern reformers to join the party that thus included states' rights planters. Issues could matter.[17]

Others became Whigs for different reasons, mostly centered on matters of family or local politics. Power can create resentment and opposition. In some places, those on the political outside organized to get inside. In Maryland, anti-Jackson dissidents from a host of groups constituted the Whigs. In Kentucky, regional politics pushed people into one party— the peripheral areas went Democratic, the richer central core went Whig. In North Carolina, local rivalries and group identification operated; in Mississippi, family ties and county politics defined the political culture in many places.[18]

Class and occupational differences also emerged. The heart of Whiggery beat most strongly in the middle and upper classes of more prosperous, commercially oriented areas. Overall, a majority of wealthy businessmen, large planters, rising professionals, successful merchants, and growing manufacturers generally voted with the party of Clay's American System. The soul of the Democrats lay in yeoman farmers trying to eke out a life on a subsistence income in marginal, underdeveloped areas. Yet, even though the elite in Massachusetts and Michigan and the wealthiest of New York City were almost invariably Whigs, simple class divisions are misleading. The working class in urban areas, for example, tended to divide in its party allegiance, with mechanics, artisans, and manufacturing workers often casting their ballots for the Whig Party. And in the South, Whigs tended to be strongest in the high-slave areas, but slaveholding overall did not define the parties. In Arkansas and Kentucky, for example, slaveholders tended to be Whig, but in North Carolina and Virginia, the reverse occurred. Thus, while generally more of the wealthier might vote Whig and more of the poorest vote Democratic, many variations on that theme existed. All that meant that Clay had to appeal to a wide and diverse Whig base when he campaigned.[19]

More than class, it was basic belief systems and principles that divided Whigs and Democrats. The diverse Whig coalition of northern protectionists and southern free-traders, nationalists and nullifiers, manufacturers and laborers, slaveholders and antislavery advocates, wealthy and poor, reactionaries and reformers—all resulted from anti-Jackson anger to some degree.

On questions touching morality, including temperance, numerous Whigs sought a government that took a more active role in shaping the conduct of people. Perhaps motivated, in part, by a fear of the lower classes, many of the party faithful stressed the need for self-reform, self-control, and self-restraint. When they found such qualities absent in others, Whigs often sought to use the power of authority to wage "moral war" and shape individual behavior. At the extreme, that could produce a form of moral absolutism and some calls for cultural uniformity, or it could instead provide needed aid for the debilitated and the helpless. If Whigs could be morally obnoxious at times, Democrats could be morally callous at other times. If Whigs saw government as a positive force in such matters, Democrats viewed the people as the "best judges in their own affairs." If Whigs favored public charity, Democrats looked more to private aid. If Whigs wanted to move the debate on religious issues into the public sphere, Democrats pushed to further separate church and state. If Whigs said a paternalistic father knew best, Democrats answered that the populace knew best and should be left alone. But on some of those matters, the leader of the Whigs, the very human and not always self-controlled Henry Clay, often found himself closer to the Democrats than to members of his own party. That situation would sometimes put him into uncomfortable positions and cause him to lose support from those who saw such questions as the most important factors in their electoral decisions.[20]

On governmental questions, both parties portrayed themselves as the true patriotic offspring of the Revolutionary era's "old republicans," and their opposition as the enemy of republicanism. Both spoke disparagingly of corrupt Europe. Both advocated progress, as they envisioned it. But they held different views of where the power to govern resided and who should control it. Whigs saw suffrage as a privilege, while Democrats viewed it as a right (at least for white males). The party of Clay looked to Congress as the best spokesman for the people's will and as the proper forum to limit the tyranny of the executive; the party of Jackson regarded the president as the protector of the voter and his veto as the way to counter congressional attempts to defeat majority rule. Whigs considered parties more as a necessary evil, a way to combine to oppose presidential excesses; Democrats presented parties as a way to protect the people from powerful combinations inside and outside of government.[21]

Yet Whigs, while often seeking to preserve order, harmony, and stability in the existing social and political order, did not fear change per se. Whereas traditionalist Democrats opposed greater governmental power generally as a dangerous thing, and while they worried that the wealthy— "the dwellers in splendid city palaces, surrounded by all the luxuries of life," in James Buchanan's words—would dominate and control, Whigs expected a wise governance would be a progressive, positive force in improving American life. Activist Whigs thus wanted to guide national progress; limited-government Democrats wanted the country to find its own, best way. Clayites worried most about powerful presidents and dishonest officials; Democrats most feared corrupt corporations and aristocratic control. Whigs sought to protect the people from the executive tyranny that had "disrupted the balance of the constitution" as shown in secret cabals, a spoils system, the Force Bill, and bank wars, and a view that "the president can do no wrong"; Democrats looked to protect the people from the "power of associated wealth" as seen in the BUS, monopolies, and other concentrations of power. One party thus appealed to lasting principles, the other to the pragmatism of the people's will; one to cooperation, the other to individualism; one to insiders, the other to outsiders; one to trust, the other to distrust; one to America's hopes, the other to America's fears; one to optimism, the other to pessimism. Clay seldom doubted that, on all those options, he stood on the right side.[22]

When it came to specific programs, the party differences became even clearer. Support for or opposition to the tenets of Clay's American System party represented an obvious dividing line, but it went beyond that. Whigs, for example, supported a central, state-oriented school system to improve overall support and quality, whereas Democrats favored private, local-oriented educational institutions. The Whigs tended to be less racist but more nativist, the Democrats more white supremacist but supportive of immigrants. On the issue of territorial expansion, the party of Clay preferred to better connect America's people and their existing institutions, before expanding elsewhere. The opposition wanted to dispense individuals rapidly to relieve urban congestion and reduce class conflict. Devotees of the American System viewed the support of corporations as a sound method to spur economic growth, while the party of Jackson saw such institutions as a way of conferring special privilege on a favored few.

More broadly, Whigs pushed for a mixed economy; Democrats advocated for an agrarian-based one. The Whigs preferred enterprise; the Democrats wanted equalitarianism. In fact, the Whig advocacy of specific stands— what one Democrat called the "Abolitionist, Bankites, tarriffites, & Internal improvements party"—meant that with fewer programs to debate and divide them, the Democrats could more easily remain united. Clay held some beliefs that could move him, on occasion, closer to some Democratic positions, but his close identification with Whig Party programs would make it difficult for Clay the presidential candidate to articulate those variations.[23]

Overall, and with exceptions, Whigs took a more issue-oriented stance, Democrats a more party-oriented one. Clay supporters accepted the idea of planned progress, while Jackson allies wanted an unrestrained, laissez-faire world. Whigs sought increased opportunity; Democrats urged increased liberty. In the end, the party of Henry Clay envisioned using an interventionist government to transform the economy, promote growth, and better the lives of American citizens. It optimistically believed that a well-organized people would be virtuous, well-read, and well-behaved. To the Whigs, economic prosperity offered the best way to achieve equality, social mobility, and true freedom. Jacksonians, in turn, charged that less government, fewer rules, more local autonomy, and little federal involvement in daily life ensured real progress and freedom. For a time, those very basic difficulties would produce a furious, bitterly partisan political warfare, with Clay usually the party general in the middle of it all.[24]

Democrats and Whigs—like Jackson and Clay—often saw each other as vile, venal, and vindictive. Each feared that a victory by the other would soon bring ruin to the republic and death to free institutions. In short, they saw every election as crucial to the nation's future—and their own. In that search for votes, Democrats gained an initial advantage over the Whigs in that they organized better. An already established mass party, the well-disciplined Jacksonians better mobilized voters, especially among the rising numbers of new immigrants. In contrast, the more antiparty-oriented

Whigs saw party loyalty more as a threat to democracy than a protector of it. Such views also increased the likelihood that third parties could make more inroads in Whiggery, because that party's voters might shift loyalties easier. That would prove important in Clay's political career, as it had already with the Anti-Masonic vote in 1832.[25]

While Democrats occasionally complained of organizational weaknesses, more often Whig commentators lamented their disadvantage on that matter. Even before the upstart party's formation, Clay had observed that the Jackson forces "owe their success, mainly, to an efficient organization." A supporter in 1829 told his hero how the Jacksonians managed better and how "we *wait* for events to develope [*sic*]. . . . They *act* for the moment." In Ohio, editor Charles Hammond wrote words Clay likely did not enjoy reading: "Say what you will, these Jacksonians are excellent politicians." Some of the language may have been a too-ready response to a Whig defeat, but the core of the words rang true. In the early years of the new two-party system especially, the Democrats out-organized the Whigs. And throughout most of their life as a party, the Whigs were not as well-disciplined or as "well-drilled" as those imbued with "the Jackson Spirit." Part of that resulted from Whig antipathy to the "odious tyranny" of party discipline, part from the inability of Clay to organize a machine to match Jackson and his successors. Like other Whigs, Clay stressed the need for greater organization, but in practice, he more trusted the power of his personality. Often, Whigs—and their leader—faced an uphill electoral battle before the fight ever began.[26]

Part of the ability to organize centered on an important new device in the political toolbox of the Second Party System. Now a massive print effort sought to inform and convince an increasingly literate population. With newspapers critical to political organizations, each party worked to line up partisan editors who would render words of support to their side and heap calumnies of criticism on the other. Some new presses might specialize in foreign-language appeals, some in religious ones, but most took political sides. Congressmen used their postal franking benefit for political purposes by sending large numbers of newspapers across their districts—"I am astonished at the extent at which the franking principle is carried," wrote one. But with politics increasingly becoming the national sport, many voters eagerly spent their pennies to subscribe to a friendly newspaper. Party identification increasingly became a vital part of a person's being in antebellum America.[27]

The growth in party spirit and the emphasis on organization resulted in large voter turnouts. With almost constant electoral agitation, with the two parties nearly equal in strength in many locales, and with controversial issues or candidates constantly before them, the energized electorate surged to the polls in growing numbers during Clay's quest for the presidency. In 1840, more than 80 percent of the eligible voters cast ballots for president.[28]

Not all those votes were honestly given, however. With large bets placed on the outcomes, with patronage jobs at stake amid "the passion of office," with the certitude in their minds that one course represented evil and the other truth, some candidates or their supporters used fights and frauds to secure victory. An Election Day conflict in Lexington started when Jackson men tore down the hemp-stalk symbol of Henry Clay, an event that produced a hail of stones and numerous bloody noses. Such violence seemed all too commonplace across America. More than that, though, were the serious challenges to democracy. One politico told of receiving $200 "to assist in imparting light and knowledge among our brethren"; another related how two hundred voters had been illegally procured in just one precinct; yet another referred to a "floating vote" that moved from one place to another on Election Day, casting ballots in all; a fourth explained that to counter the thousands of Tennesseans who crossed the border to vote in Kentucky: "We shall have two or three thousand illegal ones of our own." And what held true in Clay's Kentucky could be multiplied across Clay's America. That reality of the electoral world worried Clay—rightly so, as he would find out the next time he received votes for president.[29]

Over his career, Clay would be called "the head of the Whig Party" or "its master spirit." And his will, his programs, and his oratory did help keep the diverse coalition together. Even though the party would change in composition and emphasis over the years, Clay remained its constant, its touchstone. He reminded Whiggery of why it existed as a party, beyond just opposition. But while many Americans acclaimed him as the party king, others did not accept his coronation so readily. They wanted to share or usurp the party throne. Daniel Webster stood as the leading regent-to-be.[30]

Five years younger than Clay, Webster had been born in 1782, in the same year as Calhoun, Van Buren, and Benton. Like the Kentuckian, Webster owed much of his success to his special speaking ability. But as the US senator from Massachusetts stood before an audience, this immensely talented man impressed even before he uttered a word. Most first noticed the massive head on the 5'10" frame and the "features set like stone." His swarthy, dark complexion and coal-black hair made him "Black Dan" to many. Then he would raise his head to look out at the crowd, and his brilliant, flashing, raven-like black eyes would smolder "like dull anthracite furnaces needing only to be blown." The erect, majestic bearing of Webster—making one congressman call him "the most intellectual looking man" he had ever seen—brought a sense of awe surrounding the "Godlike Daniel."[31]

Then the words came. Webster seldom spoke extemporaneously. Well-read and intelligent, he carefully planned his talks, memorized them—he had nearly total recall—and then heavily edited them before allowing their publication. In making final changes, he omitted whole sections he had spoken and added other, totally new parts. But if what people read often varied considerably from what had been said aloud, those talks, when given, still caused many to say that Webster's oratory was almost unmatched. The deep, solemn voice that uttered those words was clear, precise, and forceful. It thundered with eloquence. One newspaperman who heard him described how Webster was "a sort of human volcano, when the fires were kindled in those cavernous eyes, and he poured forth a torrent of burning words."[32]

Even those who admired the great man's many strengths, however, also recognized his many weaknesses. After Webster's death, the *North American Review* termed him "one of the largest and one of the weakest of men, of admirable genius and deplorable character." He was a great orator in Congress and an exceptional attorney before the Supreme Court; he also had a deadly flaw for an ambitious politician: he lacked humor and the human touch. While Webster could be warm and witty in the company of intimate friends, few people ever saw that side of his being in public. More often they observed a stern and somber man of overbearing manner and haughty demeanor. If a well-wisher thrust out a hand for Webster to shake, the senator often ignored it. In small gatherings, Webster's emotionally cold and taciturn attitude could repel strangers. John Quincy Adams, after spending an hour in conversation with his fellow Whig, characterized Webster's attitude the whole time as one of reserve. None of those descriptions would be applied to the convivial Clay. In fact, William Pitt Fessenden, who traveled with Webster, concluded, "If Daniel was but half as winning as either his wife or daughter, I would give more for his chances." Another contemporary noted that people admired Webster but did not love him. Those personality defects, when combined with his earlier support for the Federalists, his opposition to the War of 1812, and his modest antislavery sentiments, produced real hurdles in his search for national support.[33]

Others saw what in some ways represented more serious defects in one seeking the presidency: Webster lacked the ability and will to win. One political theorist told BUS president Nicholas Biddle, "Webster . . . has no judgment, no mercy, or boldness of character. The man has no personal courage & cannot succeed; he is made to be governed." Former cabinet member Louis McLane suggested that what courage the man from Massachusetts possesses "might be crammed into the socket of a fly's eye." When pressed on unpopular or controversial matters, Webster might equivocate so that Adams called him duplicitous; an opponent termed him "the Prince of hypocrites." But they also erred, for Webster could take courageous stands at times. Still, Clay often questioned his rival's truthfulness. In fact, while the Great Compromiser greatly admired Webster's oratorical abilities, he rarely mentioned his rival in correspondence. The sense remains that Clay simply did not respect Webster a great deal as either a politician or a statesman, did not consider him a particularly dependable congressional ally, and did not see him as a serious challenge to Clay's own presidential plans. Another of the Great Triumvirate, John C. Calhoun, offered perhaps the most damning analysis of his rival: "He has no faith in his own convictions; he can never be the head of a party. Though very superior in intellect to Mr. Clay, he lacks his moral courage and his strong convictions. . . . Mr. Clay will always be the head of the party and Mr. Webster will follow."[34]

Webster, of course, saw matters differently. He expected others to recognize his very real talents and his worth, and to support him accordingly. But while Webster certainly had ability and ambition, he lacked some of the energy and the resolve needed to achieve all his goals. Webster might work at farming at his estate of Marshfield, or at planning his talks, or at revising his orations, or at preparing for his well-paying legal cases, but most of the time he avoided hard congressional work such as creating legislation or forging compromises. As an early Clay biographer observed, "While Webster talked, Clay worked." Overall, the man from Massachusetts might rouse himself to positive action on some great controversy or diplomatic issue on occasion and gain great and deserved accolades, but more often Webster remained, as William H. Seward described him, a man of little enthusiasm. Whig John J. Crittenden explained it even more cruelly: "His ambition is a little too much mixed with *self-love*."[35]

To some Webster critics, however, self-love represented the least of Webster's faults, for they argued that he loved women, drink, and money even more. One congressman, for example, referred to Webster's "open and gross immorality," while another mentioned to his wife that one of his congressional colleagues had identified a woman who had passed by as Webster's ex-mistress. More common were the stories of Webster's intemperance, especially as he got older and more showed "the degeneration of his morals." Clay had such accounts bandied about him as well, but the Webster rumors seemingly have more substance. A diarist's reference to Webster's "love of brandy" might not mean much, but Kentuckian Thomas Marshall—an expert on the subject—reported that Webster had been "pretty high up in the wind" at a party he attended. A Tennessee representative told James K. Polk that at a recent gathering, "Webster got loudly drunk." Later, another remembered how Webster had slurred his words and muttered incoherently in a public speech. While Webster's drinking apparently had little impact on his work, it damaged his reputation.[36]

But more than any of those supposed moral failings, Webster's financial dealings raised questions about his character and ability to lead. As the editors of Webster's correspondence wrote, "He wanted very much to be President, but wanted also—perhaps even more—to amass a fortune." Yet Webster simply could not manage money. By the time of the panic of 1837, he had incurred a huge debt of some $200,000, mostly as a result of speculative ventures. Always needing funds, Webster accepted retainers, but then sometimes never commented on the cases sent him. Favors from businessmen, rumors of sales of offices when he sat in the cabinet, a $100,000 "endowment" from his friends to enable him to go back to Congress, money given to him or borrowed by him and never acknowledged or repaid—all those swirled around Webster. Near the end of Webster's life, an observer concluded, "He is a prostitute in morals. . . . Loose in money matters, tainted with fraud, fixed in profligacy, he is a living ulcer."[37]

Many of the contemporary attacks on Webster resulted from simple political propaganda, and later recollections may have been tainted by northern anger at his stand on the 1850 Compromise, but some also rang true. The "Godlike Daniel" seemed anything but divine. Yet, if Webster carried sizable political baggage in his attempts for the presidency, his exceptional talent and impressive oratory also produced a cadre of supporters, chiefly in New England. For that reason alone, Clay did not want to anger Webster or lose those allies. After all, for much of their public careers, the two had worked together closely. Over and over, Clay told public audiences and friends alike that he respected Webster and any supposed division did not represent a serious difficulty, only a temporary disagreement: "There is no permanent break between us." Clay spoke of Webster favorably, almost to prove to himself they remained allies. As the election of 1836 drew nearer,

Webster clearly wanted the new party's nomination. But Clay already had concerns about Webster's abilities and electability—and those concerns would affect Clay's own electability later.[38]

As it turned out, Clay mostly did the wrong things regarding the election of 1836. First, Clay wanted the new party to throw out the Democrats and reject Jackson's chosen successor, Martin Van Buren. But Clay saw early on that Jackson's political machine and the Whig's weak organization made his party's victory unlikely. Only months after his 1832 defeat, Clay told friends that he had "no disposition" to run in the next race unless he was absolutely certain of victory, but he doubted any Whig could win. Still, many party members expected him to seek that office and kept his name before the public. Nor did Clay quickly reject their efforts. He almost could never bring himself to say outright that he would not run, even when he did not expect to. Thus, popular journals continued to tell how this "master pilot" had taken the helm in the nation's time of need and had steered the ship of state around the shoals of nullification. But as Clay lieutenant Robert Letcher told Democrat James Buchanan in May 1835, "There is not a remote possibility of the Grand Hal running." In fact, in the quarter-century following Clay's first attempt at the presidency, the election of 1836 would be the only one in which he did not emerge as a serious candidate.[39]

That did not mean, however, that Clay would not have a major impact on the election. His real quandary was exactly what course of action he should take. The eventual Whig tactic of running three separate major candidates—Webster, William Henry Harrison, and US senator Hugh Lawson White—centered on one of them taking off and gaining enough support to win or, more likely, that they would together garner enough voters to prevent a Van Buren majority and force the election into the House once more. In that scenario, Webster would win votes in New England, Harrison in the Midwest, and White in the South. But that strategy put Clay in a multiple bind. If he supported any one of the three, he would anger the other two, and Clay needed to have as much support as possible if he wanted the presidency in 1840. But if he endorsed no one and remained above the fray, he risked antagonizing all three. Clay already opposed White, for he argued that the Tennessean's past ties to Jacksonianism and questionable commitment to the Whigs disqualified him. As for Harrison, Clay thought him honest and liked him personally, but considered the ex-general "weak, vain, and far inferior to Webster." Thus by 1835, the Kentuckian told several allies that of the three men, he had a strong preference for the man from

Massachusetts. But Clay usually added a disclaimer: "Mr. Webster does not take [with the voters]. . . . I am sorry for it; for I should greatly prefer him to either of the other two." Clay hesitated in making a formal endorsement.[40]

That inaction infuriated Webster. He needed the support of Clay and his cadre of allies to boost his fading campaign. With the Great Compromiser's refusal to end speculation on his own course of action and to come out openly for Webster, Black Dan bitterly fumed in early 1835, "It looks at present as if Mr. Clay would not do or say any thing." A month later, he complained, "Mr. Clay does nothing, and will do nothing." Clay's hesitancy to act centered on Webster's inability to generate much support on his own outside of New England. To be sure, the Kentuckian wanted Whig success, but he also sought to keep Webster's goodwill. Months before Election Day, Clay told Webster that he should leave the race because of his lack of support. That would concentrate voters on two candidates, not three. Webster refused to do so. Clay's suggestion, coupled with what Webster considered the Kentuckian's lukewarm support, irritated the proud man further. As Clay saw Whig hopes for victory becoming a bit brighter, he finally advised his friends to vote for Harrison, who had the most appeal nationally. That action alienated and infuriated Webster even more. In some ways, the widening breach between the two men would never be fully sealed.[41]

Overall, the Whigs did not do all that badly in their initial presidential race. The Democrats won the electoral vote 170–124 over the three Whig candidates, and carried fifteen of the twenty-five states. But a shift of some 2,000 votes in Pennsylvania would have given that populous state's 30 electoral votes to Harrison, throwing the election into the House once more. And Whigs lost three of the states by less than 3 percent of the vote. Hugh Lawson White also made major inroads in the formerly solid Jacksonian South, gaining 49 percent of the vote in that region. Some of that southern vote perhaps emanated from anger over the Democrats' choice as their candidate for vice president, the Kentuckian Richard M. Johnson. Stories of his mulatto mistress overrode any goodwill he gained from the election chant, "High-cockalorum rumpsey-dumpsey! Colonel Johnson killed Tecumseh!" In the end, the Democrats had won the presidency once more.[42]

Clay's actions in the race would prove to be a serious mistake on his part. Perhaps he and Webster would never have overcome their powerful presidential ambitions and become real allies. In any case, Webster openly blamed the Great Compromiser for his poor showing—he carried only his home state—and said that Clay had done him ill. As a result, when the next presidential race rolled around, and as Webster's electoral hopes grew fainter, he worked against Clay's possible nomination. Moreover, by supporting Harrison, who had done the best of the three candidates, Clay had elevated the former general as a much more viable option in 1840. And it all had been an unnecessary action. Clay had let his rising hopes of defeating the Jackson surrogate override his political instincts. Earlier, he had (correctly) expected the Whigs to lose, so he may have been better served politically either to endorse all or none. That would have still angered Webster, but at least Clay's neutrality would not have created as much resentment as did the Kentuckian's eventual support for the more electable Harrison. As it turned out, Clay's actions had produced an unexpectedly strong new challenge for 1840, and an unexpectedly angry old political rival. Both of those factors would prove important for Clay's future presidential ambitions.[43]

The 1836 campaign also had at least an indirect effect on Clay's future in two other ways. One involved Henry Clay's beloved Land Distribution Bill. After Jackson's veto in 1833, Clay had persisted in presenting it for passage. Increasingly, events made it harder to resist that call, for with the national debt paid off, the treasury's land sales and tariff revenues began producing surpluses. Those funds would go to the "pet banks," to be used mostly for speculative purposes rather than constructive ones. In December 1835, Clay had once more spoken eloquently and earnestly for his bill, noting that without the earlier veto, "What new channels of commerce and communication might have been opened! What industry stimulated, what labor rewarded! How many youthful minds might have received the blessings of education and knowledge!" Instead, the money went into the vaults of banks "for local, limited, and selfish uses," Clay said, enriching directors. But Clay's clear identification with that plan made it anathema to Democrats, even those who favored it. Calhoun rendered the proposal more palatable by introducing it as a quarterly loan, rather than a free distribution of funds. He also removed Clay's language that specified how the money would be spent. Still, in essence, the bill remained Clay's plan and he mobilized support for the measure. In that revised form, the Deposit and Distribution Act passed with bipartisan backing in June 1836. Because the states generally used the funds for schools or internal improvements, as Clay sought, and since the act took money out of the clutches of Jacksonian banks, Clay was pleased with the result. Jackson was not. But the president understood the strong support given the measure and reluctantly signed it. Of course, it did not hurt politically that the voters in the states were promised the succor of an infusion of funds.[44]

The second controversial action that election summer displeased Clay. It came after Congress adjourned and canceled some of the goodwill toward Jackson produced by the Distribution Act. In July 1836, the president ordered the issuance of a Specie Circular, which directed that, with some exceptions, federal land purchases must be made in gold or silver. Whether by design or not, the circular reduced public land sales (and correspondingly reduced the amount of money available to the just-passed Distribution Act). But it also drained specie from the East, caused others to hoard their metal coinage, thus reducing the funds available for loans, and created doubts about the soundness of the paper money issued by "pet banks." Clay openly criticized it and soon warned that it might cause a depression. In fact, by 1837 the growing pressure on the banking community produced a bipartisan attempt to relieve the problem, but Jackson pocket-vetoed the act just days before he left office. Clay considered the Specie Circular a serious mistake and saw the veto as compounding the error.[45]

Then, in the last days of the administration, the Jacksonian majority in Congress did something that shocked even some of their allies, while infuriating Clay and the Whigs. The earlier act of censure against Jackson remained on the books. A proud Andrew Jackson saw it as a continuing stain on his honor, an affront to his presidency. Accordingly, his party moved to remove the censure physically from the official record. The subsequent Expunging Resolution brought forth furious vitriol from Clay: "Must we blot, deface, and mutilate the records of the country" in order simply to satisfy the ambition and will of one man? If the act is to be done, he said, go to the people and tell them how the chief executive could "overawe Congress, trample down the Constitution, and raze every bulwark of freedom." But Clay's words went for naught. Party won out. After passage of the resolution, Whigs walked out before the journal was expunged. The next day, Clay told an ally, "The Senate is no longer a place for any decent man." Noting that the action occurred at night, he concluded, "The darkness of the deed and of the house were well suited to each other."

At least the end of the Jackson presidency was near. Perhaps Martin Van Buren would be better. After all, even though the incoming chief executive might follow what were, to Clay's view, misguided politics, and even though he would be viewed by some as Jackson's puppet, Van Buren did not raise the same fears of executive usurpation as did Jackson. The New Yorker might be a shrewd politician, but he was not a potential dictator. The Kentuckian expected to be able to work with him, even as he distrusted his politics.[46]

As it turned out, the Van Buren presidency and the panic of 1837 began almost simultaneously. That fact would immediately hamper Van Buren and quickly influence the Whigs' options—and Clay's actions—regarding the next presidential race. The Whigs made it clear who they held responsible for the depression that started in 1837. They pointed to the failed policies of Andrew Jackson and the Democrats as the reason for the distress that increasingly gripped the nation: "Truly, truly, it may be said, sir, that the evil which General Jackson did lives after him." A decade and a half later, a journal noted of Van Buren's presidency that "Jackson had sown the wind—he was to reap the whirl-wind." Clay hardly hesitated to cast blame. In truth, the depression had resulted from a series of factors, many of them not Jackson's fault. Crop prices had fallen, the balance of trade had worsened, some overseas firms had failed, and the British had demanded payment in specie. But to many Americans, the Jackson policies seemed a clear, easily understood reason for the hard times. Clay underscored how Jackson's moves had mostly spurred too-easy credit from "pet banks," an excessive issuance of paper currency, speculative ventures, and then, later, a contraction of funds.

Without the wise guiding hand of the BUS, said its one-time attorney, the arbitrary rule of Andrew Jackson produced polices that resulted in distress and depression. And the Democratic policy of limited government now seemed, in such hard times, callous and uncaring. Clay cited his opposition's "cold and heartless insensibility to the suffering of the bleeding people." Moreover, the failed policies of Jackson had caused the suspension of the distribution to the states, since a surplus no longer existed. One of Clay's chief programs had ceased as a result. But Clay also saw clearly that the Whigs had an opportunity to present their interventionist economic policy—his policy—to a more accepting nation, one desperately seeking a way out of their economic prison. The Whigs could be viewed as the group best able to handle the country's financial fortunes, the party of hope and prosperity. All that boded extremely well for the man who hoped to be the party nominee for president in 1840. Clay fully expected that he would be the person who would pull the country out of its economic morass and lead the Whigs to victory.[47]

11

Presidential Candidate III

IN 1839, HENRY CLAY FIRMLY stated, "I would rather be right than be president." But would he be either as he sought that office?[1]

Clay dearly wanted to be the nation's leader. Still, in the two years leading up to the Whig nominating convention for the 1840 election, Senator Clay did not dodge controversial issues; rather, he continued to take stands that could potentially cost him votes. One of those contentious matters involved preemption. Many Democrats favored the principle that "squatters" who settled on unsold public lands were conquerors of the wilderness and deserved the preemptive right to purchase those lands first when they were put up for sale. Many Whigs—and especially Clay—saw such squatters as wilderness trespassers who operated outside the law. Whereas Clay kinsman turned opposition leader Thomas Hart Benton, "the Political Lungs of Missouri," wanted to reduce the sale price on land not claimed, Clay wanted to restrict sales, keep prices moderately high, and use that revenue for redistribution to all the states to fund American System–style projects. If preemption passed, Clay predicted, "The national domain is gone. . . . It will require a search warrant . . . to find any part of it." While his strong opposition found support in the Eastern Seaboard states, North and South, where some citizens feared cheap land prices would lure away their workers and hasten their area's depopulation, Clay's role in the controversy hurt him elsewhere. First, as a correspondent told John J. Crittenden, even though Clay's policy might be right, it would hurt him in the West in the upcoming election. Second, in the end, the popular preemptive act passed, and that left Clay again on the losing side.[2]

Clay lost that fight, but his overall political record in the two years leading up to the convention was more mixed. He and his party did have success in beating back the new president's attempts to change the American financial system. The "pet banks" had not worked and, in fact, had probably harmed the US economy. To replace them, President Martin Van Buren proposed an independent treasury that would put banking functions under the US Treasury or, in a later plan, a system of sub-treasury federal banks to hold and distribute monies. Most Whigs and some conservative Democrats agreed with a Virginia governor who called that plan "perfect nonsense." They argued that keeping federal funds locked up in government vaults would restrict the flow of credit and hinder recovery. Clay made the matter clear. How could Democrats call the BUS unconstitutional but now want to create a national banking system? Turning to a favorite theme, he declared: "We are all—People—States—Union—Banks, bound up and interwoven together, united in fortune and destiny." Because of those connections, do not make war on banks, he counseled, for if you do, "You wage war upon the people of the United States."[3]

Whig opposition led by Clay, and the continued debate and division within the Democratic Party, caused the defeat of Van Buren's independent treasury in 1837. Clay also successfully introduced a joint resolution in 1838 that basically ended Jackson's "hard money" Specie Circular as established policy. The Kentuckian saw those victories as the first step down the road toward what he still envisioned as the best answer to federal fiscal woes—a new BUS.

But those Clay successes on national fiscal policy brought with them a political cost. John C. Calhoun ended his alliance with the Whigs. The one-time Democrat had been a reluctant ally at best, and he had been uneasy for some time, not only with the party's "federal consolidation" philosophy and its latent antislavery but also with Clay's obvious ascendancy as party leader. Now, on the issue of the sub-treasury plan, Calhoun abandoned the party and supported Van Buren, a man he had once termed a Judas and a Janus. A surprised Clay called Calhoun's speech in defense of the president typical for the South Carolinian: "plausible, abstract, metaphysical, and generalizing." And, Clay noted (as he continued to brand Calhoun as impractical), the words seemed little connected to the real-world "business of human life." Other

Whigs termed Calhoun's party switch an act of betrayal, produced by personal ambition. Somewhat ironically, John Quincy Adams referred to Calhoun's "bargain and sale of himself," while a North Carolinian accurately predicted that Van Buren would rue the day he allied with the mercurial man and the nullifiers: "They live to destroy." Nevertheless, Calhoun's actions meant another talented leader stood in opposition to Clay's politics and policies. For a few brief years, the Great Triumvirate had worked together in opposition to Jackson. Now, one by one, they had split from the Great Compromiser and stood in either silent or open opposition. It all boded ill for Clay's presidential ambitions.[4]

The break also now allowed Calhoun to vent the full fury of his frustrations with one-time cohort Clay. As the two congressional giants bandied and battled on a variety of issues, the smoldering anger could not be kept down. When an irate Clay chastised Calhoun on the floor of the Senate for deserting to the enemy, the South Carolinian responded that Clay set the standard for selling out, via the "corrupt bargain." In 1840, the break became especially clear when an indignant Clay once more noted the alliance of old enemies Van Buren and Calhoun and mentioned that without Clay's help during the Compromise of 1833, Calhoun might not even be in Congress now. An angry Calhoun shouted that Clay had needed the compromise, not he, and that he, not Clay, had dominated the action: "Events had placed him [Clay] flat on his back. . . . I had the mastery over him on the occasion." Clay quickly rose to ridicule in powerful oratory Calhoun's version of history: "The Senator from South Carolina said that [I] was flat on [my] back, and that he was my master. Sir, I would not own him as my slave. He my master! And I controlled by him! . . . Why, sir, I glorified in my strength." Calhoun, not he, had created the crisis, said Clay; Calhoun, not he, had needed it to get out of the "unwise and dangerous" situation he had produced. But he, not Calhoun, had pushed through the Compromise; he, not Calhoun, had ended the confrontation, had saved the Union, and had performed his duty. As cheers from the Senate galley greeted Clay's words, an even more embittered Calhoun plotted revenge.[5]

Henry Clay was vulnerable on the slavery issue. Calhoun used that knowledge to try to inflict serious political damage on his rival. In that fight, the South Carolinian had a decided advantage, for he had only one position—the proslavery one—to defend. So did Webster at the other extreme. But Clay tried to live in both the slavery and antislavery worlds. That stance left Clay open to attacks from all sides. Calhoun did not think a middle ground existed when it came to the slavery issue and he continually tried to force Clay to choose one side or the other, thereby hurting Clay's presidential hopes in one of the sections.[6]

A major skirmish in those developing slavery wars concerned the right of individuals to petition Congress for the restriction or abolition of slavery. Southern congressmen, led by Calhoun, with their region and their system under attack, asked the House and Senate to reject the petitions automatically, without discussion or referral to a committee. What became known as the Gag Rule would silence the antislavery voices. The issue became a test case. Calhoun intoned that "we must meet the enemy on the frontier; on the question of receiving, we must secure that important pass—it is our Thermopylae!"[7]

In 1836, Henry Clay found himself among the forces attacking the southern position. Trying to take a moderate stance, he used words and actions that—to southern eyes—still placed him in the enemy's antislavery camp. Clay stressed that the Constitution guaranteed the right of petition as "sacred," and as such, the appeals should be read and then sent to a committee for action or nonaction. "What question," he asked, "is there in human affairs so weak or so strong, that it cannot be approached by argument or reason?" Eventually, his Senate rejected both the Calhoun and the Clay plans and, in a compromise, agreed to accept the petitions but then permanently table them without discussion. Upset, Clay continued to criticize the Gag Rule over the next several years. But each time he took that stand, many in the South recoiled.[8]

Calhoun's ongoing offensive eventually took Clay down another political road, one that he did not want to travel and one with even more serious consequences for his presidential ambitions. The battle royal started in January 1838 and continued for more than a year after Calhoun introduced a set of six resolutions, which if adopted would commit the Senate to a proslavery position. Clay understood the move as an attempt by Calhoun to advance his own political future by creating an atmosphere favorable to a sectional party, led by the South Carolinian. Clay also immediately saw Calhoun's proposal as a trap. If Clay voted for or against the resolutions, he would anger one or the other section. Calling the debate abstract and unneeded, "the most unprofatable [sic] discussion that ever engrossed the attention of a deliberative body," Clay nevertheless took the bait that Calhoun dangled before him. In February 1839—only months before his party's presidential nominating convention—Clay made the fateful decision to address the issue.[9]

By then, Clay apparently had adopted a southern strategy regarding the upcoming election. He had not done well in that region in 1824 and 1832. Though a slaveholder, he uttered antislavery pronouncements, opposed the Gag Rule, and supported colonization—actions that made him suspect to many slaveholding southerners. Calhoun had led the effort to depict Clay as "soft" on slavery. And as William Preston of South Carolina wrote in 1837 regarding Clay's presidential chances, "There is already a battery opened against him in the South." A Floridian noted in 1839 that Clay's continuous actions regarding the petition issue had not helped him: "The people of the South are not satisfied with the high and noble stand he has taken as consideration of his principles. They wish him to hunt down the abolitionist, like a bloodhound. They wish him to take a stand against the reception of the petitions. . . . He will do right—let consequences be what they may." However, Clay's role in the Compromise of 1833, the growing prominence of the Whig Party in the South, and the presence of northerner Van Buren as the presumptive Democratic nominee offered some hope that Clay might run better in the region in 1840. Given his past poor history in the South, and the possibilities that now lay before him, Clay moved closer to the southern position in his new pronouncements on slavery. But if he made himself more electable in the South, he would lose some crucial northern support—support he would need to get the party's nomination.[10]

With that as background, on February 7, 1839, Clay rose to address the Senate and, in a sense, the nation. He knew full well the potential dangers in the course he was getting ready to take. He told an ally that he made the talk "after full deliberation. I expected it would encourage the Ultras more than ever against me." Clay had discussed his address with friends and when one pointed out the possible pitfalls, it had been then that Clay made his comment that he would rather be right than be president. But Clay was wrong in his words, and that error may have cost him the presidency in 1840.[11]

Now, in early 1839, Clay emphasized earlier themes, but he used language that would further alienate some northern antislavery supporters. He reiterated that slavery remained a state issue, that Congress had no power at present to regulate the interstate slave trade, and that slavery could be abolished in the District of Columbia, but that it was not expedient to do so. The most controversial part of that February talk involved what he said regarding the "ultra Abolitionists" of the North. To Clay, their "reckless" pursuit of immediate abolition risked civil war. It seemed as if Clay now blamed abolitionists more than proslavery extremists for the growing divide in America. And by emphasizing that emancipation without compensation would be an unconstitutional seizure of property, by stressing that immediate abolition would produce race warfare, by attacking abolitionists' "mad and fatal course" as one that had set back the antislavery cause, Clay had forsaken the moral high ground and had cultivated the safer soil of gradualism and legalism. One unfortunate line in his talk would haunt him politically among abolitionists the rest of his career. After decrying the "unnatural amalgamation" of the races and repeating his general opposition to slavery, Clay declared: "I prefer the liberty of my own country to that of any other people, and the liberty of my race to that of any other race."[12]

Perhaps Clay thought he had nothing to lose by his attacks on abolitionists. After all, abolitionist Lewis Tappan had told him only months before that no abolitionist would vote for a slaveholder, even a distinguished one with antislavery tendencies. Perhaps Clay thought the gains in the South would more than offset any losses in the North. Perhaps he truly feared that abolitionism represented as great a threat to the Union as proslavery radicalism. Perhaps he simply wanted to reestablish his bona fides in the South, to be a candidate for all sections. Or perhaps Calhoun's strategy regarding Clay had worked. Perhaps Clay had compromised too often and had lost support from both extremes. Whatever the reason, Clay had taken a stand and would have to live with the political ramifications of that decision.[13]

As expected, many southerners, including Calhoun, praised Clay's stance. But others in the South cautioned that Clay had just masked his true antislavery feelings. On the other side of the argument, some northerners noted that Clay had said that if he were in the Deep South, surrounded by large numbers of slaves, he would probably not favor emancipation at any cost. The harshest reaction, reflecting abolitionist views, came from the *New York Colored American*. After Clay's speech, the paper termed Clay "a great advocate of human liberty in talk, and a human enslaver in practice." This great republican in theory "trampled on men's breasts and neck with his tyrant feet," and it declared him "a monstrous outrage on humanity."[14]

At that time, Clay's America was a nation in flux. A transportation revolution, a communications revolution, and a market revolution all transformed his antebellum world. Old parties had died, new ones had been born, and others had changed. Religions rose, denominations split, and all were altered. Various "isms" emerged; different views regarding the world and America's place in it appeared; fresh ideologies and theories competed for attention. But through all the change, one institution seemed impervious to major transformation: slavery. And that fact devoured Clay's hopes for the presidency.

Clay had needed to take some bold steps in early 1839, for his campaign seemed to be faltering. Whether his anti-abolitionist speech represented the best choice is doubtful. But the electoral picture for Henry Clay had changed from a year earlier, when James K. Polk had confidently written that "you may put it down as certain that Clay is to be . . . the Federal [Whig] candidate." Two months after that, Prince Hal had told his son and others that he expected to be elected. But the fall state elections of 1838—in essence, the public opinion polls of the day—did not favor his party. Privately, a despondent Clay considered withdrawing. Publicly, others raised doubts about Clay's electability. He began to hear whispers that grew into shouts from those who opposed him, in his party and in Democratic circles. They cried out that the "worn out" Clay had lost twice and would not win now, that the opposition of abolitionists and anti-Masons meant he would not carry the North, that his land policy would doom him in the West, that his antislavery sympathies would cost him the South. Furthermore, his critics charged, his "odious" American System would drive away states' rights advocates, his supposed moral transgressions (including his role in the recent Graves duel) would hurt him with all who considered a person's moral fitness important for the presidency, and the "oft-refuted charge of bargain, intrigue, and management" would continue to damage him. Pessimists began to doubt Clay. But by the middle of 1839, the sixty-two-year-old still felt confident of being nominated, then elected. After all, Van Buren was vulnerable on many counts—his fiscal plans, several scandals, the economy, and more. But Whigs still worried. As a New York paper warned, "We must be sure Mr. Clay can be elected, or nominate somebody else."[15]

That thinking delighted the other two chief challengers at the time— Daniel Webster and William Henry Harrison. One of his two rivals did not particularly concern Clay. He did not expect Webster to beat him for the nomination, for the man from Massachusetts still had few allies south of the Mason-Dixon line and little strength outside of New England. And by early 1839, Webster also saw that the political handwriting on the wall did not include his name. He told allies that the Whigs could not win, that he would withdraw, that Clay could not gain the presidency, and that the party should "fall back on Genl. H." as their choice. Clearly, residual resentment remained over Clay's course regarding Webster in 1836. While Webster physically removed himself from the action by taking an extended European trip starting in May 1839, he did not formally withdraw until a month later, and even then his allies' actions made it obvious that their hero wanted them to oppose Clay at every stage.[16]

Webster's withdrawal seemed to leave Harrison as the only contender standing. But if Clay had correctly seen Webster as not a serious threat, he also rightly recognized that the man he had eventually endorsed in 1836—Harrison—presented a more daunting challenge. First, Harrison's campaign was partly managed by a man related to Clay by marriage—fellow Kentuckian Charles Stewart Todd. Attorney Todd, another one-time Clay supporter, now ran Harrison's race, wrote editorials, penned a campaign biography, and operated behind the scenes for his hero in homespun. In all those endeavors, he stressed Harrison's moral rectitude and military background. Both attributes continued to be important to voters. Although the nation had by now accepted parties as a legitimate part of the political process, that did not necessarily mean the voters wanted career politicians as their presidents. Many still yearned for the Jeffersonian ideal of a simple, virtuous republic, governed by selfless men above the fray. In the Second Party System, voters thus often turned to military men who seemed on the surface to eschew politics—Jackson, Harrison, Zachary Taylor, among them. As John Tyler had written in 1832, "The day is rapidly approaching when an *ounce of lead* will, in truth, be worth more than a pound of sense."[17]

Clay had already felt the sting of that outlook in his clashes with Jackson, and he did not underestimate Harrison's strengths in that arena. He had worked well with Harrison during the War of 1812, and the two men respected each other. Over the years since, Harrison had built a solid reputation as a man untainted by political infighting. At the end of 1838, several observers had concluded that Harrison's star was rising, Clay's was declining. Yet Clay also recognized that Harrison had little appeal in the South, limited charisma, and few accomplishments. Some commentators still considered a Harrison nomination out of the question.[18]

Just as the race for the Whig nomination seemed to have narrowed to two men, an unexpected new candidate emerged. He was another general, a man one paper said "has not one particle of experience in civil government," a person who rather disingenuously wrote that he was "perfectly indifferent" to the presidency and had tried to remain out of the contest until the populace demanded it. Though a huge man physically, and one who usually wore his full-dress uniform and medals to impress, General Winfield Scott did not so impress some others. Diarist George Templeton Strong, after a dinner party they both attended, penned a devastating characterization of Scott: "Any man who should listen for half an hour to the

general's bad French and flat jokes, his tedious egotisms, his agonizing ped-
antries of connoisseurship in wine and cookery, his insipid, inflated gallant-
ries, and his painful exhibitions of suspicious conceit would pronounce him
the smallest and feeblest of created men." Yet, Strong noted that this "silly
giant, a euphuistic Goliath" also had proven to be an excellent soldier: "His
faults . . . are chiefly vanity, arbitrary disposition, and an uncertain temper."
In reality, while some of General Scott's handlers hoped he would "take off"
in the race, others more realistically wanted him to slow the Clay advance
and lure pro-Clay delegates away from the Great Compromiser in regions
where Harrison had little support. As one contemporary author concluded
later, "Scott was used simply as a decoy-duck—nothing more." Political
bosses like Thurlow Weed used Scott's race for their own ends—the defeat
of Clay.[19]

By the summer of 1839, Clay observed the political landscape as he decided on his next course of action. He had certainly lost some support,
partly due to the poor Whig showing in the previous state elections.
Harrison had benefited from that to a degree, but still seemed in second
place. But Scott's entrance into the political games had complicated matters,
making a convention majority harder to achieve. And so, despite his earlier statements that he would take no trips and would follow "a position
of perfect passiveness" regarding public pronouncements, Clay made the
decision to tour the North. Perhaps that simply represented the other side of
a deliberate strategy—first to gain strength in the South through his anti-
abolitionist speech, then to secure the North with a triumphant procession.
Possibly he saw instead a need to visit the region to counter the backlash in
some places to his anti-abolitionist speech. Or perchance, he wanted to use
the opportunity to derail or slow the Scott candidacy. For whatever reason,
he decided to go. Of course, in the atmosphere of the time, his trip could
not be obviously political, for candidates should not appear to be so ambitious or grasping for the office. He warned an ally to avoid the appearance
of "all electioneering." But representatives of various groups would unfail-
ingly invite him to address them, in various cities, and good manners obviously dictated that he honor some of those requests. Restricted by tradition
from campaigning once nominated, Clay would use his upcoming trip basically to kick off his run for the White House.[20]

A few years earlier, John Quincy Adams had grumbled to his diary that
"the fashion of peddling for popularity by travelling round the country
gathering crowds together, hawking for public dinners, and spouting empty
speeches, is growing into high fashion. . . . Mr. Clay has mounted that

hobby often, and rides him very hard." Now Clay sought to follow that path to victory, and he made New York State the focus of his attention. By mid-July, Clay had reached Saratoga, where to his surprise he found himself and a vacationing Van Buren in the same hotel. In passing each other in a narrow hall, the portly president playfully remarked to his friendly and more slender opponent, "I hope I do not obstruct your way." To which Clay quickly replied, "Not here certainly." In his attempt to block Van Buren's further political advancement, Clay then traveled to New York City, Philadelphia, and Baltimore before making his way home in September.[21]

Large crowds had welcomed him everywhere he went. At Saratoga, a procession of four hundred horsemen accompanied his carriage to the front of his hotel, where cannon thundered in welcome. Some in the crowd of over four thousand—five hundred of them women waving handkerchiefs—unbuckled the horses and pulled the carriage up the hotel steps, where Clay then addressed the multitude. In New York City, the size of the welcome brought a journalist to gush, "First, there was a crowd, then again there was a crowd, and on top of that there was another crowd, . . . till half New York seemed one loud hurrah!" He thought the mile-and-a-half-long procession of some two hundred carriages, several hundred horsemen, and many thousand pedestrians the largest ever seen in the city. In the course of those travels, Clay had also made at least four speeches, as well as briefer comments in other places. Warm responses followed.[22]

Of course, the Democratic press sought to downplay his welcome in each place. In New York City, journalists wrote that "the ultras of all parties are opposed to him" and that "people get tired of old politicians almost as much as they do of old women." They predicted that ungrateful Whigs would toss Clay aside for a lesser man. Similarly, in Philadelphia, the opposition press subtly attempted to emphasize Clay's age versus the younger (by five years) Martin Van Buren, by pointing out how Clay "was completely fagged out" by the time he arrived. This man of "jaded looks," they correctly noted, "is more successful in eliciting shouts than obtaining votes." But the negativism of those reports could not obscure the fact that Clay had received enthusiastic welcomes everywhere he went. He needed that adulation to revive his spirits and his race. Yet, as would often be the case in such trips, the atmosphere deluded Clay into thinking he had more support than he did.[23]

Clay had another reason for making his trip, one beyond speaking and campaigning. He wanted to talk privately with New York Whig leaders Governor William H. Seward and editor Thurlow Weed to ascertain their stands and the situation in the state. Peter Porter, Clay's own point man in New York, had informed him a few months before that Weed and Seward were "warmly & zealously" for Clay. But circulating rumors seemed to suggest otherwise. Clay sought to determine where he stood with the two. A telltale warning that things might be amiss came when Seward tried mightily to avoid meeting Clay. A Democrat in Saratoga correctly analyzed the situation better than Clay or Porter, when he told James K. Polk that the governor "will go strongly and in good faith for the nomination of Genl. Scott." Later another New Yorker called Seward "the master spirit" against Clay in the state.[24]

But the real master of the opposition was the more powerful member of the duo, Thurlow Weed. Younger than Clay by two decades, the tall, stooped, and slow-speaking Weed had risen from meager means to become editor of an influential Rochester newspaper. Once his party had gained power, he became state printer and reportedly grew quite wealthy. A behind-the-scenes political boss, the "Wizard of the Lobby" used such tactics in ways that caused opponents to label him instead the "Lucifer of the Lobby." This man of contradictions, this person of "warm attachments and bitter hates," this journalist without ambition "save the ambition of possessing power and swaying men," had gotten Clay supporters to back his man Seward in the governor's race the year before, with the apparent understanding by them that, in exchange, Weed would back Clay for president. By 1839, things had changed, though. Weed now saw Harrison as the best chance for a Whig victory, but he also found that the general had little support in New York. How, then, could Weed keep Clay from gaining the state's delegates and from getting the nomination? The shrewdly manipulative man put Scott's name in the canvass in order, Weed said, "to keep New York away from Clay" and prevent the Kentuckian from securing a first-ballot convention victory.[25]

Clay seemed almost unaware or unbelieving that Weed would do that. But as one paper noted, Weed at least "was an honest hater." When he and Clay met at Saratoga during Prince Hal's tour, the editor clearly spelled out his belief that Clay's Masonic, slaveholding, and pro-bank background meant that he could not carry New York and could not win. Actually, that may not have been a correct analysis, and Weed may have known that. But it served his purpose well enough. Weed later admitted his role in president-making in the 1840 race. But Clay only slowly perceived that. When rumors circulated just before the convention (rumors probably instigated by Weed) that Clay would withdraw—a tactic used before with success against

Clay—an angry candidate cluelessly wrote Weed ally Seward and asked him to issue a denial of the rumor. Thus, while Weed worked for Scott and while Todd managed Harrison's campaign, Clay continued to act as his own campaign manager.[26]

The timing of Clay's tour was not accidental. Whigs had decided to hold their convention almost a year before the presidential election and so would be meeting only some three months after his tour, on December 4, 1839—very early in the game. And, despite all the problems, all the machinations, all the tours taken, the date of the convention may well have been one of the most crucial factors in Clay's failed search for the presidency in 1840.

First, the 1839 fall elections again did not favor Clay's party, and that caused some regulars to question whether the Whigs could win with him. Almost everyone could agree that Clay was the most qualified Whig candidate, but was he the most electable? Actually, had the Whigs met in the middle of the next year, as the Democrats did, their political crystal ball would have yielded many more hopes for victory, no matter who led the ticket. The 1840 races went Whig for the most part.[27]

Those votes likely reflected the nation's changing economic picture. When the Whigs met in December 1839, the business climate had seemed to be improving. But just before the convention, in a trend not yet clearly seen, the economy began to sink again. By mid-1840, when Webster returned to America, he now noted that the fall in prices and the decline in business made Whigs more enthusiastic about their chances. For he and other party members recognized that in the short term, swing voters and new members of the electorate tended to blame the party in power—the Democrats—for the situation. Thus, had the Whigs met six months later, in a more typical timing, the economic climate would have made them much more certain of victory with a Clay candidacy.[28]

But as the convention date drew nearer, Clay had to deal with the reality of the present, and he did not face a particularly pleasant reality. In October he saw the unexpected Democratic electoral success. By the next month it had become clear that the Webster forces had turned to Scott—this man who said he had not voted for the last thirty-one years—as they, too, attempted to derail a Clay nomination. Weed and Seward now openly operated for Scott. Harrison still seemed strong. Clay's stances on several issues remained under attack. Rumors circulated of his withdrawal. But, despite the negative signs, Clay continued to be reasonably confident. Most southern states had endorsed him—his southern strategy seemed to be working—and he had gained the delegate support of several northern states, such as Connecticut. He also had sizable blocs of delegates in large-vote states, including New York. Despite all the attacks, all the schemes, all the talk of a rebound in the economy, Clay still went into the convention as the strongest candidate. But all those questions had raised doubts about his electability as the doors of the Harrisburg Lutheran Church, the site of the Whig convention, opened.[29]

The forces of Henry Clay came to Harrisburg with the most votes of any candidate. But, in one sense, bad luck again stalked the Clay camp. Clay had almost the entire southern vote in his pocket. But four slave states—South Carolina, Georgia, Tennessee, and Arkansas—had no voting delegates at the convention. That situation apparently took the Clay campaign by surprise. With better information or more foresight, the allies of the Great Compromiser could have arranged to have those other delegates present, or even to have orchestrated some rump representatives to show up as the unchallenged delegates of their states. But with no votes from states in which he would have done well, Clay started out poorly.[30]

Then, early in its deliberations, the convention made a decision that basically doomed Clay's candidacy. Weed, Seward, Thaddeus Stevens, and their allies saw that Clay still had the widest base of support across the delegations. Even when Clay did not lead in a state, he usually had the next largest number of votes. Seeing that, and facing the possibility of a Clay win on the first or second ballot, the opposition outmaneuvered the Clay forces before the men of Clay knew they were under attack. The device chosen to execute the plan involved a motion to make each state delegation vote as a unit. Previously, each candidate received the votes he had in the group. The new motion would have delegations be polled by secret ballot and the majority would control the entire delegation's allotment of votes.

The unit-vote motion came before the delegates. Had the four absent states been present, the motion likely would have failed. But with them missing, and with forces of the other two candidates united against Clay on the issue, the convention adopted the unit rule. That action effectively nullified Clay's widespread secondary support, especially in big-state northern delegations. Also, by using Scott's candidacy, Weed had kept other voters from Clay—ones that otherwise would have gone to him. Belatedly, the Clay forces had understood the threat, and kinsman Cassius M. Clay made a motion that the delegates be polled individually, by voice vote, and the individual votes given to candidates. Moreover, he proposed that in states without a full delegation (as in several pro-Clay slave states) the existing members be enabled to cast the entire state's delegation vote. The convention tabled the motion. Henry Clay was in trouble.[31]

Clay, however, still retained a solid core of support that gave him a good chance for victory. But the delegates heard whispers that Clay really wanted to withdraw because he had too many enemies, and especially because the economy had improved Van Buren's chances. In opposition, the Webster forces, the abolitionists, and the anti-Masons all joined with other northern reform groups concerned about Clay's slaveholding, dueling, and moral makeup. In the South, while most delegates supported slaveholder Clay, theirs represented a soft support. Some still opposed his tariff policy, his Indian pronouncements, and his focus on a strong central government. In the West, Clay's votes regarding the land system angered others. Across the spectrum, delegates worried that Clay's BUS support, his American System, and his connection to the "corrupt bargain" charge would keep him from victory. The opposition forces touched all those buttons during the convention, and the Clay camp did not respond well. Delegates desperately wanted a Whig victory in 1840, and the words of doom regarding Clay's electability grew stronger and louder.[32]

As the time for the vote arrived, delegates huddled in separate rooms and each state sent the results of their polls to a central committee to announce the outcome. A candidate needed 128 votes to win the nomination. On the first ballot, Clay led with 103 votes from twelve states. The other two candidates, combined, had ten states. Half of Harrison's 94 votes came from two states, and most of Scott's 57 came from New York, courtesy of the unit rule. But the missing states, the unit rule, and the Scott candidacy had denied Clay the crucial first-ballot win. Over the next two ballots, one state deserted Clay, one left Harrison, and the committee announced the vote as Clay 95, Harrison 91, and Scott 68. No change occurred on the fourth ballot. Then, late at night, on the fifth ballot, Weed announced that New York's 42 votes would switch from Scott to Harrison, two other Scott states hopped on the mini-bandwagon, and Harrison won the nomination with 148 votes to Clay's 90 and Scott's 16. Clay had failed to gain the nomination—and perhaps lost his best chance to be president. Then, supposedly as a sop to Clay supporters, the convention made one of the worst decisions in Whig Party history: after making offers to others, it finally and unanimously selected John Tyler of Virginia as the candidate for vice president. A Clay supporter then read the second of the two letters from Clay that he had sent to the convention—one thanking them for the victory, the other saying he had encouraged a "free selection" and would abide by the decision. Harmony seemed to reign.[33]

Clay did not hold entirely harmonious feelings, however. In the past two tries for the presidency, he had accepted defeat gracefully, perhaps because neither came as a great surprise. But this time was different. Calhoun wrote that Clay openly seemed to take the news of his defeat well, but took it "badly at heart." A friend told Polk that Clay appeared "placid & content" but displayed a short temper. Exactly how Clay reacted remains unknown. Hints suggest some anger, understandable disappointment, and clear despondency. All those emotions grew stronger as Clay began to receive word of what had actually transpired in the convention.[34]

Almost immediately, Clay heard from friends, allies, and journalists that treachery had killed his chances.[35] Over time he concluded that "the Intriguers of 1839" and the "Webster clique" had caused his defeat and had usurped the will of the majority. He considered the Scott candidacy only a tool to defeat him. But at the same time, Clay did recognize deeper reasons for his rejection. Given the lack of overall southern support in particular, his speech on abolition had not helped him greatly in that region and had damaged him severely in northern circles. Still, the easiest thing for a political conscience was to blame the defeat not on his actions but on the actions of others. As one correspondent later wrote, "Mr. Clay never forgave the gentlemen who were instrumental in procuring the nomination of Harrison."[36]

After he found out about the events at Harrisburg, would Clay support the candidate of those who had betrayed him? He answered quickly. A week after the convention, Clay concluded to a Virginian, "No alternative remains to me but to acquiesce in it." To do otherwise would be a betrayal by him of the party and its principles. Clay soon gave a public address in favor of the nominee and called for his friends to vote "heartily, as I shall," for Harrison. As that stand became widely known, praise came Clay's way. One congressman told how "we are all in ecstasies at the noble and high toned course of our favorite Mr. Clay." A New Hampshire newspaper proclaimed that Clay's magnanimous support for Harrison had earned the admiration of many. Of course, Clay's actions also meant that since Harrison had pledged to be a one-term president, the Kentuckian already was building goodwill for the next contest. As a Connecticut paper noted, Clay's "patriotic" action clearly gave him "a new claim to the confidence and gratitude of his countrymen." Perhaps next time, in 1844, party gratitude would give him the prize denied in 1840.[37]

Clay saw his party win the presidency in 1840. Despite Democratic predictions that the Whigs were split and dying, that was not the case. One advantage Harrison enjoyed was, in fact, Henry Clay. Active candidates did not campaign, but defeated ones could, and Clay did so actively for Harrison. A journalist recalled, "Clay took the field for his rival, the people rose almost *en masse*. Banners flaunted the sky—the air rang with acclamations—the people met in armies—the pursuits of business were neglected." A Mississippi politician remarked that he had never seen such enthusiasm as displayed by the Whigs: "The 'log cabin and hard-cider' candidate is sweeping all before him." But the almost religious fervor of the mass rallies with their cries of "Tippecanoe and Tyler too" masked deeper reasons for Harrison's popularity. Whigs had learned from Democratic teachers of years before, and now they out-generaled, out-organized, and out-sloganed the opposition. New voters angry at the party in power or inspired by cultural issues flocked to the Whig standard; the energy and excitement in the race resided in that camp. And as the economic distress grew worse, the Whig option looked better.[38]

The results, however won, both pleased and disappointed Clay. He delighted in seeing his party control the White House for the first time. But he also realized that the occupant could have—should have—been one Henry Clay. As the economic recession made victory more likely, Clay mused that he would have done better than Harrison, given strengths in the South that he had but Harrison lacked. That may or may not have been true, but the thought made it a bittersweet success.

With all that had occurred in the convention and in the campaign, did Clay learn from the experience and become a better candidate? At one level, he recognized that he had trusted too much in unworthy managers and he had been outmaneuvered as a result. Clay also better understood the importance of getting out the vote—some 80 percent of the eligible voters had cast ballots. Yet in the end, he did not comprehend the fatal flaw in his own attempts to organize for political war. He could lead, but he found it hard to delegate. As an early biographer put it, "Clay was a good manager for others but a poor one for himself." The Great Compromiser would be an excellent vote counter and coalition builder with the personalities of Congress, but not a particularly good politician on the national vote-getting scene. Clay had many devoted friends, numerous supporters in all states, and loyal allies everywhere. Yet, he never had that one person or group of people who could effectively organize them to maximum advantage on his behalf. His races cried out for a Weed or Todd or Eaton or Kendall or Blair.

And Clay needed such a manager, for he often proved to be a poor judge of the overall picture. In the 1828 race, for example, he had expressed "very great" confidence in Adams's reelection, and four years later, he told family members that Jackson faced "certain" defeat. Even allies warned him that he might be too sanguine in his evaluations. Moreover, Clay (like others of his era) wrote letters or spoke out too often, and he required someone to restrain him, openly and, if needed, harshly. Clay's state-by-state advisors often added to the problem as well by giving him bad advice and faulty political intelligence. He desperately needed a trusted counselor who could contradict and confront him, and who could craft a strategy for victory.[39]

But Clay had also done reasonably well on his own, and he had such great personal appeal and such powers to convince that he hesitated to put himself in the hands of another. Too confident, he accepted the words of others with caution. He had not learned enough from the 1840 campaign and had failed to develop a strong political machine. Clay still trusted too much the force of his personality and of his programs. That Clay did as well as he did, over and over, reflects his significant strength in those areas. Yet, the presidency remained in the hands of others.

Henry Clay actually had a somewhat better opinion of the president-elect than did many of his contemporaries, though that may not be saying much. He considered the tall, gray-haired William Henry Harrison ineffectual, incompetent, and vain, but also honest, good-intentioned, and patriotic. Fellow Whig John Quincy Adams described him as a man of shallow mind who displayed a rabid thirst for lucrative political office. Democrat William L. Marcy recalled the good-hearted Harrison as a "weak and superannuated man . . . with a worthless head."[40]

Given Harrison's less than distinguished political skills and less than dominating political traits, numerous contemporary commentators expected stronger leaders to become the real powers behind the presidential throne. The question to most observers was not whether someone would eventually control the president but, rather, who that person might be. Obviously, many of the faithful expected that man to be Henry Clay, for he immediately began to get patronage requests. Opposition leaders held the same expectations; Calhoun predicted that Clay would dominate since Harrison "has neither physical nor mental powers equal to the task." But Clay worried about the general's "shattered" body and overall health. The Kentuckian also knew that while he and Harrison had been friendly on the surface, they had been rivals for the nomination and that Harrison had been given warnings Clay would seek to dominate him. The other possible

Machiavelli was Daniel Webster, who had backed Harrison early and could make good claims to political preferment as a result. In the four months between Harrison's election and his inauguration, much backstage maneuvering took place.[41]

Clay chose a careful path overall, one bound by his desire to advise the president and by Harrison's sensitivity to the whispers that Clay would lead the administration. At first, both men recognized the reality of the situation. Clay had political power, a loyal cadre, and a claim to some consideration, since he had campaigned for Harrison. The chief executive-to-be did not seek to alienate the Kentuckian. Accordingly, when the two met privately at Ashland, Harrison offered his host the post of secretary of state, but Clay declined. In fact, the senator made only modest requests for a few cabinet positions for loyal friends. Otherwise, little hint of a desire to dominate seemed evident. At the same time, Clay understood that Harrison's campaign manager represented a Kentucky faction opposed to Clay and that Webster, not Clay, was an earlier backer of the winning thoroughbred in the presidential race. The Great Compromiser told the president-elect that he had no objections to Webster's being in the cabinet—a significant concession. (But he did say that, given Webster's reputation for loose finances, he should not be secretary of the treasury.)[42]

Clay also understood that the meeting would fuel rumors: "Artful men for sinister purposes will endeavor to foster this jealousy. . . . I must avoid giving it any countenance," he wrote to a Delaware Whig. But once Harrison arrived in Washington, it became clear that Webster had the president's ear. The one Harrison appointment Clay specifically opposed was the proposal to give the important and lucrative post of collector of the port of New York City to a Weed and Webster ally. Edward Curtis had worked heartily to defeat Clay at the Harrisburg convention, by means Clay considered "base and perfidious." The Kentuckian expressed his "irrevocable" opposition to Curtis, asked that the appointment not be made, and indicated that, if done, it would be seen as an affront to him. Harrison appointed him anyway, making it clear that he listened more to Webster than to Clay.[43]

On March 4, 1841, on a gloomy, snow-flecked inauguration day, the hero of Tippecanoe and the Thames bravely refused to wear an overcoat, despite the cold, as he rode a white horse toward the Capitol. Twenty-six guns—one for each state—thundered a welcome. The bare-headed Harrison faced the fierce wind and the cheering crowd and delivered a dry, lengthy inaugural address that quickly dulled much of their enthusiasm. But the Whigs now had their own president in place. The usually optimistic Clay told a

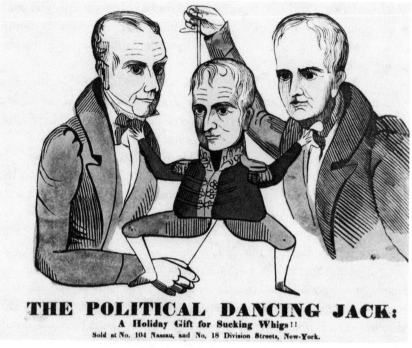

THE POLITICAL DANCING JACK:
A Holiday Gift for Sucking Whigs!!
Sold at No. 104 Nassau, and No. 18 Division Streets, New-York.

Clay (left) and Congressman Henry Wise control the strings of the toy puppet of 1840 candidate William Henry Harrison. Such perceptions later angered president-elect Harrison, but Harrison's death after only a month in office brought Vice President John Tyler, an expected Clay ally, into the executive chair. *Library of Congress, LC-USZ62-14982*

close ally, "If there be breakers ahead, they have not yet been discernible." But hidden reefs of discord would soon damage the party ship of state almost beyond repair.[44]

The oldest president and the youngest party came to power in 1841, with the country still mired in a depression. Workers had lost their jobs, farmers their lands, businesses their customers, Americans their hopes. But the Whigs took office also with a great opportunity, a good congressional majority, and a strong mandate for change. More than almost anyone else in his party, Clay recognized the necessity of seizing the moment. For the first time, Whigs controlled both houses of Congress and the presidency. If they could act boldly and productively, if they could bring the country out of the recession, if they could show the worth of their programs, the Whigs could become the dominant party on the American scene. (In fact, four score and twelve years later, in the midst of another depression, Franklin D. Roosevelt would come to office and through his words and his party's congressional actions would quickly transform the spirit—and the politics—of the nation.) In 1841, Clay saw a president who did not fully understand the situation before him. But the man with his eye on the presidency four years hence knew that if his party failed to meet the expectations, it would squander its greatest electoral opportunity and would be defeated by a disillusioned electorate. Yet, if the Whigs succeeded, if they showed their values worked, if they demonstrated their claim as the party of prosperity, then wonderful political rewards awaited the party—and Clay.

In that atmosphere, Clay tried to prod the president into a proactive response and sent a letter to Harrison, suggesting that the chief executive should adhere to his rather nebulous support for a special session to enact Whig programs and institute economic recovery. Delay would be fatal. Had Clay stopped there, repercussions might not have followed. But he went too far, for lawmaker Clay could not resist including a draft of the proposed proclamation calling for a session. It is likely that anti-Clay advisors to the president saw that letter as an attempt by their rival to supplant the Weed-Webster clique as the chief influence on Harrison. They reacted accordingly, told the president how that showed Clay's attempt to dictate to the chief executive, and convinced Harrison to write a harsh letter of response that berated Clay for his "too impetuous" communication. Moreover, the president asked that henceforth Clay contact him only in writing or in the presence of others.[45]

Harrison could not have done more to anger Clay if he had tried. First, he already had appointed Clay enemies to office; now, he had lectured the proud Clay and had even suggested his distrust of his rival. A very surprised and clearly perplexed Clay correctly saw the hand of Webster at work. Clay responded to Harrison by indicating that the president's missive had "mortified" him. How had he dictated to Harrison? Going a bit beyond the facts, he said, "I have recommended nobody for any office. I have sought none for myself, or my friends." Only in his opposition to the "perfidious" Curtis had he spoken out, and he had warned Harrison as a faithful friend, had tried to shield the president from an action that would (and did) hurt the administration. With the Senate session over, a fuming Clay left the capital. Soon after, Harrison signed a proclamation calling for the special session Clay had sought. But exactly a month after his inauguration, President Harrison died. For the first time, a vice president succeeded to the presidency as a result of the death of the chief executive. The nation faced a new situation. Exactly how that change would affect the Whig programs, Clay's relationship with the presidency, and Clay's future remained to be seen.[46]

The new president, John Tyler, remained something of an unknown quantity despite his years in politics. The son of a governor of the Old Dominion, state chief executive, and US senator himself, he had emerged from a Virginia states' rights, slaveholding background. In fact, the gaunt-looking president had been a Democrat until the actions of Andrew Jackson drove him from the party. Since then, he had been a somewhat reluctant quasi-Whig, given that his basic beliefs and those of the party often diverged. Yet, Tyler had been a loyal supporter of Clay, a man he admired. In turn, the Kentuckian, in words he likely wondered later how he ever uttered, called Tyler manly, tolerant, and "never ill-tempered," a "highly esteemed" friend. Nor were Clay's words concerning the man atypical. To many, the new president had seemed as one commentator described him: "affable, polite, and agreeable in company and conversation." The youngest man to hold the office up to that time, the fifty-one-year-old Tyler had displayed tact, charm, and geniality in his career. But some people thought that came about because he so desired not to anger anyone that he seldom expressed his true opinions, if contradictory, in person. That trait led some to think he agreed with them, when in fact he did not. But a few others saw different traits in Tyler, ones that could be warnings about the new chief executive. The Whig Crittenden considered him vain, evasive, and "too tremulous," and a Democrat told William Marcy a few years later that Tyler was "certainly the meanest man God ever made." Tyler's presidency would show him to be principled but obstinate, forceful but opinionated, proud but priggish. Theodore Roosevelt later wrote that Tyler "has been called a mediocre man, but that is unwarranted flattery. He was a politician of monumental littleness." One historian concluded that "Tyler had every quality that makes for leadership but the quality of leadership itself"; another wrote that the new president "would rather be consistent than right." Henry Clay should have been more worried than he was.[47]

Clay's actions during the first year of the Tyler presidency brought him more criticism than almost anything else he did.[48] Clay *was* more irascible, more frustrated, less compromising, more dictatorial, and less charming than usual. He certainly acted, in part, with his eye on the prize of the presidency. It was not his finest hour. But Clay's anger also grew out of the increasing likelihood that Whig hopes were going to die of a wound inflicted by the party's own chief executive. Whigs *had* to act, for if they did not, if they bickered and did little, if the president stymied their efforts, they would squander their greatest opportunity, lose elections, and face the next presidential canvass hopelessly behind. Other Whigs recognized that analysis as well and willingly followed Clay's lead. He did not have to be a dictator because the majority wanted what he did. But he did have to act, for them and for himself. Almost by default, as the president abandoned the party programs, Clay became the Whigs' leader. But his actions came at a great political cost, once more.[49]

On April 6, 1841, "His Accidency" John Tyler took the oath of office as president. A little over six weeks later the crucial special session of Congress called belatedly by Harrison would begin. In that interim, nervous Whigs worried over the chief executive's past inclination to support states' rights and oppose many of the programs they would seek to enact in that session. Clay sought to assuage their fears and wrote several allies that he did not expect the president to oppose Whig measures. But as the time neared for the senator to leave to attend the special session, his initial confidence had weakened. He left now "with strong hopes, not however unmixed with fears." If Tyler cooperated with the party, all would be fine: "Otherwise everything is at hazard," wrote Clay. A gleeful Amos Kendall told Jackson, "The political world is calm now, but some think storms are brewing." Both men were correct.[50]

On his arrival in Washington, Clay followed a daily regimen that seemed to belie any talk of his age or health issues. He went to sleep at 10:00 p.m., rose at 5:00 a.m., rode six to eight miles on horseback, then ate a hearty breakfast and read the newspapers. He would work hard the rest of the day, and party little. And they were extended work days. Not used to meeting in the muggy capital in the summer, congressmen quickly grew temperamental in the long days amid Washington's heat and humidity. Clay hoped for a short, productive session. The House elected Kentuckian John D. White as Speaker, and Clay unofficially led the Senate. The Whig majority soon passed controversial rules that limited debate in order to make it easier to pass their legislation.[51]

A week after the start of the session, Clay announced the goals of his party. He called on Congress "to go forward and re-establish the people in their lost prosperity," through a national bank and increased tariff protection, both to aid economic growth and to increase revenue. Clay also announced party support for a national bankruptcy law to provide relief to debtors and for an act to redistribute money from land sales to the states to strengthen transportation and public education. Clay offered the classic American System components. But throughout his career, Tyler had expressed his opposition to key parts of that program, especially the idea of another BUS. That issue seemed the one most likely to cause problems. Yet in his inaugural address, Tyler had indicated that he would sanction "any constitutional measure which . . . shall have for its first object the restoration of a sound circulating medium." Moreover, he had told Clay to frame a bank bill carefully "to avoid any constitutional objections." Congressional Whigs realized that the president had misgivings about the chartering of a national bank, but both sentences suggested to reasonable men that it only seemed a matter of discussion to find out the president's objections and draft a bill that would meet those concerns—a bill Tyler could sign.[52]

The ensuing debate over a national bank caused Clay much political anguish. The proposed Ewing Bill did not satisfy many Whigs, the Democrats delayed proceedings to slow the whole process, and the heat continued to take its toll. Debate grew fiercer. Clay reluctantly stepped into the growing breach and supported a mild compromise bill that he understood had received the approval of the president. The Kentuckian lobbied hard for passage of the supposed compromise. Meanwhile, Democrats reveled in the Whig infighting. By the end of July—two months into an already too long session—James Buchanan predicted that Tyler would veto the substitute bill and try to establish a new party, based on patronage, presidential power, and states' rights. Calhoun chortled that the opposition had entered the special session with much optimism, "but are now distracted and disperited [sic]." A week later, the Carolinian accurately predicted that a vote would break up the Whigs, lead to a cabinet reorganization, and defeat the party at the next election: "Discord and division have entered their ranks."[53]

Clay saw the situation that way as well. He and others continued to hear stronger and stronger warnings that Tyler would neither sign a bank bill nor let it become law without his signature. On the day the bill finally passed the House—almost two months after introduction of the proposal—a North Carolina senator told his wife that while many expected a veto, two men had spoken to the president recently and indicated that he would sign the bill: "Should he refuse . . . I fear a universal burst of indignation, and the most direful consequences to the Whig party."[54]

With the bill on his desk, Tyler delayed doing anything. The longer he held it, the more concern grew among Whigs. A congressman anticipated a veto and worried over the unknown consequences of such an action: "You may look out for a storm." Soon the tempest erupted, for on August 16, the veto came down. The president stated that to approve the unconstitutional bill would be an act of "gross moral turpitude." Unexpectedly, Tyler expressed his opposition not only to the compromise bill before him but to the original Ewing Bill as well. Yet he gave few clues about his own preferences. A Democrat told Polk of the Whig reaction: "They are in perfect confusion."[55]

But many Whigs—and Clay—still wanted a bank, so as to fill the void left by the recently deposed independent treasury and to aid economic recovery. They continued to try to craft a bill that would meet the president's constitutional objections. Various people, in and out of Congress, met with the president and certain cabinet members. They then carried back to Congress their understanding of what Tyler expected and wanted in the new bill. But Tyler either had not communicated well or had not chosen to voice his views clearly, for several individuals left with the distinct sense that with the desired modifications made—including a name change to a "Fiscal Corporation," rather than "bank"—then no veto would follow this time. One observer told how he had seen the president's handwriting on the bill, suggesting Tyler had seen, changed, and approved the new proposal.[56]

In that atmosphere, Clay had given an hour-and-a half speech regarding the veto, as the Senate decided whether to override it or not. Party fortunes may have been better served had he remained silent. But in what most contemporary observers called a typically eloquent and unexpectedly temperate speech given the circumstances, Clay spoke for the party when he only gently chided the chief executive. As a candidate, Tyler had indicated he would support some form of bank. Why did he not now? asked Clay. Congress had compromised. Why had the president not reciprocated? The chief executive had said the bank was unconstitutional, said Clay, but other presidents and the courts had indicated its legality over the years. What had changed? Reiterating his friendship with Tyler, Clay admitted the veto had surprised him and now regretted the president had not given a more explicit statement of his views. But Clay hoped that the ongoing discussions, behind the scenes, would produce a measure that could meet the country's needs: "Shall we adjourn and go home in disgust? No! No! No! . . . Let us do our duty, our whole duty, and nothing short of our duty." Had Clay left it at that, matters might have unfolded differently. But a supporter of the president rose and made an ill-advised attack on Clay. The subject of the barbs could have said nothing, but his overactive sense of honor called for a rebuttal. Clay's now harsher words accused a cabal of controlling Tyler and of trying to lure him into creating a new party, though in reality they did not have enough supporters to form "a decent corporal's guard." Those words spoken in the heat of debate wounded an overly sensitive Tyler. Besides, there may also have been too much truth in the retort.[57]

The day after Clay's speech, a new bank bill was introduced. It had been crafted to meet the president's concerns, as understood by those involved in discussions with the executive branch. Tyler's cabinet seemed confident that the plan had the president's tacit approval. But almost immediately, Tyler privately expressed reservations about the proposed "Fiscal Corporation." He had not only failed to communicate; he had also failed to lead. As a result, his actions doomed the bill and, eventually, Tyler's place in the party. What may have started as a constitutional issue to Tyler now had become, to his eyes, a matter more about power and will, about who led the party. Given the unexpected possible presidential opposition, some called on Clay to table the bill and avoid a fatal confrontation. But Clay and most Whigs considered the proposal a good compromise, supposedly endorsed by Tyler, and they moved it forward. Four days after the House passed the measure, Clay expressed his private concern that the president might leave the Whig Party: "We have made some sacrifices, may make more, to retain him, but the seeds of mutual distrust are . . . extensively sown." Soon after, the Great Compromiser told a son that he did not like the bill before the Senate, but he would support it since it had been "framed to suit the president's views, as I understood they were communicated." In that family letter, Henry Clay clearly showed that, like most Whigs, he believed the compromise bill would satisfy the chief executive. A congressman noted, however, of the president: "He . . . is changing his ground every day." When a Tyler supporter asked the chief executive how he could amend the bill to meet any possible presidential objections, Tyler told him to send the bill on as it was.[58]

Eight days after final passage of the act, John Tyler vetoed it. While the president wrote of his desire for conciliation, the message seemed to reject what others had understood the vacillating Virginian to say he would accept, and he almost appeared to be searching for reasons to disallow the measure. He had never really sought a new BUS, despite his equivocal words, and as the issue also became one of philosophy, pride, and power, he placed his stamp on the question. He could not have been more open if he had issued a formal challenge to a duel. Shocked and angry Whigs saw the veto as a dishonorable, treacherous betrayal by one of their own, "a *Judas* and *renegade* from all parties," in the words of a Democrat. They had nominated Tyler and he had accepted their platform, only to turn his back on both; they had tried to meet his constitutional objectives, only to see their efforts rejected; they had tried to work with him, only to watch as he moved away from them. No compromise, no conciliation, no peace would now follow. It was political war, with little quarter given and few prisoners taken. A Whig was heard to cry out, "The Lord took our president—the demos have taken our Vice President—and the Devil will take our party." Two days after the veto, the cabinet resigned in protest, save for Daniel Webster. While Webster pleaded that he wanted to finish some ongoing negotiations as secretary of state, "poor Daniel" also needed the income of a cabinet post. His action effectively doomed his chances for further advancement in the party. Moreover, when he not so covertly agreed to work with Tyler to ensure that Clay would not be president, that action further alienated many of the faithful.[59]

The special session sputtered to a dismal end in September. But before returning to their homes, many Whigs signed a manifesto that in effect read Tyler out of the party. At almost the same time, the president announced his cabinet replacements, which reflected a declaration of open war on Henry Clay. A bitter Clay rival from Kentucky went in as postmaster general, and the president would later appoint as the new postmaster in Lexington a man Clay strongly opposed. Clay men received dismissal notices in Pennsylvania and elsewhere, as Tyler used his patronage powers against Clay. Tyler's actions made it abundantly clear that the president expected to challenge the Kentuckian in the 1844 race. It also made it obvious that Clay had another adversary on his growing roster of enemies.[60]

The outcome of all the actions and inactions of the special session meant that the best chance for advancement of the American System had been killed by the party's own president and, as a contemporary journal noted, "That was the bitterest cup Clay ever drained." Now what the Kentuckian called "a faithful Congress and a faithless president" faced off as enemies, with "not the remotest prospect of any reconciliation." (That did not mean that Clay's playfulness left him, however. When he and the president met at a party, Clay cordially asked Tyler, "Well Mr. President, what are you for?" Confused and embarrassed by what he thought was a reference to his political stand, the chief executive hesitated. Clay laughed and continued, "Wine, Whiskey, Brandy, or Champagne? Come show your hand." For the moment, the two antagonists laughed and drank together.) But by mid-January 1842, the Great Compromiser could find little basis for political compromise and discovered instead that "all is confusion, chaos & disorder here. No system! No conceit of action! No prospect of union and harmony."[61]

When Whigs referred to Tyler as "our Crazy President," "an imbecile," "a fool," and when Tylerites called Clay "utterly demented," Democrats delighted in the Whig distress. Stephen A. Douglas saw the special-session fiasco as a "perfect windfall" for his party. Like many others of the era, including Calhoun, he predicted the dissolution of the Whigs. As a Bostonian told Webster—stuck in a state of suspended political animation—the Whigs faced a future of "bloody & exasperated war." Gloomy Whigs reconciled themselves to political defeat in the 1842 off-year elections, and it did not look promising for the party's presidential prospects in 1844, either.[62]

Most Whigs blamed the unpredictable Tyler for it all. While the president continued to make some mild conciliatory moves in the hope of keeping some party members loyal to him, very few chose that option. A Massachusetts man spoke for most of the party when he concluded that Whigs "almost universally detested" Tyler. The administration, proclaimed a congressman, could best be described as a parenthesis, which, according to one definition, was "a clause of a sentence, enclosed between black lines or brackets, which should be pronounced in a low tone of voice, and may be left out altogether without injuring the sense."[63]

Tyler's actions in 1842 and afterwards continued to widen the break. Before he finally signed the tariff of 1842, he vetoed two earlier Whig tariff bills, chiefly because they would allow Clay's redistribution of federal funds to the states. And when that issue arose in a separate bill, he pocket-vetoed it. By then, as the *New York Tribune* commented, the friends of Clay were "resolved to draw the sword and throw away the scabbard." As the division broadened, the president increasingly appointed more Democrats and southerners to office. John Quincy Adams called Tyler a man without a party, while a Whig governor termed the president "the damnest rascal and biggest fool of the age." But by then "Captain" Tyler had begun to organize what he expected to be a third-party army that he hoped would catapult him into reelection—as many had predicted even during the veto period. Clay wrote that the chief executive wanted to establish a kind of "half-way house" to gather dissidents from both parties and combine with those who wanted the existing parties to dissolve. But he found few converts to his political creed. As Clay predicted, most Democrats had no intention of leaving their party, and most Whigs stayed loyal to their new leader, Henry Clay. After hearing the president's plans for a third party, a Virginian called them "absurd, foolish" ideas, foisted on Tyler by job-hungry office-seekers and untruthful advisors. As one of those who gave counsel to the president, Daniel Webster increasingly grew disenchanted with the administration he had followed. By early 1843, he told Nicholas Biddle that the chief executive's desire to be reelected dominated everything Tyler did. Every appointment was made for political effect, and the president seemed inclined to throw himself into the arms of the Democratic Party. The next year, Webster's son read his father's words that "very unwise Counsels" had flattered Tyler and had convinced him that he could win the election in 1844: "On that subject he seems really to have lost his head."[64]

Clay had seen enough. The anger, divisions, recriminations, and lack of positive action all saddened him. From the prospect of wonderful accomplishments for the party, it had now regressed to name-calling and posturing for power. By late 1841, rumors arose that Clay might resign his Senate seat. In January 1842, he wrote his good friend Francis Brooke, "I want rest and my private affairs want attention. Nevertheless, I would make any personal sacrifices, if by remaining here, I could do any good; but my belief is that I can affect nothing, and perhaps my absence may remove an obstacle to something being done by others." Therefore, he would resign. He sent in his notice on February 16, with an effective date of March 31, 1842.[65]

On that day, he gave his valedictory speech. Most present did not expect it to be the end of Henry Clay's career, but he spoke as if it were. Clay told how he had acted for the good of his country, and as to whether he had acted correctly, "History . . . will be the best, truest, and most impartial judge." People had attacked him over the years, and friends had sustained him in return. But one recent charge he could not let pass unnoticed. The epithet of "Dictator" had been hurled at him, and he vehemently objected. What powers had he wielded? Did he have patronage, an army, or control of the purse strings of government? Had not his party acted, not he? He did admit to a temperament that, in the heat of debate, accordingly grew too ardent: For that "I now make the amplest apology." Clay concluded by wishing that he left in times better than the current one of "distrust and embarrassment" in the country, but he offered the hope that all who remained would do their duty, as he bid them "one and all, a long, a last, a friendly farewell." His emotional words touched many, and tears flowed freely. His supporters and friends cried in sorrow; his enemies, it was said, cried with joy.[66]

The Whig agenda of 1841 had mostly failed. The party expected to lose heavily at the polls in the fall. The future of the Whigs looked bleak. But the break with Tyler, which hurt deeply in the short term by revealing the party's divisions, impotence, and confusion, may in fact have started the Whigs back down the road to political rebirth. For if the hard times still continued, Tyler—not the Whigs—would be blamed for that circumstance. The party could still tout its programs as necessary and claim Henry Clay as the cure for the nation's ills. A newspaper had mused, on hearing of Clay's possible resignation: "The nation has not been in the habit of doing without the services of Mr. Clay." The resignation, said Clay's successor in the Senate, was "like the soul's quitting the body." Whigs and Henry Clay hoped that America would not be long without Clay's services, or his soul.[67]

Clay returned home to friends, farm, and family. And he returned to run for the presidency in 1844.

12

Planter and Paterfamilias

NOW-PRIVATE-CITIZEN HENRY CLAY SEEMED GENUINELY pleased to leave Washington, DC, and return to Kentucky. For the last two years he had constantly grumbled about his time away from his Ashland estate, writing to his wife in July 1840, for example: "Never was I so tired of this place; never so anxious to be with you." After the problems with President Tyler, Clay had told a friend that the capital "is ceasing to have any charms for me." (Of course, should he return with family in tow and live in the White House, that would be another matter entirely.) But in the spring of 1842, Clay had left the District in disgust.[1]

Clay needed to rest and to revive his spirits. He had remained in the capital for a month after his farewell address, saying his good-byes at a series of banquets. But by early May, the Kentuckian had made his way back to Lexington and soon afterward a crowd of some fifteen thousand formally welcomed their hero back to the Bluegrass country with a massive barbecue. When called on to address the multitude, Clay reflected on his early life, defended (again) his actions in 1825, and then turned to the present. In a preview of what might be expected in the 1844 race, he castigated Jackson for causing the current economic distress and blamed Tyler for his "dishonor and bad faith" and his failure to act. With that talk, Clay left the public arena and retired to Ashland, at least for a brief moment.[2]

Ashland represented the most public display of the success that Henry Clay had attained. He also used it as a model of the American System in action. But most of all, it offered a respite from politics, a place of quiet pleasures, a sanctuary from the world. In fact, almost all who visited Ashland saw it in those terms as well, and they wrote words of praise for what Clay had accomplished there. After going to the estate in 1835, for example, an awe-struck new Kentucky resident wrote to his brother back in Maine, "I have never yet seen anything that will at all compare with his house & its situation. Oh, it is magnificent," while diarist Philip Hone of New York concluded, "I never saw so fine a farm." Such descriptions strengthened the Clay image of the self-made man who had produced a place to which all Americans could aspire, of which all could be proud.[3]

Around the time of Clay's return, a letter writer to the *New York Tribune* told how he arrived at Clay's home via a tree-lined carriage road, and was greeted by the great man himself. As they walked in the secluded surroundings, the "prince pastoral" had picked a rose for the visitor and then later poured some delicious wine, made from grapes grown at Ashland. The writer called the place "the most delightful retreat in all the west." That

A S H L A N D

Designed by architect Benjamin Latrobe, with modifications by Clay, Ashland not only served as a place of respite for Clay but also as part of the successful model that Clay presented to the world as part of his American System. *Louis Edward Nollau Nitrate Photographic Print Collection, University of Kentucky Special Collections Research Center, 1998ua002*

same year a correspondent from the *Cleveland Herald* complimented the property even more effusively. He told of a house hidden by trees, with numerous outbuildings, "all in perfect repair, spacious, neat, and in order." In all his visits, including ones to New England, "I have never seen the same number of acres in a body, as handsome, as productive, or well fenced, and as well cultivated. His woodland is cleared of all underbrush and dead wood—his fields are enclosed with good fences." The writer then praised the excellent livestock and the general "good taste and unpretentious elegance" of the estate. But the journalist also ended with a note that had political implications. He admitted that previously he had considered Clay just another gentleman farmer, but after talking with him now he realized that Clay knew everything about his farm and his animals: "One of the best, practical, and most useful farmers, in this or any other county, is Henry Clay."[4]

Yet if Ashland's charm and efficiency could score political points for the man at Ashland, the estate had a more important political effect on Clay himself. It allowed him to clear his mind, to focus on nonpolitical matters, to relax. For Clay truly loved his land. He planted trees, fed the pigs, experimented with new breeds, and did all the little things that tied him to the soil. Ashland grounded him to the practicalities of life. In 1833, a year after his political defeat, he had happily described "our firm green sward, our natural parks, our beautiful undulating country. . . . All conspire to render home delightful." And soon after his return from the capital in 1842, he praised "this paradise of a country." Clay once said he would make a better farmer than a statesman. That could be questioned, but he *was* a better farmer than a presidential candidate. And he daily demonstrated success in the agrarian world.[5]

The making of Ashland had not occurred overnight, nor was it ever a static process. As newlyweds, the Clays had initially made their home in downtown Lexington, and Clay had built a law office near his abode. But as a young Rutherford B. Hayes later wrote of the antebellum city: "People here seem to live for the sake of living more than in most places." Fine village and country estates surrounded the urban area and Clay sought to emulate that level of living. As he later wrote (perhaps without complete fidelity to the truth): "I have never been desirous of inordinate wealth. I have been only anxious to live in a manner corresponding with the circle in which I move, and to possess the means of doing so."[6]

On his arrival in Kentucky, Clay had immediately started to gain those means, and by 1804 began acquiring the land that became Ashland. Over the years, he added various parcels until his immediate estate reached some 515 acres. There, a mile and a half from the city proper, Clay's home began to take shape. It was likely designed by Benjamin Latrobe, the nation's foremost architect, who later designed two additional wings. But if Latrobe designed, Clay modified to reflect his personal tastes.[7] The resulting brick house, painted pearl white, well represented the man who lived there. It was not extravagant but spacious, not stuffy but comfortable, not ostentatious but elegant. Traces of the political world Clay inhabited reminded visitors such as Lafayette, Monroe, Webster, Harrison, and Van Buren of the man who lived there—a bust of Clay, family portraits, a print of George Washington and his family, a rug with the woven inscription "Protection to Home Industry" all gave visual reinforcement to that fact. But many visitors noted that at home Clay took more delight in talking about his farm, land, and animals than about politics.[8]

Stepping outside the doors of the house quickly revealed the complexity and diversity of the estate. While walking the paths of that pastoral property, with its manicured lawns, shaded walks, and trees of almost every American variety, a visitor would see a series of outbuildings that, in themselves, suggested the wide variety of activities that took place on the grounds. A smokehouse, a butter house, a cheese house, a chicken coop, a dovecote, a hemp house, a greenhouse, two icehouses, a carriage house, a dairy, barns, stables, sheds, and the slave quarters filled the property. Nowhere could the existence of slave labor be ignored, for Clay at times owned more than fifty slaves, who worked to keep the grounds immaculate, the fields tilled, the animals fed, and the family supplied.[9]

A visitor to Ashland would also see wave after wave of crops, both on the immediate farm and on nearby ones Clay also owned. Clay had a diversified agricultural base. He planted corn, wheat, rye, and oats on a significant number of acres and cultivated smaller plots of potatoes, grapes, melons, and cantaloupes, not to mention a sizable garden and fruit orchard for home use. But the main cash crop was hemp. At that time, the commonwealth produced three-fourths of the nation's entire crop and chiefly shipped it outside the state for use in cotton bagging, rope, sails, ship rigging, and rough clothes. Hemp had many attractions: it did not exhaust the soil, it prevented erosion, needed no cultivation, produced an excellent return per acre, and enjoyed protection from foreign competition under the tariffs that the "Prince of Hemp" helped craft. Planted in April or May and then harvested and placed in shocks in August, the plant lay in the fields from October to January to be rotted by the dew and the snow.

The sometimes-unpleasant odors from that period could be tolerated, for the smell of money soon followed. Once the stalks rotted, a hand-operated hemp brake would crack open the plant and the fibers would be extracted.

But despite the strengths of the American crop, most authorities considered foreign-grown hemp, rotted by water rather than the dew, a superior product. Always ready to try new methods as a scientific farmer, Clay experimented with the foreign method. He had a quarter-mile-long canal dug on his grounds for use in water rotting. By either method, his hemp crops proved profitable. In 1838, for example, Clay's bagging and rope sold for $3,597, and later that year he shipped thirty-two thousand pounds of finished hemp rope to Mississippi. His agent subsequently deposited $4,148 in sales to Clay's account. Those sums represented significant amounts of money at a time when a congressman typically received under $2,000 per session. Three years later, the outlook improved even more, for amid his fights with President Tyler, Clay had managed to gain passage of a joint resolution that directed the navy to purchase American hemp for use in its ships. Hemp prices quickly rose. In short, Clay's profitable crops fed not only the farm but also his political forays.[10]

Clay's Ashland was part of a global economy—as hemp competition demonstrated. The Kentuckian also made money from his thoroughbred efforts and general animal husbandry, but more than that, he made a real contribution and greatly improved various breeds, both in Kentucky and for the nation. His American System offered a dynamic, optimistic view of what America could be, both commercially and agriculturally; Clay at Ashland represented the progressive embodiment of that ideal.

In 1833, after his presidential defeat, Clay wrote Nicholas Biddle, "In the midst of Arabian horses, English cattle, and Maltese Asses, I think I shall recover sooner than I should have done in the corrupt atmosphere of the Capital." Thoroughbreds offered the most visible display from that group, and horses had long been an integral part of the area. In 1789, Lexington had more horses than people; eleven years later, Kentucky had more horses per capita than any other state in the Union. By then, Kentuckians had begun to import stallions from England, considered at the time to be a source for the best horses. Clay entered the game early, purchasing pedigree horses by 1806. He continued to buy and breed, and his herd increased to sixty-five by 1811. Prince Hal formally established the Ashland Thoroughbred Stock Farm in 1830 and operated it until a son took it over a dozen years later and constructed a racetrack on the property. In 1831, Clay purchased a half-interest in an imported Arabian horse and soon after bought part of another

Arabian as well. The next year, one of those Arabians serviced 113 mares at a stud fee of $25 each, earning Clay, for his half-interest, over $1,400 that year. After Clay's return from Washington in 1842, admirers gave him separate gifts of three fine thoroughbreds. From those horses would descend eleven future Kentucky Derby winners. Clay succeeded as a breeder.[11]

But Clay made even more of a contribution in improving the stock of other four-legged animals, including donkeys, cattle, and sheep. In 1827, he first imported to the United States from Malta some donkey jacks and jennies. Often more valuable than thoroughbreds, jacks could fetch high prices. In 1833, Clay valued four Maltese jacks he held at $6,000; four years later, he imported from France two more jacks and seven jennies, insuring the lot for $15,400. That same year, Clay recounted the prices and profits that could be made. A good jack, he noted, would generally sell for $750 to $2,000, but one of his had gone recently for $5,000. In a society becoming more and more dependent on the ubiquitous mule (the offspring of a jackass and a mare horse), such purebred asses proved to be an excellent invest-ment. Clay sold two dozen mules in 1841 for $2,000 and fifty-two in 1849 for $6,185, for example. But more important, his efforts left a strong im-print on the quality of the work animal of America—and scientific farmers appreciated that.[12]

Clay's cattle and sheep herds reflected a similar pattern. When in England following the Treaty of Ghent he had seen fine Hereford Red cattle and he soon imported the first of that breed to the United States, in 1817. Clay also purchased full-blooded Durham bulls and cows in New York and shipped other pedigree bulls from abroad. Again, Clay found his cattle sales rather lucrative.[13] Even before the importation of the Herefords, Clay had bought Merino sheep and had shipped them west by 1813. By 1831, his flocks totaled 120 full-blooded Merino sheep. Once more, the Kentuckian sought to di-versify and experimented with cross-breeding. Despite periodic problems with dog attacks, sheep—as with thoroughbreds, jacks, and cattle—all helped make Ashland a profitable place. In 1850, Clay's livestock would be valued at $20,000—twice the worth of the house itself. The snort of a thor-oughbred, the bray of a jack, the bellow of a bull, the bleat of a sheep all showed Clay's farm to be a progressive place as well. Clay's agrarian world gave him the financial security needed to run for office, a strong reputation in the (voting) agricultural community of America, and a growing aware-ness of the interconnectivity of a global economy.[14]

Besides finding some fortune in the political world and prosperity in the agrarian one, Henry Clay sought to further his success through land

and business transactions. In those areas, he experienced a decidedly more mixed record. In regard to land—the issue that had driven so many to frontier Kentucky—Clay was active early in his career. He speculated, bought land to expand Ashland, and purchased property for family members. He secured town lots and agricultural land, houses and a hotel, mills and medicinal springs, stocks and securities. He acquired land across Kentucky and in Ohio, Indiana, Illinois, and Missouri. He invested in internal improvement enterprises—banks, bridge companies, turnpike companies, railroad companies, even a medical building for Transylvania University.[15]

Initially, it seemed to Henry Clay that everything he touched turned to gold. Just a little over a decade after his arrival in Kentucky, the thirty-one-year-old had accumulated more than 10,000 acres of land, fourteen slaves, and forty horses, along with the beginnings of an estate. By 1811, Clay had sold some of the less desirable land, but had used the proceeds in growing Lexington to procure valuable town lots. His eleven different rental properties in 1817 earned him almost $4,000 a year in income—again, more than twice a congressman's salary. By 1818, Clay had raised his taxable wealth from $44,450 just two years earlier to $75,400. His success seemed unstoppable.[16]

Then came the devastating panic of 1819. Clay's economic world collapsed. Rents fell, property values declined, debtors defaulted, and ready cash ceased. Within three years, his taxable worth may have fallen to $28,400—only about 37 percent of what it had been. That figure did not completely represent Clay's net worth—debtors owed him over $35,000 and he still had sizable holdings in valuable livestock. But the depression hit him hard, and he never again would attain a taxable worth equivalent to what he had held in 1818. By the 1830s, he had rebuilt his fortunes, but then suffered more setbacks.[17]

The panic of 1819 had a sobering effect on Clay. His speculative land transactions greatly decreased in frequency, but more than that, he had to go into significant debt to survive the distress, and that proved difficult to overcome. The time he had to devote to his finances also took away from his political life. Nor did Lexington ever fully recover from the effects, after the depression combined with Transylvania University's decline, the rise of river trade routes, the cholera deaths of 1833, and the panic of 1837. In the 1840s, the population in the city and county remained virtually stagnant, even as the nation expanded greatly. But despite the setbacks and outlook, Clay continued to take large risks, especially if it involved family members. Started in the midst of the 1837 panic, Clay's joint efforts with a son to set up a hemp rope and bagging business never proved profitable, for example. Desperate to help his son succeed, Clay poured bad money after bad money in an effort to keep the concern afloat. But it eventually failed. When an auction of assets took place, he insisted that the creditors be paid off before him. In the end, Clay received nothing from the sale and had $20,000 in debt. He had mortgaged Ashland to raise money to assist the business. With the failure of the company and no prospect of repayment, Clay had that debt hanging over his head when he returned from Washington in 1842. Financial woes often took his attention away from focusing on needed political concerns.[18]

Sometimes, his finances themselves became political issues. The panic of 1819 and its attendant problems had caused Clay to place some properties as security for a $22,000 BUS loan agreement. Political enemies heard vague rumors of that and in the election year of 1828 published stories that suggested Secretary of State Clay faced bankruptcy. An angry Clay wrote a public letter of denial, stressing that he had debts of $10,000 and (perhaps overstating the case) assets of $100,000. That issue would not be a political problem again, for he soon paid off the BUS note, but his financial issues did worry Clay at times. They also made the presidency, with its $25,000 salary, even more appealing. But in truth, had it not been for Clay's support of family members, he would have been considered very wealthy. As it was, Clay had significant assets all his life. In contrast to many southern planters, who "lived well and died broke," Clay left his descendants a good inheritance. He did navigate the financial peaks and valleys during his lifetime, but he more often stood on the high ground, surveyed his estate, and called it good.[19]

If Ashland represented the public face of the successful Clay, it did not always offer a pleasant retreat for him. Its walls also reminded Clay of the tragedies that plagued his family circle. There, his children had played, had laughed, had learned. There, Clay had experienced parental joy. But there, too, the memories of happy times past had to war with the recollections of the pain of loss. Life had not been good to Henry Clay regarding his children.

The Clays had eleven children over the first twenty-two years of their marriage. Fourteen months after their nuptials, the first offspring arrived; the last came in 1821, when Lucretia was thirty-nine and Henry forty-three. Yet within five years after greeting that last baby, Clay had experienced the deaths of four of his six daughters. Antebellum Americans almost expected death as part of the natural order; on average, one of three children did not reach adulthood. Childbirth itself, disease, and other killers took their toll. But the Clays saw the pale horse ridden by death pass their way all too often. Their first child, Henrietta, died before the age of one; daughter Laura passed away in infancy as well, a victim of whooping cough contracted while the family made the trying trip to Washington. But more heart-rending were the deaths of daughters who had survived those dangerous early years and had the promise of adulthood before them.

In 1823, fourteen-year-old Lucretia perished at Ashland, probably as a result of tuberculosis. Only two years later, an even more devastating blow came. Twelve-year-old Elizabeth, or Eliza, traveled with her parents to the capital to live, after her father took over the reins of the office of secretary of state. But fever struck her in Ohio and the family caravan stopped to let her recover. A doctor told Clay that he was confident she was recovering and that he could safely leave and assume his important duties. Lucretia would stay with Eliza, and they would make the rest of the trip and reunite with Clay later. As the patriarch traveled, about twenty miles from Washington, he picked up a newspaper to see what was happening in the world. He read of his daughter's death almost two weeks earlier. Moving faster than the reports could catch up to him, he had the sudden shock of reading of the termination of a life so young, and it stunned him. More than that, the news left him with tremendous feelings of guilt. He wrote Lucretia an explanatory letter, but told another family member how he felt extreme regret about leaving Eliza in Ohio. Left unsaid were the perhaps unspoken questions and doubts: Could he have saved her somehow, had he remained behind? Had he put pride and career over family? Whatever the answers, the fact remained that Clay had lost four daughters.[20]

That sadness had been at least somewhat tempered by the joy of his two remaining daughters' marriages. In 1822, seventeen-year-old Susan Hart Clay had exchanged vows with Martin Duralde Jr. of New Orleans. Two children—one named for her husband, one for her father—soon followed, and at age forty-five, Henry Clay was a grandfather for the first time. But five weeks after Eliza's tragic death, Susan died as well. The twenty-year-old mother of two had contracted yellow fever in Louisiana, but as a friend told Clay, "The news of the death of her sister weighed heavily on her; it depressed her spirits and perceptibly affected her health." She died on September 18, 1825, leaving behind a child not yet weaned and a two-year-old. When another correspondent described Susan's last words to Clay, the pain grew even deeper. Her parting farewell to the world had been, "I regret to die without seeing my Father & mother."[21]

Two daughters had died within weeks of each other, causing Clay great anguish. Four years after that, Clay's mother, stepfather, and brother John all passed away in the same year. Death seemed to surround Clay. But so, too, did life. His remaining daughter, Anne Brown Clay, was the joy of that life. Writers have often called Henry Clay Jr. the favorite child, but Henry Clay Sr.'s letters make it very clear that he had a special bond with Anne. Visitors and friends described her as being more like her father than any other of his children. She exuded warmth, grace, and compassion. People liked Anne when they met her, and her letters reveal a young woman mature beyond her years. Clay called her "the best of girls," for she gave great love and affection to others. She quickly attracted suitors, one being James Erwin. In October 1823, the twenty-seven-year-old former Transylvania University student and now commodities speculator married the sixteen-year-old Anne Clay. They had their first child three months after her sister Susan died in 1825. Anne had seven more pregnancies over the next decade. But of those, one was stillborn, one died before its first birthday, and another was gone by age three. All that added to her father's woes as well. Yet, by the time of her eighth pregnancy, she had four healthy children, including one named for her father and one for her mother.[22]

The Erwins had a home in New Orleans, but with Clay putting up the money in Anne's name, the Erwins purchased 108 acres of land within walking distance of Ashland. From that summer home of Woodlands, Anne continued to delight Clay: "She is one of the few sources which I have of real happiness." With his farm prospering, with his daughter and his grandchildren nearby, Clay seemed happy. Like her father, Anne delighted in horticulture. She faced her eighth pregnancy in good health and "very happy." Yet each time childbirth neared, many antebellum women feared the outcome. As one explained to her husband, "As the time is now rapidly approaching for me to give birth to a child, an event which will probably terminate my experience in this world, I take my pen to impart some of my last wishes to you and to bid you an affectionate and tender farewell."[23]

On November 2, 1835, Anne gave birth to a new boy. But the mother experienced hemorrhaging. She seemed on her way to recovery as Clay once more journeyed back to Washington. But almost as if he had a foreboding, he grew very uneasy about Anne. He told Lucretia in a letter, "My anxiety about her I cannot describe. Our only daughter—and so good a daughter." The day after he wrote these words, and five weeks after the birth of her child, Anne died, at age twenty-eight.[24]

The news of the death of his last surviving daughter almost killed Henry Clay. He had been at a gathering in Washington, laughing and joking with friends, when he opened a letter from home. His face turned ashen and he cried out, "Every tie to life is broken!" Those close to him grew concerned over his own health. If any question of Clay's deep love for his children exists, it should be dispelled by the letter he wrote his wife after hearing the news. Every line is a cry of hurt from the heart:

> Alas! My dear wife, the great Destroyer has come and taken from us our dear, dear, only daughter. . . . If the Thunderbolt of H[e]aven had fallen on me—unprepared as I fear I am—I would have submitted, cheerfully submitted . . . to have saved this dear child. She was so good, so beloving, and so beloved, so happy, and so deserving to be happy. Then, she was . . . taken from us. . . .
>
> I feel that one of the strongest ties that bound me to Earth is broken—forever broken. My heart will bleed as long as it palpitates. Never, never can its wounds be healed. . . .
>
> The dear child was so entwined around my heart; I looked forward to so many days of comfort and happiness in her company, during the remnant of my life, that I shall never, never be able to forget her.[25]

Those were not just words on paper. Various colleagues recalled that Clay cried all morning after hearing the news of Anne's death; he could not stop. On New Year's Day 1836, three weeks after his daughter's death, Clay unleashed his emotions once more in a letter to an old friend. Some wounds can never heal, he wrote, and this was one of those: "She was my nighest neighbor; all her tastes and pleasures and announcements . . . were similar to my own." She had good children, a good husband, good friends, and a good life. Anne was "the happiest female I know." Now, Clay confessed, nothing remained for him in this world "but the performance of duties." Two months following Anne's death, Clay remained secluded in his quarters, depressed and seeing almost no one except when duty demanded. Yet somehow he gathered the strength to go on, to remain positive, and to look to a better future. The will and force of Henry Clay should not be underestimated.[26]

While Clay grieved in Washington, Lucretia fought to preserve the life of Anne's newborn. She succeeded, and the boy joined the numerous other grandchildren now in and out of Ashland. Susan Duralde's two boys often shared the house with Anne's surviving children—a total of seven. At a time when Henry and Lucretia's youngest son was leaving home, the estate was hearing the sounds of even younger children once more. Clay could laugh about it and tell a friend that the house "has all the animation which was exhibited twenty years ago," but those words could not hide the hurt: "He once had daughters. Now he had none."[27]

To lose a child is a tragic, heartbreaking thing for a parent. By age fifty-seven, Henry Clay had lost six children and four grandchildren. But what happened to Clay's sons made Clay's life almost a living death in itself.

By the time of Clay's resignation and return home in 1842, all five of his sons still lived. Yet, all of them gave Clay concern, and some gave him great grief. Chief among the latter was the oldest son, Theodore, born in 1802. Clay's sons craved fame and fortune, but most lacked the ability, will, and work ethic to achieve those desires. Theodore proved no exception. Melancholy, ill-tempered, and as Henry Clay indicated, "soured with all the world," he threatened a slave with a knife, departed Harvard University without graduating, and while in Washington with his father in 1824, incurred large gambling debts and was sent home. Over the years, Clay tried to aid all his sons by providing them with funds, jobs, and support. In Theodore's case, Clay used his position as secretary of state to appoint his son as a bearer of diplomatic dispatches to Mexico. Theodore carried out the nepotistic assignment, but never could find other suitable employment. Then real problems began to arise.[28]

Theodore Clay became infatuated with a local girl who did not return his devotion as he thought she should. As a result, his father wrote, "On the subject of a certain lady he is, as we all begin to fear, quite deranged." Theodore stalked the girl and acted irrationally, and then it got worse. Finally, he entered the house of the young woman and threatened violence. A court action against Theodore was began, but the family placed him in the Lunatic Asylum of Kentucky in late 1831. That move became public knowledge and opponents occasionally used the issue against Clay. Later, family accounts would blame the insanity on an injury to the head that Theodore had suffered as a youth, but that represents rationalization more than reality. As Clay would discover, the mental illness his son displayed would not be confined to Theodore. Another son visited his brother in the asylum and reported to their father that Theodore remained "deranged upon two subjects, love and ambition." He found his brother's mind filled with suspicions, plots, and conspiracies. As it turned out, Theodore would remain institutionalized the rest of his life, getting progressively worse. He was the only son whom Clay basically gave up on.[29]

The life of second son Thomas Hart Clay caused Clay anguish as well, though with a better result. Like other male Clays, Thomas found success elusive and excesses attractive. He left the military academy at West Point in his first year. Subsequently, like all the sons, he read law, but he soon showed the effect of a dissipated life. Thomas's drinking problems grew worse and worse. By 1829, Thomas briefly went to jail in Philadelphia for nonpayment of a hotel bill—also public knowledge. Even though Clay had little confidence in Thomas's stability, he allowed the twenty-six-year-old to run a Clay-owned farm in Illinois. But absence from home apparently made the heart grow fonder for drink, and reports reached the patriarch of Thomas's bad habits and frequent "debauches." A failure as a farmer, Thomas returned to Lexington, where he again began to have problems. But Thomas became more stable, and Henry Clay continued to try and help him succeed. He later built his son the estate called Mansfield, near Ashland. By 1850, Thomas had nineteen slaves to work his land and had some success in his farming endeavors. By then, Henry Clay was almost desperate to do anything to try to bring happiness to the survivors of his once-numerous clan.[30]

Unfortunately Clay's third son, James Brown Clay, had displayed some of the same problems as his two older male siblings. He, too, found little happiness and success initially. But his father remained convinced that his son had "a remarkable business aptitude" and soon put young James in charge of yet another Clay farm in yet another state (Missouri). James eventually returned to Kentucky, married, and started a family that would grow to ten children, including one named Lucretia and one Henry. On the patriarch's return to Kentucky in 1842, he restarted his law practice to help pay off some of his debts. That also allowed the father to aid his son once more, for James had graduated from law school. Now, Henry took James as a partner to help him become better established. Around the same time that Henry Clay installed son Thomas at Mansfield, he set up James and his family at what became known as Clay Villa. That allowed the son's household to visit Ashland easily as well. But James continued to display a "roving spirit." With his father's help, James took a lucrative overseas assignment, sold his house, and on the family's return to the United States, moved back to Missouri, where he still found little happiness. Henry Clay saw another son without much purpose or promise, it seemed.[31]

The fourth son, Henry Clay Jr., appeared to have more success—West Point, profitable businesses, a law degree, and more. But the last of Clay's sons, John Morison Clay, born in 1821, did not. That son had been dismissed for bad behavior from preparatory school at Edgehill Seminary in New Jersey, then readmitted thanks to his father's intervention. After a year at Transylvania University, John entered the College of New Jersey at Princeton, only to be suspended and then dismissed in 1840. He then entered a third college, in Pennsylvania, and later privately studied some law. Called lazy and indolent, John did not have the problem of drink that some of his siblings had, but he had produced a mixed record by the time he turned twenty-one: "I almost despair of him," wrote his frustrated father. But that despair soon turned to anguish, for in the spring of 1845, John was found roaming the woods late at night, using "wild and boisterous" language, speaking incoherently, and threatening suicide. The "mental aberration" that Clay had noticed earlier now grew worse, and John was briefly institutionalized with his brother Theodore. A demoralized father found it "extremely hard to bear this last sad affliction." Happily, John got better and returned to Ashland, where he soon found his niche as the operator of the Clay horse-breeding business. Taking over supervision of those activities at age twenty-one, on Clay's return from Washington, he eventually succeeded in that arena. But he would never be free of mental illness and would be in and out of the asylum a few more times. To the very end, Henry Clay would worry that John's problem might recur at any moment.[32]

Except for Theodore, in the asylum, all the surviving Clay sons had had some limited success, often after many setbacks and failures. But none was able to stay out of the shadow of the patriarch and stand in the light of his own achievement. They could not emulate Clay; they could not meet the societal expectations of the sons of Clay; they could not be certain that he did not love politics more than them. And that reality almost destroyed some of them.

One biographer calls Clay a "wretched father." That judgment is just wrong. Clay was often an absent father. He was usually an overly indulgent father. He was frequently a distracted father. But Clay was also a loving parent, a grieving *paterfamilias*, a supportive patriarch.[33]

Many successful public men of that era spent long periods of time away from family, whether in business ventures or on the lawyer's circuit or in Congress. The first regular session of a Congress typically would run from 190 to 230 days at a time, for example. A few members, including Clay, sometimes brought their families with them, but that generally did not prove to be an acceptable option. Most did not see their families while Congress was in session. But when he was home, Clay was a caring parent who was devoted to his family. The cries of anguish upon the deaths of his children, the deep sorrows over the woes of the living, the sacrifices—many of them financial—on behalf of them reflect that love. Clay tried to balance a career that would make him worthy in the eyes of his children and their descendants, with a life that would produce funds to give his offspring an inheritance and standard of living that would ensure their well-being after his death. He thus tried to balance being a father and a politician. In those efforts, Clay did not always succeed. If anything, he was too indulgent as a parent, seldom disciplining his children. Yet he did not overlook errors, nor did he encourage irresponsibility. He might gently chastise, but in the end he forgave and brought his children home. In contrast to many of his generation, whose correspondence is filled with harsh words of criticisms or warnings of God's retribution or a dark pessimism, Clay's letters speak softer words, even when his children frequently taxed his patience.[34]

Clay's sons did have problems, as did the sons of many of the successful men in that and later generations. Some wanted to emulate their fathers but could not. Some wanted to break away from the patriarchs but in the end could not. The Hart-Clay offspring had a disposition as well to depression, alcoholism, and mental instability—no easy problems for a parent to deal with. Clay thus faced many family challenges, worked to cope with them, and tried to enable his surviving children to do well. He could have done better, as most parents could; he could have done worse, as some parents do. In short, he was not a failed father, just a typical one.[35]

But what does all that mean regarding Henry Clay the presidential candidate? First, his family situation would both give him sympathy and criticism—sympathy over the loss of his daughters and criticism, at least covertly, regarding his son in the asylum. People of his era would often blame the father for a child's misfortune. If Clay had done such a poor job of parenting, could he be trusted to be a father of his country?[36]

Death seemed ever present to him. In the last three decades of his life, he suffered the death of a mother, or brother, or child or in-law, or grandchild in almost half of those years—the loss of more than eighteen close family members.[37] That exacted a toll, physically and emotionally. Every death required him to draw deeper and deeper from the reservoir of will within him. Yet, he continued to work for family, farm, and country. Perhaps because Clay so recognized his own mortality, he worked harder for the future. He would act partly for himself and his ambitions, but also he operated for the memories of those family members now gone, for those who lived in the present, and for generations as yet unborn. If he was not as successful in his private world as he would wish, Henry Clay was further driven to succeed in the public arena—ironically, often at a further cost to his family. He almost had to live in the political world to forget the losses in the private one.

Henry Clay's family concerns did not focus only on his children. The Clays essentially raised a second family in the persons of their grandchildren. The deaths of their mothers—two Clay daughters and a daughter-in-law—resulted in ten motherless children by 1840. That year, Henry and Lucretia turned sixty-three and fifty-nine, respectively. Typically in that era, young children without mothers would be raised by other female family members rather than by the father. That would be the case with the Clays. After Anne's death, Lucretia and Henry had to care for a newborn and grandchildren aged five, six, seven, eight, eleven, and twelve, and had partial responsibility for three other motherless children as well.[38]

But if the Clays hoped for exemplary grandchildren who would bring joy in an often joyless household filled with death, if they expected new family happiness in an approaching old age, they were disappointed. In the next generation, illness, bad behavior, and drinking produced discipline problems, resentment, and also death. Over the fifteen years after Anne's death, four more grandchildren died. One did not survive infancy, but the others all had achieved adulthood. Both the Duraldes had been problem grandchildren from the start. Clay had procured Martin III a posting as a midshipman in the navy, but health problems—likely tuberculosis—soon struck. In 1846, grandson Martin Duralde III died at age twenty-three. His brother Henry Clay Duralde moved to gold-rush California, but drowned there in 1850 at age twenty-five. And in Anne's family, James Erwin Jr. died at the age of twenty, a probable suicide after a night of drinking. Clay had noted earlier that Death "has now commenced his work of destruction . . . in the second generation." His own offspring would eventually produce thirty children, twenty-five of them born in his lifetime. Of those twenty-five, eight died before Clay; nine more would pass away before Lucretia.[39]

Some of the losses occurred during crucial periods in Clay's career. One daughter died in 1823, while Clay was running for president; two passed away just as he took the office of secretary of state; a granddaughter's life ended during the 1832 presidential canvass. But other losses year after year stole from the spirit from Henry Clay. Raising a second family depleted some of his energy. Constant concerns about family members demanded his attention.[40]

Those family losses took their toll on Clay's own well-being. But he had always complained of his health and in speeches and letters had almost constantly lamented his "precarious" state, his "extremely bad" circumstances, his "prostrated" condition. He made more than a thousand references to his health over a fifty-year period. As early as age forty-six, he was telling fellow congressmen, "I am growing old." How much of that reflected real health concerns and how much represented a tendency to hypochondria is difficult to know. Clay did seem to experience problems at stressful times and would go to medicinal watering spots in Virginia or New York, or to the coast, to try to recover. The combination of rest, relaxation, and isolation from the cares of the world would restore his health.[41]

In one sense, Clay was quite lucky in regard to his health. He avoided illness during the two deadly cholera epidemics that swept Lexington, escaped serious injury when riding in a stagecoach that overturned and killed one person, eluded major harm when a bull charged him and killed his mount, and avoided death when a horse kicked him. But real illness did strike Clay, especially in 1823, 1828, and 1841–42. The first of those came in the year of Clay's daughter's death and during a presidential campaign. Next, in his time as secretary of state, he suffered the loss of two daughters and the slander of the opposition, and almost resigned his post due to persistent health issues that included numbness in one leg. In the crucial early days of the Tyler interregnum, Clay had fallen seriously ill in Baltimore. By March 1842, after the split with Tyler, Clay suffered "great pain" in the chest. He may have suffered a heart attack, but the evidence is not at all conclusive. And when ill, Clay suffered treatments that often did little to aid recovery: In 1823, he received doses of mercury; in 1834, a doctor prescribed mustard plasters on Clay's stomach; in 1842, physicians bled him copiously. Over time, health issues began to have an effect, despite the vigor and energy that Clay continued to exude in public life.[42]

In an ideal world in 1843, the sixty-six-year-old Clay would be facing the upcoming presidential campaign with all his children happy and successfully engaged in their chosen fields, with his grandchildren visiting occasionally for him to enjoy their laughter and company, with his estate producing profits and moments of relaxation, with his time free to focus on the race. But Clay's actual world featured memories of many deaths, asylums and mostly dependent adult children, a second family of grandchildren living at Ashland, a mortgage on the estate, and a very disjointed, distracted life. And so, in those circumstances, Clay faced the reality of a run for president.

13

Presidential Candidate IV

EVEN WHEN DEALING WITH FARM and family matters at Ashland, Henry Clay was never very far removed from the ever-demanding political world in which he lived. He constantly evaluated his prospects for the next presidential race and, somewhat to his surprise, found them very promising—initially. But the resulting election of 1844 would produce a perfect storm of problems. All his political baggage was once more opened to public scrutiny. New questions surfaced and demanded answers. Fresh fabrications required further responses. Fraud reared its head. In the end, no single question would decide the race or dominate the debates across the nation. Together, the old and new matters raised many doubts about the presidential caliber of Henry Clay—again.

In fact, that Clay had a real chance at victory in itself represents a tremendous testament to his abilities. After all, following the close of the divisive 1841 special session of Congress, the Whigs had lost six of the next eight contested governors' races. The midterm 1842 congressional elections had resulted in the greatest turnover in seats since the Compensation Act bloodbath of 1816. During and after those elections, the patronage of the president had also been directed against the Whigs. Some of the opposition predicted that the Whig Party might not even exist by 1844. Yet, party members had come together behind their acknowledged leader, Clay; they had repaired their hopes, and had made some inroads against the Democrats since then. Much of the credit for that rebirth from political despair resulted out of great personal loyalty to Clay by many of the core party leaders. That Clay almost won in 1844 is a testament to his political strength.[1]

Recent Whig history meant that Clay, despite his front-runner status, had much to overcome if he wanted the presidency. Tyler supporters remained outside the ranks, splintering the party coalition that had proved victorious in 1840. Additionally, the excitement and promise of that past race had been muted by the party's dismal congressional showing after Tyler's vetoes. Whigs seemingly had had a chance to prove their worth and had failed. The question of slavery also hovered over a party whose southern and northern wings stood more divided than did their Democratic counterparts. And although the Whigs had registered more new voters than the Democrats in the depression years before the 1840 race, since then the Democrats had added many more new voters than the Whigs had. For Clay's party, the saving grace in this sea of negativity seemed to be that the Democrats remained divided and uncertain as well. John Tyler might form a third party; John C. Calhoun might run as a separate, sectional candidate; and Democratic front-runner Martin Van Buren might not be able to unite the factions or generate great enthusiasm.[2]

By 1842, most commentators already expected the race to pit Van Buren against Clay. Calhoun and Tyler might bluster and bristle, and Winfield Scott might entertain hopes of challenging Clay, but few expected anyone other than the New Yorker and the Kentuckian to emerge as the major party nominees in 1844. Henry Clay welcomed such a contest, for while he both liked and respected Van Buren, he also believed he could beat him.[3]

Martin Van Buren had made a pre-campaign trip to the South and West in 1842 and had stayed at Clay's estate for several enjoyable days. When the short, pudgy, well-dressed Van Buren stood with the tall, thin, casually clothed Clay on the steps of Ashland, their contrasting appearances seemed to personify the political differences between the two. One advocated Democratic principles and admired Andrew Jackson; the other fathered the American System and hated the old general. But in many ways Van Buren and Clay were more alike than different. Both rued their lack of formal education, both liked to gamble—Van Buren had offered to bet Clay a suit of clothes on one election—and both charmed in small gatherings. (One observer called Van Buren "as polished and captivating a person in the social circle as America has ever known.") Politically, the two shared many characteristics as well. Both had served as secretary of state and, in fact, Van Buren had purchased Clay's house in Washington. Both embraced compromise to get things done. Both succeeded as coalition builders, with Van Buren better at the national level, Clay superior in Congress. And both simply loved the political game. Once when Van Buren presided over the Senate as vice president, Clay had lambasted his Democratic opponent in a speech. Afterwards, Clay had walked up to Van Buren's desk, had taken some snuff, had smiled, and said, "Van, didn't I give it to you handily today?" The New Yorker chuckled and replied, "Well, yes, you did lay it on pretty thick, but you know you were lying all the time." The two men laughed together. Clay appreciated that approach to politics and respected foes like Van Buren.[4]

Thus, while Clay detested Van Buren's political principles, he genuinely liked the man. The Kentuckian called the ex-president courteous, cordial, and amusing. But Clay also knew that Van Buren had many weaknesses, which he would exploit if a race developed between the two. Van Buren's depression-era presidency had not accomplished much, and like Clay, he had lost a presidential election. Van Buren had brokered North-South political alliances that had helped the Democracy win victories, but as a northerner, he found it hard to attract widespread southern support. Southerners also equally distrusted Clay for his moderate antislavery pronouncements, but at least he lived in what could be considered a southern state and owned slaves. One early Clay biographer called Van Buren a northern man with southern principles, Clay a southern man with northern principles. Clay expected to do well in the South against Van Buren and, at last, to be able to attack a man with a real record to defend.[5]

Van Buren had character questions and public and private liabilities that put him at political risk as well. It would be hard to attack Clay if the other party's own candidate displayed the same traits. Ambitious? So was Van Buren. A behind-the-scenes operator? So was the New Yorker. A Washington insider? So was the ex-president. And Van Buren's public image seemed at least as negative as Clay's. Even Clay opponent William Barry admitted that Clay "has traits of character that Van Buren has not." Moreover, as the "great Magician," Van Buren had a reputation as a "juggler in politics," a cunning wire-puller, an intriguing schemer, a man who put party above the people. Amos Kendall recounted a Van Buren who "glides along as smoothly as oil and as silently as a cat," while the always-quotable John Randolph noted that Van "rowed to his object with muffled oars." Van Buren might get things done, but his methods somehow did not seem honorable or open. Critics pounced on him. His flexibility would be attacked as a lack of fixed principles; he would, said a Tennessee attorney, readily "embrace any doctrine . . . which would procure him the good will of the majority." Van Buren's ability to sidestep controversial issues or to be non-committal would produce descriptions of his evasiveness. Even Van Buren's tendency to dress well would bring some to term him an effeminate dandy with perfumed whiskers. As with Clay, Van Buren's strengths could be easily reversed and presented as a weakness. That boded well for his expected opponent. Winning in 1844 looked more and more attainable to Henry Clay.[6]

Then a matter arose that changed the course of the campaign for both Clay and Van Buren. The New Yorker soon found out, as had Jackson and Clay before him, that any alliance with Calhoun would prove ephemeral, while the Kentuckian discovered that old enemy Calhoun and new opponent Tyler could still generate mischief.

Both Calhoun and Tyler wanted the presidency. By 1843, neither had yet generated much support. Some expected Tyler to make an independent bid. A few hoped the Democrats would adopt him. But most agreed that he had little real power or very good prospects. In turn, Calhoun supporters sought either to form their own party or to gain Tyler's backing for their man, should the president drop out of the race. But without much momentum, Tyler, then Calhoun, raised the issues of the annexation of the Republic of Texas into the United States as a vehicle to energize their races. Tyler wanted to use the question to restore his prestige and popularity, and to bring glory to a discredited administration. As the *United States Magazine and Democratic Review* noted later, Tyler desired to "buy his way into the Democratic party, by patronage and Texas." Calhoun expected the Texas issue would reignite the slavery debate, bring sectionalism to the forefront, and perhaps solidify the South behind his candidacy.[7]

Eventually their ambition for office brought the two men together when Tyler appointed Calhoun as secretary of state. Together, the two stressed that acquisition would furnish new markets, expand national power, and provide new lands for settlement. Texas statehood would mean greater demand for slaves and add a new slave state to support the South. And both men downplayed the possibility of war with Mexico over what Tyler would call its "silly claim to Texas." A Georgia Whig termed the appearance of the Texas issue "a miserable political humbug set up as a ruse to divide and distract the Whig party at the south." He concluded of the matter: "So far as Tyler is concerned in the [Texas] project it has been for his own aggrandizement. So far as Calhoun is concerned it has been done to [set?] up a *southern party*." And by combining the explosive Calhoun with the

Texas controversy, Tyler had made the likelihood of provocation as great as possible.[8]

By the time the Texas issue began to become a national issue, Clay had made his feelings about Texas clear for a quarter century. He had been consistent throughout. In 1819–20, Secretary of State John Quincy Adams had offered to accept a narrow definition of what the vague Louisiana Purchase included in regard to Texas, to appease then-owner Spain and to smooth the pending purchase of Florida. In Congress, Clay had vehemently disagreed with what he later called the American "abandonment" of a valid claim to Texas. Then, as secretary of state, Clay had twice tried unsuccessfully to purchase Texas. And when Texas won its independence from Mexico, Clay had supported early recognition, as he had with the South American republics and Greece. But to that point, all of Clay's efforts to secure Texas used either treaty interpretations or purchase options—in short, peaceful ones. To the one-time War Hawk, recognition and annexation represented "entirely different questions," and no actions should be taken that would produce a conflict: "I would not for one moment consent to involve this country in war to acquire that country," he wrote in 1838.[9]

If annexation could be done peacefully, then Clay had no objections to Texas entering the Union; if it remained an independent nation, he could accept that as well. Overall, Clay probably preferred the second option for the moment, for he saw before him a still-fledging United States, just emerging from a depression, with many existing structural problems, including slavery. In fact, a nineteenth-century biographer suggested that Clay did not push Texas's admission because he wanted to limit the expansion of slavery. Whatever his reasons, in the years from 1819 to 1844 Clay had not opposed bringing Texas into the Union if done by peaceful means, but once Texas had secured its independence, he could accept that status for the moment. His main concern was to avoid a controversial war that could disrupt a fragile national balance.[10]

Early on, Clay fully recognized the danger that issue might pose to his campaign. He then tried to gauge the extent of the problem, take preemptive action to minimize the threat, and remove the issue from the debate. But he either received bad information or misread the signs himself, once communications reached him regarding the issue in the South. Clay would panic, make mistakes, and lose support. But his eventual stance regarding Texas also helped him in certain places. In some ways, Texas was less a defining issue in the race than it was a symbol of all the problems Clay experienced in 1844.[11]

By late 1843, Texas annexation became an issue again. In December, Clay told allies that while Tyler and Calhoun had largely manufactured the controversy, they should do all they could to silence the debate; otherwise, it might produce unwanted "discussion, discord, and distraction." As Clay informed John J. Crittenden, America should "harmonize and improve what we have," and instead live with Texas "as good neighbors." The issue seemed to be losing power when Calhoun dropped out of the race in December 1843. But the South Carolinian had not given up on his overall goal. Texas would not go away.[12]

To gauge the effects of the Texas issue on the South and to solidify his support in a region that he expected to carry against Van Buren in 1844, Clay took one of his quasi-campaign trips. Earlier, in the fall of 1842, he had made a similar, if briefer, foray into Ohio and Indiana, with good results. In Dayton, the largest political rally ever held in the United States up to that time—as many as two hundred thousand people—gathered to hear Clay's address. Now he sought to repeat that success. For six months, from December 1843 to May 1844, Clay would literally be wined and dined across the South. In return, he made either impromptu or planned speeches in several locales. In Savannah, for example, he warned against foreign wars and stressed that "time and patience" would better produce prosperity and happiness for the nation. Clay did not mention Texas by name in his talks, but in private gatherings he did ask the opinions of those present. If his chief reason for the trip was to determine the possible effect of the Texas issue in the South, he received mixed signals. In March, he told Crittenden of the excitement in the region regarding Texas. After all, most settlers in Texas came from America and, as one paper said, "They are fighting the battles of liberty," gaining sympathy. But the next month, in a different state, Clay wrote another friend that he had discovered mostly "indifference or opposition" to annexation, "which greatly surprised me." In the nation's capital, he found not sectional divides but a united party, opposed to the "rogue leader" Tyler and annexation's threats to the Union.[13]

While Clay traveled, events accelerated. By April 1844 Calhoun had taken up his duties as secretary of state. Within weeks, he signed a treaty to annex Texas to the United States. But many commentators indicated that treaty would be a dead letter, for they expected (correctly) that the Senate would easily reject the treaty. Clay's stance seemed to be the majority view. Yet at the same time, an aging Andrew Jackson reversed his own presidential position and now wrote that Texas must be obtained "peacefully if we can, but forcibly if we must." The old general's paranoia regarding the

British and his determination to defeat Clay by any means overrode his previous stands. He now predicted (incorrectly) that annexation would not result in war. "The subject will destroy Clay even in Kentucky," he said.[14]

With a treaty signed but not ratified, with his southern trip nearly concluded, with some voters still clamoring for his views on Texas, and with the Whig presidential convention only two weeks away, Clay reached Raleigh, North Carolina. In a major speech and, four days after that, in a letter designed for widespread public consumption, Clay gave his thoughts on Texas, determined to quiet that controversy for good.

Clay's friends constantly worried about their candidate's proclivity to make needless speeches and to write too-frequent letters, both of which could produce controversy. A North Carolina Whig congressman received a communiqué asking "who the deuce among you" invited Clay to speak in that state? Such appearances, the letter writer said, would only "waken up popular animosity & prejudice. . . . If he would let himself alone, we should have less trouble in electing him. . . . If St. Paul had been a candidate for the Presidency, I should have advised him to cut the Corinthians." And Kentucky's Robert Letcher warned Crittenden as early as 1842 that Clay "must hereafter remain a little quiet and *hold his jaw*. In fact, he must be *caged*—that's the point, *cage him*! . . . I have some occasional fears that he may write too many letters." Letcher erred in one way, for no one could cage Clay. But he warned properly that when critics accused Clay of vagueness or when they attacked his vanity or his honor, he almost could not bear to remain silent, as if that taciturnity somehow proved the charge. In truth, by responding Clay just brought more attention and more credibility to the assault. As a result, people began to confuse propaganda with reality.[15]

In Raleigh in April, Clay found himself giving a fairly standard talk, in which he recounted what the Whigs represented and what the Democrats had done. The followers of Jackson abused executive power and disregarded the Constitution; they refused to protect American industry; they threatened disunion and encouraged sectionalism; they disrupted the economy. Clay wanted a land where a citizen could ask how he could "best promote the honor and prosperity of his country." That statement of Whig principles would be reprinted across the nation.[16]

A few days later, Clay finally turned to the question he had mostly avoided discussing publicly to that point: Texas. Having heard from advisors, having a proposed treaty to respond to, having ascertained sentiment in the South, Clay drafted a letter that would explain his views on the subject.

In what became known as the Raleigh letter, he started with a history of the issue at the national level, noting that annexation had been rejected as an option years before. Then came his key words: "If, without the loss of national character, without the hazard of foreign war, with the general concurrence of the nation, without any danger to the integrity of the Union, and without giving an unreasonable price for Texas, the question of annexation were presented, it would appear in quite a different light from that in which . . . it is now to be regarded." In short, if such conditions were met and things changed, annexation could occur. But Clay made it clear that now was not that time. Annexation would bring war with Mexico, and "I regard all wars as great calamities, to be avoided, if possible." As he had said for years, the nation needed "union, peace, and patience," not sectionalism, war, and passion. Moreover, Clay wrote, annexation would raise questions of national character and would proclaim to the world that America had "an insatiable and unquenchable thirst for foreign conquest." Finally, as it now stood, raising the issue would reopen the festering wounds of the slavery question and would threaten the integrity of the Union.[17]

Clay sent the letter to Crittenden in Washington, with instructions to let key allies see it, make "slight" modifications if needed, then submit it to the *National Intelligencer* for publication. Apparently, Crittenden advised delay (perhaps until after the convention), but Clay would not agree: "I entertain no fears from the promulgation of my opinion." Two days later, and with no publication yet, Clay tersely wrote Crittenden: "I *wish* it to appear accordingly." On April 27, 1844, Clay's letter appeared. Most Whigs applauded. However, many Democrats had a different reaction. After reading Clay's letter, Andrew Jackson called him "a dead political Duck." Fellow Tennessean James K. Polk, who desperately wanted the Democratic vice presidential nomination, wrote that Clay's "anti-Texas letter" meant that when Van Buren announced his support for annexation, "as I hope and believe he will," then Democratic fortunes would rise in the South, despite previous doubts about Van Buren. Both sides interpreted the Raleigh letter as helping their cause.[18]

The same day, or the next day in some cases, Jackson, Polk, and other Democrats opened their newspapers and read Van Buren's own letter regarding Texas. At first Jackson thought it a forgery. Then he grew livid at its reality. For, like Clay, the Democratic front runner had qualified and hedged but in the end had opposed immediate annexation. Moreover, since the Clay and Van Buren letters often appeared in newspapers the same day, that extremely unfortunate timing spelled trouble for both camps. The same date of the letters' publications made it seem that the two leaders, already perceived by some as behind-the-scenes manipulators, were at it again. The appearance of another bargain loomed large and benefited neither man.[19]

When they had met at Ashland two years earlier, had Clay and Van Buren agreed to take similar positions in an attempt to remove the issue from the debates? Clay's grandson, among others, seemed to imply that. But no real evidence supports the idea of an agreement, and certain factors in fact speak against it. In Clay's case, while he did apparently anticipate Van Buren's position, he acted more from a desire to meet the demands placed on him to take a stand before the convention met. Furthermore, had Crittenden promptly published the piece, it would have appeared more than a week before Van Buren's, rather than the same day. Clay and Van Buren may well have discussed Texas, as well as a host of other issues, when they had talked at Ashland over several days, but it seems likely that they made no covert or overt agreement. The matter had just not seemed that important at that time. But if the timing and content of the letters appears coincidental and accidental, their simultaneous publication proved to be an unhappy accident—another example of Clay's bad luck in elections.[20]

Van Buren had taken a courageous stand in his letter. The easiest and politically safest thing to do would have been to support annexation, to gain southern support. It might have cost him some votes in the North and in his native New York, but the South remained the party's core and another stand—or no letter at all— would have enhanced his prospects there. But Van Buren—like Clay—feared that annexation would disrupt the parties, bring war with Mexico, and perhaps even worse, place the divisive slavery issue back on the national debate stage—a very dangerous thing, indeed. Now, with a month left between the publication of the letters and the start of the Democratic convention, the political fallout from the explosive issue spread further. Tyler still remained in the contest, either as a third party choice or as the Democratic one. In turn, Calhoun told allies that he should be presented as an available choice if the convention deadlocked. And letter writers told prominent Democrats of their anger at Van Buren's stand. Some southerners wrote that on Texas rested "the very existence of our Southern Institutions" and that opposition to annexation would be a concession to abolition.[21]

But the most important letter writer was the party's patriarch, Andrew Jackson. He may well have believed that the two letters represented a collusion of Van Buren with the hated Clay. If so, that alone doomed the New Yorker in Jackson's eyes. Soon the Tennessean wrote three confidential, xenophobic letters to Francis P. Blair, complaining that Britain sought to take or buy Texas, emancipate all slaves there, and thus destroy the value of other southern slaves as a result. Because of that, Jackson emphasized, "I am for the annexation regardless of consequences." Clearly, the "firebrand of division" that Van Buren's letter had introduced in Democratic ranks had infuriated the "mortified" Jackson. Nor did he keep his opinions to himself. To complete his undercutting of his one-time protégé, Jackson wrote a public letter to the *Nashville Union*. Reprinted across the United States, the ex-president's epistle stated that while he admired Van Buren's character and patriotism, on the issue of Texas, Jackson considered his former vice president to be in error. Van Buren's road to victory now would have to run over Andrew Jackson.[22]

Clay's Raleigh letter affected his race much less than Van Buren's letter did his. Democrats portrayed Clay's communication as an attempt to placate the abolitionist wing of the Whigs and keep them in the party. Some southern Whigs raised concerns about its anti-annexation tone, but it did little damage to his candidacy before the convention. However, some Whigs, Thurlow Weed among them, worried about the long-term effect. In reply, Clay expressed no doubt about the correctness of his course: "I am firmly convinced that my opinion on the Texas question will do me no prejudice at the South." Clay may well have been right regarding strong Whigs in the region; swing voters of both parties might be another matter. But had Clay written nothing else after the Raleigh letter, and had he remained loyal to the words within, he would have been better served regarding Texas. But he did not, and was not.[23]

Believing that he and Van Buren had now disposed of the Texas issue, Clay approached the upcoming Whig convention with confidence. Part of that buoyancy also resulted from the fact that this time Webster forces would not be openly opposing him. In reality, Webster's decision to remain in the Tyler cabinet when the other Whigs had resigned had rendered him persona non grata in the party, an almost powerless pariah. A New Yorker wrote that Webster's course had doomed him: "His old substantial friends have abandoned him almost in a body." Boston rallies railed against Webster. When queried about Webster, Clay told correspondents that actions of his one-time ally had "shocked and afflicted me."[24]

Meanwhile, Webster hurriedly began to mend his political fences and move back into the Whig Party's greener political territories. He wrote Clay ally Robert Letcher, complaining like a petulant child about Clay's opposition to him in 1836 and the "ill treatment" given him by the Whig

Party since then. In turn, when an editor sought to reconcile the two, Clay noted that he had known of Webster's role in defeating Clay's nomination in 1839, yet he had supported the "Godlike Daniel" for a cabinet post nevertheless. Then Webster's surprising and shocking actions had followed, and the two had not corresponded for the past three years. Still, Clay said he would forgive and forget, and would welcome Webster back into Whig ranks, but would make no deal—such as the vice presidency—to bring that about. Webster had been severely injured politically by his dalliance with Tyler and needed to be accepted into the Whig ranks; Clay needed a united party. By April 1844, just before the convention, the two camps had temporarily reconciled in an uneasy truce. Harmony seemed everywhere.[25]

The spirit carried over to the convention itself. That Baltimore gathering could not have been much different from the one in 1839 that left Clay with such a bitter taste of treachery. This time the meeting convened at a more appropriate time in the race, open balloting occurred, and unanimity ruled. And various commentators and politicians felt sanguine about Whig chances. The *Louisville Journal* considered Clay's victory over Van Buren "a great moral fact." Party meetings at the state and local level similarly praised the expected nominee and his chances. One county committee exclaimed that Clay, the man who had stilled troubled political waters, had done so as an instrument of "Divine Providence." They added: "If such a man cannot be elected, then we can but fear for the safety of our republican institutions."[26]

On May 1, 1844, on the first ballot, the Whig convention unanimously selected Henry Clay as its nominee for president. The party adopted a very brief platform, then selected a vice president. In that process, Clay missed two important opportunities. As in the past, he left the decision completely to the delegates. On the third ballot, the group chose New Jersey's Theodore Frelinghuysen, a man of unimpeachable moral credentials. A Whig attorney noted that Clay, with the reputation of "a good deal of a runner, will run none the worse for having a deacon to ride him." While "*very much pleased*" with the vice presidential nominee, Clay would have been better served by being more involved in the decision. Someone like Millard Fillmore of New York might have helped more in the tight race, especially since Frelinghuysen proved to be another controversial choice.[27]

The second missed opportunity came when members of the convention called on the nominee to make what would have been the first acceptance speech by a presidential candidate to a convention. That unprecedented move would have upset some party purists, but Clay's oratory might have energized the Whigs. However, once nominated, candidate Clay followed the traditional protocol, citing his "duty to abstain from all solicitations, direct or indirect." He would not speak in public until the election concluded. The party, instead, would have to be satisfied to shout slogans such as "Hey—hey—de country's risin' / For Henry Clay and Frelinghuysen." Democrat James Buchanan found Whigs "high in hopes & burning with enthusiasm." The opposition *Richmond Enquirer* admitted that Democratic victory might be difficult with "Henry Clay, the roaring lion, standing in our path." A bright Whig future seemed assured.[28]

Then came the Democratic convention. What took place there did as much to cause Henry Clay's eventual defeat as any other one thing. Had the anti-annexation northerner Van Buren been nominated, a third party of proslavery, pro-annexation supporters might have split the opposition party. Or, failing that, the deep Democratic divisions and the Whig unity could have made Clay's election prospects considerably better. But none of that happened. Instead, the Democrats emerged from the convention unified, with an issue to advocate and with a candidate mostly free from the electoral history Van Buren had created.

Nearly four weeks after the Whigs convention, the divided Democrats assembled in Baltimore as well. Van Buren remained the clear favorite, but numerous forces opposed him. If delegates selected him, then supporters of both Tyler and Calhoun waited in the wings to gather angry southerners into a new party. And while some Democrats, like former governor William Marcy of New York, thought that Van Buren's response regarding Texas had quenched that fiery issue, it had not. A whole host of other politicians called on Van Buren to drop out of the contest. Amid "this storm and tempest," with infighting raging, a politician summarized the situation: "We are certainly in deep water."[29]

Van Buren had no intention of stepping down. An excellent vote counter, he expected to have enough votes to secure the nomination. But in Baltimore in 1844, the "Little Magician" for once found himself outmaneuvered by the sleight of hand of others. Southerners and northern opponents of Van Buren combined to change the rules (as they did when Clay ran in 1839). Instead of a simple majority, nomination now required receiving two-thirds of the vote. On the first ballot, Van Buren did indeed gain a majority— some 55 percent of the votes. But that was not enough. With virtually no southern support, Van Buren was a used-up man and could not gain the needed votes. More ballots followed, more stalemates occurred.[30]

The convention degenerated into what an ally of Polk called a "general pell-mell fight" and some compromise choice seemed possible. Most expected the respected Silas Wright of New York to be that person, and Van Buren offered to drop out and support him. But Wright refused to run. As the party searched for a resolution to its impasse, Polk's allies operated behind the scenes. Only weeks before the convention, Polk had been doing all he could to secure his goal of the vice presidential nomination. But after the Van Buren Texas letter, he told an ally that now "there is no telling what may occur." Given that a state of confusion existed in the party, his supporters should be prepared "to use my name in any way they may think proper." Wait for the proper time, he advised, and then act. Polk had the disadvantage of not being well known nationally and of having lost his last two attempts to be governor of Tennessee; he had the advantage of being a pro-annexation southerner and a loyal partisan of Andrew Jackson. Finally, on the ninth ballot, his name was put forward for the presidency, Van Buren turned his support to Polk, southerners followed, and Polk won the nomination. The Democrats had picked the first true "dark horse" presidential candidate in US history.[31]

A British paper referred to the selection "of a certain Mr. Polk of whom nobody ever heard." Whigs in America seemed similarly shocked. A New Yorker predicted Polk would be a "severe dose" for northern Democrats, given his adamant proslavery views; the *Whig Banner* termed the Democratic standard-bearer a "fourth rate village lawyer, the fourth rate politician." And many Democrats themselves questioned the selection of a man Amos Kendall called "unexceptional," a person not even mentioned as a candidate only a week before. They considered Polk a weak choice. They were wrong.[32]

In fact, the Democratic selection of Polk proved to be an unexpectedly brilliant political move. In one fell swoop, that nomination deflated Tyler's third-party hopes, for without Texas he had no issue and no hope for southern Democratic desertions. He would withdraw within two months and throw his support to Polk. At the same time, the selection of the proslavery Polk defeated Clay's southern strategy, crafted to vanquish the northerner Van Buren. And Polk, at age forty-eight to Clay's sixty-seven, represented young America: "The old leaders are thrown off," a supporter cheered. The effect of his nomination, wrote Polk, "has been to inspire a new spirit in our party." Even Polk's relatively thin record of accomplishments could become an asset. He would make no speeches, attend no rallies, and write only one public letter during the race. Voters likely knew little more about him and his beliefs at the end of the contest than they did at the start. Attention thus focused more on Clay.[33]

If Polk's candidacy healed Democratic divisions, Clay's presidential run also fully aroused the opposition to unity. They feared Clay more than any other Whig. They feared his policies—Clay's election, said Virginia editor Thomas Ritchie, could "ring the knell of most of our great Republican principles." They feared Clay's powers of persuasion. And they feared his ability to get things done. In short, Democrats united, as one editor recalled, on "their common hostility to Mr. Clay."[34]

Now both sides girded for a battle of epic proportions. Clay partisans echoed the words of a former congressman who proclaimed that "Polk had spent his life like a little black-jack in the depth of the forest, secured by his own insignificance from the danger of storm and tempest . . . while Henry Clay had walked the mountain tops for half a century—like a giant, baring his breast to every storm, and leaving his footprints in the living rock!" In return, Democratic partisans saw in those footprints the mark of the devil, the sign of danger to free institutions, the warning to the republic. As one nineteenth-century Kentuckian said of the Clay forces: "His friends were never more attached and enthusiastic; his enemies never more active and implacable." With an unexpected dark-horse challenger in the contest, the race was on.[35]

The campaign that followed built on the fluff and fury of 1840. As supporters of "Tippecanoe and Tyler too" had touted their log cabins and hard-cider images, published their campaign biographies, and chanted their campaign ditties, political observers had taken note. Now, in 1844, all those trends would be accelerated by both parties in ways that made the election really the first modern, media-oriented contest. But with the parties becoming more alike on some issues, such as internal improvements, races increasingly focused on process rather than principle, on propaganda rather than philosophy, on partisanship rather than perspective. The growing removal of property qualifications to vote greatly expanded the electorate, and both parties devoted much effort to mobilize new voters. Yet, as Clay pointed out in his Raleigh speech, over the years the Democrats "have been our masters, in employing symbols." With only a small margin for error in most states, by 1844 both parties engaged in a furious battle to gain the attention—and votes—of the electorate, and the Whigs took second place to no one in that contest of symbols.[36]

For those who wanted detailed information on the Whig standard-bearer, for instance, there were myriad options. Several biographies and collections of his letters and speeches appeared, giving readers various places to read Clay's own words on various subjects. For those with shorter attention spans, a one-page broadside showed images of Clay, a farmer in the field, a ship at sea, and several scantily clad classical female figures all encircling a small-print biography. "An Irish Adopted Citizen" printed *Fifty Reasons Why the Honorable Henry Clay Should Be Elected President*, and the *Ashland Text Book* offered seventy-two pages of Clay's speeches and other items. But probably the most circulated Clay book was the *Henry Clay Almanac*, with an initial print run of fifty thousand copies. Half of its thirty-two pages went to author Nathan Sargent's sketch of Clay; the rest included information on solar eclipses, the stages of the moon, and pithy sayings. A typical line referred to the Democratic monetary policy as "hard money—yes, hard to get and hard to keep!" Given the fact that the *Almanac* had been envisioned almost two years before Clay's nomination, it was obvious that the Clay forces had long planned an extensive media campaign.[37]

Similarly, the well-financed Whigs established a series of newspapers to place the Clay program and personality before the people. Endeavors like the *Missouri Mill Boy* or the *Alabama Clay Banner* were just two of the journalistic explosion of new sheets. (The number of newspapers in America would double between 1835 and 1850.) One of the strongest new voices of the Whigs would be the editor of the *New York Tribune*, Horace Greeley. A mostly self-trained child prodigy, the nearsighted, hardworking, multi-talented, eccentric Greeley strongly supported Clay all his career, and his resulting editorials thundered the Whig word in 1844.[38]

Not all party publications matched the seriousness of the newspapers, collected works, and biographies. Whig song books and sheet music touted hundreds of selections for the faithful to sing, whether in staid parlors in homes or at lively mass rallies. The almost four hundred pages of the *Clay Minstrel*, for example, contained 143 mostly eulogistic and saccharine songs. For six cents, people could purchase a copy of the Philadelphia *Whig Banner Melodist*, which included such memorable songs as "A Pig-in-a Polk." A verse of that tune ran: "A true pig-in-a Polk, both in name and action / ne'er heard of before, but is leading a faction." The *Henry Clay Almanac* asked readers to sing, to the tune of "Yankee Doodle":

> For Henry Clay and liberty
> Let all the people shout, sir;
> Let's meet the Locos [Democrats] at the polls,

And turn the *traitor* out, sir.
For Henry Clay then keep it up,
For Henry and good times, sir;
Too long by vetoes we've been ruled;
Now freedom's song will chime, sir.

Meanwhile, sheet music entitled "Here's to You Harry Clay" or "A Song for the Man" pictured Clay on the cover, and "The Whig Chief" showed Clay's boyhood home, his current residence of Ashland, and his presumed next abode, the White House.[39]

Ribbons and medals also appeared to push the Whig cause visually. The Clay Club produced a single ribbon with the image of Clay on it; others included slogans such as "Henry Clay, Pride of America," "Clay and Liberty!!!," "The People's Welfare—My Reward," and "Protector of American Industry." Medals promoted similar themes regarding the tariff and Clay's support for the common man. One even proclaimed on one side, "Henry Clay elected President A.D. 1844," while the other showed the Millboy of the Slashes and the date of the expected inauguration.[40]

Democrats did not stand by and accept that conclusion. The Whigs did have a head start in producing a positive picture, for Clay had been the expected nominee for some two years. The surprise choice of Polk left Democrats scrambling to get his story out. Most medals simply called him "Young Hickory," in an attempt to capitalize on fellow Tennessean Andrew Jackson's popularity. Newspapers like the *Ohio Coon Catcher* provided some voices to counter the Whig ones, while a series of songs attacked Clay. Broadsides like "The Mask Removed" tried to tie Clay to abolitionism, sectionalism, and Anglophilism: "Already have we seen their mission, / Is wedded close with abolition; / Such Yankee Whigs, and John Bull spies, / May prove Old England's best allies." Because of Clay's expected nomination, the Democrats had long been planning a campaign of criticism to counter the Whig onslaught of books, newspapers, pamphlets, songs, ribbons, and medals. The Democrats' most effective tool would be a series of short tracts (eight pages or so) that attacked Clay's past stands.[41]

All those different appeals from both camps mixed with barbecues, banners, betting, rallies, ratification meetings, and regalia to make the canvass colorful, loud, and lively. The campaign memorabilia, journalistic outpourings, and increased literacy of the citizens all meant that voters had more exposure to the candidates and the issues than ever before. And Clay's

CLEAR THE WAY for
OLD KENTUCKY.

I'M THAT SAME OLD COON.

The Whigs emphasized Clay's record of achievements in 1844. But the refrain may have hurt Clay in some electoral circles, for many voters wanted change, not "that same old coon." *Courtesy of Kim Gelke*

forces used the new political tactics well. In modern parlance, they tried to rebrand Clay, not as Henry but as the new Harry Clay—not as a man of either the North or South but of the West. During the ensuing race, "Harry of the West" would be criticized for certain actions he took in the campaign, but he and his allies probably won some voters because early on they took strong, proactive approaches to getting his message and his new image out to the voters of America.[42]

In the race for president, Henry Clay longed for a clear fight for once—one of policy versus policy, party versus party, candidate versus candidate. In 1824, he had faced three other challengers; eight years later, he had the third-party distraction of the anti-Masons, who took votes from his candidacy. Now, in 1844, another third party had arisen to confuse matters. Only this time the question concerned not the Masonic Order but slavery.

Clay had never been able to distance himself from that controversial matter, try as he might. On his 1842 pre-convention semi-campaign swing through parts of the Midwest, he had stopped at Richmond, Indiana, where a crowd of ten thousand waited. A Quaker named Hiram Mendenhall made his way to the front of the gathering, to hand Clay an antislavery society petition calling on him to free his slaves. Some of the angry crowd resented what they saw as an uninvited intrusion and handled Mendenhall roughly at first. But Clay quickly told them to treat the petitioner respectfully. Although he knew the presentation of the petition was designed to embarrass him, Clay made a strong, spontaneous speech regarding Mendenhall's appeal. Noting his long opposition to slavery, Clay called it, once more, "a great evil" and again stressed his support for colonization efforts. But would Mendenhall reimburse him $15,000 to buy Clay's slaves, and would he give the freed blacks land to live on in Indiana? Clay indicated that he respected the motives of "rational abolitionists" but feared the consequences of immediate emancipation: "civil war, carnage, pillage, conflagration, devastation, and the eventual extermination or expulsion of the black" would result. Had Clay closed there, the matter might have faded away, for he had simply restated earlier themes. But then he told Mendenhall to do good work in his own community, and "Go home, and mind your own business." That one line in Clay's response infuriated abolitionists, who considered it a condescending rebuke of their actions. Whigs would actually include his extemporaneous remarks in the *Ashland Text Book* as an example of Clay's strength on the issue. But abolitionists repeated the "Go home" phrase as an example of the heartless slaveholder Clay. And thousands of Mendenhalls voted in 1844.[43]

Such words had given a new third party momentum. Once more, Clay had to face possible defections from his campaign as a result. The Liberty Party growth represented the increasing move of some abolitionists from moral suasion to political action. The new party's candidate in the 1840 presidential election had earned only some seven thousand votes, but two years later the party won more than 16,000 votes in the New York governor's race alone. The Liberty men's effect on the 1844 presidential race remained uncertain, but if the election grew close, every ballot would be crucial. As early as 1842, a Boston paper opposed Clay's nomination because "it is doubtful whether he could get the vote of a single *free state*." That same year, the New York branch of the American Anti-Slavery Society resolved that it could not support Clay if he ran, for he was a slaveholder, forger of the Missouri Compromise, and a "bitter enemy of universal emancipation." By late 1843, Clay had surveyed those budding developments and warned that the Liberty Party's ambitious and selfish leaders threatened to take away Whig votes. He foresaw "exceedingly troublesome" times ahead.[44]

The Liberty Party's leader was James G. Birney, also its 1840 nominee. Clay knew him well. Born into a Kentucky slaveholding family, Birney had been educated at Transylvania and Princeton. He had moved to Alabama but then returned to Kentucky, freed his remaining slaves (which at one time numbered forty), and subsequently left to live in the North. In 1832, he had written Clay that he favored colonization as the only practical way to end slavery, and five years later still wrote of the "friendly and respectful feelings" between the two. But Clay soon warned Birney that the younger man's growing immediate emancipation views hindered the cause of eventual black freedom. Over time, they parted ways, and Birney and the Liberty Party almost seemed more interested in attacking Clay than they did the much more proslavery Polk.[45]

Democrats delighted in the situation. Contemporary estimates from members of both major parties placed the percentage of Whigs in the Liberty Party at well over 75 percent. Votes for Birney clearly took votes away from Clay. In the North, Democrats gleefully reprinted abolitionist attacks that called Clay a "Man-Stealer," "human-flesh monger," and worse. The *Concord Democrat* stressed of Clay that "the Lash Upon the Backs of women and children is heard daily. . . . The toil and sweat of his Slaves enable him to pass his days and nights in one continued scene of Gambling and Debauchery!!!" It described the Whig as "a buyer and seller of his fellow man, a dealer in flesh and blood!!!" The paper said nearly nothing about the pro-annexation Polk, a man who held almost forty men and women in bondage, and who engaged in the slave trade much more than Clay did. On the eve of the election, the Democratic *Brooklyn Eagle* recounted Clay's proslavery words and his criticism of abolition in a last effort to get northern Whigs to abandon Clay for the Liberty Party. In the South, however,

Democrats reprinted Clay's antislavery words and support for emancipation to try to get Whigs to support the party of Polk.[46]

In truth, antislavery Whigs faced a real dilemma, one that those who might vote for a minor third party would continue to confront. Should you follow your principles and oppose both major party choices? But what if that vote allows the greater evil to win? Should you compromise your principles? In 1844, that meant either voting for slaveholder Clay or not voting for him, possibly allowing the greater proslavery evil (Polk) to win.

Whig loyalists had clear answers to those queries. They saw a vote for the Liberty Party as the same as a vote for the Democracy: "Our opponents . . . are tickled to death with the prospects of using you as tools." A New York paper similarly responded: "Let it be understood, that every abolitionist who, by refusing to vote as a Whig, . . . does, in effect, vote for the maintenance of slavery." The course of those "mad abolition papers" made no sense, cried a New Bedford, Massachusetts, editor. To furious Whigs, it seemed that abolitionists said little about the proslavery expansionist Polk, but demonized Clay as a man who, as one wrote later, "exceeds any other man in responsibility for the sufferings of the negro race." Whig Abraham Lincoln, a year after the election, examined what seemed such curious, almost irrational, reasoning. Abolitionists fought the annexation of Texas and the expansion of slavery, but would not vote for the candidate who most opposed both. "If the fruit of electing Mr. Clay would have been to prevent the extension of slavery, could the act of electing have been *evil*?" Clay's own growing concern that the Liberty Party might hurt his chances in key states, especially in a close election, caused him to endorse a decision that, in the end, hurt him even more among abolitionists.[47]

Henry Clay's distant cousin Cassius Marcellus Clay had become the most outspoken and visible antislavery leader in Kentucky. Son of a wealthy slave owner, the thirty-three-year-old "Cash" Clay had been educated at Transylvania and Yale. In New Haven, he had heard abolitionist William Lloyd Garrison speak, and that argument converted him to the antislavery cause—although Clay continued to view blacks as his racial inferiors. Back in Kentucky, Clay briefly served in the state legislature, but his increasingly harsh criticism of the slave system ended his viable electoral chances. Outspoken, impetuous, and impatient, the hot-tempered Cash Clay fought a duel and engaged in several other violent confrontations. When one proslavery opponent physically assaulted him, Clay used his Bowie knife to stab his assailant, cut off an ear and part of the skull and nose, and blind him in one eye. Then he threw the man off a cliff. When (not surprisingly) the man died, Clay asked his kinsman Henry Clay to defend him. Cousin Henry did so successfully, telling the jury that had Cassius Clay not acted as he did, "He would not have been worthy of the name he bears."[48]

Cassius Clay freed his own slaves in January 1844 (though he kept the slaves his wife brought into the marriage). His fights for antislavery had given him a good reputation among northern abolitionists. Eager to help Henry, desirous of attention, and ambitious for the cause, he planned to tour the North to try to persuade antislavery advocates to vote for Clay, not Birney. Although he doubted it would do much good, presidential candidate Clay consented to the mission. But the brash Cash Clay did not always choose his words diplomatically or wisely. He told audiences that Cousin Henry held emancipationist views (true enough), but also that Henry secretly favored the abolitionist cause. In July and August letters that became public, Cassius repeated those sentiments, which quickly made their way into the southern press. Already worried about Henry Clay's commitment to the peculiar institution, undecided voters in the South now hesitated further.

A concerned Henry Clay felt that, in order to keep his fading southern support, he had to act to counter Cassius Clay's ill-chosen words. In a public letter, the candidate denied having any prior knowledge of his cousin's letters and stressed that Cash Clay had "entirely misconceived" Henry's views. Two weeks later he tried to explain to Cassius why he had written that letter: "You can have no conception . . . of the injury which your letter to the *Tribune* was doing." With the electoral vote of three or four southern states hanging in the balance, Henry Clay had written his letter "although I regretted it extremely." Citing the "great delicacy of my position," the Whig candidate noted that while northerners called him a supporter of slavery and southerners termed him an abolitionist, "I am neither the one nor the other." To compound an already messy situation, Henry Clay's private letter to Cassius Clay never made it to its intended destination and was published in a newspaper instead. All that made Henry Clay seem more political than principled and to seem more interested in appeasing the South than the North. The Cassius Clay mission proved to be an embarrassment to the campaign.[49]

While Cassius Clay toured the North, back in Kentucky, Henry Clay continued to receive disturbing intelligence about the situation in the southern states. Other concerns had arisen in the campaign—the aftereffects of the Dorr Rebellion in Rhode Island regarding who could vote and the question of American claims to the Oregon Territory—but they really had little overall effect on the way Clay ran his race. Texas did.[50]

As early as March 1844, a Democratic leader had chortled that on the annexation question, "We are forcing Clay's friends to act on the Defensive"; a few day later he added, "We attack and they must defend, thus giving us a decided advantage." Andrew Jackson, who usually had better election instincts than Clay, advised Polk in late June that the Democrats must keep pushing the issue "with energy and firmness." Clay and the Whigs found themselves in the awkward position of seeming to oppose national growth and pride, and Democrats in the South capitalized on that. The extension of US territory represented the Jacksonian alternative to the expansive economic plan of the American System. Annexation seemed the more masculine approach; it fulfilled the national vision of extending democracy to new regions and offered fresh lands for greater personal mobility. Moreover, adding Texas to the Union would protect slavery. Otherwise, more and more free states would encircle the South like "the folds of the great Boa." Not only did Clay want to derail the destiny of America, they declared, he also sought to help the hated abolitionists—and he might even be one himself.[51]

Clay read such attacks in newspapers and in letters from the South telling of the effects on Whig hopes there, and he pondered a course of action. For someone who had proved to be extremely good at reacting in a debate and thinking on his feet, Clay did not function well when confronted with changing conditions in a presidential race. The Texas issue reflected that. An ally concluded later, "A little more zigzag would have carried him into the Executive chair." But in the 1844 race, Clay tried to "zigzag" and those actions hurt his cause. Clay's campaign would have been better served had he just remained silent and held fast to the sentiments expressed in his Raleigh letter. But faced with southern defections and appeals by Whigs in that region to stop the bleeding of votes, Clay felt compelled to act.[52]

On July 1, 1844, Clay wrote what become known as the first Alabama letter. Addressed to a supporter in that state, it stated that Clay opposed abolitionism and personally had no objection to annexation. "But I certainly would be unwilling to see the existing Union dissolved or seriously jeopardized for the sake of acquiring Texas." Then he made the often-quoted comment about the Union being the key to his heart. In essence, he had not changed his stance nor said anything different, but he had tried to soothe southern feelings by emphasizing different aspects of his position. Though not really needed, the letter still did little overall damage.[53]

Southern Whigs continued to fight a defensive battle and found that Clay's letter provided them with few electoral reinforcements. Yielding to their entreaties, he penned yet another public letter almost four weeks later. Clay would write that in the second Alabama letter that he did not intend "to vary the ground in the smallest degree from which I assumed in my Raleigh letter." In that second letter, Clay reiterated that he would be glad to see annexation "without dishonor—without war, with the common consent of the United States upon just and fair terms." Stating the same conditions as before, the letter represented another unnecessary communication. But he then added that slavery "at some distant day" would be extinct and thus was really not a factor in the debate over Texas. Of course it was, and that comment angered both abolitionists and annexationists. Moreover, the apologetic tone of the language used throughout made it *seem* like Clay had equivocated. To angry abolitionists, Clay now appeared "softer" on annexation and on antislavery generally. And in his letters on the issue, Clay could be presented as trimming his sails to engage the changing political winds, rather than remaining constant in his course.[54]

Reaction to the second Alabama letter came quickly and harshly, especially in the North. Webster recounted that Clay's composition "has caused much depression & some consternation." In New York, a despondent Thurlow Weed wrote simply, "Ugly letter, that to Alabama." A memoirist recalled that the letter "took everybody . . . by surprise"; another remembered that it "fell like a wet blanket upon the Whigs." In fact, adroit Democrats played up the idea that Clay was changing his opinions in a desperate grasp for votes. One caricature showed a Janus-faced Clay with the words, "Clay's two faces," one for the North, one for the South. A newspaper poem added: "He wires in and wires out, / And leaves the people still in doubt, / Whether the snake that made the track, / Was going south or coming back." Their Clay would do anything to win.[55]

Clay reluctantly admitted that his letters left "some unfavorable impressions in particular localities." That same day, he thus wrote another letter. Addressed to the editors of the *National Intelligencer*, it sought once and for all to clear up the "unwarranted allegations . . . that the letters were inconsistent." He wrote, again, that he had remained undeviating: "I did not suppose that it was possible that I could be misunderstood." Then to appease the now-angry northerners, he emphasized that only if the conditions were met—no war, no sectional disagreements, no dishonor—would he favor annexation. In still another letter that day, Clay wrote, "I shall cease to write letters for publication." But by then it was too late.[56]

Those who have written that Clay's seemingly straddling stance on the Texas issue constituted the crucial factor in the election are mistaken. His several letters *were* a massive mistake.[57] Clay should not have written the many letters; they represented a serious error. Yet, a careful reading of the letters shows not a straddle as much as a general consistency, as Whigs said at the time. Nor were they a fatal blow to Clay's candidacy. In the delicate balancing act he was attempting, they may have hurt him in the North among some abolitionists, but they may have also served part of their purpose in the South and have helped him hold some closely contested states. The *United States Magazine and Democratic Review*, in October 1844, observed that the Texas issue represented no "influential element" in most state elections. But if the overall effect on the targeted groups ended up as something of a wash, the letters did have a more general negative effect on the race. Whether correct or not, the perception that Clay did not mean what he said and that he waffled for political effect did injure Clay in the election.[58]

One more new issue competed for Henry Clay's attention in the 1844 race. Once again, it involved a matter he really did not want injected into the campaign, but one that, in the end, he had to address by either action or inaction. The question involved the larger subjects of immigration, religion, and nativism in America and more specific concerns regarding Clay's vice presidential nominee.

Ten years younger than Clay, Theodore Frelinghuysen had served New Jersey in a number of posts, including US senator. Termed the Christian Statesman, he had supported temperance, opposed Jackson's Indian policy, and advocated various other religious and reform measures. His unexpected nomination for vice president had been seen as an attempt to bring greater moral force to the ticket headed by Clay. But the selection troubled Whig leader Thomas Ewing, for he correctly feared it would raise the controversial issue of nativism. Frelinghuysen's reputation for extreme Protestant piety and his association with rabid anti-Catholics caused Democrats to charge that he sought to enact a theocracy in order to enforce his narrow religious standards and to proscribe contrary views. The opposition pictured Clay as not sufficiently devout and Frelinghuysen as too devout.[59]

Those attacks had more force because they occurred in an era of growing criticism of immigrants and Catholics. The rising spirit of Protestant revivalism sparked a nativist movement that featured increasing hostility to the "un-American" Catholics with their loyalty to a foreign leader, demands for a larger period of residency for immigrants before they achieved citizenship, and calls for restrictions on office holding by foreign-born citizens. While nativists drew from both parties, northern Whigs made up a sizable portion of the group. In fact, lying below the Whig surface lay a strain of bias against certain groups—Catholics, immigrants, and Masons. By 1844, American nativism was growing. Would Clay lend his support to that rising force? Would he oppose it? Or would he do neither?[60]

Making the decision more complicated for Clay, reports reached him of Democratic skullduggery on the matter. Already the opposition had called Frelinghuysen and Clay enemies of Catholicism. Now numerous observers warned that the well-organized Jacksonians were making a mighty and mostly illegal effort to naturalize new immigrant voters and enlist tens of thousands of new Democrats. Those Whigs already suspicious of the foreign influence on American democracy thus moved closer to the nativist outlook. Talk spread that the Whigs and the Native American Party might combine.[61] But former New York governor William Henry Seward warned that if Whigs identified too closely with nativists, "a great evil" would result politically. For once, Clay agreed with Seward. The Kentuckian gave little support to the nativist cause. After all, early in his career he had criticized the Alien and Sedition Acts. Coming from a state he called "the Ireland of America," he had also spoken out in favor of the South American republics and their leaders when opponents in 1818 questioned whether Catholicism and liberty could exist together. He presided over a commencement at the Catholic St. Joseph College in Kentucky and counted Bishop Benedict Joseph Flaget as his friend. Later, in 1832, Clay had secured the election of the first (and to date only) Catholic priest to serve as chaplain of the Senate. The year before the campaign of 1844, Clay had indicated that neither he nor the party opposed Catholicism, and that he did not favor lengthening citizenship residency requirements, as nativists sought. Clay continued to picture the United States as a haven for those suffering political or religious persecution.[62]

But as the accounts of possible Democratic fraud poured in, Clay shifted his position slightly. Publicly, he stayed silent regarding nativism. By May 1844, he told Frelinghuysen that all foreigners currently in America should be subject to the laws in existence at their arrival, but a month before the election, Clay suggested to a man from Ohio that he remained open to discussing changes in naturalization requirements. He refused to endorse nativist rhetoric, and when allies pressed him to authorize a union of Whigs and nativists in some cities, he would not do so. But he did not forbid it, either. Pilate-like, he washed his hands of the matter. As a result, efforts to combine the two forces, particularly in Philadelphia and New York, did take place. Rumors of such alliances intensified Catholic and immigrant opposition to the Whigs, and strengthened Democrats' determination to mobilize votes in opposition, by whatever means.[63]

In addition to the relatively new issues of Texas annexation, the Liberty Party, and nativism, Clay had to deal with older questions concerning his life and career—queries that would often lie dormant for years, then emerge full-blown every time he ran for the nation's highest political office. In the 1844 race, seemingly every previously used tactic was reintroduced, every incriminating statement repeated, every weakness exposed, every suspicion mentioned. Clay had wanted to keep slavery out of the campaign; Texas had brought it in. He had sought to avoid a divisive nativist debate; Frelinghuysen's nomination had introduced it. He had hoped to avoid old issues and focus on the present; the opposition had not allowed that.

Many of the political attacks repeated timeworn accusations involving Clay's moral fitness to be president. Well over two years before the general election, when it was already clear that Clay would be the Whig nominee, northern abolitionists had opened the offensive. In a handbill, the corresponding secretary of the New York Anti-Slavery Society denounced "that notorious *Sabbath-breaking, Swearer, Gambler, Duellist, Thief, Robber, Adulterer, Man-stealer, Slave-holder*, &c.,. Henry Clay!" Northern Democrats, seeking to drive Whigs into a meaningless third-party vote, hardly hesitated to join in, condemning him as a "human-flesh monger" and "infamous Duellist." One congressman proclaimed that "the standard of Henry Clay should consist of his armorial bearings, which ought to be a pistol, a pack of cards, and a brandy-bottle."[64]

The blatant falsity of some of the charges, the staleness of others, and the exaggeration of most angered Clay: "I believe I have been charged with every crime enumerated in the Decalogue. . . . Shrinking from all the issues, arising out of the great questions of National policy which have hitherto divided the Country, they have no other refuge left but in personal abuse, detraction, and defamation." He told a Clay Club that "fabrication and forgery are and will continue to be employed to vituperate and vilify me." It had been twelve years since his last presidential race, and many new voters had entered the electorate in that time. They may have heard the outline of charges against Clay, but those new voters had not been exposed to the full fury of the anti-Clay rhetoric. Now, Democrats made certain that the fresh faces at the polling place knew the dangers Clay posed and the evil he represented, "as a political Lucifer that ought to be driven headlong from the garden of our Republican Eden." What they called informing the electorate, the Whigs termed misrepresentations and slander. Clay had different words for it all: "detestable libels and lies." The likelihood of a high-minded campaign seemed remote.[65]

To Clay, the rhetoric on the dueling issue represented a perfect example of the unfairness of the attacks on him. Yes, he had fought two duels, the last almost two decades earlier, a fact that even a campaign biography termed "a mark of weakness." But he had also voted to outlaw dueling in the District of Columbia. Besides, said his partisans, how could Democrats attack him when Polk's mentor Jackson had killed a man in an affair of honor? Did the Polk people condemn that? But the opposition in 1844 mostly focused not on any duel Clay fought; instead, they blamed Clay for his role in the Graves-Cilley affair, which ended in the Maine congressman's death. Clay's failed role as would-be peacemaker in that duel now was reversed by the opposition. Amos Kendall wrote an eight-page pamphlet, *Henry Clay's Duels*, in which he called Clay "an accomplice in the murder" of Cilley. It got worse. In the tightly contested state of Pennsylvania, Democrat James Buchanan spoke under a banner that pictured a bloody hand and the words "Henry Clay the murderer of the lamented Cilley." Antislavery advocates took up that theme as well. The Rev. Lyman Beecher preached against Clay's selection, saying Clay's hands were stained with blood: "The duellist is a murderer." A flurry of published letters defended Clay's denials of wrongdoing, but each just brought the matter before the public once more.[66]

Charges of Clay's dueling, along with ones concerning his alleged gambling, drinking, and swearing, more often appeared in the northern press, for such attacks seemed less viable in the more hedonistic, cavalier South. But in the more evangelical, reform-minded North, where such matters of morality might have greater effect, both the Democratic and Liberty Parties played up those stereotypes of Clay. The *Washington Globe* reprinted the 1838 charge that Clay had yelled in Congress, "Go home, God damn you! where you belong!" Similarly, a Boston paper had long called on voters to reject such an intemperate, profane man whose habits, if he were elected president, would weaken the moral fiber of the country. Another newspaper published a letter from an enemy of Clay's in Kentucky, who wrote that he had seen Clay gambling twice recently, a charge the candidate denied, with observers at both places backing his denial. Enemies of the Whig leader even proclaimed that, if elected, Henry Clay would set up a gambling table in the White House. To the sixty-seven-year-old Clay, who probably drank in moderation, seemingly swore no more than the average American, and apparently no longer gambled, the attacks on him, not his life, seemed immoral.[67]

And then there was the never-dying "corrupt bargain" charge. John Quincy Adams labeled the revival of the "stale and base calumny" an attempt to defeat Clay and tarnish "my honest fame." A Clay paper termed the attacks "old and threadbare, dirty and rotten." Both were correct in that the matter had been rehashed ad nauseam over the last two decades and it seemed impossible to say anything more. But Democratic publicists created an issue by calling on Clay to publish the 1825 letter he had written to Francis P. Blair concerning the House selection of a president. Editors suggested that since the letter would reveal the "foul alliance," Clay had thus concealed the contents. All of that had come up before, in the 1828 Adams-Jackson race. At the time, Clay had asked Blair if he wanted to release the correspondence, but the one-time Clay ally had become a firm Jacksonian by then and pleaded with Clay not to make public the "undesirable" contents. Clay had honored that wish, saying he would not violate the sanctity of a private correspondence. Besides, the letter could injure Adams's feelings, for Clay had playfully made fun of him and termed him the "choice of evils." But Clay had also written in the letter that he would act in his deliberations only for the public good. In that sense, the letter helped Clay's cause, but he accepted Blair's position and the letter remained private into 1844.[68]

But Democrats continued to charge Clay with withholding vital, incriminating evidence of corruption. An Alabama paper indicated that the missive must show Clay's "conscious guilt." Such attacks apparently had enough force that two North Carolinians wrote from that swing state, indicating that the issue was hurting Clay's candidacy there. Other advisors warned Clay to ignore the old issue. The candidate did not directly respond, for a change, but his growing fear of failure finally led him, late in the race, to write to the ally who currently held the letter and who had allowed "hundreds" to see it. Clay gave him approval to publish it, if he thought it would help. He did. Disappointed Democrats made the most of the situation, even then. Their sixteen-page pamphlet, *The Coalition of 1825 or Henry Clay's Bargain with John Quincy Adams*, selectively used quotes that supported the Democratic version of the story and omitted language that presented Clay in a positive light. The opposition would not let the charge die.[69]

Probably the most unsettling, and in some ways most important, old topic concerned what Clay considered a real issue: the tariff. On that score, the Whig candidate expected to gain much support in crucial northern

states. After all, the Whig tariff of 1842 had proved popular in the important state of Pennsylvania, Clay had fathered the protectionist American
System that the state favored, and Polk had constantly voted against high
tariffs in his career. Whig prospects looked bright in the Keystone State as
a result. Democratic advisors to Polk came to the same conclusion. Robert
Walker correctly wrote Polk, "We must have the vote of Pennsylvania in
order to succeed." The next day, Andrew Donelson advised his standard-
bearer to deliberate prudently and then issue a rare public letter on the
matter.[70]

Polk carefully prepared a letter that greatly helped his cause in that state.
Almost unanimously decried since then as an audacious, duplicitous, and
deliberate fraud, the resulting politically brilliant letter made free-trader
Polk appear to favor protection. Writing to John Kane in June 1844, Polk
said that he had previously sanctioned "moderate discriminating duties"
that not only raised revenue but also offered "reasonable incidental protection" to industry. He indicated that the government had the duty to provide
a "fair and just protection to all the great interests of the whole Union."
The careful choice of words meant that Polk would not offend his free-
trade allies in the South, while Pennsylvania Democrats who needed a more
protectionist stance from their candidate could choose words that made
him appear to favor a high tariff. As a result of the letter, wrote Polk's vice
presidential candidate George Dallas of Pennsylvania, all of the Democrats
in that state stood united and "eminently happy." Buchanan praised Polk
for his "discreet & well-advised letter" and now gave speeches proclaiming
Polk a better friend of the protective tariff than Clay. Another letter writer
told Polk, "Your Kane letter makes you President, by securing the North,
especially New York & Pennsylvania."[71]

Clay worried that the Kane letter might indeed keep Pennsylvania in the
Democratic column and make Polk president. But the letter represented a
hoax, a ruse, a falsification of Polk's views. How could the electorate believe
that Polk's message reflected his past votes or present views? In August 1844,
Clay wrote that nothing had surprised him in the campaign so much as the
apparent acceptance of Polk's letter as fact. If newspapers did not challenge
the Democrat, then "I shall distrust the power of the press and of truth."
The popularity of the Kane letter and brazen Democratic attacks that implied Clay no longer favored a protective tariff, caused Clay to issue still
another letter. As editor Horace Greeley later wrote, "Lies lost the votes of
thousands of Protectionists, who were unfairly induced to believe Polk as
much as Protectionist as Clay!"[72]

Both campaigns were well funded and both effectively used symbols and songs to get their messages across. But as in other contests, the Democratic propaganda machine proved far superior to Whig efforts in 1844. Part of that was simply because the Jacksonians had more ammunition for their attacks, in that Clay had served long and run often. But when Democrats criticized the Whig candidate, they also mentioned, in a more secondary way, a host of other of Clay's faults. In one of the strangest, they labeled him a sympathizer with the disgraced Federalist Party and its supposed anti-democratic views. Since Clay had been a fervent opponent of the Federalists, that seemed odd indeed. The Democrats also charged Clay with violating the Sabbath by gambling on horse races on a Sunday—he had not—and by encouraging Sabbath breaking, when he permitted a loud procession to welcome him in New Orleans on a Sunday visit there. The opposition further declared that Clay had committed perjury by swearing an oath that he was qualified to be senator when, at age twenty-nine, he was not. (On that point, Clay wrote friends, noting that he never took an oath regarding his qualifications as senator.) The Jacksonians published a private letter of Clay's, in which he had criticized Georgia's actions regarding Indians, and they then concluded that Clay had thus supported the Indians' "deeds of blood and murder." Democrats further condemned what they called Clay's "unhallowed ambition," his dictatorial nature, and his long lust for office.[73]

Some of the attacks on Clay did have a more policy-based origin. A Democratic journal criticized the Whig's "bold and elastic latitudinarianism of construction" of the Constitution and his "narrow restrictive commercial policy." Another pamphlet, *Henry Clay and the Laboring Classes,* portrayed him as favoring "the *land* over the *laborer*," opposing preemption rights for foreigners, and seeking to make workers "his white slaves." Other writers averred that the American System favored the privileged classes over the masses. Democrats also revitalized an older, clever, hypothetical question-and-answer session with a supposed banker, who exaggerated Clay's stance on that question. And they threw asides. To make the point to immigrants, they asked: "Does Henry Clay love the Irish?" The fictional answer: "Yes, just as much as he loves Andrew Jackson." But, overall, while Clay may not have liked some of the language used in those tracts—"The snake must be killed"—he could accept such rhetoric on those subjects as valid exaggerations in the political game. The personal attacks, however, he could not forgive, nor could he ignore the obvious falsifications on several matters.[74]

Whigs responded to the charges against Clay by calling them worn-out words, hypocritical utterances, and outright lies. More often, they pointed to Clay's history and positions—his self-made-man status, his accomplishments, his nationalism, his leadership. But they also took the low road at times as well, with a widely reprinted forgery regarding Polk's purchase of slaves, for instance. They fell back on the Harrison strategy of slogans and songs over substance. One ballad, for example, referred to "The fine Kentucky gentleman, / Whose heart is in his hand; / The rare Kentucky gentleman, / The noblest in the land." Whigs happily proclaimed to the opposition: "Get out of the way, you're all unlucky / Clear the track for old Kentucky."[75]

More effective, however, were Democratic messages like the one in the *Brooklyn Eagle* and elsewhere. Among the "Fifty Reasons why Henry Clay should not be President" were Clay's "corrupt bargain" (reason number one), his stands on the tariff, his support of the BUS, his policy on internal improvements, his "life of wickedness," his "electioneering" for the office through tours, his position on Texas, his role in the Cilley duel, his tyranny in Congress, his encouragement of "drunken

Clay's expected victory in 1844 was intended to bring financial security through creation of a new BUS. Election literature suggests the institution would soon pay the bearer "in whig glory," bank notes, or "Generous Confidence." *Courtesy of Kim Gelke*

revelry and bacchanalian songs" in campaigns, and lastly, his "war with all moral and political progress." Whether such approaches and tactics would be rewarded, and thus would be repeated in later races, would be decided by the electorate. Once more, the voters held the political fate of Henry Clay in their hands.[76]

Balloting for president still took place over the course of almost two weeks, at different times in different states, so the results became known at a frustratingly sporadic pace. Some optimistic Whigs already referred to Clay as "the President" and commented, "Polk thank Heavens has no chance." Clay expressed his typical confidence in his cause, but also correctly gauged the potential closeness of the election. And even though other states voted after New York, it soon became clear that the voters of that state would decide who the next president would be. At Ashland, Clay awaited word of his fate.[77]

Accounts differ as to whether Clay received the crushing news of the New York vote at a party or at home. But they all agree that to those who saw him, Clay accepted his defeat with a calmness and serenity that astonished observers. If Clay had a propensity to swear, that would have been the time to do so, but his daughter-in-law wrote that she heard no loud, angry words from him. Close ally Leslie Combs visited his friend a few days afterwards and found Clay calm but "evidently deeply wounded by the result." The defeated man might accept the voice of the electorate, said Combs, but he had "high consciousness of unrewarded public service and unappreciated merit." But, most of all, Clay told Combs, with tears in his eyes, he hurt not as much for himself but for those friends who had worked on his behalf. Later, when a supporter wrote Clay, telling how crushed and depressed he was by the result, Clay answered with an acknowledgment that "My own heart bled and still bleeds for my country, for my friends, and for myself." While Clay may have written of the hurt he felt, he presented a calm exterior to the world. But that may have all been a carefully constructed façade. Clay's grandson told how in the privacy of Ashland, Lucretia took Henry in her arms "and they wept together." An emotional man, Clay somewhere had to release the tears of lifelong dreams now defeated.[78]

Democrats, of course, delighted in the "glorious news" and in the plight of the prostrated and "pitiful" Whigs. The results did strike the defeated and demoralized party extremely hard. Over and over, report after report stressed how thousands wept openly at the news. Greeley "sobbed like a child"; Millard Fillmore lamented, "All is gone. A cloud of gloom hangs over the futu[re]." Some shocked Whigs took to their beds, while others closed their businesses, as if a national disaster had struck. Clay's friend Octavia Walton LaVert told how she cried upon hearing that the president now would be "a Pigmy, when the Giant should rule." Leslie Combs wrote that he felt like a man in a bad dream: James K. Polk, a person "without a single great act in peace or war," had defeated the great man, Henry Clay, "whose whole life has covered himself & his country with immortal glory. . . . God help us preserve the people, for they seem not to know what they do."[79]

Clay supporters blamed his defeat on various causes. "The Texas question did more to beat us than anything," one Whig concluded. New York's Millard Fillmore told Clay that "abolitionists and foreign Catholics have defeated us." One editor believed that the Democrats' ability to get the electorate to look at "irrelevant and unimportant matters," instead of the issues, had decided the race. The *New Orleans Bee* pointed in its state to the injustice of "a fraud so palpable in itself as to require no proof, so stupendous as to startle many who profit by it, and so apparent as to defy concealment." After hearing from allies in several places, Clay blamed his loss on the nativist and immigrant issues, on the abolitionist third-party vote, and on the frauds. But he insightfully noted that a combination of adverse issues had to occur: "It required the union of all these elements . . . to defeat us." Was he right? Why exactly did Clay lose, or, more correctly perhaps, why did he fail to win?[80]

In answering that second question, many contemporaries pointed to the obvious—the Texas annexation issue. Given that Clay lost New York State—and thus the election—by only five thousand votes and the third party count in that state totaled over fifteen thousand, that seemed an apparent answer. And in one sense, that argument had much to recommend it, though not necessarily in the way most observers saw it. Overall, the Texas issue may have won Clay as many votes overall as it lost him. But its emergence defined the race by bringing about the nomination of proslavery southerner Polk. As a congressman concluded, "It will . . . *unite* the *hitherto divided South*." Polk's candidacy cemented the cracks in Democratic unity in the region. In that indirect way, the annexation issue did injure Clay. Still, the Whigs officially took five of the thirteen slave states and, in reality, probably won six—nearly half. But the presence of the southerner Polk, not the northerner Van Buren, on the Democratic ticket may have been more important than the specific issue itself.[81]

Clay's Alabama letters, in response to annexation, also had an effect on the race. Convention wisdom blamed those missives for his defeat, but the letters may actually have won Clay as many ballots as they caused him to lose. Yet on the larger issue of presidential decisiveness, firmness, and discipline, Clay's letters did injure his cause. More of the single-minded (if sometimes wrong-headed) focus of a Jackson or the resolute determination of a Polk would have served Clay well in 1844.[82]

Other observers also blamed the annexation question, Clay's response to it, and the Cassius Clay imbroglio as factors in turning Whig anti-slavery voters toward the Liberty Party. A Whig woman termed such Liberty Party votes "treacherous and detestable," since they had allowed the election of Polk. An angry Horace Greeley cried out to Liberty men that "on your guilty heads shall rest the curses of unborn generations," for they had done nothing but elect the proslavery candidate. Frelinghuysen fumed about the "invincibly obstinate" third-party voters, while various party leaders also denounced Thurlow Weed for his relative inaction in New York.[83]

However, despite the obvious numbers, the Liberty Party may have been less important than many at the time indicated. Some newspapers stressed that the Texas controversy actually pushed abolitionists away from the Liberty Party toward the Whigs. And a third-party core would have voted outside the regular party apparatus, no matter the candidate or the issue. Moreover, some antislavery Democrats deserted Polk and voted for the Liberty Party. One study suggested that twice as many former Liberty Party voters switched to Clay, as did Clay voters go to Birney. Certainly, had that third party not been in the field, most of those ballots would have been cast for Clay—had they voted at all, an uncertain thing—and he would have won. But in the reality of the race, Clay would, in the end, do quite well in keeping the Liberty Party vote lower than it had been recently. No new serious antislavery defections occurred. While the Texas question had an effect, it did not deal a death blow to Clay's hopes; it produced only one of the several wounds that slowly led to his political demise.[84]

Other problems had hurt Clay in different places, in various ways. In the South, what a Democrat called Clay's "wild & reckless schemes of Whig policy" generally and Clay's tariff views specifically cost him votes. But, more important, Polk's Kane letter on the tariff had probably made the difference in Pennsylvania, with its 26 electoral votes. One despairing Philadelphia Whig could not believe how the Democrats, "with an audacity unparalleled," claimed Polk as a friend of protection: "Thousands really believed it." Clay lost Pennsylvania by some 6,000 votes out of more than 330,000 ballots cast.[85]

The Pennsylvania results came four days before the New York vote, and may have influenced the way some New Yorkers cast their ballots, but other factors proved more crucial in that key state. Because the more radical abolitionists would not likely have voted for any slaveholder, and since the Liberty Party count remained static from earlier races, a better explanation of why Clay lost New York lies in a triad of causes—the use of patronage by President Tyler, the personnel in the parallel governor's race, and the fraudulent voting.[86]

Democrats early on focused on New York as the key state. Tyler, seeking to defeat Clay, used his limited governmental largess to aid the Democrats there. But party advisors still feared Polk might well lose the state. His prospects, however, grew much brighter with the nomination of Silas Wright for governor. Before Wright agreed to run, there was a schism among Democrats. Van Buren supporters remained angry over his treatment at the national convention, while anti-annexation Democrats and nativist Democrats questioned whether they should support a third party. But Van Buren, still a good party man, persuaded his ally, the much respected Wright, to allow his name to be put forth for governor. Whigs quickly realized the importance of that move. One called Wright "the hardest man for us to beat. . . . With *any other* nomination our success was assured." They realized that Wright's selection united the opposition factions and stimulated greater turnout by the Democrats. Van Buren told Jackson that the nomination made New York safe for the Democrats, "beyond all doubt." But other Democrats were not so sanguine. They feared the Whigs' use of Wall Street money, the possibility that the Liberty Party vote might prove smaller than expected, and the power of a nativist-Whig alliance.[87]

In fact, those Democratic concerns may have produced fraud in the 1844 presidential race. While Wright's presence in the race helped mightily—he carried the state with twice the margin as did Polk—Democrats did not trust their fate to Wright alone. Already they had capitalized on Frelinghuysen's presence on the opposition ticket and the rumors of a nativist-Whig alliance; the bishop of New York reportedly urged his flock to defeat Frelinghuysen. But still Whigs seemed confident of winning the state, "if the vote is *honestly* cast" and the opposition did not cheat "too much." Whigs had good reason to worry, for the Democrats went beyond simple appeals. Some in that party believed their propaganda and saw a possible Clay presidency as the personification of evil, while others simply wanted to win, no matter the candidate. For whatever the reason, Democrats systematically met new immigrants, almost literally as they stepped off the ship, and naturalized them instantly, without the required five-year residency period. The new citizens were then allowed to express their gratitude for such unexpected good fortune by registering to vote and casting a Democratic ballot. Over the last three months before the election, between five thousand and fifteen thousand immigrants thus illegally became voters—a number sufficient to defeat Clay in New York. The large and sudden increase in the number of voters in the city itself brought one historian to record that "observers commented that the city's dogs and cats must have been affected by an unusual dose of civic pride." Whigs at the time blamed Clay's New York defeat on "fraud, falsehoods, & foreigners" and the "purchased suffrage of a Foreign legion." Webster publicly attributed the loss to the votes of illegally naturalized or even unnaturalized citizens and called for the "error" to be corrected. But in 1844, the result seemed to indicate that crime did indeed pay.[88]

The wages of political sin paid well in other places, as well. In one state, and perhaps two, fraud in the balloting cost Clay additional electoral votes. Charges of widespread bribery and unparalleled fraud came from Georgia, which went Democratic by fewer than 2,000 votes. Supposedly, 90 percent of the eligible voters went to the polls, with supporters of Clay polling some 2,000 votes more than in 1840, while the Democratic count increased by more than twelve thousand from the previous presidential race. Perhaps the winners had organized better, or the Texas issue had energized them more. Or perhaps the Whig accusations were correct.[89]

If the charges of corruption in Georgia rested on more uncertain evidence, the Plaquemines scandal in Louisiana proved to be one of the most outrageous frauds in that state's storied history. In the 1840 and 1843 elections, no more than 340 people had voted in Plaquemines parish. Only 538 white males inhabited the place. Except on Election Day 1844. Anticipating a close statewide vote, Democratic leader John Slidell chartered two steamboats, put New Orleans "roughs" on them, conveyed the eager voters to the parish, and then had the well-paid passengers vote several different times. It worked. The parish officially cast 1,044 votes, 1,007 of them for Polk. He came out of Plaquemines parish with a 970-vote majority and won Louisiana with a 699-vote majority, thus taking the state's electoral votes. When confronted with the obvious fraud, a Democratic paper blandly attributed the turnout to the excellent weather. One Louisiana correspondent told Clay that "the grossest, the most infamous frauds" had robbed him of votes there.[90]

Texas, the tariff, character concerns, immigration and nativist questions, Oregon, the American System, the Wright candidacy, the slaveholder topic, voting fraud—all contributed to Clay's defeat. Little things meant much in such a close race, and Clay could point to a series of mistakes on his part, together with the charges put forth by the opposition, as possible factors in changing the votes of the few who ended up deciding the election. Once more, he could look back at what might have been.[91]

Each time Clay ran for president, he garnered a larger percentage of the vote than in his previous attempts. Of the twenty-five states that conducted a popular vote in 1844, Clay's total exceeded Harrison's in all but eight (and three of those were virtual toss-ups). Turnout seemed about equal to 1840 as well. But Clay's overall percentage of the vote dropped some 3 percent from Harrison's. That resulted from two factors: the decrease in Whig votes in the South and the greater Democratic vote in all sections except New England. While some of those Democratic ballots might have been illegally counted, that party simply had been more aggressive in reaching out to new voters. And the Whigs' dismal 1841 congressional performance had hurt as well. Clay had much to overcome. In one sense, Polk's victory represented not a win by the person but by the party.[92]

Despite all his problems, Clay almost won—and if illegal votes are factored out, perhaps did win. Even excluding New York, Clay could still have won by carrying Pennsylvania, Georgia, and Louisiana—all states where the opposition used questionable tactics against him. A switch in voting by some 4,500 individuals in those three states would have given the race to the Whigs as well. In Georgia's ninety-three counties, for example, a shift in votes by a dozen people per county would have given Clay the state. The "what ifs" could go on, but basically a multiplicity of matters defeated Clay. The Texas issue doomed Van Buren—whom Clay would likely have defeated—and brought in a southern candidate; Polk's Kane letter on the tariff hurt Clay in a key state; the morality charges against Clay put him constantly on the defensive; the selection of Frelinghuysen aroused antipathy in the Catholic and immigrant communities; the American System and Clay's own record in Congress gave enemies a target to attack; the fraudulent votes hurt. Polk's narrow margin of victory in many states meant that across America, in each precinct, if just one Whig had stayed away or voted for the Liberty Party, or if one undecided voter changed his mind, or if a single person feared the Whig dalliance with the nativists, that could have been enough to defeat Clay.[93]

But Clay barely won several states that he did carry. He secured Tennessee, Delaware, and New Jersey by fewer than a thousand votes in each. Had Polk lost, he could have been asking himself "What if" in regard to those states. In that very close presidential race in 1844, every action, every decision, every voter counted. And in that count, Clay came up just short. For the third time, he had lost a presidential election. But this one hurt the most because victory had been so tantalizingly close.[94]

On hearing the news of Polk's victory, a fading Andrew Jackson declared, "The Republic is safe." A Democratic diarist consigned Clay "to the political tomb forever. He is now too old to run again. . . . He is forever silenced. . . . I am frank enough to admit him to be a great man, and he has served his country for a long time." In the same spirit, the *United States Magazine and Democratic Review,* in "a last word about Mr. Clay," proclaimed his career at an end. The "very worst man in the Union" still had been a foe "well worthy of our steel," but this "badly great man" now no longer would challenge them. Another member of the victorious party told the new president-elect "that Heaven has ordained it in its wisdom that Mr. Clay is not to rule over us." Clay, too, may have questioned whether a higher power had forsaken him. As it was, he told a newspaper, "Now, I hope to spend the remainder of my days in peace and quiet."[95]

If that indeed represented Clay's desire, he fell short of achieving that goal.

14

Presidential Candidate V

CLAY DID NOT ACCEPT HIS 1844 defeat well. But he quickly received an out-pouring of condolences, tributes, and gifts, as many Whigs sought to ease his pain, to honor the work of the person they considered America's greatest statesman, and to praise a man whose career now seemed ended. Mostly they just wanted to thank the sixty-seven-year-old Henry Clay for his long years of service to party and country. But part of that heartfelt adoration also came out of a sense of sadness and even pity. Supporters of the Great Compromiser appeared genuinely sorry for Clay and argued that he had been cheated out of his rightful and overdue victory. Some simply refused to believe that the lesser James K. Polk could defeat the great Henry Clay except through unfair or fraudulent practices. But most just suffered vicariously with Clay as he experienced one more great hurt in a life of many hurts.[1]

In an attempt to mitigate the anguish and to pay homage to their long-time leader, people sent many gifts to Clay—silver pitchers, cut-glass vases, a silver cane, a silver service, a diamond bracelet, $500 from a whaling captain, and even a pair of socks. Perhaps more rewarding than the physical favors were the letters Clay received from allies and supporters. As a Tennessean wrote of Clay: "Had he not been defeated he should never have known the sincere devotion of his friends." The greatest example of that came about in a financial way.[2]

Clay's major losses in the failed hemp factory he owned with his son, and now the lack of a sizable presidential salary to look forward to, caused Clay to consider selling off part or all of his Ashland estate to satisfy his creditors. Friends warned others of that situation and they quietly addressed the issue. A bank began to inform Clay that anonymous donors were making payments on his note of indebtedness. They did not want their names known, both so that Clay could not return the money and because they did not want him politically indebted to them. According to one account, on hearing the news, Clay burst into tears and cried out, "Did any man ever have such friends?" Other Clay acquaintances, on learning of such generosity, acted in a similar manner and forgave debts he owed them. A grandson estimated that obligations up to $50,000 were cleared from the books overall. The amount likely was less than that, but still was sizable. Clay had feared an old age filled with debts, constant toil, and even the loss of his homestead. But now, probably for the first time since before the panic of 1819, Clay experienced a sense of financial freedom. He did not have to spend his remaining days trying to earn attorney fees to keep the bill collector at bay.[3]

The belief that Clay's career had ended sparked the widespread gift-giving and expressions of gratitude. Ironically, however, the support might have helped reinvigorate him. The larger gifts allowed him more freedom, should he reenter the political arena. The smaller favors convinced him that he still enjoyed much political love. Those sentiments might remain dormant in the immediate moment after his defeat, but they could quickly mature under the right conditions. After all, there would be another presidential campaign in 1848.

But that moment remained far distant in political time. In March 1845, the new president's presence in the White House worried Henry Clay, for he knew James K. Polk all too well from their time in Congress. He did not anticipate much personal goodwill from a man whose legal mentor had been Clay's old enemy Felix Grundy or whose political idol had been Andrew Jackson. Nor did Clay expect to agree with the president's ardent proslavery, pro-annexation, anti-bank, and low-tariff policies. In fact, Polk would sign a new low-tariff act (much to the disgust of Pennsylvanians who had voted for Polk). But the president's personality and passion also bothered Clay. Polk certainly brought several positives to the presidency—a courteous spirit, impeccable character, and an ability to organize his thoughts. A hardworking, secretive person who mostly followed his own counsel, Polk thus would become sure of his decisions and would be strong-willed in pursuit of any course of action he adopted. However, those same qualities might result in a presidency that delegated little, listened to few contrary voices, and acted unilaterally. Convinced of American exceptionalism, confident that Manifest Destiny "was not a matter of it but merely one of how," certain of his rightness, and totally focused on his goals, James K. Polk was self-righteous. Such unquestioned passion disturbed Henry Clay.[4]

Clay watched as events unfolded in the way he had generally predicted. As a result of President Tyler's last-minute actions, the Texas annexation process had already begun when Polk took office. With the formal conclusion of that effort months later, Texas entered the Union, and the likelihood of war with Mexico increased. Given Polk's designs on large parts of Mexican territory, especially California, war seemed the most likely way to achieve that goal. He sent General Zachary Taylor, a former Kentuckian, to the Rio Grande border that Polk called the boundary of Texas. (Historians generally concur that the United States had questionable claims to a clearly contested region.) By most indications, Polk expected his actions to provoke an incident that could create a pretext for conflict. The impatient Polk and his cabinet, however, had agreed to ask for a declaration of war even before any hostilities broke out. Fortunately for them, the Mexican military—who saw themselves as expelling invaders from their territory—did strike. That bloodshed gave Polk a reason to call for war. For the moment, most members of Congress accepted the president's version of events. Only later would opponents term Polk's order an unauthorized, provocative invasion that precipitated the war. Either way, the fighting had begun.[5]

Very quickly, Clay and his Whigs faced a dilemma. Many people, especially in the North, opposed the conflict as an immoral act done, as Webster wrote, out of "greediness for more Slave Territory." With the latest introduction of the Wilmot Proviso, calling for any newly acquired territory to be free from slavery, the war reintroduced that divisive issue into the national debate. Other Whigs across America also grew concerned over the specter of a huge expansion of national territory. Such a large nation, they predicted, would produce a collection of neighborhoods, not a country. The *Louisville Journal* warned that American identity would be lost in the vastness of the new land, and the not-so-united States would fragment further. Party outcries grew louder as it became clear that Polk sought to insert politics into the military. The president had to turn to the Whig generals Zachary Taylor and Winfield Scott as the senior commanders, but he gave both men little praise and eventually little support. Polk would try to appoint Democrat Thomas Hart Benton as overall commander, but failed. Still, of his some thirteen appointments as generals, all were Democrats. Such actions made it seem to worried Whigs—of all sections—that the president wanted to create an army filled with sycophants—the very thing Clay had so feared.[6]

The Whig dilemma—Clay's dilemma—centered on the role of a loyal opposition in a time of war. Open and defiant Federalist opposition to the War of 1812 had basically killed that party. Overly strenuous comments of criticism might be viewed by the electorate as traitorous words in wartime. So, not for the last time in American history, the Whig opposition criticized the administration's conduct of the war, and even the legitimacy of the conflict itself, but praised the efforts of the soldiers at the front. Democrats tended to divert attention from critical questions by focusing on Manifest Destiny or by attacking the character of the Mexican people, their government, and their weaknesses. A Democratic journal referred to Mexico "with all its degeneracy and anarchy." Others countered the Whigs' criticism of the strain the new territory could put on the nation by noting how new inventions like the railroad and telegraph could tie the greater land together. But above all, Polk simply accused Whigs of giving "aid and comfort" to the enemy.[7]

Henry Clay observed all those happenings from his Ashland estate and publicly remained remarkably quiet. But he voiced to friends and acquaintances his strong opposition to what he saw taking place in his America. More than a year before the war broke out, he had written that annexation would prolong slavery's existence by opening new lands for expansion. That, in turn, would produce greater abolitionist anger. The next month, he had warned that the looming conflict might produce "some Military Chieftain who will conquer us all." Once the fighting erupted in earnest, Clay acknowledged that the "Trumpet of War" called young men to the service, and he supported their sacrifice for country. But this "unfortunate war" had been illegally conceived and had given birth to an abomination he could not support. He clearly saw that the conflict of conquest had produced feelings of distrust and worry in South America. Countries there feared the eyes of Manifest Destiny would wander to them next. But most of all, Clay simply opposed war in general, except in extreme cases: "What a waste of precious human life it occasions." At the same time, he could not forgive—or forget—the narrow vision of those he held partly responsible: "I wonder what the violent portion of the abolitionists now think . . . having contributed to produce the present state of things." Clay could have been president, and if that had been the case, he wrote, there would be no low tariff, no Texas annexation, no Mexican war, no heated debates about the expansion of slavery, and "no imputation against us, by the united voice of all the nations of the earth, of a spirit of aggression and inordinate territorial aggrandizement." The nation had made its choice and now had to deal with the consequences.[8]

When Clay voiced his support for the troops, his words were more than philosophical. For among the some 4,842 of Kentucky's sons who fought in the Mexican-American War was Henry Clay Jr. The young man had earned a bachelor's degree from Transylvania University, and then he had graduated second in his class at West Point. He had turned to the law after that. A bit aloof, somewhat reclusive, and certainly unsure of himself, Henry Jr. competed with his sister Anne for paternal affection and constantly wanted Henry Sr.'s approval. Over and over, the son would downplay his abilities in order to elicit a compliment. Again and again, Henry Jr. asked his father to tell him what he should do with his life. Time after time, Henry Clay refused to do so, telling his namesake that he must make that decision himself and that he would support him, whatever his choice. But the father's frankness did put some pressure on Henry Clay Jr. For with all the problems faced by the other male members of the family—mental instability, bouts of depression, and alcohol abuse—Henry Clay Jr. represented, said his father, the family's best promise for future achievement: "On you my hopes are chiefly centered."[9]

In truth, Henry Clay Jr. did not have the personality, the drive, or the work ethic to emulate his father's success. He had ability, but was basically a solid, successful citizen who wanted to be more than that. In 1832, Henry Jr. married, and his wife's family's largess allowed him also to make good real estate investments and grow quite wealthy at a young age. He traveled overseas, served in the Kentucky General Assembly, and developed into a man his father called "one of my greatest comforts." Moreover, Henry Clay Jr.'s wife Julia became almost a surrogate daughter to a father-in-law who had lost all his own daughters. But she died in childbirth in 1840. That death hit Clay hard and left a devastated Henry Clay Jr. a widower with three children, just ten days before his thirtieth birthday.[10]

Henry Clay Jr. almost could not go on. To the father's despair, the son grew depressed, even suicidal, wandered aimlessly, and read endlessly. When the war with Mexico started, he entered the service as a lieutenant colonel of the Second Kentucky Infantry. Perhaps he did so out of patriotic reasons, or perhaps for the opportunity to win the acclaim he sought, or perhaps for the possibility of intentionally putting himself in harm's way. Earlier, at the military academy, Henry Clay pointed to some nearby hills and told his son, "Remember . . . that from these heights the spirits of our revolutionary heroes are the witnesses of your conduct." For a Clay, expectations ran high.[11]

Henry Clay Jr. found his unit poorly organized and ill-disciplined—like most in the war—but once in the army of Zachary Taylor, he grew restless: "I long for a battle." Back in the states, the rumors of a brewing conflict gave his father a sense of foreboding. The Clay family returned to Ashland after a trip, and the next day as they sat down to dinner, another son entered and told them that Henry Clay Jr. had been killed at the Battle of Buena Vista. He would be buried as a hero in the Frankfort cemetery. A young John C. Breckinridge gave the funeral oration, and Clay wept openly at his loss.[12]

The father was reminded daily of his son's death. When he walked the grounds of Ashland, he passed through the shade of trees planted by his son. When he went into the house, his son's chair remained vacant. When he saw the three orphaned grandchildren, he would think of their parents. Perhaps Clay also felt some personal guilt, for he had encouraged his son to attend West Point. Had the martial spirit learned there driven Henry Clay Jr. to join? For many reasons, then, the father grew despondent. The

Several lithographs memorialized the 1847 death of Henry Clay Jr. at the Battle of Buena Vista in the Mexican-American War. The loss of Clay's best-known son was particularly painful because it came in a war the father bitterly opposed. *Library of Congress, LC-USZ62-62237*

political world seemed far distant. But what hurt also was the needless aspect of it all. As Clay told a friend, his loss would not have hurt as much had it not come in a conflict of such "unnecessary and . . . aggressive nature." Webster, too, would later lose a son in the war, causing a Whig journal to cry out that the children of Whig leaders "are shedding their blood for the sake of their country, in a most unholy war."[13]

Those words—"unholy war"—reflected the growing religious spirit in antebellum America. But over the years, matters holy had not generally engaged Henry Clay's deep attention. He had been respectful of religion and never irreligious, but he had not joined a church. Despite the presence of the nearby Cane Ridge Revival, Clay had not yielded to the enthusiasm or seemingly even mentioned it in his correspondence. Ecumenical in his words and actions, he did act in support of persecuted religions. Clay helped the Shakers, calling them "worthy of all respect and confidence." Not man but only a higher power could, said Clay, determine if the Shaker creed was in error. The Kentuckian also told Mormon leaders that he supported their right to have petitions heard in Congress, for their unpopular religion deserved the same protection all other Americans received. Clay further commented that those who followed different religions in different lands would also ultimately "secure an abode in those regions of bliss." But Clay had never joined a church himself. He had observed how religious forces had driven off Transylvania's outstanding president, had probably heard of a witch trial in a neighboring county, had seen the religious wars between various Christian sects, and seemed to want no part of that: "Deliver me from Church dissentions and from Church tribunals!"[14]

When Clay was a young man, the Federalists had attacked Thomas Jefferson as an agnostic or atheist, and questions about a leader's religion had grown more plentiful since then. In Clay's case, the fact that he did not belong to any church became an issue in his presidential races. By the 1820s, one letter writer called Clay a "Godless" politician who devoted more attention "to the trump card, than to the Holy Bible." Had Clay just joined a church, despite his reservations, it would have aided his political cause. He did not. In 1832, he admitted in a speech to Congress that he was not a member of any religious sect: "I regret that I am not. I wish that I was, and do trust I shall be." An early biographer, in anticipation that his book would chart the life of *President* Clay, spent several pages detailing the importance of religion in Clay's life, including quotes that indicated Clay's belief in a higher being. Yet, even though Clay attended church regularly and perused theological works often, that was not enough for some voters.

But the combination of a growing awareness of his own mortality and the death of his son apparently changed Clay religiously. On June 27, 1847, in the parlor at Ashland, he became a member of the Episcopal Church. Even then, some opponents continued to attack him on the issue, now saying that he had joined "an aristocratic church," not one attended by the "meek and lowly." But had Clay joined three years earlier, before the 1844 election, and had he freed his slave Charles Dupuy before that contest instead of the month after, those actions might have had a positive effect on more morally oriented voters. But for Clay, principle dictated his course on those questions more than expedient politics.[15]

Perhaps his son's death also sparked Clay's subsequent actions regarding the Mexican-American War. Or perhaps his anger had been building and now finally erupted. For whatever reason, Henry Clay determined to speak out publicly and forcibly in opposition to the war. By the time he did, the United States had already won the major battles and had occupied Mexico City. But no peace had emerged, and the debate grew fiercer over whether the victors should seize all of Mexico. Thus, on November 13, 1847, before a Lexington crowd of some three thousand (likely including Abraham Lincoln), the seventy-year-old Clay summoned forth some of his youthful passion and vocal fervor once more. Sculptor Joel Tanner Hart heard the one-hour speech and wrote in his diary that it represented "the greatest address, both in argument & eloquence that I have ever heard." Another listener later recalled how Clay's "eyes burned like bulbs of fire. I have never heard such a speech."[16]

The fierce, ardent War Hawk of 1812 had changed and matured. And the situation had altered as well. Over time, Clay had seen the harsh realities of the earlier conflicts, had watched the rise of military-hero worship, and had observed a nation now fighting not for honor in a "just" war but for conquest in an unjust one. On a rainy day, he thus rose to vent his anger and sadness about the current situation. He sadly noted, "This is a gloomy day and like it our nation is shrouded in gloom." Clay apologized to the audience, acknowledging that "in the autumn of my years" he did not have his rhetorical powers of the past. Then Clay gave a strong talk that gave eloquent voice to all the Whig and antiwar sentiments and arguments.[17]

He warned, "War unhinges society, disturbs its peaceful and regular industry, and scatters poisonous seeds of disease and immorality." It produced the "glitter, pomp, and pageantry" that generated a false spirit of "wild adventure and romantic enterprise." It took lives, seizing that irreplaceable "human treasure." It turned in directions "infinite and unknown."

It brought carnage, debt, and death. It threatened the unity and stability of the Union and wasted the country's energy. In this case, a president almost single-handedly had fomented the conflict by ordering troops to a disputed place where fighting would almost certainly erupt, causing war. That made the United States the culpable aggressor: "It is Mexico that is defending her fire-sides, her castles, and her altars." Clay stressed that he did not oppose adding new territory to the Union, if done by diplomacy or by purchase. But he did not support acquisition through violent conquest. Nor did he favor adding new slave territory to the nation. The fruits of war might be new lands added to the American empire, but those came, he averred, at the cost of sectional discord (as the Wilmot Proviso debate already showed) and at the risk of creating a standing army led by some "unprincipled chieftain" who might use it to destroy American liberties. Clay concluded by proposing a series of resolutions: that annexation had produced the war "without the previous consent and authority of Congress," that the United States should not yield to those who sought to seize all of Mexico, and that any land taken should not be made slave territory. It was a courageous oration.[18]

Whigs, especially in the North, predictably applauded the speech, for Clay had clearly articulated the party's position. William Henry Seward called it "surpassingly beautiful," a talk that would influence many. Democratic papers, on the other hand, called Clay a "coward and knave" and criticized the talk for giving "aid and comfort" to the enemy, for siding with the "barbarous and treacherous Mexicans," and for opposing a cause for which "his own gallant son had shed his life blood." In fact, the continuing antiwar sentiment may have hastened the end of the conflict. When presented with a proposed peace treaty that clearly did not go as far as he wanted, President Polk may have accepted it in part to still the growing dissatisfaction with the war. Whigs agreed to the treaty because they feared another might be worse, while Democrats went with the document for they worried about later results if they did not. It was a peace, editorialized the *National Intelligencer*, "which everyone will be glad of, but no one will be proud of." Three months after Clay's antiwar speech, the peace treaty was ratified by the Senate. A year later, a Mexico City periodical wrote that had Clay been elected president, "perhaps he would not have lost his son, nor we California." It concluded, "His name should be forever pronounced with praise among us." But Clay *had* lost, and the ramifications of that continued and continued.[19]

Despite the Democratic verbiage, President Polk commended "Mr. Clay's generous and manly conduct" and restraint during his administration. In fact, Clay had considered Jackson irrational and dangerous; he viewed Tyler as irresponsible and traitorous. But Van Buren and now Polk—though dangerously misguided in policy matters—he generally respected. Both had given long service, both knew how the game was played—in a sense, better than Clay—and both had some appealing personal qualities. He might express full political rage over their policy decisions, but they still retained from Clay at least a measure of respect. Perhaps for that reason, in February 1848, Clay met with Polk, who received him with "the greatest civility." They exchanged memories of times past, of fights fought, of political wars won—and lost. Some two weeks later, a pleased Polk then held a dinner as a "mark of respect for Mr. Clay." What the overworked president called an "exceedingly pleasant" time followed.[20]

During the repast, Clay sat by the accomplished First Lady. He complimented her, saying all spoke highly of her management of the White House. Then he laughingly noted, however, that "some little differences of opinion" existed regarding her husband's actions. The very politically minded Sarah Polk replied in the same light spirit, saying that if a Whig happened to win the presidency that year, no one's election could please her more than Clay's. He thanked her and she then added that should he become president and move to the White House, he would find it in perfect order. "I'm certain of that," he laughed. That exchange meant nothing in the larger scheme of things, but once more it showed Clay's charm, even among the ranks of the enemy, and at the same time, it indicated the respect others gave him and that he could return. It also demonstrated that some still considered Clay presidential material for 1848.[21]

Clay's eventual course regarding the presidency in 1848 can be viewed in two very contradictory ways. One cynical scenario features a Clay who had determined, shortly after his 1844 defeat, to seek the office once more. Everything he did in the ensuing years—his religious conversion, his antiwar speech, his stronger antislavery stance—had been done with an eye toward the voters. Always ambitious, the elderly statesman thus made a deluded, pathetic last attempt, even though all could see he could not win. But his attempt divided the party, alienated allies, and reduced his prestige.

Another explanation, however, portrays a Clay who initially neither expected nor anticipated another run. He told people his career had ended and that he had suffered enough disappointments. As he got older, Clay also better realized that he carried considerable electoral baggage. He understood that many considered him stale, elderly, and unelectable. Moreover, his antiwar speech had alienated many voters. In this version of events, only when it appeared that the Whigs might nominate a person who seemingly rejected party principles, a man who represented all the things that Clay opposed in a presidential candidate, did a still not-so-reluctant Clay begin to reconsider his earlier decision. Clay's long career had been focused on keeping the nation united and strong. Now he would try to do the same for his Whigs.

The man who produced such an adverse reaction in Clay was someone the Kentuckian had known—though not well—for years. But in that time, the two had apparently never talked politics. That was understandable, for until late 1846, General Zachary Taylor had shown virtually no interest in things political. He had never held civil office, nor even voted. But the unexpected military success of this "child of chance" in the war with Mexico had awakened the general's sleeping political aspirations. In June 1846, Taylor had told his son-in-law that he would not accept a nomination, but by February 1847, just days before his death, Henry Clay Jr., who served under Taylor, had written his father that his commander now had political ambitions: "The Presidency begins to loom before him." Polk also noted that Taylor had become "giddy with the idea of the Presidency" and marveled at the political rise of the formerly unknown military man. The president later called Taylor uneducated, "exceedingly ignorant of public affairs, and . . . of very ordinary capacity," a person of limited judgment and narrow mind.[22]

Yet he misjudged the general, and by 1847 the Taylor boom had begun, to the dismay of many politicians, including Henry Clay. The man at the center of the attention had been born in Virginia seven years after Clay; had come to Louisville, Kentucky, with his distinguished family when he was only a few months old; and had resided in the commonwealth most of his life. Though Taylor left in 1841 to live on his Louisiana and Mississippi plantations, served by more than a hundred slaves, he still considered Kentucky his home state. Most of his key advisors had Kentucky ties as well. In some ways, the ensuing struggle for supremacy in the national Whig Party would be one of Kentucky versus Kentucky. A military man almost all his adult life, Taylor had commanded troops in the Second Seminole War and then led the first battles in the Mexican-American War. His victories at Palo Alto, Resaca de la Palma, Monterey, and Buena Vista likely owed more to enemy weaknesses, superior American artillery, and strong US subordinate leadership than to Taylor's own generalship. He may have been lucky, but he became a winner. And Clay was not.[23]

An unimposing figure, and one whose casual dress reinforced that impression, the sixty-three-year-old, bowlegged, tobacco-chewing general who sometimes spoke with a stammer did not seem impressive compared to Henry Clay. But if almost no one called Taylor a great man, numerous people termed him a good one. Enemies and allies alike stressed his calm courage under fire, his decided firmness, his "plain common sense." Troops loved their unpretentious and unassuming "Old Rough and Ready"; non-military men (including Clay) praised the honesty and frankness of this simple man.[24]

Seemingly a modest man, Taylor also had much to be modest about. Political figures as diverse as Daniel Webster and Jefferson Davis agreed that Taylor "knew little of public affairs, and less of public men." Ill-educated in a formal sense, Taylor took quick exception to any criticism or slight, and he operated with the blunt certainty of the outsider sure of his correctness and critical of the establishment. A man who spoke privately with Taylor reported that the general said little of substance, seemed unable to converse for very long, and offered only "the most uncommon plain replies." In short, to many, Taylor seemed a man of modest virtues, limited political knowledge, and significant military achievement. Critics did not see those as the credentials of a president. Yet they missed the point: Taylor had just the virtues many voters sought. They wanted simplicity, plainness, and certainty. Unspoiled and anti-party, Taylor represented the innocence of the outsider—like many of them. He was the great military hero whom many antebellum men wanted to be. Zachary Taylor was a formidable foe.[25]

Yet Taylor made numerous errors in his search for the presidency—ones that almost derailed his candidacy. One historian wrote that the general "could pen without a blush a page-long sentence which violated all the rules of syntax." Despite his problems with the King's English, Taylor persisted in writing public letters. His advisors constantly tried to draft replies that Taylor could sign; at times they succeeded, but the stubborn candidate—like Clay—often hesitated to accept advice. A mixture of political sagacity and raw naïveté, Taylor initially tried to portray himself as a man above party, who could appeal to both sides. He sought to unite the nation behind his personal, issue-less campaign, one tied to no faction or party. Saying that he "owed it to the country" to follow the people's wishes that he run, Old Rough and Ready—or his handlers—often skillfully made those points in nebulously worded communiqués. But Whigs wondered if Taylor would accept their party's nomination. His answer might decide the race.[26]

In a July 1847 letter reprinted in newspapers, Taylor stated his refusal to be the candidate of any party. Then in September, the general indicated he would not become "the slave of a party" and again stated that he would not accept a nomination from either one. Over the next months, he repeated that declaration. But that stance increasingly antagonized the Whigs, and Taylor's chances for a victory achieved outside a party apparatus grew fainter over time. In April 1848, two of his letters appeared in print at almost the same time, further confusing the issue. In the first, to the editor of a Virginia paper, Old Rough and Ready now wrote that he would accept the nomination by the Whigs, but still affirmed that if they chose someone else, he would not withdraw from the race. Two different sets of his advisors tried to correct that somewhat defiant tone by drafting a message two days later to Taylor's brother-in-law—what became known as the first Allison letter. Taylor openly and finally declared himself a Whig, though not "an ultra Whig." He promised to follow the elusive "will of the people" on such matters as the tariff and internal improvements. The general still insisted on the inclusion of the declaration that, though a Whig, he would act independently of party once in office. But the Allison letter generally accomplished its dual purpose of deemphasizing Taylor as a no-party man who would run outside of party ranks and of making him instead seem a good Whig. Not coincidentally, that made Zachary Taylor the front runner for the Whig nomination.[27]

Taylor's status in the race resulted in large part from the efforts of a man who had long been Henry Clay's staunch friend, ally, and advisor, Kentucky's John J. Crittenden. Most observers saw the younger man—by almost a decade—as Clay's clear protégé, his chosen successor, and his most trusted confidant. He even looked like Clay—tall, slender, erect—and spoke like Clay. A US senator described Crittenden as "a man of fine genius. . . . He is really eloquent and when he chooses can seal his adversary by sarcasm." A modest, patient, knowledgeable man of solid judgment and strong integrity, Crittenden impressed many. On Clay's recommendation, Crittenden had been nominated—though not confirmed—for a seat on the US Supreme Court, at the end of John Quincy Adams's presidency. In return, when Crittenden had seemed poised to enter the Senate again in 1831, Clay suddenly decided he needed to be in Washington as the election neared, and Crittenden graciously stepped aside. Not for the last time, Clay's wishes trumped Crittenden's. But with Clay's support, he had taken that seat following Clay's retirement, then had served briefly in the Harrison-Tyler cabinet, before going back to the Senate after Clay's resignation in 1842. Throughout those years, Clay solicited Crittenden's suggestions, entrusted him with the introduction of important public letters, and viewed him as one of his key advisors. No one was closer to Henry Clay politically than John Jordan Crittenden.[28]

Yet Crittenden remained in the political shadow of his mentor: "Kept in the shade by Henry Clay, he became somewhat crabbed and sardonic," recalled one political observer. Though some now spoke of Crittenden as a possible presidential choice in 1848, the careful Kentuckian did not think the time right. Instead, he became the man perhaps more responsible than any other for the rise of Zachary Taylor, a kinsman of Crittenden's first wife. Speculation arose that the sixty-year-old Crittenden expected to advise and control the inexperienced general. Then, after Taylor's one-term presidency, the full powers of that office could be marshaled in support of Crittenden as Taylor's chosen successor.[29]

When Clay, just weeks after his 1844 race, told his protégé that, with that defeat, he sought only "peace and retirement," Crittenden had, not surprisingly, taken that as a signal he was free to run himself or support any candidate he chose. Unfortunately, he backed exactly the kind of person Clay could not tolerate for president. Crittenden stated several times that Clay—or any civilian—could not win in the postwar atmosphere and that only General Taylor could take the party to victory. The Whigs must not lose again, he averred. For purely practical reasons, then, Crittenden supported the politically untested, almost anti-party, military man. Not only did he back Taylor—quietly at first—but when the general grew hesitant to run, Crittenden apparently persuaded him to enter the race. Without his support, Taylor's candidacy likely would have failed. But with the promise of the presidency, with its visions of power and patronage dancing in their heads, various Whig party operatives followed Crittenden's lead. He enlisted Clay biographer and *Louisville Journal* editor George D. Prentice, President Harrison's campaign manager Charles Todd, and even many of Clay's factional enemies from Kentucky. Crittenden had hitched his future to Taylor's success.[30]

Unfortunately, from early on Crittenden did not clearly communicate his intentions to his mentor. Clay heard rumors that Crittenden supported Taylor, but initially seemed to be in denial that such accounts could be correct. He could not believe that his friend would support a man who operated outside of party, a person who represented, to Clay, all that was wrong with American popular politics. As Taylor's strength grew, Clay's concerns increased exponentially. Correspondents asked Clay if he endorsed Crittenden's actions. Finally, owing to "our mutual friendship," Clay sent one such letter of inquiry to Crittenden to give him the opportunity to respond to the rumors. A few days later, in late September 1847, Clay rather coolly informed his erstwhile ally that the Kentuckian's support for Taylor caused him "some mortification." He noted that rallies for Taylor had included Clay's enemies in their ranks; Clay made it clear that he would "regret exceedingly" any collusion between his friends and Taylor's forces.[31]

When Crittenden nevertheless continued to serve as the de facto campaign manager for Taylor, Clay grew angrier. He saw such actions as a dishonorable, traitorous betrayal of their friendship. The trusted man whose career he had promoted had gone over to support an enemy of much that Clay held dear. But on a less personal level, Clay also recognized the political importance of Crittenden's actions, should Clay decide to run. That his ally had abandoned him, had declared him unelectable, and had organized Kentucky against him would be a serious political liability. The practical implications of Crittenden's involvement became clear in February 1848, when Whigs met in Frankfort to select delegates to the national convention. Taylor forces aggressively pushed their man's cause; Clay allies expected Whig leaders to endorse the supporters of a founder of their party. More as an act of respect for Clay than an indication of sentiment, the convention voted for a delegation unpledged to any candidate. But beyond that, Taylor's supporters immediately reassembled and endorsed the general's candidacy. Confusing news accounts made it appear to some that Kentucky had in fact gone for Taylor. Crittenden's role in all that, and his later comments that Taylor neither drank nor played cards—seen as an affront to Clay—so infuriated Clay that the two men rarely spoke again. To have the voters reject Clay was one thing; to have friends do so was quite another matter.[32]

The rational part of Clay could see the signs favoring Taylor—the general had hero status, an excellent organization, and the mass of the South behind him because he was a slaveholder from the region. Clay, in contrast, had his legacy of losing, his own allies and home state opposing him, and his long history operating against him. Yet, Clay did not want the Democrats and their doctrines to be victorious, nor did he want "a mere Military man" to win the presidency. Besides, Taylor—to Clay—simply had no qualifications for the office and might become the military despot that Clay constantly feared—or at least said he feared. The prospects of a Taylor presidency pained him immensely. The Great Compromiser now found himself, in his words, facing "only a choice of evils."[33]

Clay first reacted to his quandary by vacillating. Initially, he had told friends that he would not run. In September 1846, Clay indicated to Mary

Bayard that he had no desire to have his name put again before the people as a candidate: "I have had my turn." More than a year later, he informed an Ohio congressman that he did not expect to be a candidate and might refuse the nomination if offered—though he did not expect that situation to occur. To a Louisiana ally, just prior to autumn 1847, Clay repeated his intention not to run again.[34]

Yet, over those same months, Clay gave more nebulous and qualified responses to others. The Kentuckian told his strong supporter Horace Greeley in November 1846 that party support and his health might dictate whether he would run. Five months later, writing to a US senator from Delaware, Clay provided even more specific conditions: he must be of good health and unimpaired mind, and he must be the choice "by an unquestionable majority of the country"—a condition Clay admitted was not likely to exist. In November 1847, Clay told Greeley that he might not decide on a course of action until the following spring. All those mixed signals slowed organizing for Clay, confused Taylor supporters, and fueled constant speculation. Clay seemed almost to want to resist the temptation to run, but with the lure of the presidency dangling before him, he just could not take his eyes off the prize.[35]

A conflicted Clay thus acted as he often did in such situations—he took trips. He spent the winter of 1846–47 again in warmer New Orleans; then, in late 1847, he journeyed to White Sulphur Springs, West Virginia, for almost two weeks. From there he went to the ocean vacation spot of Cape May, New Jersey, after stops in Maryland, Delaware, and elsewhere. Every place Clay went, crowds greeted him with great enthusiasm. On board a boat on the Delaware River, he received such a demonstration of affection that it drove him to tears; a journalist wrote that Clay then thanked the crowd "in tones that thrilled and in words that melted the hearts of all present." Once, at Cape May, Clay frolicked in the surf, swam in the ocean, rested—and held court for the reporters who visited him there. Greeley's *Tribune* reported that while Clay bore the burden of the loss of his son, the tall, erect, silver-haired patriarch still displayed the vigor of a much younger man. Another account recorded that Clay walked with and talked to almost anyone he met, and how, when several hundred Connecticut supporters arrived by boat, he greeted them, thanked them, and told them that he had come there to relax, to try to forget his personal losses, and not to campaign. His words and evident sadness left many in tears.[36]

On his return to Lexington, Clay made his widely reprinted antiwar speech, and his hometown paper soon began touting him for the presidency. But Clay himself remained uncertain of his course. Then on the day before Christmas 1847, he arrived in Washington, DC, ostensibly to try a case before the Supreme Court and to give his valedictory as president of the American Colonization Society. But Clay also came to talk to Whig members of Congress to gauge their reactions to Zachary Taylor's bid for the presidency. Apparently, Clay had expected to find strong support for Taylor, but he discovered that many Whig political insiders had serious concerns about Taylor. Clay did not withdraw. By early 1848, he now seemed like a man much more certain of his course of action. Clay decided to make another trip, though this time less for personal refreshment of body and mind and more for rebuilding his political soul.[37]

In February 1848, as the Whigs gathered in Frankfort, Kentucky, to select delegates to the convention, Henry Clay left Washington for Philadelphia and New York City—two key states. In the City of Brotherly Love, however, Clay's campaign almost came to a sudden end. At the mayor's house where Clay stayed, a servant blew out the gas flame in Clay's room rather than turning off the gas. Clay slept in a room filling with gas. But he miraculously awoke in the morning unharmed. Aside from that potentially fatal mishap, everything else in Philadelphia exceeded expectations. More than 100,000 people lined the streets to welcome their special visitor. All seemed to want to see, touch, and perhaps even hear the greatness that was Henry Clay. Friendly papers noted the excellent health and vigor of the "Sage of Ashland," this man "without power or office—but not without honor."

Then, on a sunny March day in New York City, the scene was repeated. The fact that a lone eagle soared before Clay's boat as the craft arrived in the city seemed to many a positive omen for Clay. Huge assemblies of people welcomed Clay as a man who had devoted most of his life to the service of his country. Van Buren greeted him as well, and together the two toured institutions for the visually and mentally impaired. Clay shook hands with the residents, signed autographs, and kissed some of the girls. Once more, the trip allowed him to bask in the adoration of the masses. Their enthusiasm reinvigorated the elder statesman for one last campaign.[38]

But during that same time, events reminded him of his own mortality, and not just by his own brush with death. Two days before Clay had planned to leave on his trip, eighty-year-old John Quincy Adams had suffered a massive stroke. The ex-president had asked for his old secretary of state. Clay had gone to him, had held his hand, and had spoken to him one last time. Adams died the day Clay left Washington. In Philadelphia, the Kentuckian offered a eulogy to the man he had served well and had grown to respect, and in New York he paid a final tribute to him, as the body of the departed statesman made its way to Massachusetts for burial. That somber event took some of the joy away from Clay's tumultuous welcome in both places, but by the time Clay returned home at the end of March, he had finally decided what he would do. Though a peace had ended the Mexican-American War—removing that part of the issue—Taylor's devotion to Whiggery and its principles still remained unclear, and Clay's trips had convinced him of his own popularity. Accordingly, on April 10, 1848—just two months before the convention—Clay announced that he would permit his name to be placed in nomination. In his public letter, he told how his friends had indicated that he alone of the Whigs could carry crucial northern states and thus he should allow them to place his name before the convention. As the election had neared, Clay had once more looked around him and seen no candidate his superior or, perhaps, even his equal. Others, of course, viewed matters from a very different perspective. Be that as it may, Clay was in the race, at least. He would try a fifth time for the presidency.[39]

It was not just a two-man race. Understudies lurked in the wings, ready to spring forth and become the main actors if the convention deadlocked. Polk's example in 1844 loomed large. But Clay considered most of them mere pretenders and none of them serious rivals. Winfield Scott—another general!—had been a factor in 1840 and might be again, but he would not win, Clay felt, for he had no southern base; Daniel Webster garnered no support outside of a small part of New England; John McLean of Ohio, cabinet secretary under three presidents, bore the stigma of loyally serving Andrew Jackson. Of the three candidates, Scott worried Clay most. Like Taylor, he wore the laurels of military victory. But Clay recognized that the ambitious Scott had limited personal appeal and that Taylor hated him, and the other general's forces would thus not support Scott. Yet, Clay also understood that if Scott's chances faded in the convention, he likely would turn his forces over to Clay. As for the grieving Webster, whose son had died of typhoid fever in Mexico, the Whig divisions in Massachusetts meant that he had only lukewarm support in his home territory and tepid enthusiasm outside it. McLean, as Adams had earlier written, "thinks of nothing but the Presidency by day and dreams of nothing else by night." But Greeley considered the Ohioan "unloved" by voters; most saw his only hope of realizing his dreams would be an impasse at the convention. Thus, both Clay and Taylor viewed each other as the key contender. The rest remained bothersome minor characters more full of sound and fury than of real substance.[40]

At one time, Zachary Taylor had written Clay that if the Great Compromiser entered the race, he would drop out. Clay's early indecision might have been complicated by that knowledge. But as Taylor grew more convinced that the people's will dictated that he run—and with Crittenden strengthening Taylor's resolve on that point—the general withdrew that commitment. When Clay finally allowed his name to be placed in nomination, that action infuriated Old Rough and Ready. Earlier, he had grumbled that the Kentuckian seemed "more anxious for office than for the interest of the country, or the success of the Whig party." But with significant questions about his own party loyalty still unaddressed, Taylor and his advisors realized they had to do something or Clay might outflank them and win the party's nomination. To counter Clay, the Taylor camp had quickly issued the general's Allison letter, in an attempt to place Taylor firmly in the Whig ranks.[41]

Clay's announcement and Taylor's letter meant that both sides removed any restraints regarding criticism of the other. The Clay forces offered the simplest message: Taylor had no qualifications for the office, no Whig principles, and no loyalty to the party. He would be another Tyler. Horace Greeley wrote that "if we nominate Taylor, we may elect him, but we destroy the Whig party." Many political regulars told Clay the same thing— he must run or the party would be ruined. A magazine made the issue clear for the Whigs: "If they are anxious for success alone . . . without any reference to principle, consistency, or their future well-being as a party, they will nominate General Taylor." In short, the Whigs faced a dilemma. Should they nominate the qualified, principled party leader Clay and possibly lose the race, while keeping their political faith and honor, or should they nominate a politically untested military man and possibly win the contest but lose the party in the process?[42]

Much more complex and wide-ranging criticisms of Clay came from the Taylor forces. They called Clay too aged—he was seven years older than Taylor—too stale on the issues, too tied to antislavery, and unelectable. A Georgia paper referred to the "imbecility of old age" that governed the actions of this "rejected petitioner"; a factional Kentucky opponent emphasized that Clay's stances on internal improvements and the bank no longer had any force. The young Whigs cried out: "We are tired of old issues and old names." On the matter of antislavery, Taylor's southern allies struck Clay hard for his supposed surrender to abolitionism. The things northern Whigs found more acceptable—his adoption of religion, opposition to the Mexican-American War, and antagonism to the expansion of slavery—Clay had adopted. He would not go so far as to write off the South completely—he still had hopes there—and thus would not support the Wilmot Proviso. But he saw that the election would once more be lost or won in the North. However, Clay's words in his antiwar speech against the expansion of slavery did turn many southern Whigs toward Taylor, who had expressed few public thoughts on that—or any—issue. A Tennessee Whig wrote that Clay's words had "ruined" the Kentuckian's prospects in that region; Georgia's Robert Toombs said Clay had sold himself body and soul to the North. And throughout it all, Taylor's managers drew attention to his own soundness on slavery. They also underscored that nothing would heal the splits and unite the seriously divided Democrats more than a Clay candidacy. In contrast, Taylor had alienated no voters over the years.[43]

All those messages were tied to the chief criticism of Clay—the "distressing doubt" that he could win. Even former allies agreed. Abraham Lincoln sadly wrote of his idol's chances: "We can elect nobody but Gen: Taylor." A Kentuckian told Crittenden, "I would rather take a certain triumph with another than to risk being . . . defeated with Mr. Clay." Different Whigs accepted those statements as fact, for various reasons. Some grew concerned that Clay could carry no southern states. Conversely, northern Whigs shied away because he would not take a stronger stance against slavery. A Louisianan wrote that the question "is narrowing fast & surely, down to the slavery or no slavery question." But, most of all, the opposition to Clay came from those who valued party success over party principles; they wanted victory at any cost.[44]

But if Clay became the nominee, would that automatically mean the Whigs would lose, as his detractors claimed? Clay and others at the time—perhaps correctly—argued that as the Whig nominee he would actually have an excellent chance at winning, especially given the different circumstances from 1844. Should the opposition, for example, select a northern Democrat—as they did—then slaveholder Clay might well win several southern states, and at least likely retain those border slave states he had carried four years earlier. Moreover, if New York Democrats remained badly divided—as they did—then Clay could carry that crucial state that he had barely lost in the last race. And Clay's strong pro-tariff views might well win him Pennsylvania, given that state's anger over the Democratic tariff. Finally, while most agreed that as a Deep South slaveholder Taylor could not carry Ohio, Clay would have a much better chance of doing so. Thus, to some observers, Clay offered a better opportunity for victory than Taylor did. Clay was far from being the certain loser opponents pictured.[45]

At the same time, numerous unknown answers confused such scenarios. Would Clay's recent antislavery pronouncements still drive away potential southern votes, even if he became the only slaveholder in the race? If Clay received the Whig nomination, would that action unite divided Democrats against this man they saw as a dangerous evil? Would Taylor, if rejected by the Whigs, then rise as a third-party candidate and split that party's vote? Or, if Clay were the nominee, would he again do something politically hurtful, and again lose? Those queries fed the doubters who feared Clay's nomination would take the party down the road to defeat once more. But despite the questions and the criticisms, the fact remained: if Clay received the Whig nomination, he would indeed have a real chance for victory. As the *New York Herald* observed, Clay had "as good a prospect, if not a better [one], than he ever had during his career, for the White House."[46]

The prospects for Clay—or any Whig—grew brighter after the Democratic convention concluded in late May. It selected former Jackson secretary of war and now-senator Lewis Cass of Michigan, an aging, heavy-set man identified with his newly stated doctrine to let each territory decide the fate of slavery within its borders, no matter the Missouri Compromise—what became known as popular sovereignty. That proposal would aid northerner Cass in the South, but hurt him drastically in the North. The question of slavery now divided the Democrats more than ever before. Antislavery members of the party balked at Cass's nomination. In the New York contingent, the so-called Barnburners, prompted by antislavery motives, walked out of the convention. They would later form the core of the Free Soil Party, with Martin Van Buren as its nominee. In 1844, the Liberty Party had drawn most of its voters from the Whig ranks, but in 1848, the Free Soilers would take more ballots from the Democrats, especially in New York. That reversal made the possibility of a Whig victory much greater. If Clay could just gain the nomination, it well could be his year—at last. In the twilight of life, he might finally realize his long-deferred hope for the presidency.[47]

The decision would be made by the 279 delegates who assembled in Philadelphia on June 7, 1848. The winning candidate would need 140 votes. Just before the convention opened, Clay wrote that he did not expect to win, but was saddened that the party seemed "willing to cast overboard so many of the cherished measures and principles for which we have been so long . . . contending." But for once, Henry Clay was too pessimistic.[48]

Ohio and Kentucky were the bellwethers for the nomination. If Clay could show strength in those two places, he would likely be the leading vote-getter. As the first balloting concluded, the count stood as Taylor 111, Clay 97, Scott 43, Webster 22, and two others 6 each. On that critical first ballot, Taylor led, chiefly by taking most of the slave-state votes. Not a single vote from that region went to a northerner. But had Clay led on that ballot, it would have demonstrated his wide support across the sections and his ability to win. And, in some ways, he easily could have led. Ohio's governor had begged Clay to run and had, on more than one occasion, promised to deliver most of that state's 22 votes to Clay. Other leaders in the Buckeye State had made similar commitments to him. Clay wrote that he had "numerous assurances, in every form, and from the highest sources" that Ohio would vote for him. But on the first ballot, 20 of that state's votes instead went to General Scott. Some suggested that Clay ally Thomas Corwin of Ohio saw himself as a potential compromise choice and tried to keep Clay from winning outright. Others pointed to Scott's northern ties. Still more emphasized the hidden hand of Thurlow Weed, again. For whatever reason, Ohio disappointed Clay. Had he received those 20 votes, Clay would have led Taylor 117–111, a strong, symbolic vote.

But as much as the Ohio vote hurt, the actions of the twelve-man Kentucky delegation pained him even more. If he could not carry his own state's votes, that would be interpreted as a sign of weakness. On the first ballot, Kentucky had given Taylor 7 votes, Clay 5. Crittenden's influence was clear. Had Clay been able to secure the unanimous vote of Kentucky, along with the Ohio delegation, he would have had 124 votes, with Taylor having 104, Scott with 23, and Webster with 22. With that lead, on a second ballot either the vote of the Scott or Webster forces would have given Clay the nomination. But in reality, he trailed Zachary Taylor, and that provided fuel to those who said Clay could not win.[49]

A second factor, revealed only later, further damaged Clay's chances. Before the convention, candidate Scott (who disliked Taylor intensely) had told a political ally that if his bid faltered, then the ally was authorized to tell Clay managers that Scott would give his support to Clay, in exchange for the vice presidential nomination. That would ensure Taylor's defeat, advance Scott's own fortunes, and perhaps gain the support of Clayites for a later Scott presidential race. Clay allies would have a military hero on the ticket, as well. For unknown reasons, however, the Scott spokesman never conveyed that offer. They almost certainly would have accepted the proposition, for Scott's 43 votes would have given Clay the nomination, no matter the Ohio and Kentucky vote. On the other hand, more adroit Clay managers could have sought out the Scott leaders and been proactive in offering such a deal, as well.[50]

But the absence of the Scott offer, the "malign influence" of the divided Kentucky vote, and the unexpected Ohio defection all doomed Clay's chances. His vote fell during the next two ballots. Then, on the fourth ballot, Weed turned several of New York's formerly Clay votes to others, Pennsylvania joined them, and Kentucky went 11–1 for Taylor. The die was cast, for Taylor now had 171 votes, Scott had 63, Clay had 32, and an "obstinate" Webster had 14. It was over. Zachary Taylor had won the Whig nomination; Henry Clay had been defeated once more.[51]

Taylor's opponents refused to make the nomination unanimous. Divisions regarding slavery and uncertainty about Taylor's policies resulted in no party platform. Greeley called the whole affair "a slaughterhouse of Whig principles." In the end, Clay's allies, and Clay himself, all agreed on why he lost—Kentucky's votes, Ohio's reversal, and Webster's refusal of support. But the greatest cause of his defeat was the Taylor forces' successful portrayal of the military man as a winner and of politician Clay as a loser. As a Whig delegate wrote later in the *Southern Literary Messenger*: "Gunpowder again prevailed. . . . The old trick of an inexpedient expediency was revived, and the last chance of electing Clay to the Presidency thrown away."[52]

Clay had made his last run for the presidency. Or had he? That an untested political neophyte had defeated the political idols of the Whigs galled some party partisans. In New England, disappointed Whigs pouted over the results. Webster wrote that he would ignore the nominee and quietly vote for the party. But others, including convention delegate (and later US vice president) Henry Wilson of Massachusetts, refused to approve the "wicked nomination" of an unprincipled slaveholder, "brought forth from the obscurity of a frontier camp." And such criticisms came not just from antislavery New Englanders. A worried Georgia Whig told Crittenden that "*real Clay*men" had become open in their opposition to the general's cause, while a journal found Clay's friends "greatly dissatisfied, not to say exasperated" by the nomination. One observer sarcastically noted that in rejecting Clay and Webster, the Whigs had taken up "General Availability."[53]

Henry Clay did not accept his rejection very well. He had usually been a good loser. But the 1848 defeat finally seemed to release Clay's pent-up fury—at political machinations, at fate, at himself. He would not go quietly into the political night in 1848; he could not, in clear conscience.

THE ASSASINATION OF THE SAGE OF ASHLAND.

In Clay's failed attempt to seize the 1848 Whig nomination from Zachary Taylor, Clay supporters felt betrayed. In a cartoon that recalls Shakespeare's *Julius Caesar*, Clay reads Horace Greeley's *Tribune* in the peace of Ashland as ten men with daggers prepare to assassinate the unsuspecting candidate. On the left is Daniel Webster; on the right are former ally John J. Crittenden of Kentucky and New York party boss Thurlow Weed. *Library of Congress, LC-USZ62-1422*

A convention delegate had suggested that Clay might see his defeat as "an act of ingratitude by the party founded, and built up and defended, consolidated, kept together, loved, and led by himself." In fact, Clay viewed the action exactly that way. All his years of service had been tossed aside for political expediency. Clay was more than sad; he was mad. In truth, Clay should not have run in 1848. But with the ascendancy of Taylor and Scott, Clay had foreseen problems ahead for the party. Only when a reluctant (but still ambitious) Clay received assurances of support that made his nomination seem likely, had he yielded to the call and entered the fray. He had no desire to lose again. The eventual outcome made him feel betrayed and used by party leaders. Most of all, he was "mortified" by the vote of the Kentucky delegation and severely criticized Crittenden for his course. Clay even drafted a fifteen-page manuscript to go to the *Louisville Journal* opposing the election of Crittenden for governor. In it, Clay decried Crittenden's "faithless and ungrateful" betrayal of a friend, the act of a man whose heart had been eaten away by ambition. But one of Clay's sons asked his father to reflect more before sending the letter, and Clay never published it. Still, the outpouring of anger represented the hurt Clay still felt. In truth, Crittenden had committed to Taylor at a time when he believed Clay was not going to run, and once in the Taylor camp he remained loyally there. Besides, Crittenden wanted to be on the winning side. But Clay allies continued to attack what they called Crittenden's "double dealing and treachery."[54]

Despite his angst, Clay still had to decide if he would support the nominee, as he had in the past. This time he would not. In letter after letter, he gave the same reasoning. Clay would not "give the lie to myself" and reject all that he had valued over the years. He would not in good conscience support for president a duplicitous and "wholly incompetent" man who had no civil experience, who had repudiated Whig principles, and who had threatened to run as a third-party candidate if denied the Whig nomination. Soon after the convention, Clay again wrote that he feared Taylor's nomination would mean the dissolution of the Whigs and the rise of a Jackson-like "mere *personal* party." When a delegation arrived at Ashland asking for an endorsement of Taylor, a bitter Clay recalled the Taylor forces' attacks on Clay's electability and responded, "I think his availability will carry him along without any assistance from unavailable men." The next month, Clay admitted that nothing in the contest caused him to want "to stimulate my exertions or to animate my patriotism." With Cass and Taylor as the chief contenders, he saw a choice "between the frying pan and the fire."[55]

Clay's open refusal to endorse Taylor, or even to say that he would vote for him, encouraged those Whigs who questioned the general's qualifications or his commitment to their party. By late August, they began publicly urging Clay to become an independent candidate. They reasoned that such an action would put four candidates in the field (as in 1824) and might allow a Clay win outright. At worst, it would send the election to the Whig-controlled House of Representatives, where Clay's long connections might produce victory. Cincinnati Whigs wrote Clay asking approval to proclaim his candidacy, while a New York City rally attended by some ten thousand people called on Clay to rescue their party from its crisis of conscience.[56]

A single word from Clay would put him back in the presidential mix once more. Ironically, Democrats began to praise Clay, to lionize his past accomplishments, and to emphasize his betrayal by the convention in an attempt to divide the Whigs. In one clever piece, a newspaper rewrote *Hamlet* with "the Millboy" being stabbed in the back by an underling while a white-faced General Taylor watched and asked, "Is it done?" When confronted by the ghost of the Millboy, Taylor cried out that he had not done the killing himself. But such Democratic efforts failed. Clay would not endorse Taylor, but he also would not countenance a separate race for the presidency by Henry Clay. He understood that with four candidates in the race, utter chaos would result, and no one could foretell the results. Certainly, his candidacy would divide the Whigs—his party—and might produce a Democratic victory. Or, if the election went into the House for a decision, a political bloodbath could ensue; American democracy might not survive the stress. So, as much as he disliked the choices before him, Clay would not agree to become a third-party candidate. In a public letter in September, Clay stated that such actions had no support from him and that he would not accept a nomination by any group or party. Reluctantly, regretfully, sadly, Clay finally recognized that his presidential hopes had ended. He would never be president.[57]

Zachary Taylor became president instead. The Deep South had its first chief executive (and the last until the 1960s). For once, Clay had accurately predicted the outcome. Taylor had barely won, losing Ohio as Clay had expected, but carrying Pennsylvania and New York. Had either of those states rejected him, Taylor would have lost. In fact, Taylor's percentage of the overall popular vote fell below Clay's of four years earlier; he would be a minority president. Several commentators suggested that had Clay been the candidate, he would have done better than Taylor. After looking at the results, Clay agreed. In the first election when all Americans voted for president on the same day—a reform furthered by the Louisiana frauds in 1844—Henry Clay did not vote for the man who had never voted. On Election Day, word came that Clay was ill and could not go to the polls. Whether he was actually sick, whether he used that as an excuse, or whether the prospects of a Taylor presidency had created a psychosomatic illness, Clay would not endorse Taylor by voting for him.[58]

In June, Clay had asked his friends to leave him "undisturbed in the quiet shade of Ashland. . . . My race is run." Two months later, he reiterated that sentiment: "I consider my public career as forever terminated." But if Clay no longer held presidential aspirations, he still cared for his country and feared for its future. His public career would continue.[59]

15

Pacificator—and Peace

FOLLOWING HIS FAILURE TO GAIN the presidential nomination in 1848, Clay could easily have retreated to the repose of Ashland, to enjoy his remaining years. But serious threats on the national horizon brought him to the realization that he should not—could not—do that. In fact, Clay's words and actions over the last years of his life reveal much about him as politician and man. Every rational part of his political being told him he had no real hopes for future high office; he now spoke only for himself, consequences be damned. Those lingering times in a long life epitomize the basic beliefs that guided Henry Clay during the years of his presidential quests.

In 1849, Kentucky decided to revise its fifty-year-old constitution. That gave both proslavery and antislavery forces the opportunity to elect delegates to the upcoming convention. Kentucky could strengthen the hold of slavery on the state or, alternatively, craft a document that might even end slavery over time. In many ways, the ensuing discussion marked the last significant debate on antislavery in the South before the Civil War. What an observer called a "very much agitated" dialogue followed. Henry Clay, now freed from the politics of trying to balance and explain his antislavery views to the South and his slaveholding to the North, decided to voice his stand on the issue in an attempt to influence the delegate selection.[1]

Wintering in the warmer weather of New Orleans, Clay had suffered an injury in a serious fall, another sign of his advancing age. But as he recovered, he penned a letter to his friend Richard Pindell. Clay may have been influenced by an event that occurred in Kentucky in 1848, when a college student named Patrick Doyle had organized a sizable number of slaves in an attempt to escape captivity and cross the Ohio River into free territory. Just a few miles short of the river, they had been surrounded and, after a fight, retaken. Some of the leaders were sentenced to be hanged, but the slave-holding judge at the trial implored the governor for mercy, writing, "They are property and yet they are men. . . . Think of what history may say. . . . I had rather you pardon all." The governor heeded that plea. But Doyle received a twenty-year sentence and died in prison, a forgotten martyr to the antislavery cause. The episode demonstrated to Clay, once more, that the desire for freedom ran deep in all races.[2]

With that background, with the campaign for constitutional convention delegates just beginning and with nothing to gain politically, Clay penned his Pindell letter on February 17, 1849. In it, he took a firm and clear anti-slavery, antiestablishment stand. Completely rejecting the "positive good" theory of slavery, Clay answered those who called the black race inferior and unworthy of freedom. He wrote that if that condition justified slavery, "then the wisest man in the world would have a right to make slaves of all the rest of mankind." Those of greater intellectual ability, white or black, should fulfill their obligation to their fellow man and raise them up, not subjugate them. Then, turning to the specific moment, Clay called for the election of delegates who would produce a constitution that provided for "cautious and gradual" emancipation, followed by colonization. According to his plan, by 1860 at the latest, all the slaves would be declared free, once they had reached the age of twenty-five and had earned enough money under an apprentice system to pay their way to Africa. Under that scenario, he indicated, Kentucky would be free of slavery within forty years. Rid finally of that great evil that held people in servitude, Kentuckians would prosper and live with a clear conscience at last.[3]

His own conscience perhaps soothed by writing the letter, Clay asked a son back in Kentucky to show it to several allies for comment. They did not encourage its publication, but Prince Hal once more ignored their advice and wrote his son that his letter "will bring me some od[ium]. I nevertheless wish it published. I owe that to the cause, and [to] myself, and to posterity." The letter appeared in state newspapers in March and immediately received national attention. Predictably, those on both extremes criticized Clay. Abolitionist William Lloyd Garrison termed it a cowardly, cruel, and remorseless missive, while proslavery "fire-eaters" used even harsher words. Clay, however, aimed his words not at northern abolitionists but at Kentucky voters. In an open discussion of the wisdom of slavery—a rare thing in a slave society—slaveholder Clay lent his name and prestige to the emancipation cause. The *Covington Journal* called his words fresh, clear, and positive, while the *Louisville Courier* asked for an end to that "incubus upon the public prosperity." From farther afield, the British *Spectator* praised Clay and concluded that "the internal canker of the republic is its slavery."[4]

In the end, however, voters heard loudest the voices of those who feared a world without slavery. The state that was once at the frontier of change now shunned it, at least on matters of race. When the votes were counted, just one in ten Kentuckians had voted for emancipationists as delegates to the convention. Only two delegates represented that cause. The resulting constitutional revision actually strengthened the peculiar institution in Kentucky. Observers grew stronger in their conviction that antislavery in the South had no chance, since even moderate Kentucky would not adopt it. A discouraged Clay blamed timid politicians who would not speak out, the false fears voiced by proslavery leaders, and the worries left by abolitionist rhetoric from outside the state. To Clay, the vote meant that "for a long time to come," slavery would continue in Kentucky. But still he stressed that slavery must end eventually. Such a wrong could not endure.[5]

Twice in his lifetime—in the vote for a new constitution in 1799 and now in 1849—Clay had openly spoken out for an end to slavery when the matter had come up for public vote. Twice he had been on the losing side. In the half century after his first public stance on the subject, he had sometimes lost his way and retreated from the strongest elements of those stands. Yet as the southern resistance to slavery's end grew stronger, Clay never recanted his basic stance that slavery was evil. But in the end, when it concerned slavery in Kentucky, voters chose white supremacy over party and loyalty to the racial status quo over their devotion to Henry Clay.

After still another defeat, it is a wonder that Clay did not become a bitter old man. Trusting in the people's will, he had seen them twice deny him regarding slavery and the Kentucky constitution and thrice reject him for president. Supporting the party he had helped found, he had watched its delegates turn down his candidacy two more times. Believing in the nation's destiny for greatness, he had observed other leaders tear down his programs and imperil the Union itself. He had suffered not only political losses but also personal ones, with the deaths of seven children. But Clay did not lose hope. He worried about the United States, as a concerned parent might, but he seldom descended into pessimism. Instead of rejecting the populace who had denied his dreams, he gained energy from the political adoration of his allies and emerged optimistic in the end.

Yet Clay could not ignore the threats to his country, and he had over the years worked again and again to quiet the tensions and unite the nation. Now, in 1849, another such threat loomed. As Clay had predicted, the huge expanse of new territory taken in the Mexican-American War had brought the slavery issue once more to the forefront, with a ferocity not seen before. Just as some northerners wanted all the new lands free of permanent servitude, some southerners called for the expansion of slave power into the several potential states. The presence of political novice Zachary Taylor in the White House did not bode well for a resolution, either. Harsh words erupted. From Georgia, one writer predicted the flowing of "civil blood," and another concluded that "sectional feeling is stranger than I ever saw it before." A former South Carolina governor told John C. Calhoun that a dissolution of the nation was certain "and the sooner we can get rid of it the better." Southerners made plans for a convention in Nashville—possibly to declare for secession. And while some northerners did not want to believe that such a danger existed, others preferred division to the continued expansion of slavery. Overall, as one politician noted, "We have . . . too much demagoguism and too little statesmanship."[6]

Clay heard the angry words and understood the seriousness of the situation. But his national career had seemed over just a year before. After his controversial Pindell letter, enemies had proclaimed that Clay was "done up in Kentucky" as well. Moreover, his energies had declined and his infirmities had increased. When asked three years earlier if he would return to the Senate, Clay had admitted that he could not conceive "of a state of things in which I would consent to go back." As tensions rose, Kentucky Whig Governor William Owsley offered to appoint Clay to fill a Senate vacancy, but in June 1848 Clay had declined, saying that only a "great emergency" would force him back. When friends offered his name for a seat in early 1849, Clay had written from New Orleans, "God knows I have no personal desire to return to that body" and regretted that his name was being presented. But he did not issue a unilateral rejection, either. Perhaps he realized that statesmanship was indeed needed or the Union might well be threatened. Perhaps he just could not wean himself from the mother's milk of politics. But perhaps, as he had said many years earlier, "There are no sacrifices too great for one to make, when necessary, for his country." The General Assembly once more elected Clay to the Senate, as he defeated

Richard M. Johnson by a vote of 93–49. The people wanted Henry Clay and his voice of reason.[7]

New senator Henry Clay took his time in making his way to the December 1849 opening of Congress. Before Clay left Kentucky, he had written a friend that he opposed the extension of slavery into the new lands, but he also feared that northern agitation on that issue might drive the South into an extreme position. The Millboy of the Slashes hoped that would not occur: "We are fellow-citizens of one common and glorious country." He traveled for a month, gauging public opinion along the way. Finally, by the first day of December, Clay arrived in the District of Columbia, back after a seven-year hiatus from political office. At the opening of the Thirty-First Congress, two days later, he arrived on the Senate floor dressed in his traditional black, with a high white-collared shirt. It was as if a ghost had returned to revisit his previous haunts. Out of his past, old enemies and allies joined him as they took their seats—Benton, Calhoun, Cass, Houston, and Webster, among others. Younger senators came to welcome the suddenly invigorated Clay as well—Stephen A. Douglas, the Illinois Democrat who Clay would come to admire because he could get things done, and Jefferson Davis, a man Clay had known when Davis had been a student at Transylvania, who had served with Clay's son in the Mexican-American War, and who now sat next to Clay. A former son-in-law of President Taylor, Davis would not, however, gain Clay's admiration during the session.[8]

Almost immediately, Clay discovered that the "feeling for division . . . is stronger than I supposed it could be." By early January 1850, Clay had grown more fearful as he measured the situation. He told a son: "Some Hotspurs of the South are openly declaring themselves for a dissolution of the Union . . . if the Wilmot Proviso be adopted. This sentiment of disunion is more extensive than I had hoped." Three weeks later, Clay told allies in the West that he found a "bad state of things" in Washington, where slavery seemed the "all-engrossing theme."[9]

Meanwhile, actions by the president were not helping calm the passions. With a mediocre cabinet and no congressional majority in either house, Taylor had found governing hard enough. Added to that was the administration's lack of social skills. A Whig congressman admitted, "I have never been able to converse one minute with the President upon politics without his changing the Subject." Nor did Taylor see in the return of the experienced Clay an opportunity for help. In fact, members of both parties worried about the presence of the Kentuckian in the capital.

Democrats like Davis feared that Clay would use his "evil influence" against their programs and party. In turn, Taylor supporters grew concerned that Clay would try to wrest party control from the chief executive. But, in fact, Clay remained politically quiet, at least initially. Privately (and a bit unfairly), he complained—as did Webster and other congressmen—that his friends received no patronage rewards from the new administration, even though their votes had elected Taylor. The only sop given Clay occurred before Clay came to Washington, when he had surprisingly asked the president to appoint his son James to a diplomatic post. Perhaps as a peace offering to Clay, the president made James B. Clay the chargé d'affaires to Portugal. However, the father told a friend, "This little affair will have no effect upon my relations to the Administration." And seemingly it did not. His son's appointment may have muted Clay's open statement of his growing concerns, but it did not halt them.[10]

Soon after his arrival in the capital, Clay dined with Taylor, who treated him with "much consideration." By contrast, Clay found the president's advisors "all civil with me but nothing more." Supporters of other Whig leaders continued to be cut out of administrative councils and appointments, and various party members grew uneasy. As they turned more and more to their old leader for advice and support, Taylor became more distant and cooler. He was president, not Clay. But leadership does not automatically come with the position of chief executive, and the times needed a leader.[11]

As Clay and others saw it, several issues demanded resolution. The foremost question was whether slavery would be extended into the new lands of California, New Mexico, and Utah. Another distraction concerned the hotly disputed Texas–New Mexico boundary, a matter that had already produced bloodshed and threatened to cause conflict between these two neighbors or between federal and state forces. Southerners also wanted a stronger law regarding the return of runaway slaves, while antislavery northerners had begun to call for the abolition of slavery, or at least of the slave trade, in the District of Columbia. And there remained the bonded debt Texas had incurred as a result of its independent status. Those bondholders sought to have their speculative ventures fully funded by the federal government. Congress looked to slaveholder and unionist Taylor for guidance on these matters.[12]

On January 21, 1850, the president submitted a special message to Congress outlining his plans. He supported the immediate admission of California and New Mexico as free states, but said nothing about other matters of concern. Taylor stated his hope that "exciting topics of a sectional nature" would not be discussed. It was not a bad plan. It just had no hope of success. Feeling betrayed by the slaveholder they had elected, southerners angrily opposed the proposal, which would in effect limit the expansion of slavery and add more free-state votes in Congress. A former Georgia senator called Taylor "a perfect automaton in the hands of others," specifically Seward, now a key advisor to Taylor. Speaker of the House Howell Cobb of Georgia later wrote that the president's plan had virtually no support in the South. If the chief executive pushed that option and northern votes passed it, the "common opinion" in the South, said Calhoun, would favor leaving the Union in order to protect slavery. Another Georgia politician just days before had expressed the same sentiment, predicting that admission of the states would leave the South "powerless" and produce "a tide of fanaticism." Open talk of secession began to be heard in the halls of Congress. The dangers of separation seemed very real.[13]

In 1848, the *New York Tribune* had asked, "Who . . . is better prepared to . . . safely guide the Ship of State beyond the reach of the impending storm than Henry Clay?" The voters had answered otherwise. But now the nation needed a pilot, and the people turned once more to the Great Pacificator. They may not have deemed him good enough to be president, but they wanted him to preserve the country and the presidency. Almost as soon as Clay had arrived in the capital, union men of both parties had approached him, with "hope that I may be able to calm the raging elements." For more than ten months, Clay had remained publicly silent about his concerns regarding the administration and its course involving the controversy. He had not openly attacked the president's appointment and patronage decisions, even though he—and other Whigs—had been upset by them. Prince Hal had not said or done anything publicly to challenge the president as party leader. Over the next three months that would change.[14]

Clay had a mixed history of working with presidents. The Kentuckian served well under John Quincy Adams and would do so under Millard Fillmore. By definition, he led the opposition when presidents of the other party held office. But the Whigs Tyler and Taylor present a more complicated picture. Clay would eventually break with both men because the chief executives either seemed to be abandoning Whig doctrines or their actions—or nonactions—created concern. Nor was Clay alone in that response. In both instances, the majority of the party ultimately supported Clay. When it came down to a choice of policy or the president, Clay chose to follow his philosophy over the politician each time.

Many judged that the Taylor plan had only made the crisis worse by feeding the fears of the South. Nor did the chief executive's action over the next month improve matters. When a delegation of three southerners warned Taylor of the growing danger of separation if he pursued his limited policy, the old general angrily replied, Jackson-like, that if that occurred, he would personally lead a force to crush such a movement and would hang the leaders as traitors. He expected that threat to be enough. He provided no words of conciliation or compromise. But in Jackson's time, South Carolina had remained alone, without allies. By 1850, much of the South stood united in their shared attitude. Unless something changed, a military man soon might be leading an army against his fellow Americans in a civil war.[15]

That possibility was unacceptable to Henry Clay. Almost two months after his arrival in Washington, and a month after Taylor had presented his plan, Clay realized—as did others—that something else had to be done to end the crisis. Only then did Clay take action. First, the Great Pacificator made a difficult decision. He had barely spoken to Daniel Webster since the Tyler administration. But now, on a snowy Washington night, seventy-two-year-old Henry Clay made an unannounced visit to Webster, told him of his ideas for a compromise, and asked for his cooperation, or at least his nonopposition. Over the next six weeks, Webster mostly observed events, but in the end, he would support Clay's strategy. After talking to others, Clay presented his own proposal to end the confrontation and remove the possibility of disunion. In doing so, he intentionally did not openly break with the administration but, rather, proffered an alternative to its solution. But Taylor would not budge from his stance, and he saw Clay's efforts as an attack on his proposal. Increasingly concerned about Clay's growing leadership role, the president used what powers his administration had to oppose the compromise. But Clay had expected that, when he rose to offer what he called a "comprehensive plan of adjustment" to answer "this distracting question."[16]

On January 29, 1850, Clay presented his compromise and a week later, over a two-day period, he explained his ideas for "an amicable arrangement of all the questions in controversy between the free and the slave states." Although his voice in private conversations had grown weaker and softer, as he now rose to offer his proposal, the old, clear, magical tones once more enthralled. Clay understood that for a compromise to be successful, both sides must feel they would receive something in honorable exchange for relenting on other matters. Accordingly, he offered the South a stronger

Fugitive Slave Law and the statement that Congress could not regulate the interstate slave trade. For the North, he proposed admission of California as a free state and the ending of the slave trade in the District of Columbia. On the murky Texas–New Mexico border controversy, which seemed about to produce a clash of arms between the Texas military and the federal army in New Mexico, Clay proposed that in return for an agreement generally favorable to New Mexico, the federal government would reward Texas by assuming its debt.

That left only the issue of whether slavery would be allowed in New Mexico and Utah territories. In Clay's view, that was a moot matter because Mexico had abolished slavery, and those ex-Mexican lands retained that status. The Great Pacificator's interpretation meant that neither North nor South would "win" on that issue, though the practical effect would favor the northern position. Clay argued that everyone should want that proposal to pass: the Texas bondholders would profit from their speculation (not coincidentally also providing an important lobbying force for the compromise); the South would gain more protection of slavery where it existed; the North would gain a free state and the recognition that the other territories would not have slaves, as well as the end of the slave trade in Washington itself. Clay stressed that the proposed law "is founded upon mutual forbearance, originating in a spirit of conciliation and concession."[17]

Clay sought to accomplish two things by his compromise. First, he consciously tried to shift the focus of the discussion away from the question of slavery and instead to the issue of the preservation of the Union. By doing that, he especially hoped to appeal to southern Whigs who, as a former congressman wrote, would "fight for slavery but die by the union." Overall, Clay expected that radicals on either side would not yield. But he sought to win over moderates of both parties, in both sections. In the end, a strange combination of northern Democrats and southern Whigs would form the core of votes for compromise. The second thing that Clay wanted to do was simply to get the dialogue started and the debate going by combining the elements into a comprehensive design. Adrift before, Congress now had a plan that might work. Clay had established the agenda, had provided direction to the discussion, and had given Congress the hope that a resolution could occur.[18]

The next seven months proved to be some of the most frustrating of Clay's career. He told his wife that he had never worked harder in his life. A newspaper noted that Clay's very presence in the debate greatly increased the possibilities of resolution, while an abolitionist reluctantly conceded that

Clay had "a peculiar power." Charles Sumner wrote admiringly that "Clay is determined . . . & he is daily showing what a strong *will* can do." Observers mostly knew that the Great Compromiser did not have the energy, the fire, or the force he once possessed. Yet, they saw that when no one else seemed able to act, Clay stepped up and, with a younger man's spirit, took the lead.[19]

If he symbolized the behemoth in the debate, Clay also had constant political attack dogs nipping at his heels. A month after presenting his proposals, he complained that he had been listening all day "to the grating and doleful sounds of dissolution of the Union, Treason, and War." Many southerners had immediately termed Clay's plans too pro-northern and, led by Davis and others, had criticized point after point, offering amendment after amendment. On March 4, 1850, a frail, dying Calhoun came to the Senate chambers to have his speech read for him. He yielded on nothing, impractically calling for a constitutional amendment to guarantee slavery's existence in the United States—forever. Three days later, Webster finally spoke out in what became known as his Seventh of March Speech. His courageous—if flawed—support for the basis of the compromise brought forth howls of protests from northern abolitionists. Then four days after Webster, antislavery advocate William H. Seward gave his maiden major speech in the Senate, explaining that the laws of man must be superseded by a "higher law." Seward called all legislative compromises "radically wrong." In combination, the speeches by Calhoun on the one side and Seward on the other, when compared to Clay's and Webster's calls for calm, turned some moderate northerners toward the compromise position. In the South, Clay's plans for compromise had slowed the secession train. Still, each extreme fought resolution on Clay's terms.[20]

But some enemies did turn to Clay in support, for they, like him, saw the dangers to the Union. Thomas Ritchie, his one-time friend from Virginia and longtime editorial enemy, made a strong call for union. He attacked the "voice of fanaticism" and the "torch of discord" that threatened to overwhelm "the grandest experiment which has ever been seen in the annals of man." Ritchie then asked, "Have we no great men among us, whose spirits are equal to the storm which threatens our institutions?" Taylor had "shrunk from his responsibility" and was not such a man, but someone must take the helm. Ironically, Ritchie's editorial appeared the same day Clay offered his plan to Congress. When he later read the editor's words, the senator asked for an interview with his old enemy. Sharing his longtime adversary's fears about division and secession, Ritchie agreed to meet in Clay's rooms in the National Hotel.

According to the editor's version, "He received us with the most winning courtesy and kindness. He treated me as if no unpleasant relations had ever existed between us." They talked specifics, with frankness and calm, and the whole discussion left Ritchie "deeply impressed" with Clay's love of his country, devotion to his union, and dedication to a compromise. He promised to support Clay's proposals in his widely circulated paper. The two left the meeting as friends, joined by respect and a common cause. At the same time, Clay and another former ally-turned-opponent, Francis Preston Blair, also mended their political palisades and restarted their friendship. Clay needed all the support he could get.[21]

On March 31, 1850, the death of John C. Calhoun temporarily halted the debate. When Clay slowly rose to offer his thoughts on the life of his longtime adversary, he praised Calhoun's "clear, concise, compact logic." Noting their differences as well, Clay concluded with kind words that may or may not have reflected his true feelings: "I was his senior . . . in years—in nothing else." He then turned to the empty chair and asked who would fill that vacancy. But Calhoun's death did not appreciably change the southern position, for even before that, younger men like Davis had led the fight for slavery. Meanwhile the Taylor administration continued to push its doomed strategy, with Clay's old enemy, Benton, as its chief advocate in the Senate. No consensus existed. Harsh words continued. Anger still raged. Clay and other leaders had hoped to push through the various elements of his plan via separate bills (as they had done in the Missouri Compromise). But influential southerners insisted that the package be kept together, to ensure that their concerns would not be rejected. Clay opposed that approach but reluctantly agreed at last, saying that he was "wedded to no particular plan of . . . tranquillizing this country" as long as the compromise passed. In April, the proposal went to the Committee of Thirteen—six northerners, six southerners, and Clay, the man above sectionalism. After some three weeks, the committee issued its report and supported a so-called omnibus bill. Clay had yielded, or been outvoted on several key matters—in truth, making the compromise weaker—yet the core elements remained. But the committee report now had more pro-southern elements, and that sparked another round of debates.[22]

On top of the still-fierce discussions about the revised compromise, Taylor continued to oppose any agreement. When the administration-backed newspaper printed friendly words about Clay's compromise efforts, Taylor replaced its editor. To Clay, that action apparently ended his uneasy peace with the administration, for the president appeared to be using his office to try to discredit the Committee of Thirteen report. Taylor and his advisors seemed like amateurs in a serious game that was hard enough for the professionals to master. Finally, in mid-May, Clay openly broke with the administration. Speaking in the Senate, the Kentuckian said that Taylor's plan would bind only one of the five bleeding wounds of the country, and would wreck the "delicate balance" between the sections. The nation would bleed to death. The break intensified a month later, when "A Friend of the Union" published a sixteen-page pamphlet, *Henry Clay and the Administration*. It bitterly assailed the Taylor presidency for its "deliberate and cold-blooded assault" on Clay, who was only trying to calm the "fierce sectional discord." The pamphlet emphasized that Taylor's inaction had only widened the breach between North and South and had left the country despairing of a solution. Instead, the "inexperienced" Taylor should have invited and learned from the counsel of Clay, Webster, and other leaders rather than have "repulsed" their advice. In answer, an understandably angry administration more forcibly opposed the compromise efforts. As Clay commented the day before the nation celebrated its independence, it now was "war, open war, undisguised war."[23]

The debates dragged on into early July. The heat, the delaying tactics, the endless amendments, and the lack of statesmanship increasingly grated on Clay. The oldest senator, he grew more impatient, irritable, and inflexible: "The body politic cannot be preserved unless this agitation, this distraction, this exasperation . . . between the two sections . . . shall cease." Clay wrote to a son telling him that the fate of the bill remained uncertain, while to Lucretia he expressed his fear that the compromise would fail and the Union would dissolve. In late July, Clay—who had already spoken some seventy times in defense of the compromise plan—now made a last appeal. Fear the "fatal consequences" if nothing was done, he told his colleagues. Remembering that a compromise requires "mutual sacrifice," they must pass this "great measure of reconciliation and harmony." Once more, Clay concluded by asking the senators to embrace the "dove of peace" and rid themselves of passions, jealousies, and resentments. They should think instead of "our country, our conscience, and our glorious Union." The *Brooklyn Eagle* proclaimed: "Never, never, was Old Hal as great as he has been today." But, despite Clay's words, the whole carefully constructed plan for compromise fell apart. The votes of southern secessionists, northern abolitionists, and some Taylor supporters killed Clay's compromise.[24]

Worn out, distraught, and defeated, a weary Clay departed the capital for the refreshing waters of Newport, Rhode Island, for a little over two weeks' respite. But he did not leave Washington full of despair. The combination of a tragedy and a change of strategy had modified the equation, and had given hope to pro-compromise forces. The tragedy—the unexpected death of President Taylor—had removed a major obstacle to passage of the compromise. (In fact, Crittenden's biographer would write later that had Taylor lived, war would have followed.) After serving as a pallbearer in Taylor's funeral, Clay soon paid a visit to the new president, Millard Fillmore, a close friend of Clay and Webster, and found him supportive. The strategic change involved returning to the original plan to pass the various parts individually. Just before he left for Newport, Clay endorsed that strategy: "I am willing now to see them pass separate and distinct." Democrat Stephen A. Douglas took over management of that matter and began the process. The "Little Giant" would be helped tremendously by the fact that Clay had been successful in turning the debate to the question of union and thus had helped convince a majority of voters that some kind of compromise should emerge. Clay may have also understood that he had become so identified with the compromise that some in Congress opposed it simply for that reason. By removing himself from the battlefield, the country might yet win the war.[25]

Ambitious, impulsive, and hard-working, Douglas personified "Young America" with the energy of a believer in Manifest Destiny. His huge head and strikingly blue eyes drew attention more than did his stature and stoutness. Now, with the aid of Fillmore and Webster, Douglas began getting the individual pieces of the compromise puzzle passed by the Senate. Each region could vote for or against the part it supported or opposed, while abstentions would allow passage of controversial parts. In this way, much of the compromise had passed by Clay's return on August 27; within three weeks, the last bill made it through the House as well. (Ironically, in the House, a "little omnibus" strategy had succeeded, in contrast to the Senate strategy.) The final version differed from Clay's original proposal and the Committee of Thirteen's plan in ways that favored the South. Those significant changes took away from the balance Clay had sought and added elements that would soon create more controversy.[26]

Clay had stated that slavery no longer existed in the new territories by virtue of its abolishment under Mexican law. The final version, however, rejected that interpretation and left the question of slavery open for residents of the territories to decide—a process of popular sovereignty. Furthermore, the bill stated that, whatever the territorial decision, a future Congress could not refuse admission to the Union on those grounds. (If New Mexico, for example, chose to adopt slavery, the more numerous northern votes could not keep it out.) The final compromise also gave slave-state Texas more of the disputed territory with New Mexico than Clay had proposed. More controversially, the Fugitive Slave Law expunged Clay's proposal that any alleged escaped slave be given a trial to decide if the person in question should be returned to slavery. The harsher wording thus gave slave owners a much freer hand in retaking runaway slaves. In time the law became a fierce political and polemical flashpoint. Still, the compromise package had finally passed, after the longest session of Congress to that date. In the end, the final act had been the product of many congressional hands. But even before the adoption of the compromise, Clay had written to a family member that, if passed, the result "will be substantially mine"—and it was.[27]

Most white Americans reacted to the passage of the compromise with relief and joy; for them, the crisis had ended. But not all praised the results. Abolitionists termed it too pro-southern, while "fire-eaters" favoring a separate southern nation opposed any conciliatory actions. But the chorus of support from the majority of the nation drowned out those voices. The Compromise of 1850 satisfied voters, for a time. The results proved, in the end, less of a compromise and more of a truce or armistice. But a compromise, by nature, is seldom permanent. And even a truce means no war, civil or otherwise—it allows for further negotiations; it brings peace for the moment. In this case, it left a still-united nation.[28]

Clay may have erred in several ways in the crisis, but if he made mistakes, he did so for the right reasons. Most of those living amid the dangerous days of 1850 praised the settlement, and while they acknowledged the roles of Fillmore, Douglas, and Webster, they chiefly credited Clay. Even those opposed to him politically recognized his key role. Ritchie wrote that "No man in the Republic could as successfully take the lead in the needed work of pacificator as Mr. Clay." A Mississippi senator remembered that Webster, Cass, and Clay "sacrificed everything like personal rivalry, disregarded everything like party ascendancy, . . . uniting themselves as a band of brothers . . . in support of their common country." Another Democrat, Stephen A. Douglas, recognized that the Kentucky Whig could be a catalyst for the opposition but later concluded that "from the moment that Clay arrived among us he became the leader of all the Union men, whether Whigs or democrats [sic]." Douglas spoke to posterity, calling out, "Let it always be said of old Hal that he fought a glorious & a patriotic battle. No man was ever governed by higher & purer motives." Martin Van Buren, perhaps, best put it into context. He termed Clay's role in 1850 "more honorable

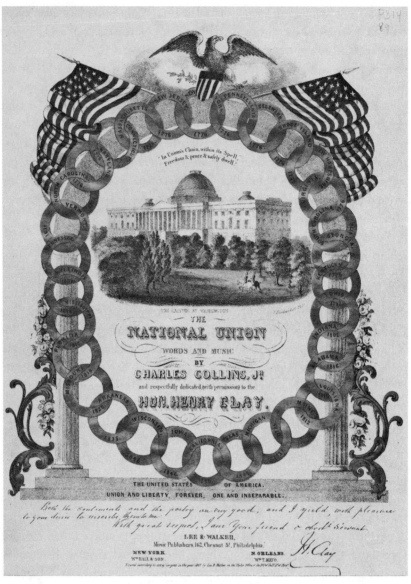

A song dedicated to Clay honors his efforts in the Compromise of 1850. The chain linking the states together, the olive branch, and the inscriptions regarding "the union and liberty, forever" all reflect the optimistic spirit following the Compromise. *Frances G. Spencer Collection of American Popular Sheet Music, Crouch Fine Arts Library, Baylor University, Waco, TX*

and durable than his election to the presidency could possibly have been." Clay never attained the presidency, but he had won something more important: the respect of the nation.[29]

Henry Clay again basked in the adulation of the masses. The temporary euphoria after the end of the crisis brought the people's plaudits for his role. And when he continued to reiterate what others knew as reality—that he had "no wish or thought of ever again consenting to the use of my name in connection with the office of President"—then those in both parties praised his compromise efforts. Accordingly, when Clay made his way back to Kentucky after the long session of Congress had ended, it seemed almost like the triumphant procession of a Roman commander after a victory. On his arrival in Lexington, plebeians urged Clay to speak, but he did so only briefly, telling the crowd, "There lives an old lady about a mile-and-a half from here, whom I would rather see than any of you." Later, Clay addressed a joint session of the Kentucky legislature, and thunderous applause filled the chamber. It all seemed a love feast for Henry Clay.[30]

Still, Clay remained acutely aware that while the immediate danger had passed, it lay only dormant, ready to erupt, for "malcontents, at the North and in the South, may seek to continue or revive agitation." And, in fact, abolitionists blamed Clay for the "infamous" compromise that had yielded so much to slaveholders. Frederick Douglass termed Clay "the most popular and, at the same time, the most wicked man in the US Senate." While southern extremists initially remained mostly quiet as the compromise spirit swept the region, increasing northern resistance to the Fugitive Slave Law soon rekindled their radical efforts to raise the sectional specter once more.[31]

As Clay turned to survey the political state of America, he also worried about his Whig Party. In 1851, he trudged through the rain to vote, but saw Kentuckians elect a Democrat as governor for the first time in some two decades. In the North, Whigs lost members to growing abolitionist third-party movements; in the South, the Democrats' stronger identification with the defense of slavery diluted Whig strength over time as well. Clay saw the signs of party problems. As talk about the 1852 presidential election began, allies once more called on the now-popular Great Compromiser to run, but this time he continually stated his "unconquerable repugnance" to the idea. For the only time in three decades, a presidential election approached without Clay's name being mentioned as a serious candidate. His ambition, if not totally burned out, he kept well-hidden under a bushel of denials. But without their leader, could the party survive?[32]

Some of that debate lay in the near future. Clay remained a US senator from Kentucky and after only a brief respite at home, he returned to Washington in December 1850 for the start of the second session of the Thirty-First Congress. He took his seat, but spoke seldom. Still, despite his attempt to remain above partisan debate, Clay could not resist when a states' rights advocate spoke of the nation exercising only powers found in the Constitution. Prince Hal rose and asked what part of that document gave a state the power to secede, as the "fire-eaters" had threatened. Clay also spoke out against northern resistance to the new Fugitive Slave Law. But mainly he was just tired and ailing. In March 1851, Henry wrote Lucretia: "I can't live a great deal longer." Once the session concluded, Clay traveled to Cuba in a three-week attempt to restore his health. On his arrival in Havana, a crowd in the main square of the city surrounded the famous American. He could not escape his celebrity. His health did benefit some from his stay in what he called a "very different" kind of place, but Clay continued to cough constantly. He returned to Kentucky by April. and by November, he had gone back to Washington, DC, his symbolic home.[33]

But by then Henry Clay was dying. The Great Compromiser could not compromise that situation. He returned to Congress to do his duty as senator and also to argue a potentially lucrative case before the US Supreme Court. But almost immediately on his return, Clay began to experience increasingly bad health. He made a brief appearance in the Senate on December 1, 1851, but returned no more; he turned over his oral arguments before the court to an ally with whom he split the resulting sizable fee that followed a favorable decision. All the while, Clay's health worsened. A national death watch began. He continued to spit up blood and could not sleep because of incessant coughing. The man who once exuded energy and vitality now complained of a lack of strength, no appetite, and a constant cold. Clay took opiates to help him get some rest, and displaying his famous wit amid the adversity, noted that he had "nearly emptied an apothecary shop" with the various medicines he took. Seldom venturing from his room in the National Hotel, he resigned his Senate seat in December, effective the next September. Ever the politician, Clay had taken that action in order to ensure that a Whig administration would choose his successor early, rather than leaving the task to the Democrats who would soon take the reins of office.[34]

By January 1852, Clay told a fellow member of Congress that his situation remained "very critical." Two months after that, he reported to his wife back in Kentucky that "I may linger on for months, but I cannot get well." Yet at the same time, a newspaper described Clay as a man in poor health but one who still displayed a "hopeful" spirit, strong intellect, and firm affection for others. By the next month, Crittenden and Clay had made a peace of sorts; the younger man called on his one-time mentor, but found him "very low & his fate inevitable." As his last days more obviously approached, Clay admitted that he was ready to go, though, he said with a smile perhaps, "I welcome death but do not desire an exciting one." Finally, on the rainy morning of June 29, 1852, at the age of seventy-five, Henry Clay died, in the arms of his country, in the national capital, hoping that his last compromise would bind the sections and keep his beloved Union intact, but fearful that it would not.[35]

Reaction to the loss of one of the nation's most revered—and most reviled—leaders came almost immediately. Congress adjourned on hearing the news. That evening a procession marched through the streets of the capital in Clay's honor. But the Librarian of Congress found

Clay was the first person to lie in state in the Capitol rotunda in Washington; as the body made its way from there to Kentucky, massive numbers of Americans honored him along the way, reportedly the greatest outpouring of public mourning since the death of George Washington. In Lexington, Clay's funeral hearse then made its way to his burial plot. *Courtesy of Ashland, the Henry Clay Estate*

their actions ironic: "They commenced firing a salute of some hundred guns, in honor of the dead patriot, as if he had been 'a military chieftain': Nitre, sulphur, and smoke to honor such a man as Clay! Alas!" Over the next days, private condolences poured in to the family, calling Clay a man above party, a unifier, a great leader. Public tributes to the statesman came from across America. Crittenden, Seward, and Lincoln, among others, offered eulogies, and most newspapers assessed his career as well. A Texas paper noted that "the history of his country will be his eulogy," and the *New York Times* later remarked that the many tributes seemed almost unnecessary: "The facts of his life are engraved on the public memory."[36]

On July 1, 1852, the body of the man whose life had ended made its way from the National Hotel to the Senate chamber of the Capitol. All across America, stores closed, cannons thundered, flags flew at half-mast, and bells tolled. After the funeral services, the iron and mahogany casket with silver handles was moved to the rotunda. For the first time in the nation's history an American lay in state in the Capitol rotunda. Clay's face was exposed so those who passed to say good-bye could see him one last time. Near the end of the hot July day, "vivid lightning and deep rolling thunder, and a gale of wind" swept the city, as if Nature itself roared in tribute. Then it was over.[37]

Like a sacred political relic, the casket made a roundabout two-week trip to Kentucky, covering 1,200 miles and passing through six states, so even more Americans could offer their farewell tributes. Contemporaries termed it the greatest outpouring of public mourning in the nation's history, save that accorded George Washington. On July 10, the body was interned in Lexington Cemetery, before a crowd of some thirty thousand. Already a group of Clay supporters had begun planning for a monument to honor him but, in truth, as a former Clay enemy said in a eulogy, through Clay's lifetime of work, "He carved his *own* statue, he built his own monument."[38]

Two days later, Clay's will was probated. It left most of his assets of some $65,000 to his wife, with specific bequests to his sons, grandchildren, and friends. His will also directed that any slave children born after 1850 would be freed, at age twenty-eight for males, twenty-five for females. Until that time, they would be taught to read and given the opportunity to earn money for passage to Africa.[39]

But Clay's service to his country did not conclude with his death. The United States would need his spirit again and again.

16

Postscript

WITH CLAY IN WASHINGTON, DC, no more, with his ability to craft workable plans now absent, with his eloquent voice calling for reason now stilled, could the nation remain one and united? The answer to that question seemed to be symbolized by the fate of Clay's own estate, Ashland. A son had purchased the property after Clay's death, but the home had been deemed structurally unsound and it was razed—an act perhaps with some psychological overtones. When a *Cincinnati Gazette* reporter visited in the late summer of 1854, he found just a brick wall of the parlor still standing, and workmen had begun to level even that: "All . . . that remains of the old homestead of the statesman is a pile of bricks and rubbish." Only trees and a carriage reminded the visitor of the man who had lived there. Angry, the journalist wrote that the edifice should have been repaired instead, preserved as one of America's "shrines of liberty." The house would, in fact, be rebuilt by 1857, supposedly using a similar floor plan. But by then, the sectional passion present at the time of Clay's death had grown stronger, the rhetoric shriller, the possibilities of resolution dimmer. At Ashland, the brick walls that had seen the warm sun of many summers and the soft rain of many autumns had been dismantled. Would the edifice that was the nation suffer the same fate? And if it did, could it emerge, like Ashland, as a reborn, stronger place, built on a new, firmer foundation, looking forward to a better future? Or would the country lie in ruins, a grim reminder of the failures of a generation that did not include Clay?[1]

Even before his death, Henry Clay's carefully constructed political world had begun to collapse. His party fell first. Clay had been its leader, the spiritual and philosophical core of the Whigs; without him its collective heart grew weaker every day. It soon stopped beating. As a journal noted just a few years later, "Clay was spared one sorrow. He did not live to see the party that he loved, and which loved him, degraded and broken up." The resulting party chaos and fragmentation only added to the dangerous instability of the times. All that would be personified at Ashland. One of Clay's sons would support the new American, or Know-Nothing, Party, another the Democratic Party. And in the 1860 presidential election, Southern Democratic candidate John C. Breckinridge of Kentucky stood in the symbolic shadow of nationalist and Whig Henry Clay and gave a major address at Ashland. As Clay had feared, sectional parties had begun to replace national ones.[2]

Then, on April 12, 1861, guns echoed across the waters of Charleston Harbor. Federal soldiers in Fort Sumter felt the first shock waves from the impact. Soon more shocks would be felt across America. The Civil War had begun—on Henry Clay's birthday. Numerous other ironies abounded. Not only did the cannon thunder on a day when some citizens across the nation still celebrated the memory of the great peacemaker, as they had since his death, but the commander of the fort, Robert Anderson, also hailed from Kentucky. Moreover, the leaders of the two warring sides—Abraham Lincoln and Jefferson Davis—had both been born in the commonwealth.

Kentucky appeared to be in the middle of the crisis, whether it wanted to be or not. On the Washington Monument, begun in the District of Columbia in the late 1840s, the state had inscribed the Clay-inspired words: "Under the auspices of heaven & the precepts of Washington, Kentucky will be the last to give up the Union." But in April 1861 would that be the case? Various forces pulled Kentucky to support one side or the other as the commonwealth sought to find its way in the crisis of the Union. This land that had been a middle ground between competing cultures during its formative frontier period now became that kind of place once more.[3]

While Confederate president Davis had mostly opposed Clay earlier, US president Lincoln had tried instead to follow the lead of his fellow Kentuckian, calling Clay his "beau ideal of a statesman." Lincoln invoked his hero's name numerous times and declared again and again that the Great Compromiser's visions reflected his own. But more than that, Clay's antiwar speech and criticism of the slave power in the same talk strengthened in Lincoln a sense of moral mission. And after his election, the president-elect took four references into a room with him as he composed his inaugural address. One of the four was Clay's 1850 speech on the Compromise. A part of Clay, who never became president, lived on in President Lincoln.[4]

Yet importantly, there was a major difference between Clay and Lincoln. To Clay, union was most important and he therefore would compromise on the moral issue of slavery and the lives of millions of humans held in bondage in order to still the southern dissent, to try to avoid war, and to keep the nation one. Lincoln differed on that score. If Clay wanted to preserve the Union he knew, Lincoln wanted to defend a different kind of union. He recognized that sometimes an evil is so great that a people or a nation cannot compromise on the issue. The expansion of slavery was just such an evil. He could not—would not—allow the peculiar institution to spread. To yield on that issue would be a retreat from the ethical high ground into a moral morass. Clay never understood that.[5]

With the coming of war after Fort Sumter, then, Kentucky had to decide on a course of action. The allies of Lincoln and Davis voiced their appeals, worked to influence the decisions, and labored to move the commonwealth to their side. And in those crucial, desperate days, the voice of Henry Clay once more echoed across Kentucky and the nation. His words, his beliefs, his advice became a clarion call to guide the citizenry. People could read Clay's warnings in his collected speeches, and newspapers reprinted key parts of the Great Pacificator's past talks. Individuals could even purchase an envelope bearing Clay's picture with words regarding secession printed on the image. Many Kentuckians were well inculcated in Clay's vision of America and accepted it as their own. And so as the waves of fear about the future surged across the state and nation, would Clay's spirit help keep Kentucky in the Union, or would his state reject him?[6]

Like Banquo's ghost, Henry Clay haunted the secession crisis, warning of evil. In one sense, Clay had done his job too well in life, for his actions still remained vivid in the psyche of much of the populace. When earlier crises had arisen, and when the nation had seemed to be on the verge of conflict, Clay had stepped up and defused the situation. As a Clay friend later stated, the Great Compromiser would never have accepted the notion of an irrepressible conflict looming in 1861. A senator who served with Clay wrote that had Clay been in Congress at the time, "There would, I feel sure, have been no civil war." In that secession spring of 1861, Kentuckian John J. Crittenden had tried wear the Clay cloak of compromise and had invoked both the spirit and the name of Clay: "What do I ask of you more than

Mr. Clay himself did?" But Crittenden's efforts, like those of many others, failed. Circumstances had changed, and different solutions were needed. No new Clay with the same foresight, will, and force came forward.[7]

But Clay's spirit lived on in other ways. His words would be quoted in the crisis, not just in Kentucky but also across the nation, and others paraphrased his sentiments without directly citing the author. Clay's own language made it clear how he would have stood on the issue before the people. Almost three decades before the Civil War, Clay had all too accurately foreseen what the future could hold, if his generation did not act constructively:

> I wish to see war of no kind; but, above all, do I not desire to see a civil war. When war begins . . . no human foresight is competent to foresee when, or how, or where it is to terminate. But when a civil war shall be lighted up . . . , and armies are marching, and commanders are winning their victories, and fleets are in motion . . . tell me, if you can—tell me, if any human beings can tell its duration? . . . In what state will be left our institutions? In what state our liberties? I want no war; above all, no war at home.[8]

Six years later, Clay had again warned of what could occur without wise actions: war would produce "desolated fields, conflagrated cities, murdered inhabitants, and the overthrow . . . of human government." No one could win a fratricidal war: "It would be a conquest without laurels, without glory—a self, a suicidal conquest—a conquest of brothers over brothers."[9]

But if a division did occur, which side would Clay have taken? After Clay had finished a speech in 1850, a South Carolinian arose to take exception to his characterization of one of the "fire-eaters" in that state. Clay's quick response had left little doubt of the contempt he held: "If he pronounced the sentiment attributed to him of raising the standard of disunion and of resistance to the common Government . . . , if he follows that declaration by corresponding overt acts, he will be a traitor, and I hope he meets the fate of a traitor." A few days later, the Kentuckian faulted those who threatened secession: "I said, and I repeat—and I wish all men who have pens to record it—that if any single State, or the people of any State, choose to raise the standard of disunion and to defy the authority of the Union, I am for maintaining the authority of the Union," by force, if necessary. Even if his own state of Kentucky hoisted the disunion banner, he would oppose it: "I would go against Kentucky herself in that contingency, much as I love her."

That sentiment by a slaveholding southerner represented a very significant statement. And to those who spoke of their state as their country, Clay had forcefully rejoined, "This Union is my country; the thirty States are my country," all together as one, as the United States of America.[10]

In the last year before his death, Clay had gone even further in his denunciation of secessionist doctrine. He had written several letters on the subject, many of which would reemerge in newspapers later. In October 1851, for example, Clay had advocated putting down illegal resistance to the Union, "at every hazard." Revolution, he agreed, was a fundamental right, but not so secession. People could revolt against a government only if an "intolerable" tyranny so oppressed them and a blatant injustice so tormented them that they had no other option. But in America, no such situation existed. Citizens voted freely, enjoyed wide rights, and possessed a voice in government. "Metaphysical" secession theorists and "rash men, promoted by ambition" suggested that a state could leave the Union even if it only differed from the view the majority held. To Clay, dedicated to the idea of majority rule, such a theory represented extreme error. Secession would be an "atrocious," unconstitutional act of madness that would fragment the nation and bring constant conflict. Such words made a difference when Kentucky took action a decade later.[11]

In early 1861, Kentucky remained torn, distraught, and divided. It first adopted a policy of neutrality, making it a kind of "domestic Switzerland," as one historian put it. But after a four-month period, the General Assembly finally ended the policy of neutrality and declared Kentucky a loyal member of the United States. Angry pro-southern Kentuckians formed their own rump government, with their own governor and, eventually, own congressmen. With that group's admission into the Confederacy, Kentucky had a star on both flags. And as Clay had foreseen, it became a Brothers' War—more so perhaps than anywhere else.[12]

Kentucky's decision to remain a loyal state proved to be one of the most decisive victories the Union achieved. Lincoln's observation that "to lose Kentucky is nearly the same as to lose the whole game" has often been noted. But the rest of that comment reveals much as well: "Kentucky gone, we cannot hold Missouri, nor, I think, Maryland. These all against us, and the job on our hands is too large for us." Lincoln knew that Kentucky's decision could mean the difference between Union success and failure. In fact, the border slave states that remained loyal—Kentucky, Missouri, Maryland, and Delaware—may have provided the key to Union success. Three of the South's four largest cities—Baltimore, St. Louis, and Louisville—lay in that area. And those four loyal border states had a large population that could have greatly enlarged the Confederate States of America (CSA) fighting pool and made the South much more competitive on that score. In short, the lingering impact of Henry Clay on Kentuckians' decision making, and the Bluegrass State's resulting influence on the other border states may have been one of the crucial factors in the Civil War.[13]

Henry Clay had warned of the costs of a conflict, and his descendants would feel the divisive effects firsthand. One son (and a son-in-law) supported the North, one the South, and one vacillated. The pro-Confederate sibling would die in exile during the fight. Beyond that, five of Henry Clay's grandchildren took up arms—for both sides. Of those who fought, three—including Henry Clay III—never returned. Nor was Clay's old estate and rebuilt house spared the ravages of war. In October 1862, a skirmish took place on the grounds, literally bringing the war home to the Clays.[14]

That battle between Blue and Gray in some ways reinforced the fact that Clay had failed. In the end, he had not framed a political system capable of withstanding the stresses placed on it after his death. His compromises had delayed the conflict enough so that the North gained strength, but in the end, they failed to quiet the sectional controversy and had not succeeded in preventing war. His attempts to end the divisive question of slavery as an issue had not borne fruit. And his inability to win the presidency had kept him from strengthening the course of the nation that way. Yet Clay succeeded better than that record indicates. The continuing influence he had on the mindset of his home commonwealth and other border states proved crucial. Defeated in life in his presidential bids, Clay may have achieved one of his greatest victories after his death.

While Henry Clay's words and spirit continued to inform and influence those of the next generation, he could have been even more instrumental in shaping history. For he could have been president of the United States. After all, as the *New York Times* noted in 1852, "to be head of the Government—to be the President—is the summit of all political hopes." And as a Democratic journal wrote, in relief, after a Clay defeat, "Had he succeeded, it would have stamped him, his ideas, and his character, upon the future history of our government."[15]

If Henry Clay had been elected president, what would that have meant for the United States? Would a Clay presidency have been, as John Quincy Adams once said, "a perpetual succession of intrigue and management with the legislature," and an administration ruled by impulsive actions? Or, would he have been a strong, imaginative leader? At the worst, he certainly would have been better than the two Whig generals who received the nominations in his place. And in the best of worlds, President Clay could have gotten his American System adopted, two decades before his disciple Lincoln did so in large part. The BUS, the protective tariff, the planned and federally funded internal improvements, even a plan for gradual emancipation—all could have been established by the man an 1853 journal called one of the two best in antebellum America "in the practical business of statesmanship." But beyond that, a Clay presidency might have greatly changed the eventual course of American history. Many historians argue, for example, that had Clay won in 1844, there would have been no conflict with Mexico, and possibly no Civil War.[16]

But why did Clay not win? Commentators ranging from contemporaries of Clay to modern-day writers have offered an array of explanations. Some argue that it was the fault of antebellum voters, who selected the less talented politicians over Clay, while others point to Clay's own inability to gauge the electorate's mood and his mistakes made in his races. Some voters never forgave Clay for what they perceived as his acceptance of the office of secretary of state after the 1824 election—what was termed the "corrupt bargain."

Other critics have pointed out that Clay, long a fixture in Washington, DC, and in public life, also represented the political insider at a time when voters sought changes and fresh faces. Similarly, as a member of Congress and as a public figure over a long period of time, Clay took stands on a variety of controversial issues, including his American System, and those actions alienated various constituencies. But other narrators have noted that election fraud and just bad luck denied him key states and victory.

And, finally, certain commentators have indicated that as a candidate's morals became increasingly important to some voters, Clay's reputation as a dueler, drinker, womanizer, swearer, and gambler hurt him. Additionally, issues did matter. As a man who sought to appeal to both sections and as an antislavery slaveholder, Clay found he could not transcend those matters as he sought votes. His compromises gained him acclaim, but also angered those on the extremes, costing him ballots from both ends of the political spectrum. Given all those explanations, what really caused Clay's defeats?

A Kentucky leader told his diary in 1832, with Jackson's impending defeat of Clay, that he hoped voters of the future would choose a president more by "the contents of his head and heart and not the scars on his body." But between 1828 and 1848, only two nonmilitary heroes won election to the office of the presidency—Van Buren, on Jackson's coattails, and Polk in a militaristic mode—and neither served a second term. Military leadership bested political statesmanship. In 1834, Clay himself told Congress that voters must not choose presidents based on "a single grievance, real or imaginary" (such as anti-Masonry) but, rather, should look at a candidate's entire "private character, conduct, and habits," as well as his principles, motives, "passions, prejudices, and temper of mind."[17]

Despite his losses, Clay seemingly never lost faith in the American voter and in democracy as the best system. He felt the electoral cuts deeply, despaired of the results, and worried about the qualifications and actions of those who defeated him. But he did not long retreat from that rugged, often ungrateful political world, back to the serenity of Ashland. He shook off his temporary depression and continued to act for what he deemed the good of the nation, even for those voters who had denied him thrice. Gifted with superb oratorical powers and great personal charisma, Clay could win over almost any gathering. But he failed to grasp why some of those he so charmed in the moment would later shatter the spell he cast and vote against him. Nor did he fully comprehend that things he saw as his strengths—his long service in the capital, for example—might be seen by others as a weakness. The ultimate Washington insider, Clay would be perceived by some voters as the problem, not the solution—too tied to the past, too committed to the system, too identified with the establishment. Nor did Clay quickly recognize the power of different rising forces in politics. If the electorate sometimes misunderstood Clay, he often misread the electorate as well.

Yet if Clay largely tended to absolve the voters and the party delegates for his defeats, that does not mean they should be given a free historical pass. Clay did not adapt well to the changes in democracy in his era, and he did not fully reinvent his image (to put it in more modern terms). But at the same time, he faced voters easily swayed by propaganda and falsehoods, and delegates readily bedazzled by the prospects of victory. The questions that a democracy continues to face operated then as well: Will voters accept the partisan rhetoric, or focus on actual actions? Will they look at a single issue or a single part of the past of a person, or examine the overall candidate? Will they follow the allure of the untested and the unknown, or go for the experienced record? The voters did not always answer those questions in a way conducive to victory for Henry Clay.

Some observers ascribed Clay's losses simply to bad luck: "Mr. Henry Clay . . . is certainly the most unlucky man in the world," an Arkansas critic noted with some sarcasm in 1840. But he was right. Clay *was* unlucky, and that may be the worst burden any presidential candidate has to bear. Yet, had Clay been more efficient, had he been more proactive, had he handled misfortune more wisely, he might have better overcome the hand that fate dealt him. Many political leaders also blamed Clay's losses—especially in 1824 and 1844—not on bad luck but, rather, on significant fraud by the opposition. Some commentators also pointed to Whig political betrayal in the years he did not secure his party's nomination. But if Clay was unlucky, and if fraud was a factor, those should only be sidebars in his story, not a major chapter detailing his defeats. Other matters proved more crucial.[18]

Clay made key mistakes in his array of races. In fact, critics have generally blamed Clay's losses on his own miscalculations and missteps more than any other factor. Clay misread Jackson's strength in 1824, and then made the serious error of accepting the office of secretary of state from the man he had made president, thus creating the perception of evil. His decision to run in 1832 proved a poor one, and his subsequent identification with defense of the BUS represented a fatal fault. Moreover, before the 1839 convention, Clay's attacks on abolitionists cost him the votes he needed to gain his party's nomination. Then, in 1844, Clay so waffled on Texas that he satisfied no one, losing crucial votes either to apathy or the Liberty Party. And in the 1848 fight for the Whig nomination, his detractors said he should not have run—that he was too old, too out-of-touch, and too many times defeated.

Some of those criticisms have varying degrees of validity. On the one hand, Clay certainly made a mistake regarding the "corrupt bargain," assuredly erred in attacking abolitionists in 1839, and absolutely penned too many letters in the 1844 race. On the other hand, numerous otherwise intelligent people advised him to accept the cabinet post from John Quincy Adams. Moreover, if Clay wrote letters that hurt his cause, so too did other politicians of his era, including Van Buren and Taylor. And if Clay's 1839 anti-abolitionist words hurt him in the North, they probably helped him in the South. Similarly, the Texas issue both aided and hindered Clay in 1844. Finally, Clay should not have made the race for office in 1848, but he did so reluctantly when it became clear that Zachary Taylor might win if Clay did not enter the fray. Taylor represented all that Clay thought presidential candidates should not be—a general, a man without political experience or programs, a person who was not even a good Whig. In each case, Clay ran and made mistakes—as do virtually all candidates. But those errors generally did not represent fatal flaws.

THE "IM*BODYMENT*."

" Henry
Clay, the liv-
ing personification
and imbodyment of
Whig principles."
Whig address.
IN 1777
born: In
1805 quarrelled
with Col. Davis of Ken-
tucky, which led to his first duel:
In 1808 he challenged Humphrey Marshall, and fired three times at his heart:
In 1825 he challenged the great Jo hn
Ran dolph, and fired once at his he art,
but without effect: In 1838 he plan ned
the CILLEY DUEL, by wh ich
A MURDER was perpe tra-
ted, and a wife made a ma-
ni ac: In 1841, wh en
65 years old, and gr ey
hea ded, is under 5000 dollars BONDS to KEEP T HE
P EACE ! At the age of 29
h e PERJURED himself t o
s ecure a Seat in the Unite d
S tates Senate. In 1824 he mad e
an infamous bargain with John Quin cy
Adams, by which he SOLD OUT
for a £1200 a-year OFFICE. He
is also well kn own as a GAM-
BLER, and SA BBATH BREA-
KER. His P OLITICS
are precisely and exactly
those of the Hartfordcon-
vention fed eralist: op-
posed to e qual rights,
e q u a l l a w s;
and in favour
of mono polising
l a w s a n d
char tered
priv i l e-
ges. Also
h e sus-
tai n s
the fe-
roci ous
Alge rines
in their deeds of
BLOOD AND MURDER.

A calligram called "The 'Embodyment'" ties together many of the charges directed at Clay over the years—how he helped "murder" Congressman Cilley in a duel, how he "perjured" himself when he took a seat in Congress when too young to do so, how he "sold out" in his "infamous bargain" with Adams, how he was a gambler "and Sabbath-breaker," and how he "sustained" the Indians in their "deeds of blood." *Courtesy of George McGee*

More crucial to understanding why Clay did not win the presidency are a series of other factors. He could never really satisfactorily solve the questions of slavery and antislavery, he could never fully recover from the effect his compromises had on some voters, and he could never adequately overcome the fact that his nationalism, principles, and programs hurt him politically. Different elements, at different times, thus combined to defeat him.

Clay proved to be an excellent leader in the congressional arena. There, he knew the players, their personalities, their individual strengths and weaknesses, their specific hopes and fears. Though it might come at a political cost to him, Clay could analyze, argue, cajole, plead, and dazzle with oratory in order to get things done. But outside of Congress, Clay more often seemed a poor politician in his national races. As an 1849 paper put it: "Mr. Clay has been the most un-politic of politicians." Because of his success in Congress, Clay became too certain of his abilities and operated basically as his own campaign manager. Moreover, many of those minions he trusted to work for his interests in key states did not always turn out to be good choices and would be constantly outmaneuvered. Clay also tended to respect the older republican ideas regarding a presidential candidate's conduct—essentially that, once nominated, the person should not campaign, should write a few public letters, and should trust the electorate. Only slowly did Clay adjust to the changes taking place in his era. And if he never completely broke free of the traditional mentality of his youth, or from his conviction that he understood the political world better than any manager would, at the same time, Clay did learn from many of his mistakes. His share of the vote increased each time he ran, he grew to understand the need for a political press, and he did embrace the newer imagery and popular campaign tactics.[19]

A critical determinant of Clay's losses involved what might be termed the "paradox of Henry Clay." Pictured by both contemporary and later critics as a wildly ambitious, unprincipled politician who would do anything to win the nation's highest office, Clay actually lost many votes because he openly and forcefully advocated specific programs, voted his conscience on controversial issues, and voiced key principles. While it is easier to criticize, it is harder to push a program. As a biography that appeared in Clay's lifetime explained, "All his aspirations are to build up, not to tear down—to create, not to destroy."[20]

But constructive actions and words of advocacy have their cost, and Clay knew that all too well. In 1838, a Kentucky legislator recognized what that meant: Clay "is held to a strict account for every opinion and sentiment he may pronounce as well as every vote he may give." That politician expected Clay to lose the votes of two states in an upcoming expected race because of that: "I think he did right, because he acted according to the dictates of his judgment and his boldness was in accordance with the tenor of his whole life." Over his long career, Henry Clay proved relatively consistent in his support of the American System, antislavery, colonization, and other programs. He took stands while many of his opponents remained mute or spoke in meaningless platitudes. And some in his time appreciated and praised Clay for the "frank, manly, and undisguised manner [in which] you have always expressed your political views & opinions." But Clay's words could be removed from context and used against him.[21]

Taking a stand, defending a bill or a compromise or a principle, voting on a controversial issue may make it more difficult for a member of Congress to win the presidency instead of someone who has neither the opportunity, nor perhaps the will, to do so. Since 1832, only fifteen incumbent senators have received their party's nomination for president and only three—Warren G. Harding, John F. Kennedy, and Barack Obama—have won. In fact, since the 1980s some sixty sitting members of Congress have sought the nation's highest office and all but one failed in that quest. Only one Speaker of the House—Polk—has gone on to serve as president. Does that mean that ambitious politicians should be silent servants rather than bold leaders? Should they so gauge opinion to take the most popular course rather than follow the course they deem correct? Should they surrender their independence and follow the course of least resistance and less controversy? Clay's answer to those questions would be obvious. As a rule, he would not be silent, would act as he thought right, and would not avoid confrontation. But could Clay have been president if he had answered—and acted—otherwise? Perhaps. He, however, would not see that as the honorable thing to do. The answer to those questions also depends on what a person seeks in public life. If the presidency and its powers is the goal, then nonaction might or might not aid in the pursuit of that goal. But without action, without a distinguishing program, one individual might be no different from another. And perhaps the accomplishment is greater than any mere office. Clay's fame lies less in the races that he ran than in the life that he lived.[22]

Had Clay desired the presidency so much that he would do anything to win it, he would have taken different stands and muted his views on controversial issues. Had he become a candidate for just one section, he might have won, but he would not, for he sought to be president for *all* the nation. Had he become either fully proslavery or antislavery, he might have achieved higher office, but he would not abandon the moderate course he advocated. Clay did work hard—terribly hard—to win the presidency that he so wanted. Yet he seldom turned his back on the beliefs he valued, even if they potentially could injure his chances for victory. Clay had the political courage to voice his views and to stand by them under the glare of public scrutiny. Contrary to the image of a Clay who would forfeit anything to win, his entire life story reveals a more mixed picture. Henry Clay wanted to be president badly, but he also wanted his life to mean something, no matter the political cost.

But the chief reason that Henry Clay did not win the presidency is the fact that so many factors were at play. He fought too many battles over too many issues for too many years. The longer Clay stayed in the public eye, the more groups he angered and the more people he provoked. One voter may have opposed Clay because he disliked the candidate's stance on the tariff or the role of government or the sale of public lands or even a particular bill; another might object to Clay's compromises. One might reject Clay for high office because the Kentuckian held slaves, or, conversely, because he voiced antislavery views; another might spurn the Great Pacificator because he seemed too much the insider, too tied to past politics, too out of touch with rising American sentiment. One might cast a ballot for the opposition because he perceived Clay to be too ambitious or too immoral or too tied to a corrupt bargain; another might repudiate the Whig leader because the loser Clay had made too many mistakes to be trusted with the reins of the presidency. And some simply voted for others out of party loyalty or the promise of a job. As a newspaperman explained, "Mr. Clay has too many classes of opponents, all acting from different motives, and yet uniting in opposing him, that he has fearful odds to encounter." All that taken together meant that Clay had too many defensive fires to fight, and in race after race he could not respond adequately to all the burning problems he faced.[23]

Yet, Clay *almost* won. He had a chance in 1824 and barely lost two decades later. Had he received his party's nomination in 1840, he very likely would have achieved his dream; he might have done so had he taken the nomination in 1848. But voters' continuing support for Henry Clay for president in virtually every election after 1824 showed the force of his appeal and the loyalty of his allies. After all, the factors that contributed to his losses also operated in a more positive way as well. Clay's stands on slavery and his colonization plan, for instance, wounded his hopes for the presidency with some voters. But he gained the aid of others as a slaveholder who called slavery wrong or a leader who proposed a plan to end slavery over time. Similarly, Clay's political beliefs and creeds may have impaired his prospects, but many others praised them as sound ways to promote American growth. Clay's stands in Congress on controversial issues may have marred his presidential possibilities, but that he took public stands on matters of importance impressed others. In Clay's era, many worshiped the military hero ideal and praised a militant, expansionist spirit, but others lauded Clay's opposition to the Mexican-American War as the correct response. His compromises may have limited Clay's appeals among those on the extremes of an issue, but his era more often honored his efforts and praised his accomplishments and leadership.

While a simple answer might be desired, in truth, Clay lost the two nominations and the three presidential races chiefly owing to a multiplicity of matters, each of which contributed to his defeat. Every election had different circumstances, characters, and dynamics. But in each, whether trying to persuade delegates to select him or voters to elect him, Clay failed. Politically, he did not die from a single fatal wound, but bled to death from a thousand cuts. And so he remained a fingertip away from the presidency.

Given his setbacks, would the man one paper labeled "The Napoleon of Defeat" be honored and remembered, or would he, as a contemporary feared, "pass unmerited and unrewarded in this world"? For many in Henry Clay's era, the answer to that question was easy and obvious. Even his enemies grudgingly recognized Clay's strengths. A Democratic journal in 1838 admitted to "a certain kind of liking for Mr. Clay," for his "manly" boldness, vast popularity, and frank openness. In fact, writer after writer sounded the same theme. After visiting the United States, a Norwegian journalist told his fellow citizens about this man Henry Clay: "For more than thirty years, he has stood out in his country as . . . a statesman of unusual perspicacity, prescience, wisdom, and energy, as a citizen of outstanding talents . . . , as a man of strictest honor . . . , and as the chivalrous friend of Liberty everywhere. . . . His fame . . . belongs to the nation." In his eulogy to Clay, Abraham Lincoln noted that with defeat, most men pass into memory, often to be forgotten; not so Henry Clay. Lincoln could agree with a contemporary biographer of Clay—if not president, Clay nevertheless was "the chief citizen of the republic."[24]

"Loser" Clay did not seem overly concerned about his own place in history. In 1840, he told the Senate that if a person performed his duty to the best of his abilities, then ambition should be satisfied, with no higher reward needed. Two years later, again to Congress, Clay stressed to them,

"History . . . and posterity . . . will be the best, truest, and most impartial judge." A man who did not fear the future, Clay trusted in the judgment of those who would evaluate him in the years ahead.[25]

At Clay's death, the United States had been a nation less than a year longer than Clay had lived; for almost half a century of that time, he had served as a leader in that new country's development. An 1846 letter writer concluded of Clay: "His history constitutes a large portion of our national renown." Clay and the country had grown up together, and he had played a vital role in that maturation process. After all, leadership extends beyond the Oval Office. Henry Clay the politician may never have won the nation's highest honor, but much of the United States certainly gave its approval to Henry Clay, the man and the leader. Given Clay's service and influence on the course of the country, perhaps posterity should no longer call it the Jacksonian Era, or the Age of Jackson, and instead term it the Clay Era, or the Age of Henry Clay.[26]

In the twentieth and twenty-first centuries, Henry Clay's legacy produced mixed results. To one Kentucky governor, ever since Clay said "he would rather be right than [be] president, the American people have believed that their public officials couldn't be both." Yet parts are clear. If the United States truly became a nation only after it emerged from the crucible of the Civil War, then Clay in his antebellum era represented the anomaly, as an advocate for nationalism and unionism at a time when most spoke for section. Moreover, Clay's diplomatic, political, and economic vision for America eventually prevailed. The present-day United States looks more like Clay's view of the future than the perspective offered by Andrew Jackson. Clay won that fight at least.[27]

Yet for modern-day politicians, the words and spirit of Henry Clay often have less force. At a roundtable discussion in 2011, former Speaker of the House Democrat Nancy Pelosi and the then-Speaker Republican John Boehner both acknowledged how Clay had influenced them, yet critics questioned whether their actions indicated that. Senate Majority Leader Mitch McConnell from Kentucky wrote his senior thesis on Clay, had an image of Clay in his office, and had commented in 2009 that, like Clay, "you have to learn to compromise" to be successful. Yet, critics have complained that McConnell has not acted enough like his hero. And when new US senator Rand Paul from the commonwealth of Kentucky rose from his seat at Henry Clay's original desk in his maiden speech, he criticized the man who had once sat there. Faulting Clay for being a compromiser, the new senator suggested that would not be his way.[28]

There are more images of Clay in the US Capitol building than of any other American save one. Are we still influenced by the spirit of Henry Clay? *Bronze by Charles H. Niehaus, National Statuary Hall, Office of the Architect of the Capitol*

Others have recognized Clay's importance, both in his time and as an example in their own era. In 1957, a Senate committee named the five most influential senators in American history. The first of those was Henry Clay. Historians, a bit more belatedly perhaps, have reached the same conclusion. An 1986 survey of a hundred scholars ranked senators in regard to leadership, ability to compromise, value to the Senate in their era, and legislative creativity. The historians placed Clay first overall. Two decades after that, *Atlantic Monthly* polled a smaller group of scholars for their list of the hundred most influential Americans—in all fields. Clay stood in the top third of that list, ahead of all the men who defeated him—save Andrew Jackson. Long after their deaths, both men continue to fight for place. And as of 2010, there were more images of Henry Clay in the US Capitol than those of any other person, except George Washington.[29]

As those actions suggest, the 1850 *New York Herald* proved prescient: "Henry Clay may never reap the reward of his devotion to the United States, to the Union, and to the Constitution, but posterity will do him justice if the present generation do not." Later generations would write biographies of "the Great Rejected," and include him in pantheons of national heroes by placing memorials to him in cemeteries, public squares, and capitol rotundas. But the best monument is the fact that the United States remains one country, one people, one example of a successful democracy, still working, still changing, still trying to reflect the enduring spirit of Henry Clay.[30]

NOTES

———————

ABBREVIATIONS

AC	*Annals of Congress*
Adams, *Memoirs*	Charles Francis Adams, comp., *Memoirs of John Quincy Adams*, 12 vols. (Philadelphia, 1874–77)
Apple, *Family Legacy*	Lindsey Apple, *The Family Legacy of Henry Clay* (Lexington: University Press of Kentucky, 2011)
Calhoun Papers	Robert Meriwether et al., eds., *Papers of John C. Calhoun*, 28 vols. (Columbia: University of South Carolina Press, 1989–2003)
CG	*Congressional Globe*
Clay and Oberholtzer, *Clay*	Thomas Hart Clay and Ellis Oberholtzer, *Henry Clay* (Philadelphia: George W. Jacobs, 1910)
Coleman, *Crittenden*	Ann Mary Crittenden Coleman, *The Life of John J. Crittenden*, 2 vols. (Philadelphia, 1871)
Colton, *Clay*	Calvin Colton, *The Life and Times of Henry Clay*, 2 vols. (New York, 1846)

CP	James Hopkins et al., eds., *The Papers of Henry Clay*, 10 vols. and Supplement (Lexington: University Press of Kentucky, 1959–92)
FCHQ	*Filson Club History Quarterly*
FHS	Filson Historical Society, Louisville
Graham Papers	J. G. de Roulhac Hamilton, ed., *The Papers of William Alexander Graham*, 8 vols. (Raleigh, NC: State Department of Archives and History, 1957)
Heidler and Heidler, *Clay*	David Heidler and Jeanne Heidler, *Henry Clay: The Essential American* (New York: Random House, 2010)
Jackson Correspondence	John Spencer Bassett, ed., *Correspondence of Andrew Jackson*, 7 vols. (Washington, DC: Carnegie Institute of Washington, 1926–35).
Jackson Papers	Sam Smith and Harriett Owsley et al., eds. *Papers of Andrew Jackson*, 10 vols. to date (Knoxville: University of Tennessee Press, 1980–).
JAH	*Journal of American History*
JER	*Journal of the Early Republic*
JSH	*Journal of Southern History*
KHS	Kentucky Historical Society, Frankfort
LC	Library of Congress
Mangum Papers	Henry Shanks, ed., *The Papers of Willie Person Mangum*, 5 vols. (Raleigh, NC: State Department of Archives and History, 1950–56).
OVH	*Ohio Valley History*
Polk Papers	Herbert Weaver et al., eds., *Correspondence of James K. Polk*, 13 vols. to date (Nashville, TN: Vanderbilt University Press, 1969–).
Presidential Elections	Arthur Schlesinger and Fred Israel, eds., *History of American Presidential Elections, 1789–1968*, 4 vols. (New York: Chelsea House, 1971).
RD	*Register of Debates*
Register	*Register of the Kentucky Historical Society*

Remini, *Clay*	Robert Remini, *Henry Clay: Statesman for the Union* (New York: W. W. Norton, 1991).
Schurz, *Clay*	Carl Schurz, *Henry Clay*, 2 vols. (Boston, 1899 ed.).
UK	University of Kentucky Special Collections, Lexington
VHS	Virginia Historical Society, Richmond
Webster Papers	Charles Wiltse and Michael Birkner, eds., *Papers of Daniel Webster*, 14 vols. (Hanover, NH: University Press of New England, 1974–89).
Works of Buchanan	John Bassett Moore, ed., *The Works of James Buchanan*, 12 vols. (repr., New York: Antiquarian Press, 1960).

Prologue

1. Cited in William H. Townsend, *Lincoln and the Bluegrass* (Lexington: University of Kentucky Press, 1955), 91–92.
2. *New York Herald,* cited in Holman Hamilton, *Zachary Taylor: Soldier in the White House* (1951; repr., Hamden, CT: Archon Books, 1966), 66.

Preface

1. Burton Milward, *A History of the Lexington Cemetery* (Lexington, KY: Lexington Cemetery Co., 1989), 35–42; "Statue of Henry Clay Shattered by a Storm," *Register* 1 (1903): 110; *Frankfort State Journal,* May 1, 1910.
2. Schurz, *Clay*; Joseph Rogers, *The True Henry Clay* (Philadelphia: J. B. Lippincott, 1904); Clay and Oberholtzer, *Clay*; George Poage, *Henry Clay and the Whig Party* (Chapel Hill: University of North Carolina Press, 1936); Bernard Mayo, *Henry Clay: Spokesman of the New West* (Boston: Houghton Mifflin, 1937); Glyndon G. Van Deusen, *The Life of Henry Clay* (Boston: Little, Brown, 1937).
3. See, for example, Arthur Schlesinger Jr., *The Age of Jackson* (Boston: Little, Brown, 1945).
4. Clement Eaton, *Henry Clay and the Art of American Politics* (Boston: Little, Brown, 1957); Daniel Walker Howe, *The Political Culture of the American Whigs* (Chicago: University of Chicago Press, 1979); Thomas Brown, *Politics and Statesmanship: Essays on the American Whig Party* (New York: Columbia University Press, 1985); Michael Holt, *The Rise and Fall of the American Whig Party* (New York: Oxford University Press, 1999); Merrill Peterson, *The Great Triumvirate: Webster, Clay, and Calhoun* (New York: Oxford University Press, 1987); "Introduction," in *A Political Nation: New Directions in Mid-Nineteenth Century American Political History,* ed. Gary Gallagher and Rachel Shelden (Charlottesville: University of Virginia Press, 2012), 3; Kimberly Shankman,

Compromise and the Constitution: The Political Thought of Henry Clay (Lanham, MD: Lexington Books, 1999); Robert Pierce Forbes, *The Missouri Compromise and Its Aftermath* (Chapel Hill: Universty of North Carolina Press, 2007); John Waugh, *On the Brink of Civil War: The Compromise of 1850 and How It Changed the Course of American History* (Wilmington, DE: Scholarly Resources, 2003); Robert Remini, *At the Edge of the Precipice: Henry Clay and the Compromise That Saved the Union* (New York: Basic Books, 2010); Fergus Bordewich, *America's Great Debate: Henry Clay, Stephen A. Douglas and the Compromise That Preserved the Union* (New York: Simon and Schuster, 2012); Sean Wilentz, *The Rise of American Democracy* (New York: W. W. Norton, 2005); Daniel Walker Howe, *What Hath God Wrought: The Transformation of America, 1815–1848* (New York: Oxford University Press, 2007); Remini, *Clay*; Heidler and Heidler, *Clay*; Harlow Giles Unger, *Henry Clay: America's Greatest Statesman* (Boston: Da Capo Press, 2015); Maurice Baxter, *Henry Clay and the American System* (Lexington: University Press of Kentucky, 1995); Maurice Baxter, *Henry Clay the Lawyer* (Lexington: University Press of Kentucky, 2000): Peter Knupfer, *The Union as It Is: Constitutional Unionism and Sectional Compromise, 1787–1861* (Chapel Hill: University of North Carolina Press, 1991); Amy Greenberg, *A Wicked War: Polk, Clay, Lincoln, and the 1846 US Invasion of Mexico* (Princeton, NJ: Princeton University Press, 2012); Apple, *Family Legacy*. The Unger biography appeared too late for full inclusion in this work, but presents only a general view for a popular audience.

5. James Traub, "A Realist in the White House," *Wall Street Journal*, July 13–14, 2014; Thomas DiLorenzo, "Henry Clay: National Socialist," *Free Market* 16 (1998); Tom Eblen, "Books Show Our Need for Another Henry Clay," *Lexington Herald-Leader*, May 9, 2010.

6. Review of *The Life, Correspondence, and Speeches of Henry Clay*, in *North American Review* 102 (1866): 176–77.

7. "The Statesman of America in 1846," *Littell's Living Age* 12 (1847): 571; transcript of interview by Terry Birdwhistell with Alex Humphrey, September 24, 1974, Louie B. Nunn Center for Oral History, UK.

8. Kenneth Williams and Melba Porter Hay, eds., "Henry Clay Represents What This Country Is About: A Roundtable Discussion with the Biographer and Editors," *Register* 100 (2002): 455n; "They Made America," *Atlantic Monthly*, December 2006, 59–65, 72–78; William Ridings Jr. and Stuart McIver, "1990's Presidential Poll: Presidential Election Re-Evaluations" (copy in author's possession).

9. Stanley Renshon, "The Corporation Psychoanalytic Study of Political Leaders," in *Profiling Political Leaders: Cross-cultural Studies of Personality and Behavior*, ed. Ofer Feldman and Linda Valenty (Westport, CT: Praeger, 2001), 233–53.

10. Leslie Combs to Phillip Phoenix [?], November 20, 1844, Leslie Combs Papers, UK.

Chapter 1

1. Clay to Robert Chilton, October 29, 1839, *CP*, 9:353; *An American System for the Protection of American Industry* (Cincinnati, 1824), 15; Colton, *Clay*, 1:18; George Robertson, *Scrap Book on Law and Politics, Men and Times* (Lexington, KY, 1855), 155; Epes Sargent, *Life and Public Service of Henry Clay*, ed. Horace Greeley (Auburn, NY, 1852), 13–14; *New York Daily Times*, March 24, 1852; *Richmond Whig*, cited in *Portsmouth New-Hampshire Gazette*, May 2, 1843; "Life of Henry Clay," *Henry Clay Almanac . . . 1844* (New York, 1844), 17; *Boston Patriot and Mercantile Advertiser*, August 6, 1830; Horace Greeley, *Recollections of a Busy Life* (New York, 1868), 168. Both Daniel Walker Howe, *The Political Culture of the American Whigs* (Chicago: University of Chicago Press, 1979), 129, and Stephen Oates, "Harry of the West, Henry Clay," [Ohio Historical Society] *Timeline* (October–November 1991), 5, credit Clay with coining the term the "self-made man."

2. Speech on Surveys for Roads and Canals, 1824, *CP*, 3:621; *RD*, 24th Cong., 1st Sess. (1835–36), 52.

3. *Speech of the Hon. Henry Clay of Kentucky . . .* [n.p., n.d.], 3; ". . . State of the Country . . . ," in Calvin Colton, *The Works of Henry Clay*, 10 vols. (New York: G. P. Putnam's Sons, 1904), 8:197–214; Clay to Lucretia Clay, March 6, 1840, *CP*, 9:394–95; Sargent, *Clay*, 225; *RD*, 23rd Cong., 1st Sess. (1833–34), 1484; *CG*, 23rd Cong., 1st Sess. (1833–34), 345; W. A. W., "Henry Clay, the Slashes, and Ashland Again," *The Century* 34 (1887): 958.

4. Speech in Lexington, 1842, and Clay to W. L. Woodward, January 3, 1846, both in *CP*, 9:709, 10:255; Zachary Smith and Mary Rogers Clay, *The Clay Family* (Louisville, KY, 1899), 88–89; Susan Clay and Lucretia Clay, "Henry Clay and His Slanders . . . ," boyhood chapter, Box 55, Papers of Henry Clay and Family, LC; Speech in Indianapolis, 1842, *CP*, 9:783.

5. Clay and Clay, "Clay and Slanders," boyhood chapter; Glyndon G. Van Deusen, *The Life of Henry Clay* (Boston: Little, Brown, 1937), 6; Bible, Clay Family Papers, VHS; Remini, *Clay*, 3; Bernard Mayo, *Henry Clay: Spokesman of the New West* (Boston: Houghton Mifflin, 1937), 4, 13, 41; Heidler and Heidler, *Clay*, 10–12; Clay and Oberholtzer, *Clay*, 18. Both Mayo and Remini indicate Henry Watkins was twenty-six, Elizabeth thirty-three, at the time of marriage. "D.W.B," in "Henry Clay's Mother," unidentified clipping in Box 64, Papers of Henry Clay and Family, says Watkins was twenty-three at the time.

6. Clay to H. Hays, July 13, 1842, *CP*, 9:733; Colton, *Clay*, 1:19; Smith and Clay, *Clay Family*, 88–89; Clay and Oberholtzer, *Clay*, 18. In contrast to most sources, Henry's brother Porter said the second marriage produced only six children. See *Lexington Herald*, January 4, 1925, in Samuel Wilson Collection, UK. The erroneous figure of eleven children produced by the second marriage appears in Irving Stone's caustic *They Also Ran: The Story of the Men Who Were Defeated for the Presidency* (Garden City, NY: Doubleday, 1945), 37.

7. Clay and Clay, "Clay and His Slanders," boyhood chapter; "Rev. Porter Clay," Box 57, Clay Family Papers, LC; Colton, *Clay*, 1:26; Smith and Clay, *Clay Family*, 88–89; Clay and Oberholtzer, *Clay*, 21.

8. Adams, *Memoirs*, 5:59; Robert Winthrop, *Memoirs of Henry Clay* (Cambridge, MA, 1880), 28; Quentin Scott King, *Henry Clay and the War of 1812* (Jefferson, NC: McFarland, 2014), 7; J. Drew Harrington, "Henry Clay and the Classics," *FCHQ* 61 (1987): 238, 246; Clay to Henry Clay Jr., October 21, 1828, and April 19, 1829, both in *CP*, 7:511, 8:30.

9. David Dearinger, "The Diary of Joel Tanner Hart, Kentucky Sculptor," *FCHQ* 64 (1990): 23; Clay Account with John and Thomas P. Hart, and Clay to James B. Clay, December 15, 1837, both in *CP*, 2:707, 9:108; *Galveston Weekly Journal*, August 13, 1852; Samuel Orth, *Five American Politicians* (Cleveland, OH: Burrows Brothers, 1906), 186; *CP*, 3:451n; Joseph Ficklin to Clay, September 5, 1829, *CP*, 8:94.

10. "Adams, *Memoirs*, 5:59, 325; Leon Tyler, *Letters and Times of the Tylers*, 2 vols. (Richmond, VA, 1884), 1:290; Samuel Foot, *Autobiography*, 2 vols. (New York, 1873), 2:262; review of *The Speeches of Henry Clay*, in *North American Review* 25 (1827): 444; "Modern Oratory," *Southern Literary Messenger* 18 (1852): 375.

11. Colton, *Clay*, 1:21–22; James Swain, "Memories of Henry Clay," in *Life and Speeches of Henry Clay* (New York, 1844), 8; Mayo, *Clay*, 20–22; Harrison, "Henry Clay," 180; George Prentice, *Biography of Henry Clay* (Hartford, CT, 1831), 8; Clay and Oberholtzer, *Clay*, 18–19; Sargent, *Clay*, 15.

12. James Hopkins, "A Tribute to Mr. Clay," *Register* 53 (1955): 284; Mayo, *Clay*, 24–25; Colton, *Clay*, 1:25. On Wythe, see Imogene Brown, *American Aristides: A Biography of George Wythe* (Rutherford, NJ: Farleigh Dickinson University Press, 1981).

13. Mayo, *Clay*, 26; Harrington, "Clay and Classics," 237; Clay to Benjamin Minor, May 3, 1851, *CP*, 10:886–89. Clay would name a son for Wythe.

14. Prentice, *Clay*, 8; Mayo, *Clay*, 40–44; License to Practice Law [November 6, 1797], Henry Clay Foundation Papers, UK.

15. David Hackett Fischer and James Kelly, *Bound Away: Virginia and the Westward Movement* (Charlottesville: University Press of Virginia, 2000); *RD*, 23rd Cong., 1st sess. (1831–32), 1099; James Klotter, *The Breckinridges of Kentucky* (Lexington: University Press of Kentucky, 1986), 13, 4; Patricia Watlington, *The Partisan Spirit: Kentucky Politics, 1779–1792* (New York: Atheneum, 1972), 200, 211; Arthur Moore, *The Frontier Mind: A Cultural Analysis of the Kentucky Frontiersman* (Lexington: University of Kentucky Press, 1957), 4, 23–24, 30, 67.

16. Merrill Peterson, *The Great Triumvirate: Webster, Clay, and Calhoun* (New York: Oxford University Press, 1987), 7; A. D. Kirwan, *John J. Crittenden: The Struggle for the Union* (Lexington: University of Kentucky Press, 1962), 27–29.

17. William Connelley and E. Merton Coulter, *History of Kentucky*, ed. Charles Kerr, 5 vols. (Chicago: American Historical Society, 1922), 2:730; Mary

Wharton and Edward Bowen, *The Horse World of the Bluegrass* (Lexington, KY: John Bradford Press, 1980), vii, ix, 13–15, 19, 27–30; William Leavy, "A Memoir of Lexington and Its Vicinity," *Register* 40–42 (1942–44): 8; Elizabeth Perkins, *Border Life: Experience and Memory in the Revolutionary Ohio Valley* (Chapel Hill: University of North Carolina Press, 1998), 4, 94–99; Craig Friend, *Along the Maysville Road: The Early American Republic in the Trans-Appalachian West* (Knoxville: University of Tennessee Press, 2005), 32–35, 209; Lee Shai Weissbach, "The Peopling of Lexington, Kentucky: Growth and Mobility in a Frontier Town," *Register* 81 (1983): 119; J. D. DeBow, *Statistical View of the United States* (Washington, DC, 1854), 40; James Klotter and Freda Klotter, *A Concise History of Kentucky* (Lexington: University Press of Kentucky, 2008), 102.

18. Richard Wade, *The Urban Frontier: The Rise of Western Cities, 1790–1830* (Cambridge, MA: Harvard University Press, 1967), 170, 20. Soon after Clay arrived, Lexington had 1,475 people, 360 of them slaves. See *Lexington Kentucky Gazette*, March 28, 1798.

19. Timothy Flint, *Recollections of the Last Ten Years*, ed. C. Hartley Gratton (New York: A. A. Knopf, 1932), vi–vii; Flint, *Recollections of the Last Ten Years* (Boston, 1826), 67–68.

20. John Melish, *Travels in the United States of America . . .* , 2 vols. (Philadelphia, 1812), 2:184; Godfrey Vigne, *Six Months in America*, 2 vols. (Philadelphia, 1832), 2:27; Harry Toulmin, *A Description of Kentucky in North America* (London, 1792[1793]), 17, 93.

21. Stephen Aron, *How the West Was Lost: The Transformation of Kentucky from Daniel Boone to Henry Clay* (Baltimore: Johns Hopkins University Press, 1996), 171; John Boles, *The Great Revival, 1787–1805* (Lexington: University Press of Kentucky, 1972), 55–63; Ellen Eslinger, *Citizens of Zion: The Social Origins of Camp Meeting Revivalism* (Knoxville; University of Tennessee Press, 1999), 193–97, 214, 226, 239; Paul Conkin, *Cane Ridge: America's Pentecost* (Madison: University of Wisconsin Press, 1990), 58–62, 3, 115, 87, 132, 171, 149.

22. Alexander Wilson, quoted in J. Winston Coleman Jr., "Lexington as Seen by Travellers, 1810–1835," *FCHQ* 29 (1955): 267–68; Elias Fordham, *Personal Narrative of Travels . . .* , ed. Frederic Ogg (Cleveland, OH: Arthur R. Clarke, 1906), 177; Patrick Lee Lucas, "It's All Greek to Me: Re-examining the 'Athens of the West' Claims of Lexington, Kentucky, 1820–1829" (MA thesis, University of Kentucky, 1998), 153, 101; Mary Jean Elliott, "Lexington, Kentucky, 1792–1820: The Athens of West" (MA thesis, University of Delaware, 1973), 26; E. MacKenzie, *An Historical, Topographical, and Descriptive View of the United States of America*, 2nd ed. (Newcastle, UK, 1819), 233.

23. Leavy, "Memoir," 40:373; Charles Staples, *The History of Pioneer Lexington, 1779–1806* (1939; repr., Lexington: University Press of Kentucky, 1996,), 31; Wade, *Urban Frontier*, 20; Clement Eaton, *Henry Clay and the Art of American Politics* (Boston: Little, Brown, 1957), 10; Kim Gruenwald, *River of Enterprise: The Commercial Origins of Regional Identity in the Ohio Valley, 1790–1850* (Bloomington: Indiana University Press, 2002), 88.

24. Leavy, "Memoir," 41:320, 129–33; F. Cuming, *Sketches of a Tour of the Western Country...*, in Thwaites, *Early Western Travels*, 6:188; Wade, *Urban Frontier*, 115, 131; Julius MacCabe, *Directory of the City of Lexington... for 1838 &'39* (Lexington, KY, 1838), 18–19; George Ranck, *History of Lexington* (Cincinnati, OH, 1872), 303; J. Lewis Peyton, *Over the Alleghanies and Across the Prairie* (London, 1870), 99.

25. Wade, *Urban Frontier*, 236; F. Garvin Davenport, *Ante-Bellum Kentucky: A Social History, 1800–1860* (1943; repr., Oxford, OH: Mississippi Valley Press, 1983), 46; Ranck, *History of Lexington*, 45–48; Niels Henry Sonne, *Liberal Kentucky, 1780–1828* (1939; repr., Lexington: University of Kentucky Press, 1968), 191n; John Thelin, *A History of American Higher Education* (Baltimore: Johns Hopkins Press, 2004), 46–47; Coleman, "Lexington," 278; Horace Holley, "To the Board of Trustees," December 23, 1823, Papers of the Governors: John Adair, Kentucky Department for Libraries and Archives, Frankfort; *Lexington Kentucky Gazette*, March 21, 1839; "A Memoir," in Haskell Monroe et al., eds., *The Papers of Jefferson Davis*, 14 vols. (Baton Rouge: Louisiana State University Press, 1971–2015), 1:lxxviii. For a decade after 1818, Clay served on the school's Board of Trustees, after having sat in that post for seven years in an earlier stint.

26. Samuel Brown, *The Western Gazetteer; or Emigrant's Directory* (Auburn, NY, 1817), 93; Coleman, "Lexington," 273; West Hill Jr., *The Theatre in Early Kentucky* (Lexington: University Press of Kentucky, 1971), 116; Fordham, *Personal Narrative*, 223; Wade, *Urban Frontier*, 21, 233, 236, 240.

27. Lee Soltow, "Kentucky's Wealth at the End of the Eighteenth Century," *Journal of Economic History* 43 (1983): 620, 624. See also Joan Wells Coward, *Kentucky in the New Republic* (Lexington: University Press of Kentucky, 1979), 55; Fredricka Teute, "Land, Liberty, and Labor in the Post-Revolutionary Era: Kentucky and the Promised Land" (PhD diss., Johns Hopkins University, 1988), 263, 275; Perkins, *Border Life*, 85; Aron, *How the West Was Lost*, 203; Friend, *Maysville Road*, 107, 284.

28. Matthew Schoenbachler, "The Origins of Jacksonian Politics: Central Kentucky, 1790–1840" (PhD diss., University of Kentucky, 1996), 60; Lowell Harrison, *Kentucky's Road to Statehood* (Lexington: University Press of Kentucky, 1992), 121; Coward, *Kentucky in the New Republic*, 27.

29. Toulmin, *Description of Kentucky*, 121; Thomas Appleton Jr., "An Englishman's Perspective of Antebellum Kentucky," *Register* 79 (1981): 62; John David Smith, "Slavery and Antislavery," in *Our Kentucky: A Study of the Bluegrass State*, 2nd ed., ed. James Klotter (Lexington: University Press of Kentucky, 2000), 112–19; Aron, *How the West Was Lost*, 89–95; Wade, *Urban Frontier*, 125; Vigne, *Six Months in America*, 2:34; Brown, *Emigrant's Directory*, 92.

30. Sonne, *Liberal Kentucky*, 205; *Paris (KY) Literary Pamphleteer* 1 (1823): 15; *Lexington Western Luminary*, February 10, 1825; Leavy, "Memoir," 42:53, 41:120–21; Charles Murray, *Travels in North America*, 2 vols., 3rd rev. ed. (London, 1854), 1:189; John Wright Jr., *Transylvania: Tutor to the West*

(Lexington, KY: Transylvania University, 1975), 74–75. See also Tom Eblen and Mollie Eblen, "Horace Holley and the Struggle for Kentucky's Mind and Soul," in *Kentucky Renaissance: The History and Culture of Central Kentucky, 1792–1852*, ed. James Klotter and Daniel Rowland (Lexington: University Press of Kentucky, 2012): 204–21. The law school would later reopen, but again closed in 1895.

31. Wade, *Urban Frontier*, 182, 170, 53, 169–70, 84; *CP*, 2:665; Randolph Hollingsworth, *Lexington: Queen of the Bluegrass* (Charleston, SC: Arcadia, 2004), 71; John Wright Jr., *Lexington: Heart of the Bluegrass* (Lexington, KY: Lexington-Fayette County Historic Commission, 1987), 51–52; Samuel D. McCullough's Reminiscences of Lexington," *Register* 27 (1929): 422–25; Vigne, *Six Months in America*, 2:28.

32. *Lexington Observer and Kentucky Reporter*, June 22, July 19, 1833; Andrew Reed and James Matheson, *Narrative of the Visit to the American Churches...*, 2 vols. (New York, 1835), 1:129; Leavy, "Memoir," 42:26–28; Friend, *Maysville Road*, 277; Ranck, *History of Lexington*, 325–26; W. Harrison to Jillson Harrison, Harrison Family Papers, KHS; Nancy Baird, "Asiatic Cholera's First Visit to Kentucky," *FCHQ* 48 (1974): 230–33; MacCabe, *Directory for 1838*, 22–23; Wright, *Lexington*, 45, 84; Robert Letcher to Orlando Brown, July 31, 1849, Orlando Brown Papers, KHS.

33. *Frankfort Commonwealth,* June 18, 1833; Reed and Matheson, *Narrative*, 1:129.

34. Colton, *Clay*, 1:31; Mayo, *Clay*, 91.

35. *Brooklyn Eagle*, July 6, 1852; Colton, *Clay*, 1:31; George Poage, *Henry Clay and the Whig Party* (Chapel Hill: University of North Carolina Press, 1936), 3: *CP*, 1:427n, 447n; Mayo, *Clay*, 91.

36. Susan Clay, "Lucretia Hart Clay," typescript, 7–10, Box 57, Clay Family Papers, LC; William Floyd, "Lucretia Hart Clay," *Ashland: The Henry Clay Estate*, September 1997, [2]; Mayo, *Clay*, 90; Henry Clay Simpson Jr., *Josephine Clay* (Louisville, KY: Harmony House, 2005), 7; John Neagle to John Saratain, November 15, 1842, John Neagle Papers, FHS; Amos Kendall to [J. L. Kimmel], May 14, 1814, Amos Kendall Miscellaneous Papers, FHS; Gaillard Hunt, ed., *The First Forty Years of Washington Society* (New York: Charles Scribner's Sons, 1906), 85–86, 88, 157, 246, 332; William Storrs to Susannah Stone, December 22, 1831, William Storrs Letter, LC.

37. James Brown to Clay, September 16, 1804, Clay to James B. Clay, December 29, 1849, Clay to Henry Clay Jr., March 29, 1830, Clay to James Brown, May 9 and January 23, 1825, Clay to Dolley Madison, December 13, 1836, and Clay to Lucretia Clay, November 19, 1835, all in *CP*, 1:149; 10:639; 8:184; 4:336, 38; 8:871, 803; Hunt, *Forty Years*, 332. See also Sarah Agnes Wallace, comp., "Last Letters of Henry Clay," *Register* 50 (1952): 308.

38. Lucius Little, *Ben Hardin* (Louisville, KY, 1887), 352–53; Maurice Baxter, *Henry Clay the Lawyer* (Lexington: University Press of Kentucky, 2000), 32.

39. Peterson, *Great Triumvirate*, 9; Schurz, *Clay*, 1:23; George Dangerfield, *The Era of Good Feelings* (New York: Harcourt, Brace, and World, 1952), 11; Baxter, *Clay the Lawyer*, 32; Clay and Oberholtzer, *Clay*, 21; Joel Tanner

Hart Diary, June 1, 1847, Box 6, Joel Tanner Hart Papers, Reuben T. Durrett Collection, University of Chicago; Little, *Ben Hardin*, 25; Amos Kendall, *Autobiography* (Boston, 1872), 144.

40. "Memoirs of Micah Taul," *Register* 27 (1929): 367; Harrison Recollection of Clay, Box 12, Papers of James O. Harrison, LC; W. F. G. Shanks, "Tom Marshall of Kentucky," *Harper's New Monthly Magazine* 35 (1867): 356.

41. "Henry Clay," Edward F. Buckley Papers, FHS.

42. J. Winston Coleman Jr., *Henry Clay's Last Criminal Case* (Lexington, KY: Winburn Press, 1950), 8; Hart Diary, July 4, 1846; Mayo, *Clay*, 102; Colton, *Clay*, 1:79, 86, 96; Sue Bullitt to John Bullitt, May 1849, Bullitt Family Papers, Oxmoor Collection, FHS.

43. Baxter, *Clay the Lawyer*, 72, 75; Memorandum of Suits Given to Clay by John Breckinridge, February 20, 1800, Thomas Todd to Clay, May 23, 1807, and Thomas Jefferson to Clay, August 28, 1822, all in *CP*, 1:22, 296; 3:280–81; Wright, *Transylvania*, 52; Thomas Clark, ed. *The Voice of the Frontier* (Lexington: University Press of Kentucky, 1993), 239; Adams, *Memoirs*, 7:78–83.

44. Aron, *How the West Was Lost*, 82, 84; Eslinger, *Citizens of Zion*, 65; James Brown to Clay, October 31, 1805, *CP*, 1:206; Baxter, *Clay the Lawyer*, 23; Tax Bill [October 1809], *CP*, 1:402.

45. Baxter, *Clay the Lawyer*, 21, 20; Memorandum, July 20, 1816, Thomas Hart Papers, UK; Petition of Henry Clay, House of Representatives Report No. 505 (22nd Cong., 1st Sess.); Note Account, Private, with Morrison Estate, July 16, 1827, and Memorandum on Legal Profession in Kentucky, ca. 1817, both in *CP*, 6:788; Supp.: 57. See also Henry Clay Papers, Special Collections, Transylvania University.

46. Baxter, *Clay the Lawyer*, 22; Clay to Lucretia Clay, January 4, 1852, *CP*, 10:943; Sandra Day O'Connor, "Henry Clay and the Supreme Court," *Register* 94 (1996): 357, 360; Jeremy McLaughlin, "Henry Clay and the Supreme Court," *Journal of Supreme Court History* 34 (2009): 28–55; Robert Slaughter and Rice Ballard to Clay, January 9, 1841, and Clay to Lucretia Clay, March 13, 1847, both in *CP*, 9:475–76; 10:313–14.

47. Prentice, *Clay*, 16, 18; Coleman, *Last Case*, 9; Sargent, *Clay*, 18; Baxter, *Clay the Lawyer*, 32; *Lexington Reporter*, cited in Mayo, *Clay*, 87; James Brown to Clay, March 12, 1805, *CP*, 1:180. On the debate over whether Clay's clients ever received the death penalty, see Eaton, *Clay*, 13, Coleman, *Last Case*, 22, and William LaBach to James Keller, November 20, 1996, Fayette County Bar Association *Bar News*, January/February 1997, 10–14.

Chapter 2

1. Joan Wells Coward, *Kentucky in the New Republic: The Process of Constitution Making* (Lexington: University Press of Kentucky, 1979), 26–33, 107–108, 113; *Kentucky Gazette*, February 21, May 9, 1798, April 11, 1799; John

Breckinridge to Samuel Meredith, August 7, 1796 (copy), Vol. 14, Papers of the Breckinridge Family, LC; Breckinridge to Shelby, March 11, 1798, Isaac Shelby Papers, Reuben T. Durrett Collection, University of Chicago.

2. *Kentucky Gazette*, April 25, 1798, February 28, 1799; *CP*, 1:3–8, 10–14; Colton, *Clay*, 1:187.

3. James Klotter, *The Breckinridges of Kentucky* (Lexington: University Press of Kentucky, 1986), 26–27; Coward, *Kentucky in the New Republic*, 140, 159, 167; Ellen Eslinger, *Citizens of Zion: The Social Origins of Camp Meeting Revivalism* (Knoxville: University of Tennessee Press, 1999), 135–36. Samuel Orth, *Five American Politicians* (Cleveland, OH: Burrows Brothers, 1906), 358, mistakenly says Clay was a member of the constitutional convention.

4. George Prentice, *Biography of Henry Clay* (Hartford, CT, 1831), 24. For other accounts with other details, see Ethelbert Warfield, *The Kentucky Resolution of 1798*, 2nd. ed. (New York, 1894), 43; Epes Sargent, *Life and Public Services of Henry Clay*, ed. Horace Greeley (Auburn, NY, 1852), 23; Remini, *Clay*, 28–29; and review of *Life of Henry Clay*, in *North American Review* 33 (1831): 358.

5. Clay to James Taylor, May 26, 1800, *CP*, 1:31, 31n; *Frankfort Palladium*, November 4, 1800.

6. Prentice, *Clay*, 25–26. On life at the springs, see J. Winston Coleman Jr., *The Springs of Kentucky* (Lexington, KY: Winburn Press, 1955), 84–93.

7. Robert Ireland, *The County Courts in Antebellum Kentucky* (Lexington: University Press of Kentucky, 1972), 172, 3, 7, 9, 64–67, 5; Christopher Waldrep, "Opportunity on the Frontier South of the Green," in Craig Friend, ed., *The Buzzel about Kentucky: Settling the Promised Land* (Lexington: University Press of Kentucky, 1999), 165; Richard McCormick, *The Second American Party System* (Chapel Hill: University of North Carolina Press, 1966), 211–12; Thomas Clark, *The Rampaging Frontier* (Indianapolis, IN: Bobbs-Merrrill, 1939), 123, 120.

8. 1806 Mason County Circular, cited in Noble Cunningham Jr., *The Jeffersonian Republicans in Power: Party Operations, 1801–1809* (Chapel Hill: University of North Carolina Press, 1963), 211; "Memoirs of Michah Taul," *Register* 27 (1929): 364–65; Jasper Shannon and Ruth McQuown, *Presidential Politics in Kentucky, 1824–1948* (Lexington: Bureau of Government Research, University of Kentucky, 1950), 7.

9. 1806 Mason County Circular; McCormick, *Second Party System*, 211; William Connelley and E. Merton Coulter, *History of Kentucky*, 5 vols. (Chicago: American Historical Society, 1922), 1:477; Harry Laver, *Citizens More than Soldiers: The Kentucky Militia and Society in the Early Republic* (Lincoln: University of Nebraska Press, 2007), 15, 5, 102, 22, 47, 22, 10, 4, 68; Anthony Hunn to Clay, [ca. July 2, 1808], *CP*, 1:358–59. Bernard Mayo, *Henry Clay: Spokesman of the New West* (Boston: Houghton Mifflin, 1937), 148–49, says Clay had been "cocksure and had to make the dramatic appearance to save his victory."

10. *Kentucky Gazette*, August 14, 1804, August 13, 1805; *Kentucky House Journal* (1807–08), 46; "Life of Henry Clay," *Henry Clay Almanac for . . . 1844* (New York, 1844), 20.

11. Mayo, *Clay*, 161–62.

12. William Littell, *Festoons of Fancy* (1816; repr., Louisville: John P. Morton, 1940). 17; *Kentucky House Journal* (1804), 95–103; Mayo, *Clay*, 164; Stephen Aron, *How the West Was Lost: The Transformation of Kentucky from Daniel Boone to Henry Clay* (Baltimore: Johns Hopkins University Press, 1996), 158–60. On Grundy, see Joseph Parks, *Felix Grundy* (University: Louisiana State University Press, 1940) and J. Roderick Heller III, *Democracy's Lawyer* (Baton Rouge: Louisiana State University Press, 2010).

13. Glyndon G. Van Deusen, *Life of Henry Clay* (Boston: Little, Brown, 1937), 36–37; Aron, *How the West Was Lost*, 150–60; Remini, *Clay*, 43.

14. Credentials as US Senator, November 19, 1806, *CP*, 1:254–55; Remini, *Clay*, 43; Everett Brown, *William Plumer's Memorandum of Proceedings in the United States Senate, 1803–1807* (New York, Macmillan, 1923), 552–53, 565, 570.

15. US Constitution, Article I, Section 3; *AC*, 9th Cong., 2nd Sess. (1806–7), 24; Clay and Oberholtzer, *Clay*, 45; Clay to Thomas Bond, September 10, 1844, *CP*, 10:111; Robert Winthrop, *Memoir of Henry Clay* (Cambridge, MA, 1880), 5.

16. Paul Salamanca and James Keller, "The Legislative Privilege to Judge the Qualifications, Elections, and Returns of Members," *Kentucky Law Journal* 95 (2006–7): 307–10; Clay to Thomas Hart, February 1, 1807, and Clay to William Prentiss, February 13, 1807, both in *CP*, 1:274, 280. He is the third youngest senator. John Henry Eaton was younger when he became senator in 1818 and Armistead Mason in 1816 was also younger. See Don Ritchie to James Klotter, July 14, 2009 (email) and "Youngest Senator," US Senate, www.senate.gov/artandhistory/history/minute/Youngest_Senator.htm.

17. *Kentucky Reporter*, January 6, February 17, 1810.

18. Daniel Walker Howe, *What Hath God Wrought: The Transformation of America, 1815–1848* (New York: Oxford University Press, 2007), 564, 61; Emmeline Stuart Wortley, *Travels in the United States* (New York, 1851), 88; "Memoirs of Judge William Wallace Trimble," typescript in possession of Cassandra Trimble; John Silva Meehan Diary, May 13, March 24, May 9, 1846, Box 2, John Silva Meehan Papers, LC; Gaillard Hunt, ed., *The First Forty Years of Washington Society* (New York: Charles Scribner's Sons, 1906), 284, 9, 11; James Young, *The Washington Community, 1800–1828* (New York: Harcourt, Brace, 1966), 43; "American Statesmen," in *Fraser's Magazine*, reprinted in *Littell's Living Age* 36 (February 19, 1853): 341. See also Rachel Shelden, *Washington Brotherhood: Politics, Social Life, and the Coming of the Civil War* (Chapel Hill: University of North Carolina Press, 2013), 9–13, 67–72, 102–17.

19. Thomas Ewing to Maria Ewing, January 24, [1828], Thomas Ewing Family Papers, LC; "Lord Carlisle's Lecture at Leeds," *Littell's Living Age* 28 (February

1, 1851): 198; Young, *Washington Community*, 5, 42; Hunt, *Forty Years*, 158; Charles Sydnor, *The Development of Southern Sectionalism, 1819–1848* (Baton Rouge: Louisiana State University Press, 1948), 19; Claude Bowers, *The Party Battles of the Jackson Period* (New York: Houghton Mifflin, 1922), 29, 6.

20. David Johnson, *John Randolph of Roanoke* (Baton Rouge: Louisiana State University Press, 2012), 49; Young, *Washington Community*, 98–99, 94; "Lord Carlisle's Lecture," 19; Rachel Selden, "Not so Strange Bedfellows: Northern and Southern Whigs and the Annexation Controversy, 1844–1845," in Gary Gallagher and Rachel Shelden, eds., *A Political Nation: New Directions in Mid-Nineteenth Century American Political History* (Charlottesville: University of Virginia Press, 2012), 13–15, 23–24; Thomas Hubbard to Phebe Hubbard, December 7, 11, 22, 1821, Papers of Thomas H. Hubbard, LC.

21. Young, *Washington Community*, 46–47, 89; A. D. Kirwan, *John J. Crittenden* (Lexington: University of Kentucky Press, 1962), 101; Clay to George Thompson, March 14, 1810, *CP*, 1:458; Madison to Richard Cutts, February 27, 1841, in David Mattern and Holly Shulman, eds., *The Selected Letters of Dolley Payne Madison* (Charlottesville: University of Virginia Press, 2003), 357; Thomas Hubbard to Phebe Hubbard, December 22, 1821, Hubbard Papers; T. A. Marshall to Eliza Marshall, February 19, 1835, Marshall Family Papers, FHS; Thomas Hubbard to Phebe Hubbard, January 13, 1822, Hubbard Papers; Joshua Leavitt to R. Hooker Leavitt, December 10, 1841, Joshua Leavitt Papers, LC. See also Padraig Riley, "The Lonely Congressman: Gender and Politics in Early Washington, DC," *JER* 34 (2014): 243–73.

22. "Lord Carlisle's Lecture," 199; "American Statesmen," 341; *RD*, 22nd Cong., 2nd. Sess. (1832–33), 689; Meehan Diary, April 5, 30, 1846, April 1852, Boxes 1–2, Meehan Papers; Young, *Washington Community*, 45, 97.

23. *Kentucky Reporter*, March 17, 1810; Speech on Proposed Repeal of Non-Intercourse Act, February 22, 1810, *CP*, 1:448–49. Quentin Scott King, *Henry Clay and the War of 1812* (Jefferson, NC: McFarland, 2014) provides a detailed look at Clay in this era.

24. *Kentucky Reporter*, March 17, 1810; Speech on Non-Intercourse Act, *CP*, 1:449–50.

25. Speech on the Occupation of West Florida, December 28, 1810, *CP*, 1:316, 514. For other Clay actions, see, for example, *Kentucky Reporter*, March 10, 14, April, 21, 5, May 12, 1810.

26. Clay to Caesar Rodney, May 27, 1810, *CP*, 1:472; *Kentucky Reporter*, May 19, August 18, 1810; Clay to Adam Beatty, May 31, 1810, and Clay to James Monroe, November 13, 1810, both in *CP*, 1:473, 498. In contrast to one story that appeared in *Kentucky Reporter* (September 8, 1810), Clay did not resign his Senate seat and served until the term ended.

27. *AC*, 12th Cong., 1st Sess. (1811–12), 330; Colton, *Clay*, 1:141; Robert Remini, *The House: The History of the House of Representatives* (New York: HarperCollins, 2006), 90; Office of the Speaker of the House of Representatives, "Selection of the Speaker," http://speaker.house.gov/features/selection.asp. The other

instance came in 1860 when freshman William Pennington of New Jersey won the post.

28. Clerk of the House, "Speakers of the House," http://clerk.house.gov/histHigh/Congressional_History/Speakers.html; Office of the Speaker, "Appendix 1: Speakers of the House of Representatives," http://speaker.house.gov/features/app1.asp; Leon Tyler, *The Letters and Times of the Tylers*, 2 vols. (Richmond, VA, 1884), 1:289–90.

29. Clerk of the House, "Party Divisions," http://clerk.house.gov/histHigh/Congressional_History/partyDiv.html; William Brock, *Parties and Political Conscience: American Dilemmas, 1840–1850* (Millwood, NY: KTO Press, 1979), 75; Young, *Washington Community*, 128; Mary Parker Follett, "Henry Clay as Speaker of the House," *New England Magazine* 12 (1892): 344.

30. Prentice, *Clay*, 63; Neil MacNeil, *Forge of Democracy: The House of Representatives* (New York: David McKay, 1963), 66, 46, 64, 47, 65; Sargent, *Clay*, 111; Comment in the Senate, April 17, 1850, *CP*, 10:702. For a study that downplays Clay's role more, see Gerald Gamm and Kenneth Shepsie, "Emergence of Legislative Initiative: Standing Committees in the House and Senate, 1810–1825," *Legislative Studies Quarterly* 14 (1989): 39–66.

31. Sargent, *Clay*, 110; Mangum to Duncan Cameron, December 10, 1823, *Mangum Papers*, 1:82–83. See also *AC*, 16th Cong., 1st Sess. (1819–20), 2250.

32. Randall Strahan et al., "The Clay Speakership Revisited," *Polity* 32 (2000): 567, 580–87; MacNeil, *Forge of Democracy*, 68. See also Kenneth Shepsle, "Studying Institutions: Some Lessons from the Rational Choice Approach," *Journal of Theoretical Politics* 1 (1989): 141, and for a contrasting view, Remini, *The House*, 91.

33. MacNeil, *Forge of Democracy*, 69; Theodore Burton, "Henry Clay, Secretary of State," in *The American Secretaries of State and Their Diplomacy*, 12 vols., ed. Samuel Flagg Bemis and Robert Ferrell (New York: Pageant Books, 1927–64), 4:115; Follett, "Clay," 347; Remini, *The House*, 92; Schurz, *Clay*, 1:254.

34. Sean Wilentz, *The Rise of American Democracy: Jefferson to Lincoln* (New York: W. W. Norton, 2005), 147; Comment in Senate, April 1, 1850, *CP*, 10:692.

35. *AC*, 12th Cong., 1st Sess. (1811–12), 159, 600, 601, 599; Clay to Caesar Rodney, August 6, 1810, *CP*, 1:481; *Kentucky Gazette*, July 28, 1807; Speech on the Occupation of West Florida, December 28, 1810, *CP*, 1:515; *Niles Weekly Register* 2 (April 18, 1812): 105–106; Eunice Fuller Barnard, "To Henry Clay Comes Paradoxical Fame," *New York Times Magazine*, April 10, 1927; Harry Ward, *Charles Scott and the 'Spirit of '76'* (Charlottesville: University Press of Virginia, 1988), 186–87.

36. Clay to Joseph Nicholson, December 21, 1811, *CP*, Supp.:18; Mayo, *Clay*, 504; After Dinner Remarks, July 27, 1812, *CP*, 1:696–97; *Kentucky Gazette*, August 4, 1812; Ronald Hatzenbuehler, "Party Unity and the Decision for War in the House of Representatives, 1812," *William and Mary Quarterly*, 3rd Series, 29 (1972): 372, 379, 383; and Hatzenbuehler, "The War Hawks

and the Question of Congressional Leadership in 1812," *Pacific Historical Review* 45 (1976): 3–4, 21.

37. *AC*, 12th Cong., 1st Sess. (1811–12), 596–97; *Washington National Intelligencer*, April 14, 1812.

38. Hunt, *Forty Years*, 59, 300; Garry Wills, *Explaining America: The Federalist* (Garden City, NY: Doubleday, 1981), 3, 10; Clay to Rodney, December 29, 1812, and Clay to Monroe, August 25, 1812, both in *CP*, 1:751, 719; *AC*, 12th Cong., 2nd. Sess. (1812–13), 674; "Life and Times of Robert B. McAfee . . . Part Four," *Kentucky Ancestors* 43 (2007): 25; James Hammack Jr., *Kentucky and the Second American Revolution: The War of 1812* (Lexington: University Press of Kentucky, 1976), 111–12; James Russell Harris, "Kentuckians in the War of 1812: A Note on Numbers, Losses, and Sources," *Register* 82 (1984): 277–86; Clay to Thomas Bodley, December 18, 1813, Thomas Bodley Collection, KHS.

39. Monroe to Clay, September 17, 1812, *CP*, 1:727; *AC*, 12th Cong., 2nd. Sess. (1812–13) 661, 664; Full Powers to Commissioners to Negotiate a Treaty of Commerce, *CP*, 1:853; Young, *Washington Community*, 183–84; Clay to James Taylor, April 10, 1813, *CP*, 1:782; Isaac Shelby to Clay, May 16, 1813, *CP*, Supp.:26–27; Shelby to John J. Crittenden, April 1814, in Coleman, *Crittenden*, 1:31.

40. *AC*, 13th Cong., 1st Sess. (1813–14), 1057; *Keene New Hampshire Sentinel*, January 29, 1814; *Washington Federal Republican*, January 29, 1814. See also King, *Clay and War of 1812*, 265–402.

41. Clay and Russell to James Bayard and Albert Gallatin, April 14, 1814, *CP*, 1:875; King, *Clay and War of 1812*, 268; Van Deusen, *Henry Clay*, 97; Gallatin to Clay, April 22, 1814, Clay to William Crawford, April 14, 1814, Clay to Russell, May 1, 1814, Clay to Bayard and Gallatin, May 2, 1814, account with Joseph and Olof Hall, June 2, 1814, and Clay to Charles Tait, August 19, 1814, all in *CP*, 1:883–84, 877, 888, 890, 930; Supp.:36.

42. George Dangerfield, *The Era of Good Feelings* (New York: Harcourt, Brace, and World, 1952), 7, 4; Jonathan Russell to Clay, July 2, 1814, *CP*, 1:940; Wilentz, *American Democracy*, 167; Adams, *Memoirs*, 3:39, 78.

43. Remini, *Clay*, 121; George Herring, *From Colony to Superpower: US Foreign Relations since 1776* (New York: Oxford University Press, 2008), 130, 129; Joseph Rogers, *The True Henry Clay* (Philadelphia: J. B. Lippincott, 1902), 77.

44. Jonathan Russell to Clay, October 15, 1815, *CP*, 2:76; Adams, *Memoirs*, 3:103; Schurz, *Clay*, 1:108.

45. The American Commissioners to James Monroe, December 25, 1814; Adams, *Memoirs*, 3:126; *American State Papers: Foreign Relations*, 3:745–48, 732–33; Clay to James Monroe, December 25, 1814, *CP*, 1:1007; Herring, *Colony to Superpower*, 130; Howe, *What Hath God Wrought*, 72–73. News of the peace treaty arrived in Lexington on February 23, 1815, for example. See Amos Kendall, *Autobiography* (Boston, 1872), 137.

46. Commercial Convention with Great Britain, July 3, 1815, *CP*, 2:54–59, 59n; Remini, *Clay*, 125, 128; Clay and Oberholtzer, *Clay*, 402–403; Account as Minister Plenipotentiary, ca. January 1, 1816, *CP*, 2:117; Joseph Anderson to Clay, July 12, 1822, *CP*, 3:258, www.senate.gov/reference/resources/pdf97-1011.pdf.

47. Clay to Lucretia Clay, July 14, 1815, *CP*, 2:60–61; *Washington National Intelligencer*, September 11, 1815; *Lexington Western Monitor*, November 6, 1815.

48. *Lexington Observer and Kentucky Reporter*, November 20, 1847; Speech on the Direct Tax, *CP*, 2:141–42, 148–49; *AC*, 14th Cong., 1st Sess. (1815–16), 777; Heidler and Heidler, *Clay*, 104; *RD*, 18th Cong., 2nd. Sess. (1824–25), 238; *AC*, 12th Cong., 1st Sess. (1811–12), 912; 14th Cong., 1st Sess. (1815–16), 776–77.

49. Clay to Martin D. Hardin, October 13, 1815, *CP*, 2:71–72, 72n; Sargent, *Clay*, 63; *AC*, 14th Cong. 1st Sess. (1815–16), 374; James Madison to Clay, August 30, 1816, and Clay to Madison, September 14, 1816, *CP*, 2:226, 233; "Life of Henry Clay," *North American Review* 33 (1831): 366.

50. *AC*, 14th Cong., 1st Sess. (1815–16), 1174, 1188; Rogers, *True Henry Clay*, 95; C. Edward Skeen, "Vox Populi, Vox Dei: The Compensation Act of 1816 and the Rise of Popular Politics," *JER* 6 (1986): 253–74; William Bianco, David Spence, and John Wilkerson, "The Electoral Connection in the Early Congress: The Case of the Compensation Act of 1816," *American Journal of Political Science* 40 (1996): 147–48.

51. George Blakey, "Rendezvous with Republicanism: John Pope vs. Henry Clay in 1816," *Indiana Magazine of History* 62 (1966): 234–40; Orval Baylor, *John Pope, Kentuckian* (Cythiana, KY: Hobson Press, 1943), 2, 5, 36, 87; Lucius Little, *Ben Hardin* (Louisville, 1887), 247, 250; *Lexington Western Monitor*, July 19, 1816.

52. Campaign Speech at Sandersville, *CP*, 2:219–21; Blakey, "Pope vs. Clay," 241, 245–46, 250; Baylor, *Pope*, 114, 116, 121–22; *Middletown* (CT) *American Sentinel*, October 30, 1832; *Brattleboro* (VT) *Messenger*, October 13, 1832; Skeen, "Compensation Act"; Bianco, Spence, and Wilkerson, "Compensation Act," 149. Colton, *Clay*, 1:99; Sargent, *Clay*, 69; "Henry Clay," *Harper's* 5 (1852): 395; and Orlando Brown, "The Governors of Kentucky," *Register* 49 (1951): 215–16, all have varied versions of the "flint" story, while Blakey, "Pope vs. Clay," 250, has a slightly different vote than the 2,495 for Clay, 1,838 for Pope, cited here.

53. Robert Pierce Forbes, *The Missouri Compromise and Its Aftermath* (Chapel Hill: University of North Carolina Press, 2007), 18, 17; Dangerfield, *Era of Good Feelings*, 97.

54. Adams, *Memoirs*, 4:242; Forbes, *Missouri Compromise*, 24; Schurz, *Clay*, 1:141; *AC*, 15th Cong., 1st Sess. (1817–18), 1379; Young, *Washington Community*, 188; Clay to Thomas Bodley, December 3, 1817, Bodley Papers.

55. Clay to Peter Irving, August 13, 1817, *CP*, Supp.: 62–63; Wilentz, *American Democracy*, 206, 215; Maurice Baxter, *Henry Clay and the American*

System (Lexington: University Press of Kentucky, 1995), 34–35; Thomas Brown, *Politics and Statesmanship: Essays on the American Whig Party* (New York: Columbia University Press, 1985), 123; Kim Gruenwald, *River of Enterprise: The Commercial Origins of Regional Identity in the Ohio Valley, 1790–1850* (Bloomington: Indiana University Press, 2002), 99, 110–11, 113; Daniel Feller, *The Public Lands in Jacksonian Politics* (Madison: University of Wisconsin Press, 1984), 24; Charles Sellers, *The Market Revolution: Jacksonian America, 1815–1846* (New York: Oxford University Press, 1991), 135–36; Kim Phillips, "The Pennsylvania Origins of the Jackson Movement," *Political Science Quarterly* 91 (1976): 493: Stephen Fackler, "John Rowan and the Demise of Jeffersonian Republicanism in Kentucky," *Register* 78 (1980): 1; *An American System for the Protection of American Industry* (Cincinnati, OH, 1824), 2, 5.

56. Matthew G. Schoenbachler, "The Origins of Jacksonian Politics: Central Kentucky, 1790–1840" (PhD diss., University of Kentucky, 1996), 125, 137, 145; *American System*, 4; Receipted Tax Bill, 1818, *CP*, 2:665; Receipted Bill from William Gilliam, ca. May 1, 1822, *CP*, 3:203; Clay to Langdon Cheves, March 15, 1820, *CP*, 2:795. On the Clay debt, see *CP*, 2:877, 4:38, 5:282, 6:362, 7:298, 303, 553.

57. Harry Stevens, "Henry Clay, the Bank, and the West in 1824," *America Historical Review* 60 (1955): 843, 846; Clay to Langdon Cheves, March 15, 1820 (*CP*, 2:794), February 10, 1821 (*CP*, 3:25–26), September 8, 1821 (*CP*, 3:113), December 3, 1821 (*CP*, 3:144); Harry Watson, *Andrew Jackson vs. Henry Clay: Democracy and Development in Antebellum America* (Boston: Bedford/St. Martin's, 1998), 56; Donald Ratcliff, "The Role of Voters and Issues in Party Formation: Ohio, 1824," *JAH* 59 (1973): 859–60, 859n.

58. Thomas Blakemore, "The Blakemore Family: Personal History," 1, Blakemore Family Papers, VHS; Johnson to Morgan Neville, June 1833, in "The Letters of Richard M. Johnson of Kentucky," *Register* 38–40 (1940–42), ed. James Padgett, 40:80; Jonathan Jones, "The Making of a Vice President: The National Political Career of Richard M. Johnson of Kentucky" (PhD diss., University of Memphis, 1998), 203, 209–15, 222–25. For Johnson's career generally, see Leland Meyer, *The Life and Times of Colonel Richard M. Johnson of Kentucky* (New York: Columbia University Press, 1932).

59. Emily Ford, "Richard Mentor Johnson: Thirty Years in Congress" (MA thesis, University of Kentucky, 1929), 21; Jones, "Making of Vice President," 42, 44, 49, 49n; Meyer, *Johnson*, 309; "Reception of Col. R. M. Johnson at Springfield, May 19, 1843," *Journal of the Illinois State Historical Society* 13 (1920–21): 204, 196. For the debate on the killing of Tecumseh, good, concise sources are Lewis and Richard Collins, *History of Kentucky*, 2 vols. (Covington, KY, 1874), 2:403–10, and Stuart Sprague, "The Death of Tecumseh and the Rise of Rumpsey Dumpsey," *FCHQ* 59 (1985): 455–56.

60. Clay to Langdon Cheves, ca. February 1820 (*CP*, 2:773) and October 3, 1821 (*CP*, 3:124); Clay to John Berrien, September 22, 1843, *CP*, 9:859; Clay to

Crittenden, March 10, 1826, in Coleman, *Crittenden*, 1:64. Clay to Langdon Cheves, July 21, 1821, *CP*, 3:102; Jones, "Making of Vice President," 100–105, 113, 131–38, 143; R. M. Johnson to Andrew Jackson, April 26, 1819, in Padgett, "Letters of Johnson," 39: 37; *CP*, 3:89n. For Johnson's financial woes, see also Papers of Richard Mentor Johnson, passim, LC, and Richard Mentor Johnson Correspondence, passim, FHS.

61. R. M. Johnson to Andrew Jackson, August 4, 1819, and Johnson to James Monroe, July 11, 1819, both in Padgett, "Letters of Johnson," 39:178, 174; Johnson to Thomas Wilson, November 16, 1824, Johnson Correspondence (FHS); Adams, *Memoirs*, 6: 240; Padgett, "Letters of Johnson," 38:187; Wallace Turner, "Henry Clay and the Campaign of 1844" (MA thesis, University of Kentucky, 1933), 5.

62. Meyer, *Johnson*, 319–21; Jones, "Making of Vice President," 396–97, 286–88; Ford, "Johnson," 16; *Washington Globe*, July 7, 1835; Wilentz, *American Democracy*, 448.

63. Warden Pope to Andrew Jackson, May 31, 1829, in *Jackson Papers* 7:256; Ford, "Johnson," 16; Jones, "Making of Vice President," 297, 395; Meyer, *Johnson*, 321; *Washington Globe*, July 7, 1835; John Catron to Andrew Jackson, in *Jackson Correspondence,* 5:331. For comments on Johnson having other mistresses, see *Polk Papers*, 5:286, 376, 580; 7:30; Catherine Bragg to Catherine Gould, October 8, 1840, Catherine L. Bragg Letters, FHS; Jones, "Making of Vice President," 303–305.

64. *Kentucky Reporter*, May 3, 7, June 14, 1820; *AC*, 16th Cong., 2nd Sess. (1820–21), 434–35.

65. Major Wilson, *Space,Time, and Freedom: The Quest for Nationality and the Irrepressible Conflict, 1815–1861* (Westport, CT: Greenwood, 1974), 51; Dangerfield, *Era of Good Feelings*, 175, 204; Feller, *Public Lands*, 24–25; Forbes, *Missouri Compromise*, 5, 35–36, 43, 47; Glover Moore, *The Missouri Controversy, 1819–1821* (Lexington: University of Kentucky Press, 1953) 36; Richard Brown, "The Missouri Crisis, Slavery, and the Politics of Jacksonianism," *South Atlantic Quarterly* 65 (1966): 55; Matthew Mason, *Slavery and Politics in the Early American Republic* (Chapel Hill: University of North Carolina Press, 2006), 8; *AC*, 15th Cong., 2nd Sess. (1818–19), 1204; William Freehling, *The Road to Disunion: Secessionists at Bay, 1776–1854* (New York: Oxford University Press, 1990), 149.

66. *AC*, 16th Cong, 1st Sess. (1819–20), 704; Moore, *Missouri Controversy*, 94; Speech on the Missouri Bill, Clay to Amos Kendall, January 8, 1820, and Clay to Adam Beatty, January 22, 1820, all in *CP*, 2:777, 752, 766.

67. Moore, *Missouri Controversy*, 88, 95, 102–103; John Van Atta, *Wolf by the Ears: The Missouri Crisis, 1819–1821* (Baltimore: Johns Hopkins University Press, 2015), 98–100; *AC*, 16th Cong., 1st Sess. (1819–20), 835–42; Clay to John J. Crittenden, January 29, 1820, Clay to Martin Hardin, February 5, 1820, Clay to Leslie Combs, February 5 and 15, 1820, and Clay to Horace Holley, February 17, 1820, all in *CP*, 2:769, 775, 774, 780, 781; Alfred Lightfoot, "Henry Clay and the Missouri Question, 1819–1821,"

Missouri Historical Review 61 (1967): 154, 153; Everett Somerville Brown, ed., *The Missouri Compromise and Presidential Politics, 1820–1825, From the Letters of William Plumer, Junior* (St. Louis: Missouri Historical Society, 1926), 30–33; Merrill Peterson, *The Great Triumvirate: Webster, Clay, and Calhoun* (New York: Oxford University Press, 1987), 61; Clay to Adam Beatty, March 4, 1820, *CP*, 2:788. See also Matthew Mason, "The Maine and Missouri Crisis: Competing Priorities and Northern Slavery Politics in the Early Republic," *JER* 33 (2013): 675–700.

68. Peterson, *Great Triumvirate*, 65.

69. Forbes, *Missouri Compromise*, 108, 110; Van Atta, *Wolf by the Ears*, 116–21; Joseph Gales Jr. to Clay, December 7, 1820, *CP*, 2:911; Lightfoot, "Clay and Missouri," 157–58; Remini, *The House*, 110; Adams, *Memoirs*, 5:91.

70. *AC*, 16th Cong., 2nd Sess. (1820–21), 872; Wilentz, *American Democracy*, 235; Clay to Greenberry Ridgely, January 23, 1821, Clay to Langdon Cheves, February 15, 1821, and Clay to William Woods, July 16, 1835, all in *CP*, 3:14, 41; 8:786–87.

71. Forbes, *Missouri Compromise*, 112, 115, 117–18; Clay to William Woods, July 16, 1835, *CP*, 8:787; Moore, *Missouri Controversy*, 155–57; Robert Seager II, "Henry Clay and the Politics of Compromise and Non-Compromise," *Register* 85 (1987): 8; Committee Report, February 26, 1821, *CP*, 3:49; Kimberly Shankman, *Compromise and the Constitution: The Political Thought of Henry Clay* (Lanham, MD: Lexington Books, 1999), 18; Peter Knupfer, *The Union as It Is: Constitutional Unionism and Sectional Compromise, 1787–1861* (Chapel Hill: University of North Carolina Press, 1991), 100.

72. Brown, ed. *Missouri Compromise*, 38; Moore, *Missouri Controversy*, 158, 154; John Marshall to Charles Hammond, December 28, 1823, in William Henry Smith, *Charles Hammond and His Relations to Henry Clay and John Quincy Adams* (Chicago, 1885), 19–20.

73. Michael Morrison, *Slavery and the American West* (Chapel Hill: University of North Carolina Press, 1997), 52; William Birney, *James G. Birney and His Times* (New York, 1890), 408; Wilentz, *American Democracy*, 851n; Moore, *Missouri Controversy*, 342.

Chapter 3

1. Madeline McDowell, "Recollections of Henry Clay," *The Century* 50 (1895): 767; Lida Mayo, "Henry Clay, Kentuckian," *FCHQ* 32 (1958): 171; Remini, *Clay*, 626; Joel Tanner Hart Diary, November 21, 1846, Box 6, Joel Tanner Hart Papers, Reuben T. Durrett Collection, University of Chicago; Thomas Brown, *Politics and Statesmanship: Essays on the American Whig Party* (New York: Columbia University Press, 1985): 118; "Mr. Clay," *American Monthly Magazine* 1 (1829): 341, 343; George Dangerfield, *The Era of Good Feelings* (New York: Harcourt, Brace, and World, 1952), 10; [Joseph Baldwin], "Representative Men: Part I," *Southern Literary*

Messenger 19 (1853): 522; Henry Clay Passport, March 8, 1851, Henry Clay Miscellaneous Papers, FHS; "Isaac Bassett: A Senate Memoir," www.senate. gov/artandhistory/art/special/Bassets/+detail.ctm?it=3; "Reminiscences of Washington," *Atlantic Monthly* 45 (1880): 292.

2. George Bancroft, "A Few Words about Henry Clay," *The Century* 30 (1885): 479; Merrill Peterson, *The Great Triumvirate: Webster, Clay, and Calhoun* (New York: Oxford University Press, 1987), 10; "Henry Clay," *Harper's New Monthly Magazine* 5 (1852): 393; Hector Green to Ellen Green, October 6, 1840, Box 2, Green Family Papers, FHS; *Whig Banner Melodist* 1 (September 1844): n.p.; George Prentice, *Biography of Henry Clay* (Hartford, CT, 1831), 272; "Henry Clay," Edward F. Berkley Papers, FHS.

3. Gaillard Hunt, ed., *The First Forty Years of Washington Society* (New York: Charles Scribner's Sons, 1906), 146; J. O. Harrison, "Henry Clay," *The Century* 33 (1886): 178; Horace Greeley, *Recollections of a Busy Life* (New York, 1868), 168; *Whig Banner Melodist* 1 (September 1844): n.p.; Schurz, *Clay*, 1:327; James Hopkins, "A Tribute to Mr. Clay," *Register* 53 (1955): 284.

4. "Henry Clay as an Orator," *Putnam's Monthly Magazine* 3 (1854): 498–99; Harrison, "Clay," 179; James G. Harrison's Recollections of Henry Clay, Box 12, Papers of James G. Harrison, LC; Arthur Schlesinger Jr., *The Age of Jackson* (Boston: Little, Brown, 1945), 82; Dangerfield, *Era of Good Feelings*, 10; "Reminiscences of Washington," 292; J. W. Watson, "With Four Great Men: Henry Clay," *North American Review* 147 (1888): 589.

5. Clay and Oberholtzer, *Clay*, 15; *Mobile Advertiser*, in *Galveston Weekly Journal*, August 13, 1852; *New York Times*, March 24, 1852; "Henry Clay as Orator" (*Putnam's*), 499; Edward McDermott, "Fun on the Stump: Humors of Political Campaigning in Kentucky," *The Century* 50 (1895): 826.

6. Bancroft, "Few Words about Clay," 479; Hector Green to Ellen Green, October 6, 1840, Green Family Papers; US Senate, "About Henry Clay," www.senate.gov/artandhistory/art/special/Clay/Introduction/ HenryClay.htm.

7. Remini, *Clay*, 2, 541; Daniel Walker Howe, *What Hath God Wrought: The Transformation of America, 1815–1848* (New York: Oxford University Press, 2007), 26; *Macon Weekly Georgia Telegraph*, August 9, 1859; E. S. Abdy, *Journal of a Residence and Tour in the United States of North America . . . ,* 3 vols. (London, 1835), 2:115.

8. Colton, *Clay*, 1:65; "Henry Clay" (*Harper's*), 5:393; "Henry Clay as Orator" (*Putnam's*), 497; Peterson, *Great Triumvirate*, 383; Edgar DeWitt Jones, *The Influence of Henry Clay upon Abraham Lincoln* (Lexington, KY: Henry Clay Memorial Foundation, 1952), 17; "Henry Clay as Orator," *New Englander and Yale Review* 2 (1844): 105.

9. David Dearinger, "The Diary of Joel Tanner Hart, Sculptor," *FCHQ* 64 (1990): 24; *CP*, 8:240n; William Greene to Clay, August 19, 1830, and Speech in Senate, February 14, 1851, both in *CP*, 8:253, 10: 857; review of "Speeches of Henry Clay," *North American Review* 25 (1827): 443–44;

"Henry Clay as Orator" (*New Englander*), 110; "Modern Oratory," *Southern Literary Messenger* 18 (1852): 375. See, for example, Robert Remini, *Daniel Webster: The Man and His Times* (New York: W. W. Norton, 1997), 186, 329–30.

10. "Schurz's Life of Henry Clay," *Overland Monthly and Out West Magazine* 10 (1887): 213; William Brock, *Parties and Political Conscience: American Dilemmas, 1840–1850* (Millwood, NY: KTO Press, 1979), 79; James Jasinski, "The Forms and Limits of Prudence in Henry Clay's (1850) Defense of the Compromise Measures," *Quarterly Journal of Speech* 81 (1995): 454; Jones, *Clay and Lincoln*, 17, 2; Abraham Lincoln, Eulogy on Henry Clay, July 6, 1852, in Roy Basler, ed., *Collected Works of Abraham Lincoln*, 9 vols. (New Brunswick, NJ: Rutgers University Press, 1959), 2:127.

11. "Henry Clay as Orator" (*Putnam's*), 501; review of "Life, Correspondence, and Speeches of Henry Clay," *North American Review* 102 (1866): 149.

12. Christopher Morgan to Edwin Morgan, March 31, 1840, Papers of Christopher Morgan, LC; unidentified clipping, Papers of Henry Clay and Family, LC; Remini, *Clay*, 20; Adams, *Memoirs*, 9:505–506; Nathan Sargent, *Public Men and Events*, 2 vols. (Philadelphia, 1875), 2:38–41.

13. "Editor's Drawer," *Harper's New Monthly Magazine* 17 (1858): 426. Colton, *Clay*, 1:113 has a different version.

14. Colton, *Clay*, 1:107; *Works of Buchanan*, 4:296; James Buchanan to Robert Letcher, April 17, 1842, Coleman, *Crittenden*, 1:176; "Editor's Drawer," *Harper's New Monthly Magazine* 48 (1873): 155; Clay and Oberholtzer, *Clay*, 421–23. For a different version of the "posterity" quote, see Hart Diary, July 17, 1847.

15. William Preston to Willie Mangum, March 28, 1838, *Mangum Papers*, 2:517; Sargent, *Public Men*, 2:129; *Polk Papers*, 6:58n.

16. Bassett, "Senate Memoir"; Prentice, *Clay*, 222, 94

17. Unidentified clipping, Clay Family Papers; *New London (CT) Gazette and General Advertiser*, October 10, 1832; *Columbus Ohio State Journal*, October 6, 1832; *New York Mercury*, February 15, 1832; *CG*, 26th Cong., 2nd Sess. (1840–41), 332; *RD*, 23rd Cong., 2nd Sess. (1834–35), 300; John Belohlavek, "Henry Clay and the Historian: A One-Hundred-Year Perspective," *Florida Historical Quarterly* 71 (1993): 483; "Representative Men: Part I," 596; Craig Friend and Lorri Glover, eds., *Southern Manhood: Perspectives on Masculinity in the Old South* (Athens: University of Georgia Press, 2004), viii–ix.

18. Samuel Brown, *The Works of Rufus Choate with the Memoir of His Life* (Boston, 1862), 56; *CG*, 27th Cong., 2nd Sess. (1841–42), 377; Remini, *Clay*, 58.

19. *Macon Weekly Georgia Telegraph*, August 9, 1859; Harrison, "Clay," 179; Clay and Oberholtzer, *Clay*, 399; Robert Winthrop, *Henry Clay* (Cambridge, MA, 1880), 30–31, 35; McDowell, "Recollections," 770.

20. See James David Barker, *The Presidential Character: Predicating Performance in the White House*, 3rd ed. (Engelwood Cliffs, NJ: Prentice-Hall, 1985), 532.

21. Greeley, *Recollections*, 168; "Autobiography of Harrison," October 1880, Box 12, Harrison Papers; Prentice, *Clay*, 11; "Modern Oratory," 375; Charles Sumner to Richard Milnes, May 1, 1844, in Beverley Wilson Palmer, ed., *The Selected Letters of Charles Sumner*, 2 vols. (Boston: Northeastern University Press, 1990), 1:137; "Editor's Drawer" (1873), 316.

22. *Sing-Sing (NY) Hudson River Chronicle*, August 27, 1839; *Keene New Hampshire Sentinel*, October 10, 1850; Henry Foote, *Casket of Reminiscences* (1874; repr., New York: Negro Universities Press, 1968), 29; John Neagle to John Sartain, November 15, 1842, John Neagle Papers, FHS; Edward Bates to Julia Bates, February 25, 1828, Edward Bates Papers, VHS; Williams Storrs to Susannah Storrs, December 22, 1831, Letter of Williams Storrs, LC; *Galveston Weekly Journal*, July 9, 1852; Hart Diary, November 27, 1846; Watson, "With Four Great Men," 589.

23. Hunt, *First Forty Years*, 285–86; "Lord Carlisle's Lecture at Leeds," *Littell's Living Age* 28 (1851): 199; Henry Clay Simpson Jr., *Josephine Clay: Pioneer Horsewoman of the Bluegrass* (Louisville, KY; Harmony House, 2006), 6.

24. Clay and Oberholtzer, *Clay*, 403; Edward Bates to Julia Bates, February 25, 1828, Bates Papers; Remini, *Clay*, 532; Greeley, *Recollections*, 250.

25. Hart Diary, November 27, 1846.

26. Bancroft, "Few Words about Clay," 479.

27. *Middleton Connecticut Constitution*, March 15, 1848; review of "The Last Seven Years of the Life of Henry Clay," *New Englander and Yale Review* 14 (1856): 544; Thomas Blakemore, "The Blakemore Family," 5, Blakemore Family Papers, VHS; unidentified clipping, Box 64, Clay Family Papers; "Editor's Drawer," *Harper's New Monthly Magazine* 20 (1860): 419.

28. *New York Times*, July 1, 1852; Schurz, *Clay*, 1:328.

29. Michael Holt, *The Rise and Fall of the American Whig Party* (New York: Oxford University Press, 1999), 185–86.

30. Adams, *Memoirs*, 5:496; *Louisville Public Advertiser*, August 20, 1828; "First Word After the Election," *United States Magazine and Democratic Review* 15 (1844): 429; *Brooklyn Eagle*, March 11, 1848, December 19, 1842; *Portland (ME) Eastern Argus*, September 21, 1832; Thomas Marshall to Louis Marshall, April 19, 1842, in Margaret Caldwell, comp., "A Web of Family Letters from a Kentucky Family, 1816–1865," 72, typescript, Newberry Library, Chicago; *Richmond Enquirer*, October 5, 1832; Jackson to D. G. Goodlett, March 12, 1844, *Jackson Correspondence*, 6:275.

31. Ethan Fishman, *The Prudential Presidency: An Aristotelian Approach to Presidential Leadership* (Westport, CT: Praeger, 2001), 114, 122.

32. Bancroft, "Few Words About Clay," 479; Winthrop, *Clay*, 26; *Macon Georgia Telegraph*, August 1, 1843; Foote, *Casket of Remembrances*, 364; Lucius Little, *Ben Hardin* (Louisville, KY, 1887), 348; "First Word," 429, Adams, *Memoirs*, 6:258, 8:445; *Portsmouth New-Hampshire Gazette*, October 22, 1844; Webster to Franklin Havin, July 4, 1850, and to Edward Everett, December 15, 1844, *Webster Papers*, 7:121, 6:63; "Daniel Webster," *North America Review* 104 (1867): 66.

33. "Daniel Webster," 66.

34. "Journal Kept for the Children of a Journey to the West in June 1839," Journal of T. R. Sullivan, LC; *Washington Globe*, August 7, 1838; *Portsmouth New-Hampshire Gazette*, February 13, 1838; *Portland* (ME) *Eastern Argus*, September 18, 1838; David Smiley, "An Emissary from Cousin Henry: Cassius M. Clay and Henry Clay in the Election of 1844," *Register* 53 (1955): 121.

35. Matthew Schoenbachler, "The Origins of Jacksonian Politics: Central Kentucky 1790–1840" (PhD diss., University of Kentucky, 1996), 44; Francis Fessenden, *Life and Public Services of William Pitt Fessenden*, 2 vols. (Boston: Houghton Mifflin, 1907), 1:14; "Editor's Easy Chair," *Harper's New Monthly Magazine* 59 (1879): 142; http://Washington.intercontinental.com/washa/dining_03.html; "Kentucky in Washington," *Kentucky Monthly*, January 2009, 44. On Clay's purchases of liquor, see *CP*, 1:133–34; 4:707; 9:231; 10:302; 9:18.

36. Adams, *Memoirs*, 4:40; "Suggestions of the Past: John Tyler's Administration," *The Galaxy* 13 (1872): 348; Charles Sellers, *The Market Revolution: Jacksonian America, 1815–1846* (New York: Oxford University Press, 1991), 266; Daniel Walker Howe, *The Political Culture of the American Whigs* (Chicago: University of Chicago Press, 1979), 159; Clay to Harrison Otis, January 24, 1839, *CP*, 9:275.

37. *Lexington Herald-Leader*, July 9, 2000; Kentucky Horse Park, *Kentucky Bloodlines: The Legacy of Henry Clay* (Lexington, KY: Horse Park, 2005), 9; Everett Brown, *William Plumer's Memorandum of Proceedings in the United States Senate, 1803–1807* (New York: Macmillan, 1923), 608; Adams, *Memoirs*, 5:59, 3:60; *Portsmouth New-Hampshire Gazette*, November 21, 1843; Joseph Rogers, *The True Henry Clay* (Philadelphia: J.B. Lippincott, 1902), 63; Little, *Ben Hardin*, 34; review of "Life, Correspondence, and Speeches of Clay," 172; *Louisville Commercial*, August 10, 1890.

38. Review of "Life, Correspondence, and Speeches of Clay," 172; Adams, *Memoirs*, 3:101; Little, *Ben Hardin*, 33; Colton, *Clay*, 1:47; Clay to James B. Clay, May 22, 1839, *CP*, 9:318; Peterson, *Great Triumvirate*, 381.

39. *New Bedford* (MA) *Mercury*, December 9, 1842; *The Liberator*, November 4, 1842; *Portsmouth New-Hampshire Gazette*, March 12, 1832; *Newport Rhode-Island Republican*, October 2, 1832; *Bennington Vermont Gazette*, August 27, 1844; *CP*, 5:417n.

40. Bertram Wyatt Brown, *Southern Honor: Ethics and Behavior in the Old South* (New York: Oxford University Press, 1982), xv, 369, 353, 357; Kenneth Greenberg, *Honor and Slavery* (Princeton, NJ: Princeton University Press, 1996), xi–xii, 9; Spencer O'Brien to Willie Mangum, February 26, 1832, *Mangum Papers*, 1:495; *Easton Maryland Gazette*, May 4, 1839; Foote, *Casket of Reminiscences*, 186; Friend and Glover, *Southern Manhood*, x; James Klotter, *Kentucky Justice, Southern Honor, and American Manhood: Understanding the Life and Death of Richard Reid* (Baton Rouge: Louisiana State University Press, 2003), 48–49; David

Chaney, "The Spectacle of Honour: The Changing Dramatization of Status," *Theory, Culture, & Society* 17 (1995): 152. See also Richard Bell, "The Double Guilt of Dueling: The Stain of Suicide in the Anti-Dueling Rhetoric in the Early Republic," *JER* 29 (2009): 383–410.

41. Clay to James Clark, January 19, 1809, *CP*, 1:400. See also *Kentucky House Journal* (1808–09), 93, 103; Mayo, *Clay*, 338; Clay to Thomas Hart Jr., January 4, 1809, Clay to Humphrey Marshall, January 4, 1809, and Humphrey Marshall to Clay, January 4, 1809, all in *CP*, 1:398–99; H. Blanton letter fragment, KHS; *Kentucky Reporter*, January 26, 23, 1809; R. U. Major to T. M. Green, March 15, 1889, typescript, and H. Blanton Recollection, June 5, 1879, typescript, both in "Henry Clay," Vertical Files, KHS.

42. "Edmund Ruffin's Visit to John Tyler," *William and Mary College Quarterly Historical Magazine* 14 (1906): 195; Sargent, *Public Men*, 1:125–28; John Chavis to Willie Mangum, July 30, 1833, *Mangum Papers*, 2:37; "Henry Clay" (*Harper's*), 396; William Cabell Bruce, *John Randolph of Roanoke*, 2 vols. (New York: G. P. Putnam's Sons, 1922), 2:357, 313–14; Dangerfield, *Era of Good Feelings*, 206, 354–55; Thomas Holmes to Clay, August 24, 1826, *CP*, 5:645–46; "John Randolph of Roanoke," *Harper's New Monthly Magazine* 5 (1852): 536; Hugh Garland, *The Life of John Randolph of Roanoke*, 13th ed. (1850; New York, 1866), 374–75; Adams, *Memoirs*, 8:64; Sargent, *Clay*, 120; Louis McLane to Kitty McLane, May 7, 13, 1824, Papers of Louis McLane, LC. See also David Johnson, *John Randolph of Roanoke* (Baton Rouge: Louisiana State University Press, 2012), 3–6, 141, 29, 183.

43. Debate on Revenue Proposals, January 20, 1816, *CP*, 2:136; Robert Remini, *The House: The History of the House of Representatives* (New York: HarperCollins, 2006), 92; Peterson, *Great Triumvirate*, 141; Bruce, *Randolph*, 2:203; Paul Corts, "Randolph vs. Clay: A Duel of Words and Bullets," *FCHQ* 55 (1981): 155, 157; *RD*, 19th Cong., 1st Sess. (1825–26), 389–406; Thomas Jessup to J. R. Underwood, March 4, 1853, Box 2, Clay Family, Henry Clay Memorial Foundation Papers, UK; Clay to Randolph, March 31, 1826, and Randolph to Clay, April 1, 1826, both in *CP*, 5:208, 209n, 211–12.

44. "Memorandum of the Terms of the Contemplated Meeting Between Messers. Randolph and Clay," Box 35, Papers of Clay and Family; Jessup to Underwood, March 4, 1853, Clay Family; Thomas Hart Benton to "Dear Sir," March 24, 1844, Thomas Hart Benton Letters, LC; Thomas Hart Benton, *Thirty Years View*, 2 vols. (New York, 1883), 1:70–77; *Kentucky Reporter*, April 24, 1826; Sargent, *Public Men*, 1:124; "Henry Clay" (*Harper's*), 397; Peterson, *Great Triumvirate*, 141. Different versions exist concerning the words uttered, as are cited in, for example, Johnson, *John Randolph*, 212. I have used the ones given closest to the date of the event, by those present.

45. Clay to Francis Brooke, April 19, 1826, Clay to Henry Bascom, April 10, 1826, Henry Warfield to Clay, May 5, 1826, John J. Crittenden to Clay, April 27, 1826, Christopher Hughes to Clay, April 12, 1826, James Brown to Clay, May 10, 1826, Sylvester Southworth to Clay, April 20, 1826, Charles King to Clay, April 12, 1826, Clay to Francis Brooke, April 19, 1826, and Clay to

Crittenden, May 11, 1826, all in *CP*, 5:253, 227, 307, 277, 231, 356, 259, 233, 253, 36.

46. "Randolph" (*Harper's*), 536–37; Johnson, *John Randolph*, 226; Clay to Francis Brooke, March 11, 1833, *CP*, 8:631; Sargent, *Public Men*, 1:129; George Peake to Willie Mangum, April 21, 1843, *Mangum Papers*, 3:444–45; unknown to Clay, May 31, 1833, *CP*, 8:645; Bruce, *Randolph*, 47.

47. Bruce, *Randolph*, 197; Alben Barkley, *That Reminds Me* (Garden City, NY: Doubleday, 1954), 259. On at least four or five other occasions, Clay nearly fell victim to the dueling virus as well, but was able to avoid the infection. See Prentice, *Clay*, 29–30; *Kentucky Reporter*, February 9, 1824; Ichabod Bartlett to Clay, January 29, 1824, Clay to Bartlett, January 29, 1824, and Clay to Charles Hammond, February 22, 1824, all in *CP*, 3:616, 618, 655; William M. Meigs, *Life of Thomas Hart Benton* (Philadelphia: J. B. Lippincott, 1904), 221; William Buckner to Thomas Buckner, October 6, 1835, Box 3, Buckner Family Papers, FHS; *Portland* (ME) *Eastern Argus*, October 13, 1835; Thomas Coit to Williams Lakier, October 23, 1835; Richard Gantz, "Henry Clay and the Harvest of Bitter Fruit: The Struggle with John Tyler, 1841–1842" (PhD diss., Indiana University, 1986), 49–50; "Reminiscences of Washington," 376; A. O. P. Nicholson to James K. Polk, March 9, 10,1841, *Polk Papers*, 5:654–55.

48. A. D. Kirwan, *John J. Crittenden: The Struggle for the Union* (Lexington: University of Kentucky Press, 1962), 119–20; Melba Porter Hay, "Compromiser or Conspirator? Henry Clay and the Graves-Cilley Duel," in *A Mythic Land Apart: Reassessing Southerners and Their History*, ed. John David Smith and Thomas Appleton Jr. (Westport, CT: Greenwood, 1997), 60–68; John Wilson, *The Code of Honor* (Charleston, SC, 1858), 6–15; J. M. Foltz to Henry Wise, February 28, 1842, Barton H. Wise Papers, VHS; Blakemore, "Personal History," Blakemore Family Papers.

49. Henry Wise to J. L. O'Sullivan, n.d., Wise Papers; Thomas Marshall to mother, August 4, 1842, Marshall Family Papers, FHS; *CP*, 9:153n; *Henry Clay's Duels*, Tract No. 1 (n.p., 1844), 1, 4; *Brooklyn Eagle*, October 22, 1844; Hay, "Compromiser or Conspirator," 68–76, 78n.

50. Hector Green to Ellen Green, October 6, 1840, Green Family Papers; *Norwich Connecticut Courier*, January 25, 1832; George Bancroft to Sarah Bancroft, January 11, 1832, in M. A. DeWolfe Howe, *The Life and Letters of George Bancroft*, 2 vols. (New York: Charles Scribner's Sons, 1908), 1:197; Louis McLane to Kitty McLane, January 17, 1825, Box 1, McLane Papers; Charles Davis to Clay, October 4, 1844, *CP*, 10:130; *CP*, 4:431, 8:101, 240; Clay to Charles Hall, March 7, 1845, and Clay to Charles Ridgely, March 7, 1845, both in *CP*, 10:206; *Lexington Observer and Reporter*, November 14, 1846; Elizabeth Varon, " 'The Ladies Are Whigs': Lucy Barbour, Henry Clay, and Nineteenth-Century Virginia Voters," *Virginia Cavalcade* 42 (1992): 76, 74–75, 81; review of Sarah Maury, "The Statesmen of America in 1846," *Littell's Living Age* 12 (1847): 570; Howe, *What Hath God Wrought*, 606–607; Ronald Formisano, "The New Political History and

the Election of 1840," *Journal of Interdisciplinary History* 23 (1993): 682n; Sargent, *Public Men*, 2:246.

51. *Boston Bee*, January 9, 1843; *Lexington Observer and Reporter*, November 14, 1846; Peterson, *Great Triumvirate*, 379; Speech in Lexington, June 9, 1842, *CP*, 9:709; Hunt, *First Forty Years*, 145, 304, 277–78, 285–86, 299–303; unidentified clipping, Box 64, Clay Family Papers.

52. Clay and Oberholtzer, *Clay*, 426; Bassett, "Senate Memoir," February 2, 1832; Howe, *What Hath God Wrought*, 290; Hunt, *First Forty Years*, 183; Harrison, "Clay," 765; Job Pierson to Clarissa Pierson, January 13, 1832, Box 1, Pierson Family Papers, LC; Thomas Marshall to Eliza Marshall, February 14, 1835, Marshall Family Papers, William Henry Harrison to Clay, September 20, 1839, *CP*, 9:342; "Reminiscences of Washington" *Atlantic Monthly* 47 (1881): 241; *New York Herald*, March 10, 1848.

53. Job Pierson to Clarissa Pierson, September 17, 1831, Box 1, Pierson Family Papers; *Concord New-Hampshire Patriot*, July 9 and January 2, 1832; *Newport Rhode-Island Republican*, October 2, 1832; *Portsmouth New-Hampshire Gazette*, July 9, 1832; *Portland Maine Eastern Argus*, September 4, 1832; *National Intelligencer*, October 29, 1844.

54. For a sampling of historians' comments, see Sellers, *Market Revolution*, 63; Dangerfield, *Era of Good Feelings*, 10; Remini, *Clay*, 252; Kenneth Williams and Melba Porter Hay, eds., " 'Henry Clay Represents What This Country Is About': A Round Table Discussion with His Biographer and Editors," *Register* 100 (2002): 430.

55. George McDuffie, in *RD*, 19th Cong., 1st Sess. (1825–26); L. Smith to B. W. Smith, May 25, 1844, L. Smith Papers, FHS; Rogers, *True Henry Clay*, 164; Carol Bleser, ed., *Secret and Sacred: The Diaries of James Henry Hammond* . . . (New York: Oxford University Press, 1988), 172; Remini, *Clay*, 252; Margaret Bailey to her sister, June 15 [1850?], UK; Clement Eaton, *Henry Clay and the Art of American Politics* (Boston: Little, Brown, 1957), 59.

56. Rebecca Smith Blodget, ca. October 1828, and Charcila Owings, December 10, 1826, both in *CP*, 7:477–78, 5:986–87, 987n.

57. Eliza Johnston to Clay, July 14, 1828, Josiah Johnston to Clay, July 14, 1828, and Clay to Josiah Johnston, October 5, 1829, all in *CP*, 7: 384–86; 8:110; Williams and Hay, "Clay Round Table," 430–31, 431n; Clay to Mary Bayard, July 17 and June 19, 1848, both in *CP*, 10:509, 494–95; Anthony Kaye, "The Second Slavery: Modernity in the Nineteenth-Century South and the Atlantic World," *JSH* 75 (2009): 648; Clay to Octavia Walton LeVert, n.d. [1844?], and Clay to LeVert, February 28, 1847, both in *CP*, 10:69, 312.

58. Sean Wilentz, *The Rise of American Democracy* (New York: W. W. Norton, 2005), 267; Elizabeth Hanson, "Clay Papers Project Completes Its Final Chapters," *Odyssey: The Magazine of University of Kentucky Research* 9 (Summer 1991): 4.

59. S. Ann Garrett, *Cursory Family Sketches* (Albany, NY, 1870), 89.

60. *Washington National Journal*, September 7, 1831; *Concord New-Hampshire Patriot*, July 9, 1832; Belohlavek, "Clay and the Historians," 490.

Chapter 4

1. T. H. Bennett to Clay, May 19, 1828, *CP*, 7:280–81; *Niles Weekly Register* 15 (September 5, 1818): 32; Carl Hicks, "Henry Clay and His South American Relations" (MA thesis, University of Kentucky, 1955), 65; unidentified clipping, post 1921, Samuel M. Wilson Collection, UK; *Caracas, Venezuela El Nuevo Diario*, August 13, 16, 1927, in "Henry Clay" Vertical Files, KHS.

2. Address to the Public, December 29, 1827, *CP*, 6:1395; Kimberly Shankman, *Compromise and the Constitution: The Political Thought of Henry Clay* (Lanham, MD: Lexington Books, 1999), 2.

3. Halford Hoskins, "The Hispanic American Policy of Henry Clay, 1816–1828," *Hispanic American Historical Review* 7 (1927): 468; William Spencer Robertson, "The Recognition of the Hispanic American Nations by the United States," *Hispanic American Historical Review* 1(1918): 240–45, 250–52, 257; George Herring, *From Colony to Superpower: US Foreign Relations since 1776* (New York: Oxford University Press, 2008), 154.

4. *AC*, 14th Cong., 1st Sess. (1815–16), 724, 2nd Sess. (1816–17), 742; Hicks, "Clay and South America," 7; Speech on Bill for Enforcing Neutrality, and Motion and Speech in Recognition of the Independent Provinces of the River Plata, both in *CP*, 2:291, 512, 514, 530.

5. *AC*, 14th Cong., 2nd Sess. (1816–17), 742, 16th Cong. (1817–18), 1426; River Plata Speech, *CP*, 2:520, 522; George Dangerfield, *The Era of Good Feelings* (New York: Harcourt, Brace, and World, 1952), 271–72; L. H. Butterfield, "The Jubilee of Independence, July 4, 1826," *Virginia Magazine of History and Biography* 61 (1953): 14; *Lexington Kentucky Reporter*, June 14, 1820; *AC*, 16th Cong., 1st Sess. (1819–20), 2224.

6. Adams, *Memoirs*, 4:15, 30–31, 6:224; Robert Forbes, *The Missouri Compromise and Its Aftermath* (Chapel Hill: University of North Carolina Press, 2007), 206–207.

7. Merrill Peterson, *The Great Triumvirate: Webster, Clay, and Calhoun* (New York: Oxford University Press, 1987), 58; Glyndon G. Van Deusen, *The Life of Henry Clay* (Boston: Little, Brown, 1937), 132.

8. *AC*, 18th Cong., 1st Sess. (1823–24), 1174–77, 1173. See also *Charleston Mercury*, February 9, 1824, and *Newport Rhode-Island Republican*, June 19, 1832.

9. Clay's Address to Young Men's National Republican Convention, *New-England Magazine* 3 (1832): 68; *AC*, 15th Cong., 2nd Sess. (1818–19), 361; Speech on the Seminole War, January 20, 1819, *CP*, 2: 659; Larry Klein, "Henry Clay, Nationalist" (PhD diss., University of Kentucky, 1977), 82; *Niles Weekly Register* 36 (April 18, 1829): 125; Calhoun Speech in Support of the Veto Power, February 28, 1842, in *Calhoun Papers*, 16:135.

10. Marc Kruman, "The Second American Party System and the Transformation of Revolutionary Republicanism," *JER* 12 (1992): 510; *RD*, 23rd Cong., 1st Sess. (1833–34), 1480; Shankman, *Compromise and the Constitution*, 42; Seminole War Speech, *CP*, 2:658.

11. *AC*, 16th Cong., 1st Sess. (1819–20), 2041; 12th Cong., 2nd Sess. (1812–13), 666; *RD*, 24th Cong., 1st Sess. (1835–36), 1135; Speech in Senate, July 22, 1850, *CP*, 10:776, 774; Peter Knupfer, *The Union as It Is: Constitutional Unionism and Sectional Compromise, 1787–1861* (Chapel Hill: University of North Carolina Press, 1991), x, xi, 5; Lawrence Kohl, *The Politics of Individualism: Parties and the American Character in the Jacksonian Era* (New York: Oxford University Press, 1989), 84–85; Lonnie Maness, "Henry Clay and the Problem of Slavery" (PhD diss., Memphis State University, 1980), 156.

12. Knupfer, *Union as It Is*, 21.

13. Speech on Tariff, March 30–31, 1824, and Speech in Senate, April 8, 1850, both in *CP*, 3;727, 49n; 10:698.

14. Shankman, *Compromise and the Constitution*, 13; Daniel Feller, *The Jacksonian Promise: America, 1815–1840* (Madison: University of Wisconsin Press, 1995), 72; Theodore Benditt, "Compromising Interests and Principles," in *Compromising in Ethics, Law, and Politics*, ed. J. Roland Pennock and John Chapman (New York: New York University Press, 1979), 26; Speech in Raleigh, NC, April 13, 1844, *CP*, 10:31.

15. Joseph Pearson, "The Whig Promise: The Antebellum Rise of Middle-Class Political Culture" (PhD diss., University of Alabama, 2015), 203; Sarah Bischoff Paulus, "America's Long Eulogy for Compromise: Henry Clay and American Politics, 1854–58," *Journal of the Civil War Era* 4 (2014): 29–31; Martin Golding, "The Nature of Compromise," in Pennock and Chapman, *Compromising in Ethics*, 16; David Zarefsky, "Henry Clay and the Election of 1844: The Limits of a Rhetoric of Compromise," *Rhetoric & Public Affairs* 6 (2003): 80.

16. *New York Times*, November 30, 1964; A. D. Kirwan, *John J. Crittenden: The Struggle for the Union* (Lexington: University of Kentucky Press, 1962), 129; Dangerfield, *Era of Good Feelings*, 312; Joseph Carens, "Compromise and Politics," in Pennock and Chapman, *Compromising in Ethics*, 139; Golding, "Nature of Compromise," 5, 7.

17. *AC*, 15th Cong., 1st Sess. (1817–18), 1166–67, 362–64, 1165, 1362.

18. Schurz, *Clay*, 1:134; Speech on Internal Improvements, March 13, 1818, *CP*, 2:470; *AC*, 18th Cong., 1st Sess. (1823–24), 2001, 1315; 11th Cong., 3rd Sess. (1810–11), 216; *RD*, 22nd Cong., 2nd Sess. (1832–33), 741; Speech on Bill to Recharter the Bank of the United States, February 15, 1811, and Speech on the Bank of the United States, June 3, 1816, both in *CP*, 1:537; 2:202; Major Wilson, *Space, Time, and Freedom: The Quest for Nationality and the Irrepressible Conflict, 1815–1861* (Westport, CT: Greenwood, 1974), 57.

19. *AC*, 15th Cong., 1st Sess. (1817–18), 1362, 1166, 1366, 1167; Speech on Internal Improvements, March 13, 1818, *CP*, 2:473; Speech in Senate, January 24, 1842, *CP*, 9:639; Peterson, *Great Triumvirate*, 315.

20. Review of *Biography of Henry Clay*, *North American Review*, 33 (1831): 385–86; Speech in Senate, June 4, 1840, *CP*, 9:419.

21. "One Last Word before the Election," *United States Magazine and Democratic Review* 15 (1844): 326; "First Word after the Election," *United States Magazine and Democratic Review* 15 (1844), 429; "Henry Clay" review, 378–79; *Portland* (ME) *Eastern Argus*, September 21, 1832; "Pitt" to Clay, June 21, 1816, *CP*, 2:210; *RD*, 19th Cong., 1st Sess. (1825–26), 1955.

22. Carter Goodrich, "National Planning of Internal Improvements," *Political Science Quarterly* 63 (1948): 16–22; Maurice Baxter, *Henry Clay and the American System* (Lexington: University Press of Kentucky, 1995), 27; Dangerfield, *Era of Good Feelings*, 13.

23. *CP*, 2:860n; *AC*, 16th Cong., 1st Sess. (1819–20), 2228, 2041; 18th Cong., 1st Sess. (1823–24), 1997–98, 1040, 1964. Clay would also have nationalized the telegraph, on its invention, by having Congress purchase the rights. See "Henry Clay on Nationalizing the Telegraph," *North American Review* 154 (1892): 382.

24. Colton, *Clay*, 1:149; Peterson, *Great Triumvirate*, 71.

25. *AC*, 18th Cong., 1st Sess. (1823–24), 1027, 1036; 14th Cong., 1st Sess. (1815–16), 427; James Winkler, "Henry Clay: A Current Assessment," *Register* 70 (1972): 180; Remini; *Clay*, 228; Richard McCormick, "The Party Period and Public Policy: An Explanatory Hypothesis," *JAH* 66 (1979): 283–84; Speech on Internal Improvements, March 7, 1818, *CP*, 2:458; *RD*, 18th Cong., 2nd Sess. (1824–1825), 234, 239; Clay to Francis Brooke, August 28, 1823, *CP*, 3:480; Carl Degler, *The Other South: Southern Dissenters in the Nineteenth Century* (New York: Harper and Row, 1974), 106; Stephen Aron, *How the West Was Lost* (Baltimore: Johns Hopkins University Press, 1996), 135; Wilson, *Space, Time, and Freedom*, 63, 53.

26. Heidler and Heidler, *Clay*, 229; "First Word after the Election," 427; *Brooklyn Eagle*, March 15, 1848; Craig Friend, *Along the Maysville Road: The Early American Republic in the Trans-Appalachian West* (Knoxville: University of Tennessee Press, 2005), 22, 261; Kirwan, *Crittenden*, 49.

27. *Macon Georgia Telegraph*, June 18, 1838; Harry Watson, *Liberty and Power: The Politics of Jacksonian America* (New York: Hill and Wang, 1990), 114; *Concord New Hampshire Patriot*, September 2, 1839; Herbert Ershkowitz and William Slade, "Consensus or Conflict? Political Behavior in the State Legislatures during the Jacksonian Era," *JAH* 58 (1971): 61

28. John Larson, "'Bind the Nation Together': The National Union and the Struggle for a System of Internal Improvements," *JAH* 74 (1987): 365; Brooke to Clay, August 14, 1823, *CP*, 3:468–69; *AC*, 18th Cong., 1st Sess. (1823–24), 1308; Forbes, *Missouri Compromise*, 223; Thomas Jefferson to John Holmes, April 22, 1820, in Merrill Peterson, *Thomas Jefferson: Writings* (New York: Viking, 1984), 1434; Matthew Mason, *Slavery and Politics in the Early American Republic* (Chapel Hill: University of North Carolina Press, 2006), 8.

29. Speech on Domestic Manufactures, March 26, 1810, *CP*, 1:459, 461; Kohl, *Politics of Individualism*, 97; Remini, *Clay*, 139; Daniel Walker Howe, *The Political Culture of the American Whigs* (Chicago: University of Chicago Press,1979), 120; Thomas Brown, *Politics and Statesmanship: Essays on the*

American Whig Party (New York: Columbia University Press, 1985), 177–78; F. W. Taussig, *The Tariff History of the United States*, 8th rev. ed. (1892; New York: Capricorn Books, 1964), 68.

30. Taussig, *Tariff History*, 70, 73; *AC*, 18th Cong., 1st Sess. (1823–24), 1560.

31. *AC*, 18th Cong., 1st Sess. (1823–24), 1962, 1988, 1963–64, 1978–80, 1984–85, 1993–94, 1999, 1997, 1978, 2001; Bettie Boyd, "Henry Clay and the Tariff" (MA thesis, University of Kentucky, 1938), 1–5, 31; *An American System for the Protection of American Industry* (Cincinnati, [1824?]).

32. E. Merton Coulter, "The Genesis of Henry Clay's American System," *South Atlantic Quarterly* 25 (1926): 50–51, 54; Theodore Gronert, "Trade in the Blue-Grass Region, 1810–1820," *Mississippi Valley Historical Review* 5 (1918): 315–16; James Hopkins, *A History of the Hemp Industry in Kentucky* (Lexington: University of Kentucky Press, 1951), 67–71, 109; J. D. B. DeBow, *Statistical View of the United States . . . being a Compendium of the Seventh Census* (Washington, DC, 1854), 177; *AC*, 18th Cong., 1st Sess. (1823–24), 1673.

33. Harry Watson, *Andrew Jackson vs. Henry Clay: Democracy and Development in Antebellum America* (Boston: Bedford/St. Martin's, 1998), 46–48; Charles Sellers, *The Market Revolution* (New York: Oxford University Press, 1991), 45–46; Kim Gruenwald, *River of Enterprise: The Commercial Origins of Regional Identity in the Ohio Valley, 1790–1850* (Bloomington: Indiana University Press, 2002), 106–109.

34. Vote as Bank Director, April 5, 1808, *CP*, 1:325, 325n; *AC*, 11th Cong., 3rd Sess. (1810–11), 210, 219, 218, 213, 211–12, 361.

35. Clay to Andrew Broaddus Jr., June 5, 1843, *CP*, 9:825; *RD*, 23rd Cong., 1st Sess. (1833–34), 1590; Speech in Norfolk, April 22, 1844, *CP*, 10:49; *AC*, 14th Cong., 1st Sess. (1815–16), 1193; 18th Cong., 1st Sess. (1823–24), 1312.

36. Emerson, "Self-Reliance," in *Essays: First Series* (1841), www.emersoncentral.com/selfreliance.htm; *AC*, 14th Cong., 1st Sess. (1815–16), 1193, 1190–92; *RD*, 22nd Cong., 1st Sess. (1831–32), 1268; Schurz, *Clay*, 1:133; Prentice, *Clay*, 121.

37. Clay to unknown, March 24, 1816, and "Pitt" to Clay, ca. June 21, 1816, both in *CP*, 2:181, 210.

38. James Atherton to Charles Atherton, January 18, 1832, in Samuel Wilson, "Letters of 1831–'32 about Kentucky," *FCHQ* 16 (1942): 222; Daniel Walker Howe, *What Hath God Wrought: The Transformation of America, 1815–1848* (New York: Oxford University Press, 2007), 564.

39. McCormick, "Party Period," 284; James Klotter, "Two Centuries of the Lottery in Kentucky," *Register* 87 (1987): 422–24.

40. *Kentucky House Journal* (1804), 96; *CP*, 1:162; Report on Ohio Rapids Canal, *CP*, 1:285, 86; Everett Brown, ed., *William Plumer's Memorandum of Proceedings in the United States Senate, 1803–1807* (New York: Macmillan, 1923), 628, 593, 595; Karl Raitz and Nancy O'Malley, "Local-Scale Turnpike Roads in Nineteenth Century Kentucky," *Journal of Historical Geography* 33 (2007): 2.

41. Colton, *Clay*, 1:441; Nelson Nicholas to James Madison, September 2, 1812, in J. C. A. Stagg et al., eds., *Papers of James Madison: Presidential Series*, 8 vols. to date (Charlottesville: University Press of Virginia, 2004), 5:256–57.

42. Raitz and O'Malley, "Local-Scale Turnpike Roads," 3; Gronert, "Trade in the Blue-Grass Region," 317, *AC*, 14th Cong., 1st Sess. (1815–16), 791–92.

43. Stephen Minicuccci, "Internal Improvements and the Union, 1790–1860," *Studies in American Political Development* 18 (2004): 164, 177; Goodrich, "National Planning," 32; Larson, "Bind the Republic Together," 363, 377–78, 365, 380; *AC*, 14th Cong., 2nd Sess. (1816–17), 868, 867.

44. *AC*, 15th Cong., 1st Sess. (1817–18), 1360, 1166-67, 1180, 1170, 1365, 1178; 18th Cong., 1st Sess. (1823–24), 1037, 1027 1030.

45. George Baker, ed., *The Works of William H. Seward*, 3 vols. (New York, 1853), 3:107.

46. Quoted in Peterson, *Great Triumvirate*, 305; Abraham Lincoln, Eulogy on Henry Clay, July 6, 1852, in Roy Basler, ed., *Collected Works of Abraham Lincoln*, 9 vols. (New Brunswick, NJ: Rutgers University Press, 1959), 2:125–26; Mary Follett, "Henry Clay as Speaker of the House," *New England Magazine* 12 (1892): 347; William Barry to daughter, February 22, 1834, in "Letters of William T. Barry," *William and Mary College Quarterly Historical Magazine* 14 (1906): 239.

47. Unidentified clipping, Box 64, Papers of Henry Clay and Family, LC; Thomas Ewing to Maria Ewing, March 7, 1832, June 7, 1834, Box 155, Thomas Ewing Family Papers, LC; J. W. Binckley, "The Leader of the House," *The Galaxy* 1 (1866): 496.

48. Margaret Bailey to sister, June 15, [1850], UK.

49. Peterson, *Great Triumvirate*, 382; Ben Perley Poore, "The Capitol at Washington," *The Century* 25 (1853): 808; George Bancroft, "A Few Words about Henry Clay," *The Century* 30 (1885): 479; Thomas Ewing to John J. Crittenden, May 20, 1848, Box 156, Ewing Family Papers.

Chapter 5

1. *Charleston City Gazette and Commercial Daily Advertiser*, January 16, 1822; *CP*, 3:415n; *Edwardsville (IL) Spectrum*, November 23, 1822; *Boston Daily Advertiser*, December 14, 1822; *Lexington Kentucky Reporter*, January 13, 1823. For a good, concise discussion of the race and the candidates, see James Hopkins, "Election of 1824," in *Presidential Elections*, 1:349–81. Donald Ratcliffe's good and detailed *The One-Party Presidential Contest: Adams, Jackson, and the 1824's Five-Horse Race* (Lawrence: University Press of Kansas, 2015) arrived too late for a full inclusion in the text, but many of the themes in the work had been presented earlier in Ratcliffe articles.

2. Chase Mooney, *William H. Crawford, 1772–1834* (Lexington: University Press of Kentucky, 1974), 78, 91, 211; Schurz, *Clay*, 1:223; Langdon Cheves to Clay, November 9, 1822, *CP*, 3:314; George Robertson to Eleanor Robertson,

November 26, 1817, George Robertson Papers, KHS; George Dangerfield, *The Era of Good Feelings* (New York: Harcourt, Brace, and World, 1952), 104; *The Times and Hartford Advertiser*, July 20, 1824; William Plumer to William Plumer Jr., November 15, 1820, in *The Missouri Compromises and Presidential Politics, 1820–1825*, ed. Everett Brown (St. Louis: Missouri Historical Society, 1926), 56; Adams, *Memoirs*, 4:241. On Crawford's unusual size for the era, he stood between 6'3" and 6'6" and weighed some 275 pounds at the time, according to Clairborne Gooch to Thomas Ritchie, April 24, 1824, Gooch Family Papers, VHS, and Thomas Hubbard to Phebe Hubbard, December 26, 1822, Thomas Hubbard Papers, LC.

3. Mooney, *Crawford*, 1–3, 10–11, 236; Clay to Charles Tait, August 19, 1814, and Clay to John Sloan, October 28, 1822, both in *CP*, Supp.:37, 121; A. D. Kirwan, "Congress Elects a President: Henry Clay and the Campaign of 1824," *Kentucky Review* 4 (1983): 8; William Shade, *Democratizing the Old Dominion: Virginia and the Second Party System, 1824–1861* (Charlottesville: University Press of Virginia, 1996), 84–85.

4. *The Times and Hartford Advertiser*, September 23 and October 28, 1823; Auburn Wells, "Henry Clay and the Bargain and Corruption Incident . . . " (MA thesis, University of Kentucky, 1935), 22; Mooney, *Crawford*, 241; Gaillard Hunt, ed., *The First Forty Years of Washington Society* (New York: Charles Scribner's Sons, 1906), 162, 172; Clay to William Creighton Jr., January 1, 1824, *CP*, Supp.:166; Adams, *Memoirs*, 6:265.

5. Clay to George Featherstonhaugh, May 26, 1824, Clay to Francis Brooke, May 28, 1824, and Josiah Johnston to Clay, September 11 and August 9, 1824, all in *CP*, Supp.:176; 3:767, 837, 808; Adams, *Memoirs*, 6:428, 395; Brown, *Missouri Compromises*, 108; Clairborne Gooch to Thomas Ritchie, April 24, 1824, Gooch Family Papers; Albert Ray Newsome, *The Presidential Election of 1824 in North Carolina* (Chapel Hill: University of North Carolina Press, 1939), 109.

6. Kirwan, "Congress Elects a President," 11–12; *Charleston Mercury* February 28 and 16, 1824; Adams, *Memoirs*, 6:240; *The Times and Hartford Advertiser*, September 9, 1823.

7. David F. Musto, "The Youth of John Quincy Adams," *Proceedings of the American Philosophical Society* 113 (1969): 269; *The Times and Hartford Advertiser*, October 7 and September 9, 1823; "Patrick Henry" to Clay, April 21, 1822, *CP*, 3:196; Daniel Walker Howe, *The Political Culture of the American Whigs* (Chicago: University of Chicago Press, 1979), 44; *Charleston Mercury*, February 6, 1824; *RD*, 19th Cong., 1st Sess. (1825–26), 1989; Henry Shaw to Clay, April 4, 1822, *CP*, 3: 185; Dangerfield, *Era of Good Feelings*, 7.

8. William Freehling, *The Road to Disunion: Secessionists at Bay, 1776–1854* (New York: Oxford University Press, 1990), 342; Glyndon G. Van Deusen, *The Life of Henry Clay* (Boston: Little, Brown, 1937), 171; Brown, *Missouri Compromises*, 64; Schurz, *Clay*, 1:103; Remini, *Clay*, 109; George Prentice, *Biography of Henry Clay* (Hartford, CT, 1831), 255; Daniel Walker Howe, *What*

Hath God Wrought: The Transformation of America, 1815–1848 (New York: Oxford University Press, 2007), 245; Mary Hargreaves, *The Presidency of John Quincy Adams* (Lawrence: University Press of Kansas, 1985), 22; Sean Wilentz, *The Rise of American Democracy: Jefferson to Lincoln* (New York: W. W. Norton, 2005), 257; Howe, *Political Culture*, 45.

9. Adams, *Memoirs*, 5:58; Ratcliffe, *One-Party Contest*, 72–79, 216–23.

10. Ratcliffe, *One-Party Contest*, 36–40. See, for example, John T. W. Walworth, February 22, 1824, John Telemachus Johnson Misc. Papers, FHS; *Niles Weekly Register* 26 (March 27, 1824): 50.

11. *Boston Commercial Gazette*, October 25, 1824.

12. *Lexington Kentucky Reporter*, February 10, 1823; Clay to Peter Porter, April 14, 1822, Clay to Return Jonathan Meigs, June 8, 1822, Clay to Thomas Dougherty, December 7, 1821, Clay to William Creighton Jr., April 12, 1822, Clay to Francis Brooke, January 31, 1823, and Clay to Peter Porter, March 18, 1823, all in *CP*, 3:191, 226, 145, 359, 401, and Supp.:106; *Village Record*, in *Arkansas Gazette*, June 17, 1823; John Johnson to R. W. Walworth, February 22, 1824, Johnson Papers; *Philadelphia Aurora*, in *Lexington Kentucky Reporter*, June 30, 1823.

13. Samuel Overton to Andrew Jackson, August 1, 1822, and Jackson to Andrew Jackson Donelson, May 2, 1822, both in *Jackson Papers*, 5:178; John Overton to Clay, January 16, 1822, and Andrew Hynes to Clay, June 30, 1822, both in *CP*, 3:156, 243; Supp.:116n.

14. Remini, *Clay*, 213; Van Deusen, *Clay*, 168; Clement Eaton, *Henry Clay and the Art of American Politics* (Boston: Little, Brown, 1957), 49; Clay to Return Jonathan Meigs, August 21, 1822, *CP*, Supp.:117; Calhoun to Ninian Edwards, August 20, 1822, *Calhoun Papers*, 9:249; Clay to Peter Porter, October 22 and August 10 1822, and Clay to Adam Beatty, July 6, 1823, all in *CP*, 3:300, 274; Supp.:146; *RD*, 19th Cong., 1st Sess. (1825–26), 1990.

15. *AC*, 15th Cong., 2nd Sess. (1818–19), 631.

16. "Philo Jackson," *The Presidential Election . . .* (Frankfort, KY, 1823), 14, 16; Wilentz, *American Democracy*, 169; Jon Meacham, *American Lion: Andrew Jackson in the White House* (New York: Random House, 2008), xx; John Marszalek, *The Petticoat Affair* (New York: Free Press, 1997), 7–8; Andrew Burstein, *The Passions of Andrew Jackson* (New York: Alfred A. Knopf, 2003), 241–48: Van Deusen, *Clay*, 168; Kirwan, "Congress Elects a President," 10; William Anderson to Jackson, October 24, 1828, *Jackson Papers*, 6:519; Adams, *Memoirs*, 7:383; Clay to Richard Wilde, April 27, 1833, *CP*, 8:640; Jefferson quoted in Howe, *What Hath God Wrought*, 205.

17. Frances Dugan and Jacqueline Bull, eds., *Bluegrass Craftsman: Being the Reminiscences of Ebenezer Hiram Stedman, Papermaker 1808–1885* (1959; Lexington: University of Kentucky Press, 2006), 71; Wilentz, *American Democracy*, 169, 301, 248; Marszalek, *Petticoat Affair*, 102; William Barry to James Harrison, May 20, 1831, Box 11, Papers of James O. Harrison, LC; William Barry to daughter, February 22, 1834, "Letters of William T. Barry," *William and Mary College Quarterly Historical Magazine* 14

(1906): 239; Robert Remini, *The Election of Andrew Jackson* (Philadelphia: J. B. Lippincott, 1963), 67; Hargreaves, *Presidency of Adams*, 20; Dangerfield, *Era of Good Feelings*, 122–24; Burstein, *Passions of Jackson*, 54, 235.

18. Speech on the Direct Tax, January 29, 1816, and Resolution Concerning Military Academy, March 10, 1820, both in *CP*, 2:157, 794; *AC*, 14th Cong., 1st Sess. (1815–16), 783; 12th Cong., 1st Sess. (1811–12), 598; 18th Cong., 1st Sess. (1823–24), 1971.

19. Jackson to William Fulton, December 21, 1823, *Jackson Papers*, 5:329; Speech on the Non-Intercourse Act, February 22, 1810, and Speech on Bill to Raise an Additional Military Force, December 31, 1811, both in *CP*, 1:450, 605.

20. Daniel Richter, *Facing East from Indian Country: A Native History of Early America* (Cambridge, MA: Harvard University Press, 2001), 232–33; Howe, *What Hath God Wrought*, 75, 70, 100–107. See also Matthew Warshauer, *Andrew Jackson and the Politics of Martial Law* (Knoxville: University of Tennesse Press, 2006).

21. Remini, *Clay*, 166; Edwin A. Miles, "The Whig Party and the Menace of Caesar," *Tennessee Historical Quarterly* 27 (1968): 364; *AC*, 15th Cong., 2nd Sess. (1818–19), 634, 633, 637–38, and *CP*, 2:636–60.

22. *AC*, 15th Cong., 2nd Sess. (1818–19), 641, 648, 645, 653–55; Adams, *Memoirs*, 6:501.

23. Harry Watson, *Andrew Jackson vs. Henry Clay: Democracy and Development in Antebellum America* (Boston: Bedford/St. Martin's, 1998), 55; Clay to Josiah Johnston, October 6, 1827, CP, 6:1115; Clay to Charles Hammond, October 30, 1827, and Clay to Peter Porter, [December] 1823, both in *CP*, 6:1203, 3:535.

24. Wilentz, *American Democracy*, 248; Daniel Feller, *The Jacksonian Promise: America, 1815–1840* (Baltimore: Johns Hopkins University Press, 1995), 74; Watson, *Jackson vs. Clay*, 38; Lynn Parsons, *The Birth of Modern Politics* (New York: Oxford University Press, 2009), 93, 195.

25. Samuel Orth, *Five American Politicians* (Cleveland, OH: Burrows Brothers, 1906), 190.

26. Marszalek, *Petticoat Affair*, 14; Robert Hay, "The Case for Andrew Jackson in 1824: Eaton's *Wyoming Letters*," *Tennessee Historical Quarterly* 29 (1970): 140–50; Richard John, "Affairs of State: The Executive Departments, the Election of 1828, and the Making of the Democratic Party," in Meg Jacobs, William Novak, and Julian Zelizer, eds., *The Democratic Experiment: New Directions in America Political History* (Princeton, NJ: Princeton University Press, 2003), 58; Richard Latner, "A New Look at Jacksonian Politics," *JAH* 61 (1975): 946.

27. Kim Phillips, "The Pennsylvania Origins of the Jackson Movement," *Political Science Quarterly* 91 (1976): 495, 499, 501, 508; "Jackson," in *Presidential Elections*, 15; Harry Laver, *Citizens More Than Soldiers: The Kentucky Militia and Society in the Early Republic* (Lincoln: University of Nebraska Press, 2007), 80–88; Edward Pessen, *Jacksonian America: Society, Personality, and Politics* (Homewood, IL: Dorsey, 1969), 209; Latner, "New Look," 946; *RD*,

19th Cong. 1st Sess. (1825–26), 1990. See also *St. Louis Enquirer*, May 3, 1823; *Lexington Kentucky Gazette*, October 29 and November 13, 1823.

28. Peter Knupfer, *The Union as It Is: Constitutional Unionism and Sectional Compromise, 1787–1861* (Chapel Hill: University of North Carolina Press, 1991), 137; E. D. Mansfield, *Personal Memories . . . 1803–1843* (Cincinnati, OH, 1879), 203; Charles Sellers, *The Market Revolution: Jacksonian America, 1815–1846* (New York: Oxford University Press, 1991), 107, Michael Holt *The Rise and Fall of the American Whig Party* (New York: Oxford University Press, 1999), 8; Ronald Formisano, *The Transformation of Political Culture: Massachusetts Parties, 1790s–1840s* (New York: Oxford University Press, 1983), 33; Frank Mathias and Jasper Shannon, "Gubernatorial Politics in Kentucky, 1820–1851," *Register* 88 (1990): 249; Kimberly Shankman, *Compromise and the Constitution: The Political Thought of Henry Clay* (Lanham, MD: Lexington Books, 1999), 85. By 1824, six states also chose presidential electors by a district vote, so in those states, a divided count could result. For a good discussion of the evolution of the electorate, see Donald Ratcliffe, "The Right to Vote and the Rise of Democracy, 1787–1828," *JER* 33 (2013): 219–54, and his "Popular Preferences in the Presidential Election of 1824," *JER* 34 (2014): 45–77.

29. Kirwan, "Congress Elects a President," 13; Stephen Minicucci, "Internal Improvements and the Union, 1790–1860," *Studies in America Political Development* 18 (2004): 165n; *Petersburg Republican*, quoted in Paul C. Nagel, "The Election of 1824: A Reconsideration Based on Newspaper Opinion," *JSH* 26 (1960): 319–20; Clay to Josiah Johnson, September 3, 1824, *CP*, 3:827.

30. David Hackett Fischer and James Kelly, *Bound Away: Virginia and the Westward Movement* (Charlottesville: University Press of Virginia, 2000), 202–203, 284; Harry Ammon, "The Richmond Junto, 1800–1824," *Virginia Historical Magazine* 61 (1953): 395, 399, 407–408, 417; George Sheppard to Andrew Stephenson [*sic*], April 20, 1824, Stevenson Family Papers, LC.

31. Wilentz, *American Democracy*, 851n; John Sloan to Clay, October 16, 1822, *CP*, 3:294; Ratcliffe, "Ohio, 1824," 851; Thomas Reed to Clay, September 5, 1822, Gabriel Johnston to Clay, May 27, 1823, and Josiah Johnston to Clay, August 19, 1824, all in *CP*, 3:284, 423, 816; *Lexington Reporter*, February 25, 1822; Nagel, "Election of 1824," 324, 321, 317.

32. "Life of Henry Clay," *North American Review* 33 (1831): 392; "Representative Men, Part I," *Southern Literary Messenger* 19 (1853): 529; *Richmond Enquirer*, in *Kentucky Gazette*, March 13, 1823; Langdon Cheves to Clay, November 9, 1822, Clay to Peter Porter, December 7, 1824, and Clay to George Featherstonhaugh, December 9, 1824, all in CP, 3:314, 892; Supp.:182–83; *Providence Gazette*, November 3, 1824; Hargreaves, *Presidency of Adams*, 21. It should be noted that in the West, Clay did have numerous advantages, in contrast to the East. See Donald Ratcliffe, "The Role of Voters and Issues in Party Formation: Ohio, 1824," *JAH* 59 (1973): 861.

33. Adams, *Memoirs*, 5:304; Langdon Cheves to Clay, November 9, 1822, *CP*, 3:314; *Lexington Kentucky Reporter*, April 21, 1823. See also *Kentucky Gazette*, April 24, 1823.

34. John McKinley to Clay, June 3, 1823, and Benton to Clay, July 23, 1823, both in *CP*, 3:427, 460.

35. Thomas Wharton to Clay, August 13, 1823, John McKinley to Clay, September 29, 1823, and Clay to Benjamin Leigh, October 20, 1823, all in *CP*, 3:466–67, 490–91, 501.

36. William Plumer Jr. to William Plumer, December 3, 1823, in Brown, *Missouri Compromises*, 84–85; Clay to James Erwin, December 29, 1823, and January 7, 1824, Clay to Francis Brooke, January 22, 1824, Clay to Peter Porter, January 31, 1824, Clay to Richard Bache, February 17, 1824, Clay to Charles Hammond, February 22, 1824, Clay to Josephus Stuart, December 19, 1823, and March 24, 1824, all in *CP*, Supp.:164–68; 3:603, 630, 645, 654, 545, 676.

37. Clay to Peter Porter, April 26, 1824, *CP*, 3:743; Adams, *Memoirs*, 6:417; Clay to Francis Blair, February 29, 1824, *CP*, Supp.:171.

38. *Alexandria (VA) Herald*, October 18 and 25, 1822; *The Times and Hartford Advertiser*, December 2, 1823.

39. Clay to Peter Porter, February 3, 1823, *CP*, 3:364; Andrew Jackson to John Coffee, January 10 and April 28, 1823, and April 17, 1824, *Jackson Papers*, 5:234, 273, 395–96; Clay to Peter Porter, June 15, 1823, *CP*, 3:432; Adams, *Memoirs*, 6:265, 264, 241; William Plumer Jr. to William Plumer, February 5, 1824, in Brown, *Missouri Compromises*, 96; Ratcliffe, *One-Party Contest*, 196; Donald Cole, *Martin Van Buren and the American Political System* (Princeton, NJ: Princeton University Press, 1984), 124; Clay to Josiah Johnston, September 3 and 10, 1824, Johnston to Clay, October 20, 1824, and Clay to Charles Hammond, October 25, 1824, all in *CP*, 3:826, 832–33, 869, 870–71.

40. Adams, *Memoirs*, 5:326.

41. Clay to Josephus Stuart, March 24, 1824, Clay to Francis Brooke, March 16, 1824, and from Josiah Johnston, September 22, 1824, all in *CP*, 3:676, 674, 845; *Haverhill (MA) Gazette*, October 30, 1824; Epes Sargent, *Life and Public Service of Henry Clay*, ed. Horace Greeley (Auburn, NY, 1852), 102; Clay to George Featherstonhaugh, December 9, 1824, *CP*, Supp.:182–83.

42. Clay to Charles Hammond, October 25, 1824, *CP*, 3:870; Ratcliffe, "Popular Preferences in 1824," 65, 54–64; Dangerfield, *Era of Good Feelings*, 336. For election statistics, as referenced throughout, see *Congressional Quarterly's Guide to US Elections*, 4th ed. (Washington, DC: CQ Press, 2001), 1:644. The *Guide* numbers are taken from the Historical Archive of the Inter-University Consortium for Political Research, but for a critique of that source, see Ratcliffe, "Popular Preferences in 1824," 53, 54n. Using a variety of sources, Ratcliffe, 55–66, formulated somewhat different vote totals for most of the states.

43. Ratcliffe, "Ohio, 1824," 848–63; Ratcliffe, "Popular Preferences in 1824," 55, 63. See also Anthony Gene Carey, *Parties, Slavery, and the Union in Antebellum Georgia* (Athens: University of Georgia Press, 1997), 22.

44. Clay to Francis Brooke, November 26, 1824, Box 37, Papers of Henry Clay and Family, LC.

45. Adam Beatty to Clay, April 17, 1822, *CP*, 3:193; William Creighton to Clay, May 1822, *CP*, 3:205; Richard M. Johnson to John J. Crittenden, March 7, 1824, in "The Letters of Richard M. Johnson of Kentucky," *Register* 39 (1941), ed. James Padget, 187; Peter Porter to Clay, May 26, 1823, Clay to Charles Hammond, August 21, 1823, and Josiah Johnston to Clay, June 27, 1824, all in *CP*, 3:421, 472, 787. For more on Porter, see Daniel Dean Roland, "Peter Buell Porter and Self-Interest in American Politics" (PhD diss., Claremont Graduate School, 1990), and Papers of Peter B. Porter, Buffalo and Erie County Historical Society.

46. Clay to Peter Porter, September 2, 1824, and Porter to Clay, October 6, 1824, both in *CP*, 3:825, 860.

47. Dangerfield, *Era of Good Feeling*, 334–35; Martin Van Buren, *Autobiography* (Washington, DC: Government Printing Office, 1920), 145; Cole, *Van Buren*, 135–37; Porter to Clay, January 14, 1825, *CP*, 4:17; Wilentz, *American Democracy*, 250; Ratcliffe, *One-Party Contest*, 224–27.

48. James Swain, *The Life and Speeches of Henry Clay* (New York, 1844), 1:133; Sargent, *Clay*, 106n, 196; Heidler and Heidler, *Clay*, 170–74.

49. John Sacher, *A Perfect War of Politics: Parties, Politicians, and Democracy in Louisiana 1824–1861* (Baton Rouge: Louisiana State University Press, 2003), 15–18; Thomas Robertson to Clay, July 5, 1822, *CP*, 3:249; *Baltimore Patriot*, April 11, 1823; Clay to Francis Brooke, February 26, 1823, Clay to Peter Porter, April 26, 1824, Clay to Josiah Johnston, August 31, 1824, and Clay to George Featherstonhaugh, October 10, 1824, all in *CP*, 3:387, 743, 821; Supp.:180.

50. Clay to Josephus Stuart, December 6, 1824, *CP*, 3:891; David Ker to Jackson, November 23, 1824, *Jackson Papers*, 5:450; Clay to George Featherstonhaugh, December 9, 1824, and Clay to Peter Porter, December 26, 1824, both in *CP*, Supp.:183; 3:904; Adams, *Memoirs*, 6:446.

51. Clay to Francis Brooke, December 22, 1824, *CP*, 3:900; also in Clay Family Papers, LC.

52. Clay to Peter Porter, December 26, 1824, and Clay to James Brown, January 23, 1825, both in *CP*, 3:904; 4:38; Colton, *Clay*, 1:291; Sargent, *Clay*, 196; Orth, *Five American Politicians*, 196; Sacher, *Perfect War*, 20–21.

Chapter 6

1. Everett Brown, ed., *William Plumer's Memorandum of Proceedings in the United States Senate, 1803–1807* (New York: Macmillan, 1923), 37, 41–43; Thomas Metcalfe to Robert Poage, February 8, 1823, UK; Auburn Wells, "Henry Clay and the Bargain and Corruption Incident" (MA thesis, University of Kentucky, 1935), 54; Clay to Benjamin Leigh, December 22, 1824, *CP*, 3:901; Willie Mangum to Duncan Cameron, January 10, 1825, in *Mangum Papers*, 1:173; William Plumer Jr. to William Plumer,

December 16, 1824, in *The Missouri Compromises and Presidential Politics, 1820–1825,* ed. Everett Brown (St. Louis: Missouri Historical Society, 1926), 123.

2. David Feller, *The Jacksonian Promise: America, 1815–1840* (Baltimore: Johns Hopkins University Press, 1995), 1; *RD,* 18th Cong., 2nd Sess. (1824–25), 4; Address to Lafayette, December 10, 1824, and Clay to James Brown, January 23, 1825, both in *CP,* 3:894, 894n; 4:39. For Clay-Lafayette letters, see *CP,* 2:112; 3:311; 4:893, 905; 5:202, 283, 400; 6:872; 7:520; 8:7. On Lafayette's visit to the Clay estate, see J. Winston Coleman Jr., *Lafayette's Visit to Lexington* (Lexington, KY: Winburn Press, 1969), 5–16.

3. James Heaton to Charles Morrell, March 2, 1825, Papers of James Heaton, LC; Clay to Francis Blair, January 8, [1825], *CP,* 4:9.

4. Louis McLane to Kitty McLane, January 13, 1825, Box 1, Papers of Louis McLane, LC.

5. Willie Mangum to Duncan Cameron, January 10, 1825, *Mangum Papers,* 1:174; Buchanan to Thomas Elder, January 2, 1825, in *Works of Buchanan,* 1:120; Clay to George Featherstonhaugh, January 21, 1825, and Clay to Francis Brooke, January 28, 1825, both in *CP,* 4:34, 45–46; *CG,* 26th Cong., 1st Sess. (1839–40), 97.

6. Clay to Charles Hammond, October 30, 1827; Address to the People of the Congressional District, March 26, 1825, William Plumer Jr. to Clay, January 8, 1828, Clay to George McClure, December 28, 1824, Clay to Francis Brooke, January 28, 1825, Clay to George Featherstonhaugh, January 21, 1825, Clay to Francis Blair, [January 8, 1825], and January 29, 1825, all in *CP,* 6:1204; 4:152–53; 7:19; 3:906; 4:45–46, 34, 10, 47.

7. Harrison Munday to Clay, July 24, 1827; Address to Congressional District, *CP,* 7:817, 4:161.

8. Claiborne Gooch to Thomas Ritchie, April 24, 1824, Gooch Family Papers, VHS.

9. For examples of letters telling of Clay's early support of Adams, see Colton, *Clay,* 1:381–82, 388; James Davidson to Clay, October 20, 1827, *CP,* 6:1172; Thomas Hart Benton, *Thirty Years View,* 2 vols. (New York, 1854–55), 1:48; Crittenden to Clay, September 3, 1827, Charles Todd to Clay, January 16 and February 18, 1828, Lafayette to Clay, October 10, 1827, James Barbour to Clay, August 14, 1827, Josiah Johnston to Clay, November 17, 1827, Dominique Bouligny to Clay, December 8, 1827, and Clay to George McClure, December 28, 1824, all in *CP,* 6:992; 7:43–44, 105–106; 6:1133–34, 900, 1274–77, 1346–47; 3:906.

10. Adams, *Memoirs,* 6:446–47, 452, 455; Will Gilliam Jr., "Robert Perkins Letcher, Whig Governor of Kentucky," *FCHQ* 24 (1950): 6.

11. Adams, *Memoirs,* 6:457, 464–65; Clay to Blair, January 8, 1825, and Clay to Adams, January 9, 1825, both in *CP,* 4:9–11; George Dangerfield, *The Era of Good Feelings* (New York: Harcourt, Brace, and World, 1952), 339. See also Kristofer Ray, "The Corrupt Bargain and the Rise of the Jacksonian

Movement, 1825–1828," in Brian McKnight and James Humphreys, eds., *The Age of Andrew Jackson* (Kent, OH: Kent State University Press, 2011), 28–29.

12. William Plumer Jr. to William Plumer, January 11, 1825, in Brown, *Missouri Compromises*, 131; *Kentucky Acts* (1824–25), 279; Louis McLane to Kitty McLane, January 13, 1825, Box 1, McLane Papers; Adams, *Memoirs*, 6:446, 455; Amos Kendall to Clay, December 22, 1824, *CP*, 3:902.

13. *AC*, 14th Cong., 1st Sess. (1815–16), 1190; Campaign Speech at Sandersville, July 2, 1816, *CP*, 2:216–17.

14. Mary Hargreaves, *The Presidency of John Quincy Adams* (Lawrence: University Press of Kansas, 1985), 46; *Boston Commercial Gazette*, February 3, 1825; *Nashville Republican*, in *New Haven Connecticut Herald*, February 8, 1825; *Boston Patriot*, February 5, 1825.

15. William Plumer Jr. to William Plumer, January 24, 1825, in Brown, *Missouri Compromises*, 134–35; *Portland* (ME) *Eastern Argus*, February 7, 1825; Adams, *Memoirs*, 6:478, 485; Louis McLane to Kitty McLane, January 17 and February 6, 1825, in Box 1, McLane Papers.

16. Jackson to Andrew Jackson Donelson, April 17, 1824; David Corbin Ker to Jackson, November 23, 1824, Jackson to Chandler Price, January 9, 1825, and Jackson to Berkeley Lewis, December 27, 1824, January 24 and 29, 1825, all in *Jackson Papers*, 5:396, 450; 6:11; 5:459; 6:20–23; John Sacher, *A Perfect War of Politics: Parties, Politicians, and Democracy in Louisiana, 1824–1861* (Baton Rouge: Louisiana State University Press, 2003), 21.

17. Colton, *Clay*, 1:353; Andrew Jackson to the Public, July 18, 1827, and Jackson to Carter Beverly, June 5, 1827, both in *Jackson Papers*, 6:363, 331; *New York Times*, June 9, 1856.

18. James Buchanan to the Editor of the Lancaster Journal, August 8, 1827, in Colton, *Clay*, 1:352–55; Buchanan to Andrew Jackson, August 10, 1827, *Jackson Papers*, 6:374; *New York Times*, July 10 and June 9, 1856; *Louisville Times*, in *Dallas Weekly Herald*, August 9, 1856; *Louisville Journal*, July 21, 1856; Robert Letcher to John J. Crittenden, December 8, 1842, in Coleman, *Crittenden*, 1:195; James Buchanan to Robert Letcher, June 27, 1844, and Buchanan to W. B. Reed, September 8 and July 7, 1856, both in *Works of Buchanan*, 6:59–60; 10:85–86, 911.

19. Andrew Jackson to William Lewis, September 1, 1827, and Jackson to Amos Kendall, September 4, 1827, both in *Jackson Papers*, 6: 387–88; Jackson to William Lewis, February 28, 1845, and Jackson to D. G. Goodlet, March 12, 1844, both in *Jackson Correspondence*, 6:375, 273.

20. Stenberg, "Jackson, Buchanan," 65; *Columbian Observer*, in *Richmond Enquirer*, February 3, 1825.

21. Edward Ayers, *Vengeance and Justice: Crime and Punishment in the 19th Century American South* (New York: Oxford University Press, 1984), 11, 16; *National Intelligencer*, in *Richmond Enquirer*, February 3, 1825. A report would go out, in fact, that Clay had been killed in a duel with his accuser. See, for example, *Concord (NH) Patriot*, February 14, 1825.

22. *Salem (MA) Gazette*, February 15, 1825; *The Calumny Refuted . . .* (n.p., 1828?), 9; Adams, *Memoirs*, 6:497; Clay to John Eaton, March 30 and April 1, 1825, Eaton to Clay, March 28 and 31, April 2, 1825, all in *CP*, 4:196, 201–202, 191–92, 198–200, 207–208. An early Clay biographer said that Eaton had written the letter, but others have noted the possible role of Samuel Ingham. See Joseph Rogers, *The True Henry Clay* (Philadephia: J. B. Lippincott, 1904), 131; James Parton, *Life of Andrew Jackson* (New York, 1860), 3:102–20; and Sean Wilentz, *The Rise of American Democracy* (New York: W. W. Norton, 2005), 852n, 862n.

23. Clay Appeal to the House, February 3, 1825, *CP*, 4:52; Frederick Jackson Turner, *Rise of the New West, 1819–1829* (1906; New York: Collier Books, 1962), 187; *Report of the Committee to whom was referred the Communication of the Speaker . . .* , House Report 64, 18th Cong., 2nd Sess. (1825), 1–5; Albany Argus, *The Coalition of 1825 . . .* (Albany, NY, 1844), 11; *Salem* (MA) *Gazette*, February 15, 1825; *Kentucky Reporter*, July 18, 1827; *CP*, 6:770.

24. *The Times and Hartford Advertiser*, February 10, 1825; *Richmond Enquirer*, February 22, 1825; *Coalition of 1825*, 8; Clay to Francis Blair, January 29, 1825, *CP*, 4:47; Clay to Blair, February 4, 182, Box 37, Papers of Henry Clay and Family, LC.

25. Adams, *Memoirs*, 6:475–76; Gaillard Hunt, ed., *The First Forty Years of Washington Society* (New York: Charles Scribner's Sons, 1906), 185; Hargreaves, *Presidency of Adams*, 39; Clay to Daniel Cook, March 12, 1827, *CP*, 6:295; *Macon* (GA) *Weekly Telegraph*, June 25, 1844; Donald Ratcliffe, *The One-Party Presidential Contest: Adams, Jackson, and the 1824's Five-Horse Race* (Lawrence: University Press of Kansas, 2015), 244–45. It should be noted that Missouri congressman Scott had previously been involved in a land transaction with Clay. See *CP*, 2:579n.

26. Hunt, *Forty Years*, 186; Louis McLane to Kitty McLane, February 5, 1825, Box 1, McLane Papers; Adams, *Memoirs*, 6:476; John Eaton to John Overton, February 7, 1825, *Jackson Papers*, 6:27.

27. *Salem (MA) Gazette*, February 8, 1825; Martin Van Buren, *Autobiography* (Washington, DC: Government Printing Office, 1920) 2:152; Ratcliffe, *One Party Contest*, 2; Robert Pierce Forbes, *The Missouri Compromise and Its Aftermath* (Chapel Hill: University of North Carolina Press, 2007), 327n; Henry Warfield to Clay, May 30, 1822, *CP*, 3:210–11; Louis McLane to Kitty McLane, February 9 and 11, 1825, Box 1, McLane Papers; Daniel Walker Howe, *What Hath God Wrought* (New York: Oxford University Press, 2007), 240; Hunt, *Forty Years*, 195; *Salem (MA) Gazette*, January 28, 1825.

28. Adams, *Memoirs*, 6:508–509.

29. Clay to Francis Brooke, January 31, 1823, and Clay to Michah Taul, June 7, 1825, both in *CP*, 3:359; 4:418; A. D. Kirwan, "Congress Elects a President: Henry Clay and the Campaign of 1824," *Kentucky Review* 4 (1983): 22; Robert Seager II, "Henry Clay and the Politics of Compromise

and Non-Compromise," *Register* 85 (1987): 10; William Plumer Jr. to William Plumer, February 16, 1824, in Brown, *Missouri Compromises*, 101.

30. Clay to Francis Brooke, February 14 and 18, 1825, John J. Crittenden to Clay, February 15, 1825, William Creighton Jr. to Clay, February 19, 1825, Amos Kendall to Clay, March 7, 1825, Clay to Charles Hammond, April 4, 1825, and Clay to George Featherstonhaugh, February 26, 1825, all in *CP*, 4:67, 74, 68, 76, 91, 211, 83; Louis McLane to Kitty McLane, February 14, 1825, Box 1, McLane Papers; William Plumer Jr. to William Plumer, February 16, 1825, in Brown, *Missouri Compromises*, 140; Commission as Secretary of State, March 7, 1825, *CP*, 4:90, 90n; Adams, *Memoirs*, 6:515, 525.

31. "Introduction," *Jackson Papers*, 6:xxix; Hargreaves, *Presidency of Adams*, 45, 248; Speech in Senate, February 19, 1838, *CP*, 9:146; "Representative Men, Part I," *Southern Literary Messenger* 19 (1853): 529; "Life of Henry Clay," *Henry Clay Almanac . . . 1844* (New York, 1844), 24; Forbes, *Missouri Compromise*, 189–90; William Nowell to J. B. Harrison, May 30, 1824, Box 1, Burton N. Harrison Papers, LC.

32. Henry Foote, *Casket of Reminiscences* (1874; repr., New York: Negro Universities Press, 1968), 5; "Introduction," *Jackson Papers*, 6:xiii; *Washington Gazette*, in Harry Watson, *Andrew Jackson vs. Henry Clay: Democracy and Development in Antebellum America* (Boston: Bedford/St. Martin's, 1998), 161; *RD*, 19th Cong., 1st Sess. (1825–26), 1953–1954. See also *New-Bedford* (MA) *Mercury*, February 18, 1825.

33. Jeptha Garrigus to Clay, January 8, 1828, and Address to the People, March 26, 1825, both in *CP*, 7:17, 4:163. Donald Ratcliffe, "Popular Preferences in the Presidential Election of 1824," *JER* 34 (2014): 67–74, using the candidates' legislative vote percentages, has suggested that those states' votes would have been 92,000 for Adams, 91,000 for Crawford, 51,000 for Clay, and only 34,000 for Jackson. Combining those estimates with the actual vote would give Adams a plurality and almost a majority.

34. Wells, "Clay and Corruption," 87–88; Andrew Jackson to Berkeley Lewis, February 15, 1825, *Jackson Papers*, 6:29–30; "Representative Men, Part I," 525.

35. "Representative Men, Part I," 525; *RD*, 19th Cong., 1st Sess. (1825–26), 1958.

36. Clay to William Blackford, August 24, 1827, and Charles Hammond to Clay, October 29, 1827, both in *CP*, 6:957, 1199.

37. William Henry Smith, *Charles Hammond and His Relations to Henry Clay and John Quincy Adams* (Chicago, 1885), 39; Epes Sargent, *Life and Public Service of Henry Clay*, ed. Horace Greeley (Auburn, NY, 1852), 103; Bertram Wyatt-Brown, *The Shaping of Southern Culture: Honor, Grace, and War, 1760s–1880s* (Chapel Hill: University of North Carolina Press, 2004), 70.

38. Colton, *Clay*, 1:343.

39. Clay to Maurice Langhorne, May 23, 1825, Speech at Louisville, July 9, 1825, Speech at Lexington, July 13, 1827, and David Ogden to Clay, January 8, 1828, all in *CP*, 4: 389, 521; 6:776; 7:18; Andrew Jackson to Samuel

Swartwout, February 22, 1825, *Jackson Papers*, 6:41–42, 86; Address to the People of the Congressional District, March 26, 1825, *CP*, 4:163.

40. Address to the People of the Congressional District, March 26, 1825, *CP*, 4:145, 154, 152, 161, 155–57, 163. See also Clay, *To the People of the Congressional District . . .* (n.p., [1825]), 2–13 and *Lexington Kentucky Reporter*, April 11, 1825.

41. Lewis Cass to Clay, April 14, 1825, Clay to John Sloan, April 7, 1825, Clay to Fielding Turner, April 28, 1825, Daniel Breck to Clay, June 13, 1825, and Toast at Maysville Banquet, May 24, 1825, all in *CP*, 4:257, 226–27, 301, 437, 393; E. D. Mansfield, *Personal Memories . . . 1803–1843* (Cincinnati, OH, 1879), 210–11.

42. Charles Hammond to Thomas Ewing, March 2, 1825, Ewing Family Collection, University of Notre Dame, Reel 1, microfilm edition; James Buchanan to Robert Letcher, July 27, 1844, *Works of Buchanan*, 6:64; "Representative Men, Part I," 529.

43. Merrill Peterson, *The Great Triumvirate: Webster, Clay, and Calhoun* (New York: Oxford University Press, 1987), 129; Seager, "Politics of Compromise," 10.

44. George Prentice, *Biography of Henry Clay* (Hartford, CT, 1831), 293; *CP*, 8:25; "Mr. Markley's Letter to the Public," in Colton, *Clay*, 1:357; Schurz, *Clay*, 1:257; Seager, "Politics of Compromise," 10; Remini, *Clay*, 270; Watson, *Jackson vs. Clay*, 64; Howe, *What Hath God Wrought*, 211; Wilentz, *American Democracy*, 255.

45. *Henry Clay Almanac, 1844*, 26; Speech in Lexington, June 9, 1842, *CP*, 7:710.

46. Jeffrey Jenkins and Brian Sala, "The Spatial Theory of Voting and the Presidential Election of 1824," *American Journal of Political Science* 42 (1998): 1175–78; Clay to William Crawford, February 18, 1828, *CP*, 7:99–101; 1842 speech, in Larry Klein, "Henry Clay, Nationalist" (PhD diss., University of Kentucky, 1977), 60; Foote, *Casket of Reminiscences*, 27–28.

Chapter 7

1. Clay to John Mason, March 9, 1826, Clay to James Erwin, April 28, 1826, Statement of Auction Sale, June 24, 1825, Memorandum to Robert Scott, July 6, 1825, Clay to James Erwin, August 30, 1825, and April 21, 1827, Rental Agreement, October 11, 1825, Clay to James Brown, May 22, 1826, and Receipt from Susan Decatur, June 5, 1827, all in *CP*, 5:155–56, 283; 4:457–61, 512–13, 601; 6:471; 4:729; 5:388–89; 6:649.

2. Richard Cutts to John Fairchild, July 8, 1839, Cutts Family Papers, LC; Clay to James Brown, December 14, 1826, *CP*, 5:1001.

3. Clay to Louis McLane, January 14, 1826, Clay to Webster, February 16, 1826, and Clay to the House of Representatives, January 11, 1827, all in *CP*, 5:33–35, 35n, 109–10; 6:42; Mary Hargreaves, *The Presidency of John Quincy Adams* (Lawrence: University Press of Kansas, 1985), 211–12.

4. Clay to George Thompson, September 23, 1826, Clay to Elisha Whittlesey, March 26, 1825, Clay to John J. Crittenden, April 26, 1825, Clay to

James Brown, December 12, 1825, and March 27, 1827, Webster to Clay, September 28, 1825, and James Brown to Clay, April 28, 1825, all in *CP*, 5:707; 4:179, 289, 896; 5:361; 4:699, 302.

5. Schurz, *Clay*, 1:308–10.

6. Clay to James Brown, March 27, 1827, Clay to John Sloane, April 7, 1825, Clay to Francis Brooke, April 6, 1825, John Quincy Adams to Clay, August 23, 1827, and Clay to Crawford, February 18, 1828, all in *CP*, 6:362; 4:227, 221; 6:952; 7:100–101; Adams, *Memoirs*, 7:217, 254, 257; Merrill Peterson, *The Great Triumvirate: Webster, Clay, and Calhoun* (New York: Oxford University Press, 1987), 132.

7. *New London Gazette*, October 10, 1832; Colton, *Clay*, 1:131–33; Clay to John J. Crittenden, May 11, 1826, and Clay to Robert Walsh Jr., April 25, 1836, both in *CP*, 5:360; 8:845; Norman Graebner, "Henry Clay, Realist," *Register* 107 (2009): 552–53; *RD*, 22nd Cong., 1st Sess. (1831–1832), 1354; Clay to Antonio José Cañaz, April 18, 1825, Clay to Joel Poinsett, March 26, 1825, and March 15, 1827, and Clay to Thomas Robertson, December 7, 1825, all in *CP*, 4:264, 171; 6:308; 4:882–83; Remini, *Clay*, 299. For an overview of Clay as secretary of state, see Theodore Burton, "Henry Clay, Secretary of State," in *The American Secretaries of State and their Diplomacy* (1928; New York: Cooper Square, 1964), 4:115–58.

8. George Herring, *From Colony to Superpower: US Foreign Relations since 1776* (New York: Oxford University Press, 2008), 143–44; George Dangerfield, *The Era of Good Feelings* (Boston: Harcourt, Brace, and World, 1952). 372–74, 377–79; Hargreaves, *Presidency of Adams*, 102, 107. For an example of the attacks on Clay on this issue, see *Richmond Enquirer*, February 11, 1832.

9. Halford Hoskins, "The Hispanic American Policy of Henry Clay, 1816–1828," *Hispanic American Historical Review* 7 (1927): 473, 475.

10. Dangerfield, *Era of Good Feelings*, 361; Clay to James Brown, February 21, 1826, and Clay to John J. Crittenden, March 10, 1826, both in *CP*, 5:122, 158; Adams, *Memoirs*, 7:111; Herring, *From Colony to Superpower*, 162–63; Donald Cole, *Martin Van Buren and the American Political System* (Princeton, NJ: Princeton University Press, 1984), 148.

11. *RD*, 19th Cong, 1st Sess. (1825–26), 1955, 1958, 1988, 395, 401, 403; Dangerfield, *Era of Good Feelings*, 357; Paul Corts, "Randolph vs. Clay: A Duel of Words and Bullets," *FCHQ* 43 (1969): 153–56.

12. Hoskins, "Hispanic American Policy," 475; Dangerfield, *Era of Good Feelings*, 371, 363.

13. Herring, *From Colony to Superpower*, 160–63; Clay to Richard Anderson Jr. and John Sergeant, May 8, 1826, *CP*, 5:313–44; Remini, *Clay*, 297, 285.

14. Dangerfield, *Era of Good Feelings*, 348, 350; Daniel Walker Howe, *What Hath God Wrought* (New York: Oxford University Press, 2007), 259; E. Malcolm Carroll, *Origins of the Whig Party* (1925; repr. Gloucester, MA: Peter Smith, 1964), 3; Adams, *Memoirs*, 7:61; Michael Holt, *The Rise and Fall of the American Whig Party* (New York: Oxford University Press, 1999), 7; Claiborne Watkins to Clay, September 30, 1826, *CP*, 5:738; Thomas

Brown, *Politics and Statesmanship: Essays on the American Whig Party* (New York: Columbia Univeristy Press, 1985), 17.

15. Henry Warfield to Clay, July 5, 1826, Thomas Mitchell to Clay, November 10, 1826, Daniel Webster to Clay, March 25, 1827, William Rochester to Clay, October 9, 1827, and Porter Clay to Clay, February 22, 1827, all in *CP*, 5:523–24, 891; 6:355, 1129, 222.

16. Thomas McGiffin to Clay, February 19, 1827, *CP*, 6:210; Adams, *Memoirs*, 7:349, 544, 8:32; Ronald Formisano, *The Transformation of Political Culture: Massachusetts Politics, 1790s–1840s* (New York: Oxford University Press, 1983), 16; Thomas Smith to Clay, October 7, 1827, *CP*, 6:1121–22; Richard John, "Affairs of Office: The Executive Departments, the Election of 1828, and the Making of the Democratic Party," in *The Democratic Experiment: New Directions in American Political History*, ed. Meg Jacobs, William Novak, and Julian Zeliger (Princeton, NJ: Princeton University Press, 2003), 58, 60; Charles Hammond to Clay, October 18, 1827, *CP*, 6:1161.

17. Clay to James Brown, September 4, 1825, *CP*, 4:618; Richard McMillan, "Election of 1824: Corrupt Bargain or the Birth of Modern Politics?," *New England Journal of History* 57 (2001): 36; *Jackson Papers*, 6:92; Adams, *Memoirs*, 7:113; Mary Hamilton to Joseph Hamilton, May 31, 1827, Box 2, Mary H. Orr Collection, Tennessee State Library and Archives.

18. Adams, *Memoirs*, 7:439, 379–83; *Address to the Public . . .* (n.p., 1827); Peterson, *Great Triumvirate*, 148–49; Address to the Public, June 29, 1827, *CP*, 6:728. See also *The Calumny Refuted . . .* (n.p., n.d.).

19. Sandra Van Burkleo, "'The Paws of Banks': The Origins and Significance of Kentucky's Decision to Tax Federal Banks, 1818–1820," *JER* 9 (1989): 462; "Hamilton" [Mathew Carey], *Some Notices of Kentucky . . .* (Philadelphia, 1828), n.p.; Elisha Plumb to William Plumb, April 28, 1821, Plumb Collection, KHS; Alfred Tischendorf and E. Taylor Parks, eds., *The Diary and Journal of Richard Clough Anderson Jr., 1814–1826* (Durham, NC: Duke University Press, 1964), 102; John Brown to Orlando Brown, March 4, 1820, Orlando Brown Papers, KHS.

20. Sean Wilentz, *The Rise of American Democracy* (New York: W. W. Norton, 2005), 209, 288; *Kentucky Acts* (1819–20), 811–13, 917–21; Billie Hardin, "Amos Kendall and the 1824 Relief Controversy," *Register* 64 (1966): 197; Journal of Joseph Rogers Underwood (typescript), December 30, 1826, Underwood Collection, Western Kentucky University; Charles Sellers, *The Market Revolution* (New York: Oxford University Press, 1991), 169. References to the Old Court–New Court struggle generally come from Arndt Stickles, *The Critical Court Struggle in Kentucky, 1819–1829* (Bloomington: Graduate Council of Indiana University, 1929); Dale Royalty, "Banking, Politics, and the Commonwealth of Kentucky, 1800–1825" (PhD diss., University of Kentucky, 1971); Tom Barton, "Politics and Banking in Republican Kentucky, 1805–1824" (PhD diss., University of Wisconsin, 1968); Sandra Van Burkleo, "'That

Our Pure Republican Principles Might Not Wither': Kentucky's Relief Crisis . . . 1818–1826" (PhD diss., University of Minnesota, 1988); and Matthew Schoenbachler, *Murder and Madness: The Myth of the Kentucky Tragedy* (Lexington: University Press of Kentucky, 2009), 61, 102–103, 105.

21. Charles Bussey, "Joseph Desha," in Lowell Harrison, ed., *Kentucky's Governors*, new ed. (2004), 29–32; Paul Doutrich III, "A Pivotal Decision: The 1824 Gubernatorial Election in Kentucky," *FCHQ* 56 (1982): 23.

22. Matthew Schoenbachler, "The Origins of Jacksonian Politics: Central Kentucky, 1790–1840" (PhD diss., University of Kentucky, 1996), 197; Stephen Fackler, "John Rowan and the Demise of Jeffersonian Republicanism in Kentucky, 1819–1831," *Register* 78 (1980): 21.

23. Clay to Amos Kendall, October 18, 1825, and Clay to John J. Crittenden, March 10, 1826, and August 22, 1825, all in *CP*, 4:748; 5:159; 4:585.

24. William Barry to Clay, January 10, 1825, Francis Blair to Clay, February 11, 1825, and Amos Kendall to Clay, March 23, 1825, all in *CP*, 4:12, 64, 135.

25. John J. Crittenden to Clay, November 25, 1826, and April 27, 1826, Clay to Crittenden, May 11, 1826, and Robert Wickliffe to Clay, September 13, 1826, all in *CP*, 5:950, 278, 360, 685; Harry Volz III, "Party, State, and Nation: Kentucky and the Coming of the American Civil War" (PhD diss., University of Virginia, 1982), 28; William Lucy, "An Essay on the Want of Common Schools in Kentucky" (1832), 1, Bemiss Family Papers, VHS.

26. Adams, *Memoirs*, 7:217; Howe, *What Hath God Wrought*, 278; *Niles Weekly Register* 32 (April 28, 1827): 149–50; Brown, *Politics and Statesmanship*, 18–19; Harry Watson, *Andrew Jackson vs. Henry Clay* (Boston: Bedford/St. Martin's, 1998), 70–71; Ann Toplovich, "Marriage, Mayhem, and Presidential Politics: The Robards-Jackson Backcountry Scandal," *OVH* 5 (2005): 18, 17; Andrew Burnstein, *The Passions of Andrew Jackson* (New York: Alfred A. Knopf, 2003), appendix.

27. Toplovich, "Marriage, Mayhem, and Presidential Politics," 15, 3–22; John Marszalek, *The Petticoat Affair: Manners, Mutiny, and Sex in Andrew Jackson's White House* (New York: Free Press, 1997), 7–9; Jackson to James Polk, in *Polk Papers*, 1:181; John Eaton to Jackson, December 22, 1826, and Jackson to Richard Keith Call, May 3, 1827, both in *Jackson Papers*, 6:245–46, 315; Charles Hammond to John Eaton, January 3, 1827, in William Smith, *Charles Hammond and His Relation to Henry Clay and John Quincy Adams* (Chicago, 1885), 50–51. Clay did alert Hammond that Eaton was accusing Clay of instigating the attack. See Clay to Hammond, December 23, 1826, *CP*, 5:1023–24, which Wilentz, *American Democracy*, 306, interprets as a sign of Clay's guilt.

28. Clay to Hammond, June 1, 1827, *CP*, 6:631.

29. [Joseph Baldwin], "Representative Men: Part I," *Southern Literary Messenger* 19 (1853): 521, 529; W. C. Rives to Thomas Gilmer, July 22, 1827, in "Letters of William C. Rives, 1823–1829," *Tyler's Quarterly Historical and Genealogical Magazine* 5 (1924): 234; James Brown to Clay, May 10, 1828, *CP*, 7:266.

30. Henry Shaw to Clay, November 17, 1827, *CP*, 6:1279; Hargreaves, *Presidency of Adams*, xiii; Richard McCormick, *The Second American Party System* (Chapel Hill: University of North Carolina Press, 1966), 215; Chris Sperry and Sox Sperry, "Media Construction of Presidential Campaigns," *Social Education* 71 (2007): 366; Francis Blair to Joseph Desha, October 30, 1828, Vol. 1, Papers of Joseph and John R. Desha, LC. See also John Rowan to James Morrison, April 14, 1828, John Rowan Letter, FHS.

31. Heidler and Heidler, *Clay*, 208; Henry Shaw to Clay, November 17, 1827, *CP*, 6:1278; Robert Remini, *The Election of Andrew Jackson* (Philadelphia: J. B. Lippincott, 1963), 129; *CP*, 6:239, 353, 402n, 1072.

32. "George Washington" (pseud.), "People of Kentucky" (pamphlet, 1828), [1].

33. Clay to William S. Dallam, September 1, 1827, Clay to Francis Brooke, March 10, 1828, Clay to James Erwin, May 22, 1828, Clay to Adam Beatty, June 20, 1828, Joseph Johnston to Clay, July 14, 1828, and James Brown to Clay, August 12, 1828, all in *CP*, 7:985, 155, 290, 357, 386, 424; McCormick, *Second Party System*, 218–20; Howe, *What Hath God Wrought*, 50.

34. *Congressional Quarterly's Guide to US Elections*, 2 vols. (4th ed., Washington, DC: CQ Press, 2001), 1:645, 728; Wilentz, *American Democracy*, 309, 308; Sellers, *Market Revolution*, 297, 299; Clay to Robert Breckinridge, October 31, 1828, Vol. 55, Breckinridge Family Papers, LC.

35. Donald Cole, *Vindicating Andrew Jackson: The 1828 Election and the Rise of the Two-Party System* (Lawrence: University Press of Kansas, 2009), 196–99, 203.

36. Margaret Smith to J. Bayard Smith, November 30, 1828, Margaret Smith to Maria Boyd, February 16, 1829, and Margaret Smith to Mrs. Kirkpatrick, January 12, 1829, all in *The First Forty Years of Washington Society*, ed. Gaillard Hunt (New York: Charles Scribner's Sons, 1906), 246, 277, 259; James Polk to Lucius Polk, January 3, 1829, in *The Filson* 8 (2008): 3; Clay to John Q. Adams, March 3, 1829, *CP*, 7:633.

37. Speech at Farewell Dinner, March 7, 1829, and Speech at Frederick, MD, March 18, 1829, both in *CP*, 8:5–6, 11–13; Adams, *Memoirs*, 8:111.

38. Clay to Philip Fendall, March 31, 1829, Clay to James Erwin, April 9, 1829, Speech at Fowler's Garden, May 16, 1829, and Clay to James Brown, November 12, 1828, all in *CP*, 8:19, 23, 53; 7:535.

39. Quoted in Robert Pierce Forbes, *The Missouri Compromise and Its Aftermath* (Chapel Hill: University of North Carolina Press, 2007), 215.

40. John J. Crittenden to Clay, February 15, 1829, *CP*, 7:620; review of *The Life, Correspondence, and Speeches of Henry Clay*, *North American Review* 102 (1866): 183.

41. "Memoirs of Michah Taul," *Register* 27 (1929): 502; "Senator Benton and Gen. Jackson," September 10, 1823, Thomas Hart Benton Papers, LC; William Freehling, *Road to Disunion: Secessionists at Bay, 1776–1854* (New York: Oxford University Press, 1990), 541–42; Ben Perley Poore, "The Capitol at Washington," *The Century* 25 (1883): 808; Henry Foote, *Casket of Reminiscences* (1874; repr., New York: Negro Universities Press, 1968),

330–31, 338; John Tyler to Robert Tyler, June 3, 1858, in Leon Tyler, *The Letters and Times of the Tylers*, 2 vols. (Richmond, VA, 1884), 2:19; Allan Nevin, ed., *Polk: The Diary of a President, 1845–1849* (London: Longmans, Green, 1929), 274, 356; Comment in Senate, June 13, 1850, *CP*, 10:748.

42. Bertram Wyatt-Brown, *Southern Honor* (New York: Oxford Universsity Press, 1982), 318; Clay to James Brown, March 27, 1827, Clay to Benton, December 6, 1827, and James Brown to Clay, May 29, 1827, all in *CP*, 6:362, 1342, 604.

43. Heidler and Heidler, *Clay*, 61: *RD*, 23rd Cong., 1st Sess. (1833–34), 2114; William Barry to Clay, January 11, 1810, *CP*, 1:435–36; "Autobiography of Harrison," October 1880, Box 12, Papers of James O. Harrison, LC; G. Glenn Clift, *Governors of Kentucky, 1792–1942* (Cynthiana, KY: Hobson Press, 1942), 168–69; John Pope to Jackson, February 19, 1829, *Jackson Papers*, 7:50; John, "Affairs of Office," 56, 62–63; William Barry to Susan Taylor, June 11, 1829, in "Letters of William T. Barry," *William and Mary College Quarterly* 13 (1905): 241–42.

44. David Lee Child to Clay, April 11, 1829, *CP*, 8:25; *Kentucky Reporter*, June 3, 1829; Speech at Fowler's Garden, May 16, 1829, and Clay to Josiah Johnston, October 5, 1829, both in *CP*, 8:54, 43, 47–48, 50, 54, 110, 101.

45. Marszalek, *Petticoat Affair*, 140, 47.

46. Marszalek, *Petticoat Affair*, 35–36, 40–42, 47, 49, 48; Thomas Ewing to Maria Ewing, March 5, 1831, Thomas Ewing Family Papers, LC; Duff Green to John Helm, May 20, 1831, *Calhoun Papers,* 11:389.

47. Marszalek, *Petticoat Affair*, 238, 111, 54–56, 85, 135, 184; Duff Green to John Helm, May 20, 1831, *Calhoun Papers*, 11:386; Thomas Ewing to Maria Ewing, March 5, 1831, Ewing Papers

48. Ezra Stiles Ely to Andrew Jackson, March 18, 1829, Jackson to Ely, March 23, 1829, Jackson to John McLemore, April [26], 1829, and Jackson to John Coffee, May 30, 1829, all in *Jackson Papers*, 7:103, 114, 184, 249.

49. Clement Eaton, *Henry Clay and the Art of American Politics* (Boston: Little, Brown, 1957), 167; Marszalek, *Petticoat Affair*, 161, 158, 162–63.

50. *RD*, 18th Cong., 2nd. Sess. (1824–25), 285–86; Speech at Wheeling, March 31, 1829, *CP*, 8:20; Speech on Cumberland Road, January 17, 1825, *CP*, 4:22; Carlton Jackson, "The Internal Improvement Vetoes of Andrew Jackson," *Tennessee Historical Quarterly* 25 (1966): 262.

51. James Richardson, *Compilation of the Messages and Papers of the Presidents,* 10 vols. (Washington, DC, 1897), 2:483–93: Jackson, "Internal Improvement Vetoes," 273.

52. Jon Meacham, *American Lion: Andrew Jackson in the White House* (New York: Random House, 2008), 140; Michael Korzi, "The Seat of Popular Leadership: Parties, Elections, and the Nineteenth-Century Presidency," *Presidential Studies Quarterly* 29 (1999): 366n; Jackson, "Internal Improvement Vetoes," 261, 266; Stephen Minicucci, "Internal Improvements and the Union," *Studies in American Political Development* 18 (2004): 166.

53. Clay to Peter Porter, June 13, 1830, *CP*, 8:223; Leslie Combs to Andrew January, February 16, 1831, Leslie Combs Letters, FHS; *CP*, 8:221n; Peterson, *Great Triumvirate*, 195.

54. *CP*, 8:235–44. For a list of Clay's travels over the years, see Charles Muntz, "Henry Clay's Travels, 1830–1852," http://henryclay.org/wp-content/uploads/2014/04/Henry-Clays-Travels.pdf.

55. John J. Crittenden to Clay, February 15, 1829, *CP*, 7:620; *Kentucky Reporter*, November 16, 1831; Remini, *Clay*, 373.

Chapter 8

1. Jackson to Van Buren, May 23, 1829, *Jackson Papers*, 7:239; "Mr. Clay," *American Monthly Magazine* 1 (1829): 344.

2. Clay to Francis Brooke, January 10, 1829, *CP*, 7:595; *Macon Telegraph*, April 11, 1829; review of *The Speeches of Henry Clay*, in *North American Review* 25 (1827): 425; Junius Browne, "George D. Prentice," *Harper's New Monthly Magazine* 50 (1875): 193; George Prentice, *Biography of Henry Clay* (Hartford, CT, 1831).

3. Betty Congleton, "Prentice's Biography of Henry Clay and John Greenleaf Whittier," *FCHQ* 37 (1963): 325–26; Browne, "Prentice," 194–96, 199.

4. W. C. Rives to Thomas Gilmer, July 22, 1827, "Letters of William C. Rives, 1823–1829," *Tyler's Quarterly Historical and Genealogical Magazine* 5 (1924): 235; Edwin Miles, "Andrew Jackson and Senator George Poindexter," *JSH* 24 (1958): 56; James Brown to Clay, November 30, 1829, Josiah Johnston to Clay, December 20 and 12, 1829, "Alexis de Sarcy" to Clay, February 11, 1830, Robert Letcher to Clay, December 21 and 26, 1829, and John Sergeant to Clay, July 20, 1829, and June 25, 1830, all in *CP*, 8:131, 158, 135, 174, 159–60, 164, 78, 229–30, 177n; Clay to Thomas Metcalfe, September 9, 1831, Metcalfe Papers, KHS; *Washington Globe*, January 22, 1831.

5. Webster to Clay, April 4, 1831, *CP*, 8:331; J. F. H. Claiborne, *Life and Correspondence of John A. Quitman*, 2 vols. (New York, 1860), 1:106.

6. Clay to Edward Everett, August 20, 1831, *CP*, 8:387, 332n; *Baltimore Patriot*, August 26, 1831; *Boston Courier*, in *New-Hampshire Patriot and State Gazette*, August 29, 1831; Clay to Josiah Johnston, August 20, 1831, and Clay to Thomas Speed, August 23, 1831, both in *CP*, 8:389, 390.

7. Francis Blair to Maria Gratz, April 20, 1831, in Thomas Clay, "Two Years with Old Hickory," *Atlantic Monthly* 60 (1887): 193.

8. Calhoun to Christopher Vanderventer, May 25, 1831, Calhoun to Samuel Ingham, July 31, 1831, and John Floyd to Calhoun, April 16, 1831, all in *Calhoun Papers*, 11:395, 443, 370; Francis Brooke to Clay, May 26, 1831, *CP*, 8:351; *New-Hampshire Patriot and State Gazette*, March 5, 1832.

9. Colton, *Clay*, 110; Clay to Hezekiah Niles, November 25, 1828, *CP*, 7:548; Schurz, *Clay*, 1:xxiii; Clay to George Watterson, July 21, 1829, and William Brent to Clay, December 5, 1829, both in *CP*, 8:79, 133. For a concise

summary of the race, see Robert Remini, "Election of 1832," in *Presidential Elections*, 1:495–516.

10. Joseph Tillinghast to H. A. S. Dearborn, December 16, 1831, Joseph Tillinghast Papers, FHS; R. M. Johnson to John McLean, December 15, 1831, in James Padgett, ed., "The Letters of Colonel Richard M. Johnson of Kentucky," *Register* 40 (1942): 78.

11. Jon Meacham, *American Lion: Andrew Jackson in the White House* (New York: Random House, 2008), 215; Tyler to Mary Tyler, December 28, 1831, in Leon Tyler, *The Letters and Times of the Tylers*, 2 vols. (Richmond, VA, 1884), 1:428–29.

12. *Pennsylvania Whig*, in *Poughkeepsie* (NY) *Independence*, June 6 and February 8, 1832; Ronald Formisano, "Political Character, Antipartyism, and the Second Party System," *American Quarterly* 21 (1969): 692, 690; Formisano, *The Transformation of Political Culture: Massachusetts Parties, 1790s–1840s* (New York: Oxford University Press, 1983), 197–202; Donald Ratcliffe, "Antimasonry and Partisanship in Greater New England, 1826–1836," *JER* 15 (1995): 200, 210, 214. On anti-Masonry generally, see William Vaughn, *The Antimasonic Party in the United States, 1826–1843* (Lexington: University Press of Kentucky, 1983), and Paul Goodman, *Toward a Christian Republic* (New York: Oxford University Press, 1988).

13. Amanda Salyer, "Henry Clay's Campaign for the Presidency in 1832" (MA thesis, University of Kentucky, 1934), 47; *Poughkeepsie* (NY) *Independence*, June 6, 1832; *Providence Rhode-Island American*, May 15 and October 5, 1832; *Newport Rhode-Island Republican*, October 2, 1832; *Concise History of Lexington Lodge No. 1 . . .* (Lexington, KY: n.p., 1913), 21; *CP*, 2:916n; *Keene New-Hampshire Sentinel*, January 6, 1832; Richard Rush to Clay, June 1, 1831, *CP*, 8:354–55; Adams, *Memoirs*, 8:535.

14. Clay to Peter Porter, June 13, 1830, Clay to Samuel Southard, September 30, 1831, Clay to Joseph Gales, August 2, 1831, Clay to Ambrose Spencer, May 12, 1832, and Clay to Francis Brooke, July 18 and June 23, 1831, all in *CP*, 8:222, 409, 381, 513, 373, 364; Clay to Thomas Metcalfe, September 9, 1831, Metcalfe Collection; Salyer, "Clay's Campaign," 47; Calhoun to Christopher Vandeventer, August 5, 1831, *Calhoun Papers*, 11:450; Remini, "Election of 1832," 1:502.

15. Merrill Peterson, *The Great Triumvirate: Webster, Clay, and Calhoun* (New York: Oxford University Press, 1987), 198; Clay to James Conover, August 3, 1831, Josiah Johnston to Clay, September 20, 1830, Peter Porter to Clay, October 6, 1830, and William Lawrence to Clay, November 8, 1830, all in *CP*, 8:384, 268, 278, 291; Webster to Jeremiah Mason, March 19, 1830, *Webster Papers*, 3:36; Daniel Walker Howe, *What Hath God Wrought* (New York: Oxford Univeristy Press, 2007), 268; Thomas Brown, *Politics and Statesmanship* (New York: Columbia University Press, 1985), 23.

16. *Brattleboro* (VT) *Messenger*, March 24, 1832; Ambrose Spencer to Webster, October 24, 1831, *Webster Papers*, 3:132; *Boston Advocate*, in *Providence Rhode-Island American*, June 12 and 29, 1832.

17. Charles McCarthy, "The Antimasonic Party," *Annual Report of the American Historical Association for the Year of 1902*, 2 vols. (Washington, DC: Government Printing Office, 1903), 1:413–16; J. Blount to Caleb Cushing, June 27, 1832, Caleb Cushing Papers, LC; Thomas Ewing to [unknown] Pease, May 10, 1832, Box 156, Ewing Family Papers; Calhoun to Samuel Ingham, May 25, 1831, *Calhoun Papers*, 11:392.

18. Charles Hammond to Thomas Ewing, June 17, 1832, (microfilm), Thomas Ewing Papers, Ewing Family Collection, University of Notre Dame; *Providence Rhode-Island American*, October 15, 1832, cited in *Richmond Enquirer*, October 12 and 30, September 28, 1832.

19. For this discussion of the Second Bank of the United States, see George Dangerfield, *The Era of Good Feelings* (Boston: Harcourt, Brace, and World, 1952), 179, 187; Howe, *What Hath God Wrought*, 374–76; Sean Wilentz, *The Rise of American Democracy* (New York: W. W. Norton, 2005), 205–207; Charles Sellers, *The Market Revolution* (New York: Oxford University Press, 1991), 313; Edward Pessen, *Jacksonian America: Society, Personality, and Politics* (Homewood, IL: Dorsey, 1969), 329, 145; Harry Watson, *Andrew Jackson vs. Henry Clay* (Boston: Bedford/St. Martin's, 1998), 22, 80–81; Bray Hammond, *Banks and Politics in America . . .* (Princeton, NJ: Princeton University Press, 1957), 198–254, 294–304, 358–383; Jean Wilburn, *Biddle's Bank: The Crucial Years* (New York: Columbia University Press, 1967), passim; John McFaul, *The Politics of Jacksonian Finance* (Ithaca, NY: Cornell University Press, 1972), 1–14.

20. Clay to William Jones, December 17, 1816, *CP*, 2:262; Wilentz, *American Democracy*, 365; Clay to William Jones, February 4, 1818, *CP*, 2:433–34; Maurice Baxter, *Henry Clay the Lawyer* (Lexington: University Press of Kentucky, 2000), 55–56, 59; Clay to Langdon Cheves, February 10, 1821, June 23, and September 13, 1822, and Clay to Nicholas Biddle, March 8, 1825, all in *CP*, 3:25, 238, 286; 4:93; *RD*, 23rd Cong., 1st Sess. (1833–34), 1531.

21. Charles Sellers, "Banking and Politics in Jackson's Tennessee, 1817–1827," *Mississippi Valley Historical Review* 41 (1954): 61–84; Watson, *Jackson vs. Clay*, 79n; Charles Jared Ingersoll to Nicholas Biddle, February 2, 1832, in Reginald C. McGrane, ed., *The Correspondence of Nicholas Biddle* (Boston: Houghton Mifflin, 1919), 172.

22. Clay to Biddle, September 11, 1830, and Biddle to Clay, November 3, 1830, both in *CP*, 8:263–64, 287.

23. James Brown to Clay, *CP*, 8:434; William Lewis to Biddle, May 25, 1830, Robert Smith to Biddle, December 13, 1830, Edward Shippen to Biddle, December 6, 1831, and Daniel Webster to Biddle, December 31, 1833, all in McGrane, *Biddle Correspondence*, 104, 117, 136, 178, 218.

24. Samuel Smith to Biddle, December 7 and 17, 1831, Webster to Biddle, December 10, 1831, Thomas Cadwalader to Biddle, December 21, 1831, and Biddle to Samuel Smith, January 4, 1832, all in McGrane, *Biddle Correspondence*, 143–45, 148–52, 162–64; Webster to Clay, January 8, 1832, *CP*, 8:443. See also Maurice Baxter, *Henry Clay and the American System*

(Lexington: University Press of Kentucky, 1995), 90, and Robert Remini, *Daniel Webster* (New York: W. W. Norton, 1997), 345.

25. Biddle to Webster, February 16, 1826, and December 2, 1828, and Biddle to Charles Jared Ingersoll, February 11, 1832, all in McGrane, *Biddle Correspondence*, 39, 179, 58; Wilentz, *American Democracy*, 365; Howe, *What Hath God Wrought*, 375; Pessen, *Jacksonian America*, 146; Biddle to James Harper, January 9, 1829, William Lewis to Biddle, May 3, 1830, Biddle to Thomas Cooper, May 6, 1833, and Biddle to Joseph Hemphill, December 14, 1830, all in McGrane, *Biddle Correspondence*, 68, 98–99, 209, 119.

26. *Advocate*, quoted in *Newport Rhode-Island Republican*, April 9, 1834.

27. Howe, *What Hath God Wrought*, 378.

28. Donald Cole, *A Jackson Man: Amos Kendall and the Rise of American Democracy* (Baton Rouge: Louisiana State University Press, 2004), 2, 1, 63; Donald Cole, "A Yankee in Kentucky: The Early Years of Amos Kendall, 1789–1828," *Proceedings of the Massachusetts Historical Society*, 3rd series 109 (1997): 25, 28; *Easton* (MD) *Gazette*, May 4, 1839; Robert Tinkler, review of *A Jackson Man*, H-Tennessee@h-net.msu.edu; Thomas Stevenson to Clay, August 29, 1848, *CP*, 10:529.

29. "Political Portraits with Pen and Pencil: Amos Kendall," *United States Democratic Review* 1 (1838): 403–407; Amos Kendall, *Autobiography* (Boston, 1872), 101–15, 158–80; Amos Kendall to [J. L. Krimmel], May 14, 1814, and August 16, 1815, and Kendall to [F. G. Flugal], April 4, 1839, all in Amos Kendall Papers, FHS; Receipt from Amos Kendall, July 1, 1815, *CP*, 2:53; Arthur Schlesinger Jr., *The Age of Jackson* (Boston: Little, Brown, 1945), 68. See also Cole, *Jackson Man*, 13, 34, 38, 44.

30. Billie Hardin, "Amos Kendall and the 1824 Relief Controversy," *Register* 84 (1966): 205; Cole, *Jackson Man*, 63, 55, 61, 77; Kendall to Clay, March 23, February 19, and April 28, 1825, all in *CP*, 4:135–36, 77, 306.

31. Kendall to Joseph Desha, April 9, 1831, in James Padgett, ed., "Correspondence Between Governor Joseph Desha and Amos Kendall, 1831–1835," *Register* 38 (1940): 8; Clay to Kendall, October 18, 1825, *CP*, 4:747; Mary Hargreaves, *The Presidency of John Quincy Adams* (Lawrence: University Press of Kansas, 1985), 257; Glyndon Van Deusen, *The Life of Henry Clay* (Boston: Little, Brown, 1937), 217; Clay to Kendall, October 18, 1825, Kendall to Clay, May 28, 1828, and July 8, 1826, and William Worley to Clay, December 11, 1826, all in *CP*, 4:747; 7:306; 5:534, 959; Daniels, "Kendall," 55, 58–62; *Argus of Western America*, January 10 and February 21, 1827; Richard Johnson to Martin Van Buren, September 22, 1827, in James Padgett, ed., "The Letters of Colonel Richard M. Johnson of Kentucky," *Register* 39 (1941): 268; Clay to John Harvie, June 5, 1828, *CP*, 7:327.

32. Kendall to Jane Kendall, January 4, February 25, and April 6, 1829, in Kendall, *Autobiography*, 278, 285, 290; Kendall to [F. G. Flugel], April 4, 1839, Kendall Papers.

33. Cole, "Yankee in Kentucky," 24; Robert Gibbs to Nicholas Biddle, December 11, 1831, McGrane, *Biddle Correspondence*, 139; Thomas Ewing

to "Dear Sir," January 9, 1833, Box 156, Thomas Ewing Family Papers, LC; Speech at Hagerstown, March 20, 1829, *CP*, 8:15; Remini, *Clay*, 404. See also Stephen Campbell, "The Spoils of Victory: Amos Kendall, the Antebellum State, and the Growth of the American Presidency," *OVH* 11 (2011): 3–25.

34. "Frances Preston Blair, Sr.," in John Kleber, ed., *The Kentucky Encyclopedia* (Lexington: University Press of Kentucky, 1992), 85–86; Clay, "Two Years with Old Hickory," 187; Elbert B. Smith, *Francis Preston Blair* (New York: Free Press, 1980), 3–53, 73.

35. *Washington Globe*, June 23, 1856; Cole, "Yankee in Kentucky," 73; Van Deusen, *Jacksonian Era*, 33.

36. For the Clay-Blair correspondence, 1821–28, see *CP*, 3:10–11, 4:860–61, 5:4–6, 6:1106–107, 7:140–41, 6:1261; 5:440; Supp.: 193–94; 6:1163, 7:30, 194.

37. Clay, "Two Years with Old Hickory," 192; Julius Caesar, Act I, scene ii, 191.

38. On the divisions, see William Barry to Joseph Desha, February 8, 1831, Amos Kendall to Desha, April 9, June 2, and September 12, 1831, and Desha to Kendall, May 6 and June 19, 1831, all in Vol. 1, Papers of Joseph and John R. Desha, LC. See also Desha to Kendall, February 21, 1833, vol. 2; William Barry to Susan Taylor, February 22, 1834, in "Letters of William T. Barry," *William and Mary College Quarterly Historical Magazine* 14 (1906): 238; Cole, *Jackson Man*, 238, 242.

39. William Biddle to Charles Jared Ingersoll, February 11, 13, and 26, 1832, all in McGrane, *Biddle Correspondence*, 180, 182, 187; Edwin J. Perkins, "Lost Opportunities for Congress in the Bank War: A Reassessment of Jackson's Veto Message," *Business History Review* 61 (1987): 532–40; William Barry to Susan Taylor, July 4, 1832, "Barry Letters"; *Vermont Gazette*, October 30, 1832.

40. Richard Latner, "A New Look at Jacksonian Politics," *JAH* 61 (1975): 954; Wilentz, *American Democracy*, 369, 876n; Cole, *Jackson Man*, 165–70; John Ashworth, *"Agrarians" and "Aristocrats": Party Political Ideology in the United States, 1837–1846* (London: Royal Historical Society, 1983), 3; Michael F. Holt, *The Rise and Fall of the American Whig Party* (New York: Oxford University Press, 1999), 16. The veto appears in James Richardson, comp., *A Compilation of the Messages and Papers of the Presidents, 1789–1897*, 10 vols. (Washington, DC, 1897), 2:577–91.

41. Watson, *Jackson vs. Clay*, 181–82, 186, 185.

42. Watson, *Jackson vs. Clay*, 183–85.

43. "Representative Men, Part II," *Southern Literary Messenger* 19 (1853): 588; James David Barker, *Politics by Humans: Research in American Leadership* (Durham, NC: Duke University Press, 1988), 7; Watson, *Jackson vs. Clay*, 181–82, 184, 187.

44. Daniel Feller, *The Jacksonian Promise: America, 1815–1840* (Baltimore: Johns Hopkins University Press, 1995), 170.

45. Howe, *What Hath God Wrought*, 375; Sellers, *Market Revolution*, 322; *RD*, 22nd. Cong., 1st Sess. (1831–32), 1221–40, 1273, 1269; Wilentz, *American Democracy*, 373.

46. *Washington Globe*, in *Portland Eastern Argus*, October 3 and 8, 1832; *Richmond Enquirer*, September 28 and October 9, 1832; *Providence (RI) Patriot*, September 1, 1832; *Hartford Times*, October 15, 1832; *Vermont Gazette*, September 11, 1832; *Concord (NH) Patriot*, September 10, 1832.

47. *Newport (RI) Republican*, September 18, 1832; Wilentz, *American Democracy*, 373; Elisha Whittlesey to Clay, September 19, 1832, *CP*, 8:577.

48. *Richmond (VA) Enquirer*, October 5, 1832; *Washington Globe*, in *Portsmouth New-Hampshire Gazette*, October 9, 1832; *Hartford Times*, October 15, 1832; *Washington Globe*, January 11, 1832; *Concord New-Hampshire Patriot*, September 22, 1832; *Providence Rhode-Island American*, September 18 and August 3, 1832.

49. *Vermont Gazette*, June 19, 1832; *Hartford Times*, October 15, 1832; *Richmond (VA) Enquirer*, October 5, 1832.

50. *Easton (MD) Argus*, July 20, 1832; *Concord New-Hampshire Patriot*, May 7, October 22, and July 4, 1832; *Portland (ME) Eastern Argus*, June 1 and September 4, 1832; *Portsmouth New-Hampshire Gazette*, March 12, 1832; *Vermont Gazette*, October 9, 1832; *Providence Rhode-Island Republican*, July 10, 1832.

51. *Washington Globe*, January 10, 1832; *Portsmouth New-Hampshire Gazette*, March 12 and October 9, 1832; John Cuddy to Francis Blair, May 12, 1832, McDonald Family Papers, VHS; *Vermont Gazette*, June 19, 1832; *Richmond (VA) Enquirer*, June 29, 1832; *Concord New-Hampshire Patriot*, October 22, 1832; *Augusta (ME) Argus*, October 31, 1832; *Albany Argus*, November 3, 1832.

52. *Pennsylvania Whig*, in *Poughkeepsie (NY) Independence*, August 6, 1832; Howe, *What Hath God Wrought*, 334; *Keene New-Hampshire Sentinel*, June 15, 1832; *Columbia Ohio State Journal*, October 27, 1832; *New York Spectator*, October 1, 1832.

53. Lynn Marshall, "The Strange Stillbirth of the Whig Party," *American Historical Review* 72 (1967): 448, 447; Holt, *Whig Party*, 17; *New London (CT) Gazette*, January 25, 1832; Salyer, "Clay's Campaign in 1832," 49; *Hallowell (ME) American Advocate*, October 26, 1832.

54. *Keene New-Hampshire Sentinel*, June 15, 1832; *Columbus Ohio State Journal*, October 27 and 6, 1832; *Baltimore Gazette*, January 19, 1832; *New-London (CT) Gazette*, January 25, 1832; "Freedom and Clay: A New Patriotic Song," (1831), LC Music Division.

55. Letcher to George C. Washington, August 26, 1830, Robert Perkins Letcher Papers, FHS; John Sergeant to Clay, July 7, 1830, *CP*, 8:233; James Heaton to Charles Heaton, August 23, 1831, Papers of James Heaton, LC; Calhoun to S. D. Ingham, December 22, 1831, *Calhoun Papers*, 11:526; Gaillard Hunt, ed., *The First Forty Years of Washington Society* (New York: Charles Scribner's Sons, 1906), 332; Willie Mangum to William Polk, February 11, 1832, *Mangum Papers*, 1:481; Calhoun to Bolling Hall, February 13, 1832, *Calhoun Papers*, 11:554; *Easton (MD) Gazette*, July 28, 1832; Clay to William Teagarden, September 15, 1832, *CP*, 8:576; Joseph Sprague to H. A. Dearborn, October 23, 1832, Joseph E. Sprague Letter, LC.

56. *Congressional Quarterly's Guide to US Elections*, 2 vols. (4th ed., Washington, DC: CQ Press, 2001), 1:646, 729; *Richmond (VA) Enquirer*, October 4, 1832; Jonathan M. Atkins, "The Presidential Candidacy of Hugh Lawson White in Tennessee, 1832–1836," *JSH* 58 (1992): 28; Clay to Samuel Lyman, October 22, 1832, *CP*, 8:586; John Sacher, *A Perfect War of Politics: Parties, Politicians, and Democracy in Louisiana, 1824–1861* (Baton Rouge: Louisiana State University Press, 2003), 59–60, 63–64.

57. *Salem Gazette*, November 27, 1832; Ratcliffe, "Antimasonry," 226; *Congressional Quarterly Guide*, 646, 645; Wilentz, *American Democracy*, 373.

58. Henry Shaw to Clay, January 9, 1829, and John Lawrence to Clay, August 21, 1830, both in *CP*, 7:593; 8:254; Peterson, *Great Triumvirate*, 384; Calhoun to S. D. Ingham, December 22, 1831, *Calhoun Papers*, 11:526; review of *The Life, Correspondence, and Speeches of Henry Clay*, in *North American Review* 102 (1866): 186.

59. Clay to Charles Hammond, November 17, 1832, *CP*, 8:599; *Hartford Connecticut Mirror*, December 15, 1832; *Portsmouth New-Hampshire Gazette*, December 4, 1832. See also Andrew Kincannon to James Polk, November 26, 1832, *Polk Papers*, 1:536: "Clay and the Bank Are Done, I Think Forever."

Chapter 9

1. Zachary Smith and Mary Clay, *The Clay Family* (Louisville, KY, 1899), 56; Epes Sargent, *Life and Public Service of Henry Clay*, ed. Horace Greeley (Auburn, NY, 1852), 145; Tax Bill, ca. February 1, 1806, ca. February 1, 1809, and ca. February 1, 1812, all in *CP*, 1:171, 402, 628; Fayette County Kentucky Tax Records, 1800, 1801 (microfilm, KHS); Annela Rose, *Fayette County Kentucky 1810–1820 Census* (Irvine, KY: Printed by the author, 1982), 65; Rowena Lawson, *Fayette County Kentucky 1810–1840 Census* (n.p.: Heritage Books, 1986), 61, 44–87; Clay to Joshua Giddings, October 6, 1847, *CP*, 10:356; Marion Lucas and George Wright, *A History of Blacks in Kentucky*, 2 vols. (Frankfort: Kentucky Historical Society, 1992), 1:4, 2; William Freehling, *The Road to Disunion: Secessionists at Bay, 1776–1854* (New York: Oxford University Press, 1990), 495.

2. Joan Wells Coward, *Kentucky in the New Republic: The Process of Constitution Making* (Lexington: University Press of Kentucky, 1979), 43; Lucas, *Blacks in Kentucky*, 1:xv; Allan Kulikoff, "Uprooted Peoples: Black Migrants in the Age of the American Revolution," in Ira Berlin and Ron Hoffman, eds., *Slavery and Freedom in the Age of the American Revolution* (Charlottesville: University Press of Virginia, 1983), 149; Fredrika Teute, "Land, Liberty, and Labor in the Post-Revolutionary Era: Kentucky as the Promised Land" (PhD diss., Johns Hopkins University, 1988), 275; *1850 Fayette County Kentucky Census* (Lexington, KY: Fayette County Genealogical Society, n.d.), iv, 230; *Statistical View of the United States . . . Being a Compendium of the Seventh Census* (Washington, DC, 1854), 236.

3. Ivan McDougle, *Slavery in Kentucky, 1792–1865* (Lancaster, PA: New Era Printing, 1918), 39; *AC*, 18th Cong., 1st Sess. (1823–24), 1979; Clay to Cornelius Baldwin, August 28, 1838, and Clay to Jacob Gibson, July 25, 1842, both in *CP*, 9:222, 745; Harold Tallant, *Evil Necessity: Slavery and Political Culture in Antebellum Kentucky* (Lexington: University Press of Kentucky, 2003), 2.

4. Colton, *Clay*, 1:190–91; Joseph Rogers, *The True Henry Clay* (Philadelphia: J. B. Lippincott, 1902), 30; Comment in Senate, March 9, 1836, *CP*, 8:837; "Down the Ohio to the Underworld," *Littell's Living Age* 92 (1867): 37. Clay also apparently represented slaves without charging a fee in cases when they sought freedom, and according to a biographer, "always" received a favorable decision. Sargent, *Life of Clay*, 21; *New York Times*, July 20, 1852.

5. *Kentucky Gazette*, April 25, 1798; Coward, *Kentucky in the New Republic*, 136, 138. Scaevola was a legendary Roman hero who had burned off his right hand in a show of courage. It means "left-handed" in Latin.

6. Remini, *Clay*, 28; Stephen Aron, *How the West Was Lost: The Transformation of Kentucky from Daniel Boone to Henry Clay* (Baltimore: Johns Hopkins University Press, 1996), 95–96; Clay to John Sloane, August 12, 1823, and Clay to Richard Pindell, February 17, 1849, both in *CP*, Supp.:148–49; 10:574–81.

7. Clay to Daniel Huey, May 30, 1837, *CP*, 9:47; *Tenth Annual Report of the American Society for Colonizing Free People of Colour of the United States* (Washington, DC, 1827), 21, 19; Speech to the Kentucky Colonization Society, August 26, 1836, *CP*, Supp.:266; MS Speech on Slavery, John Payne Papers, LC; Clay to Cornelius Baldwin, August 28, 1838, and Speech to the General Assembly of Kentucky, both in *CP*, 9:222, 829.

8. Speech in Lexington, November 13, 1847, Clay to Colonization Society of Kentucky, December 17, 1829, and Speech before the American Colonization Society, January 20, 1827, all in *CP*, 10:373; 8:142, 140; 6:94.

9. Alfred Hunt, *Haiti's Influence on Antebellum America* (Baton Rouge: Louisiana State University Press, 1988), 2; *New York Colonial American*, June 1, 1839; *AC*, 16th Cong., 1st Sess. (1819–20), 2228; Remarks in Senate, March 23, 1840, and February 1, 1841, Clay to Benjamin Coates, October 18, 1851, and Clay to Robert Hamilton, October 2, 1849, all in *CP*, 9:399, 495, 925, 845, 10:621.

10. James Freeman Clarke, *Autobiography, Diary, and Correspondence,* ed. Edward Everett Hale (Boston, 1891), 103, 98; Clarke, "George D. Prentice and Kentucky Thirty-Five Years Ago," *Old and New* 1 (1870): 743; William Birney, *James G. Birney and His Times* (New York, 1890), 131; William Townsend, *Lincoln and the Bluegrass: Slavery and Civil War in Kentucky* (Lexington: University of Kentucky Press, 1955), 118. See also July 1839, Journal of T. R. Sullivan, LC.

11. Freehling, *Road to Disunion*, 18, 35, 74; Lucas, *Blacks in Kentucky*, 1:140, 86, 42; *Compendium of Seventh Census*, 95; Peter Bardaglio, *Reconstructing*

the Household: Families, Sex, and the Law in the Nineteenth-Century South (Chapel Hill: University of North Carolina Press, 1995), 30; J. Winston Coleman Jr., *Slavery Times in Kentucky* (1940; repr. New York: Johnson Reprint, 1970), vii.

12. Tallant, *Evil Necessity*, 63–64; Lucas, *Blacks in Kentucky*, 5, 42–43; Ken Emerson, *Doo-Dah! Stephen Foster and the Rise of American Popular Culture* (New York: Simon and Schuster, 1997), 193–95, 15; Frederic Bancroft, *Slave-Trading in the Old South* (Baltimore: J. M. Furst, 1931), 128–31, 389, 392; James Klotter, *The Breckinridges of Kentucky* (Lexington: University Press of Kentucky, 1986), 64–65; Freehling, *Road to Disunion*, 65; Townsend, *Lincoln and the Bluegrass*, 73; Clay to Joseph Berry, January 15, 1833, *CP*, 8:650; Jared Stone to Thomas Thomas, March 4, 1836, in Alfred Thomas, ed., *Correspondence of Thomas Ebenezer Thomas* (Dayton, OH: n.p., 1909), 8.

13. Clay to Edmund Pendleton, July 27, 1833, Account with Robert Scott, July 16, 1827, Statement of Farm Receipts, July 15, 1827, Clay to Joshua Giddings, October 6, 1847, and Deed of Emancipation, December 9, 1844, all in *CP*, 8:659; 9:52n; 6:794, 786; 10:356, 106n; Richard Troutman, "The Emancipation of Slaves by Henry Clay," *Journal of Negro History* 40 (1955): 179; Colton, *Clay*, 1:34; *New York Daily Times*, February 5, 1853; Clay and Oberholtzer, *Clay*, 288. For purchases of spouses and children, see *CP*, 8:85n–87n; 9:52n; 10:106n.

14. *CP*, 5:1035n (see also 4:7n; 8:184, 319, 675; 9:90 on overseers); Stephen Oates, "Harry of the West: Henry Clay," *Timeline* 8 (1991): 7; Clay to Sidney Gay, December 1, 1847, *CP*, 10:383; *Lexington Observer and Reporter*, June 5, 1846.

15. Bill of Sale, June 4, 1824, Clay to Thomas McGriffins, October 4, 1828, and James Erwin to Clay, January 6, 1829, all in *CP*, 3:773, 7:483, 590.

16. Clay to Sidney Gay, June 28 and December 1, 1847, both in *CP*, 10:336, 383; *St. Louis Daily Missouri Republican*, October 14, 1849; Clay to James B. Clay, September 3, 1849, *CP*, 10:614; *Boston Daily Bee*, September 5, 1849; Frank Severance, *Old Trails on the Niagara Frontier* (Buffalo, NY, 1899), 245. Joel Strangis, *Lewis Hayden and the War against Slavery* (North Haven, CT: Linnet Boooks, 1999), 9–10, accepts Hayden's charges without critical inquiry. Randolph Paul Runyon, *Delia Webster and the Underground Railroad* (Lexington: University Press of Kentucky, 1996), 113–16, provides a more careful examination of the issue.

17. Sargent, *Clay*, 148; Clay to Sydney Gay, December 27, 1847, Deed of Emancipation, July 11, 1808, and Robert Scott to Clay, January 5, 1824, all in *CP*, 10:391; 1:370; 3:563. For Clay slave purchases cited in the *Clay Papers*, see *CP*, 1:54, 370, 374, 384, 395, 554, 581, 725, 766, 786, 824–25, 949–50; 2:417, 892–93; 3:73, 127, 310, 773, 872; 4:721; 8:85n–87n; 9:52n; 10:106n; Sarah Wallace, "Lost Letters of Henry Clay," *Register* 50 (1952): 308. For slave sales, see *CP*, 3:310, 563; 8:85n–87n; 10:106n; Supp.:196. Typically, Clay also hired out some half-dozen slaves a year, realizing significant income from that practice. See, for example, *CP*, 1:72, 326; 2:86, 128;

3:520; 7:587; 8:85n–87n; James Hopkins, ed., "Henry Clay, Farmer and Stockman," *JSH* 15 (1949): 94.

18. Power of Attorney to John Polland, December 24, 1814, and John Bradford to Clay, October 3, 1816, both in *CP*, 1:1006; Supp.:56; *Washington National Intelligencer*, November 6, 1817; Clay to US Circuit Court for the District of Columbia, February 18, 1829, and Clay to Philip Fendall, September 10, 1830, both in *CP*, 7:623; 8:261; Wiley Cassidy, "Henry Clay's Attitude on Slavery" (MA thesis, University of Kentucky, 1939), 17–18; Deed of Emancipation, October 12, 1840, *CP*, 9:52n; *New York Times*, February 5, 1853.

19. L. Smith to B. W. Smith, May 25, 1844, L. Smith Papers, FHS; *Cleveland Gazette*, June 27, 1891. A story of another such liaison with a New Orleans woman has even less evidence to support her claim. Again, however, that does not mean that her account was not correct; it just cannot be authenticated. Lindsey Apple to author, August 2013.

20. Clay to William Russell, July 18, 1835, *CP*, 8:789.

21. Freehling, *Road to Disunion*, 133; Daniel Walker Howe, *What Hath God Wrought: The Transformation of America, 1815–1848* (New York: Oxford University Press, 2007), 497; Charles Sellers, *The Market Revolution: Jacksonian America, 1815–1846* (New York: Oxford University Press, 1991), 127; David Reynolds, *Waking Giant: America in the Age of Jackson* (New York: HarperCollins, 2008), 27; Birney, *Birney*, 159 Edward Pessen, *Jacksonian America: Society, Personality, and Politics* (Homewood, IL: Dorsey, 1969), 65; Andrew Cayton, "Artery and Border: The Ambiguous Development of the Ohio Valley in the Early Republic," *OVH* 1 (2005): 24; Keith Griffin, *Front Line of Freedom* (Lexington: University Press of Kentucky, 2004), 31.

22. *Compendium of the Seventh Census*, 63; Speech to Colonization Society, January 21, 1851, Speech to Colonization Society, December 17, 1829, and Speech to Organization of American Colonization Society, December 21, 1816, all in *CP*, 10:845; 8:147, 151; 2:264, 263; *Baltimore Sun*, August 14, 1851; Colton, *Clay*, 1:196–97.

23. Hunt, *Haiti's Influence*, 2; Colton, *Clay*, 1:198; Clay to Jacob Gibson, July 25, 1842, *CP*, 9:745; *Compendium of the Seventh Census*, 85; *AC*, 18th Cong., 1st Sess. (1823–24), 1979; Robert Pierce Forbes, *The Missouri Compromise and Its Aftermath* (Chapel Hill: University of North Carolina Press, 2007), 29; Lonnie Maness, "Henry Clay and the Problem of Slavery" (PhD diss., Memphis State University, 1980), 31.

24. *Concord New Hampshire Observer*, May 26, 1823; Daniel Walker Howe, *The Political Culture of the American Whigs* (Chicago: University of Chicago Press, 1979), 137, 134; Howe, *What Hath God Wrought*, 265, 264; Thomas Brown, *Politics and Statesmanship: Essays in the American Whig Party* (New York: Columbia University Press, 1985), 138, 140; Harry Watson, *Andrew Jackson vs. Henry Clay* (Boston: Bedford/St. Martin's, 1998), viii.

25. Speech to the ACS, January 17, 1829, *CP*, 7:601; 8:874n; *Lexington Observer and Reporter*, January 31, 1849; Thomas Jones, "Henry Clay and Continental

Expansion, 1820–1844," *Register* 73 (1978): 247; Griffin, *Front Line of Freedom*, 21; Speech Before ACS, January 20, 1827, *CP*, 6:87, 85.

26. David Streifford, "The American Colonization Society: An Application of Republican Ideology to Early Antebellum Reform," *JSH* 45 (1979): 201; Speech on Organization of ACS, December 21, 1816, *CP*, 2:263; Maness, "Clay and Slavery," 30; Speech Before ACS, January 20, 1827, *CP*, 6:93; Douglas Egerton, "Averting a Crisis: The Proslavery Critique of the American Colonization Society," *Civil War History* 43 (1997): 145; Tallant, *Evil Necessity*, 51; *Baltimore Sun*, August 14, 1851.

27. Tallant, *Evil Necessity*, 27; Eric Burin, *Slavery and the Peculiar Solution: A History of the American Colonization Society* (Gainesville: University Press of Florida, 2005), 18; Richard John, "Affairs of Office: The Executive Department, the Election of 1828, and the Making of the Democratic Party," in *The Democratic Experiment*, ed. Meg Jacobs, William Novak, and Julian Zeliger (Princeton, NJ: Princeton University Press, 2003), 74.

28. Speech to Annual Meeting, ACS, January 12, 1851, Clay to James Brown, July 7, 1833, Clay to Joseph Berry, January 15, 1833 and Clay to Cornelius Baldwin, August 28, 1838, all in *CP*, 9:845, 8:656, 650; 9:222.

29. Speech before the ACS, January 20, 1827, Clay to Gentlemen of the Colonization Society of Kentucky, December 17, 1829, and Clay to Thomas Speed, June 19, 1833, all in *CP*, 6:87, 90; 8:149, 154, 653; Egerton, "Averting a Crisis," 153. The statistics come from Bureau of the Census, *Historical Statistics of the United States, 1789–1945* (Washington, DC: Bureau of the Census, 1949), 25, 27. Two articles in the *African Repository and Colonial Journal* 3 (1827): 86, and 4 (1828): 262, estimate passage costs at twenty-five and thirty dollars per person, the latter slightly higher than Clay's figures.

30. Clay to Samuel Wilkenson, April 26, 1839, *CP*, 9:310; Howe, *What Hath God Wrought*, 409.

31. Forbes, *Missouri Compromise*, 217; Merrill Peterson, *The Great Triumvirate: Webster, Clay, and Calhoun* (New York: Oxford University Press, 1987), 285; *Charleston Mercury*, April 24, 1830; *Louisville Daily Democrat*, March 26, 1851; J. D. B. DeBow, "Kentucky," *Commercial Review* 7 (1849): 205; C. Ray Bennett, "All Things to All People: The American Colonization Society in Kentucky, 1829 –1860" (PhD diss., University of Kentucky, 1980), 87.

32. Burin, *Peculiar Solution*, 17, 26, 64, 66, 61; Speech to ACS, January 18, 1848, *CP*, 10:397.

33. *Rochester North Star*, January 28, 1848; Howe, *Political Culture*, 136; Streifford, "American Colonization Society," 208; Burin, *Peculiar Solution*, Table 2. Burin estimates that only eleven thousand free blacks went to Africa. P. J. Staudenraus, *The African Colonization Movement, 1816-1865* (New York: Columbia University Press, 1961), 251, puts the figure higher, at over fifteen thousand colonists to Liberia.

34. Freehling, *Road to Disunion*, 122; *Rochester North Star*, April 27, 1849; Maness, "Clay and Slavery," 33; Ronald Formisano, *The Transformation*

of Political Culture: Massachusetts Politics, 1790s–1840s (New York: Oxford University Press, 1983), 326.

35. *Liberator*, in *Rochester North Star*, February 11, 1848; Lewis Tappan to Clay, July 20, 1835; James Birney to Clay, December 22, 1837, both in *CP*, 8:793; 9:111–12, 297; Birney, *Birney*, 148, diary entry of September 16, 1834; *Rochester North Star*, March 2, 1849, June 9, 1848, April 20, 1849, *New Bedford (CT) Mercury*, December 9, 1842; *Whig Banner*, March 15, 1844.

36. Clay to Joseph Berry, June 15, 1833, *CP*, 8:650; J. F. Clarke to the Boston Observer, August 15, 1836, in *African Repository and Colonial Journal* 12 (1836): 321; John Irvin Jr. to John Irvin Sr., February 26, 1839, John Irvin Jr. Letters, FHS. Similar sentiments appeared in a letter from Thomas Waring to D.W. Murphy, dated December 4, 1845, Thomas Waring Collection, KHS. Waring predicted that within two years a Kentucky convention would end slavery *"entirely"* if "our Northern friends will only be quiet."

37. Clay in *Tenth Annual Report of the ACS*, 131; Speech to the ACS, December 15, 1836; Speech to Kentucky Colonization Society, August 26, 1836; Clay to Harrison Otis, November 14, 1838, John Russ to Clay, December 22, 1838; Clay to John Whittier, July 22, 1837; Remark in Senate, March 1, 1841; Clay to Colonization Society of Kentucky, December 17, 1829, all in *CP*, Supp.: 262, 266; 9:248, 259, 64, 509; 8:142.

38. Schurz, *Clay*, 2: 235; Howe, *Political Culture*, 64; *Keene New-Hampshire Sentinel*, September 6, 1849; Clay and Oberholtzer, *Clay*, 289n; Brown, *Politics and Statesmanship*, 143.

39. Tallant, *Evil Necessity*, 62; Kimberly Shankman, *Compromise and the Constitution: The Political Through of Henry Clay* (Lanham, MD: Lexington Books,1999), 101. The "no compromise with dishonor" quotation would come from Kentucky editor Henry Watterson on July 13, 1896. See Arthur Krock, *The Editorials of Henry Watterson* (Louisville, KY: Courier-Journal, 1923), 76.

40. Schurz, *Clay*, 2:164.

41. Birney, *Birney*, 148; David Smiley, *Lion of White Hall: The Life of Cassius Clay* (1962; repr., Gloucester, MA: Peter Smith, 1969), 49.

42. The following discussion of Calhoun comes from a series of sources, but chiefly these works: Richard Hofstadter, *The American Political Tradition and the Men Who Made It* (New York: Alfred A. Knopf, 1948); Margaret Coit, *John C. Calhoun* (Boston: Houghton Mifflin, 1950); Peterson, *Great Triumvirate*; John Niven, *John C. Calhoun and the Price of Union* (Baton Rouge: Louisiana State University Press, 1988); Irving Bartlett, *John C. Calhoun* (New York: W. W. Norton, 1993); and parts of the *Calhoun Papers*.

43. John Tyler, "The Deed of the Cabinet," April 24, 1856, in *The Letters of the Tylers*, 2 vols., ed. Leon Tyler (Richmond, VA, 1884), 2:397; Clay to Willie Mangum, July 11, 1842, *CP*, 9:732; James Graham to William Graham, April 16, 1834, in *Graham Papers*, 1:307; Freehling, *Road to Disunion*, 266; Webster to Joseph Hopkinson, February 9, 1833, in *Webster Papers*, 3:213;

Howell Cobb to James Buchanan, June 17, 1849, and Cobb to Mary Cobb, February 1, 1849, in "The Correspondence of Robert Toombs, Alexander H. Stephens, and Howell Cobb," *Annual Report of the American Historical Association for the Year 1911*, 2 vols., ed. Ulrich Phillips (Washington, DC: Government Printing Office, 1913), 2:164–65.

44. Gamaliel Bradford, *As God Made Them: Portraits of Some Nineteenth-Century Americans* (Boston: Houghton Mifflin, 1929), 89; Freehling, *Road to Disunion*, 265; *Macon Georgia Telegraph*, August 9, 1859; "American Statesman," *Littell's Living Age* 36 (1853): 342; Albert Kirwan, *John J. Crittenden: The Struggle for the Union* (Lexington: University of Kentucky Press, 1962), 115; M.A. DeWolfe Howe, *The Life and Letters of George Bancroft*, 2 vols. (New York: Charles Scribner's Sons, 1908), 1:196.

45. J. O. Harrison, "Henry Clay," *The Century* 33 (1886): 182; *The Republican*, May 17, 1850, clipping in Papers of Henry Clay and Family, LC.

46. James Read, *Majority Rule versus Consensus: The Political Thought of John C. Calhoun* (Lawrence: University Press of Kansas, 2009), 55, 83, 2, 222; Major Wilson, "'Liberty and Union': An Analysis of Three Concepts Involved in the Nullification Controversy," *JSH* 33 (1967): 332.

47. Read, *Majority Rule*, 5, 27–29, 57, 161, 218, 113; Freehling, *Road to Disunion*, 258–59; Merrill Peterson, *Olive Branch and Sword—The Compromise of 1833* (Baton Rouge: Louisiana State University Press, 1982), 41; Peter Knupfer, *The Union as It Is* (Chapel Hill: University of North Carolina Press, 1991), 106–107, 213.

48. Read, *Majority Rule*, 41, 172, 67, 88, 179, 185–87, 118, 122; Jon Meacham, *American Lion: Andrew Jackson in the White House* (New York: Random House, 2008), 185; Adams to Clay, September 7, 1831, *CP*, 8:397; Clay and Oberholtzer, *Clay*, 182; Clay to citizens of New York City, October 3, 1851, to Thomas Speed, May 1, 1831, both in *CP*, 10:920; 8:344; George Bancroft, "A Few Words about Henry Clay," *The Century* 30 (1885): 481; Freehling, *Road to Disunion*, 156; Schurz, *Clay*, 2:161.

49. *Calhoun Papers*, 16: xxviii; Forbes, *Missouri Compromise*, 216; Matthew Mason, *Slavery and Politics in the Early American Republic* (Chapel Hill: University of North Carolina Press, 2006), 303n.

50. John Long to Willie Mangum, April 5, 1832, in *Mangum Papers*, 1:532; Chilton Allan to "Dear Sir," February 4, 1832, Chilton Allan Collection, FHS; *New York Mercury*, February 15, 1832; Hezekiah Niles to Clay, February 28, 1832, *CP*, 8:469; Lacy Ford, "Republican Ideology in a Slave Society: The Political Economy of John C. Calhoun," *JSH* 54 (1988): 419; Speech in Raleigh, April 13, 1844, *CP*, 10:27; *RD*, 22nd Cong., 1st Sess. (1831–32), 288, 292, 67, 258, 257.

51. Freehling, *Prelude to Civil War*, 43; George Dangerfield, *The Era of Good Feelings* (New York: Harcourt, Brace, and World, 1952), 410–11; Sean Wilentz, *The Rise of American Democracy* (New York: W. W. Norton, 2005), 859n; Freehling, *Prelude to Civil War*, 43, 179, 184, 106–107, 138. Gavin Wright, *The Political Economy of the Cotton South* (New York: W. W. Norton, 1978), 131; Peterson, *Olive Branch*, 37–38.

52. Samuel Smith to John Speed Smith, April 27, 1832, Smith Family Papers, VHS; Alexander Claxton to Francis Sorrell, May 24, 1832, Papers of Alexander Claxton, Naval Historical Foundation Collection, LC; Job Pierson to Samuel Pierson, December 14, 1832, oversized, to Clarissa Pierson, December 27, 1832, Box 2, Job Pierson Family Papers, LC. See also Peter Coclanis, *The Shadow of a Dream: Economic Life and Death in the South Carolina Low Country, 1670–1920* (New York: Oxford University Press, 1991).

53. Watson, *Jackson vs. Clay*, 90–91; Peterson, *Olive Branch*, 47; Hugh Garland, *The Life of John Randolph of Roanoke*, 13th ed. (1850; New York, 1866), 358; Job Pierson to Clarissa Pierson, December 27, 1832, Pierson Family Papers; Meacham, *American Lion*, 239.

54. *Register of Debates*, 22nd Cong., 2nd Sess. (1832–33), 470; Clay to Henry Clay Jr., December 30, 1832, Clay to Thomas Helm, January 5, 1833, and Clay to Charles Faulkner, January 11, 1833, all in *CP*, 8:606, 609, 611; Howe, *What Hath God Wrought*, 405; [Joseph Baldwin], "Representative Men, Part I," *Southern Literary Messenger* 19 (1853): 524.

55. Patricia Watlington, *The Partisan Spirit* (New York: Atheneum, 1972), 140–44, 253–60; John Brown to Thomas Jefferson, August 10, 1788, and Jefferson to Archibald Stuart, January 25, 1786, both in Julian Boyd, ed., *The Papers of Thomas Jefferson* (Princeton, NJ: Princeton University Press, 1950–), 13:494; 9:218; Teute, "Law, Liberty, and Labor," 8, 16, 21, 26, 29, 83–84; Andro Linklater, *An Artist in Treason: The Extraordinary Double Life of General James Wilkinson* (New York: Walker, 2009), 85–89, 93–101.

56. Richard Lowitt, "Activities of Citizen Genet in Kentucky, 1793–1794," *FCHQ* 22 (1948): 252–67; Lowell Harrison and James Klotter, *A New History of Kentucky* (Lexington: University Press of Kentucky, 1997), 73–74, 83–85; Clay to John Breckinridge, November 21 and December 30, 1803, both in *CP*, 1:122, 124–25.

57. Thomas Perkins Abernathy, *The Burr Conspiracy* (New York: Oxford University Press, 1954), vii, 15–100; Milton Lomask, *Aaron Burr: The Conspiracy and Years of Exile, 1805–1836* (New York: Farrar, Straus, and Giroux, 1982), 13–86, 123–49 Burr to Clay, November 7 and December 1, 1806, Clay to William Pindell, October 15, 1828, Clay to Thomas Todd, January 24 and February 1, 1807, and Clay to William Prentiss, February 13, 1807, all in *CP*, 1:253, 256; 7:501; 1:272–73, 280; Mayo, *Clay*, 222, 225–26, 261, 266, 270; Nicholas Warfield to John Payne, January 14, 1807, Payne Papers.

58. *AC*, 12th Cong., 2nd Sess. (1812–13), 664; Clay to Langdon Cheves, March 5, 1821, and Toast, May 19, 1821, both in *CP*, 3:58–59, 81–82; Forbes, *Missouri Compromise*, 94.

59. Knupfer, *Union as It Is*, 123. See also Rogan Kersh, *Dreams of a More Perfect Union* (Ithaca, NY: Cornell University Press, 2001).

60. James Hopkins, "A Tribute to Mr. Clay," *Register* 53 (1955): 285; Clay to Francis Lathrop et al., February 17, 1851, *CP*, 8:622; 9:713.

61. Clay to Mathew Carey, October 25, 1830, and Clay to John Proud, November 26, 1849, both in *CP*, 8:281; 10:628; Schurz, *Clay*, 2:160; Speech, April 13 and 22, 1844, and August 30, 1828, all in *CP*, 10:31, 49; 7:450–51.

62. Adams, *Memoirs*, 8:332; Peterson, *Olive Branch*, 49; Donald Cole, *Martin Van Buren and the American Political System* (Princeton, NJ: Princeton University Press, 1984), 238.

63. Peterson, *Olive Branch*, 20; Howe, *What Hath God Wrought*, 405; *Charleston Courier* in *Easton (MD) Gazette*, May 4, 1839; Garland, *Randolph*, 361–62; Forbes, *Missouri Compromise*, 264; Arthur Cole, *The Whig Party in the South* (1914; repr., Gloucester, MA: Peter Smith, 1962), 24; Tyler, *Tylers*, 1:467.

64. *Richmond Enquirer*, January 1, 1831; *Hartford (CT) Times*, August 13, 1832.

65. Schurz, *Clay*, 2:8; Watson, *Jackson vs. Clay*, 92; Clay to Peter Porter, February 16, 1833, *CP*, 8:624; *CG*, 25th Cong., 3rd Sess. (1838–39), 173; *Richmond Enquirer*, June 29, 1832; Peterson, *Olive Branch*, 52.

66. Schurz, *Clay*, 2: 10; *RD*, 22nd Cong., 2nd Sess. (1832–33), 462–73; 723; Clay to Peter Porter, February 16, 1833, Clay to Francis Brooke, January 17, 1833, Clay to Henry Brackenridge, November 12, 1843, and Clay to Nathaniel Beverley Tucker, October 10, 1839, all in *CP*, 8:24, 613–14; Supp.:291, 276; Bettie Boyd, "Henry Clay and the Tariff" (MA thesis, University of Kentucky, 1938), 69–70; Meacham, *American Lion*, 251; Clay and Oberholtzer, *Clay*, 210–11. For the talk, see *RD*, 22nd. Cong., 2nd. Sess. (1832–33), 462–82.

67. William Hammet to T. W. White, February 12, 1833, William Hammet Letters, VHS; Peterson, *Olive Branch*, 65; Speech in Senate, February 25, 1837, *CP*, 9:31–32; Boyd, "Clay and Tariff," 70.

68. E. D. Mansfield, *Personal Memoirs . . . 1803–1843* (Cincinnati, OH, 1879), 251; Thomas Corwin to James Heaton, January 28, 1832, James Heaton Papers, LC; Martin Golding, "The Nature of Compromise," in J. Roland Pennock and John Chapman, eds., *Compromise in Ethics, Law, and Politics* (New York: New York University Press, 1979), 23; *Jackson Correspondence*, 5:53.

69. Clay to Nicholas Biddle, February 16, 1833, Clay to Francis Brooke, February 14, 1833, and Clay to Peter Porter, February 16, 1833, all in *CP*, 8:624, 623.

70. Clay to John Claxton, August 22, 1844, Clay to James Madison, May 28, 1833, and Speech in Senate, February 23, 1833, all in *CP*, 10:101; 8:643, 626.

71. Daniel Webster to Joseph Hopkinson, February 21, 1833, *Webster Papers*, 3:220; Speech in Milledgeville, March 19, 1844, and Clay to Biddle, April 10, 1833, both in *CP*, 10:10; 8:636; Maurice Baxter, *Henry Clay and the American System* (Lexington: University Press of Kentucky, 1995), 84; Freehling, *Road to Disunion*, 284.

72. Job Pierson to Clarissa Pierson, February 12 and 13, 1833, Box 1, Pierson Family Papers; Sol Clark to Francis Blair, March 20, 1833, Sol. Clark Collection, FHS; Calhoun to James Hammond, November 27, 1842, *Calhoun Papers*, 16:555.

73. William Hammet to T. W. White, February 11, 1833, Hammet Letters; Clay to Francis Brooke, February 14, 1833, *CP*, 8:623.

74. Heidler and Heidler, *Clay*, 255; Baxter, *Clay and American System*, 114–18; Sargent, *Clay*, 150; Peterson, *Olive Branch*, 11; *RD*, 22nd. Cong., 1st Sess. (1831–1832), 70, 68; *CG*, 26th Cong, 1st Sess. (1839–40), 97.

75. *RD*, 22nd Cong., 2nd. Sess. (1832–33), 68–79, 464; Baxter, *Clay and American System*, 117–19; Edward Jackson, "Henry Clay's Attitude Toward the Public Land Problem in the United States, 1831–1842" (MA thesis, University of Kentucky, 1934), 36–37; William Hammet to T. W. White, January 11, 1832, Hammet Letters; Peterson, *Olive Branch*, 83.

76. Daniel Feller, *The Public Lands in Jacksonian Politics* (Madison: University of Wisconsin Press, 1984), 169.

77. *Vermont Phoenix*, December 2, 1842; S. A. Douglas to Virgil Hickox, May 10, 1861, in Robert Johannsen, ed., *The Letters of Stephen A. Douglas* (Urbana: University of Illinois Press, 1961), 513.

Chapter 10

1. *Hartford Connecticut Courant*, June 15, 1839; Clay to Francis Brooke, August 2, 1833, and Speech in Senate, April 30, 1834, both in *CP*, 8:661, 722.

2. *AC*, 15th Cong., 2nd Sess. (1818–19), 640, 634–35; *RD*, 23rd Cong., 2nd Sess. (1834–35), 308; *Henry Clay Almanac for the Year . . . 1844* (New York, 1844), 30; Clay to the Gentlemen of the Colonization Society of Kentucky, December 17, 1829, *CP*, 8:139; Ricky Hendricks, "Henry Clay and Jacksonian Indian Policy," *FCHQ* 60 (1986): 221.

3. Alfred Cave, "Abuse of Power: Andrew Jackson and the Indian Removal Act of 1830," *Historian* 65 (2003): 1330–39; Larry Klein, "Henry Clay, Nationalist" (PhD diss., University of Kentucky, 1977), 96–97; Clay to James Conover, June 13, 1830, and Clay to John Gunter, June 6, 1831, both in *CP*, 8:222, 358; Daniel Walker Howe, *What Hath God Wrought: The Transformation of America, 1815–1848* (New York: Oxford University Press, 2007), 353.

4. Cave, "Abuse of Power," 1349–50; Klein, "Henry Clay, Nationalist," 226; Edward Pessen, *Jacksonian America* (Homewood, IL: Dorsey, 1969), 317; Howe, *What Hath God Wrought*, 423.

5. *RD*, 23rd Cong., 1st Sess. (1833–34), 1773; 2nd Sess. (1834–35), 308, 291, 294, 297–98; Hendricks, "Jacksonian Indian Policy," 237.

6. Robert Remini, *The Election of Andrew Jackson* (Philadelphia: J. B. Lippincott, 1963), 75; Howe, *What Hath God Wrought*, 420; Clement Vann to Clay, December 7, 1848, *CP*, 10:561.

7. For a convenient summary of the Removal of the Deposits, see Terry Corps, *Historical Dictionary of the Jacksonian Era and Manifest Destiny* (Lanham, MD: Scarecrow Press, 2006), 253–55. The following discussion has been informed by these works, among others: Howard Bodenhorn, *A History of Banking in Antebellum America* (Cambridge, UK: Cambridge University Press, 2000); Frank Gatell, "Spoils of the Bank War: Political Bias in the Selection of Pet Banks," *American Historical Review* 70 (1964): 35–58; and Peter Temin, *The Jacksonian Economy* (New York: Norton, 1969).

8. Jon Meacham, *American Lion: Andrew Jackson in the White House* (New York: Random House, 2008), 256–57, 268; Willie Mangum to

Duncan Cameron, February 7, 1834, *Mangum Papers*, 2:74; William Barry to daughter, February 27, 1834, in "Letters of William T. Barry," *William and Mary Quarterly Historical Magazine* 14 (1906): 239; Clay to Roger Huntington, June 5, 1834, in possession of the William Lambert Huntington Family, Seattle; *RD*, 23rd Cong., 1st Sess. (1833–34), 547, 1579, 92.

9. *RD*, 23rd Cong., 1st Sess. (1833–34), 59, 1177, 68, 94, 76, 61; *CG*, 23rd Cong., 1st Sess. (1833–34), 57.

10. Charles Sellers, *The Market Revolution* (New York: Oxford University Press, 1991), 336; Biddle to William Appleton, January 27, 1834, and Biddle to Joseph Hopkinson, February 21, 1834, both in Reginald McGrane, ed., *The Correspondence of Nicholas Biddle . . . 1807–1844* (Boston: Houghton Mifflin, 1919), 219, 222; Jackson to Andrew Jackson Jr., February 16, 1824, *Jackson Correspondence*, 5:249.

11. Jonathan Jones, "The Making of a Vice President: The National Political Career of Richard M. Johnson of Kentucky" (PhD diss., University of Memphis, 1998), 253, 260; Donald Cole, *Martin Van Buren and the American Political System* (Princeton, NJ: Princeton University Press, 1984), 244, 272, 286.

12. *RD*, 23rd Cong., 1st Sess. (1833–34), 831–32; Howe, *What Hath God Wrought*, 389.

13. Glyndon G. Van Deusen, *Thurlow Weed: Wizard of the Lobby* (1947; repr., New York: Da Capo Press, 1969), 69; Arthur Cole, *The Whig Party in the South* (1914; repr., Gloucester, MA: Peter Smith, 1962), 12, 18, 30; *Charleston Mercury*, December 17, 1832; Schurz, *Clay*, 2:45; Sean Wilentz; *The Rise of American Democracy* (New York: W. W. Norton, 2005), 448.

14. Thomas Jeffrey, "National Issues, Local Interests, and the Transformation of Antebellum North Carolina Politics," *JSH* 50 (1984): 43–45, 49; Richard McCormick, "Ethno-Cultural Interpretations of Nineteenth-Century American Voting Behavior," *Political Science Quarterly* 89 (1974): 351–77; B. W. Crowninshield to Clay, March 14, 1827, *CP*, 6:304.

15. David Reynolds, *Waking Giant: America in the Age of Jackson* (New York: HarperCollins, 2008), 112; Michael Holt, *The Rise and Fall of the American Whig Party* (New York: Oxford University Press, 1999), 117–18; James Brewer Stewart, "Reconsidering the Abolitionists in an Age of Fundamentalist Politics," *JER* 26 (2006): 1; Harry Volz, "Party, State, and Nation: Kentucky and the Coming of the American Civil War" (PhD diss., University of Virginia, 1982), 34; Thomas Redard, "The Election of 1844 in Louisiana: A New Look at the Ethno-Cultural Approach," *Louisiana History* 22 (1981): 431.

16. Holt, *Whig Party*, 115; Mark Haller, "The Rise of the Jackson Party in Maryland, 1820–1829," *JSH* 28 (1962): 325; Ronald Formisano, "The New Political History and the Election of 1840," *Journal of Interdisciplinary History* 23 (1993): 679; Donald Ratcliffe, "Politics in Jacksonian Ohio," *Ohio History* 88 (1979): 29–31; Michael Holt, "The Election of 1840, Voter Mobilization, and the Emergence of the Second American Party

System," in William Cooper Jr., Michael Holt, and John McCardell, eds., *A Master's Due: Essays in Honor of David Herbert Donald* (Baton Rogue: Louisiana State University Press, 1985), 52; William Shade, *Democratizing the Old Dominion: Virginia and the Second Party System, 1824–1861* (Charlottesville: University Press of Virginia, 1996), 10–11; Donald Cole, "The Presidential Election of 1832 in New Hampshire," *Historical New Hampshire* 21 (1966): 36–37.

17. Shade, *Democratizing the Old Dominion*, 112–13; Holt, *Whig Party*, 30; Wilentz, *American Democracy*, 509; Cole, *Whig Party*, 67. See also Paul Goodman, "The Social Basis of New England Politics in Jacksonian America," *JER* 6 (1986): 30–31.

18. Ronald Formisano, *The Transformation of Political Culture: Massachusetts Parties, 1790s–1840s* (New York: Oxford University Press, 1983), 283; Formisano, "New Political Theory," 674; Shade, *Democratizing the Old Dominion*, 11; Haller, "Jackson Party in Maryland," 307; Volz, "Party, State, and Nation," 31–32; Jeffery, "North Carolina Politics," 49; Christopher Olsen, *Political Culture and Secession in Mississippi: Masculinity, Honor, and the Antiparty Tradition, 1830–1860* (New York: Oxford University Press, 2000), 6, 14.

19. Reynolds, *Waking Giant*, 112; Holt, *Whig Party*, 83, 118, 116–17; Holt, "Election of 1840," 52–53; Formisano, *Transformation of Political Culture*, 283; Pessen, *Jacksonian America*, 264–65; Frank Otto Gatell, "Money and Party in Jacksonian America: A Quantitative Look at New York City's Men of Quality," *Political Science Quarterly* 82 (1967): 235–52; Cole, *Whig Party*, 104; Gene Boyett, "The Whigs of Arkansas, 1831–56" (PhD diss., Louisiana State University, 1972), 259; Marc Kruman, *Parties and Politics in North Carolina, 1836–1865* (Baton Rouge: Louisiana State University Press, 1983), 15, 271; Jeffery, "Antebellum North Carolina Politics," 49n. See also Christopher Waldrep, "Who Were Kentucky's Whig Voters? A Note on Voting in Eddyville Precinct in August 1850," *Register* 79 (1981): 326–32.

20. *Concord New Hampshire Patriot and State Gazette*, September 1, 1834; Wilentz, *American Democracy*, 488, 490–91; Bradley Bond, *Political Culture in the Nineteenth-Century South: Mississippi, 1830–1900* (Baton Rouge: Louisiana State University Press, 1995), 86; Laurence Fredrick Kohl, *The Politics of Individualism: Parties and the American Character in the Jacksonian Era* (New York: Oxford University Press, 1989), 63, 97, 115–17; Sean Wilentz, "Bush's Ancestors," *New York Times Magazine*, reprinted in *Louisville Courier-Journal*, October 23, 2005; Thomas Brown, *Politics and Statesmanship: Essays on the American Whig Party* (New York: Columbia University Press, 1985), 46; John Ashworth, *"Agrarians & Aristocrats": Party Political Ideology of the United States, 1837–1846* (London: Royal Historical Society, 1983), 79; Formisano, *Transformation of Political Culture*, 268; Daniel Walker Howe, *The Political Culture of the American Whigs* (Chicago: University of Chicago Press, 1979), 37; Stewart, "Reconsidering the Abolitionists," 1.

21. *Sing-Sing Hudson River Chronicle*, August 27, 1839; Speech in Wilmington, NC, April 9 or 10, 1844, *CP*, 10:18; Redard, "The Election of 1844," 422; Major Wilson, "The 'Country' versus the 'Court': A Republican Consensus and Party Debate in the Bank War," *JER* 15 (1995): 641, 633; Marc Kruman, "The Second American Party System and the Transformation of Revolutionary Republicanism," *JER* 12 (1992): 521, 528; Anthony Gene Carey, *Parties, Slavery, and the Union in Antebellum Georgia* (Athens: University of Georgia Press,1997), xiii.

22. Kohl, *Politics of Individualism*, 83, 22, 132; Speech, August 5, 1840, *Works of Buchanan*, 4:288; Brown, *Politics and Statesmanship*, 182; Remini, *Clay*, 462; Ashworth, *Agrarians & Aristocrats*, 54–55; Speech in Raleigh, NC, April 13, 1844, and Speech on the State of the Country, June 27, 1840, both in *CP*, 10:34; 9:427; *Washington National Intelligencer*, December 2, 1833; Wilson, "Country Versus the Court," 635–36, 641; Kimberly Shankman, *Compromise and the Constitution: The Political Thought of Henry Clay* (Lanham, MD: Lexington Books, 1999), 93; Daniel Feller, *The Jacksonian Promise: America, 1815–1840* (Baltimore: Johns Hopkins University Press, 1995); Marvin Meyers, *The Jacksonian Persuasion: Politics and Belief* (Stanford, CA: Stanford University Press, 1957), 13.

23. James Heaton to A. E. Varmest [?], August 25, 1831, Papers of James Heaton, LC; Carl Kaestle and Maris Vinovskis, *Education and Social Changes in Nineteenth-Century Massachusetts* (Cambridge, MA: Cambridge University Press, 1980), 220–31; Howe, *What Hath God Wrought*, 585, 582; Harry Watson, *Andrew Jackson vs. Henry Clay* (Boston: Bedford/ St. Martin's, 1998), 103–105; Michael Morrison, "Martin Van Buren, the Democracy, and the Partisan Politics of Texas Annexation," *JSH* 61 (1995): 712–13; Michael Morrison, "Westward the Curse of Empire: Texas Annexation and the Whig Party," *JER* 10 (1990): 226; Kruman, "Special Privilege," 56; Formisano, *Transformation of Political Culture*, 277, 272; Richard Latner, "A New Look at Jacksonian Politics," *JAH* 61 (1975): 968; Wilson, "Country versus the Court," 641; David Hubbard to James K. Polk, February 23, 1840, *Polk Papers*, 5:392; Lex Renda, review of *The Republican Vision of John Tyler*, in *JAH* 90 (2004): 239.

24. Howe, *Political Culture of Whigs*, 187, 19, 21; Kohl, *Politics of Individualism*, 115, 121, 98; Browne, *Politics and Statesmanship*, 217.

25. Kruman, "Second American Party System," 521–23; Schurz, *Clay*, 1:321; Richard John, "Affairs of Office: The Executive Departments, the Election of 1828, and the Making of the Democratic Party," in *The Democratic Experiment: New Directions in American Political History*, ed. Meg Jacobs, William Novak, and Julian Zelizer (Princeton, NJ: Princeton University Press, 2003), 51; Ronald Formisano, "Political Character, Antipartism, and the Second Party System," *American Quarterly* 21 (1969): 684, 700, 709.

26. *Polk Papers*, 4:424; 5:578, 669; Clay to John Henry, September 27, 1827, Williams Brent to Clay, December 5, 1829, and Peter Porter to Clay, January 8, 1828, all in *CP*, 6:1074; 8:133; 7:22; William Smith, *Charles Hammond and*

His Relations to Henry Clay and John Quincy Adams (Chicago, 1885), 47; *Louisville Journal*, February 18 and June 10, 1851; Thomas Ewing to John J. Crittenden, May 20, 1848, Box 156, Thomas Ewing Family Papers, LC; Journal of Joseph Rogers Underwood, December 4, 1826, Series I, Box 2, Kentucky Library, Western Kentucky University.

27. Formisano, *Transformation of Political Culture*, 16; John Sergeant to Clay, September 26, 1827, *CP*, 6:1072; Howe, *What Hath God Wrought*, 237; Wilentz, *American Democracy*, 303; Job Pierson to Clarissa Pierson, December 4, 1831, Box 1, Job Pierson Family Papers, LC; Howe, *Political Culture of Whigs*, 15.

28. Howe, *Political Culture of Whigs*, 14, 12; Thomas Alexander, "The Dimension of Voter Partisan Constancy in Presidential Elections from 1840 to 1860," in William Gienapp et al., eds., *Essays in American Antebellum Politics, 1840–1860* (College Station: Texas A&M Press, 1982), 70–71, 92; Holt, "Election of 1840," 16–17.

29. Zenas Preston Diary, October 10, 1844, Papers of Zenas Preston, LC; James Blaine to Philemon Ewing, October 9, 1848, James Gillespie Blaine Papers, FHS; Allan Nevins, ed., *Polk: The Diary of a President, 1845–1849* (New York: Longmans, Green, 1929), 58; Kruman, "Second American Party System," 526; Elizabeth Boggs to "brother," August 10, 1827, Lilbum W. Boggs Papers, Missouri Historical Society; Albert Hodges to Orlando Brown, October 17, 1836, Box 6, Orlando Brown Papers, FHS; John Brown Diary, January 26, 1821, Southern Historical Collection, University of North Carolina (microfilm); James Clark to Clay, October 20, 1828, and David Trimble to Clay, October 22, 1828, both in CP, 7:508, 513; Frank Mathias and Jasper Shannon, "Gubernatorial Politics in Kentucky, 1826–1851," Register 88 (1990): 258; Tracy Campbell, Deliver the Vote: A History of Election Fraud . . . 1742–2004 (New York: Carroll and Graf, 2005), 12–26.

30. "Alas, Poor Henry Clay," *United States Magazine and Democratic Review* 7 (1840):100.

31. James Graham to William Graham, January 5, 1834, *Graham Papers*, 1:281; Brown, *Politics and Statesmanship*, 49; "Henry Clay as an Orator," *Putnam's Monthly Magazine* . . . 3 (1854): 493; Job Pierson to Clarissa Pierson, December 16, 1831, Box 1, Pierson Family Papers; "American Statesman," *Littell's Living Age* 36 (1853): 341; *New York Times*, March 24, 1852; Holt, *Whig Party*, 487.

32. Irving Bartlett, *Daniel Webster* (New York: W. W. Norton, 1978), 23; Ben Perley Poore, "The Capitol at Washington," *The Century* 25 (1883): 808; Robert Remini, *Daniel Webster* (New York: W. W. Norton, 1997), 53, 186, 329–30; "American Statesman," 343; "Modern Oratory," *Southern Literary Messenger* 18 (1852): 375; Horace Greeley, *Recollections of a Busy Life* (New York, 1868), 251; *Macon Weekly Georgia Telegraph*, September 9, 1859.

33. "Daniel Webster," *North American Review* 104 (1867): 121; Greeley, *Recollections*, 250; Howe, *Political Culture of Whigs*, 214; Merrill Peterson, *The Great Triumvirate: Webster, Clay, and Calhoun* (New York: Oxford

University Press, 1987), 37, 249; review of the *Life, Correspondence, and Speeches of Henry Clay, North American Review* 102 (1866): 149; Francis Fessenden, *Life and Public Services of William Pitt Fessenden*, 2 vols. (Boston: Houghton Mifflin, 1907), 1:12,15; Adams, *Memoirs*, 10:379; Brown, *Politics and Statesmanship*, 51; *Bennington Vermont Gazette*, June 19, 1832.

34. Thomas Cooper to Nicholas Biddle, July 1, 1837, in McGrane, *Biddle Correspondence*, 282; Louis McLane to Kitty McLane, February 21, 1825, Box 1, Papers of Louis McLane, LC; Adams, *Memoirs*, 10:347; John Pierson to Clarissa Pierson, December 22, 1832, Box 2, Pierson Family Papers; Nathaniel Beverly Tucker to Clay, December 25, 1844, *CP*, 10:183; Clay and Oberholtzer, *Clay*, 253.

35. Remini, *Webster*, 347–55, 107; Joseph Rogers, *The True Henry Clay* (Philadelpha: J. B. Lippincott, 1904), 379; "Eulogy of Webster," December 14, 1852, in *The Works of William H. Seward*, ed., George Baker, 3 vols. (New York, 1853), 3:112, 115; Robert Letcher to John J. Crittenden, May 3, 1836, in Coleman, *Crittenden*, 1:99.

36. George Poage, *Henry Clay and the Whig Party* (Chapel Hill: University of North Carolina Press, 1936), 100–11; Nicholas Carroll to Willie Mangum, October 28, 1841, *Mangum Papers*, 3:248; Job Pierson to Clarissa Pierson, December 10, 1831, Box 1, Pierson Family Papers; Remini, *Webster*, 51, 309; Bartlett, *Webster*, 201, 283; "Webster," 114; Allan Nevins and Milton Thomas, eds., *Diary of George Templeton Strong*, 4 vols. (New York: Octagon Books, 1952), 2:107; Thomas Marshall to Eliza Marshall, February 26, 1832, Box 1, Marshall Family Papers, FHS; Cave Johnson to James K. Polk, August 15, 1841, *Polk Papers*, 5:725; Peterson, *Great Triumvirate*, 394.

37. *Webster Papers*, 4:xi–xiii; "Webster," 121; Sam Casey to C. A. Wickliffe, February 23, 1842, Letter, FHS; Holt, *Whig Party*, 526–27.

38. E. Malcolm Carroll, *Origins of the Whig Party* (1925; repr., Gloucester, MA: Peter Smith, 1964), 81–82, 93–97; *RD*, 22nd Cong., 2nd Sess. (1832–33), 808; Clay to James Brown, March 26, 1828, Clay to Nicholas Biddle, April 10, 1833, and Clay to Francis Brooke, February 28, 1833, all in *CP*, 7:188; 8:637, 628.

39. Clay to Francis Brooke, May 30, 1823, and Clay to [John Bailhache], July 14, 1835, both in *CP*, 8:645, 782; Willie Mangum to David Swain, December 22, 1833, Orlando Brown to Mangum, December 21, 1834, and Duncan Cameron to Mangum, February 15, [1835], all in *Mangum Papers*, 2:52, 250–51, 313; George Tucker, "A Discussion on the Progress and Influence of Philosophy," *Southern Literary Messenger* 1 (1835): 416; James Buchanan to Martin Van Buren, May 21, 1835, *Works of Buchanan*, 2:442.

40. Clay to [John Bailhache], July 14, 1835, Clay to Samuel Southard, July 31, January 27, and April 2, 1835, and Clay to Francis Brooke, June 27, 1835, all in *CP*, 8:783, 795, 776, 770, 775.

41. Webster to Jeremiah Mason, January 1 and February 1, 1835, *Webster Papers*, 4:5, 25; Clay to Hugh White, August 27, 1838, *CP*, 9:221; Heidler and Heidler, *Clay*, 273.

42. *Congressional Quarterly's Guide to US Elections*, 2 vols.(4th ed., Washington, DC: CQ Press, 2001), 1:730, 647; *Frankfort Argus of Western America*, November 25, 1835, and March 2, 1836; Jonathan Atkins, "The Presidential Candidacy of Hugh Lawson White in Tennessee, 1832–1836," *JSH* 58 (1992): 28; Williams Moseley to John Moseley, May 22, 1836, Moseley Family Papers, KHS; Noah Brooks, "American Politics II: The Passing of the Whigs," *Scribner's Magazine* 17 (1895): 209.

43. Webster to Robert Letcher, October 23, 1843, in Coleman, *Crittenden*, 1:204–206; Harrison Gray Otis to Clay, January 11, 1839, *CP*, 9:269; Remini, *Webster*, 479, 487.

44. Magdalen Eichert, "Henry Clay's Policy of Distributing the Proceeds from Public Land Sales," *Register* 52 (1954): 27–28; Edward Jackson, "Henry Clay's Attitude Toward the Public Land Problem in the United States, 1831–1842" (MA thesis, University of Kentucky, 1934,) 49–50, 53; Speech in Lexington, June 9, 1842, *CP*, 9:711; Harry Watson, *Liberty and Power: the Politics of Jacksonian America* (New York: Hill and Wang, 1990), 162–63; Garret Wall to "Dear Sir," December 29, 1835, Letter of Garret D. Wall, LC; *RD*, 24th Cong., 1st Sess. (1835–36), 50–52, 1096; Daniel Feller, *The Public Lands in Jacksonian Politics* (Madison: University of Wisconsin Press, 1984), 183; Clay and Oberholtzer, *Clay*, 245–46; Remini, *Clay*, 487.

45. Heidler and Heidler, *Clay*, 275; Howe, *What Hath God Wrought*, 503; Speech in Senate, January 11, 1837, *CP*, 9:4, 3; *RD*, 24th Cong., 2nd Sess. (1836–37), 366, 370, 431; Watson, *Liberty and Power*, 164; Sellers, *Market Revolution*, 347. Clay was reelected as US senator in December 1836. *Lexington Observer and Reporter*, December 21, 1836.

46. *RD*, 24th Cong., 2nd Sess. (1836–37), 438–40; Peterson, *Great Triumvirate*, 251–52; Clay to Letcher, January 17, 1837, *CP*, 9:14.

47. *CG*, 25th Cong., 1st Sess. (1837), 247; [Joseph Baldwin], "Representative Men: Part II," *Southern Literary Messenger* 19 (1853): 593; Brown, *Politics and Statesmanship*, 34, 1162; Wilentz, *American Democracy*, 441, 396; Watson, *Jackson vs. Clay*, 106; Cole, *Van Buren*, 292–93, 301; Feller, *Jacksonian Promise*, 193; *RD*, 25th Cong., 1st Sess. (1837), 251–69 (quotation on 269); Holt, *Whig Party*, 61.

Chapter 11

1. *Washington Daily National Intelligencer*, March 30, 1839; *Niles Weekly Register* 56 (March 23, 1839): 55; Nathan Sargent, *Public Men and Events,* 2 vols. (Philadelphia, 1875), 2:74. Michael Holt, in *The Rise and Fall of the Whig Party* (New York: Oxford University Press, 1999), 89, calls the comment "apocryphal," and Heidler and Heidler, *Clay*, 300, note the doubts expressed about it. But different versions exist, Clay did not deny it, and in fact, it sounds like something Clay might have said, with an eye to posterity.

2. Daniel Feller, *The Public Lands in Jacksonian Politics* (Madison: University of Wisconsin Press, 1984), 127, 68, 79–80, 122; John Ashworth, "*Agrarians*

& Aristocrats": Party Political Ideology in the United States, 1837–1846 (London: Royal Historical Society, 1983), 77; Clay to S. Lisle Smith, June 22, 1838, and Clay to John Dillon, July 28, 1838, both in CP, Supp.:272; 9:214; RD, 24th Cong., 2nd Sess. (1836–37), 662; Charles Morehead to Crittenden, May 19, 1838, Charles Morehead Letters, UK. See also John Van Atta, "'A Lawless Rabble': Henry Clay and the Cultural Politics of Squatters' Rights, 1832–1841," JER 28 (2008): 327–78.

3. David Campbell to Jacob Lynch, April 16, 1838, Papers of David Campbell, LC; Charles Sellers, The Market Revolution (New York: Oxford University Press, 1991), 333; RD, 25th Cong., 1st Sess. (1837), 521; Lawrence Frederick Kohl, The Politics of Individualism: Parties and the American Character in the Jacksonian Era (New York: Oxford University Press, 1989), 114.

4. Lacy Ford, "Republican Ideology in a Slave Society: The Political Economy of John C. Calhoun," JSH 54 (1988): 406; Heidler and Heidler, Clay, 280; Remini, Clay, 513; Adams, Memoirs, 9:398; James Graham to William Graham, October 10, 1837, Graham Papers, 1:529; John J. Crittenden to Willie Mangum, October 11, 1837, Mangum Papers, 2:511.

5. Merrill Peterson, Olive Branch and Sword—The Compromise of 1833 (Baton Rouge: Louisiana State University Press, 1982), 106–11; CG, 26th Cong., 1st Sess. (1839–40), 97–98.

6. William Freehling, The Road to Disunion: Secessionists at Bay, 1776–1854 (New York: Oxford University Press, 1990), 339.

7. Freehling, Road to Disunion, 308, 311; William Van Deburg, "Henry Clay, the Right of Petition, and Slavery in the Nation's Capital," Register 68 (1970): 132–33; Schurz, Clay, 2:155; CG, 24th Cong., 1st Sess. (1835–36), appendix, 225.

8. Comment in Senate, April 12 and March 9, 1836, Speech in Senate, February 7, 1839, and Remarks in Senate, February 13, 1840, all in CP, 7:841, 833; 9:278, 387; Freehling, Road to Disunion, 326, 325; Van Deburg, "Clay," 133–35; Clay and Oberholtzer, Clay, 292; Lonnie Maness, "Henry Clay and the Problems of Slavery" (PhD diss., Memphis State University, 1980), 155–56. See also New Bedford Mercury, December 16, 1842.

9. Maness, "Clay and Slavery," 156, 159, 157; Clay to Francis Brooke, January 13, 1838, Clay to Peter Porter, January 10, 1838, and Clay to Francis Brooke, January 13, 1838, all in CP, 9:129, 127; Van Deburg, "Clay," 136–37, 139.

10. William Preston to Willie Mangum, [October 4, 1837], Mangum Papers, 2:510; Charles Lathrop to John Johnson, April 29, 1839, Charles C. Lathrop Papers, FHS. See also Charles Sellers, "Who Were the Southern Whigs?" American Historical Review 59 (1954): 336, who notes the virtual dead heat between the two parties in the South between 1836 and 1848, with the two dividing the state vote and the Whigs winning around 2 percent more of the popular vote in those presidential elections.

11. Clay to Alexander Hamilton, February 24, 1839, CP, 9:291.

12. CG, 25th Cong., 3rd. Sess. (1838–39), 167, appendix, 354–59.

13. Lewis Tappan to Clay, May 1, 1838, and Clay to Tappan, July 6, 1838, both in *CP*, 9:182, 212.

14. Van Deburg, "Clay," 146; *Charleston Mercury*, February 12, 1839; Sargent, *Public Men*, 2:75; *Concord New-Hampshire Patriot*, March 11 and May 6, 1839; *New York Emancipator*, November 10, 1842; *New York Colored American*, June 1, 1839.

15. Polk to A. O. P. Nicholson, January 13, 1838, John Catron to Polk, October 27, [1838], John Bills to Polk, August 25, 1838, and George Jones to Polk, March 19, 1838, all in *Polk Papers* 4:330, 590, 533, 394; Clay to Henry Clay Jr., March 2, 1838, and Clay to Francis Brooke, November 3, 1838, both in *CP*, 9:152, 245; Holt, *Whig Party*, 98; 442; James Graham to William Graham, October 14, 1838, *Graham Papers*, 2:24–26; Richard Gantz, "Henry Clay and the Harvest of Bitter Fruit: The Struggle With John Tyler, 1841–1842" (PhD diss., Indiana University, 1986), 8; Oliver Smith to Clay, September 28, 1839, *CP*, 9:249–50; *Portsmouth (NH) Journal of Literature and Politics*, June 29, 1839. For a concise summary of the ensuing race, see William Nisbet Chambers, "Election of 1840," in *Presidential Elections*, 1:643–84.

16. William Preston to Willie Mangum, October 4, 1837, Hamilton Jones to Mangum, December 22, 1837, and John Owen to Mangum, January 11, 1841, all in *Mangum Papers*, 2:510, 513–14, 3:92; "Alas, Poor Henry Clay," *United States Magazine and Democratic Review* 7 (1840): 101; *Portsmouth New Hampshire Gazette*, September 10, 1839; Webster to Samuel Jaudon, March 29, 1839, and Webster to Hiram Ketchum, February 10, 1838, both in *Webster Papers*, 4:355, 269; Gantz, "Clay," 23–24.

17. G. W. Griffin, *Memoir of Col. Chas. S. Todd* (Philadelphia, 1873), 20–21, 33, 35, 45; Richard Carwardine, "Evangelicals, Whigs, and the Election of William Henry Harrison," *American Studies* 17 (1983): 56, 62; John Tyler to Henry Curtis, April 13, 1832, in Leon Tyler, *The Letters and Times of the Tylers*, 2 vols. (Richmond, VA, 1884), 1:439. On Todd, see Sherry Jelsma, *Political Quickstep: The Life of Kentucky's Colonel Charles S. Todd* (Louisville: Butler Books, 2017).

18. Harrison to Clay, September 20, 1839, *CP*, 9:342–43; David Reynolds, *Waking Giant: America in the Age of Jackson* (New York: HarperCollins, 2008), 320; Adam Huntsman to James K. Polk, December 16, 1838, *Polk Papers*, 4:652: James Graham to William Graham, December 14, 1838, *Graham Papers*, 2:24–25; Richard Hawes to Orlando Brown, December 13, 1838, Box 6, Orlando Brown Papers, FHS; Thomas Cooper to Nicholas Biddle, October 10, 1838, in Reginald McGrane, ed., *The Correspondence of Nicholas Biddle . . .* (Boston: Houghton Mifflin, 1919), 333.

19. *Sing-Sing (NY) Hudson River Chronicle*, June 25, 1839; Winfield Scott to Benjamin Leigh, August 29, 1839, Benjamin Watkins Leigh Papers, VHS; Allan Nevins and Milton Thomas, eds., *The Diary of George Templeton Strong: The Turbulent Fifties, 1850–1859* (New York: Octagon Books, 1974), 21; Sargent, *Public Men*, 2:81.

20. Clay to Gulian Verplanck, June 8, 1838, Clay to John Kerr, May 22, 1838, and Clay to Peter Porter, June 6, 1839, all in *CP*, 9:201, 188, 324.

21. Adams, *Memoirs*, 9:25; Donald Cole, *Martin Van Buren and the American Political System* (Princeton, NJ: Princeton University Press, 1984), 350. On the trip, see *CP*, 9:330–39, *Boston Weekly Messenger*, August 14, 1839, and Isaac Fletcher to James K. Polk, September 4, 1839, *Polk Papers*, 5:229.

22. *Columbus Ohio Statesman*, August 23, 1839; *Baltimore Sun*, August 26, 1839; *Sing-Sing* (NY) *Hudson Valley Chronicle*, August 27, 1839; *Charleston Southern Patriot*, August 26, 1839; *CP*, 9:335–39.

23. *Macon Georgia Telegraph*, October 15, 1839; *Concord New Hampshire Patriot and State Gazette*, September 2, 1839.

24. Peter Porter to Clay, February 16, 1839, *CP*, 9:287; Glyndon G. Van Deusen, *The Life of Henry Clay* (Boston: Little, Brown, 1937), 327–29; John Cramer to James K. Polk, August 18, 1839, *Polk Papers*, 5:193; Fitzwilliam Byrdsell to John C. Calhoun, June 5, 1849, *Calhoun Papers*, 26:419.

25. Glyndon G. Van Deusen, *Thurlow Weed: Wizard of the Lobby* (1947; repr., New York: Da Capo Press, 1969), 4, 31, 55, 105, 227, 98–101, 111; T. B. Thorpe, "Thurlow Weed," *Appleton's Journal* 12 (August 8, 1874): 161–62; unidentified clipping, 1855, Papers of Thurlow Weed, LC; *New York Daily News*, August 8, 1855; Schurz, *Clay*, 2:179.

26. *Buffalo Daily Republic*, August 14, 1855; Henry Watson, *Liberty and Power: The Politics of Jacksonian America* (New York: Hill and Wang,1990), 213: Van Deusen, *Weed*, 111; Clay to Peter Porter, September 27, 1839, and Peter Porter to Clay, December 16, 1839, both in *CP*, 9:347, 366; Gantz, "Clay," 10.

27. Holt, *Whig Party*, 103, 88; Clay to Nathan Sargent, October 25, 1839; Epes Sargent, *Life and Public Service of Henry Clay*, ed. Horace Greeley (Auburn, NY, 1852), 5; "The Dissolution of the Whig Party," *United States Magazine and Democratic Review* 6 (1839): 355; Arthur Cole, *The Whig Party in the South* (1914; repr., Gloucester, MA: Peter Smith, 1962), 62.

28. Joel Silbey, *Martin Van Buren and the Emergence of American Popular Politics* (Lanham, MD: Rowman and Littlefield, 2002), 122; Heidler and Heidler, *Clay*, 292; Webster to Joshua Bates, May 26, 1840, *Webster Papers*, 5:24; Michael Holt, "The Election of 1840, Voter Mobilization, and the Emergence of the Second Party System," in *A Master's Due: Essays in Honor of David Herbert Donald*, ed. William Cooper Jr., Michael Holt, and John McCardell (Baton Rouge: Louisiana State University Press, 1985), 36, 52–55. For a critique of Holt's economic argument, see Ronald Formisano, "The New Political History and the Election of 1840," *Journal of Interdisciplinary History* 23 (1993): 661–82.

29. Clay to Nathan Sargent, October 25, 1839, and from Willis Hall, November 20, 1839, both in CP, 9:352, 355, Winfield Scott to Joel Poinsett, February 4, 1839 (copy), Leigh Papers; E. Malcolm Carroll, *Origins of the Whig Party* (1925; repr., Gloucester, MA: Peter Smith, 1964), 153; Cole, *Whig Party in the South*, 56.

30. *Proceedings of the Democratic Whig Convention . . . 1839* (Harrisburg, PA, 1839), 5–7; Gene Boyette, "The Whigs of Arkansas, 1836–1856" (PhD diss., Louisiana State University, 1972), 106n; Anthony Carey, *Parties, Slavery, and the Union in Antebellum Georgia* (Athens: University of Georgia Press, 1997), 47.

31. Horace Greeley, *Recollections of a Busy Life* (New York, 1868), 130–31; *Brooklyn Eagle*, October 26, 1841; Daniel Walker Howe, *What Hath God Wrought: The Transformation of America, 1815–1848* (New York: Oxford University Press, 2007), 103; Remini, *Clay*, 552–53; *Baltimore Sun*, December 9, 1839; Carroll, *Whig Party*, 162; *1839 Whig Convention*, 18; *Easton (MD) Gazette*, December 21, 1839; *New York Daily Tribune*, March 3, 1848.

32. Peter Porter to Clay, December 16, 1839, *CP*, 9:365; Schurz, *Clay*, 2:176; *Easton (MD) Gazette*, December 12, 1839; Magdelen Eichert, "Henry Clay's Policy of Distribution of the Proceeds From Public Land Sales," *Register* 52 (1954): 29.

33. *Vermont Phoenix*, December 13, 1839; *Hartford Connecticut Courant*, December 14, 1839; *Baltimore Sun*, December 9, 1839; *1839 Whig Convention*, 20, 22; *Boston Weekly Messenger*, December 11, 1839; *Easton (MD) Gazette*, December 12, 1839; "Mr. Leigh and The Vice Presidency," *Tyler Quarterly Historical and Genealogy Magazine* 3 (1922): 215; E. D. Mansfield, *Personal Memories* (Cincinnati, OH, 1879), 317. The votes on the various ballots remain in controversy. The official report only gave the final vote, but Gantz, "Clay," 11, offers a different count even on that. Various others give Harrison 91 rather 94 on the initial vote, as did a story in the *Boston Atlas*, but the *Courant, Messenger*, and *Phoenix* (see above) have state-by-state breakdowns, and their count seems more reliable.

34. Calhoun to A. P. Calhoun, December 20, 1839, *Calhoun Papers*, 15:22; James Catron to Polk, January 3, 1840, *Polk Papers*, 5:367.

35. Leslie Combs to Clay, December 6, 1839, and Peter Porter to Clay, December 16, 1839, and November 29, 1840, all in *CP*, 9:362, 365, 455; *New York Daily Tribune*, March 3, 1848, *Columbus Ohio Statesman*, December 14, 1839.

36. Clay to Benjamin Leigh, June 20, 1843, and Speech in Raleigh, April 13, 1844, both in *CP*, 9:827; 10:35; Clay and Oberholtzer, *Clay*, 265; "Suggestions of the Past: John Tyler's Administration," *The Galaxy* 13 (1872): 348.

37. Clay to J. S. Barbour, December 14, [18]39, Clay Family Papers, VHS; *Keene New-Hampshire Sentinel* December 25 and 23, 1839; Charles Wintersmith to Willis Green, December 20, 1839, Willis Green Papers, FHS; Gantz, "Clay," 15–16; *Hartford Connecticut Courant*, February 1, 1840.

38. "Alas, Poor Henry Clay," 99–100; Alexander Hunter to Bushrod Hunter, March 17, 1840, Blow Family Papers, VHS; Sargent, *Public Men*, 1:85; [Joseph Baldwin], "Representative Men, Part II," *Southern Literary Messenger* 19 (1853): 593; John Quitman to J. G. H. Claiborne, February 24, 1840, in J. F. H. Claiborne, *Life and Correspondence of John A. Quitman* (New York, 1860), 188–89; Christopher Morgan to Henry Morgan, March 5, 1840, Papers of Christopher Morgan, LC; Burton Folsom II, "Party

Formation and Development in Jacksonian America: The Old South," *Journal of American Studies* 7 (1973): 228–29.

39. Merrill Peterson, *The Great Triumvirate: Webster, Clay, and Calhoun* (New York: Oxford University Press, 1987), 384; Rogers, *Clay*, 197; Clay to James Brown, May 30, 1827, Clay to Henry Clay Jr., August 5, 1832, from Charles Hammond, October 18, 1827, from Caspar Wever, August 22, 1829, and from John J. Crittenden, November 15, 1827, all in *CP*, 6:612, 8:560, 6:1161, 8:89, 6:1265.

40. Clay to Samuel Southard, July 31, 1835, Clay to Christopher Hughes, August 25, 1839, and Clay to Harrison Otis, December 28, 1840, all in *CP*, 8:795, 799; 9:468; Adams, *Memoirs*, 7:273, 229, 530; William Marcy Diary, July 23, 1843, Vol. 81, Papers of William L. Marcy, LC.

41. Calhoun to Virgil Maxey, February 19, 1841, *Calhoun Papers*, 15:508; Clay to Leverett Saltonstall, November 22, 1840, *CP*, 9:454.

42. Clay to John Clayton, December 17, 1840, Clay to James Watson Webb, October 27, 1843, Clay to Francis Brooke, December 8, 1840, and Clay to Peter Porter, December 8, 1840, all in *CP*, 9:465, 875, 458, 459.

43. Clay to John Clayton, December 17, 1840, *CP*, 9:466; Remini, *Clay*, 556, 575; Clay to Peter Porter, February 7, 1841, *CP*, 9:497; George Poage, *Henry Clay and The Whig Party* (Chapel Hill: University of North Carolina Press, 1936), 27; Van Deusen, *Weed*, 119; Nicholas Carroll to William Graham, April 7, 1841, *Graham Papers*, 2:184–85.

44. "Reminiscence of Washington," *Atlantic Monthly* 46 (1880): 372–73; Clay to John Clayton, March 3, 1841, *CP*, 9:510.

45. Gantz, "Clay," 54; Christopher Morgan to Henry Morgan, January 26, 1841, Morgan Papers; Clay to Harrison, March 13, 1841, and Harrison to Clay, March 13, 1841, both in *CP*, 9:514–16; Holt, *Whig Party*, 125, 127; Sargent, *Public Men*, 2:115–16.

46. "Reminiscences of Washington," 376; Clay to Harrison, March 15, 1841, *CP*, 9:516; Gantz, "Clay," 57–58.

47. Robert Morgan, *A Whig Embattled: The Presidency of John Tyler* (Lincoln: University of Nebraska Press, 1954), xii–xiii; "Edmund Ruffin's Visit to John Tyler," *William and Mary Quarterly Historical Magazine* 14 (1906): 196, 204; Freehling, *Road to Disunion*, 357; John Tyler to Clay, March 27, 1825, Clay to Charles Faulkner, January 26, 1833, and Speech in Senate, August 19, 1841, all in *CP*, 4:189; 8:616; 9:587, 591; Sargent, *Clay*, 222; Poage, *Clay and Whig Party*, 33; Henry Foote, *Casket of Reminiscences* (1874; repr. New York: Negro Universities Press, 1968), 57; Gantz, "Clay," 58, 77; Crittenden to Clay, March 3, 1827, *CP*, 6:258; J. D. Stevenson to William Marcy, March 17, 1844, Vol. 9, Marcy Papers ; Edward Crapol, *John Tyler* (Chapel Hill: University of North Carolina Press, 2012 ed.), xvii; Margaret Coit, *John C. Calhoun* (Boston: Houghton Mifflin, 1950), 358; Charles Wiltse, *The New Nation, 1800–1845* (New York: Hill and Wang,1961), 175.

48. For examples of critical words regarding Clay, see Glyndon G. Van Deusen, *The Jacksonian Era* (New York: Harper, 1959), 151, 155; Clement Eaton, *Henry*

Clay and the Art of American Politics (Boston: Little, Brown, 1957), 147; Robert Seager II, "Henry Clay and the Politics of Compromise and Non-Compromise," *Register* 85 (1987): 19; Remini, *Clay*, 586, 581, 583; William Shade, *Democratizing the Old Dominion: Virginia and the Second Party System, 1824–1861* (Charlottesville: University Press of Virginia, 1996) 292; Sellers, *Market Revolution*, 312. For more balanced views, see Gantz, "Clay," 94; Holt, *Whig Party*, 130, 123, 126; and Peter Knupfer, *The Union as It Is* (Chapel Hill: University of North Carolina Press, 1991), 152–53.

49. Holt, *Whig Party*, 123, 130.

50. Seager, "Clay and Compromise," 19–20; Clay to Samuel Starkweather, April 15, 1841, and Clay to Francis Brooke, May 14, 1841, both in *CP*, 9:519, 534; Amos Kendall to [Andrew Jackson], undated fragment, Amos Kendall Miscellaneous Papers, FHS.

51. Clay to Lucretia Clay, June 6, 1841, *CP*, 9:539; William Graham to Susan Graham, June 26 and July 24, 1841, *Graham Papers*, 2:205, 217; Calhoun to Thomas Clemson, July 11, 1841, *Calhoun Papers*, 15:607; David Kruger, "The Clay-Tyler Feud, 1841–1842," *FCHQ* 42 (1968): 167.

52. Shade, *Democratizing the Old Dominion*, 246; Holt, *Whig Party*, 128; William Brock, *Parties and Political Conscience; American Dilemmas, 1840–1850* (Millwood, NY: KTO Press, 1979), 90; Kruger, "Clay-Tyler Feud," 165.

53. Gantz, "Clay," 101, 154–61, 144–46; Kruger, "Clay-Tyler Feud," 168; James Osborne to William Graham, August 15, 1841, *Graham Papers*, 2:228; Speech in Senate, July 27, 1841, *CP*, 9:575; Buchanan to Bedford Brown, July 30, 1841, *Works of Buchanan*, 5:21; Calhoun to Thomas Clemson, July 23, 1841, and Calhoun to James Hammond, August 1, 1841, both in *Calhoun Papers*, 15:647, 659. For views more sympathetic to Tyler, see Robert Seager II, *And Tyler Too: A Biography of John and Julie Gardiner Tyler* (New York: McGraw Hill, 1963), and Dan Monroe, *The Republican Vision of John Tyler* (College Station: Texas A&M Press, 2003).

54. William Graham to Susan Graham, August 8, 1841, *Graham Papers*, 2:224–25.

55. James Morehead to Orlando Brown, August 11, 1841, Orlando Brown Papers, FHS; Gantz, "Clay," 201; J. G. M. Ramsey to Polk, August 25, 1841, *Polk Papers*, 5:737.

56. Gantz, "Clay," 166, 170–76, 78–79, 88; "Documents: Diary of Thomas Ewing, August and September, 1841," *American Historical Review* 18 (1912): 99–102, 111; Brock, *Parties and Political Conscience*, 96; Speech in Indianapolis, October 5, 1842, *CP*, 9:783; William Graham to James Bryan, September 13, 1841, *Graham Papers*, 2:241.

57. William Graham to Susan Graham, August 22, 1841, *Graham Papers*, 2:234; Garrett Davis to John Payne, August 30, 1841, John Payne Papers, LC; Clay and Oberholtzer, *Clay*, 279; Poage, *Clay and Whig Party*, 73–74; "Ewing Diary," 103; Speech in Senate, August 19, 1841, *CP*, 9:587–91; Gantz, "Clay," 182–84; 115; *Daily Missouri Republican*, September 2, 1841; Calhoun to Andrew Pickens Calhoun, July 31, 1841, *Calhoun Papers*, 15:656–57.

58. Holt, *Whig Party*, 134; Kruger, "Clay-Tyler Feud," 171; Morgan, *Whig Embattled*, 36; "Ewing Diary," 105, 107; Clay to Ambrose Spencer, August 27, 1841, and Clay to Henry Clay Jr., August 31, 1841, both in *CP*, 9:594, 599; William Graham to Susan Graham, August 27, 1841, *Graham Papers*, 2:235.

59. Second Bank Veto Message, Tyler, *Letters of the Tylers*, 2:102; Maurice Baxter, *Henry Clay and the American System* (Lexington: University Press of Kentucky, 1995), 167; Thomas Brown, *Politics and Statesmanship: Essays on the American Whig Party* (New York: Columbia University Press,1985), 167; William Graham to James Bryan, September 13, 1841, and April 11, 1842, both in *Graham Papers*, 2:241; 286; Clay to Pierce Butler, August 8, 1842, *CP*, 9:752; Turney to Polk, August 12, 1841, and George Harris to Polk, September 3, 1841, both in *Polk Papers* 5:722, 752; Thomas Ewing to Maria Ewing, September 10, 1841, Box 158, Thomas Ewing Family Papers, LC; John J. Crittenden to W. Thompson, September 11, 1841, John Jordan Crittenden Papers, FHS; "Ewing Diary," 109, 111–12; Kruger, "Clay-Tyler Feud," 172; Poage, *Clay and Whig Party*, 47, 104; John Tyler Jr. to Lyon Tyler, January 29, 1883, in Tyler, *Letters of the Tylers*, 2:122.

60. Holt, *Whig Party*, 137; Gantz, "Clay," 234–38, 246; Morgan, *Whig Embattled*, 162; Calhoun to James Hammond, February 4, 1842, *Calhoun Papers*, 16:108; Brock, *Parties and Political Conscience*, 107; *CP*, 9:529n.

61. "Representative Men," 593; Clay to Robert Swartwout, January 14, 1842, Clay to James Watson Webb, February 7, 1842, and Clay to Porter, January 16, 1842, all in *CP*, 9:631, 648, 632; William Graham to Susan Graham, August 29, 1841, *Graham Papers*, 2:236. For a slightly different account of the Tyler-Clay meeting, see James Simmons to wife, August 29, 1841, James Francis Simmons Papers, FHS.

62. P. M. Wetmore to William Marcy, April 24, 1844, Marcy Papers; William Graham to James Bryan, February 10, 1842, *Graham Papers*, 2:225–26; Thomas Marshall to Louis Marshall, April 19, 1842, Marshall Papers, FHS; *Brooklyn Eagle*, October 26, 1841; Charles Story to William Greenough, February 8, 1842, Charles W. Story Jr., Papers, FHS; Douglas to William Prentice, August 30, 1841, in Robert Johannsen, ed., *Letters of Stephen A. Douglas* (Urbana: University of Illinois Press, 1961), 99; Calhoun to Virgil Maxey, December 26, 1841, *Calhoun Papers*, 16:21.

63. Jeremiah Mason to Webster, August 28, 1842, *Webster Papers*, 5:240; Edward McDermott, "Fun on the Stump: Humors of Political Campaigning in Kentucky," *The Century* 50 (1895): 41.

64. Feller, *Public Lands*, 187–88; Holt, *Whig Party*, 147–48; Edward Jackson, "Henry Clay's Attitude toward the Public Land Problem . . . 1831–1842" (MA thesis, University of Kentucky, 1934), 88–91; *CP*, 9:628n; *New York Tribune*, March 20, 1842; Adams to Clay, September 20, 1842, *CP*, 9:769; Robert Letcher to Crittenden, June 21, 1842, Coleman, *Crittenden*, 1:183; Richard Thompson, *Recollections of Sixteen Presidents*, 2 vols. (Indianapolis, IN, 1896), 2:245, 250–52; Gantz, "Clay," 274; Brock, *Parties and Political*

Conscience, 98–99; Clay to John Sloan, October 23, 1841, *CP*, 9:615; Robert Corbin to Robert Beverly, March 5, 1843, Beverly Family Papers, VHS; Webster to Biddle, March 11, 1843, in McGrane, *Biddle Correspondence*, 345–46; Webster to Daniel Fletcher Webster, April 1, 1844, *Webster Papers*, 6:43.

65. *St. Louis Daily Missouri Republican*, November 22, 1841; Clay to John Berrien, October 7, 1841, Clay to Nathaniel Tallmadge, October 30, 1841, Clay to Brooke, January 27, 1842, and Clay to the General Assembly of Kentucky, February 16, 1842, all in *CP*, 9:612, 619, 641, 656.

66. *CG*, 27th Cong. 2nd Sess. (1841–42), 377. Gantz, "Clay," 94, 330, 304, notes that the dictatorship of the caucus would be more correct, for they often moved ahead of Clay.

67. *St. Louis Daily Missouri Republican*, November 22, 1841; Crittenden to Robert Letcher, May 1, 1842, in Coleman, *Crittenden*, 1:177.

Chapter 12

1. Clay to Lucretia Clay, July 7, 1840, and Clay to Christopher Hughes, November 15, 1841, both in *CP*, 9:430, 622; Merrill Peterson, *The Great Triumvirate: Webster, Clay, and Calhoun* (New York: Oxford University Press, 1987), 317.

2. Richard Gantz, "Henry Clay and the Harvest of Bitter Fruit: The Struggle with John Tyler, 1841–1842" (PhD diss., Indiana University, 1986), 305–10; Clay to James Morehead, June 11, 1842, and Speech in Lexington, June 9, 1842, both in *CP*, Supp.:287; 9:708–10.

3. Daniel Walker Howe, *The Political Culture of the American Whigs* (Chicago: University of Chicago Press, 1979), 130; Philemon Mitchell to Isaac Mitchell, October 27, 1835, Mitchell Family Papers, KHS; Bayard Tuckerman, ed., *The Diary of Philip Hone*, 2 vols. (New York, 1889), 2:314.

4. *Niles Weekly Register* 68 (June 21, 1845): 246–47; *Niles Weekly Register* 69 (October 11, 1845): 93; *Charleston Southern Patriot*, October 8, 1845.

5. *Niles Weekly Register* 64 (July 1, 1843): 279; Joseph Rogers, *The True Henry Clay* (Philadelphia: J. B. Lippincott, 1902), 48; Clay to Francis Brooke, May 30, 1833, Clay to John Clayton, May 27, 1843, and Clay to Brooke, April 19, 1830, all in *CP*, 8:644; 9:821; 8:194.

6. *CP*, 1:31, 96–97; Charles Williams, ed., *Diary and Letters of Rutherford Birchard Hayes*, 5 vols. (Columbus: Ohio State Archaeological and Historical Society, 1922–26), 1:484; Clay to Abbot Lawrence, March 20, 1845, *CP*, 10:209. Given the many transactions Clay engaged in regarding land, animals, and houses, the full citations of those are not given, just the relevant pages in the *Clay Papers*.

7. *CP*, 1:148–49, 114, 683; 2:212; 3:886; 7:414; 8:209–10; Clement Eaton, *Henry Clay and the Art of American Politics* (Boston: Little, Brown, 1957), 63; Patrick Snadon, "Benjamin Henry Latrobe and Neoclassical Lexington," in James Klotter and Daniel Rowland, eds., *Kentucky Renaissance: The History and Culture of Central Kentucky, 1792–1852* (Lexington: University Press of

Kentucky, 2012), 308–15, 339n; Latrobe to Clay, August 15 and 24, 1813, and September 5, 1813, and Agreement with John Fisher, [April 28, 1813], all in *CP*, 1:818, 820, 823, 791. The Clay estate is commonly referred to as being 600 acres, a figure given by one visitor. But other records indicate it at around 515 acres. In a July 5, 1831, letter (*CP*, 8:371), Clay said he had 500 acres; in a 1840s statement of assets (*CP*, Supp.:280), he listed it as 515 acres, the same number he included in an 1851 statement of assets (*CP*, 10:904). In 1851, he was taxed for 510 acres (*CP*, 10:838). See also *CP*, 7:414 and 8:310n.

8. Henry Clay Jr. to Clay, May 19, 1832, *CP*, 8:518; Thomas McCormack, ed., *Memoirs of Gustave Koerner*, 2 vols. (Cedar Rapids, IA: Torch Press, 1909), 1:349; *Niles National Register* 68 (June 21, 1845): 246–47; Lida Mayo, "Henry Clay, Kentuckian," *FCHQ* 32 (1958): 173; Joel Tanner Hart Diary, November 27, 1846, Reuben T. Durrett Collection, University of Chicago.

9. *Niles National Register* 68 (June 21, 1845): 247; *Niles National Register* 69 (October 11, 1845): 93; "Ashland, The Home of Henry Clay," *Century Magazine* 33 (1886): 163–64, 169; Mayo, "Clay," 173; Clay to Mrs. McMahon, [March] 1817, and Clay to Nicholas Berthoud, November 14, 1819, both in *CP*, 2:333, 720; Richard Troutman, "Henry Clay and His 'Ashland' Estate," *Register* 54 (1956): 161, 164. See also Amelia Rogers, "Ashland, the Home of Henry Clay" (MA thesis, University of Kentucky, 1934).

10. *CP*, 8:529, 488; *Niles National Register* 68 (June 21, 1845):247; 1850 Agricultural Census, in *Kentucky Bloodlines: The Legacy of Henry Clay* (Lexington: Kentucky Horse Park, 2005), 9; James Hopkins, *A History of The Hemp Industry in Kentucky* (Lexington: University of Kentucky Press, 1951), 68, 5, 21–22, 6, 14, 20, 45–47, 54, 103, 145–47, 171–74; *Vincennes (IN) Western Sun*, June 5, 1824; *CP*, 8:272–78; 9:671–72; 10:237; 9:794, 123, 242; *AC*, 18th Cong., 1st Sess. (1823–24), 1672. The congressional estimate, which does not include travel, was calculated at the $8/day rate for a session lasting from December 4, 1843, to June 17, 1844.

11. Clay to Biddle, April 10, 1823, *CP*, 8:637–38; Maryjean Wall, "'A Richer Land Never Seen Yet': Horse Country and the 'Athens of the West,'" in Klotter and Rowland, *Kentucky Renaissance*, 131–57; Lee Soltow, "Horse Owners in Kentucky in 1800," *Register* 79 (1981): 206; Jeff Meyer, "Henry Clay's Legacy to Horse Breeding and Racing," *Register* 100 (2002): 473, 475n, 477–81; *CP*, 1:113, 234, 282, 322, 171, 628; 8:371, 582; *Lexington Herald-Leader*, July 9, 2000.

12. *CP*, 6:1296, 1296n; 8:668n; 9:2, 140, 53, 622; 10:247. As Troutman, "Ashland Estate," 168, notes, George Washington received jacks and jennies as gifts from abroad, but Clay first imported them and used them extensively.

13. Troutman, "Ashland Estate," 166–67; *CP*, 2:329, 345; 8:371, 668, 864, 804; 9:219, 236. In 1836, one of Clay's bulls charged Clay, killing his horse but not seriously injuring the rider. See *Salem (MA) Gazette*, September 9, 1836.

14. J. D. B., "Kentucky," *Commercial Review* 7 (1849): 199; *CP*, 8:37, 336, 663, 352; 9:325; 10:326; *Kentucky Bloodlines*, 9; James Hopkins, "Henry Clay, Farmer and Stockman," *JSH* 15 (1949): 89; Peterson, *Great Ttriumvirate*, 373.

15. *Stewart's Kentucky Herald*, February 8, 1797; *CP*, 8:41, 754; Supp.:280; Henry Clay Estate folder, Box 15, Papers of James O. Harrison, LC; Robert Wright, "Corporations and the Economic Growth and Development of the Antebellum Ohio River Valley," *OVH* 9 (2009): 61. For the full references to the land/lease agreements, contact the author at james_klotter@georgetowncollege.edu.

16. *CP*, 1:402, 628; 2:367, 306, 665. Taxes were paid on land, slaves, and the trappings of wealth—pianos, gold watches, stud horses, and carriages, among other things. But Clay's full wealth was larger than his taxable worth. For comparisons to Kentuckians generally, see Lee Soltow, "Kentucky Wealth at the End of the Eighteenth Century," *Journal of Economic History* 43 (1983): 617–33.

17. *CP*, 3:203, 345; 7:207; 9:238n.

18. *RD*, 24th Cong., 2nd Sess. (1836–37), 774; . . . *Compendium of the Seventh Census* (Washington, DC, 1854), 236; Robert Peter, *History of Fayette County Kentucky . . .* (Chicago, 1882), 272; *CP*, 2:159, 169, 249–50; 9:790–93, 791n, 806–807; 10:209–10; Apple, *Family Legacy*, 58–59.

19. *CP*, 2:876; 7:303; 3:886; 7:298; Daniel Walker Howe, *What Hath God Wrought: The Transformation of America, 1815–1848* (New York: Oxford University Press, 2007), 60.

20. Apple, *Family Legacy*, 64–66; Howe, *What Hath God Wrought*, 37; Clay to Christopher Hughes, December 8, 1816, *CP*, 2:259–60; Supp.:143n; Heidler and Heidler, *Clay*, 180, 153; Colton, *Clay*, 31; *Lexington Kentucky Reporter*, June 23, 1823, and September 12, 1829; Clay to John Quincy Adams, July 21, 1825, Clay to John J. Crittenden, July 25, 1825, Clay to Francis Brooke, September 25, 1825, Clay to Lucretia Clay, August 24, 1825, and Clay to James Erwin, August 28, 1825, all in *CP*, 4:546, 551, 615, 589, 598, 586n.

21. Marriage Bond for Susan Hart Clay, [April 22, 1822], *CP*, 3:198; Heidler and Heidler, *Clay*, 155; Apple, *Family Legacy*, 67–68; *Kentucky Gazette*, October 14, 1825; Clay to James Brown, November 14, 1825, George Eustis to Clay, September 20, 1825, and Clay to Etienne Majureau, September 19, 1825, all in *CP*, 4:822, 665, 658–59.

22. Adams, *Memoirs*, 7:52; Remini, *Clay*, 360; Colton, *Clay*, 1:32; James Brown to Clay, July 28, 1828, *CP*, 7:409; Margaret Bayard Smith to Mrs. Samuel Boyd, December 25, 1835, in Gaillard Hunt, ed., *The First Forty Years of Washington Society* (New York: Charles Scribner's Sons, 1906), 375; Clay to Daniel Webster, June 13, 1828, and Clay to Henry Clay Jr., June 3, 1830, both in *CP*, 7:350; 8:231; Henry Clay Simpson Jr., *Josephine Clay: Pioneer Horsewoman of the Bluegrass* (Louisville, KY: Harmony House, 2005), 31–32; Apple, *Family Legacy*, 68. Erwin's sister would later marry Tennessee Whig leader John Bell. See Burton Folsom II, "The Politics of Elites . . . ," *JSH* 39 (1973): 36.

23. Simpson, *Josephine Clay*, 32; Clay to Henry Clay Jr., October 31, 1830, Anne Clay to Clay, April 11, 1832, and Clay to Francis Brooke, August 2, 1833, all in *CP*, 8:284–85, 491, 661; Maria Gooch to Claiborne Gooch, August 27, 1820, Gooch Family Papers, VHS.

24. Simpson, *Josephine Clay*, 33; Clay to Lucretia Clay, November 19 and December 9, 1835, both in *CP*, 8:803, 805.
25. Margaret Bayard Smith to Mrs. Samuel Boyd, December 25, 1835, in Hunt, *First Forty Years*, 375; Clay to Lucretia Clay, December 19, 1835, *CP*, 8:808–809.
26. Unidentified clipping, 1835, Box 64, Papers of Henry Clay and Family, LC; Clay to Lucretia Clay, December 19, 1835, and Clay to Francis Brooke, January 1, [1836], both in *CP*, 8:809, 813–14.
27. James Erwin to Clay, December 15, 1835, and Clay to Christopher Hughes, June 18, 1827, both in *CP*, 8:807; 9:50; Colton, *Clay*, 1:32. Clay may have been partly so attracted to women, because they replaced, in a sense, the daughters he had lost. See Madeline McDowell, "Recollections of Henry Clay" *The Century* 50 (1895): 766.
28. Apple, *Family Legacy*, 32–34; *CP*, 8:489, 213; 7:217; 6:307; Amos Kendall, *Autobiography*, (Boston, 1872), 123; *Lexington Kentucky Reporter*, March 3, 1823.
29. Apple, *Family Legacy*, 69–71; Heidler and Heidler, *Clay*, 234–35; *CP*, 8:284, 442–43, 453–54, 530–31, 675–76, 603; Colton *Clay*, 1:33; Zachary Smith and Mary Clay, *The Clay Family* (Louisville, KY, 1899), 35; Theodore Clay to Henry Clay, May 20, 1832, Box 38, Clay Family Papers; *Macon (GA) Daily Telegraph*, July 22, 1865. But Clay, even then, left funds in his will for Theodore, should he recover.
30. On Thomas, see *CP*, Supp.:100n; 3:83n; 4:13n, 705; 6:385; 7:81; 8:3, 31–32, 132n, 213, 284, 675; 9:87n, 187; 8:843n; 10:215n; Apple, *Family Legacy*, 24, 34–36; Elizabeth Simpson, *Bluegrass Homes and Their Traditions* (Lexington, KY: Transylvania Press, 1932), 379; Seventh Census (1850) Slave Inhabitants, Kentucky, Fayette County (microfilm), 673.
31. On James, see *CP*, 5:188; 8:285, 602, 704, 801; 9:324; 10:215n, 824, 583, 836n; Colton, *Clay*, 1:33; Apple, *Family Legacy*, 40–41.
32. For John, see *CP*, 8:285, 752, 761, 847, 848n; 9:133n, 309, 133, 213, 208, 215, 881; Colton, *Clay*, 1:33; *Boston Bee*, July 24, 1845; Simpson, *Josephine Clay*, 55–57; Myers, "Clay's Legacy," 481, 481n; "Clay Papers Project Completes Its Final Chapter," *Odyssey* 9 (1991): 5.
33. Remini, *Clay*, 201.
34. Kendall, *Autobiography*, 115–18; J. O. Harrison, "Henry Clay," *The Century* 33 (1886): 175; McDowell, "Recollections of Henry Clay," 767.
35. For samples of problems various important figures of Clay's era experienced with their sons, see, for example, Peterson, *Great Triumvirate*, 389, 403–404; Paul Nagel, *Descent from Glory: Four Generations of the John Adams Family* (New York: Oxford University Press, 1983), 157–60, 167–68, 171–73; James Klotter, *The Breckinridges of Kentucky* (Lexington: University Press of Kentucky, 1986), 77, 89.
36. Word also spread through private letters. Harriet Martineau in 1835 told how one son was in the asylum, another was a "sot," a third was "jealous & irritable in his temper," and the two youngest boys "give no great promise

of steadiness." John Gatton, " 'Mr. Clay & I got Stung': Harriet Martineau in Lexington," *Kentucky Review* 1 (1979): 52.

37. See author at james_klotter@georgetowncollege.edu for a list of the deaths.

38. Apple, *Family Legacy,* 75; *CP*, 9:312, 396n; 8:871.

39. Apple, *Family Legacy,* 77–80; *CP*, 9:449n; 10:377; 8:732, 753; 9:801; 8:864; 10:912–13; G. Schmidt to Clay, December 13, 1851, Box 11, Harrison Papers; *CP*, 9:310; 10:259, 279–80, 278n, 808; *Middletown (CT) Constitution*, April 19, 1848.

40. Hunt, *Forty Years,* 259.

41. Clay to Frederick Ridgely, January 17, 1811, Clay to Francis Brooke, August 28, 1823, and April 17, 1834, Clay to James Brown, October 8, 1826, and Clay to John Quincy Adams, July 7, 1828, all in *CP*, Supp.:16; 3:481; 8:715; 5:761; 7:375; Apple, *Family Legacy,* 64; *AC*, 18th Cong., 1st Sess. (1823–24), 1312.

42. *CP*, 8:649, 654, 736; Supp.:274; 4:489; 7:262; 9:518n, 688; Supp.:151; 8:715–16; Remini, *Clay*, 601; Heidler and Heidler, *Clay*, 363; *AC*, 18th Cong., 1st Sess. (1823–24), 1312.

Chapter 13

1. Michael Holt, "The Election of 1840, Voters Mobilization and the Emergence of the Second American Party System," in *A Master's Due*, ed. William Cooper, Michael Hold, and John McCardell (Baton Rouge: Louisiana State University Press, 1985), 56-57; Daniel Walker Howe, *What Hath God Wrought: The Transformation of America, 1815–1848* (New York: Oxford University Press, 2007), 594; Charles Sellers, *The Market Revolution* (New York: Oxford University Press, 1991), 412. For predictions of the dissolution of the Whig Party, see Stephen Douglas to William Prentice, August 30, 1841, in Robert Johannsen, ed., *The Letters of Stephen A. Douglas* (Urbana: University of Illinois Press, 1961), 99; Hopkins Turney to Polk, August 12, 1841, *Polk Papers*, 5:722; Calhoun to Virgil Maxey, December 26, 1841, *Calhoun Papers*, 16:21. For a good summary of the race, see Charles Sellers, "Election of 1844," in *Presidential Elections*, 1:747–98.

2. Holt, "Election of 1840," 23, 58; Michael Holt, *The Rise and Fall of the American Whig Party* (New York: Oxford University Press, 1999), 150, 75, 196, 199, 163; William Brock, *Parties and Political Conscience 1840–1850* (Millwood, NY: KTO Press, 1979), 106, 121; Armistead Burt to Nathan Griffin, January 10, 1844, in Milledge Bonham Jr., "Documents: A Carolina Democrat on Party Prospects in 1844," *American Historical Review* 42 (1936): 82.

3. On the certainty of Van Buren's nomination, see Thomas Hart Benton to Jackson, March 10, 1842, and Jackson to Van Buren, November 22, 1843, both in *Jackson Correspondence*, 6:143, 177; Silas Wright to John Law, November 5, 1842, Letters of Silas Wright, LC; Cave Johnson to Polk, October 21, 1842, and Archibald Yell to Polk, October 31, 1843, both in *Polk Papers*, 6:127, 355; Clay to Peter Porter, September 17, 1843, *CP*,

9:857; Jonathan Atkins, *Parties, Politics, and Sectional Conflict in Tennessee, 1832–1861* (Knoxville: University of Tennessee Press, 1997), 126.

4. Clay to Van Buren, March 17, 1842, Clay to Nathan Sargent, May 31, 1842, and Clay to Francis Brooke, March 23, 1834, all in *CP*, 9:680, 704; 8:706; Donald Cole, *Martin Van Buren and the American Political System* (Princeton, NJ: Princeton University Press, 1984), 188; Henry Foote, *Casket of Reminiscences* (1874; repr. New York: Negro Universities Press, 1968), 59; Joel Silbey, *Martin Van Buren and The Emergence of American Popular Politics* (Lanham, MD: Rowman and Littlefield, 2002), xiii, 60; Sean Wilentz, *The Rise of American Democracy* (New York; W. W. Norton, 2005), 295; Remini, *Clay*, 617; *Brooklyn Eagle*, May 23, 1842. Van Buren has attracted a number of good biographers and in-depth studies. See, for example, the above, plus Robert Remini, *Martin Van Buren and the Making of the Democratic Party* (New York: Columbia University Press, 1959), James Curtis, *The Fox at Bay:Martin Van Buren and the Presidency, 1837–1841* (Lexington: University Press of Kentucky, 1970), John Niven, *Martin Van Buren* (New York: Oxford University Press, 1983), Major Wilson, *The Presidency of Martin Van Buren* (Lawrence: University Press of Kansas,1984), and Jerome Mushkat and Joseph Rayback, *Martin Van Buren* (DeKalb: Northern Illinois University Press, 1997).

5. Clay to Francis Brooke, August 28, 1838, and Clay to Nathan Sargent, May 31, 1842, both in *CP*, 9:224, 704; *St. Louis Missouri Republican*, September 18, 1849; *Louisville Journal*, January 5, 1844; William Freehling, *The Road to Disunion* (New York: Oxford University Press,1990), 340; Schurz, *Clay*, 2:244.

6. "Letters of William T. Barry," *William and Mary College Quarterly Historical Magazine* 14 (1906): 239; John Tyler to Littleton Tazewell, May 8, 1831, in Leon Tyler, *The Letters and Times of the Tylers*, 2 vols. (Richmond, VA, 1884), 1:423; *Washington Globe*, January 9, 1832; William Brent to Clay, November 11, 1829, Henry Shaw to Clay, February 11, 1823, and Henry Warfield to Clay, May 30, 1822, all in *CP*, 8:123; 3:373, 211; *Portsmouth (NH) Journal*, June 29, 1839; Sellers, *Market Revolution*, 317; George Dangerfield, *The Era of Good Feelings* (New York: Harcourt, Brace, and World, 1952), 359; Silbey, *Van Buren*, 24, 56, 218; Terry Cahol to Polk, January 31, 1831, *Polk Papers*, 1:387; Cole, *Van Buren*, 172–73.

7. Holt, *Whig Party*, 164, 170; Freehling, *Road to Disunion*, 402; Robert Corbin to Robert Beverly, March 5, 1843, Beverly Family Papers, VHS; *New-Bedford (MA) Mercury*, December 30, 1843; Robert Hunter to Calhoun, August 21, 1843, *Calhoun Papers*, 17:373; Michael Morrison, "Westward the Curse of Empire: Texas Annexation and the American Whig Party," *Journal of the Early Republic* 10 (1990): 225, 227; Edward Crapol, *John Tyler* (2006), 177, 183–85, 222; "The Last Acting President," *United States Magazine and Democratic Review* 16 (1845): 212.

8. *Columbus Ohio Coon Catcher*, September 28, 1844; Ellis Hartford, "Henry Clay and the Texas Question" (MA thesis, University of Kentucky, 1934),

40–41; Tyler to John Mason, August 23, 1845, Mason Family Papers, VHS; Alexander Stephens to James Thomas, May 17, 1844, in Ulrich Phillips, ed., "The Correspondence of Robert Toombs, Alexander H. Stephens, and Howell Cobb," *Annual Report of the American Historical Association for the Year 1911*, 2 vols. (Washington, DC: Government Printing Office, 1913), 2:57–58.

9. Hartford, "Clay and Texas," 1–10, 13–17; Clay to Jonathan Russell, January 29, 1820, *CP*, 3:371; Clay to Crittenden, January 29, 1826, Coleman, *Crittenden*, 1:40; *AC*, 16th Cong., 1st Sess. (1819–20), 1719, 1727–29; *RD*, 24th Cong., 1st Sess. (1835–36), 1848; 2nd Sess., 982; Speech in Senate, April 3, 1820, Remark in Senate, March 1, 1837, and Clay to Peter Porter, January 26, 1838, all in *CP*, 3:814; 9:35, 135.

10. Schurz, *Clay*, 2:93.

11. Heidler and Heidler, *Clay*, 381.

12. Clay to Leverett Saltonstall, December 4, 1843, and Clay to Crittenden, December 5, 1843, both in *CP*, 9:896, 898; Holt, *Whig Party*, 169; Calhoun to Robert Hunter, December 22, 1843, *Calhoun Papers*, 17:636–37; Garrett Davis to Brutus Clay, December 21, 1843, Box 4, Martha Clay Lewis Series, Clay Family Papers, UK; "Introduction," *Calhoun Papers*, 16:xiv; Matthew Fitzsimmons, "Calhoun's Bid for the Presidency, 1841–1844," *Mississippi Valley Historical Review* 38 (1951): 55–59.

13. Stephen Oates, "Harry of the West, Henry Clay," *Timeline* 8 (1991): 17; *CP*, 9:761, 776; Darman Pickelsimer Jr., "To Campaign or Not Campaign: Henry Clay's Speaking Tour Through the South," *FCHQ* 42 (1968): 275–42; Epes Sargent, *Life and Public Services of Henry Clay*, ed. Horace Greeley (Auburn, NY, 1852), 213–18; Speech in Savannah, March 22, 1844, Clay to Crittenden, March 24, 1844, and Clay to Willie Mangum, April 14, 1844, all in *CP*, 9:833n; 10:3n, 12, 14, 39; George Poage, *Henry Clay and the Whig Party* (Chapel Hill: University of North Carolina Press, 1936), 123–24; Rachel Selden, "Not So Strange Bedfellows: Northern and Southern Whigs and the Annexation Controversy, 1844–1845," in Gary Gallagher and Rachel Shelden, eds., *A Political Nation: New Directions in Mid-Nineteenth Century American Political History* (Charlottesville: University of Virginia Press, 2012), 12, 16–17.

14. Jackson to William Lewis, April 8, 1844, and Jackson to Francis Blair, May 7, 1844, both in *Jackson Correspondence*, 6:278, 283–84.

15. Edward William Johnston to Willie Mangum, September 14, 1843, *Mangum Papers*, 3:468; Letcher to Crittenden, June 21, 1842, in Coleman, *Crittenden*, 1:183.

16. Speech in Raleigh, NC, April 13, 1844, *CP*, 10:18–38.

17. *Washington Daily National Intelligencer*, April 27, 1844; To the Editors . . . , April 17, 1844, *CP*, 10:41, 43–44, 46.

18. Clay to Crittenden, April 17, 19, and 21, 1844, *CP*, 10:40, 46–47; Jackson to Francis Blair, May 7, 1844, *Jackson Correspondence*, 6:283; Polk to Cave Johnson, May 4, 1844, in "Documents: Letters of James K. Polk to Cave Johnson, 1833–1848," *Tennessee Historical Magazine* 1 (1915): 238–39.

19. Brock, *Parties and Conscience*, 120; Heidler and Heidler, *Clay*, 389; Michael Morrison, "Martin Van Buren, the Presidency, and the Partisan Politics of Texas Annexations," *JSH* 61 (1995): 710; Freehling, *Road to Disunion*, 409–10; Merrill Peterson, *The Great Triumvirate: Webster, Calhoun, and Clay* (New York: Oxford University Press, 1987), 347; Wilentz, *American Democracy*, 566.

20. Clay and Oberholtzer, *Clay*, 309; [E. Merton Coulter], "Henry Clay," *Dictionary of American Biography*, 10 vols. (1928–34), 178; Clement Eaton, *Henry Clay and the Art of American Politics* (Boston: Little, Brown,1937), 173; 309; Glyndon G. Van Deusen, *The Jacksonian Era, 1828–1848* (New York: Harper and Row, 1959), 182; Cole, *Van Buren*, 393; Heidler and Heidler, *Clay*, 387.

21. Wilentz, *American Democracy*, 568; Brock, *Parties and Conscience*, 121; Calhoun to Robert Hunter, May 1844, Dixon Lewis to Franklin Elmore, May 9, 1844, James Gadsden to Calhoun, May 3, 1844, and Levoritt Coe to Calhoun, May 11, 1844, all in *Calhoun Papers*, 18:385, 465, 411, 484.

22. Jackson to Blair, May 7, 11, and 18, 1844, Jackson to William Lewis, May 11 and August 1, 1844, and Jackson to Editors of the Nashville *Union*, May 13, 1844, all in *Jackson Correspondence*, 6:283–87, 287–88, 307, 289–91; Polk to Cave Johnson, May 4 and 14, 1844, in "Letters of Polk," 238; Andrew Jackson to B. F. Butler, May 14, 1844, in "Letters of Gideon Pillow to James K. Polk, 1844,"*American Historical Review* 11 (1906): 833–34; Robert Seager II, "Henry Clay and the Politics of Compromise and Non-Compromise," *Register* 85 (1987): 24.

23. *Bennington Vermont Gazette*, April 18, 1844; *Covington* (KY) *Western Visiter*, May 23, 1844; Poage, *Clay and Whig Party*, 139; Clay to Weed, May 6, 1844, *CP*, 10:54.

24. Clay to Peter Porter, September 17, 1843, *CP*, 9:857; Nicholas Carroll to Willie Mangum, October 28, 1841, *Mangum Papers*, 3:247–48; Robert Rhett to Calhoun, October 3, 1842, *Calhoun Papers*, 16:486; Clay to John Sargent, July 29, 1843, *CP*, 9:841.

25. Webster to Letcher, October 23, 1843, Coleman, *Crittenden* 1:204–206; Clay to James Watson Webb, October 27, 1843, Clay to Nathaniel Tucker, January 11, 1845, Clay to John Lawrence, October 5, 1843, and Clay to Peter Porter, October 3, 1843, all in *CP*, 9:875; 10:189; 9:866, 865; Webster to Edward Everett, January 29 and April 1, 1844, and Webster to Daniel Fletcher Webster, April 1, 1844, all in *Webster Papers*, 6:23–24, 41, 43.

26. *Congressional Quarterly's Guide to US Elections*, 2 vols. (4th ed., Washington, DC: CQ Press, 2001), 1:446–47; Charles Sumner to Richard Milner, May 1, 1844, in Beverly Palmer, ed., *The Selected Letters of Charles Sumner*, 2 vols. (Boston: Northeastern University Press, 1990), 1:137; Thomas Ewing to Maria Ewing, January 12 and 23, 1844, Box 158, Thomas Ewing Family Papers, LC; *Louisville Daily Journal*, January 4 and 9, 1844.

27. *Covington (KY) Licking Valley Register*, August 10, 1844, "Henry Clay and Frelinghuysen Whig Principles!!" Henry Clay Misc. Papers, FHS;

Henry Clay Almanac . . . 1844 (New York, 1844), 3; Holt, *Whig Party*, 189; Allen Nevins and Milton Thomas, eds., *Diary of George Templeton Strong* (New York: Octagon Books, 1974), 232; Hugh Waddell to William Graham, May 7, 1844, *Graham Papers*, 2:495.

28. Clay to Reverdy Johnson, April 29, 1844, and Clay to the editors of the *Washington Daily National Intelligencer*, May 4, 1844, both in *CP*, 10:51–53; *Enquirer* cited in Wallace Turner, "Henry Clay and The Campaign of 1844" (MA thesis, University of Kentucky, 1933), 515.

29. William Marcy to P. M. Wetmore, May 2, 1844, Vol. 9, Papers of William L. Marcy, LC; Robert Hunter to "My Dear Sir," February 20, 1843, Robert M. T. Hunter Papers, VHS; Buchanan to Cornelia Roosevelt, May 13, 1844, *Works of Buchanan*, 6:2; Gideon Pillow to Polk, May 22, 1844, in "Pillow Letters," 835–36.

30. Silbey, *Van Buren*, 176–77; *Guide to Elections*, 447, 574; J. D. Stevenson to William Marcy, May 5, 1844, Vol. 9, Marcy Papers; Gideon Pillow to Polk, May 24, 1844, "Pillow Letters," 837–38; Robert Armstrong to Polk, June 3, 1844, *Polk Papers*, 7:188.

31. Gideon Pillow to Polk, May 28, 1844, "Pillow Letters," 840–41, 841n; Gary Kornblith, "Rethinking the Coming of the Civil War: A Counterfactual Exercise," *JAH* 90 (2003): 81; J. D. Stevenson to William Marcy, April 21, 1844, and Silas Wright to Marcy, September 13, 1844, both in Vol. 9, Marcy, Papers; Allan Nevins, ed., *Polk: The Diary of a President, 1845–1849* (London: Longmans, Green, 1929), xiii–xix;; Powell Moore, "James K. Polk: Tennessee Politician," *JSH* 17 (1951): 509, 493, 50–68; Howe, *What Hath God Wrought*, 683.

32. *Brooklyn Eagle*, September 4, 1844; Nevins and Thomas, *Strong Diary*, 237; *Whig Banner*, June 7, 1844; George Yerby to Willie Mangum, June 29, 1844, *Mangum Papers*, 4:141; Kornblith, "Coming of Civil War," 82; Kendall to Jackson, August 28, 1844, *Jackson Correspondence*, 6:316; Horace Greeley, *Recollections of a Busy Life* (New York, 1868), 161.

33. Wilentz, *American Democracy*, 573; Howe, *What Hath God Wrought*, 685; Peterson, *Great Triumvirate*, 361; Jackson to Francis Blair, August 29, 1844, *Jackson Correspondence*, 6:317; John Catron to Polk, June 8, [1844], *Polk Papers*, 7:214; Polk to Cave Johnson, June 8, 1844, "Cave Johnson Letters," 244; "Preface," *Polk Papers*, 8:xvi.

34. J. D. Stevenson to William Marcy, June 3, 1844, Vol. 9, Marcy Papers ; "Political Calculations," *Littell's Living Age* 16 (1848): 421; Roy Curry, "James A. Seddon: A Southern Prototype," *Virginia Magazine of History and Biography* 63 (1955): 126; Thomas Ritchie to Howell Cobb, February 8, 1844, in Phillips, "Correspondence," 2:55; Greeley, *Recollections*, 151.

35. Lucius Little, *Ben Hardin* (Louisville, KY, 1887), 351, 345.

36. *Louisville Daily Journal*, February 3 and January 26, 1844; Harry Watson, *Liberty and Power: The Politics of Jacksonian America* (New York: Hill and Wang, 1990), 6; Wilentz, *American Democracy*, 15; Howe, *What Hath God Wrought*, 74–75; Speech in Raleigh, April 13, 1844, *CP*, 10:36.

37. "The Life and Public Services of Henry Clay" (1844); *Louisville Daily Journal*, January 8, 1844; *Henry Clay Almanac*, 3; Nathan Sargent to Clay, August 6, 1842, *CP*, 9:751. For full biographical citations to the materials, see J. Winston Coleman Jr., *A Bibliography of Kentucky History* (Lexington: University of Kentucky Press, 1949), 173–78.

38. *Louisville Daily Journal*, January 9, 1844; Sellers, *Market Revolution*, 370; Glyndon Van Deusen, *Horace Greeley* (1953; New York: Hill and Wang, 1964), 6, 19, 39, 55, 51, 83, 95.

39. Arthur Moore, "Anti-Clay Songs from the Campaign of 1844," *FCHQ* 26 (1952): 223–24; *Whig Banner Melodist* 1 (September 1844): n.p.; *Henry Clay Almanac*, 4; "Here's to You Harry Clay" (1844), "A Song for the Man" (1844), and "The Whig Chief" (1844), all in LC.

40. Ribbons in Henry Clay Misc. Papers, FHS; Gustav Kobbe, "Presidential Campaign Medals," *Scribner's Magazine* 4 (1888): 341.

41. Kobbe, "Campaign Medals," 341; Moore, "Anti-Clay Songs," 225–33; "The Mask Removed" (1844), 1; *Henry Clay's Duels*, Tract No. 1 (n.p., 1844), reprints one example.

42. John Sacher, *A Perfect War of Politics: Parties, Politicians, and Democracy in Louisiana, 1824–1861* (Baton Rouge: Louisiana State University Press, 2003), 121.

43. "Henry Clay at Richmond," *Indiana Magazine of History* 4 (1908): 124, 118, 121, 128; Schurz, *Clay*, 2:231–32; Clay and Oberholtzer, *Clay*, 305; Peterson, *Great Triumvirate*, 351–52; Speech at Richmond, Indiana, October 1, 1844, *CP*, 9:777–81; Kimberly Shankman, *Compromise and the Constitution: The Political Thought of Henry Clay* (Lanham, MD: Lexington Books, 1999), 103; Leonard Kenworthy, "Henry Clay at Richmond," *Indiana Magazine of History* 30 (1934): 353–59; *Ashland Text Book*, 70–72, Two variations of Clay's concluding words appear in "Clay at Richmond" (1908), 125, 128.

44. *Guide to Elections*, 1:648; William Birney, *James G. Birney and His Times* (New York, 1890), 355; *Boston Daily Courier*, December 29, 1842; *The Liberator* 12 (December 30, 1842): 2056; Clay to Thomas Ewing, November 1, 1843, *CP*, 9:878; Clay to L. Saltonstall, December 4, 1843, Box 35, Papers of Henry Clay and Family, LC. See also *New York Emancipator and Free American*, November 10, 1842.

45. Birney, *Birney*, 4, 11, 25, 30, 33, 40, 139; Betty Fladeland, *James Gillespie Birney* (1955; repr., New York: Greenwood, 1969), 34, 8, 13, 16–19, 44, 71, 83, 93–95: Birney to Clay, August 28, 1832, and December 22, 1837, and Clay to Birney, November 3, 1838, all in *CP*, Supp.:241; 9:111, 244; Wilentz, *American Democracy*, 573.

46. John Galbraith to Polk, September 14, 1844, *Polk Papers*, 8:57; Ambrose Spencer to Clay, November 21, 1844, and Leverett Saltonstall to Clay, December 10, 1844, both in *CP*, 10:156, 177; *New York Tribune*, September 3, 1847; *New Bedford Mercury*, December 9, 1842; *Concord (NH) Democrat*, in Turner, "Clay and 1844," 62; *Brooklyn Eagle*, November 2, 1844.

47. Stanley Carton, "Cassius Marcellus Clay, Antislavery Whig in the Presidential Campaign of 1844," *Register* 68 (1970): 18, 29; *New York Emancipator and Free American*, November 17, 1842; *New Bedford (MA) Mercury*, December 9, 1842; *Bennington Vermont Gazette*, April 9, 1844: *Rochester North Star*, August 4, 1848; Lincoln to Williamson Durley, October 3, 1845, in Roy Basler, ed., *Collected Works of Abraham Lincoln*, 9 vols. (New Brunswick, NJ: Rutgers University Press,1959), 1:347.

48. David Smiley, *Lion of White Hall: The Life of Cassius M. Clay* (1962; repr., Gloucester, MA: Peter Smith,1969), 16, 20–21, 30–31, 36, 52, 73, 63; *The Life of Cassius Marcellus Clay: Memoirs, Writings, and Speeches* (Cincinnati, OH, 1886), 55–57, 74, 81–85; *Writings of Cassius Marcellus Clay*, ed. Horace Greeley (1848; repr. New York: Negro Universities Press, 1969), 137–45, 157–72; Speech at Defense of Cassius M. Clay, ca. September 1843, *CP*, Supp.:291.

49. Smiley, *Lion of White Hall*, 66–78; Jane Pease and William Pease, *Bound with Them in Chains: A Biographical History of the Antislavery Movement* (Westport, CT: Greenwood, 1972), 68; Clay, *Writings*, 158, 170-72; Clay to Daniel Wickliffe, September 2, 1844, and Clay to Cassius Clay, September 18, 1844, both in *CP*, 10:1089, 118; Carton, "Cassius Clay," 33; Holt, *Whig Party*, 183, For an earlier example of a paper calling Cassius Clay Henry's son, see *Haverhill* (MA) *Gazette*, January 9, 1841.

50. On the Dorr Rebellion, see Howe, *What Hath God Wrought*, 599, and Wilentz, *American Democracy*, 540–44. For Clay's stance on Oregon, see Clay to Thomas Worthington, June 24, 1843, *CP*, 9:828–29.

51. J. D. Stevenson to William Marcy, March 17 and 24, 1844, Marcy Papers; Jackson to Polk, June 27, 1844, *Jackson Correspondence*, 6:299; Peterson, *Great Triumvirate*, 361; Major Wilson, *Space, Time, and Freedom . . . 1815–1861* (Westport, CT: Greenwood, 1974), 95; Gene Boyette, "The Whigs of Arkansas, 1831–1856" (PhD diss., Louisiana State University, 1972), 224; Michael Morrison, *Slavery and the American West: The Eclipse of Manifest Destiny and the Coming of the Civil War* (Chapel Hill: University of North Carolina Press, 1997), 5; Holt, *Whig Party*, 207; Handbill, 1844, Archer Family Papers, VHS.

52. Stephen Miller to Clay, June 20, 1844, John J. Crittenden to Clay, November 15, 1827, and Robert Wickliffe to Clay, March 26, 1828, all in *CP*, 10:72; 7:191; 8:89; Robert Winthrop, *Memoirs of Henry Clay* (Cambridge, MA, 1881), 28; Boyette, "Arkansas Whigs," 226, 229.

53. Clay to Stephen Miller, July 1, 1844, *CP*, 10:79; Holt, *Whig Party*, 180.

54. Clay to Edgar Atwater, September 18, 1844, Clay to Lemuel Moffitt and James Bloss, September 30, 1844, Clay to Joshua Giddings, September 11, 1844, and Clay to Thomas Peters and John Jackson, July 27, 1844, all in *CP*, 10:117, 129, 114, 89; Schurz, *Clay*, 2:264.

55. Webster to Edward Curtis, September 1, 1844, *Webster Papers*, 6:53; Wilentz, *American Democracy*, 573; Nathan Sargent, *Public Men and Events*, 2 vols.

(Philadelphia, 1875), 2:244; "Reminiscences of Washington," *Atlantic Monthly* 46 (1880): 674; *Columbus* (OH) *Coon Catcher*, September 28, 1844; Seller, *Market Revolution*, 417. See also "State Central Committee of Whigs . . . to Henry Clay," *Quarterly Publication of the Historical and Philosophical Society of Ohio* 10 (1915): 18–19.

56. Clay to Willis Green and Garrett Davis, September 23, 1844, Clay to John Purdue, September 19, 1844, Clay to the editor of the *National Intelligencer*, September 23, 1844; and Clay to James Watson Webb, September 23, 1844, all in *CP*, 10:124, 119, 122–24, 136.

57. Glyndon G. Van Deusen, *Life of Henry Clay* (Boston: Little, Brown, 1937), 375; Holt, *Whig Party*, 180.

58. Joel Silbey, *Storm over Texas: The Annexation Controversy and the Road to Civil War* (New York: Oxford University Press, 2005), 76–77; Thomas Jones, "Henry Clay and Continental Expansion," *Register* 73 (1975): 266; Freehling, *Road to Disunion*, 436; Peter Knupfer, *The Union as It Is* (Chapel Hill: University of North Carolina Press, 1991), 154; review of *The Last Seven Years of the Life of Henry Clay*, *New Englander and Yale Review* 14 (1856): 545–46; Van Deusen, *Jacksonian Era*, 188; Vernon Volpe, "The Liberty Party and Polk's Election, 1844," *Historian* 53 (1991), at http://web.ebscohost.com; *United States Magazine and Democratic Review* 15 (1844): 323.

59. Peterson, *Great Triumvirate*, 361; Wilentz, *American Democracy*, 569; Clay to Thurlow Weed, May 6, 1844, *CP*, 10:53; Thomas Ewing to Clay, *CP*, 10:74; Thomas Redard, "The Election of 1844 in Louisiana," *Louisiana History* 22 (1981): 426; Heidler and Heidler, *Clay*, 389.

60. For the broad context, see, for example, Dale Knobel, *America for the Americans: The Nativist Movement in the United States* (New York: Twayne, 1996).

61. Heidler and Heidler, *Clay*, 391; *Frankfort Campaign for 1844*, July 20 and September 7, 1844; *Louisville Journal*, July 31 and August 27, 1844; John Swift to James Pegram, September 22, 1844, Pegram-Johnson-McIntosh Papers, VHS; Holt, *Whig Party*, 187, 204; Gregory Borchard, "The *New York Tribune* and the 1844 Election," *Journalism History* 53 (2007): 56; Greeley, *Recollections*, 165.

62. Seward to Clay, November 7, 1844, *CP*, 10:141–42; Holt, *Whig Party*, 205; *RD*, 22nd Cong., 1st Sess. (1831–1832), 267; Speech in Recognition of the Independent Provinces . . . , March 24, 1818, *CP*, 2:522; Mary Ellen Doyle, *Pioneer Spirit: Catherine Spalding, Sister of Charity of Nazareth* (Lexington: University Press of Kentucky, 2006), 77, 258n; Gaillard Hunt, ed., *The First Forty Years of Washington Society* (New York: Charles Scribner's Sons, 1906), 340n; "Senate Chaplain," www.senate.gov/artandhistory/history/common/briefing/senate-chaplain,htm; Clay to James Simpson, August 15, 1843, and Clay to James Watson Webb, October 25, 1844, both in *CP*, 9:845; 10:176.

63. Clay to Theodore Frelinghuysen, May 22, 1844, Clay to Thomas Ewing, June 19, 1844, and Clay to Andrew Burt, October 9, 1844, all in *CP*, 10:13, 71, 131; Holt, *Whig Party*, 207; Borchard, "Tribune," 56; George Dallas to Polk,

September 20 and October 8, 1844, and Barnabas Bates to Polk, September 21, 1844, all in *Polk Papers*, 8:97, 169, 103; J. W. Edmonds to William Marcy, October 12, 1844, Vol. 9, Marcy Papers; Francis Blair to Jackson, October 27, 1844, *Jackson Correspondence*, 6:328; Nicholas Carroll to Willie Mangum, September 8, 1844, *Mangum Papers*, 4:182; Charles Davis to Clay, October 4, 1844, *CP*, 10:130.

64. *CP*, 9:754n; Holt, *Whig Party*, 185; *New Bedford (MA) Mercury*, December 9, 1842; Adams, *Memoirs*, 12:45.

65. Clay to John Clayton, August 22, 1844, and Clay to Clay Club, May 11, 1844, both in *CP*, 10:102, 59; *Macon Georgia Telegraph*, June 21, 1844; Clay to Willie Mangum, September 11, 1844, *CP*, 10:115.

66. James Swain, *Life and Speeches of Henry Clay* (New York, 1844), 141; Clay to Alexander Plumer, August 1, 1844, and Kendall to Clay, August 6, 1844, both in *CP*, 10:92, 94–95; *Clay's Duels*, 4; *New Orleans Daily Creole*, September 4, 1856; *Bennington Vermont Gazette*, August 27, 1844. On the duel, see notes in chapter 3 and Melba Porter Hay, "Compromiser or Conspirator? Henry Clay and the Graves-Cilley Duel," in John David Smith and Thomas Appleton Jr., eds., *A Mythic Land Apart: Reassessing Southerners and Their History* (Westport, CT: Greenwood, 1997), 57–79.

67. *Washington Globe*, in *Macon Georgia Telegraph*, July 2, 1844; *Boston Courier*, December 29, 1842; *CP*, 10:103n; *Frankfort Campaign for 1844*, September 21, 1844; Rogers, *Clay*, 187.

68. Adams, *Memoirs*, 12:21, 7:461–62; *Little Rock Arkansas Gazette*, May 29, 1844; *Ohio Statesman* in *Macon Georgia Telegraph*, July 18, 1843; Blair to Clay, March 28, 1828, Clay to John Harvie, June 5, 1828, Clay to Benjamin Leigh, July 20, 1844, Clay to Francis Brooke, March 10. 1838, and Clay to Blair, January 8, [1825], all in *CP*, 7:194, 327; 10:88; 7:154; 4:910; Clay to Edmund Taylor, September 17, 1844, Henry Clay Papers, UK.

69. *Huntsville Democrat* in *Macon Georgia Telegraph*, June 27, 1844; Major Willcox and W. H. Hardee to Clay, August 27, 1844, Letcher to Clay, July 6, 1844, Clay to Willie Magnum, September 11, 1844, and Clay to Benjamin Leigh, September 30, 1844, all in *CP*, 10:103, 81–82, 115, 128; *The Coalition of 1825 or Henry Clay's Bargain with John Quincy Adams* (Albany, NY, 1844), 516.

70. Robert Walker to Polk, May 30, 1844, and Andrew Donelson to Polk, May 31, 1844, both in *Polk Papers*, 7:168, 169.

71. *New York Tribune*, September 3, 1847; Holt, *Whig Party*, 184; Schurz, *Clay*, 2:258; Peterson, *Great Triumvirate*, 363; Wilentz, *American Democracy*, 573; Clay and Oberholtzer, *Clay*, 313; Polk to John Kane, June 19, 1844, George Dallas to Polk, July 6, 1844, both in *Polk Papers*, 7:267, 321–23; Buchanan to Polk, September 23, 1844, *Buchanan Correspondence*, 6:71; *New Orleans Daily Creole*, September 4, 1856; J. George Harris to Polk, July 25, 1844, *Polk Papers*, 7:395.

72. Clay to Joseph Ingersoll, August 29, 1844, and Clay to Thomas Miller, September 9, 1844, both in *CP*, 10:106, 110; *Bennington Vermont Gazette*, November 14, 1843; Greeley, *Recollections*, 165.

73. Broadside, "Electors of Michigan," at http://infoweb.newbank.com; Clay to F. M. Wright, October 21, 1844, *CP*, 10:134; *New York Plebeian*, in *Bennington Vermont Gazette*, March 5, 1844; *Macon Georgia Telegraph*, July 18 and 23, 1843, and June 14, 1842; Clay to Thomas Bond, September 10, 1844, *CP*, 10:111; Broadside, "The Em*body*ment," copy in possession of George McGee; *Concord New Hampshire Gazette*, October 22, 1844.

74. "One Last Word before The Election," *United States Magazine and Democratic Review* 15 (1844): 326, 325; *Henry Clay and the Laboring Millions*, Tract No. 8 (n.p., 1844), 38, 40; *An Essay on the American System* . . . (n.p., 1844), 3, 5, 8, 14; *Concord New Hampshire Gazette*, July 9, 1844; *Richmond Enquirer*, June 15, 1832.

75. "Mr. Clay—The Texas Question," *American Review: A Whig Journal* 1 (1845): 75–76, 79; Sellers, "Election of 1844," 1:791; Peterson, *Great Triumvirate*, 354; Clay and Oberholtzer, *Clay*, 313.

76. *Brooklyn Eagle*, October 22, 1844.

77. Holt, *Whig Party*, 1012n; Broadside, *Presidential Chart* (n.p., 1844); R. T. Allison to John Bullitt, September 3, 1844, Bullitt Family Papers–Oxmoor Collection, FHS; John Swift to James Pegram, September 22, 1844, Pegram-Johnson-McIntosh Papers; Clay to William Campbell, October 26, 1844, *CP*, 10:137.

78. Madeline McDowell, "Recollections of Henry Clay," *The Century* 50 (1895): 768; *Charleston Southern Patriot*, November 25, 1844; Susan Clay "Henry Clay and His Slanderers," in the chapter "Henry Clay and The Presidency," Box 55, Clay Family Papers; Leslie Combs to Phillip Phoenix[?], November 20, 1844, Leslie Combs Papers, UK; Peterson, *Great Triumvirate*, 366; Joseph Hoxie to Clay, November 26, 1844, and Clay to Hoxie, December 4, 1844, both in *CP*, 10:159, 171; Clay and Oberholzer, *Clay*, 321.

79. Mildred [unknown] to Eliza Holladay, November 11, 1844, Holladay Family Papers, VHS; Zenas Preston Diary, November 20, 1844, Papers of Zenas Preston, LC; *New York Times*, July 3, 1852; E. O. Mansfield, *Personal Memories* (Cincinnati, OH, 1879), 211: "The Statesmen of America . . . ," *Littell's Living Age* 12 (1847): 571; Van Deusen, *Horace Greeley*, 95; Fillmore to Clay, November 11, 1844, *CP*, 10:144–45; Mary Robertson to John Bullitt, November 24, 1844, Bullitt Family Papers; John Freeman to Sally Hamilton, November 28, 1844, Box 2, Orr Collection, Tennessee State Library and Archives; George Julian, "Some Ante-Bellum Politics," *North American Review* 163 (1896): 198; D. D. Mitchell to James B. Clay, November 22, 1844, Box 41, Clay Family Papers; Octavia LaVert to Clay, December 6, 1844, *CP*, 10:174; Combs to Phillip Phoenix, November 20, 1844, Combs Papers.

80. Morrison, "Westward the Curse of Empire," 221; Millard Fillmore to Clay, November 11, 1844, *CP*, 10:144; Holt, *Whig Party*, 195: *New Orleans Bee*, November 7, 1844; Clay to John Clayton, December 2, 1844, *CP*, 10:167.

81. Holt, *Whig Party*, 201; Dixon Lewis to [Richard Cralle], March 19, 1844, *Calhoun Papers*, 17:879; Anthony Gene Carey, *Politics, Slavery, and the*

Union in Antebellum Georgia (Athens: University of Georgia Press, 1997), 81; Peterson, *Great Triumvirate,* 766; Volpe, "Liberty Party," 10.

82. Shelden, "Not So Strange Bedfellows," 21–23; Robert Merry, *A Country of Vast Designs: James K. Polk, the Mexican War, and the Conquest of the American Continent* (New York: Simon and Schuster, 2009), 110.

83. William Marcy to Polk, June 28, 1844, William Cramer to Polk, September 17, 1844, and Gansevoort Melville to Polk, October 3, 1844, all in *Polk Papers,* 7:297; 8:79, 146; John Walker to Willie Mangum, April 24, 1844, and Louisa Childs to Mangum, February 10, 1845, both in *Mangum Papers,* 4:119, 262; Theodore Frelinghuysen to Clay, November 9, 1844, *CP,* 10:143; Van Deusen, *Horace Greeley,* 136; Glyndon G. Van Deusen, *Thurlow Weed* (1947; repr. New York: Da Capo Press, 1969), 133, 136; *Portland (ME) Advertiser,* clipping, 1855, in Scrapbook, Papers of Thurlow Weed, LC.

84. Volpe, "Liberty Party," 910; Lex Renda, "Retrospective Voting and the Presidential Election of 1844: The Texas Issue Revisited," *Presidential Studies Quarterly* 24 (1994): 837–40; Joel Silbey, *Party over Section: The Rough and Ready Presidential Election of 1848* (Lawrence: University Press of Kansas, 2009), 10, 14; Holt, *Whig Party,* 201.

85. John Blair to Polk, March 11, 1843, and Alfred Balch to Polk, July 9, 1844, both in *Polk Papers,* 6:243; 7:326; Nathan Sargent to Willie Mangum, August 21, 1844, *Mangum Papers,* 4:180.

86. Greeley, *Recollections,* 165; John McKeon to Polk, November 2, 1844, *Polk Papers,* 8:279.

87. Seager, "Clay and Compromise," 26; P. M. Wetmore to William Marcy, July 24, 1844, Vol. 9, Marcy Papers; Cole, *Van Buren,* 399; Nicholas Carroll to Willie Mangum, September 8, 1844, *Mangum Papers,* 4:181; Jackson to Polk, September 26, 1844, *Jackson Correspondence,* 6:322; Alfred Balch to Polk, August 12, 1844, William Marcy to Polk, September 11, 1844, and James McKisick to Polk, September 15, 1844, all in *Polk Papers,* 7:448; 8:44, 65.

88. Cole, *Van Buren,* 399; John Wendell to Clay, March 11, 1848, *CP,* 10:414; Nicholas Carroll to Willie Mangum, October 7, 1844, and James Auchincloss to Mangum, October 15, 1844, both in *Mangum Papers,* 4:205, 213; Tracy Campbell, *Deliver the Vote: A History of Election Fraud . . .* (New York: Carroll and Graf, 2005), xvi, 20, xvii; Mark Summers, *The Plundering Generation* (New York: Oxford University Press, 1987), 58–59; Zachary Taylor to R. C. Wood, February 18, 1848, in *Letters of Zachary Taylor* (Rochester, NY: Genesee Press, 1908), 153; *Niles Register* 67 (November 2, 1844): 144; Leverett Saltonstall to Clay, December 10, 1844, Central Clay Committee to Clay, March 4, 1845, and Frelinghuysen to Clay, November 9, 1844, all in *CP,* 10: 177, 20–34, 143; Leslie Combs to W. W. Boardman, November 28, 1844, Leslie Combs Misc. Letters, FHS; George Davis to Clay, November 19, 1844, *CP,* 10:151; *Boston Weekly Messenger,* November 13, 1844. An *Atlanta Constitution* story, circa 1884 (Box 64, Clay Family Papers), indicated that the Clay Club of New York City reported that Clay ally Leslie Combs had rejected an offer to give Clay 5,000 New York City votes in exchange for $50,000.

89. William Gould to Clay, December 18, 1844, *CP*, 10:180; Carey, *Parties, Slavery, and the Union*, 77–78.

90. Holt, *Whig Party*, 198; Sacher, *Perfect War of Politics*, 124–25; Turner, "Campaign of 1844," 60; "Reminiscences of Washington," *Atlantic Monthly* 46 (1880): 674; Sargent, *Public Men*, 2:248–49; Rednard, "Election of 1844," 429; Daniel Walker Howe, *The Political Culture of The American Whigs* (Chicago: University of Chicago Press, 1979), 129; Remini, *Clay*, 665; Heidler and Heidler, *Clay*, 394; Andre Roman to Clay, December 2, 1844, *CP*, 10:169; Campbell, *Deliver the Vote*, 24–25. Democrats made charges of fraud as well, with the strongest case being in Tennessee, where Clay carried his opponent's home state by a mere 113 votes. But Clay's overall vote in Tennessee—which had twice defeated Polk for the governorship—basically matched Harrison's of four years earlier, while Polk's count was 11,000 greater than the Democratic vote of 1840. See *Frankfort Campaign for 1844*, June 4, 1845, and *Guide to Elections*, 1:649.

91. Freehling, *Road to Disunion*, 438.

92. Seager, "Compromise and Non-Compromise," 4; Holt, *Whig Party*, 332, 197–99; Brock, *Parties and Political Conscience*, 25, 154. Statistics generally come from the *Frankfort Campaign for 1844*, June 4, 1845, which has county-by-county figures for the nation and indicated it used "the official returns." Slightly different totals sometimes appear in *Guide to Elections*, 1:649. As Holt, *Whig Party*, 1012n, notes, some of the decline in the Whig vote in the South could be explained by the fact that several southern states voted after the election results seemed clear and thus Whigs had not gone to the polls as they might otherwise have.

93. *Frankfort Campaign for 1844*, September 28, 1844; Edmund Wiltse et al. to Samuel Burke, October 25, 1844, Burke Family Papers, VHS; Gansevoort Melville to Polk, October 26, 1844, *Polk Papers*, 8:225, 327–28, Volpe, "Liberty Party," 698–703; Wilentz, *American Democracy*, 574. Polk won these states in close votes: Pennsylvania—6,332 (26 electoral votes); New York—5,106 (36); Michigan—3,466 (5); Indiana—2,314 (12); Georgia—2,047 (10); and Louisiana—699 (6). Howe, *Political Culture*, 17, notes that because of racially inspired property tests, ten thousand free blacks in New York State could not vote. Had they voted, would Clay have won?

94. *Frankfort Campaign for 1844*, June 4, 1845; Thomas Alexander, "The Dimensions of Voter Partisan Constancy in Presidential Elections From 1840 to 1860," in William Gienapp et al., *Essays on American Antebellum Politics, 1840–1860* (College Station: Texas A&M Press, 1982), 71–73. In fact, a shift of a total of under 15,000 votes from Polk to Clay in five states other than New York would have given the Kentuckian a huge victory in the electoral college. Those votes and New York's would have made the numbers 200–75 in favor of Clay rather than the 105–170 that resulted.

95. Jackson to Andrew J. Donelson, November 18, 1844, *Jackson Correspondence*, 6:329; Preston Diary, November 20, 1844, Zenas Preston Papers; *United States Magazine and Democratic Review* 15 (1844): 430, 427; Joseph Southall

to Polk, November 11, 1844, *Polk Papers*, 8:309; *Charleston Southern Patriot*, November 25, 1844.

Chapter 14

1. For expressions to Clay, see *CP*, 10:144–86.
2. For gifts to Clay, see *CP*, 10:212, 217, 286, 163, 204, 253n, 198, 185; M. E. Bailey to Mary Eccles, January 13, [1845], in possession of Betty Jones, Richmond, KY.
3. Clay to Octavia LeVert, May 20, 1845, *CP*, 10:226; 846n, 200, 202, 207n, 221, 221n; Merrill Peterson, *The Great Triumvirate: Webster, Clay, and Calhoun* (New York: Oxford Univeristy Press, 1987), 372; Remini, *Clay*, 673; Heidler and Heidler, *Clay*, 395–96; Clay and Oberholtzer, *Clay*, 324.
4. Michael Holt, *The Rise and Fall of the American Whig Party* (New York: Oxford University Press, 1999), 233; Horace Greeley, *Recollections of a Busy Life* (New York, 1868), 161; William Marcy Diary, June 19–20, 1849, Vol. 82, Papers of William L. Marcy, LC; William Dusinberre, *Slavemaster President: The Double Career of James Polk* (New York: Oxford University Press, 2003), 119; Robert Merry, *A Country of Vast Designs: James K. Polk, the Mexican War, and the Conquest of the American Continent* (New York: Simon and Schuster, 2009), 17,159, 337, 269; William Brock, *Parties and Political Conscience: American Dilemmas, 1840–1850* (Millwood, NY: KTO Press, 1979), 164–65; Amy Greenberg, *A Wicked War: Polk, Clay, Lincoln, and the 1846 US Invasion of Mexico* (New York: Alfred A. Knopf, 2012), 36.
5. John Tyler, "A Statement of What Transpired . . . ," Davis Family Papers, VHS; Allen Nevins, ed., *Polk: The Diary of a President, 1845–1849* (London: Longmans, Green, 1929), 5, 83, 91; Dusinberre, *Slavemaster President*, 133–75; Charles Sellers, *The Market Revolution* (New York: Oxford University Press, 1991), 422, 427; Merry, *Country of Vast Designs*, 327; Augustus Storrs to Webster, October 23, 1847, *Webster Papers*, 6:243. Greenberg, *A Wicked War*, has an excellent discussion of the conflict and the personalities involved. See also Scott Silverstone, *Divided Union: The Politics of War in the Early American Republic* (Ithaca, NY: Cornell University Press, 2004).
6. Brock, *Parties and Political Conscience*, xi, 170–71; Webster to Robert Winthrop, December 13, 1844, and James Kent to Webster, October 13, 1847, both in *Webster Papers*, 6:62, 243, 247; Charles Sumner to Francis Lieber, March 22, 1847, in *The Selected Letters of Charles Sumner*, 2 vols., ed. Beverly Wilson Palmer (Boston: Northeastern University Press, 1990), 189; Nolan Fowler, "Territorial Expansion—A Threat to the Republic," *Pacific Northwest Quarterly* 53 (1962): 36; *Lexington Observer & Reporter*, April 2, 1845; *Louisville Journal*, December 11, 1844; Daniel Walker Howe, *The Political Culture of the American Whigs* (Chicago: University of Chicago Press, 1979), 93; Norman Graebner, "Party Politics and the Trist Mission," *JSH* 19 (1957): 150–52; Daniel Walker Howe, *What Hath God Wrought: The Transformation of America, 1815–1848* (New York: Oxford University Press, 2007), 750.

7. Joseph Pearson, "The Dilemma of Dissent: Kentucky's Whigs and the Mexican War," *OVH* 12 (2012): 24–47; *United States Magazine and Democratic Review* 22 (1848): 2; Fowler, "Territorial Expansion," 42; Merry, *Country of Vast Designs*, 322–23.

8. Clay to Martha Buckingham, March 31, 1845, Clay to John Thompson, April 23, 1845, and Clay to Octavia LeVert, June 25, 1846, all in *CP*, 10:212, 219, 274; *Lexington Observer & Reporter*, November 14, 1846; John Bassett Moore, "Henry Clay and Pan-Americanism," *Columbia University Quarterly* 17 (1915): 357: Clay to Octavia LeVert, November 6, 1846, Clay to Horace Greeley, June 23, 1846, and Clay to Epes Sargent, February 15, 1847, all in *CP*, 10:285, 272–74, 308.

9. Norman Tutorow, *Texas Annexation and the Mexican War* (Palo Alto, CA: Chadwick House, 1978), 280; Apple, *Family Legacy*, 24, 27, 30, 38–39, 70; *Richmond Enquirer*, August 23, 1831; *CP*, 6:366, 385; 7:80–81, 969, 571; 8:18, 91, 117, 231, 346–47; Clay to Clay Jr., June 30, 1830, *CP*, 8:231.

10. *Lexington Observer & Reporter*, October 18, 1832; Apple, *Family Legacy*, 46–47, 50; *CP*, 8:648, 771, 9:152n; Clay to Clay Jr., November 14, 1828, and February 20, 1840, both in *CP*, 7:538; 9:391.

11. Clay to Lucretia Clay, April 25, 1840, *CP*, 9:409; Apple, *Family Legacy*, 75; John C. Breckinridge, *An Address on the Occasion of the Burial of the Kentucky Volunteers Who Fell at Buena Vista* (Lexington, KY, 1847), 8.

12. Henry Clay Jr. Journal, July 8 and 23, September 21, and October 6, 1846, and February 1847, Box 7, Henry Clay Foundation Papers, UK; Mary Black, "'The Stoutest Son': The Mexican-American War Journal of Henry Clay Jr.," *Register* 106 (2008): 12–37, 40; Clay Jr. to Clay, February 12, 1847, *CP*, 10:305: Clay to James B. Clay, February 24, 1847, and Clay to Lucretia Clay, March 13, 1847, both in Box 39, Papers of Henry Clay and Family, LC; *Covington Licking Valley Register*, May 14, 1847; Clay to Mary Bayard, April 16, 1847, *CP*, 10:321; "Battle of Buena Vista," *Littell's Living Age* 13 (1847): 235; Joel Tanner Hart Diary, July 20, 1847, Box 6, Hart Papers, Reuben T. Durrett Collection, University of Chicago.

13. *New York Tribune*, August 23, 1847; *Covington (KY) Licking Valley Register*, May 14, 1847; Clay to John Clayton, April 16, 1847, *CP*, 10:322; Merry, *Country of Vast Designs*, 355; Greenberg, *A Wicked War*, 167; Remini, *Clay*, 685; *Columbus Ohio Statesman*, April 12, 1847.

14. Schurz, *Clay*, 2:288; Heidler and Heidler, *Clay*, 415; Paul Conkin, *Cane Ridge: America's Pentecost* (Madison: University of Wisconsin Press, 1990), 3; Speech to Shakers, October 15, 1829, Remarks in Senate, January 28, 1840, Clay to Joseph Smith, November 15, 1843, and Speech in Lexington, November 12, 1847, all in *CP*, 9:794n; Supp.:228; 9:384, 890; 10:369; Niels Henry Sonne, *Liberal Kentucky, 1780–1828* (1939; repr., Lexington: University of Kentucky Press, 1968), 196–97; Craig Friend, *Along the Maysville Road: The Early American Republic in the Trans-Appalachian West* (Knoxville: University of Tennessee Press, 2005), 37, 39; Clay to Horace Holley, September 8, 1818, *CP*, 2:596.

15. *Kentucky Gazette*, August 1, 1828; *RD*, 22nd Cong., 1st Sess. (1831–32), 1130–31; Colton, *Clay*, 1:53–59; "Mr. Clay at Home," *Niles Weekly Register* 64 (July 1, 1843): 279; *St. Louis Daily Missouri Republican*, June 26, 1852; Clay to Mary Bayard, February 4, 1845, *CP*, 10:197; Edward Berkley to C. M. Butler, August 2, 1852, Edward F. Buckley Papers, FHS; *Boston Bee*, July 16, 1847; J. B. Mower to Willie Mangum, October 18, 1847, *Mangum Papers*, 5:84; Deed of Emancipation of Charles Dupuy, December 9, 1844, *CP*, 10:176; Heidler and Heidler, *Clay*, 415.

16. Hart Diary, November 13, 1847; Joseph Rogers, *The True Henry Clay* (Philadelphia: J. B. Lippincott, 1904), 199.

17. Speech in Lexington, November 13, 1847, *CP*, 10:362–63; *Frankfort Commonwealth*, November 16, 1847; Hart Diary, November 13, 1847; Merry, *Country of Vast Designs*, 396; Remini, *Clay*, 697.

18. Speech in Lexington, November 13, 1847, *CP*, 10:361–75; Greenberg, *A Wicked War*, xv, xviii, 231–34, 237.

19. Joel Silbey, *Party over Section: The Rough and Ready Presidential Campaign of 1848* (Lawrence: University Press of Kansas, 2009), 27; "A Hawk Becomes a Dove: Henry Clay's Speech on the Mexican War . . . ," *Lincoln Lore*, October 1974, 4; *Columbus Daily Ohio Statesman*, November 15, 1847; *Brooklyn Eagle*, March 15 and 11, 1848; Howe, *American Whigs*, 95; R. R., "Henry Clay," *El Album Mexican* 2 (1849): 83–84 (trans. Hensley Woodbridge).

20. Henry Foote, *Casket of Reminiscences* (1874; New York: Negro Universities Press, 1968), 22; Clay to Lucretia Clay, February 18, 1848, *CP*, 10:403; Nevins, *Polk Diary*, 300; Merry, *Country of Vast Designs*, 419–20, 424.

21. Greenberg, *A Wicked War*, 30–31; *Bennington Vermont Gazette*, March 28, 1848.

22. Clay to Daniel Ullman, May 12, 1847, and Clay to Roland Houghton, July 4, 1848, both in *CP*, 10:329, 507; Greeley, *Recollections*, 211; Holman Hamilton, "Election of 1848," in *Presidential Elections*, 1:867: Holman Hamilton, *Zachary Taylor*, 2 vols. (1941; 1951; repr., Hamden, CT: Archon Books, 1966), 2:92; 1:112; Taylor to Jefferson Davis, August 16, 1847, in Haskell Monroe et al., eds., *Papers of Jefferson Davis*, 14 vols. (1971–2015), 3:211; Taylor to R. C. Wood, September 27, 1847, and June 21, 1846, *Letters of Zachary Taylor from the Battle-Fields of the Mexican War . . .* (Rochester, NY: Genesee Press, 1908), 134, 14; Henry Clay Jr. to Clay, February 12, 1847, *CP*, 10:306; Nevins, *Polk Diary*, 174, 389.

23. Bill Roberts to "Dear Sir," September 8, 1846, William O. Robertson Collection, KHS; Hamilton, *Taylor*, 1:21, 33, 72, 112, 122; 2:32, 52; *Taylor Letters*, xv; K. Jack Bauer, *Zachary Taylor* (Baton Rouge: Louisiana State University Press, 1985), 214; *Webster Papers*, 6:268n.

24. Hamilton, *Taylor*, 2:21, 218; Silbey, *Party over Section*, 100; Bauer, *Taylor*, 322, 327; Richard Thompson, *Recollections of Sixteen Presidents*, 2 vols. (Indianapolis, 1896), 2:350; Orth to Schuyler Colfax, May 9, 1847, in J. Herman Schavinger, ed., "The Letters of Godlove S. Orth, Hoosier

Whig," *Indiana Magazine of History* 39 (1943): 386–87; "Buena Vista," 235; Charles De Lavan to Calhoun, October 24, 1848, *Calhoun Papers*, 26:106–107; Malcolm McMillan, ed., "Joseph Glover Baldwin Reports on the Whig National Convention of 1848," *JSH* 25 (1959): 376; "The Nomination of General Taylor," *American Review* 2 (1848): 2–3; Clay to John Clayton, April 16, 1847, *CP*, 10:322.

25. Robert Remini, *Daniel Webster* (New York: W. W. Norton, 1997), 659; Davis to John J. Crittenden, January 30, 1849, in *Davis Papers*, 4:9; Heidler and Heidler, *Clay*, 460, 426; Elbert Smith, *The Presidencies of Zachary Taylor and Millard Fillmore* (Lawrence: University Press of Kansas, 1988), 20.

26. Glyndon G. Van Deusen, *Life of Henry Clay* (Boston: Little, Brown, 1937), 385; Van Deusen, *Thurlow Weed* (1947; repr. New Yprk: Da Capo Press, 1969), 158; Taylor to Clay, April 30, 1848, *CP*, 10:452; Holt, *Whig Party*, 270.

27. *New York Tribune*, September 11, 1847; Taylor to R. C. Wood, September 27 and October 19, 1847, *Taylor Letters*, 134, 143; Taylor to Orlando Brown, December 18, 1847, Zachary Taylor Papers, KHS; Taylor to Editors of Richmond Republican, April 20, 1848, Preston Family Papers, VHS; Hamilton, *Taylor*, 2:80–81; "The True Whig Sentiments," (1848), 1–2.

28. A. D. Kirwan, *John J. Crittenden: The Struggle for the Union* (Lexington: University of Kentucky Press, 1962), 3, 15, 323, 90–91, 98; Underwood Journal, November 7, 1825, Series I, Box 2, Underwood Collection, Kentucky Library, Western Kentucky University; Francis Blair to Clay, January 30, 1826, *CP*, 5:70; Crittenden to John Young, June 9, 1848, John Jordan Crittenden Papers, FHS; "Reminiscences of Washington," *Atlantic Monthly* 46 (1880): 371.

29. "Reminiscences of Washington," 371; George Bancroft to John Appleton, February 13, 1847, in M. A. De Wolfe Howe, *The Life and Letters of George Bancroft*, 2 vols. (New York: C. Scribner's Sons, 1908), 2:13: John Coffin, "The Whig Party in Kentucky," chap. 6:27, 38, UK.

30. Clay to Crittenden, November 28, 1844, and Crittenden to A. T. Burney, January 8, 1848, both in Coleman, *Crittenden*, 1:225, 290; Crittenden to John Young, June 9, 1848, Crittenden Papers, FHS; Holt, *Whig Party*, 269; Taylor to R. C. Wood, July 20, 1847, *Taylor Letters*; Hamilton, *Taylor*, 2:64; Kirwan, *Crittenden*, 218; Betty Congleton, "Contenders for the Whig Nomination in 1848 and the Editorial Policy of George D. Prentice," *Register* 67 (1969): 121, 123; Joseph White to Clay, May 26, 1848, *CP*, 10:472; Heidler and Heidler, *Clay*, 421; Coffin, "Whig Party," chap. 6:51, 54.

31. Joseph White to Clay, September 4, 1847, Clay to White, September 20, 1847, and Clay to Crittenden, September 21 and 26, 1847, all in *CP*, 10:349, 352, 350, 355. See also Coleman, *Crittenden*, 1:282.

32. *New York Herald*, March 1, 1848; *New York Daily Tribune*, June 2, 1848; *CP*, 10:393n; Kirwan, *Crittenden*, 223. The convention also named Crittenden as the Whig candidate for governor.

33. Clay to John Clayton, April 16, 1847, Clay to Daniel Ullman, May 12, 1847, and Clay to William Worsley et al., June 27, 1847, all in *CP*, 10:323, 329, 504.

34. Clay to Mary Bayard, May 7, 1846, Clay to Joshua Giddings, October 6, 1847, and Clay to William Mercer, December 14, 1847, all in *CP*, 10:267, 356, 390.

35. Clay to Greeley, November 21, 1846, Clay to John Clayton, April 16, 1847, Clay to Greeley, November 22, 1847, and Thomas Stevenson to Clay, April 8, 1848, all in *CP*, 10:294, 322, 378, 427.

36. Clay to Mary Bayard, August 7 and September 22, 1847, Clay to J. B. Clay, August 6, 1847, and Clay to Lucretia Clay, August 18, 1847, all in *CP*, 10:343, 354, 340; *New York Tribune*, August 26 and 27, September 25, August 23, and September 7, 1847; *Lexington Observer & Reporter*, August 28, 1847.

37. *Macon (GA) Weekly Telegraph*, November 16, 1847; George Poage, *Henry Clay and the Whig Party* (Chapel Hill: University of North Carolina Press, 1936), 168–69; Clay to William Mercer, February 7, 1848, *CP*, 10:400.

38. *New York Herald*, February 28 and March 8, 1848; *Boston Bee*, March 1, 1848; "Reminiscences of Washington," 809; *Brattleboro (VT) Semi-Weekly Eagle*, February 29, 1848; *Amherst (NH) Farmer's Cabinet*, March 2, 1848; *New York Daily Tribune,* March 1, 1848; *Baltimore Sun*, March 10, 1848; *Middletown (CT) Constitution*, March 15, 1848; *New York Herald*, March 10, 1848.

39. Sean Wilentz, *The Rise of American Democracy* (New York: W. W. Norton, 2005), 614; *Concord New-Hampshire Patriot*, March 16, 1848; *Keene New-Hampshire Sentinel*, March 2, 1848; *New York Daily Tribune*, March 3, 1848; *Easton (MD) Gazette*, March 18, 1848; Holt, *Whig Party*, 311; Clay to the Public, April 10, 1848, *CP*, 10:430–31.

40. Clay to Horace Greeley, December 10, 1847, Clay to John Clayton, April 16, 1847, Clay to Octavia LeVert, December 19, 1846, Charles Morehead to Clay, May 2, 1848, and Joseph White to Clay, May 26, 1848, all in *CP*, 10:387, 322, 299, 458, 471; Hamilton, *Taylor*, 2:59; Taylor to R. C. Wood, June 23, 1847, *Taylor Letters*, 108; Taylor to Jefferson Davis, April 20, 1848, *Davis Papers*, 3:306; Crittenden to Robert Letcher, March 9, 1846, in Coleman, *Crittenden*, 1:275; Merry, *Country of Vast Designs*, 253; Howe, *What Hath God Wrought*, 867; Wilentz, *American Democracy*, 616; Adams, *Memoirs*, 8:537; Greeley to Clay, November 30, 1847, and Thomas Stevenson to Clay, May 18, 1848, both in *CP*, 10:382, 467.

41. Taylor to Clay, November 4, 1847, *CP*, 10:360; Bauer, *Taylor*, 229; Taylor to R. C. Wood, October 19, 1847, *Taylor Letters*, 143. Taylor would write that he had no recollection of having written Clay saying he would step down, but the above letter makes it clear that he did so. For Taylor's denial, see Taylor to Orlando Brown, March 15, 1848, Zachary Taylor Papers, KHS.

42. Glyndon G. Van Deusen, *Horace Greeley* (1953; New York: Hill and Wang, 1964), 121; "Political Calculations," *Littell's Living Age* 16 (1848): 422; *New York Daily Tribune*, September 7, 1847, and March 3, 1848.

43. *Macon Georgia Telegraph*, April 25, 1848; Richard Hawes to Calhoun, May 5, 1848, *Calhoun Papers*, 25:392; J. B. Mower to Willie Mangum, September 21, 1847, *Mangum Papers*, 5:81; Holt, *Whig Party*, 276, 281;

Thomas Corwin to William Bebb, January 23, 1848, Papers of William Bebb, LC; Heidler and Heidler, *Clay*, 439; Logan McKnight to John Bullitt, November 25, 1847, Bullitt Family Papers–Oxmoor Collection, FHS; Robert Toombs to James Thomas, April 16, 1848, in U. B. Phillips, ed., "The Correspondence of Robert Toombs, Alexander H. Stephens, and Howell Cobb," *Annual Report of the American Historical Association for the Year 1911*, 2 vols. (Washington, DC: Government Printing Office, 1913), 2:104; "Political Calculations," 421.

44. Thomas Stevenson to H. T. Duncan, April 12, 1848, Letters of Thomas B. Stevenson, LC; C. M. Clay to Horace Greeley, December 20, 1847, Cassius Marcellus Clay Collection, Chicago Historical Society; Lincoln to Archibald Williams, April 30, 1848, in Roy Basler, ed., *Collected Works of Abraham Lincoln*, 9 vols. (New Brunswick, NJ: Rutgers University Press, 1959), 1:468; G. B. Kinkead to Crittenden, January 2, 1847, in Coleman, *Crittenden*, 1:266; Logan McKnight to John Bullitt, February 5, 1848, Bullitt Family Papers-Oxmoor Collection.

45. Hamilton Fish to Willie Mangum, February 22, 1848, and Mangum to William Graham, January 23, 1848, both in *Mangum Papers*, 5:100, 94; *New York Daily Tribune*, April 24, 1848; Clay to Seargent Prentiss, April 12, 1848, *CP*, 10:432; Gene Wells Boyette, "The Whigs of Arkansas, 1836–1856" (PhD diss., Louisiana State University, 1972), 305.

46. *New York Herald*, March 8, 1848.

47. Willard Klunder, "Lewis Cass and Slavery Expansion," *Civil War History* 32 (1986): 295–96, 298–99; Wilentz, *American Democracy*, 608; Holt, *Whig Party*, 376. On Cass, see Willard Klunder, *Lewis Cass and The Politics of Moderation* (Kent, OH: Kent State University Press, 1996). Noah Brooks, "American Politics III," *Scribner's Magazine* 17 (1895): 840, described the origin of the "Barnburners" name: "Men . . . accused them of being ready to destroy the Union to kill slavery, like the foolish farmer who burned his barn to exterminate the rats that plagued him."

48. Peterson, *Great Triumvirate*, 440: Clay to Phillip Fendall, June 6, 1848, *CP*, 10:480.

49. Michael Holt, "Winding Roads to Recovery: The Whig Party from 1844 to 1848," in William Gienapp et al., *Essays in American Antebellum Politics, 1840–1860* (College Station: Texas A&M Press, 1982), 126; Holt, *Whig Party*, 297, 321–23; Clay to Christopher Hughes, June 14, 1848, John Botts to Clay, August 23, 1848, Clay to Thomas Stevenson, October 29, 1848, and Joseph White to Clay, May 26, 1848, all in *CP*, 10:487, 523, 556, 472; John Mosely to J. Quincy Smith, April 1848, Mosely Family Papers, KHS; McMillan "Baldwin Reports," 372. The various convention votes can be followed in *Congressional Quarterly's Guide to U. S. Elections*, 2 vols. (4th ed., Washington, DC: CQ Press, 2001), 1:576.

50. Holt, *Whig Party*, 319; *New York Tribune*, September 14, 1848; *CP* 10:514n.

51. John Lawrence to Clay, June 9, 1848, and Leslie Combs to Clay, June 10, 1848, both in *CP*, 10:481, 483. Weed later commented, "Our humble

agency in President-making has been limited to Harrisburg in 1840 and Philadelphia in 1848." Unidentified clipping, c. 1855, Papers of Thurlow Weed, LC. In 1849, another New Yorker blamed Seward. See F. W. Byrdsall to Calhoun, June 5, 1849, *Calhoun Papers*, 26:419.

52. Hamilton, *Taylor*, 2:97: *New York Tribune*, June 14, 1848; Clay to Greeley, June 15, 1848, Leslie Combs to Clay, June 10, 1848, John Lawrence to Clay, June 9 and 23, 1848, and James Harlan to Clay, June 2 and 15, 1848, all in *CP*, 10:489, 481, 503, 478, 490; McMillan, "Baldwin Reports," 372, 375; John Collins to "Jim," July 27, 1847, John Armstrong Collins Papers, FHS; [Joseph Baldwin], "Representative Men, Part II," *Southern Literacy Messenger* 19 (1853): 596.

53. *Middletown (CT) Constitution*, June 27, 1848; Webster to Daniel Fletcher Webster, June 19, 1848, *Webster Papers*, 6:299; *Rochester North Star*, June 30, 1848; Alexander Stephens to Crittenden, September 26, 1848, in Phillips, "Correspondence," 127; "Henry Clay," *Harper's New Monthly Magazine* 5 (1852): 397; Eustis Prescott to Calhoun, September 6, 1848, *Calhoun Papers*, 26:37.

54. McMillan, "Baldwin Reports," 376; Clay to Mary Bayard, June 19, 1848, *CP*, 10:494; "A Louisville Whig," Ms. Box 39, and Ms. dated December 14, 1862, Box 44, both in Clay Family Papers; Ellwood Fisher to Calhoun, July 21, 1848, *Calhoun Papers*, 25:608; *Brooklyn Eagle*, July 21, 1848. Poage, *Henry Clay and the Whig Party*, 181, 181n, suggests that had the letter been published, Crittenden would have lost his race for governor and Taylor's chances would have been significantly lessened. Moreover, Clay might not have been able to garner support to return to the Senate later.

55. Clay to Morton McMichael, September 16, 1848, Clay to James Lynch et al., September 20, 1848, and Clay to William Worsley et al., June 27, 1848, all in *CP*, 10:542, 545, 504; Clay to J. M. Harris, August 18 and September 14, 1848, Henry Clay Papers, FHS; *Clarksville (TX) Northern Standard*, August 26, 1848.

56. Chesselden Ellis to Calhoun, July 5, 1848, *Calhoun Papers*, 25:674; Clay to Cincinnati Whigs, September 1, 1848, *CP*, 10:529; *Rochester North Star*, September 15, 1848; *New York Daily Tribune*, September 7 and 8, 1848.

57. *Henry Clay and the Administration* (Philadelphia, 1850), 3; *Richmond Examiner*, July 4 and 11, 1848; Clay to James Lynch et al., September 20, 1848, *CP*, 10:544. For other Clay letters rejecting appeals to run as an independent, see *CP*, 10:504, 525, 529, 534, 537, 544.

58. William Freehling, *Road to Disunion: Secessionists at Bay, 1776–1854* (New York: Oxford University Press, 1990), 477; Silbey, *Party over Section*, 144–45; *Guide to Elections*, 656, 733; Clay to Christopher Hughes, December 16, 1848, *CP*, 10:563; Howe, *What Hath God Wrought*, 832; Clay to Nicholas Bean, August 24, 1848, *CP*, 10:527, 559n.

59. Clay to William Worley et al., June 27, 1848, and Clay to Nicholas Dean, August 24, 1848, both in Box 39, Clay Family Papers.

Chapter 15

1. William Freehling, *The Road to Disunion: Secessionists at Bay, 1776–1854* (New York: Oxford University Press, 1990), 467; Joseph Hodges to William Hodges, June 29, 1849, Hodges Family Papers, KHS. For the convention struggle, see Asa Martin, *The Anti-Slavery Movement in Kentucky Prior to 1850* (1918; repr., New York: Negro Universities Press, 1970), 111–38; Lowell Harrison, *The Anti-Slavery Movement in Kentucky* (Lexington: University Press of Kentucky, 1978), 56–60; and especially Harold Tallant, *Evil Necessity: Slavery and Political Culture in Antebellum Kentucky* (Lexington: University Press of Kentucky, 2003), 133–60.

2. *Columbus Ohio Statesman*, January 20, 1849; Frederick Douglass to Clay, December 3, 1847 (typescript copy), Frederick Douglass Papers, LC; Marion Lucas, *A History of Blacks in Kentucky* (Frankfort: Kentucky Historical Society, 1992), 1:73; J. Winston Coleman Jr., *Slavery Days in Kentucky* (1940; repr. New York: Johnson Reprint, 1970), 88–92; James Prichard, "The Doyle Conspiracy of 1848" (paper delivered at Ohio Valley History Conference, 1998, copy in author's possession at james_klotter@georgetowncollege.edu), 8.

3. Clay to Pindell, February 17, 1849, *CP*, 10:574–81, 575, 576; Carl Degler, *The Other South* (New York: Harper and Row, 1974), 83; Freehling, *Road to Disunion*, 494.

4. Clay and Oberholtzer, *Clay*, 341; Clay to James B. Clay, March 3, 1849, and William Lloyd Garrison to Clay, March 16, 1849, both in *CP*, 10:582, 584–85; *Boston Daily Bee*, March 19, 1849; *Covington (KY) Journal*, March 9, 1849; *Louisville Weekly Courier*, March 3, 1849; *Spectator*, in *Littell's Living Age* 22 (1849): 562. See also Robert Breckinridge, "The Question of Negro Slavery and the New Constitution of Kentucky," *Princeton Review* 21 (1849): 583.

5. Tallant, *Evil Necessity*, 149; Richard Hawes to Orlando Brown, July 28, 1849, Box 6, Orlando Brown Papers, FHS; *Rochester North Star*, August 31, 1849, Clay to Morton McMichael, April 9, 1849, and Clay to Robert Hamilton, October 2, 1849, both in *CP*, 10:588. 621, As Tallant notes, incomplete returns make the numbers confusing. Of those counties with extant statistics, emancipationists won 35 percent of the vote.

6. Michael Holt, *The Rise and Fall of the American Whig Party* (New York: Oxford University Press, 1999), 459; U. B. Phillips, ed., "The Correspondence of Robert Toombs, Alexander H. Stephens, and Howell Cobb," *Annual Report of the American Historical Association for the year 1911*, 2 vols. (Washington, DC: Government Printing Office, 1913), 2:153, 184; James Hammond to Calhoun, February 19, 1849, *Calhoun Papers*, 26:295; C. S. Morehead to J. J. Crittenden, March 30, 1850, in Coleman, *Crittenden*, 1:363; Michael Birkner, "Daniel Webster and the Crisis of Union, 1850," *Historic New Hampshire* 37 (1982): 155.

7. Richard Hawes to Orlando Brown, July 28, 1849, Box 6, Orlando Brown Papers; Clay to Thomas Stevenson, December 19, 1846; William Owsley

to Clay, June 20, 1848, Clay to Owsley, June 22, 1848, and Clay to James Harlan, January 26, 1849, all in *CP*, 10:299, 498, 501–502, 567; *New York Times*, October 14, 1852; George Poage, *Henry Clay and the Whig Party* (Chapel Hill: University of North Carolina Press, 1936), 191.

8. *Brooklyn Daily Eagle*, July 16, 1848; *Floridian & Journal*, August 11, 1849; "Reminiscences of Washington," *Atlantic Monthly* 47 (1881): 241; *CG*, 31st Cong., 1st Sess. (1849–50), 1; Joseph Rogers, *The True Henry Clay* (Philadelphia: J. B. Lippincott, 1904), 343; Haskell Monroe et al.eds., *Papers of Jefferson Davis*, 14 vols. (1971–2015), 1:135n, 136n; "Jefferson Davis: The Ex-Confederate President at Home," *Tyler's Quarterly Magazine* 32 (1951): 171.

9. Clay to Leslie Combs, December 22, 1849; Clay to J. B. Clay, January 2, [1850], and Clay to Thomas Stevenson, January 26, 1850, all in *CP*, 10:635, 647, 655, 653. In a brief story on December 12, 1849, the *Boston Weekly Messenger* reported that a man named Robinson had attempted to assassinate Clay six days earlier.

10. Rachel Shelden, *Washington Brotherhood: Politics, Social Life, and the Coming of the Civil War* (Chapel Hill: University of North Carolina Press, 2013), 76; Holman Hamilton, *Zachary Taylor*, 2 vols. (1941; 1951; repr., Hamden, CT: Archon Books, 1966), 2:167; K. Jack Bauer, *Zachary Taylor* (Baton Rouge: Louisiana State University Press, 1985), 297, 266, 79: William Lynch, "Zachary Taylor as President," *JSH* 4 (1938): 290–91; *Crittenden*, 1:340; Holt, *Whig Party*, 406, 412, 429, 457–58; *Columbus, Ohio Daily Statesman*, January 30, 1849; Robert Toombs to Crittenden, January 3, 1849, in Phillips, "Correspondence," 2:140; Webster to Jonathan Hall, May 18, 1850, *Webster Papers*, 7:99; Edward Morris to George Fisher, December 1, 1849, Box 1, Papers of George P. Fisher, LC; "Many Whigs" to "Sirs," October 1849, Box 158, Thomas Ewing Family Papers, LC; Clay to James Harlan, March 13, 1849, and Clay to Mary Bayard, June 16, 1849, both in *CP*, 10:596; 603; Sara Bearss, "Henry Clay and the American Claims Against Portugal," *JER* 7 (1987): 167–80.

11. Clay to Susan Clay, December 15, 1849, Box 39, Papers of Henry Clay and Family, LC; Clay to Lucretia Clay, December 28, 1849, *CP*, 10:633, 638; Peter Knupfer, *The Union as It Is* (Chapel Hill: University of North Carolina Press, 1991), 180; Poage, *Clay and Whig Party*, 229.

12. Elbert Smith, *The Presidencies of Zachary Taylor and Millard Fillmore* (Lawrence: University Press of Kansas, 1988), 97–99. On the compromise process generally, see Holman Hamilton, *Prologue to Conflict: The Crisis and Compromise of 1850* (1964; Lexington: University Press of Kentucky, 2005), John Waugh, *On the Brink of Civil War* (Wilmington, DE: Scholarly Resources, 2003), Robert Remini, *At the Edge of the Precipice: Henry Clay and the Compromise That Saved the Union* (New York: Basic Books, 2010), and Fergus Bordewich, *America's Great Debate: Henry Clay, Stephen A. Douglas, and the Compromise That Preserved the Union* (New York: Simon and Schuster, 2012). Bordewich has the fullest discussion overall.

13. Robert Brent, "Between Calhoun and Webster: Clay in 1850," *Southern Quarterly* 9 (1970): 294; Holt, *Whig Party*, 475; William Lumpkin to Calhoun, August 17, 1849, *Calhoun Papers*, 27:38; Cobb to William Hull, July 17, 1850, in Phillips, "Correspondence," 2:199–200; Hamilton, *Prologue to Conflict*, 44, 139; H. V. Johnson to H. S. Foote, January 19, 1850, in Percy Flippin, "Herschel V. Johnson Correspondence," *North Carolina Historical Review* 4 (1927): 199.

14. *New York Tribune*, March 3, 1848; Clay to Mary Bayard, December 14, 1849, *CP*, 10:633.

15. Poage, *Clay and Whig Party*, 191; Mark Stegmaier, "Zachary Taylor versus the South," *Civil War History* 33 (1987): 219–25; Bauer, *Taylor*, xxii; Hamilton, *Prologue to Conflict*, 50.

16. Holt, *Whig Party*, 477; Poage, *Clay and Whig Party*, 204, 207, 229; Clay to Thomas Stevenson, April 3, 1850, and Clay to James Harlan, January 24, 1850, both in *CP*, 10:695, 653.

17. "Henry Clay the Statesman," unidentified clipping, Box 64, Clay Family Papers; *Cong. Globe*, 31st Cong., 1st Sess. (1849–50), 344–46; appendix, 115–27. For Clay's proposed division of Texas, see Hamilton, *Prologue to Conflict*, 57. On the Texas bondholders, who included abolitionists and proslavery advocates, see "Texas Debt Note Books," Record Group 56; "Texas Debt #29," "Texas Debt 1856–70," and "Register of Certain Claims . . . Under the Act of 9 September 1850," all in Record Group 217, Dept. of the Treasury, National Archives.

18. Birkner, "Webster and Union," 156; John McHenry to Robert Hunter, February 21, 1850, in "Correspondence of Robert M. T. Hunter," *Annual Report of the American Historical Association for the Year 1916*, 2 vols., ed. Charles Ambler (Washington DC: S.N., 1918), 2:104; Remini, *Clay*, 733; Heidler and Heidler, *Clay*, 477; Knupfer, *Union as It Is*, 181, 185.

19. Clay to Lucretia Clay, February 19, 1850, Box 39, Clay Family Papers; Holt, *Whig Party*, 476; Beverly Wilson Palmer, ed., *The Selected Letters of Charles Summer*, 2 vols. (Boston: Northeastern University Press, 1990), 1:298.

20. Clay to John Pendleton Kennedy, February 24, 1850, *CP*, 10:682; Thomas Brown, *Politics and Statesmanship: Essays on The American Whig Party* (New York: Columbia University Press, 1985), 110–12; Bordewich, *America's Great Debate*, 178, 258.

21. Henry Foote, *Casket of Reminiscences* (1874; repr., New York: Negro Universities Press, 1968), 24; Thomas Ritchie, *Letter Containing Reminiscences of Henry Clay and the Compromise* ([Richmond, VA?], 1852), 2, 5, 6, 8–10, 12; *New York Daily Times*, September 18, 1852. For charges that Clay "bought off" Ritchie, see Smith, *Presidencies of Taylor and Fillmore*, 132.

22. *CG*, 31st Cong., 1st. Sess. (1849–50), 624–25, appendix, 1400; "Henry Clay as Orator," *Putnam's Monthly Magazine* 3 (1859): 493; Heidler and Heidler, *Clay*, 469; Richard Thompson, *Recollections of Sixteen Presidents*, 2 vols. (Indianapolis, 1896), 2:356; Speech in the Senate, May 8, 1850, *CP*, 10:713–17. For the byzantine maneuvering on the bills, see Frank Hodder, "The

Authorship of the Compromise of 1850," *Mississippi Valley Historical Review* 22 (1936): 525–36. A variation of the quote regarding Calhoun is in "Clay as Orator," 493 ("He was my junior in years—in nothing else").

23. Stegmaier, "Taylor vs. the South," 227; Holt, *Whig Party*, 497, 508; Speech in Senate, May 13 and 21, 1850, *CP*, 10:718–21, 725–30; A Friend of the Union, *Henry Clay and the Administration* (Philadelphia, 1850), 3–6; Comment in Senate, July 3, 1850, *CP*, 10:760. For a different interpretation of Taylor's actions than presented here, see Smith, *Presidencies of Taylor and Fillmore*, 141–46, 189.

24. Remini, *At the Edge of the Precipice*, 153; *Brooklyn Eagle*, June 13 and July 25, 1850; Waugh, *Brink of Civil War*, 176; Comment in Senate, June 13, 1850, Clay to Thomas Clay, May 31 and July 1, 1850, Clay to Lucretia Clay, July 6, 1850, Comment in Senate, July 22, 1850, and Clay to James Harrison, June 19, 1850, all in *CP*, 10:747, 736, 759, 763, 772–75, 781,754; Douglas to Charles Lanphier and George Walker, August 3, 1850, in Robert Johannsen, ed., *The Letters of Stephen A. Douglas* (Urbana: University of Illinois Press, 1961), 192.

25. "Monthly Record of Current Events," *Harper's Monthly Magazine* 1 (1850): 563; *Boston Weekly Messenger*, August 7, 1850; "Hon. James B. Clay to His Constituents" (July 8, 1858 Pamphlet); Kirwan, *Crittenden*, 264; *Keene New-Hampshire Patriot*, July 18, 1850; Clay to James Clay, July 18 and August 15, 1850, both in *CP*, 10:767, 795; Glyndon G. Van Deusen, *The Life of Henry Clay* (Boston: Little, Brown, 1937), 413; Comment in Senate, August 1, 1850, *CP*, 10:789.

26. Foote, *Casket of Reminiscences*, 92; Robert Johannsen, *Stephen A. Douglas* (New York: Oxford University Press, 1973), vii–viii; William Graham to James Graham, August 29, 1850, *Graham Papers*, 3:369; Holt, "Introduction" to Hamilton, *Prologue to Conflict*, xviii; Holt, *Whig Party*, 543.

27. Robert Russell, "What Was the Compromise of 1850?" *JSH* 22 (1956): 304; Holt, *Whig Party*, 532; William Freehling, "Sidebar" (typescript in author's possession); Clay to James Clay, March 6, 1850, *CP*, 10:685. Keith Griffler, in *Front Line of Freedom: African Americans and the Forging of the Underground Railroad in the Ohio Valley* (Lexington: University Press of Kentucky, 2004), 107, calls the Fugitive Slave Law of 1850 "the brainchild of Kentucky's Henry Clay." But the idea did not originate with Clay nor did the resulting act include some key features that Clay had proposed in his original plan.

28. Martin Golding, "The Nature of Compromise," 18, and Joseph Carens, "Compromise in Politics," 128, both in J. Roland Pennock and John Chapman, eds., *Compromise in Ethics, Law, and Politics* (New York: New York University Press, 1979); Sean Wilentz, *The Rise of American Democracy* (New York: W. W. Norton, 2005), 637; Freehling, *Road to Disunion*, 509.

29. Foote, *Casket of Reminiscences*, 25; Bauer, *Taylor*, 397; Senator Douglas's Speech, September 18, 1858, in Roy Basler, ed., *The Collected Works of Abraham Lincoln*, 9 vols. (New Brunswick, NJ: Rutgers University Press,

1959), 3:169; Douglas to Charles Lanphier and George Walker, August 3, 1850, *Douglas Letters*, 192–93; Jon Meacham, *American Lion: Andrew Jackson in the White House* (New York: Random House, 2008), 351.

30. Clay to Thomas Clay, August 6, 1850, *CP*, 10:791; Poage, *Clay and Whig Party*, 243; Clay to Donald MacLeod, November 14, 1851, MacLeod Family Papers, VHS; *Lexington Kentucky Statesman*, October 5 and 19, 1850; *Mr. Clay's Speech to the General Assembly of Kentucky 1850* (Frankfort, KY, [1850]), 3, 7, 10.

31. Clay to Union Meeting, January 30, 1851, in *St. Louis Daily Missouri Republican*, February 15, 1851; E. D. Mansfield, *Personal Memories . . . 1803–1843* (Cincinnati, 1879), 214; *Rochester North Star*, October 31, 1850. Another concern for Clay involved the course of the US Supreme Court. Already, in a Kentucky case, the court had seemed to support the idea that slavery could not be restricted. See Robert Schweman, "*Strader v. Graham*: Kentucky's Contribution to National Slavery Litigation and the *Dred Scott* Decision," *Kentucky Law Journal* 97 (2008–09): 353–438.

32. *Baltimore Sun*, August 21, 1851; Michael Holt, "The Mysterious Disappearance of the American Whig Party," in Michael Holt, *Political Parties and American Political Development . . .* (Baton Rouge: Louisiana State University Press, 1992), 237–64; *St. Louis Daily Missouri Republican*, August 28, 1851; Clay to Daniel Ullman, June 14, 1851, *CP*, 10:896.

33. Speech in Senate, February 24, 1851, and Comment in Senate, February 18, 1851, both in *CP*, 10:873, 863; Clay to Lucretia Clay, March 7, 8, and 18, 1851, Box 39, Clay Family Papers; *Macon Georgia Telegraph*, April 1, 1851; *St. Louis Daily Missouri Republican*, April 17, 1851.

34. J. Winston Coleman Jr., *Last Days, Death, and Funeral of Henry Clay* (Lexington, KY: Winburn Press,1951), 27n, 3–4; Clay to James Clay, January 3, [1852], Box 39, Clay Family Papers; Clay to Lucretia Clay, February 27 and November 18, 1851, and January 4 and 12, 1852, Clay to John Clay, February 28, 1852, and Clay to the General Assembly of Kentucky, December 17, 1851, all in *CP*, 10:896, 933, 943, 947, 956, 928.

35. Clay to Garrett Davis, January 12, 1852, and Clay to Lucretia Clay, March 22, 1852, both in *CP*, 10:943, 961; *St. Louis Daily Missouri Republican*, April 12, 1852; Crittenden to Orlando Brown, May 5, 1852, Box 6, Orlando Brown Papers, FHS; Clay to James Clay, February 18, 1851, Box 39, Clay Family Papers; Poage, *Clay and Whig Party*, 275–77.

36. Meachem Diary, June 29, 1852, Papers of John Silva Meachem, LC; "Condolences" folder, Box 40, Clay Family Papers; *Galveston* (TX) *Weekly Journal*, July 9, 1852; *New York Times*, July 2, 1856.

37. Pierson Diary, July 1, 1852, Job Pierson Family Papers, Box 1, LC; *New York Times*, June 3 and July 1, 1852; *St. Louis Daily Missouri Republican*, June 3 and July 9, 1852; J. Winston Coleman Jr., "Opening of The Henry Clay Sarcophagus . . . January 5th, 1951," J. Winston Coleman Collection, Transylvania University Library; Merrill Peterson, *The Great Triumvirate: Webster, Clay and Calhoun* (New York: Oxford University Press, 1987), 487; Meachem Diary, July 1, 1852.

38. Sarah Purcell, "All that Remains of Henry Clay: Political Funerals and the Tour of Henry Clay's Corpse," *Common Place* 12 (2012), www.common-place.org; Heidler and Heidler, *Clay*, xvii–xxiv; *New York Times*, July 21, 1852; Tom Marshall Eulogy, Box 55, Clay Family Papers.

39. "Henry Clay's Last Will," *University of Kentucky Libraries Bulletin* 1 (1949): 3–9; Statement of Assets, 1851, and Memoranda of H. Clay, June 1852, both in *CP*, 10:904, 968.

Chapter 16

1. *Cincinnati Gazette*, in *New York Times*, October 3, 1854 and July 21, 1855; *Macon (GA) Weekly Telegraph*, July 22, 1865; J. Winston Coleman Jr., *Last Days, Death, and Funeral of Henry Clay* (Lexington, KY: Winburn Press, 1951), 23; Charles Coleman Jr., "Ashland, The Home of Henry Clay," *Century Magazine* 33 (1886): 168–69; *Remembering Barry Bingham* (n.p.: Privately printed, 1990), 109.

2. Michael Holt, "The Mysterious Disappearance of the American Whig Party," in *Political Parties and American Political Development*, ed. Michael Holt (Baton Rouge: Louisiana State University Press, 1992), 338; "Mr. Clay's Private Correspondence," *Littell's Living Age* 48 (1856): 251; Apple, *Family Legacy*, 103–104, 107; William Davis, *Breckinridge: Statesman, Soldier, Symbol* (Baton Rouge: Louisiana State University Press, 1974), 239; Clay to James Harvey, August 18, 1848, *CP*, 10:408. In the Memoirs of Thomas Clay, December 14, 1862, Box 44, Papers of Henry Clay and Family, LC, Thomas indicated that he voted Democratic in 1856, but in a letter at the time, he said he supported the Know-Nothings. See *New Orleans Daily Creole*, August 30, 1856, and also *Austin Texas State Gazette*, October 18, 1856.

3. Image of Washington Monument inscription, www.nps.gov/wamo/photosmultimedia/upload/WAMC/.

4. Eulogy for Henry Clay, July 6, 1852, First Debate with Stephen A. Douglas at Ottawa, IL, August 21, 1858, Lincoln to Daniel Ullman, February 1, 1861, Lincoln to Edward Wallace, October 11, 1859, Speech at Rushville, IL, October 20, 1858 and Speech at Petersburg, IL, October 29, 1858, all in Roy Basler, ed., *The Collected Works of Abraham Lincoln*, 9 vols. (New Brunswick, NJ: Rutgers University Press, 1953–55), 2:122–32; 3:29–30; 4:184; 3:487, 329, 333; Amy Greenberg, *A Wicked War: Polk, Clay, Lincoln, and the 1846 US Invasion of Mexico* (New York: Alfred A. Knopf, 2012), 237–38; Edgar Dewitt Jones, *The Influence of Henry Clay upon Abraham Lincoln* (Lexington, KY: Henry Clay Memorial Foundation, 1952), 29, 32, 1.

5. Andrew Cayton, "To Save the Union," *New York Times Book Review*, July 4, 2010; Robert W. Johannsen, *Lincoln and the South in 1860* (Ft. Wayne, IN: Louis A. Warren Lincoln Library and Museum, 1989), 51; Ronald White, *A. Lincoln: A Biography* (New York: Random House, 2009), 349, 449–51. William Cooper, in his "Where Was Henry Clay? President-Elect

Abraham Lincoln and the Crisis of the Union, 1860–1861," in *A Political Nation: New Directions in Mid-Nineteenth American Political History*, ed. Gary Gallagher and Rachel Shelden (Charlottesville: University of Virginia Press, 2012), 126–40, is critical of Lincoln for not being more Clay-like in seeking compromise.

6. Envelope ca. 1861–65, available at http://infoweb.newsbank.com/iw-search/we/HistArchive?p_action=doc&f_content=image. See also James C. Klotter, "Kentucky, the Civil War, and Henry Clay," *Register* 119 (2012): 243–63. For a sample of the range of newspapers reproducing Clay's words, compare *New York Times*, December 26, 1860, with the *Warren (OH) Western Reserve Chronicle*, January 9, 1861, with the obscure *Egg Harbor City (NJ), Atlantic Democrat*, May 15, 1861.

7. *Macbeth*, Act 1, scene 3; Robert Winthrop, *Memoir of Henry Clay* (Cambridge, MA, 1880), 2; Henry Foote, *Casket of Reminiscences* (1874; repr., New York; Negro Universities Press, 1968), 30; "Address of the Rev. Ed. F. Berkley, Funeral of the Hon. H. Clay, July 10, 1852," Edward F. Berkley Papers, FHS; Coleman, *Crittenden*, 2:273, 278, 313.

8. *RD*, 22nd Cong., 2nd Sess. (1831–33), 472.

9. *CG*, 25th Cong., 3rd Sess. (1838–39), appendix, 359.

10. Speech in Senate, July 22, 1850, and Comment in Senate, August 1, 1850, both in *CP*, 10:789–90; William Freehling, *The Road to Disunion: Secessionists at Bay, 1776–1854* (New York: Oxford University Press, 1990), 506; *Mr. Clay's Speech to the General Assembly of Kentucky 1850* (Frankfort, KY [1850]), 13; *CP*, 10:830.

11. Clay to Francis Lathrop, February 17, 1851, Clay to Thomas Stevenson, May 17, 1851, and Clay to Fellow Citizens of New York City, October 3, 1851, all in *CP*, 10:861, 891, 923; *Baltimore Sun*, October 18, 1851.

12. Thomas Mackey, "Not a Pariah, but a Keystone: Kentucky and Secession," in Kent Dollar, Larry Whitaker, and W. Calvin Dickinson, eds., *Sister States, Enemy States: The Civil War in Kentucky and Tennessee* (Lexington: University Press of Kentucky, 2009), 34–36; Henry Volz III, "Party, State, and Nation: Kentucky and the Coming of the Civil War" (PhD diss., University of Virginia, 1982), 458–62.

13. Lincoln to O. H. Browning, September 22, 1861, in Basler, *Collected Works*, 4:532–33; William Freehling, *The South Versus The South* (New York: Oxford University Press, 2001), 23; Mackey, "Kentucky and Secession," 26–28; *1860 US Census*, 598–99.

14. Apple, *Family Legacy*, 109; Henry Clay Simpson Jr., *Josephine Clay* (Louisville, KY: Harmony House, 2001), 60, 37, 51, 60; *CP*, 10:823n; e-mail from Eric Brooks to author, December 2011; Basil Duke, *History of Morgan's Cavalry* (Cincinnati, OH, 1867), 383–85.

15. *New York Times*, March 24, 1852; "First Word After the Election," *United States Magazine and Democratic Review* 15 (1844): 436.

16. Schurz, *Clay*, 1:201; Leslie Southwick, *Presidential Also-Rans and Running Mates, 1788–1980* (Jefferson, NC: McFarland, 1984), 73; [Joseph Baldwin],

"Representative Men, Part I," *Southern Literary Messenger* 19 (1853): 525; William Dusinberre, *Slavemaster President: The Double Career of James K. Polk* (New York: Oxford University Press, 2003); A. D. Kirwan, *John J. Crittenden* (Lexington: University of Kentucky Press, 1962), 169; Michael Holt, *The Rise and Fall of the American Whig Party* (New York: Oxford University Press, 1999), 982; Remini, *Clay*, 668; Daniel Walker Howe, *What Hath God Wrought: The Transformation of America, 1815–1848* (New York: Oxford University Press, 2007), 689–90; Joel Silbey, *Storm over Texas: The Annexation Controversy and the Road to Civil War* (New York: Oxford University Press, 2005), xvii. The best exploration of what a Clay presidency might have meant is Gary Kornblith, "Rethinking the Coming of the Civil War: A Counterfactual Exercise," *JAH* 90 (2003): 76–105.

17. Journal of Joseph Rogers Underwood, September 27, 1852, Series I, Box 2, Underwood Papers, Kentucky Library, Western Kentucky University; *RD*, 23rd Cong., 1st Sess. (1833–34), 1283.

18. *Portsmouth New Hampshire Gazette*, February 4, 1840.

19. Sandra Moats to the Editor, *New York Times*, July 25, 2010; *Rochester North Star*, April 27, 1849; Peter Knupfer, *The Union as It Is: Constitutional Unionism and Sectional Compromise, 1787–1861* (Chapel Hill: University of North Carolina Press, 1991), 135, 156.

20. "Henry Clay as an Orator," *New Englander and Yale Review* 2 (1844): 107; James Swain, *Life and Speeches of Henry Clay*, 2 vols. (New York, 1844), 1:197.

21. Charles Morehead to John J. Crittenden, May 19, 1838, Charles Morehead Letters, UK; Thomas Nevitt to Clay, November 23, 1844, *CP*, 10:157.

22. Senate Historical Office, "1801–1850," www.senate.gov/artandhistory/history/minutes/celebrating_a_first.htm; David Brooks, "How to Run for President," *Atlantic Monthly* 298 (October 2003): 33; *Louisville Courier-Journal*, November 14, 2011.

23. *Charleston Courier*, in *Macon Georgia Telegraph*, October 15, 1839.

24. *Rochester North Star*, April 27, 1849; J. G. Hornburgen to John Bullitt, August 15, 1846, Bullitt Family Papers–Oxmoor Collection, FHS; "The Coming Session," *United States Democratic Review* 3 (1838): 298; Johan Reiersen, "A Biographical Sketch of Henry Clay," ca. 1844–45, trans. Frank Nelson (1980), 1; Lincoln, "Eulogy on Henry Clay," July 6, 1852, in Basler, *Collected Works*, 2:126; Swain, *Clay*, 1:26.

25. *CG*, 26th Cong. 1st Sess. (1839–40), 98; 27th Cong., 2nd Sess. (1841–42), 377.

26. J. B. Mower to Willie Mangum, August 2, 1848, *Mangum Papers*, 4:469; *New York Times*, July 3, 1852; Greenberg, *A Wicked War*, 8.

27. Louie Nunn, "Crusade versus Crime Luncheon," March 29, 1971, in Robert Sexton, ed., *The Public Papers of Governor Louie B. Nunn* (Lexington: University Press of Kentucky, 1975), 452; Remini, *Clay*, 644; Howe, *What Hath God Wrought*, 825; Harry Watson, *Andrew Jackson vs. Henry Clay* (Boston: Bedford/St. Martin's, 1998), 117.

28. "Present and Former House Speakers Honor Henry Clay," *Transylvania University Magazine*, Summer 2011, C2; John David Dyche, *Republican Leader: A Political Biography of Senator Mitch McConnell* (Wilmington, DE: ISI Books, 2009), 14; *Louisville Courier-Journal*, November 9, 2014; Fergus Bordewich, "The Rescue of Henry Clay," *Smithsonian*, November 2009, 79; Jay Newton-Small, "Let's Make a Deal," *Time*, June 13, 2011, 28; Senate Resolutions 89 (106th Cong., 1st Sess.) and 630 (109th Cong., 2nd Sess.), and Speech (112th Cong., 1st Sess., 5433-34), all in *Congressional Record*. See also Scot Lehigh, "Henry Clay's Lesson for Today," http://bostonglobe.com/opinion/2015/03/31/henry-clay-lesson-for-today.

29. Senate Historical Office, "1941–1967 ... The Famous Five," www.senate.gov/artandhistory/history/minutes/the_Famous_Five.htm; Kenneth Williams and Melba Porter Hay, eds., "Henry Clay Represents What This Country Is About: A Round Table Discussion with His Biographer and Editors," *Register* 100 (2002): 455n; "They Made America," *Atlantic Monthly* 298 (December 2006): 59–65, 72–78; Apple, *Family Legacy*, 84; https://www.senate.gov/artandhistory/art/common/collection_list/Sittername_List.htm#C; https://www.aoc.gov/blog/artfully-yours-george-washington

30. *New York Herald*, November 21, 1850; cited in Holman Hamilton, *Zachary Taylor: Soldier in the White House* (1951; repr., Hamden, CT: Archon Books, 1966), 66.

INDEX

———◦◦◦———

Figures and notes are indicated by *f* and *n* following the page number.